PREFACE

The present volume was begun seventeen years ago. At the time of the discussion of the income tax which culminated in the law of 1894, when practically nothing had been written on the subject in this country, I undertook to make researches into the history of taxation in the American colonies and states which might throw light on the question. The results of some of these studies were published in 1894–5, and constitute the earlier chapters of Part II of the present work. I proposed at the time to continue these studies and to publish a book on the general subject. The income tax decisions of 1895, however, were at once recognized as putting a temporary quietus on any legislative programme, and I turned aside from the project until the time should seem more propitious. The renewed agitation looking toward a federal income tax which eventuated in the submission of the Sixteenth Amendment afforded this opportunity, and accordingly my earlier researches have been completed and brought up to date, with the results herewith presented. As it seems probable that we shall before long have an income tax in the United States, my chief object in writing this book has been to set the subject in a somewhat clearer light and to aid the legislator in constructing a workable scheme.

It may appear to some that too much attention has been paid to the historical side of the subject. It seemed to me, however, that the most important lesson to be learned from experience was the gradual transition in public sentiment from a position of uncompromising hostility to one of virtual acquiescence. Such a lesson, however, can be impressed only after a full and thorough presentation of the facts.

This, apart from the inherent interest of the matter, must be my excuse for attempting an exhaustive statement, not only of the legislation and of the parliamentary history, but also of the scientific as well as of the more ephemeral literature of the topic, in the most important countries from which we have a lesson to learn. In this investigation, especially so far as England is concerned, virtually no help was secured from any existing investigation, and I have therefore been compelled to make a pioneer study, with all its inevitable defects.

Some will no doubt take up this volume in the hope of securing a general survey of the question. To such readers it is suggested that the main outlines of the problem will be found in the Introduction and the Conclusion, and that they may do well to confine their attention to these portions of the work, referring to Parts I and II only in so far as they may be interested in securing a more detailed confirmation of the points there presented.

So much help has been afforded by friends, both at home and abroad, in scientific as well as in official circles, that it would be hopeless to attempt any record here of my indebtedness to individuals. I cannot, however, refrain from acknowledging a deep obligation to my colleague, Professor H. R. Mussey, and to my son, Eustace J. Seligman, for the invaluable assistance they have afforded in the dreary task of reading the proof.

EDWIN R. A. SELIGMAN.

COLUMBIA UNIVERSITY, NEW YORK,
January 10, 1911.

PREFACE TO THE SECOND EDITION

In the present edition a chapter has been added on the new Federal income tax, the chapter on the state income taxes has been rewritten so as to include a description of the Wisconsin income tax, and not a few additions and corrections have been made in the other chapters. The bibliography has also been enlarged.

E. R. A. S.

March, 1914.

TABLE OF CONTENTS

INTRODUCTION

THE FUNDAMENTAL PROBLEMS

PART I

THE INCOME TAX ABROAD

PREFATORY NOTE

THE INCOME TAX IN THE MIDDLE AGES

BOOK I

THE INCOME TAX IN ENGLAND

CHAPTER I

THE WAR TAX. 1798–1816

CHAPTER II

The Income Tax on Trial. 1842–1862

CHAPTER III

The Modern Income Tax: A Half Century of Achievement. 1862–1911

BOOK II

THE INCOME TAX ON THE CONTINENT

CHAPTER I

Germany

THE INCOME TAX

A STUDY OF THE HISTORY, THEORY, AND PRACTICE OF

INCOME TAXATION AT HOME AND ABROAD

BY

EDWIN R. A. SELIGMAN
McVickar Professor of Political Economy
Columbia University

SECOND EDITION, REVISED AND ENLARGED WITH A NEW CHAPTER

THE LAWBOOK EXCHANGE, LTD.
Clark, New Jersey

ISBN 9781584773856 (hardcover)
ISBN 9781616191641 (paperback)

Lawbook Exchange edition 2011

The quality of this reprint is equivalent to the quality of the original work.

THE LAWBOOK EXCHANGE, LTD.
33 Terminal Avenue
Clark, New Jersey 07066-1321

Please see our website for a selection of our other publications and fine facsimile reprints of classic works of legal history:
www.lawbookexchange.com

Library of Congress Cataloging-in-Publication Data

Seligman, Edwin Robert Anderson, 1861-1939.
The income tax : a study of the history, theory, and practice of income taxation at home and abroad / by Edwin R.A. Seligman.— 2nd ed., rev. and enl. with a new chapter.
p. cm.
Previously published: 2nd ed., rev. and enl. with a new chapter. New York: Macmillan, 1914.
Includes bibliographical references and index.
ISBN 1-58477-385-5 (cloth: alk. paper)
1. Income tax—Law and legislation—United States. 2. Income tax—Law and legislation—Europe. 3. Income tax—United States. 4. Income tax—Europe. I. Title.

KF6369.S455 2003
343.7305'2—dc21 2003044247

Printed in the United States of America on acid-free paper

THE INCOME TAX

A STUDY OF THE HISTORY, THEORY,
AND PRACTICE OF

INCOME TAXATION AT HOME AND ABROAD

BY

EDWIN R. A. SELIGMAN

McVickar Professor of Political Economy
Columbia University

SECOND EDITION, REVISED AND ENLARGED WITH A NEW CHAPTER

New York
THE MACMILLAN COMPANY
1914

Set up and electrotyped. Published February, 1911.

New revised and enlarged edition. Published May, 1914.

Norwood Press
J. S. Cushing Co. — Berwick & Smith Co.
Norwood, Mass., U.S.A.

CHAPTER II

FRANCE

CHAPTER III

OTHER COUNTRIES

PART II

THE INCOME TAX AT HOME

CHAPTER I

THE INCOME TAX IN THE AMERICAN COLONIES

CHAPTER II

State Income Taxes

CHAPTER III

The Civil War Income Tax

APPENDIX

CHAPTER IV

The Income Tax of 1894

CHAPTER V

The Constitutionality of the Income Tax

CHAPTER VI

The Proposed Sixteenth Amendment

CONCLUSION

A PRACTICABLE PROGRAMME

APPENDIX

The Income Tax of 1913

INTRODUCTION

THE FUNDAMENTAL PROBLEMS

THE FUNDAMENTAL PROBLEMS

§ 1. *The Development of the Norm of Taxation*

THE income tax has come into the forefront of public discussion with comparative rapidity. In France it is now the centre of political agitation. In the United States it is looming large on the political horizon. In Great Britain it has only recently been accepted as a permanent part of the tax system, and important problems of reconstruction have been occupying the centre of the political stage. In Germany the success of the Prussian tax during the last two decades has engendered a strong movement in its favor throughout the remaining commonwealths. Among the smaller states, both of Europe and of other continents, many have already adopted the system, while others are preparing to adopt it. Everywhere, in short, there seems to be a trend toward the income tax.[1]

[1] The literature in English on the subject of the income tax is exceedingly meagre. Bastable, *Public Finance*, and H. C. Adams, *Science of Finance*, give only summary accounts. K. K. Kennan, *Income Taxation, Methods and Results in Various Countries*, Milwaukee, 1910, published since the first edition appeared, contains an account of existing systems.

In Germany good summaries will be found in the text-books on Finance by Wagner, Cohn, Roscher, Stein, and v. Heckel. The best special book devoted to the subject, although now somewhat antiquated, is that of Held. This, as well as the more recent works of Neumann and Fuisting, will be analyzed later.

In France the recent active discussion of the subject has led to a more abundant literature. Apart from the general text-books on Finance by Leroy-Beaulieu, Stourm, and Jèze, which contain succinct accounts of the subject, a large number of special volumes have recently appeared. Among the most important are those of Denis, Philippe, Gaston-Gros, Ingenbleeck, and Haristoy. These will be discussed in the chapter on France.

For fairly good bibliographies see Edith M. Phelps, *Selected Articles on the Income Tax with Special Reference to Graduation and Exemption*. Minneapolis, 1909; and two works issued by the Library of Congress in 1907 and 1911.

Why is this so? What is the explanation of this essentially modern phenomenon? For what reason are the fiscal systems that have so well served their purpose in the past now everywhere being brushed aside, and being replaced or supplemented by the income tax? What, in short, is the real significance of the movement?

In order fully to comprehend this, it would be necessary to trace the development of taxation and to study the fundamental ideas which lie at the basis of this development. As the general phase of this development, however, has been elaborated in another place,[1] it will be necessary here only to recall the broad lines of the evolution, and to remember the process through which voluntary offerings gradually change into compulsory payments, and the primitive fees and tolls evolve into indirect taxes, to be followed, only at a much later stage, by a system of direct taxes. Without going into the details of that development, we may be permitted to recall the conclusion. Amid the clashing of divergent interests and the endeavor of each social class to roll off the burden of taxation on some other class, we discern the slow and laborious growth of standards of justice in taxation, and the attempt on the part of the community as a whole to realize this justice. The history of finance, in other words, shows the evolution of the principle of faculty or ability to pay—the principle that each individual should be held to help the state in proportion to his ability to help himself.

Premising a general acquaintance with the main lines of fiscal evolution, what interests us here is the tracing of the fundamental ideas on which the evolution was based. In other words, taking it for granted—what indeed cannot fail to be granted, after a study of the facts—that there has been a progressive attempt to realize the demands of fiscal justice and a more or less unconscious tendency to work out the principle of ability to pay, the question presents itself as to what are the historic forms of the test of this ability. Granted that in some more or less rough way an endeavor is

[1] Seligman, *Essays in Taxation*, 8th ed. (1913), chap. I.

made, almost from the beginning, to apportion public burdens in accordance with the presumed capacity of individuals or classes, the problem arises as to how the capacity to bear this burden is to be measured. Even where it is difficult to recognize any conscious attempt on the part of government to carry this principle into practice, and even where actual fiscal institutions represent more or less thinly disguised efforts of the dominant economic class to roll the burdens on the shoulders of the weak, — even here it is rare to find a cynical disregard of all considerations of equity; and even here a more or less successful effort is made to clothe the hard facts of economic oppression in the garb of some specious explanation. Thus, whether it be actually realized or not, it is possible to interpret the successive stages of fiscal development in terms of an attempt to enforce various criteria of ability to pay.

From this point of view, namely that of the norm or test of faculty, it may be said that no less than five answers have been given in the course of history. At the outset, the individual as such was selected as the norm. Mere numbers suffice in primitive society to answer the requirements of justice. Thus it is that everywhere the beginnings of direct taxation take the form of the poll or capitation tax. In a primitive community where private property has but slightly developed or where the differentiation in economic conditions is insignificant, where there are no very rich and no very poor, where every man works and where individual revenue is derived almost exclusively from individual exertion, it is indeed true that polls form an approximately satisfactory test of ability in taxation. Wherever we have primitive economic and democratic conditions, whether it be in the early stages of Teutonic civilization or in the beginnings of Puritan New England, we find that the poll tax forms an essential ingredient of the fiscal system.

With the development of private property, however, and with the differentiation of economic classes, a change sets in. The original equality of wealth is followed by an inequality of possessions. The distribution of ownership, in other words, is now gradually divorced from the mere accumulation of numbers. A poll tax responds less and less well to the demands of faculty until it finally becomes, at all events as the sole test of ability, almost wholly a mockery. Efforts may indeed be made to improve the situation for a time by graduating the poll tax according to outward signs so that the poll tax in some cases becomes a class tax, the assessment being graded roughly in accordance with the social position of the individual. But this class or classified poll tax, as we find it in the early Middle Ages, is only a makeshift, and before long the poll tax is either supplemented or supplanted by a property tax.

§ 2. *Property as the Test of Faculty*

In this second stage of development, property is accepted as the test of faculty in taxation. For many centuries it forms an admirable test. Amid the rude conditions of ownership that we find at this stage of economic life, private property consists very largely of land and of appurtenances to land, so that the property tax is virtually a tax on real estate. Gradually, as primitive industry and commerce develop, various forms of personal property come into prominence and are added to the tax lists, until finally the two elements are fused together in order to form the general property tax, which is universally found in this stage of economic development. Property becomes the only possible general test of faculty in taxation because it is the specific mark of distinction between classes and between individuals within each class. At first the property tax is shyly and cautiously added to the poll tax, as an unimportant feature of the system; then the property tax grows in significance while the poll tax slowly recedes; until finally the poll tax disappears and the property tax remains in possession of the field. The general property tax is found wherever a primitive democracy is accompanied by a moderate agricultural and commercial development.

For a long time the general property tax functions satisfactorily and responds fairly well to the canons of justice in taxation. But in the inevitable course of economic development, with the growing differentiation of economic classes and with the increasing complexity of economic life, certain difficulties make themselves felt, not only in the practical application of the system but also in the theoretical basis of the tax. With the practical difficulties of the system, this is not the place to deal. The causes of the breakdown of the general property tax and the reasons why it everywhere disappeared in the later Middle Ages in Europe and why it is beginning to disappear in its last stronghold — the United States — have been sufficiently expounded elsewhere.[1] What interests us in this place is the theoretical shortcomings of property as a test of faculty in taxation.

These shortcomings may be summarized as follows: In the first place, a gap often discloses itself between property and product. It is indeed true that in the long run the value of a piece of property stands in a close relation to its yield. To use a modern phrase that has become familiar, capital is nothing but capitalized income. That is to say, what a piece of property will fetch in the market represents nothing but a capitalization of its present and prospective yield. While this is, however, true in the long run, it is not true in the short run. The value of a piece of property may bear only a slight relation, or no relation at all, to the yield of that property in any particular year, or even for a term of years. Two farmers may possess homesteads of equal value. The one may have bad luck and suffer drought or inundation, while the other may enjoy a bountiful harvest. With property as a test of faculty, the two farmers will pay the same, although the produce of their farms may differ enormously. Again, of two house owners desiring to rent their property, one may succeed and the other may fail for the year, or for a term of years. Although the unsuccessful owner has no income, he must, with property as the test of faculty, pay the

[1] See Seligman, *Essays in Taxation*, chap. ii.

same amount as the other. Instances might be multiplied, all tending to show that property and product may frequently diverge.

In the second place, a distinction is gradually observable between property incomes and labor incomes. In the early stages of the development, where property owners bear the greater part of the public burdens, the man who has no property either is reached by the poll tax, or is of such slight taxable capacity that he is entirely omitted. In modern times, however, with the growth of lucrative professions and with the great opportunities for rich salaried positions, labor incomes assume an importance which did not exist in earlier times. It may well be granted that the recipient of a modest salary should be put on a different plane from the individual who receives a like income from invested property; but that is a different thing from claiming that lawyers or doctors or engineers or railway presidents with salaries or professional earnings of from twenty-five to one hundred thousand dollars a year should not be called upon to contribute at all to the public charges. The acceptance of property as the sole test of ability to pay would result in a complete exemption of such classes, and would give rise to countless well-founded complaints.

In the third place, the recognition of property as the test of ability to pay raises a difficulty connected with indebtedness. There is a well-defined distinction between the legal and the economic conceptions of property. By property in the legal sense is meant the ownership of individuals in things or in rights to things, irrespective of the ulterior division of the produce of the property. By property in the economic sense — usually denominated wealth — is meant the control of the services of the thing possessed. If a part of the services or produce has to be handed over by the individual to some one else, it does not really form a part of his wealth. The owner of a ten-thousand-dollar farm who has mortgaged it for five thousand dollars possesses wealth, or property in the economic sense, to the extent of five thousand dollars. That wealth represents the amount that he is worth. His debts are a part not of his assets, but of his liabilities, and must be deducted from the assets in order to strike a correct balance sheet. Legally, however, — at all events under the modern law of mortgage — his property amounts to ten thousand dollars. If the government, as is usually the case, looks at the piece of property rather than at the individual condition of the property owner, it will assess the taxpayer on the full ten thousand dollars. In other words, in a property tax the expenses incurred in maintaining the property are ordinarily not considered.

This insistence upon the legal rather than the economic conception of property dates from the period when virtually all existing credit consisted of consumption credit rather than production credit and when indebtedness played a very small rôle in the social economy. In modern times, however, credit has become the very basis of business enterprise. Under these circumstances the problem of indebtedness assumes a new significance. It was but natural, therefore, that the property tax, where it still existed, should take some account of this new condition and should endeavor to make allowance for debts. But experience soon showed that this attempt was fraught with great practical difficulties. As we have seen in the United States, the creation of fictitious debts became such a paying investment that most of the states which introduced the system were compelled again to abolish it. As a consequence, some states today deduct mortgage debts from real estate; others deduct general indebtedness from personal estate; a few permit deduction for indebtedness in general; while most of the states allow either for no deduction at all, or for deduction in only personal or real estate. Such a situation is bound to be unsatisfactory.

In the fourth place, property as a test of faculty fails to draw the correct distinction between the constituent elements of wealth. In former times, when property was scanty and almost entirely used for productive purposes, the situation was simple. But in modern times a sharp line must be drawn between consumption property and productive capital, between property utilized primarily for purposes of enjoyment and property utilized for the securing of a money income. Take as an example of the first case a private library or art gallery or park which, instead of being the source of a money income, is really the occasion of a distinct expenditure. To put such things on the same footing as property which yields a money income is, to say the least, a procedure open to grave doubt. To tax property as a unit, irrespective of the kind of property or the income from the property or the outlay connected with the property, becomes in modern times a source of increasing embarrassment.

Finally, in the fifth place, the history of the general property tax has everywhere shown that there seem to be insuperable difficulties in reaching the multifold forms of wealth in a developed industrial society. It is everywhere conceded that universality of taxation is one of the leading fiscal principles; yet the growing difficulties of reaching all the different forms of property inevitably lead to the escape of some and to the over-assessment of others. The theory of the general property tax originally rested on the assumption that fiscal equality could be reached by taxing all individuals on their visible property. When the mass of property split up, and the myriad forms of modern intangible personalty disclosed themselves, the basis of the theory was undermined by the new conditions, and instead of equal and universal taxation there was now developed a system of partial and unequal taxation.

If we keep in mind these five different kinds of complication, we shall be able to comprehend how it was that slowly but surely property came to be regarded as a less and less satisfactory form of taxation, and we shall not be surprised to learn that it was gradually replaced by other tests of ability to pay.

§ 3. *Expenditure and Product as Tests of Faculty*

The next step in the development was the selection of expenditure as the criterion of faculty. Expenditure was first advanced as the best test of ability to pay toward the close of the Middle Ages. The great tax reformers of the sixteenth and seventeenth centuries, like Bodin, Hobbes and Petty, were influenced chiefly by the last argument. The general property tax had everywhere become a mere travesty of justice, and the system was honeycombed by abuses which seemed to be entirely ineradicable. To attain a system of taxation which no one could escape became the watchword of the tax reformers. Since every man, rich or poor, necessarily incurs expenditures, a system of taxes on expenditure was now advocated. This took the form of both direct and indirect taxes on consumption, as well as of taxes on trade and business which were supposed ultimately to reach the consumer. Indirect taxes on trade and commerce had indeed arisen, at a comparatively early period, as a development out of the mediæval system of fees and tolls. But now, in the sixteenth, seventeenth and eighteenth centuries, every European country witnessed the growth of a system of excises or expenditure taxes, which grew in importance as the old general property tax dwindled. The general excise or the single excise became the ideal of the publicists, and was in a fair way of being realized in practice.

While, however, consumption taxes succeeded in avoiding some of the worst abuses of the general property tax, it was not long before this system in turn disclosed difficulties in its operation. If the rich man stood from under in the general property tax, it was largely because the rich man's property could not be reached. With the development of expenditure as the test of faculty, however, it was inevitable that the rich man should again escape his share, because of the disparity between expenditure and revenue in the different social classes. The lower we go in the economic scale, the greater is the lack of equilibrium between revenue and expenditure. At the bottom of the scale are those whose incomes only barely suffice for their living, while at the top of the scale are those whose expenditures, no matter how large, are but a fraction of their revenue. In the one case there is absolutely no surplus available; in the other the surplus is many times greater than the expenditure. Necessarily, under such a system, a tax on expenditure becomes an increasingly heavy burden on the least wealthy classes. It is for this reason that we can explain the comparatively slight resistance to the adoption of the excise system throughout Europe at a time when political life was still controlled by the aristocracy of land or of moneyed capital. But it is evident that with the growth of democracy in more recent times a system of taxation which inevitably results in undue burdens on the less fortunate members of society was destined to become unpopular and to pass away. Expenditure becomes an unsatisfactory test of ability to pay, not only because it puts a premium on the penurious rich man, but because it imposes a crushing burden upon the average poor man. One of the first efforts of the French Revolution was to abolish not only the remains of the *taille*, or general property tax, but also the whole existing system of taxes on consumption; and the history of the nineteenth century in every progressive country has been the history of the attempt to reduce the burden of the excise taxes so far as they are still liable to the objections mentioned above. As a consequence, expenditure has been virtually abandoned as the sole test of faculty.

The next stage in the development is represented by the adoption of product or produce as the norm of taxation. We have learned of the shortcomings of property as the test of justice, and we have seen that the adoption of expenditure in lieu of property was supposed to meet the objections of lack of universality. With the failure of this system, however, tax reformers and progressive governments reverted to some of the other defects of the property tax, such as the discrepancy between the value and the yield of the property, and the inequality of the tax due to the escape of the property owner. It was reasoned — and with considerable force — that if recourse were taken to the produce of the property rather than to the property itself, several results would be achieved. In the first place, a man would be taxed only upon what he actually received, and the hardships of payment without revenue would at once be avoided; while secondly, and still more important, the tax, instead of being assessed on the whole of the property, and thus being subject to the abuses either of inquisitorial assessment or of illegitimate evasion, would be levied directly on the produce of the thing itself, which yielded a return. Property would be split up into its constituent elements, and the tax would be levied on the yield of each. Thus the tax would be levied on the produce of a piece of land, irrespective of who owned the land; the yield of the land was to be ascertained by a careful process, and if the taxes were not paid by some one, the land would be sold. In the same way as the rental of a dwelling was easily ascertainable, the house tax was now imposed upon the dwellings when they were actually rented, and only then, and if the tax were not paid by some one, the house was sold. So a business was conceived of as an entity, the product of which was to be measured by outward signs, such as the location of the business, the number of the clerks, etc., and the tax was imposed upon the business itself. A similar method was pursued with the other forms of property.

Thus there developed during the seventeenth, the eighteenth and the first half of the nineteenth century, a system of taxes on things rather than on persons, or a system of taxes on the product of the property rather than on the person of the property owner. This is the system which became known in France under the name of real taxes (*taxes réelles*) as opposed to the old personal taxes (*taxes personnelles*), and which was termed in Germany *Ertragssteuern* as opposed to the old *Vermögenssteuern*. In France it was the work of the Revolution which created a system of real taxes; in Germany and the other continental countries the movement had begun earlier and was completed somewhat later. In England, also, the same system developed, being composed, at the end of the eighteenth century, of the land tax — the last survivor of the mediæval general property tax, — the house tax, and the assessed taxes.

The adoption of product or produce as a test of faculty indeed marked a decided step forward. But as time went on, and especially after the industrial revolution, the shortcomings in the theory disclosed themselves. The very excellence of the idea of regarding only the thing rather than the person now itself gradually became a weakness. For, after all, taxes are paid by human beings and not by inanimate things. A piece of property may be assessed to taxation, but the tax must be paid out of the pocketbook or bank account — that is out of the revenue — of some person. Since, under the system of private ownership, every piece of property belongs ultimately to an individual, to tax the yield of a piece of property really means finally to tax the revenue of an individual. As soon, however, as we regard the relative condition of individuals, it becomes apparent that a system of taxes on product is painfully defective. Two adjoining pieces of property, for instance, may enjoy precisely the same yield; yet in the one case the yield may be due exclusively to the bounty of nature, and in the other case it may be the result, in large part, of the supplementary efforts of the owner. Allowance may indeed be made for this state of affairs by distinguishing the net from the gross produce, and by levying the tax on the former. Primitive land taxes, for instance, like the tithes of old, were taxes on gross produce; whereas the more approved modern form of product taxation is a tax on net produce; that is, making allowance for the expenses of cultivation. But this, although an undeniable step in advance, is not sufficient; for a system even of net produce taxes does not take account of the indebtedness of the individual. The net produce of two farmers, after allowing for the expenses of cultivation, may be precisely the same; but if the owner of one farm has purchased it on a mortgage, his final net earnings will be less than that of his neighbor. The net produce of a piece of property, in other words, is no necessary indication of the net revenue of the owner. The tax upon the thing, just because it is upon the thing, does not lend itself readily to the shifting conditions of the man who owns the thing; and yet the real ability of a person to pay taxes must be in some relation to his individual condition. Moreover, the immense increase in modern wealth and the appearance of prodigious fortunes have contributed to bring into prominence the idea of graduated taxation. Manifestly, however, a system of real taxes or taxes on product does not lend itself to the progressive principle. The larger piece of land may be owned by the poorer man, and the great wealth of the rich man may consist of a number of relatively small separate pieces of property. A system of taxation which in its very nature does not admit of progression evidently could not permanently respond to the necessities of the situation. With the revolution in the conception of faculty, the tax on product or on things thus came to be continually more unsatisfactory. Just as the gross produce system gave way to the net produce system, so now the net produce system in its turn was bound to disappear.

§ 4. *Income as the Test of Faculty*

It was thus that the fifth and final stage was reached, and that income was selected as the test of faculty in taxation. And there is no doubt that, taking it by and large, this responds more accurately to modern demands than any of the preceding tests. Accordingly, for a time, it seemed as if the new test would supplant all the other criteria, and as if all direct taxes at least would be abolished, to be replaced by a single income tax. Here again, however, more careful study disclosed certain weaknesses and disadvantages in income as the sole test of ability to pay. What are these weaknesses?

In the first place there is the difficulty of deciding with accuracy what income really means. Do we mean by income gross or net income; and, if the latter, do we include in the term everything that comes in within a definite period, or should gifts, inheritances, and speculative revenues be excluded? Furthermore, do we mean by income only money income, or also the equivalent of money income? These points will be discussed below. Even assuming, however, that a satisfactory conclusion has been reached on this matter, the next difficulty arises from the fact that all incomes do not afford equally good criteria of a man's ability to pay. Is an income of one thousand dollars derived from hard personal work to be put exactly on a par with an income of one thousand dollars derived from an inheritance, or from a lucky turn in the market? The further question arises as to whether different amounts of income present identically the same criteria of ability to pay. Is the one thousand dollars which forms the entire income of a day laborer to be treated in the same way as the fifty-thousand-dollar income of a millionnaire? Manifestly, the identical rate on all kinds and amounts of income does not constitute an ideal criterion of tax-paying ability. But still further, even if we assume that these difficulties are in some way disposed of, let us compare the two following cases: A is a bachelor, in good health, with no dependent relatives, residing in a small town where the scale of life is simple, and so little interested in charity or public affairs that he lays by a considerable amount every year. B is the recipient of precisely the same amount of income, but is a married man, with a large family; he lives in a great city with its multitudinous social demands; he is in poor health and must spend considerable sums on physicians and medicines; he has relatives dependent upon him; and he is such a model citizen that he gives largely to charities and to public purposes. Can it be said that these two men, with precisely the same income, have precisely the same ability to pay? Finally, let us take the case of two men, one of whom has invested a large sum in business or in securities which yield a definite annual revenue, while the other has invested the same amount for speculative purposes in a piece of real estate which remains unimproved and therefore unrented; or in a railway stock which happens that year to pay no dividends. Can it be said that the latter has no ability to pay at all, as compared with the former, because he receives no income?

These are but a few of the perplexing problems that confront us as soon as we make the claim that income is a perfectly satisfactory or ideal test of faculty. As a matter of fact, while income is in many respects a better test than any of the preceding criteria that have been mentioned, it is not a thoroughly adequate test, for the simple reason that no single test of ability can be found which will adjust itself to the varying needs of individuals.

It is for this reason that the early enthusiasm for the single income tax, even in theory, gradually died away, and it was realized, to an ever increasing extent, that income must be supplemented by the other tests of faculty in order to form a well-rounded whole. No modern tax system, accordingly, relies entirely upon an income tax, even as the sole direct tax. Each of the preceding tests, while unsatisfactory in itself, nevertheless possesses some advantages which can be utilized in framing a system of taxation; property, product, expenditure, nay, even polls — each in turn can be employed as a partial test of faculty in order to fill out certain gaps. For instance, property may be utilized as a partial test in the case of wealth held for enjoyment, rather than for gain; in the case of property invested for speculative purposes; in the case of property where, notwithstanding the temporary cessation of product, the money value is by no means negligible; in the case of a desire to tax property incomes at a higher rate than labor incomes; and, finally, in the case of great fiscal exigencies where it is necessary to take a part of the property itself, rather than simply its income. A tax on product may be essential where a personal tax on the individual would be impracticable. A tax on expenditure is sometimes desirable either where the income cannot be ascertained or where, because of the temporary character of the individual's sojourn, a property or income tax could not well be enforced. To assert, therefore, as is often done by superficial thinkers, that the income tax is the fairest of all taxes, is to maintain an untenable position. Purely as a matter of theory, even, an income tax is by no means always the fairest of all taxes. The most that can be said with accuracy is that, in the main, so far as direct taxes are concerned, the system of taxation ought to be so framed as to correspond roughly with the income of the various classes of taxpayers. But to say that the ideal can be reached by any single income tax is preposterous. While the system of taxation should endeavor, roughly at all events, to adjust itself to income in general, the income tax as such can form only a part, even though it may be a permanent part, of the system, the other elements of which must be based upon the remaining criteria of faculty in order to reach as close an approximation to justice as may be possible.

Finally, we are confronted by the question of the practical working of the income tax. Even if the income tax were the fairest of all taxes, — which, as we have seen, is not necessarily true, — the decision as to whether it ought to be utilized would depend largely upon whether this fairness, which is predicated of it in the abstract, would ensue in actual practice. It is notorious, however, that of all taxes the income tax is perhaps the most difficult to assess with scrupulous justice and accuracy; so that what is conceived in justice often results in crass injustice. If, therefore, we add these great practical defects to what are undeniable theoretical shortcomings, we are forced to the conclusion that the income tax is by no means the panacea which it has often been represented to be.

With all these reservations, however, there is no doubt that in the struggle for social and fiscal justice the income tax is assuming a continually more prominent part, and if we do not pitch our expectations too high, we can understand why this should be so. Under certain conditions the efficiency of the income-tax administration may gradually be improved, and under most conditions the addition to the tax system of the right kind of an income tax constitutes an undoubted step in advance. To ascertain what these conditions are, and what constitutes the right kind of an income tax, is therefore a study eminently necessary.

§ 5. *The Meaning of Income*

At the outset of such a study it is desirable to secure a clear idea of what is meant by income. Income is, of course, to be distinguished from mere receipts or gross revenue. It is more than that which simply comes in from any economic activity. By income is always meant net income, as opposed to gross income: In other words, from the receipts in any enterprise we must, in the first place, deduct the expenses of the enterprise — that is, the outlay incurred in securing the gross product. But, secondly, income as a personal category differs from net product. If a debt has been contracted in order to secure the produce of a given piece of property or of a given enterprise, the interest on the debt must be deducted. Finally, in the outlays or expenses which have been incurred to secure the product, there must also be included a compensation for wear and tear of plant; just as the investor in securities computes his actual income by deducting an amortization quota from the annual proceeds. Income, therefore, always means net income.

What has been stated is equivalent to saying that income is that which comes in to an individual above all necessary expenses of acquisition, and which is available for his own consumption. Since the income is a flow of wealth, it must always be estimated for a definite period, so that when we speak of income for purposes of taxation, we really mean annual income. Strictly speaking, income as contrasted with capital denotes that amount of wealth which flows in during a definite period and which is at the disposal of the owner for purposes of consumption, so that in consuming it, his capital remains unimpaired. The problem, however, of defining income with such precision as completely to avoid any net impairment of capital is one that almost baffles the student; and certainly no such precision can be attained for purposes of taxation.[1] Again, just as, on the one hand, income does

[1] Professor Irving Fisher, in *The Nature of Capital and Income*, New York, 1906, attempts to give a precise analysis of income; but he concedes that for purposes of taxation his scheme, while ideal in theory, would be difficult to carry out in practice. See pp. 400–403. *Cf. infra*, pp. 679–680, note.

not comprise those elements which constitute an impairment of capital, so, on the other hand, income ought not to be conceived as including those merely temporary elements which constitute an addition to capital. In a certain sense, if I receive a large gift or an unexpected inheritance, these are a part of my revenue for the year; but, strictly speaking, as they are not expected to recur, they ought to be regarded rather as additions to capital than constituent elements of income. It is for this reason that some writers desire to add to the very conception of income the idea of regularity, that is, the inflow of wealth from a more or less regular source. That this conception is not free from difficulty is undeniable; speculative gains, for instance, might be exceedingly difficult to assign with precision. The difficulty, however, is largely removed by the fact that, for purposes of taxation at least, where income is confined to the revenue from regular sources, an attempt is generally made to reach the irregular additions in other ways.

A further difficulty arises as to whether income is to include only money income, or whether it also comprises the so-called enjoyable or psychic income, that is, the pleasurable sensation or usufruct that flows in to the individual in the shape not of money, but of money's worth. That some psychic income ought to be included, goes indeed without saying. Of two house owners the one may occupy his own residence, while the other may let his out and reside with a friend. Shall the latter be taxed on the house rent and the former be exempt, simply because one receives the benefit in the shape of money, and the other in money's worth? Yet, to carry out the principle of the inclusion of psychic income in all cases would be to enunciate a principle which would be useless for fiscal purposes. Not only would there be no way of comparing the psychic income of one individual with that of his neighbor, but there is no known method of ascertaining how much psychic income any one secures. It may therefore be said that income, at least for purposes of taxation, signifies in general money income, with an occasional inclusion of such psychic income as is notorious and easily calculable.

Finally, the question arises whether the conception of net income which we have reached is adequate for fiscal purposes, and whether there ought not to be substituted for it the conception of clear income; that is, the income which remains to the individual for his own enjoyment, after deducting the charges which rest upon that income and which prevent him from disposing of the income for his own regular and individual purposes. Manifestly, such a conception of clear income cannot be accepted in its entirety; for it would practically mean that a man should be permitted to deduct from his net income all the expenses which he might deem necessary, the result being, in most cases, no income at all for revenue purposes. To a certain extent, however, as we shall see, allowance is actually made for this point of view by all modern governments, in that abatements are granted for children or other dependents, and so far as further allowances are accorded for exceptional expenditures. The conception of income which is to be utilized for fiscal purposes, therefore, is one which goes a little beyond that of net income, and which partially approximates to the character of clear income.

The conception of income which has thus been reached is one which suffers, however, two further modifications. Before the income of the individual can serve even as a half-way satisfactory test of his ability to pay, a distinction must be made between incomes as regards both their nature and their amount. The two chief principles of justice in taxation are generally regarded to be those of uniformity and of universality. Yet the endeavor to distinguish incomes in regard to their nature as well as to their amount seems to involve a departure from these two principles. The distinction between incomes with reference to their nature is commonly termed the differentiation of incomes; the distinction between incomes with reference to their amount is commonly called the graduation of incomes. In what respect, then, do differentiation and graduation really infringe upon the principles of uniformity and universality? Let us consider first the question of differentiation.

§ 6. *The Differentiation of Taxation*

Uniformity of taxation is tantamount to equality of taxation. That taxes should be uniform implies that there should be an equality in the burdens of individuals. By this, however, cannot of course be meant absolute numerical equality. Such equality would result in a poll tax, and we have seen why a poll tax becomes unjust after property itself develops. Uniformity, therefore, means relative uniformity, or relatively proportional equality. But this in itself does not solve any problem. For the question at once arises, "relative to what" or "proportional to what?" We might take some perfectly absurd criterion, like red hair, let us say, and decree that taxes should be levied only on red-haired men, and in proportion to the redness of their hair. Manifestly, this is not the kind of relative uniformity that is implied in the term. The only equality, therefore, which can possibly be intended is that which has reference to the principle that ought to govern the fiscal relations of the individual to the government. This principle, as we have seen, is that of faculty or ability to pay, and we are thus at once led back to the problem of ascertaining the correct criterion or test of this ability to pay. We have learned, however, that income as such, regarded as an absolute quantity, is not a theoretically correct criterion of faculty, and that it is necessary at all events to make a distinction between different kinds of income, since the same amount of income derived from different sources often connotes a varying degree of ability to pay. We are therefore logically forced to the conclusion that the relative equality, or the uniformity which is demanded by justice, is not only compatible with, but in reality leads to, the principle of discrimination. The only question that remains is to ascertain how far this principle of discrimination is to be carried, and where we reach the point when discrimination involves a real breach with the principles of relative uniformity.

The American courts, in interpreting the term "uniformity" as found in the state constitutional provisions affecting taxation, have decided that uniformity does not require exactly identical treatment of the different kinds of property or business subject to taxation. A reasonable classification is almost universally held to be legitimate; and a classification may, of course, involve a discrimination between the different classes. Now all that is meant by the principle of discrimination, as applied to the income tax, is that different classes of income may be treated differently. What are these classes? The distinction that has become most familiar in recent times is that between earned and unearned incomes. This distinction is based on the principle that the income is derived in the one case primarily from personal exertion, and in the other case without personal exertion. All manner of terms have been applied to this distinction. Thus temporary incomes are contrasted with permanent, labor with property incomes, spontaneous with fixed incomes, precarious with realized incomes, and even, to use Gladstone's celebrated phrase, "industrious" with "lazy" incomes. To draw a sharp line between such incomes is indeed difficult, because in incomes nominally derived from property there may be all degrees of coöperation on the part of the owner, — the strenuous exertion that may be needed to have the property yield any income at all, the more or less active superintendence of the proprietor, the exercise of only a little care in the choice of investment, or absolutely no effort at all on the part of the owner. In the great mass of business incomes where large capital is invested, the revenues undoubtedly partake in some cases almost equally of both characteristics.

Notwithstanding the difficulty, however, of drawing any hard and fast line, the distinction may undoubtedly be discerned at either end. Especially in modern times, with the immense growth of private fortunes, it has come everywhere almost instinctively to be recognized that an income derived solely from an individual's own strenuous personal exertions ought not to be treated in the same way as the income which comes, let us say, from government bonds or from the securities of a corporation in the management of which the bondholder or stockholder actually takes no part at all.

The principle of discrimination rests ultimately upon the doctrine of equality of sacrifice, but interpreted in a somewhat different way from that which has been made familiar by John Stuart Mill. The sacrifice of which he spoke is the sacrifice imposed upon the individual in parting with the amount of the tax, as compared with the residue of income that is left for purposes of enjoyment. On the other hand, the sacrifice which emerges when we are dealing with the problem of discrimination is the sacrifice involved, not with reference to the expenditure of the income, but with reference to the creation of the income. The one might be called, if we are willing to coin such phrases, a consumptional sacrifice; the other, a productional sacrifice. The sacrifice involved in earning a given amount of income is a very different thing from the sacrifice involved in receiving an equivalent amount of unearned income.

How far the principle of discrimination should be carried is, of course, a moot question. Most countries have been content with its application in a very moderate way to labor and to property incomes. In a few countries, like Italy, the distinction is carried somewhat farther, so as to classify incomes into temporary, permanent, and mixed incomes. There seems to be no reason to doubt that with the progress of time a more refined method of discrimination will be attained, and that the classes will be made more numerous.

When we leave the question of the kind of discrimination, and approach that of the amount of discrimination, we of course enter upon a field where the use of a principle may degenerate into its abuse. As soon as we depart from the doctrine of absolute numerical equality and adopt that of relative equality, the door is naturally opened to misapplications of the relation. It might, for instance, conceivably result in the complete exemption of all labor incomes, and place such a high rate upon incomes derived from property of a certain class, as virtually to confiscate that kind of property. This is, however, a danger against which we can hope to guard by a reasonable public sentiment and by the common sense of the community or, in countries where written constitutions exist, by an appeal to the underlying idea of a rational equality. If absolute uniformity is, as we have seen, really a derogation from justice, it is no objection to the introduction of a relative uniformity that the relativity may be abused. Thus far no attempt has ever been made to abuse this relativity so far as discrimination in the nature of the income is concerned. If the problem ever arises, it will be time to deal with it on the general grounds of fiscal justice and actual taxable capacity.

§ 7. *Exemption from Taxation*

The other phase of deviation from an exactly identical treatment of incomes has reference not to the nature but to the amount of the income. This problem assumes two forms, either that of the complete exemption of all incomes up to a certain point, with the same treatment of all above that point; or, on the other hand, that of a varying treatment of incomes according to their magnitude, irrespective of the amount of exemption. Naturally, also, there may be various combinations of these two plans. Fundamentally, however, the problems involved are first, that of exemption, and second, that of graduation.

The question of exemption from taxation is indeed not confined to the income tax, nor is it a modern problem. At all times and in all ages we have had examples of departure from the principle of universality of taxation. In the later Roman Empire, for instance, where the burden of local charges — the so-called *munera* — had become crushing, all kinds of more or less illegitimate privileges were granted to individuals, until exemption from taxation — *immunitas*, or freedom from the particular *munus* — became the common term for exemption in general, and has been preserved in our modern word "immunity." In the Middle Ages it is well known that the privileged classes, like the nobles, the clergy and the lawyers, secured such immunities for themselves, and that especially in France exemptions could virtually be purchased by any one who was powerful enough to do so. It is no wonder that exemption from taxation should have come into such disrepute. As we have seen above, it was the principle of universality of taxation, with the practical corollary of the general excise, that was invoked by the tax reformers of the seventeenth and eighteenth centuries to stem these enormous abuses.

In modern times, however, exemptions from taxation are of an entirely different character. The mediæval exemptions were an inversion of the principle of faculty; for those who were most able to pay were exempt, and those who were least able to pay were crushed beneath the burden. The modern principle of exemption, on the other hand, is based upon the doctrine of faculty, and is designed to lighten the burden of those who are least able to pay. Thus, from the very beginning in America, certain small amounts of property, as well as property of certain kinds, like mechanics' tools and growing crops, have been exempt from the general property tax, as was the case also in the later property taxes of the democratic communes of mediæval Europe. To these exemptions, based upon the principle that the property owners are not in a position to pay, have been added in modern times, exemptions of charitable, educational and scientific institutions, and the like, which rest on the principle that inasmuch as they fulfil a quasi-public function, they ought not to be compelled to make additional contributions to the public revenues. An interesting variation of the latter category is the exemption of church property, — a question on both sides of which much might be said but which is not pertinent here.

The modern problem of exemption, however, is of far more importance in income taxation than it is in property taxation, because in the case of the property tax the great mass of people whose earnings are entirely derived from their own exertions are *ipso facto* exempt. As they have no property, but only an income, they are not subject to the property tax. Where, however, the income tax is introduced as the chief element, or as an important part, of the tax system, the problem becomes acute, especially so far as concerns the exemption of the minimum of subsistence; that is, the exemption of an income which is deemed to be equivalent to that needed to support a family on the very lowest scale of decent subsistence.

The argument against the minimum of subsistence,[1] as it has been elaborated, especially by Professor Gustav Cohn,[2] is both economic and political in its nature. The economic argument is to the effect that from a correct point of view the expenditures for the support of government must be considered as much a part of the necessary outlays of the individual as any other kind of expense. This, it is claimed, is the only tenable ground for interpreting the relations of the individual to the state. The political argument, again, is to the effect that the exemption of a considerable class of individuals is especially dangerous in a democracy with universal suffrage; for if every one has a voice in voting how much money shall be spent and how the expenditure shall be made, and if, on the other hand, only a small class of voters contribute to the expenditures, there is grave danger of abuse and extravagance.

In answer to those objections it may be stated, first, that it is futile to speak of taxes as part of the necessary expen-

[1] For special books devoted to this purpose, see H. Schmidt, *Die Steuerfreiheit des Existenzminimums. Ein Beitrag zur Theorie der Einkommensteuern.* Leipzig, 1877; and F. Sardeman, *Das steuerfreie Existenzminimum als Beneficium Competentiae und Armutsprophylaxe.* Leipzig, 1905.

[2] *System der Finanzwissenschaft*, § 220. Stuttgart, 1889. English translation by Veblen, *The Science of Finance.* Chicago, 1895, pp. 327–330.

ditures of the individual. If wages are sufficient only for a bare minimum of subsistence, then to encroach upon this minimum by taxation is to require the minimum to be maintained in some other way. If the laborer can no longer live on his wages, he must be supported by a system of poor relief, if he is to live at all. It is difficult, therefore, to see the great advantage of taking away the money with one hand and returning it with the other. If, on the other hand, wages are, although higher than the bare minimum of subsistence, still only sufficient to maintain the laborer and his family at the customary standard of life in the particular country, the imposition of a tax upon this amount of income must necessarily lead to a lowering of the standard of life. Such an eventuality also cannot be contemplated by a modern democracy, one of whose chief concerns is to maintain and even to raise the standard of life of the mass of its citizens.

The political argument, on the other hand, has a slight degree of strength. It must, however, be remembered that it would apply at best only where the income tax is the sole source of revenue. Where, as is everywhere the case, we have other forms of taxation, resting directly or indirectly upon the less fortunate classes of the community, either exclusively or in common with the remainder of the citizens, the argument is shorn of much of its force. Even in the case of the single income tax, however, the difficulty can be overcome by putting the control of the expenditures in the hands of officials who have a certain independence in considering the best interests of the community. In the United States, for instance, where the great mass of the citizens — namely, those living on daily wages — are entirely exempt from the general property tax, we have seen but few illustrations of the dangers alluded to above. And even where such dangers have disclosed themselves, they are being averted by reforms undertaken, as in New York City, by the Board of Estimate and Apportionment, which occupies a largely independent position.

It may be said, therefore, that neither the economic nor the political argument against exemption of the minimum of subsistence is valid; while the unanswerable argument in favor of the principle is that those particular taxpayers for whom the exemption is claimed are unable to pay an income tax and at the same time to maintain themselves and their families at a decent standard of life.

What the particular figure should be at which the minimum is fixed will, of course, vary from country to country. In places where money wages are small and where the standard of life is low, a very slight minimum will suffice. In countries where wages are large, and where the laborers are accustomed to participate in the general progress of society, the minimum will naturally be much higher. With the development of the democratic idea, moreover, it may be said that the limit of exemption is apt to be raised to a continually higher figure. That the principle of exemption, like that of differentiation, is susceptible of abuse, is undoubted. There is always danger that the limit will be set too high, so as to involve unjustifiable exemptions, or that it may be made to serve sectional prejudices. The exemption of four thousand dollars in the United States income tax of 1894 comes perilously near this line, if it does not actually overstep it. But here, again, as in the case of differentiation, it must be said that we should not object to a principle because of the danger of abuse. If the principle is right, we must support it, although at the same time we must, of course, do everything in our power to give it a rational interpretation.

§ 8. *Graduation of Taxation*

The remaining form of differential treatment of incomes according to their amount is that of graduation, namely, the affixing of a different rate of taxation to different amounts of income. As this whole subject has been treated by the present writer in a separate volume,[1] it will be passed over here

[1] Seligman, *Progressive Taxation in Theory and Practice.* 2d ed., New York, 1908.

with a mere summary of the results reached in that investigation.

Graduated taxation may be of several kinds. If a tax is graduated in lieu of being proportional, the graduation may be either upward or downward. Proportional taxation in the ordinarily accepted signification means the same rate on all quantities of the thing taxed; graduated taxation may mean that the rate either decreases or increases as the amount of property or income increases. When the rate increases with the amount of the income, for instance, we have progressive taxation. When the rate decreases as the income increases, we have regressive taxation. Finally, the tax rate may increase up to a certain amount, but remain constant beyond that fixed rate. There may be progression up to a definite limit, and proportion thereafter. This is called degressive taxation. The proportional rate is here regarded as the normal one, but on all sums counted downward below this limit the tax rate gradually diminishes. Thus graduated taxation includes progressive, regressive, and degressive taxation. Practically, however, we do not find in modern times any form of regressive income taxation. All graduated income taxes are therefore either progressive or degressive. Whether we call the tax progressive or degressive depends entirely upon the point from which we count the graduation, for even in progressive taxes the progression everywhere stops at a certain limit. The precise point at which graduation commences is somewhat arbitrary. What one person would call degressive another person would call progressive taxation. Ordinarily, however, the term degressive taxation is confined to the case where the normal rate of the income tax is low, — say three or four or five per cent, — while the term progressive taxation is applied where the normal rates are considerably higher.

While many untenable claims have been presented in favor of a progressive income tax, the two chief arguments on which it may be upheld are the special compensatory and the faculty theories. The special compensatory theory, as has been pointed out,[1] applies only to an income tax which is part of a revenue system the other features of which happen to put a specifically greater burden upon the poorer classes. Thus, where there chance to exist certain indirect taxes the incidence of which is primarily upon the less fortunate classes, a progressive income tax may be defended, on the ground of its tendency to redress the inequality. This, as we shall learn, is the great argument at present advanced in France. As has been elsewhere explained, however, there are certain embarrassments connected with this theory arising from the fact that it is difficult to prove how the conceded inequality of a progressive income tax will exactly fit into, and counterbalance, the conceded inequality of the particular indirect tax. So far, however, as the circumstances warrant such a precise conclusion, the special compensatory theory is relatively defensible.

Where, however, this argument cannot be used, — and in many countries its application would be difficult, — its place can be taken by the faculty theory. The older defence of progressive taxation rested solely upon the equal sacrifice theory, in the sense of considerations connected with outlay or consumption. The attempt was made to prove that the sacrifice occasioned by the abandonment for purposes of taxation of one hundred dollars out of an income of one thousand dollars is very different from the sacrifice involved in giving up ten thousand dollars out of an income of one hundred thousand dollars. This was put on the ground that in the one case we are trenching upon necessities, and in the other we are only cutting into luxuries. The difficulty with this argument as affording a definite scale is the impossibility of measuring the precise amount of individual sacrifice in such a manner as to achieve a mathematical equality of rate. Mathematics cannot help us here because the very first conditions fail us, the power to gauge with accuracy the mathematical relations of marginal utilities. Psychological relations of such a kind cannot be reduced to exact quantita-

[1] Seligman, *Progressive Taxation*, pp. 143–149.

tive forms. The equal-sacrifice or consumption theory therefore does not lead to any definite rate of progressive taxation.

On the other hand, the conception of faculty includes more than the idea of consumption. It comprises also elements connected with acquisition or production. Modern experience especially has made it quite evident that the possession of large fortunes or incomes in itself affords the individual a decided advantage in augmenting his possessions. A rich man may be said to be subject in a certain sense to the law of increasing returns; the more he has, the easier it is for him to acquire still more. From the point of view of production, incomes may be said to differ in amount, just as we have already seen that they differ in nature. Hence, from the point of view of production, faculty may be said to increase more rapidly than fortune or income, and this element of taxable capacity would not illogically result in a more than proportionate rate of taxation.

While the sacrifice theory in itself, as we have seen, is not sufficiently cogent to lead to the demand for any definite schedule of progression, its influence in the other direction is surely not strong enough to outweigh the productive elements of faculty, which seem to imply progressive taxation. For, as we have fully explained elsewhere, the sacrifice theory or consumption element in faculty cannot be used as an argument inevitably leading to proportional taxation. If it does not necessarily lead to any definite scale of progression, much less can it necessarily lead to a fixed proportion. If we can never reach an ideal, there is no good reason, however, why we should not strive to get as close to it as possible. Equality of sacrifice, indeed, we can never attain absolutely or exactly, because of the diversity of individual wants and desires; but it is nevertheless probable that in the majority of normal and typical cases we shall be approaching more closely to the desired equality by some departure from proportional taxation. If we take a general view and treat of the average man, — and the government can deal only with classes, that is, with average men, — it seems probable that on the whole less injustice will be done by adopting some form of progression than by following the universal rule of proportion. A strictly proportional rate will make no allowance for the exemption of the minimum of subsistence. It will be a heavier burden on the typical average poor man than on the typical average rich man. It will be apt to be felt with relatively more severity by the average man who has only a small surplus above socially necessary expenses, than by the average man who has a proportionately larger surplus. It will, in short, be likely in normal cases disproportionately to curtail the enjoyment of different social classes.

Hence, if we base our doctrine of the equities of taxation on the theory of faculty, both the production and the consumption sides of the theory seem to point to progressive taxation as at all events neither more illogical nor more unjust than proportional taxation. Further than that, however, we cannot go. While the usual arguments advanced against progressive taxation are almost entirely destitute of foundation,[1] it is not a simple matter to decide how far or in what manner the principle of progression ought to be actually carried out in practice. Theory itself cannot determine any definite scale of progression whatever, and while it is highly probable that the ends of justice will be more nearly subserved by some approximation to a progressive scale, considerations of expediency, as well as the uncertainty of the interrelations between various parts of the entire tax system, should tend to render us cautious in advocating any general application, and still more cautious in proposing any radical application, of the principle. We shall see that while the principle has now been substantially accepted by most modern governments, it assumes in most countries, to a large extent, the form of taxation applied through a system of abatements, and that it is almost everywhere limited in practice by considerations of administrative expediency resting upon the particular form assumed by the income tax.

[1] Seligman, *op. cit.*, pp. 294–299.

So far, however, as the principle is concerned, we must conclude not only that graduation is valid in theory, but that it is now almost everywhere accepted as not repugnant to the doctrine of uniformity. In the United States especially, where the earlier decisions rendered under the domination of a bygone economic theory took an antagonistic attitude, a moderate graduation of taxation is now held to be no less compatible with the uniformity provisions of our constitution than is the practice of differentiation. The uniformity, in short, which modern legislation and modern economics demand is a uniformity based upon relatively proportional equality.

This, therefore, brings us to the last of the fundamental questions—the question of the kind of income tax toward which modern countries are tending; for upon the answer to this question depends not only the solution of the problem of graduation, but also the decision as to the actual success of an income tax itself.

§ 9. *The Three Types of Income Tax*

When we come to consider the various types of income taxation, we shall find that they may be reduced to three categories. The first may be called the presumptive income tax. This may be explained as follows.

It is notorious that the ascertainment of individual income is exceedingly difficult. If the attempt to reach the income of the individual rests upon the declaration of the taxpayer himself, we are putting upon him a strain which, in the present state of the relations of the individual to the government, may be characterized as exceedingly severe. It presumes a condition of integrity, a readiness to support one's share, and a complete absence of any desire to benefit oneself at the expense of one's neighbor, which is unfortunately still too rare at the present time. The place that smuggling or undervaluation takes in the customs duties is represented by the evasion and fraud which are almost inseparable concomitants of an income tax; and the difficulty is far greater in the income tax, because in the case of customs duties the officials usually have an opportunity, except in the case of crass smuggling, to inspect the property on which the tax is imposed. In the case of an income tax, however, the officials are dealing with something entirely intangible; and even where the income is derived from visible property, this property may be entirely beyond the ken of the assessor. If, therefore, the declaration of the individual is sought to be controlled by official action, officials inevitably find considerable difficulty in reaching a conclusion as to the exact amount of income. If they are lenient, the results are apt to be a farce; if they are stringent, the danger is that it will lead to a system of bureaucratic inquisition, which may end by becoming intolerable to the taxpayer.

In order to avoid these dangers, therefore, the system introduced at the outset was not to make any effort to ascertain the exact income of individuals, but to attempt to reach it approximately by a series of presumptions. People who have large incomes usually give evidence of the fact in several ways, such as the amount of rental paid for the residence, the general standard of life as shown by the equipages or automobiles, the mode of dress, especially of the female members of the family, and so on. All such criteria or indicia are patent facts, open to the observation of any one, and constitute approximate indications of relative income. In some cases the government contented itself with taking a single criterion like house rentals, so that the tax on house rentals formed a species of indirect income tax.

This system, never entirely adequate even for the more moderate grades of income, proved to be completely unsatisfactory when it came to a consideration of the higher classes of income; for the higher we rise in the scale of income, the less definite is the relation of expenditure to income. Accordingly the quasi-income taxes, in the shape of house rental taxes or expenditure taxes of various kinds, were abandoned, and the attempt was now made to ascertain not the presumptive, but the actual, income.

The simplest mode of applying this principle was to take a man's entire income and to levy the tax upon it. Since the income tax was assessed directly on the income in its entirety, or as a lump sum, it has sometimes been called the direct income tax, but might with propriety be called the lump-sum income tax.[1] The lump-sum income tax has an undoubted advantage over the tax resting on presumptions, in that, if successful, it reaches individuals on their actual income. But it is obvious that in order to overcome the difficulties adverted to above, we must have not only an admirable administrative system to which no suspicion of fraud can attach, but also a set of officials so little imbued with the bureaucratic spirit that they will refrain from inquisitorial procedure, and at the same time strike the balance between excessive rigor and undue laxity of administration. Where these dangers seemed too strong, a third method, or another form of income tax, was chosen.

All incomes are obviously derived from some source. In so far as they consist of money, they are derived from individuals who pay over the money. The idea therefore suggested itself that, instead of asking the individual to defray the tax directly out of his entire income in a lump sum, the tax should be divided into categories or schedules, each consisting of some important source of the revenue, and that an attempt should be made to catch each separate category of income while it was being paid over to the receiver. Thus a man's income might be divided into several important classes, — as the income from land or other real estate, the income from securities, the income from other forms of capital, the income from wages or professional earnings, and the like. Then, if the income, for instance, is derived from government or corporate securities, the government or the corporation might be asked, when paying out the interest or dividends, to withhold the tax. In the same

[1] This term was first suggested by the present writer a few decades ago.

way, the individual who rented a piece of real estate might be requested to pay over the tax for his lessor; the mortgagor might be obliged to pay the tax for the mortgagee; the banker might be made to pay the tax for his client; the employer for his employee; and so on. Such a system would naturally receive various names. In so far as the tax is levied separately in the different categories or schedules, it might be called a scheduled income tax instead of a lump-sum income tax. In so far as the revenues are intercepted at their source, it might be called, and in fact has been called, a system of "collection at the source," or "stoppage at source," or "taxing at the source," or "charging at the source." In so far as the tax is for the most part not collected directly from the recipient of the income, but is advanced by the payer of the income, it is sometimes called the indirect income tax, as opposed to the direct income tax. Finally, inasmuch as the tax is not collected upon the entire income of the individual, but is divided up so as to form practically a series of assessments on different kinds of income, it has sometimes been called a tax on incomes rather than a tax on income. As Great Britain is the chief, although by no means the only, example of this form of tax, it seems better to apply the term which is in common use there, namely, the "stoppage-at-source" income tax; and in England itself, where both methods have been tried, there is no doubt in the minds of the authorities as to the advantage of a stoppage-at-source income tax over a lump-sum income tax.

One of the chief points to be considered in the following investigation is to ascertain how far these claims are legitimate. It is obvious, however, that the stoppage-at-source income tax possesses disadvantages as well as advantages. If the lump-sum income tax requires admirable administrative efficiency, it possesses, at all events, the good point of permitting, without any difficulty, the application of the principles of differentiation and progression. On the other hand, while the stoppage-at-source income tax offers no obstacles to the application of the principle of differentiation, it does present very great impediments to the introduction of graduation. For it is clear that if the tax is assessed by schedules and stopped at the source, it becomes almost impossible to put definite rates upon varying amounts of total income.

Since, therefore, each of the two modern systems of income taxation possesses advantages and disadvantages of its own, it becomes necessary to probe a little deeper. It is at bottom, however, a question not alone of the particular form of tax and of administrative environment, but also of the theory embedded in the legislative provisions themselves. A mere analysis of the provisions of existing laws would be far from giving us the results which we are attempting to secure. In order to understand an existing law, it is almost always necessary to trace the origin and development of its provisions; and no judgment of the success or failure of a system can be attained without considering the manner in which the legislative provisions are actually carried out in practice. Nor, finally, can the working of a system be comprehended without a familiarity with the general attitude of the public, as reflected in the literature.

We propose, therefore, to take up the most important examples of income taxation in existence to-day; to trace the legislative and the literary history of each; to analyze the provisions of the existing law; and to explain the practical workings of the system. After we have done this for the most important foreign systems, we propose to deal with the American experiences, and with the peculiar constitutional situation in the United States. Only on the basis of such a study will it become possible to take a definite attitude on the problem of the income tax in the United States at the present time.

PART I

THE INCOME TAX ABROAD

THE MIDDLE AGES

The Income Tax in the Middle Ages

§ 1. *The Local Taxes*

The income tax played, with rare exceptions, an exceedingly insignificant rôle in the Middle Ages. Taxation itself was for a long time of minor importance when compared with the other sources of public revenue, for feudal income was derived very largely from the lucrative prerogatives of the feudal lord. When taxation did develop, it consisted, to an overwhelming extent, of taxes on trade and transportation; and when direct taxation began, first in the local communities and then in the larger divisions like departments, provinces, states and even empires, the well-nigh universal system was that of the general property tax.

The history of the general property tax has been told in another place.[1] It will be pertinent, however, to recall some points in this history so far as they bear upon the subject of the present investigation. In the first place, real estate under the feudal system was rarely bought and sold, so that practically the only method of ascertaining the value of the land was by taking account of its rents. The local property tax, so far as real estate was concerned, was therefore a tax on produce rather than on selling value; and later on, when in some cases the tax was assessed on the selling value, this was reached by capitalizing the rent. In the second place, all movables or personal property were assessed at the selling value, so that the tax became a combination of a tax on produce and on selling value. In the third place, as the expressed effort of the legislator was to reach the faculty of the tax-

[1] Seligman, *Essays in Taxation*, chap. 2. *Cf.* also Seligman, *Progressive Taxation*, part i, § 2, "The Middle Ages."

payer, the recipients of wages or salaries were considered also to possess some taxable ability, even if they had no property. We therefore frequently find an assessment on such individuals in some rough proportion to their gains. As there were virtually no important professions for a long time during the Middle Ages, this practically meant a tax upon the day laborer. In the case of official salaries, however, the same method was often pursued as in the case of real estate, and the salaries were reduced to a capital sum for purposes of taxation. In the fourth place, as trade and commerce developed, where the gains of the business man could not be approximately determined from the capital invested, we occasionally find as a supplement to the property tax, a tax upon assumed profits of business.

The mediæval system was therefore really a little more than a general property tax. The overwhelming mass of the revenue came indeed from the tax on personal property and real estate, but this was now and then supplemented by a tax on the faculties of the laborers and sometimes by a tax on the assumed faculties of the business man. Occasionally we find, in addition to the general property tax and even as a part of it, a so-called personal tax, either in the shape of a poll or capitation tax, to reach individuals who had no property, or in the shape of a graduated capitation or class tax, designed to reach certain classes whose gains were not entirely in proportion to their property.

This is not the place to deal with the history of the tax, or to point out the process by which it everywhere became virtually a tax on real estate alone. Its only interest for us in this connection is the consideration that while property was considered the best test of faculty in taxation, it was from a very early period supplemented by considerations of product. It would, however, be a mistake to consider these examples of local taxation in the Middle Ages as illustrations of a local income tax, as some scholars have carelessly asserted.[1] The

[1] *Cf.* for instance, Schönberg, p. 178; and Espinas, p. 142, in the works quoted in the next note.

conception of an income tax as the basis of the tax system was foreign to the ideas of the time. All that can reasonably be claimed is that while property was the general test of faculty, it was supplemented to a slight extent by the idea of product in those cases where property did not exist or could not be disposed of. It is the failure to distinguish between these conceptions which is responsible for the erroneous interpretations to which allusion has been made.

The numerous detailed investigations of communal finance have shown the truth of this fact beyond the peradventure of doubt. In Germany, for instance, we have such studies for the towns of Basel, Frankfort, Cologne, Brunswick, Augsburg, Osnabrück, Magdeburg, Ueberlingen, Ulm, and Dortmund.[1] In France and Belgium we have similar investigations for the towns of Douai, Amiens, Cambrai, Dinant, Luxemburg, and Senlis.[2] The same is true of local taxation in England, the

[1] G. Schönberg, *Finanz-verhältnisse der Stadt Basel im XIV und XV Jahrhundert.* Tübingen, 1879; T. Geering, *Handel und Industrie der Stadt Basel bis zum Ende des XVII Jahrhunderts.* Basel, 1886; K. Bucher, "Der öffentliche Haushalt der Stadt Frankfurt im Mittelalter," in *Zeitschrift für die gesammte Staatswissenschaft*, vol. lii (1896), pp. 1 *et seq.*; A. Henning, *Steuergeschichte von Köln in den ersten Jahrhunderten städtischer Selbständigkeit bis zum Jahre 1370.* Dessau, 1891; R. Knipping, *Die Kölner Stadtrechnungen des Mittelalters.* Bonn, 1897; H. Mack, *Die Finanzgeschichte der Stadt Braunschweig bis zum Jahr 1374.* Breslau, 1899; C. Meyer, "Der Haushalt einer deutschen Stadt im Mittelalter," in *Vierteljahrschrift für Volkswirthschaft, Politik und Kulturgeschichte*, vol. ciii (1889), pp. 48 *et seq.*; C. Stüve, *Stadtrechnungen von Osnabrück aus dem 13. und 14. Jahrhundert.* Osnabrück, 1890; C. Bielefeld, *Das Steuerwesen im Erzstift Magdeburg.* Magdeburg, 1888; Schäfer, *Wirtschafts-und Finanzgeschichte von Ueberlingen, von 1550–1628.* Breslau, 1893; A. Kölle, *Die Vermögensteuer der Reichsstadt Ulm.* Tübingen, 1896; K. Rübel, *Dortmunder Finanz-und Steuerwesen.* Dortmund, 1892. *Cf.* also, for a more general survey, K. Zeumer, *Die Deutschen Städtessteuern . . . im 12. und 13. Jahrhundert.* Leipzig, 1878; and W. Stieda, "Städtische Finanzen im Mittelalter," in Conrad's *Jahrbücher für National-Oekonomie und Statistik.* III Folge, vol. xviii (1899), pp. 1 *et seq.*

[2] G. Espinas, *Les Finances de la Commune de Douai des Origines au XVe Siècle.* Paris, 1902. This work contains some admirable comparative summaries of continental local finance and an excellent bibliography; E. Maugis, *Essai sur le Régime Financier de la Ville d'Amiens du XIVe à la Fin du XVIe Siècle.* Amiens, 1899; W. Reinecke, *Geschichte der Stadt Cambrai bis zur Erteilung der*

story of which has been told by Cannan, although he also carelessly states that "the poor rate was intended to be a local income tax upon the inhabitants of the parishes."[1] Ability is, indeed, continually mentioned as a test of taxation; but it was property or, at most, property plus product, and not income, which was taken as a criterion of ability. The history of the local rates in England, from the sixteenth and seventeenth centuries, is similar to that of the local tax or tallage of the earlier Middle Ages, where "faculties" and "chattels" (*facultates et catalla*) were considered for the most part synonymous,[2] and where product was employed as a supplement to property. So also in Scotland, where the mediæval property tax, under the name of the cess and of the stent, lasted until very recent times, the stent roll was made up according to the taxpayer's "means and substance," and we are told that the estimate of means, which comprised all the taxpayer's property, "appears to have included the incomes due to personal exertion of professional men and artisans, although no case seems to have come before the courts with reference to such incomes."[3] This tax on the so-called income of professional classes, like that on the profits of trade, was only a very subordinate part of the general stent which, as one of the laws puts it, was to be assessed upon the taxpayer "according to the avail and quantity of his rent, living, goods, and gear that he has within burgh."[4] Neither in England nor in Scotland did

lex Godefridi. Marburg, 1896; H. Pirenne, *Histoire de la Constitution de la Ville de Dinant au Moyen Age.* Gand, 1889; N. Van Wervecke, *Les Finances de la Ville de Luxembourg pendant le Règne de Philippe le Bon.* Luxembourg, 1895; J. Flammermont, *Histoire des Institutions Municipales de Senlis.* Paris, 1881. *Cf.* also in general Beaumanoir, *Coutumes de Beauvaisis.* 2 vols. Paris, 1899–1900.

[1] Edwin Cannan, *The History of Local Rates in England.* London, 1896, p. 69. *Cf.* also the admirable history contained in the *Report of the Poor Law Commissioners on Local Taxation.* London, 1843.

[2] Seligman, *Essays in Taxation*, 8th ed., p. 41.

[3] S. H. Turner, *The History of Local Taxation in Scotland.* Edinburgh, 1908, p. 38.

[4] *Ibid.*, p. 159.

the occasional assessment of professional earnings or of business profits suffice to convert the rate or stent into a "local income tax," any more than the wages tax or the business tax of the German states during the nineteenth century availed, as we shall learn, to make of the taxes on product a system of income taxation.

All over the Continent, as well as in Great Britain, the general property tax gradually shriveled up. First, personal property slipped out of the lists, and with it the few assessments on the profits of the tradespeople. A little later, the faculty tax on earnings disappeared until finally nothing was left but a tax on real estate levied, as is to a great extent still the fact, on the rental value of the land and house. Thus what was everywhere at the beginning a personal tax on the individual, measured primarily by his property and to a minor extent by the produce of the other elements of his taxable ability, turned into a real tax or a tax on the thing itself, that is, on the real estate.

To this general rule of the mediæval development there is only one important exception, namely, in the Italian towns. The Italian towns, in the early Middle Ages, were not only the centres of the new industry, but for a time witnessed a far more determined and temporarily successful struggle of democracy against aristocratic government. It is especially in Florence that we find this democratic movement, and it is accordingly there that we see the same strong tendency toward the taxation of incomes that we witness at the present day in modern democracies.

The general history of the Florentine movement, and more especially of the struggle for progressive taxation, has been told elsewhere.[1] Another aspect of the story may, however, be mentioned here, in so far as it is of importance for our

[1] Seligman, *Progressive Taxation*, part I, § 3, "The Italian Republics." The detailed history of the tax will be found in G. Canestrini, *La Scienza e l'Arte di Stato, desunta dagli Atti officiali della Republica Fiorentina e dei Medici. Ordinamenti Economici.— Della Finanza, Parte I, L'Imposta sulla Ricchezza Mobile e Immobile.* Firenze, 1862.

purposes. In the original property tax or the *estimo* of the fourteenth and the beginning of the fifteenth centuries, we find, as in the similar local taxes elsewhere in Europe, that the tax was based upon an estimate of property in general. The value of real estate, for instance, was ascertained by capitalizing the rent, and an attempt was made to reach the presumed gains of the business men, which were thereupon also capitalized at the rate of five per cent.[1] The reason, however, why the *estimo* gave way to the *catasto* in 1451 or, in other words, the reason why the property tax changed into an income tax, was the fact that in a large commercial or industrial centre, where the mass of wealth was being accumulated out of the earnings of industry and commerce rather than, as elsewhere, out of the rent of land, property was no longer so good an index of faculty as income. The democracy of Florence was as much impressed by the business earnings of the large merchant princes as are the modern democracies of Europe or America influenced by the gains of the trust magnates and of the financial kings. The democratic movement of the mediæval Italian republics is therefore responsible for the evolution of the property tax into an income tax. The *catasto* was a real income tax, and shortly afterward it was made progressive under the name of the *scala*.

From the very outset, however, the political conditions were unfavorable to efficient administration. In the struggle with the Medici the assessment of the income tax became a favorite weapon of whatever party happened to be in power; and at no other time in the world's history except, perhaps, in the later centuries of the decaying Roman Empire, was there such an orgy of corruption and of maladministration. In order to ascertain the business profits, the books of the merchants were open to inspection, and the assessors had practically unlimited scope in deciding upon the amount of the levy. Individuals might compound with the officials in a lump sum, and the frauds were accordingly overwhelming

[1] Canestrini, *op. cit.*, pp. 26, 27.

in character.[1] Everything was ruled by what was known as the *arbitrio*, that is, the arbitrary judgment of the authorities, and the income tax was utilized as the most potent engine of oppression or of favoritism.

The Florentine income tax lasted for only a relatively short time. With the final downfall of democratic liberties and with the reintroduction of the aristocratic régime in the sixteenth century, not only the income tax but all direct taxation of the wealthier classes disappeared. Before long the public revenues in Florence, as well as in most of the other Italian commonwealths, came to be derived chiefly from indirect taxes, supplemented in some cases by a kind of vague ability tax, or so-called "family" tax, the burden of which rested primarily on the poor.

§ 2. *The General or State Taxes*

The mediæval general or state taxes were a repetition on a somewhat larger scale of the local taxes. If we recall the development in England, it will be remembered that the principal tax was really a tax on property and produce.[2] It was known for some time as the fifteenth and tenth, because in the case of real estate a fifteenth was levied on the rental value or produce, while in the case of chattels a tenth of the selling value was nominally taken by the tax-gatherer. It will also be remembered how, in the hope of preventing the gradual diminution of the yield, the tax was changed from a percentage to an apportioned tax; that is, instead of actually assessing a fifteenth of the produce and a tenth of the selling value respectively, an arbitrary sum was fixed upon as representing what a fifteenth or tenth ought to yield, and this arbitrary sum was then apportioned among the various local divisions. Finally, it will be remembered how personal property slipped out of the assessment lists, and how it gradually

[1] *Cf.*, for various aspects of the situation, Canestrini, *op. cit.*, pp. 145, 164, 176, 419, 475.

[2] Seligman, *Essays in Taxation*, pp. 47 *et seq.*

became impossible to raise the required amounts. When the fifteenth and tenth disappeared, the general property tax was reintroduced in the sixteenth century under the name of the General Subsidy. After a time, however, the three phenomena repeated themselves: the change from a personal to an apportioned tax, the gradual escape of personal property, and the fading away of the yield. During the middle of the seventeenth century the old system was tried anew under the name of Commonwealth Monthly Assessments, with precisely the same results. Finally, after the Revolution, the attempt was made for the fourth time by the so-called Property Tax. The old story, however, again repeated itself, and in 1697 Parliament fixed the sum which a given rate was expected to produce; that is, it became an apportioned tax of stated amount.[1]

The English tax at the close of the seventeenth century, like all its mediæval predecessors, was a combination of property and produce tax. In the case of land, the tax was assessed on the rack rent or yearly value in 1692 at the rate of four shillings for every pound of rent.[2] In the case of personal property, the tax was assessed on the value of the property, but as the rental of land was deemed to be six per cent of its selling value, the same supposition was applied to personal property, so that four shillings on the pound of rental value would be equivalent to twenty-four shillings on every hundred pounds of capital value. The tax on "personal estates" was therefore levied at the rate of twenty-four shillings for every hundred pounds of selling value. Finally, in the case of "any person exercising any publick office or employment of profit," the tax was assessed directly upon these salaries at the rate of four shillings for every pound of salary.[3]

The tax, therefore, was a property tax, except that the value of lands was reached through their rent, and with the further

[1] 9 and 10 William and Mary, c. 10.

[2] 4 William and Mary, c. 1.

[3] Dowell, *The History of Taxation and Taxes in England*, 2d ed., London, 1888, vol. iii, p. 84, gives a very unclear and confused account of the tax.

exception that property in public offices was taxed through the salaries themselves. It was hence a combination of property and produce tax; and it is especially to be noted that no gains or profits were taxed unless, with the one exception of public salaries, they were derived from visible property. Moreover, while according to the intent of the law the chief revenue was to come from personal property, and only the necessary remainder was to be levied on the produce of real estate, in actual practice virtually nothing was assessed except real estate, so that the tax soon became a land tax. In fact, by the year 1697 it was officially termed "an aid by a land tax," or, in common parlance, the Land Tax. The salaries part of the tax lingered along during the eighteenth century, and in 1758 Pitt made an effort to increase the very scanty returns by imposing a new duty at the rate of a shilling in the pound on all offices, except naval and military offices, with a salary exceeding £100. The law, however, was more honored in the breach than in the observance, and soon became a dead letter. Thus, what was originally a general property tax with a slight element of product taxation degenerated into a land tax. Of a general income tax we find no trace at all.[1]

The only important country in which we find the development of the income tax for state purposes before the nineteenth century is France. The leading French direct tax in the Middle Ages was the *taille*, the development of a charge that was universal throughout early mediæval Europe and which, in England, had been known as tallage. The tallage was a more or less arbitrary feudal imposition upon the king's tenants, calculated primarily according to the amount of the land, but modified to some extent by general considerations of ability to pay. In England it disappeared at an early period, to merge into the general property taxes which have

[1] William Kennedy, *English Taxation, 1640–1799*, London, 1913, pp. 20, 47, thinks that I have exaggerated the distinction. But see Bruno Moll, *Zur Geschichte der englischen und amerikanischen Vermögensteuern*, München, 1912, esp. pp. 17–35, where my conclusions are confirmed.

been discussed above. In France it survived until the Revolution, and became the leading direct tax, being composed of two parts, — the *taille réelle*, levied on lands, and the *taille personnelle*, levied on individuals apart from their lands. The tax soon became honeycombed with abuses, whole classes of the population securing exemption from the burden, until it became a completely unequal and thoroughly arbitrary imposition upon the less well-to-do classes, resting upon considerations neither of property nor of income, but depending entirely upon the whim of the assessor.

At the close of the seventeenth century the fiscal situation of France had become so bad that increased revenue was imperatively necessary. France had by this time become a great industrial and commercial nation, and was far in advance not only of England, but of the adjoining countries. Accordingly, the government now thought that it would be possible to lay tribute upon these newer forms of wealth. After the elaboration of plans of tax reform in the shape of a general income tax by publicists like Vauban and Boisguilbert, the government decided to make the attempt. At first, however, it contented itself with introducing in 1697 a classified poll tax known as the *capitation*, or *capitation graduée*. This was a kind of class tax; that is to say, the tax was imposed upon individuals according to their social status, the rate for all members of the same class being identical. There were twenty-two classes, the tax ranging from one livre to two thousand livres. The capitation was suppressed in 1698, but reëstablished in 1701, and it was then gradually transformed into a tax on individual incomes, members of the same class now being rated differently. By 1705 the capitation, although still so called, had virtually become an income tax in three-fourths of the country, and lasted throughout the eighteenth century.[1]

Almost from the beginning, however, abuses disclosed themselves. In 1701, for instance, certain classes were permitted to compound for the tax, a practice known as *abonne-*

[1] For a general history of the capitation, see especially Clamageran, *Histoire de l'Impôt en France*, vol. iii, pp. 32–36 *et seq.* Paris, 1876.

ment.[1] In 1705 the capitation was in very large measure simply added to the taille,[2] just as in Massachusetts to-day the income tax is for the most part levied only on those who are already on the lists of the property tax. Then in 1708 began the period of exemptions, individuals as well as whole classes being freed from the tax, until before long all the shortcomings of the old taille reappeared in the capitation. Toward the end of the century, whenever the capitation was still levied separately, it was assessed practically on the presumptive income of the individual as measured by his house rent; and this part of the capitation was continued after the Revolution as a house-rentals tax. So far as it was levied at all on business incomes, it gave rise to the most enormous inequality and inquisition.[3] The important point to remember, however, is that what was called in France the capitation or poll tax had become, according to the theory of the law at all events, an income tax.

With the comparative failure of the capitation as a fiscal device, the government resorted to other attempts to secure a revenue from incomes. Thus, in 1710, Louis XIV enacted the so-called *dixième*, or Tenth, which was supposed to be a tax of ten per cent on all incomes throughout the country. This tax, suppressed and reënacted from time to time, was converted in 1749 into a five per cent tax, or Twentieth (*vingtième*); and this continued until the Revolution, being supplemented by a second Twentieth in 1756 and a third Twentieth from 1760 to 1763, and again from 1783 to 1786.[4]

[1] Clamageran, *op. cit.*, p. 89.

[2] Clamageran, *op. cit.*, p. 90.

[3] For the abuses connected with the capitation, see Clamageran, *op. cit.*, pp. 329 *et seq.*

[4] A detailed account of the Tenth and the Twentieth will be found in M. Houques-Fourcade, *Les Impôts sur le Revenu en France au XVIII Siècle. Histoire de la Dixième et de la Cinquantième, Leur Application dans la Généralité de Guyenne.* Paris, 1889. The *cinquantième*, or Fiftieth, referred to in the title, was a two per cent tax imposed on the produce of land in 1725. This was, however, abolished in 1727. A recent popular article on the Tenth and Twentieth, as well as on the Capitation and the Taille, is that of Charles de Lasteyrie, "L'Impôt sur le Revenu sous l'Ancien Régime" in the *Revue des Deux Mondes*, April, 1910.

The *dixième* was supposed to be a general income tax reaching incomes of four kinds; namely, from real estate, from salaries, from securities, and from business. But the tax soon showed the same weaknesses as its predecessors. One by one various individuals and classes secured exemption from the tax. Especially the so-called *vingtième d'industrie*, the income tax on business, soon became a farce. The historians tell us of the ludicrous yield (*le rendement dérisoire*),[1] of the tax, and before long not only did the Tenth and the Twentieth become quite as arbitrary as the capitation, but what was originally a percentage tax became an apportioned tax — a development entirely analogous to that of the land tax in England. It is not necessary to go into the details of the administrative system, which existed very largely only on paper. One point, however, is worth mentioning; namely, that in the few places where the tax was actually assessed, even in part, on business, it was levied not on individuals, but on groups of business men (*corps de marchands*). These made an agreement as to the total amount to be paid, which was then apportioned among their own members in a supposedly equitable ratio. The same method was also applied to certain officials and lawyers.[2] In a general way it may be said that the Tenth, and later the Twentieth, suffered from all the evils to which any tax can possibly be subject. It was, moreover, not levied in the same fashion in any two departments;[3] and the officials were for the most part so illiterate as to be unable to form the tax lists.[4] It is not to be wondered at that in the words of its historian, "the taxpayers, corrupted by the long-time practice of unlimited fiscal arbitrariness, should enter without scruple upon the path of the most extreme evasions."[5] The Tenth and the Twen-

Cf. also R. Stourm, *Les Finances de l'Ancien Régime et de la Révolution.* Paris, 1885; C. Gomel, *Les Causes Financières de la Révolution Française. Les Ministères de Turgot et de Necker.* Paris, 1892; and the same author's *Les Derniers Contrôleurs Généraux.* Paris, 1893.

[1] Houques-Fourcade, *op. cit.*, p. 167.

[2] *Op. cit.*, pp. 207–208.

[3] *Op. cit.*, p. 244.

[4] *Op. cit.*, p. 298.

[5] *Op. cit.*, p. 187.

tieth, in fact, became mere shadows or simulacra of an income tax, and the *vingtième d'industrie* especially grew to be completely absurd.

In other words, as the administrative and political customs of centuries could not be changed in a moment, the income tax, whether in the shape of the capitation or of the Tenth and the Twentieth, went the way of the old taille. Frauds, evasions, class exemptions, and the most unbounded arbitrariness soon honeycombed the system to such an extent that all personal taxation of the individual became a stench in the nostrils of the French public. One of the first acts of the Revolution accordingly was to sweep away the entire system of personal taxation.[1] Thus the two great examples of income taxation in former times, that of Florence in the fifteenth, and that of France in the eighteenth, century, were due to the same underlying economic forces, and afford eloquent proof of the danger of corrupting and destroying theoretically sound fiscal systems by deplorably inefficient administrative methods.

France was the only European country in the eighteenth century to develop an income tax, because it was the only country in which industry and commerce had attained any considerable importance. But during the eighteenth century France was being slowly overtaken by England, and by the close of the century it was England that was ready for a new attempt. With the disappearance, however, of the old régime on the continent, and with the newer conceptions of universality and equality of taxation, the way was prepared for the more modern democratic attempts to realize the principles of income taxation. With the history of the nineteenth century, first in England and then on the continent, we now have to deal.

[1] For an account of the experiments with the progressive income taxes and the forced loans of the revolutionary period, see Seligman, *Progressive Taxation*, part i, chap. 5, "The French Revolution."

BOOK I

THE INCOME TAX IN GREAT BRITAIN

CHAPTER I

The War Income Tax, 1798–1816

§ 1. *The Origin of the Triple Assessment*

The British income tax was a direct outcome of the gigantic struggle against France.[1] The reason of its introduction can be grasped only when we understand the fiscal situation of the day. Like that of most other countries, the English revenue system of the eighteenth century had come to consist almost exclusively of customs and excises. The mediæval system of taxes on property and produce had shrunk to very small dimensions, and the old general property tax had long become

[1] There is no good history of the British Income Tax. The account in Stephen Dowell, *A History of Taxation and Taxes in England from the Earliest Times to the Year 1885*, London, 4 vols., 1885, 2d ed., 1888, is neither full nor accurate. Sydney Buxton, *Finance and Politics; a historical Study, 1783–1885*, 2 vols., London, 1888, gives the general setting of the subject. Brief surveys of the legislation may be found in the *First Report from the Select Committee on the Income and Property Tax*, 1852, pp. 1–25; in the *Report from the Select Committee on Income and Property Tax*, 1861, pp. 1–10; in the *Thirteenth Report of the Commissioners of Inland Revenue on the Duties under their Management for the years 1856–1869 inclusive, with some retrospective History and Complete Tables of Accounts of the Duties from their first Imposition*, London, 1870, i, pp. 120–131, and ii, pp. 184–207; in the *Twenty-eighth Report of the Commissioners of Her Majesty's Inland Revenue on the Duties under their Management for the Year ending 31st March, 1885, with some retrospective History, and complete Tables of Accounts of the Duties from 1869–70 to 1884–5 inclusive.* London, 1885, pp. 73–85; in the *Forty-third Report of the Commissioners of Inland Revenue.* London, 1900.

Incidentally, references may also be found in the *Reports* of 1905 and 1906 mentioned *infra*, pp. 186 and 197, notes. An excellent Russian work is Oseroff, *The Income Tax in England. The Economic and Social Conditions of its Existence in the System of Taxation.* Moscow, 1898. [In the Russian language.] *Cf.* also the monograph by Manes, "Die Einkommensteuer in der englischen Finanzpolitik," in the *Festgaben für Wilhelm Lexis*, 1907.

virtually nothing but a land tax. This land tax, however, still plays so important a rôle in the administrative machinery of the present income tax that it deserves a few words of special mention.

In the preceding chapter we have called attention to the process by which the general property tax of the Middle Ages changed, by the end of the seventeenth century, into the so-called land tax, and how what was originally a percentage tax on property had become an apportioned tax, designed to yield a definite amount of revenue.[1] According to the principle of apportionment fixed in 1697, one shilling in the pound of land tax produced about half a million sterling,[2] and in that year three shillings in the pound were granted. Throughout the eighteenth century the rate varied annually from one to four shillings in the pound. The unsuccessful attempt of Grenville in 1767 to compel Townshend to accept a four-shilling rate, left the latter no alternative but to attempt to raise the necessary sums by a tax on the colonies, and thus precipitated the Revolutionary War. After the war broke out, however, four shillings became the normal rate. It proved to be impossible to increase the revenue from this source, as the landowners were in control of Parliament, and finally, in 1798, the "annual land tax," as it had now come to be called, was made a redeemable rent charge. In the course of a few decades, about one-half of the landowners in Great Britain accordingly bought themselves free of tax, and the yield of the tax is at present quite insignificant.

The machinery of the land tax has, however, been kept up from that day to this. The various land-tax acts, beginning in the seventeenth century, provided that certain individuals, especially designated, should be commissioners for executing the act in the different localities. From this fact these acts have been called "Name" acts, and have usually been enacted at the first session of each parliament, being discontinued only at the beginning of the present century. There was from the very outset a property qualification for the

[1] *Supra*, p. 48.

[2] Exactly £494,671.

position of Land Tax Commissioner, fixed at the end of the eighteenth century at the possession of an estate with an annual value of not less than £200. Justices of the Peace were *ex-officio* Land Tax Commissioners. The commissioners for the general purposes of the land tax or, as they came to be known, the General Commissioners, were empowered to divide themselves into smaller groups for the local divisions of every county or town, and in each case to select a clerk. These divisional commissioners were to appoint in every district or subdivision local commissioners, who were to nominate the assessors and collectors. The assessors and collectors were not to receive fixed salaries, but were to get a certain percentage or poundage on the amount raised. The commissioners were entirely unsalaried and, as they were chosen from the local gentry, their position was considered one of considerable dignity. With the diminution in the yield of the land tax, the duties of the commissioners became so light that by the end of the eighteenth century the tax was administered by only a few members, while the real work was done in each case by a clerk. In the majority of cases the position had thus become simply a title of honor. Yet, as we shall see later, it is these very land tax commissioners, with their clerks and assessors, who are indirectly in charge of the assessment of the present income tax.

In addition to the land tax, there had existed all through the Middle Ages a system of customs duties, at first primarily on exports and then, after the growth of the mercantilist system, on imports. Beginning in the seventeenth century, a system of excises was introduced, supplemented by a few stamp duties. After the outbreak of the American war, when larger revenues became imperative, North, following in part the suggestions of Adam Smith, turned to Holland as a model, and imposed new taxes. Among them were a tax on inhabited houses, according to rental value; the beginning of a succession duty; and a series of so-called taxes on establishments, such as men-servants, horses, and the like, designed to reach the luxury of the rich. In 1785 Pitt grouped these taxes on houses and establishments together into what afterwards became known as the assessed taxes, and put them under the management of the so-called "Commissioners for the Affairs of Taxes." The chief increase in the revenue, however, came from other sources. In 1792, just before the outbreak of the French war, out of a total tax revenue of about seventeen and a quarter millions sterling, the land tax yielded only two millions, and houses and establishments only one and one-quarter millions. Almost the entire remainder came from customs and excises. Taxes on articles of food and drink were responsible for nine millions.[1] Taxes on manufactured articles—primarily, soap, candles, leather, printed goods, glass, and drugs—yielded about one and three-quarter millions, and stamp duties yielded about one million. It will be seen, therefore, that what we have come to regard in modern times as direct taxes played a very slight rôle, and that, so far as there were any direct taxes at all, they were not personal, but real, taxes, *i.e.*, taxes not on the individual as such, but on product.

After the declaration of war in 1793, new laws were enacted, and additional taxes were laid from year to year. The old customs, excises, and stamp duties were raised from time to time, and new duties were imposed successively on tea, on stone, on salt, and on collateral successions. On the other hand, the assessed taxes, which had been increased by ten per cent in 1790, were increased by further additions of ten per cent in 1796, and again in 1797, while the system was extended from carriages, servants, and horses so to include taxes on hair-powder, dogs, watches and clocks.

All these changes, however, proved to be utterly inadequate for the great struggle, and British credit fell as the French victories increased. The country could not disguise its alarm, and by 1796 various fiscal schemes were propounded. Notwithstanding the increase in the assessed taxes, the over-

[1] Beer, three and a half millions; wine and spirits, two and a quarter millions; sugar, one and a quarter millions; tobacco and tea, about half a million; and salt a little less.

whelming mass of revenue, as we have seen, was still derived from expenditure rather than possessions. It is therefore not to be wondered at that the scheme of some direct assessment on the wealth of the individual should be advanced. One writer, who sought to inspire confidence by contrasting English and French methods,[1] suggested a "general and voluntary contribution."[2] Although in one place Bowles calls it a "Public Contribution to be furnished by the general mass of proprietors,"[3] he made it plain that he expected the yield to come primarily from the rich.[4] In the following year he returned to the scheme, lamenting the "inflexible obstinacy and the increased malignity of the Opposition," but stating that had it been adopted, "we should not now see the funds at their present low ebb."[5] Another writer even went so far as to advocate a progressive property tax. "Taxes," he tells us "should affect individuals in a progressive ratio, proportionate to their properties, for they who have the greatest interest at stake should bear the greatest charge."[6] The author was, however, willing to supplement his proposed impost by

[1] *Two Letters addressed to a British Merchant a short Time before the Meeting of the new Parliament in 1796.* By John Bowles. 4th ed., London, 1796, p. 36. A scheme of a general tax on all property had been advanced as early as 1779 in a series of letters collected in the following year under the title of *Occasional Letters upon Taxation; upon the Means of raising Supplies within the Year to answer the Expences of a necessary War; and upon such Measures as would probably tend to secure Great Britain and its natural Dependencies the Blessings of Peace upon a durable System.* By an Independent Man. London, 1780. See esp. pp. 3, 45, 72.

[2] Bowles, *op. cit.*, p. 31.

[3] *Op. cit.*, p. 63.

[4] "It should not be forgotten that the measure of Voluntary Contribution, though calculated to be general, is proposed to derive its chief effect from the wealthy and affluent." — *Op. cit.*, p. 76.

[5] *A Third Letter to a British Merchant, containing some General Remarks on the late Negociation with France, considered in Relation to Ancient and Established Principles; together with Reflections on the state of Domestic Politics, and particularly on the Mischievous Tendency of the Conduct pursued by the Opposition.* By John Bowles. London, 1797, p. 93.

[6] *A General Address to the Representatives of Great Britain on important National Subjects, agitating at the present Period.* By an Elector, M. A. London, 1797, p. 48.

indirect taxes, preferably on luxuries, as the "properest objects for taxation in time of war."[1]

By the autumn of 1797 Pitt realized the gravity of the situation. The three per cent consols, which had been nearly at par in 1792 and which had fluctuated around 70 during the next three years, fell to 55 in January, 1797, and to 47⅝ before the end of May. The Bank of England, amid universal consternation, had suspended specie payments,[2] and a French invasion under Hoche seemed imminent. The time had now come to make an appeal to the country, and in his famous budget speech of November 24, 1797, Pitt introduced his scheme for the triple assessment.

The assessed taxes, as we have learned, comprised a series of direct imposts, partly on houses and partly on so-called establishments, including carriages, servants, horses, hair-powder, dogs, watches and clocks. Pitt now decided to convert the system into what he called "a general tax on persons possessed of property commensurate as far as practical with their means." On the first reading of the bill, Pitt discussed the broad outlines of the scheme and declared the objects to be attained to be as follows: "That the plan should be diffused as extensively as possible; that it should be regulated as fairly and equally as possible, without the necessity of such investigation of property as the customs, the manners, the pursuits of the people would render odious and vexatious. That it should exclude those who are least able to contribute or furnish means of relief; that it should distinguish the gradation of classes: that it should admit of those abatements, which, in particular instances, it might be prudent to make."[3]

[1] "Those duties are preferable which the consumer pays in the purchase of the article or connectedly with the value; and which produces obliquely, rather than immediately to government." — *A General Address*, etc., p. 49. *Cf.* also the scheme of Francis Adams, *A Plan for raising the Taxes impartially and almost free of expense in War and in Peace for paying off the National Debt.* London, 1797.

[2] "A few months before payment was stopped at the Bank, any man who had predicted that event would have been pitied as a madman, or proscribed as a traitor." — *The Question as it stood in March 1798.* London, n. d. [1798], p. 22.

[3] *The Speeches of the Right Honourable William Pitt in the House of Commons.* 2d ed., London, 1808, vol. ii, p. 346.

He conceded that the "Assessed Taxes are often eluded by men of large property, who, by denying themselves many of the enjoyments of life, hoard up money and exclude themselves from assessment."[1] But Pitt contended, nevertheless, that "even though the hoards of the penurious elude our search . . . a due proportion would, at least in some cases, be forthcoming at the solicitation of self-interest and self-defense";[2] and he closed by a general appeal to this particular class of the wealthy to do their share.[3]

On the second reading of the bill, a general discussion was precipitated, and fierce opposition developed, led by Fox. Pitt replied in a brilliant speech of December 14, 1797, of which a contemporary observer, Mallet du Pan, said: "From the time that deliberative assemblies have existed, I doubt whether any man ever heard a display of this nature, equally astonishing for its extent, its precision, and the talents of its author. It is not a speech spoken by the minister; it is a complete course of public economy; a work, and one of the finest works, upon practical and theoretical finance, that ever distinguished the pen of a philosopher and statesman."[4] Pitt began by stating that it had been called a tax on property and a tax on income. It was neither, said he. Pitt

[1] *The Speeches of the Right Honourable William Pitt in the House of Commons.* 2d. ed., London, 1808, vol. ii, p. 353.

[2] *Op. cit.*, p. 354.

[3] "Then should those who, devoted to accumulation by ignorance of enjoyment, and early habits of frugality, have arisen from the lower rank and meanest employments, by rigid frugality and indefatigable industry, protected, fostered, and encouraged, by that happy system of government, and those equal laws, which enabled them and permits any man to emerge from the bottom to the top of society, — then ought they, I say, for the recollection of the benefits they have received, and for the sake of those to which they look forward, to consider themselves above all men bound to come forward, in defense of that system which afforded encouragement to their labours, nurture to their industry, vigour to their pursuits, and protection to their persons, their property and their acquisitions."— *Op. cit.*, p. 355.

[4] Quoted in *The Financial Statements of 1853, 1860–1863.* By the Right Hon. W. E. Gladstone. London, 1863, p. 15. Gladstone says, "When Pitt proposed the Income Tax to Parliament, that great man, possessed with his great idea, raised his eloquence to an unusual height and power."

declared that he did not believe in any such scheme. "If the amount of every man's property could be ascertained, it would be a most desirable thing to make the people contribute to the public exigence in proportion to their wealth. But there existed no means of ascertaining the property of individuals, except such as were of a nature that could not be resorted to. Instead, therefore, of a tax upon property, this was what he had stated it to be, — a tax upon general expenditure."[1] For the assessed taxes, he thought, were the best "visible criterion" of property.

On the third reading, Fox maintained that the bill contemplated "the most monstrous inequalities and the most gross injustice in every part,"[2] and called attention to the protests which had been made in various public meetings in London. "Is it not a dreadful thing," he asked, "to pass a bill like this against the unanimous opinion of the inhabitants of the metropolis? What is the language of this money bill? 'We give voluntarily.' — Who gives voluntarily, — the people of the metropolis, who must pay the fourth of it? No — they have unanimously declared that they cannot give it at all! that if it is attempted to be levied upon them, their ruin will be the effect of it."[3] Pitt replied in a brilliant speech. He made a crowning appeal to the patriotism of the country, and in conclusion urged his hearers to make this "great and unusual exertion," rather than to "suspend all defensive precautions and leave the country open to the ruinous projects of an insolent and overbearing enemy."[4] His appeal did not fall

[1] Pitt continued: "He had anticipated an objection which he thought would be made, viz.: that this tax applied only to such income as was in expenditure. This was an inconvenience which it was impossible to avoid, without having recourse to such a scrutiny of property as must, in every point of view, be highly objectionable. That the present plan was in its nature imperfect he was ready to admit, and had stated it to be so when he first introduced the subject; but he thought it the best and most general criterion that could be found." — Speech of December 14, 1797, in his *Speeches*, vol. ii, p. 380.

[2] *The Speech (at length) of the Right Hon. C. J. Fox, on the Third Reading of the Bill for Increasing the Assessed Taxes.* London, n. d. [1798], p. 119.

[3] *Op. cit.*, p. 121.

[4] Pitt's *Speeches*, vol. ii, p. 402.

upon deaf ears; and even though the unpopularity of the scheme was such that he was mobbed on his passage to St. Paul's,[1] the bill was enacted into law on January 12, 1798.

§ 2. *The Act of 1798*

The Aid and Contribution Act, as it was called,[2] divided the taxpayers into three categories. In the first class were comprised the presumably wealthier taxpayers, who owned establishments consisting of carriages, men-servants, or horses, and who, in Pitt's words, paid on "optional consumptions and luxuries."[3] They had their assessment for the previous year augmented as follows: If the last year's assessment was £25, it was increased three times; if £25–30, three and one-half times; if £30–40, four times; if £40–50, four and one-half times; and if over £50, five times. The second class of taxpayers included those who, while not keeping any such establishments, had been assessed on their houses, windows, clocks, or watches. In these cases the assessments of the previous year were altered as follows: —

£ 1–2	¼	£ 12½–15	2½
2–3	½	15–20	3
3–5	¾	20–30	3½
5–7½	1	30–40	4
7½–10	1½	40–50	4½
10–12½	2	Over 50	5

The third class comprised the presumably poorest individuals, who paid only on lodgings or shops. In this case the assessment was changed as follows: —

£ 3–5	1/10	£ 12½–15	¾
5–7½	⅕	15–20	1
7½–10	¼	20–25	1¼
10–12½	½	25–30	1½
		Over 30	2

[1] Cf. the "Sketch of the History of the English Income Tax," by C. A. Roberts, printed at the end of "Letter from Goldwin Smith to John V. L. Pruyn," in *Bankers' Magazine*, New York, 1866, p. 872. See also William Smart, *Economic Annals of the Nineteenth Century, 1801–1820*. London, 1910, p. 37.

[2] 38 George III, c. 16.

[3] Pitt's *Speeches*, vol. ii, p. 348.

It is clear, therefore, that, although called a triple assessment, it was in effect a system of taxation which was graduated from a slight beginning to a sum equal in one case to double, and in the other cases to five times, the original assessment. Instead of being termed a triple assessment, it should hence have been called the double and quintuple assessment.

The characteristic feature of the scheme, however, was to bring the assessments, calculated as they were according to expenditure, into some relation to income. The total payments were so arranged that incomes under £60 were exempt; incomes from £60 to £200 paid from one one hundred and twentieth to one-tenth of the respective amounts, *i.e.*, five-sixths of one per cent to ten per cent; while all incomes over £200 paid ten per cent.[1] In other words, while the normal rate of tax was supposed to be ten per cent, the rates were progressively reduced on all incomes below £200, until at £60 no tax at all was payable. In the case of incomes over £200, where the quintuple assessment fell short of reaching ten per cent of the income, the act invited the taxpayers to make additional voluntary contributions, thus realizing, in part at least, the scheme of Bowles referred to above.[2] Furthermore, additional abatements were made in

[1] The exact figures were as follows: —

On incomes from

£60–65 the tax was not to exceed $\frac{1}{120}$ of the income.
65–70 the tax was not to exceed $\frac{1}{95}$ of the income.
70–75 the tax was not to exceed $\frac{1}{70}$ of the income.
75–80 the tax was not to exceed $\frac{1}{65}$ of the income,

and so on to

£100–105 the tax was not to exceed $\frac{1}{40}$ of the income.
105–110 the tax was not to exceed $\frac{1}{38}$ of the income.
110–115 the tax was not to exceed $\frac{1}{36}$ of the income,

and so on to

£150–155 the tax was not to exceed $\frac{1}{20}$ of the income.
155–160 the tax was not to exceed $\frac{1}{19}$ of the income.
160–165 the tax was not to exceed $\frac{1}{18}$ of the income,

and so on to over

£200 the tax was not to exceed $\frac{1}{10}$ of the income.

[2] *Supra*, p. 61.

the case of large families. Parents of four to seven, eight to nine, and ten or more, children could claim ten, fifteen, and twenty per cent abatement, respectively.

The triple assessment met with considerable literary opposition, even while the bill was under discussion. One writer, who may be taken as the type of its opponents, declared it "fallacious in its view, destructive in its progress, and faulty in its completion. . . . It is not taxation, but a species of extortion. It is an experiment full of fear and danger."[1] Considerable prominence, also, was given to a letter of the celebrated radical, John Horne Tooke, who declared that "this hated impost was odious in every point of view," and who, in reply to a notice from the commissioners "that they have reason to apprehend your income exceeds sixty pounds," and that they "desire that you will reconsider your declaration of income," responded as follows: —

> "Sir : I have much more reason than the commissioners can have to be dissatisfied with the smallness of my income. I have never yet in my life disavowed, or had occasion to reconsider, any declaration which I have signed with my name. But the act of Parliament has removed all the decencies which used to prevail among gentlemen, and has given the commissioners (shrouded under the signature of their clerk) a right by law to tell me that they have reason to believe that I am a liar. They have also a right to demand from me, upon oath the particular circumstances of my private situation. In obedience to the law I am ready to attend upon this degrading occasion as novel to an Englishman, and give them every explanation which they may be pleased to require."[2]

The act, however, did not fail to find ardent supporters. One of these, who tells us that "never before did any measure meet with so sudden, so violent, and so general an opposition," wrote a work "to expostulate with my Countrymen on the inconsiderate haste with which they have suffered themselves

[1] *An Address to the Right Hon. William Pitt, etc., on some Parts of his Administration; occasioned by his Proposal of the Triple Assessment in the House of Commons in November, 1797.* London, n. d. [1798], p. 17.

[2] *Memoirs of John Horne Tooke.* By Alexander Stephens. Vol. ii, p. 157. London, 1813.

to condemn and oppose the measure."[1] He, on the contrary, was "disposed to believe it the best that could be devised under the present circumstances,"[2] holding that "a direct tax upon property would have met with a still more strenuous opposition; because it would have required a disclosure of circumstances."[3] He explained that "expenditure is taken as the criterion of ability, and, considering how few there are in this age of luxury who do not spend as much as they can afford, it must be allowed to be the best criterion that could be discovered."[4] A doubt, however, overcame him in the case of persons "whose economical dispositions keep their expenses far below the limits which the affluence of their circumstances would allow them to observe." Still he held that "such persons will have an opportunity afforded them to correct this disparity, by their voluntary contributions." He therefore concluded that this plan "is the nearest possible mode of taxing individuals according to their *real* income, without obliging them to disclose what that income is."[5]

The chief defence, however, was put forth by the Bishop of Landaff, in a pamphlet that attracted wide attention.[6] "A new system of finance," said the Bishop, "has this year been introduced; and I fairly own it has my approbation as far as it goes. It has given great discontent to many; but it has given none to me. On the contrary," he added, "instead of calling for a tenth of a man's income I wish the minister had called for a tenth, or such other portion of every man's whole property as would have enabled him not merely to make a temporary provision for the war, but to have paid off, in a few years, the whole or the greatest part of the national

[1] *An Appeal to the Head and Heart of Every Man and Woman in Great Britain, respecting the threatened French Invasion and the Importance of Immediately coming forward with Voluntary Contributions.* London, 1798, p. 30.

[2] *Op. cit.*, p. 25.

[3] *Op. cit.*, p. 30.

[4] *Op. cit.*, p. 29.

[5] *Op. cit.*, p. 31.

[6] *An Address to the People of Great Britain.* By R. Watson, Lord Bishop of Landaff. London, 1798. Another edition was published under the title of *An Address to the People of Great Britain, extracted from the Bishop of Landaff's Pamphlet.* Leeds, 1798.

debt."[1] The Bishop leaned toward the broad principle that the national debt is "a debt belonging to every individual, in proportion to the property he possesses," and that it should hence be supported by equal payments."[2] The ideal scheme, in his opinion, would be an equal property tax.[3] The objection, advanced already at that early period, to taxing the public debt in the shape of government annuities, is met by the statement: "I own that I do not see any sufficient reason why property in the funds may not be as justly as any other property subject to the disposal of the legislature."[4] The only suggestion that he made "as not undeserving of attention" is, that if a property tax be imposed, a distinction should be drawn between the owners of different classes of "permanent income." Permanent income, he thought, arises either from the rent of land, from the interest of money, or from annuities; and in each of these three cases the same income represents a varying capital value, because of the different years' purchase at which they are estimated. "Men under these different descriptions pay equally," said the Bishop, "though their properties are unequal."[5] Thus is introduced the subject of what later on came to be called the differentiation of taxation, and which was to play so great a rôle in the history of the tax.

The Bishop's address led to a wordy warfare. Wakefield replied in a work in which he wavered between respect for

[1] *An Address to the People*, etc., p. 1.

[2] "No man, relatively speaking, will be either richer or poorer by this payment being generally made, for riches and poverty are relative terms; and when all the members of a community are proportionably reduced, the relation between the individuals, as to the *quantum* of each man's property, remaining unaltered, the individuals themselves will feel no elevation or depression in the scale of society." — *Op. cit.*, p. 2.

[3] "I consider the property of men united in society so far to belong to the state, that any portion of it may be justly called for by the legislature, for the promotion of the common good; and it is then most equitably called for, when all individuals, possessing property of any kind, contribute in proportion to their possessions." — *Ibid.*

[4] *Op. cit.*, p. 4.

[5] *Op. cit.*, p. 4.

the author and contempt for his opinions.[1] As a consequence of the violent diatribes of the author against the government, the publisher was indicted for libel, and a rejoinder was made by Ranby, who denounced the *Reply* as "an ill-written and inconclusive composition."[2] Another opponent of Landaff stated that he "conceived a tax upon expenditure, or upon income which is not easily separated from expenditure, to be wrong in principle."[3] The most severe indictment of the scheme, however, is found in a work by the Earl of Lauderdale. Lauderdale especially opposed the principle that "the assessed taxes form the best evidence of property, and are, of course, the best criterion for collecting an aliquot part of men's estates." On the contrary, said Lauderdale, "I differ so far, that I regard it as the worst of all the numerous means of forming an estimate of property that has at various times been suggested."[4] There are three links in his chain of reasoning. First, he denied that "the assessed taxes can be deemed any criterion of real expenditure." Secondly, he said, "Far less do I conceive it possible that any man can deem expenditure a criterion of income." And thirdly, "In this strange chain of reasoning, . . . there is no step more ridiculous than

[1] "I protest solemnly when I observe what seems to me such absolute ignorance of the state of society in this country, and such outrageous defiance of the most notorious facts."—*A Reply to some parts of the Bishop of Landaff's Address to the People of Great Britain.* By Gilbert Wakefield. 2d ed., London, 1798, pp. 17–18.

[2] *The Examination of Mr. Wakefield's Reply to the Bishop of Landaff's Address.* By John Ranby. London, 1798, p. 3. Ranby sided with Wakefield in only one point, that of the exemption of children. *Cf.* p. 19.

[3] *A Plan for Raising the Supplies during the War, humbly submitted to the two Houses of Parliament, the Landed and Monied Interest, and to all Ranks and Conditions of the People, capable of contributing to the Expences of the State.* London, 1798, p. 11. *Cf.* also *Hints toward an improved System of Taxation extending to all Persons in exact Proportion to their Property, and without any Kind of Investigation or Disclosure of their Circumstances.* London, 1798.

[4] *A Letter on the present Measures of Finance; in which the Bill now depending in Parliament is particularly considered.* By the Earl of Lauderdale. London, 1798, p. 24.

that of considering income as a criterion of capital."[1] Lauderdale objected to all endeavors to ascertain individual property, whether directly or indirectly. "To your inquiry, whether I know of any fairer criterion, I reply, that though, undoubtedly, I know of many better, I know of none that are good, and I cannot prevail upon myself by any such suggestions to give countenance to a measure which, in the opinion of our most eminent masters of political economy, never can with propriety be adopted in a free country."[2] Lauderdale objected even to the abatements for the lower incomes, on the ground that "in the end, the lower orders will too surely discover that, though ostensibly exempted, they will be, at least, common sufferers with others, and probably greater sufferers than the classes whose assessments are augmented."[3] He characterized the law as "this offspring of Robespierre's," and maintained that "the atrocity of the measure is in every view unprecedented."[4]

The experiment with the triple assessment did not justify the hopes of its distinguished author. Instead of the four and one-half millions that had been counted upon, it yielded only two millions,[5] owing, as Pitt tells us in his budget speech of the next year, to "the difficulties which the measure encountered from the shameful evasion, or rather the scandalous frauds by which its effects were counteracted."[6] On the other hand, the voluntary contributions amounted to two millions instead of the one and one-half millions that had been anticipated, so that, in Pitt's words: "the meanness which shrunk from fair and equal contribution, has been compensated to the public by the voluntary exertions of patriotism."[7]

[1] *Op. cit.*, pp. 25–26.
[2] *Op. cit.*, p. 29.
[3] *Op. cit.*, p. 36.
[4] *Op. cit.*, pp. 32–33.

[5] In all the official records the yield of the triple assessment is put at very much lower than Pitt's figures. According to the records of the Treasury, the yield was only £1,855,996, and even that represents only the gross assessment. See *First Report from the Select Committee on the Income and Property Tax*, 1852, p. 3, and *Report of the Commissioners of Inland Revenue*. 1870, p. 120.

[6] *Speeches*, vol. ii, p. 429.

[7] "If I did not calculate the evasion, the fraud and the meanness which have struggled to defeat the operation of the assessed taxes . . . and I mention it with

As these voluntary contributions could, however, not be permanently depended upon, Pitt was led regretfully, but none the less firmly, to abandon his original project, and to propose a new tax to be levied directly on income itself.

§ 3. *Pitt's Conversion to the Income Tax*

On December 8, 1798, Pitt introduced his new scheme and touched upon the general principle which underlay it. "It is in vain," he tells us, "to disguise that, by the causes to which I have alluded, the full advantage of the principle has not been obtained. The wishes and the interest of individuals, I am sure, must unite in demanding a more comprehensive, a more equal, and a more vigorous application of a principle, the rare advantages of which we have been able to ascertain, if we have not yet been so fortunate as to enjoy."[1] Originally, we are told, he "felt it materially important to follow some durable, some apparent and sensible criterion, by which to apportion the burden." But now it had become necessary "to prevent those frauds which an imperfect criterion and a loose facility of modification have introduced; to repress those evasions so disgraceful to the country, so injurious to those who honourably discharge their equal contribution, and, above all, so detrimental to the great object of national advantage which it is intended to promote." He therefore declared it to be his intention to propose "that the presumption founded upon the assessed taxes shall be laid aside, and that a general tax shall be imposed upon all the leading branches of income," for the purpose of "obtaining, by an efficient and comprehensive tax upon real ability, every advantage which flour-

shame, that in a moment like the present, in a contest so vitally interesting to every individual and to the nation, there have been men base enough to avail themselves of the general modifications which were intended to relieve those who might have been called upon to contribute beyond their means, to avoid that fair assessment which corresponded with their circumstances, I am happy to find that the honor of the nation has been vindicated by the noble and generous aid of voluntary contribution."

[1] *Speeches*, vol. ii, p. 430.

ishing and invigorating resources can confer upon national efforts."[1]

The project of a direct tax on all incomes was novel. Very shortly after the passage of the triple assessment, an anonymous writer suggested, indeed, a "general contribution upon a broad basis."[2] But the context shows that he desired it to be restricted to the landowners and fundholders.[3] In the same way Cooke, in his so-called income tax scheme, made a distinction between different classes of revenue, and advocated a tax only on "permanent or acquired property."[4] It was reserved for Pitt, however, to suggest that all incomes, from whatever source derived, be taxed, and be taxed alike. In one of his most forceful passages, we find an eloquent defence of the justice of taxing the income from government securities, which had hitherto been exempt from taxation.[5] "I should say to the stockholders, as one of the public, if you expect from the state the protection which is common to us all, you ought also to make the sacrifice which we are called upon to make. It is not pecul-

[1] *Speeches*, vol. ii, pp. 431–433.

[2] *Consolatory Thoughts on Taxation or Contribution, in Three Letters to a Member of the House of Commons.* By the author of *Thoughts on Taxation and a new System of Funding.* London, 1798, p. 9.

[3] *Op. cit.*, p. 6.

[4] "To provide for the exigencies of the state, let property, permanent or acquired, and which produces a certain income to the possessor, be only assessed." — *The just Proportion which each Class of the People, from the Peasant to the Peer, have in the Support and Prosperity of the State. Or Test of Taxation; and a Schedule for Assessment on Income, resulting from a mathematical Investigation of the Value of Property Acquired, and that Fluctuating in Trade. Addressed to every Individual of the British Empire.* By N. Cooke. 2d ed., London, 1798, p. 24. Cooke was willing to add to the tax on permanent property a tax on annuities, pensions, and church livings (p. 25); but he held repeatedly that trade and commercial incomes must be exempt (p. 13). *Cf.* also the anonymous *Thoughts on Taxation, in the Course of which the Policy of a Tax on Incomes is impartially investigated.* London, 1798.

[5] Since the time of William and Mary, the Loan Acts had provided that government annuities should be free of all taxation. The Annual Land Tax Act, which included "annuities payable out of the public revenue," exempted "annuities of yearly payments by any Act or Acts of Parliament specifically exempted from the payment of taxes or aids." — 38 George III, c. 5, sec. 3 (1797).

iar to you, it does not belong to the quality of your income, but it is made general and required from all; you could not embark your capital in any other species of security in which it would not be subject to the same charge. I do not know what objection the stockholder could make to this appeal."[1]

On the third reading of the bill, Pitt took up in considerable detail the three chief objections urged against the scheme. Because of the great rôle that these objections played in after years, we may be pardoned for explaining Pitt's replies somewhat fully.

Referring to the contention that indirect taxes should be preferred, Pitt stated that such an increase of tax on consumption as would yield the requisite amount of revenue was not only impracticable, but would introduce "evils ten times more severe than those which are imputed to this measure."[2] In reply to the second objection, namely, the charge of inquisitorial procedure, Pitt closed his argument by putting the question. "Does the honourable gentleman really think that no precaution whatever ought to be taken to avoid those scandalous evasions which there is but too much reason to expect may be attempted?"[3] Finally, taking up the point that the proposed scheme did not discriminate between the various kinds of income according to their nature or duration, Pitt maintained that the inequalities complained of "arise out of the nature of society, and the distribution of its rank, and the classification of its property."[4] In the course of his argument Pitt advanced what later on became known as the "leave-them-as-you-find-them" theory of taxation.[5] Referring to two individuals, one of whom receives his income from land and the other from industry, Pitt asked: "What does the new tax do? Are they not left in relation to each other precisely as they were before? The tax creates no new inequality. The justice or injustice remain

[1] *Speeches*, vol. ii, p. 444.

[2] Speech of December 14, 1798, in *Speeches*, vol. iii, p. 3.

[3] *Op. cit.*, p. 6.

[4] *Op. cit.*, p. 8.

[5] As to this theory, see Seligman, *Progressive Taxation*, 2d ed., p. 231.

precisely as they were. To complain of this inequality is to complain of the distribution of property; it is to complain of the constitution of society. To attempt to remedy it, would be to follow the example of that daring rabble of legislators in another country. . . . To think of taxing these two species of incomes in a different ratio, would be to attempt what the nature of society will not admit; what has never been practised in the course of four thousand years." [1] So far as the alleged distinction between annuities and income from fixed property is concerned, Pitt replied: "A permanent estate, which is represented as never dying, and, as it were, the property of a man after his death, contributes on every exigency which may occur; the income from labour and industry is extinguished; it contributes but once; it is no longer the property of the same person; while the other, which is considered as the same property, is subject to renewed demands." This reasoning, Pitt added, "may be thought refined; but the answer is justly applicable in the case where the reason, why fixed property should contribute more, is founded on its supposed permanency, in addition to the fleeting character of the other." [2] Pitt closed his impassioned appeal in the following words: "The inequalities objected to are not peculiar to its nature; they arise from our social state itself, and the correction of that order we cannot, as we ought not, attempt to alter. It would be a presumptuous attempt to derange the order of society, which would terminate in producing confusion, havoc, and destruction, and with a derangement of property, terminate in the overthrow of civilized life." [3]

Although Pitt's eloquence carried parliament with him by a large majority, his plan aroused considerable opposition. The metropolis was not any more favorable to the new project than to the old one. The Lord Mayor, Aldermen, and Common Council of London adopted a resolution at the General Court on December 19, 1798, in which, while

[1] Seligman, *Progressive Taxation*, 2d ed., p. 9.

[2] *Speeches*, vol. iii, p. 13.

[3] *Op. cit.*, pp. 14–15.

indeed nominally approving of the principle of the bill, and acknowledging "that all taxes ought to be equitable and proportionably levied according to the property of individuals," they took exception not only to the measures devised for carrying the principle into execution,[1] but stated that the proposition to tax "the precarious and fluctuating income arising from the labour and industry of persons in trade, professions, etc., in the same proportion as the permanent annual income proceeding from landed and funded property, is most partial, cruel, and oppressive."

These ideas were taken up by Frend, who declared himself struck by the "palpable injustice" of Pitt's scheme.[2] Frend propounded his general theory that "taxation is equitable, when each member is taxed in proportion to his means of paying the tax," [3] explaining the principle further by stating, very much as Pitt did, that "taxation, to be equitable, must leave the subjects, when the tax is taken from them, precisely in the same relative situation to each other, in which they were the moment before the tax was paid."[4] In contradistinction to Pitt's contention, however, Frend attempted to show by elaborate computations that the same proportion of taxable means takes a very different rate of taxation from the various categories of income derived from property.[5] He also objected to the "peculiar progression for inferior in-

[1] "That the said bill proposes to establish an inquisitorial power unknown in this country — inconsistent with the principles of the British Constitution — and repugnant to the feelings of Englishmen." — The resolutions are printed on p. xv of the book of Frend mentioned in the next note.

[2] *Principles of Taxation*. By William Frend. London, 1799, p. iv.

[3] *Op. cit.*, p. 2.

[4] *Op. cit.*, p. 11.

[5] "To be equitable, the subjects must pay in proportion to their taxable means, and these means should be to each other, in the moments before and after the payment of the tax, in the same relative situation. They cannot be in the same relative situation, unless their taxable means of income, productive and unproductive capital, are diminished in the same proportion. This is done by assigning the value of productive and unproductive capital, and taking the income for one year: then, after the deduction from the whole of a certain sum, a certain part of the remainder is to be taken for the tax."—*Op. cit.*, p. 40.

comes" found in Pitt's scheme, and compared it to Paine's plan of graduated taxation.[1]

Pitt's project, however, was ably supported in a notable address by Lord Auckland, who considered that the bill had been, "anxiously calculated and ably and accurately framed to prevent inequality, fraud, embarrassment, and injury."[2] Auckland addressed himself particularly to two objections. It was claimed in the first place that the system of abatements on the lower incomes, which Auckland accepted, ought logically to lead to what he called the "principle of gradual rise" on the higher incomes. This Auckland denied, maintaining that progression was out of the question on account of its "levelling tendencies."[3] The other objection was that incomes like those derived from life annuities, which were supposed to be worth only ten years' purchase, ought not to be taxed at the same rate as incomes from estates in fee which were deemed to be worth thirty years' purchase. According to Auckland, however, this objection, although plausible, was equally unsound, the difficulty arising, in his opinion, entirely "from a confusion in terms, and from blending together the ideas of income and of capital."[4]

[1] "Tom Paine and Mr. Pitt are more nearly united to each other in their financial schemes, than either would be willing to acknowledge. The one is unjust to the higher, the other to the middle classes, and both affect an equal regard to the poor. The one would bring the poor and the rich together by levelling the rich; the other would increase the distance between the poor and the rich by demolishing the middle class. The one injures the mill by impairing the head of water, the other by demolishing the cogs in the smaller wheels; neither the one nor the other seems to have taken a comprehensive view of the whole machine."—*Op. cit.*, pp. iv, v.

[2] *The Substance of a Speech made by Lord Auckland in the House of Peers, on Tuesday, the 8th day of January, 1799, on the third Reading of the "Bill for Granting Certain Duties upon Income."*—London, 1799, p. 19.

[3] Graduation "would be contrary to all the safety and rights of property"; it would "be worthy only of the French Council of Five Hundred"; and it "would amount to neither more nor less than the introduction of a plan for equallizing fortunes; and to the implied inference, that because a man possesses much, therefore more shall be taken from him than is proportionably taken from others." —*Op. cit.*, p. 25.

[4] *Op. cit.*, p. 27.

§ 4. *The Act of 1799*

The supporters of the bill finally triumphed, and it was enacted into law on January 9, 1799, to come into operation on April 5.[1] It was a comprehensive enactment of 124 sections, covering 152 pages. So formidable did it seem that the government thought it wise to prepare a compendium in order to make it intelligible to the general public.[2] It was this compendium which formed the subject of one of Gillray's caricatures,[3] where John Bull is represented at his studies, attended by his guardian angel with a harp in hand, who sings, —

> "Cease, rude Boreas, blustering railer;
> Trust thy fortune's care to me."

The tax was imposed upon all residents of Great Britain in respect of their entire income, irrespective of whether this originated in Great Britain or elsewhere, and also on all absentees, — *i.e.*, British subjects not resident in Great Britain, — in respect of income from property in Great Britain. The rates, exemptions, and general abatements remained virtually the same as in the triple assessment. The abatements for children, however, were altered as follows: —

On incomes of £60–400 the abatement for each child was 5%.
On incomes of £400–1000 the abatement for each child was 4% when over 6, 3% when under 6.

[1] 39 George III, c. 13. "An Act to Repeal the Duties imposed by an Act made in the last Session of Parliament for granting an Aid and Contribution for the prosecution of the War; and to make more effectual Provision for the like Purpose, by granting certain duties upon Income, in lieu of the said Duties."

[2] *A plain, short, and easy Description of the different Clauses of the Income Tax so as to render it familiar to the meanest Capacity.* London, 1799. Various other compendiums were issued, under private auspices. One which ran through many editions was entitled: *Taxes on Income. A Correct Abridgement of the Act imposing a Tax on all Income, containing those Clauses which principally affect Landlords, Tenants, etc., exhibited in a clear and methodical Manner, etc., with a Schedule for estimating the Income of Persons liable to be Assessed.* London, n. d. [1799]. The most elaborate publication was the one mentioned in note 3 on the next page.

[3] Dowell, *The History of Taxation and Taxes in England,* 2d ed., 1888, ii, p. 226.

On incomes of £1000–5000 the abatement for each child was 3% when over 6, 2% when under 6.

On incomes over £5000 the abatement for each child was 2% when over 6, 1% when under 6.

Provision was also made for the deduction of premiums paid for life insurance, while in the case of incomes from buildings an allowance for repairs was granted, varying from three to ten per cent, according to their nature.[1]

The great change, however, consisted in the fact that the tax, instead of being calculated according to expenditure, was now imposed directly upon the entire income of the individual. The returns were required to be made under four heads,[2] comprising nineteen so-called cases, of which the first fourteen were included under head I, the next two under head II, the two following under head III, and the last under head IV.[3]

The reasons for the important change from expenditure to income as the test of taxable ability are well set forth in the semi-official publication referred to above, which explains the shortcomings of the triple assessment. "The criterion taken last year, as the means of ascertaining income, was expenditure, as evidenced by certain articles of general establishment only, and was even then admitted to be in many respects imperfect. It was fallacious, inasmuch as it included

[1] Three per cent in the case of farm buildings; eight per cent in the case of a farm with a principal messuage; ten per cent in the case of houses and buildings not occupied with a farm.

[2] The four heads were: —

I. Income from real estate.

II. Income from personal property and from trades, professions, offices, pensions, stipends, employments, and vocations.

III. Income arising out of Great Britain.

IV. Income not falling under any of the foregoing rules.

[3] The cases are printed in full in *Observations etc. upon the Act for Taxing Income; in which the Principle and Provisions of the Act are fully considered, with a View to facilitate the Execution, both with respect to Persons chargeable, and the Officers chosen to carry it into Effect. With the Act at large. Together with the Substance of the Clauses of the Assessed Tax Act that have a Reference to this, and a copious Index, referring both to the Act and Observations.* London, 1799, 220 pp. A reprint of the cases may also be found in Dowell, *op. cit.*, iii, p. 96.

some, and wholly excluded others; as it included some in different proportions to their respective means; and as from the nature of the criterion it did not embrace a large portion of the property of the community enjoyed by political bodies or persons not objects of those assessments which constituted the basis of that contribution. It was also fallacious, inasmuch as, from a regard to antecedent prejudices, it failed to enforce its principle, by compelling a disclosure of income: it left each individual to interpret the rules, and to estimate his income, without controul, according to his private bias; it involved the honest and loyal, whilst the dishonest or disaffected escaped under their own interpretation."[1] The legislature, we are told, was aided in its new task "by an almost universal conviction having pervaded the public mind of the necessity of meeting the exigencies of the times by personal taxation, in proportion to the means of the individual; and by a similar determination to suffer the prejudice, arising from the apprehension of a disclosure of circumstances to subside in favor of an effective and certain mode of enforcing the just principle of equal taxation."[2]

The administrative machinery of the act is worthy of particular mention, as much of it is still in force to-day. The revenue authorities who had been in charge of the assessed taxes, and who were then known as the Assessors for the Affairs of Taxes, were required to make lists of the Land Tax Commissioners of each locality, and to appoint a day of meeting, The Land Tax Commissioners were to appoint commissioners for the general purposes of executing the income tax act, who came to be known as the General Commissioners. In the City of London the Mayor, Aldermen, and Common Council were empowered to name six persons from whom the Mayor and Aldermen were to select three to serve as Commissioners, while others were to be chosen by the Bank of England, the East India Company, the Royal Exchange Insurance Company, and the London Insurance Company. Commissioners

[1] *Observations upon the Act for Taxing Income.* London, 1799, pp. 2, 3.
[2] *Ibid.*, p. 3.

of Appeal were to be appointed by the Grand Jurors in each locality, with similar exceptions for the City of London.

The General Commissioners were to appoint and summon the assessors or, in their default, the justices of the peace were to do so, and these assessors were to serve notice on every householder to send in lists of the people living with him. The assessors were also instructed to post notices of assessment on the church doors. Every person chargeable with the tax was to state the assessment which he "means to pay as being not less than the just rate or proportion of his income." The assessors were to make up the lists and statements, together with their own comments, and then return them to the clerks of the General Commissioners, who were to hold their meetings within a period of from fourteen to twenty-one days.

Thus far it will be seen that the entire machinery was virtually in the hands of the gentry known as the Land Tax Commissioners and their appointees. Now, however, the central government interposed with its officials known as surveyors or inspectors, appointed by the Crown. These had the right of looking at the assessment lists, of suggesting revision, and of making preliminary changes, called surcharges. The taxpayers, also, were given the right to correct any errors in their statements. If the General Commissioners found any reason to question the returns or the changes made by the surveyors or inspectors, they were empowered to examine the taxpayer or anybody else who had knowledge of the facts. The questions, however, had to be put in writing, and no taxpayer was compelled to answer any question, Moreover, the provision about calling in outsiders remained, and has remained up to the present time, a dead letter.

The General Commissioners then fixed the assessment, which might, however, still be amended by the surveyor, and in that case it went to the Commissioners of Appeal. Any taxpayer, moreover, might appeal, but he could secure no relief on appeal unless he answered the questions and volunteered to show his books. A refusal to make any lists at all was visited with a penalty of £20. The tax was payable in six annual instalments, and the assessments were made on the basis of annual income, except that in the case of incomes from professions, either the year closing, or the average of three years, might be taken. Moreover, traders who so preferred might make their returns to so-called Commercial Commissioners in the locality, rather than to the General Commissioners, and were permitted to send in sealed statements of their income. These Commercial Commissioners were in each place two in number, and were supposed to be experts in the particular matter. Every official connected with the tax was pledged to secrecy.

It will be seen, therefore, that from the very outset the administrative machinery of the income tax was designed to reduce to a minimum the immixture of the central government and the danger of inquisitorial procedure. The General Commissioners and the assessors were, in a certain sense, representatives of the taxpayers, and might naturally be supposed to defend their legitimate interests against the treasury; while on the other hand the necessary degree of government control was represented by the surveyors and inspectors who were responsible to the central government. This ingenious combination of local representatives and of government officials is found, with some modifications, in the present income tax.[1]

§ 5. *The Public Attitude toward the Income Tax*

The passage of the Income Tax Act was followed by a veritable flood of pamphlets. The question of abatements

[1] The act was amended in two unimportant particulars in May and July of the same year, by 39 George III, c. 42, and 39 George III, c. 49. The exact points may be found in the publication entitled *Income. The New Schedule, as Corrected and Altered by the Amended Act for Taxing Income. Together with an Abstract of the Clauses of the Original Act, that relate to the mode of Estimating Income, and a Brief Notice of the Provisions of the Amended Act; with a Variety of Examples calculated to shew the Mode of Estimating the different Descriptions of Income, and making the Deductions according to the Cases in the Schedule.* London, n. d. [1799]. The second part of this was also separately published under the title: *Observations*, etc. *upon the Amended Act for taxing Income.* London, n.d. [1799].

was discussed by several writers. A clergyman by the name of Beeke praised the "humane and benevolent spirit" which suggested them, but stated that he entertained considerable doubts "whether in their present form they have not created discontent and jealousy of one another, even among the persons most relieved by them; whether they apply in anything like a due proportion to the equitable reasons for abatement; and whether the present . . . scale . . . has any conveniences which can compensate for the immense diminution of the tax."[1] Rose, on the other hand, defended the principle on the ground of its "proportioning public assessments to the ability of different classes. . . . The small earnings of laborious industry are spared altogether; the progressive rise of the tax saves, in a proportional degree, the moderate incomes of the classes of all the orders below competency; and the burden of children, which always falls heaviest on the middling ranks, is considered in an abatement of the contribution of their parents."[2] But Rose urged that great care should be taken not to allow this principle to degenerate into general progressive taxation.[3] Other writers, like Lauderdale, opposed the income tax on the somewhat inconsistent grounds that it was inherently unequal, that it would discourage industry, and that it would be shifted from the tradesman to his customers and from the farmer to his landlord.[4] Lauder-

[1] *Observations on the Produce of the Income Tax, and on its Proportion to the whole Income of Great Britain: including important Facts respecting the Extent, Wealth and Population of this Kingdom. Part the First.* By the Rev. H.. Beeke. London, 1799, pp. 62–63.

[2] *A Brief Examination into the Increase of the Revenue, Commerce and Manufactures, of Great Britain, from 1792 to 1799.* By George Rose. London, 1799, p. 33 of the 4th ed.

[3] "It should always be considered, that the excessive rise of a progression of this sort is, in effect, an arbitrary levelling of situations; and that an inordinate tax on the wealthy would take from the lower classes, whom the superfluity of wealth employs, that subsistence and comfort which are bestowed by it."—*Op. cit.*, p. 34.

[4] *Plan for altering the Manner of collecting a large Part of the Public Revenue, with a short Statement of the Advantages to be derived from it.* By Lord Lauderdale. n. p., n. d. [1799], pp. 57–60.

dale suggested in its stead an inheritance tax. Others, again, called attention to the inquisitorial nature of the tax, and one ingenious author, under the *nom de plume* of Hourglass, published an amusing pamphlet supposed to be written in the year 2000, in which he recounted the exactions of the "merciless mercenaries" and the "brutes at the head of the inquisitional band, or banditti, with all the rudeness that insolence and self-important ignorance could suggest, either to distress the feelings of the indigent, or glut the bloated importance of a jack in office," to which the unhappy citizens of an earlier century had been subject.[1]

The most comprehensive discussions of the act, however, are found in two anonymous publications of the same year. One of these declared that not only consumption, but even property, is far inferior to income as a criterion of equality in taxation. It would always be difficult, the writer thought, to find means to ascertain the value of property, and furthermore, property "may be possessed without being productive; in which state it could not, with propriety, be assessed."[2] The best criterion, he held, is that of "clear income," which, he said, was the principle followed by the assessors of the local stent in Scotland.[3] He favored official valuation rather than self-assessment, and advocated rigid measures, like forfeiture, as a punishment for fraud.[4] He had, however, doubts as to the wisdom of exemptions, although he leaned on the whole to the idea of making a discrimination in the rates.[5] In the main, he was optimistic about the scheme, and concluded that "the taxation of income seems not only to possess many

[1] *The Mouse-Trap Maker and the Income Tax; a Tale, supposed, by Anticipation, to be written in the Year 2000; with an Introductory Allegory addressed to a Man in Office.* By Humphrey Hourglass. London, n. d. [1799], p. 12.

[2] *Three Essays on Taxation of Income, with Remarks on the late Act of Parliament on that Subject. On the national Debt; the Public Funds; on the probable Consequences of the Law for the Sale of the Land Tax; and on the Present State of Agriculture in Great Britain. With a Scheme for the Improvement of every Branch of it, and Remarks on the Difference between National Produce and Consumption.* [By Benjamin Bell.] London, 1799, p. 33.

[3] *Op. cit.*, p. 51. [4] *Op. cit.*, pp. 45, 53. [5] *Op. cit*, pp. 59, 61.

important advantages over every other plan of raising money that has yet been proposed, but may be easily carried into effect, without the risk of the income of individuals being disclosed, and with scarcely a possibility of its being evaded."[1]

Another warm defender of the act, after adverting to the shortcomings of expenditure as a test of taxation, considered that a "tax upon all capital" was "absolutely impracticable."[2] "Under these circumstances," he continued, "a tax upon all income has appeared to the parliament of the country to be the most equal and practicable mode of raising the necessary supplies: that it is practicable, no person has denied; that it is equal, has indeed, by a few persons, been disputed."[3] Our author vigorously denied the "injustice of taxing different sorts of income in the same proportion, and by the same rule," and repudiated with equal vigor the contention that there ought to be a "rising scale applied to incomes of different amounts."[4] He tells us that "an unfortunate prejudice prevailed in the country against anything which could lead to an investigation of the property of individuals"; but he adds that not only "a very large proportion of the landed proprietors," but also "the merchants of London, Liverpool, Norwich, Edinburgh, Glasgow and Paisley, have come forward earnestly in its support. That which in former times," he concludes, "would have been thought an intolerable calamity, is now considered as a great national advantage."[5]

After the first flood of comment, the discussion became less vigorous. A few writers, indeed, objected to the injunction of secrecy imposed on the officials. Thus Rickman

[1] *Op. cit.*, p. 55.

[2] *Review of the Arguments advanced in the House of Commons in Support of the Bill for Granting an Aid and Contribution for the Prosecution of the War, by imposing certain Duties upon Income.* London, 1799, p. 12.

[3] *Op. cit.*, p. 13.

[4] "The object of this bill is not to regulate incomes, but to tax them; and if you take from different incomes the same proportion, you leave them of course exactly in the relative state in which you find them." He agreed with Pitt that any other principle would be "destructive of all idea of property." — *Op. cit.*, p. 18.

[5] *Op. cit.*, p. 28.

said, "I do not see why the exact state of a man's pecuniary affairs should not be known, as well as the colour of his coat, or the complexion of his countenance."[1] Rickman was a warm advocate of the taxation of what he calls superflux, or the wealth of those "who acquire improperly great property; who have infinitely more than is necessary for the elegancies and superfluities, as well as the comforts, of life; who wickedly hoard, or wickedly misapply the riches they have, and who make their exorbitant wealth the constant engine of public and private misery."[2] In the same way Newbery, who made an interesting attempt to distinguish sharply between capital and income,[3] contended that the oath of secrecy imposed upon the officials "might have answered the end of quieting alarm, and of qualifying the apparent harshness of the measure, when first introduced"; but, asks he, "Is it not a prudish delicacy, and a solecism in finance?" And he adds: "Notoriety is the antidote to subterfuge and evasion."[4]

Other more prominent writers contented themselves with general censure or promiscuous praise. Thus Morgan, in 1801, attacked Pitt for continuing the tax,[5] while Wakefield declared that Morgan was entirely wrong. "Our opinions," said Wakefield, in reply to Morgan, "on the policy of that measure and of its effects are directly opposite. He singles it out as an object for censure, while I feel inclined to bring

[1] *Mr. Pitt's Democracy manifested; in a Letter to him, containing Praises of, and Strictures on, the Income Tax.* By Thomas Clio Rickman. London, 1800, pp. 9–10. *Cf.* p. 28: "It would be well if every iota of every man's income, whether in or out of business, could be known. If it could be ascertained, what property every man hath, and how he gets and applies it; it would be, like a correct chart to a mariner, a guide over the rocks, and through the mazes of society."

[2] *Ibid.*, p. 12.

[3] "Capital is a deposit for the purpose of carrying on any business or speculation; income is the emolument which arises from it."—*Observations on the Income Act; particularly as it relates to the Occupiers of Land: with some Proposals of Amendment. To which is added a Short Scheme for Meliorating the Condition of the Labouring Man.* By Francis Newbery. London, 1801, p. 13.

[4] *Op. cit.*, p. 35.

[5] *A Comparative View of the Public Finances, from the Beginning to the Close of the late Administration.* By William Morgan. London, 1801, p. 36.

it forward to public notice as an object for praise, as a measure boldly conceived and happily executed."[1] The only writer to question in detail the merits of the underlying principle was Gray, who undertook the rather arduous task of showing that "the profits on home trade and all mortgages, whether private or public, do not form any part of national income," and that they therefore ought to be exempted from the operation of the law.[2]

In his original scheme Pitt had calculated the total taxable income of the country at one hundred millions. He therefore expected to realize the sum of ten millions from the ten per cent tax. Very soon, however, it was seen that these figures were excessive, and Pitt accordingly reduced his estimate to seven and one-half millions. But even this proved too high. The tax actually yielded in 1799 only a little over six millions, producing a little more in 1800, and a little less in 1801.[3] This was, however, a very great improvement over the less than two millions produced by the triple assessment, showing the great advantages of an income tax over an expenditure tax.

The public discontent with the tax, led as usual by the metropolis, was very pronounced. In March, 1802, shortly before the conclusion of peace, the City of London submitted a petition, praying for the repeal of the tax and couched in very violent terms. The press and public meetings all over the country voiced similar sentiments, and when hostilities came to an end, by the treaty of Amiens, in May, 1802, Addington (later Lord Sidmouth), who had succeeded Pitt

1 "Nor should it be forgotten," he adds, "that it was approved, if not originally suggested, by the great body of the merchants, bankers, and traders of the capital and Liverpool." — *An Investigation of Mr. Morgan's Comparative View of the Public Finances, from the Beginning to the close of the late Administration.* By Daniel Wakefield. London, 1801, p. 24. As to this last statement of Wakefield, see also *supra*, p. 85.

2 *The Income Tax scrutinized, and some Amendments proposed to render it more Agreeable to the British Constitution.* By John Gray. London, 1802, p. 23.

3 The exact figures of the annual yield will be found in the *appendix, infra*, p. 115.

as Chancellor of the Exchequer, repealed the tax as unbefitting a time of peace, although he was compelled to make good the deficiency in the revenue by new excises and import duties, as well as by an increase of the assessed taxes. In his budget speech of April 5, 1802, he was, however, warm in its praises, stating that "it was to the wisdom which originated the tax, and the firmness which induced the House to persist in it, that the country was indebted for the comforts we now had."[1] As soon as the tax was abolished, the commissioners decided to destroy all the papers in their possession, — a fact which Frend thought "proves that honour still remains, and may it ever remain in the breast of an Englishman."[2] Morgan, writing a few months later, could not refrain from ejaculating: "Happily for the nation this odious tax has been lately repealed."[3] But Courtenay was more just, when in his reply he stated that "the income tax was among the measures which were called for at such a crisis, by an able and undaunted minister, and carried into execution by the country, with equal spirit and good sense."[4] Courtenay, however, praised Addington for his decision "to leave at liberty this

[1] *Parliamentary History*, vol. xxxvi, p. 448.

[2] We are told that the papers "were carefully collected and cut into pieces with large stationers' shears, then thrown into large bags, and conveyed with equal care to a paper manufactory, where, under the inspection of a commissioner, they were committed to the mash tub: and he did not leave them till they were reduced to a pulp." — *The Principles of Taxation: or Contribution according to Means; in which it is shewn that if every Man pays in Proportion to the Stake he has in the Country, the present Ruinous and Oppressive System of Taxation, the Custom House, and the Excise Office may be abolished, and the national Debt Gradually and Easily paid off.* By William Frend. London, 1804, p. 3. The body of this book is, with a few omissions, the same as Frend, *Principles of Taxation*, 1799, quoted above on p. 76; but the long preface of thirty pages is entirely different.

[3] *A Supplement to a Comparative View of the Public Finances, containing an Account of the Management of the Finances to the present Time.* By William Morgan. London, 1803, p. 86.

[4] *Observations upon the present state of the Finances of Great Britain; suggested by Mr. Morgan's Supplement to his "Comparative View," and by Mr. Addington's Financial Measures.* By Thomas Peregrine Courtenay. London, 1803, p. 5.

great resource, to be resorted to upon any future emergency."[1] It was not long before the emergency declared itself.

§6. *The Act of 1803*

In 1803 the war broke out anew, and Addington was soon compelled to resort to the old device. In his budget speech of June 13, 1803, he declared his intention to propose "a tax upon property," although he was careful to add: "I wish it to be distinctly understood that I consider these duties as applicable to war only, and I intend to propose that they should cease within six months after the restoration of peace."[2] He also called the tax one "on the lands and property," and again on "rents and funds." A short but important debate now took place on July 13–14. Addington had proposed to make the abatements below £150 applicable only to incomes from personal labor, but Pitt, who was now the leader of the opposition, objected, and the Chancellor finally gave way, extending the reduction to all classes.[3] In another respect, also, Pitt was successful. Addington had originally embodied his scheme in two bills, one of which dealt with the income from the funds, or government securities. Pitt objected to this dismemberment of the tax, and Addington was compelled to recast the measure and to present it in a single bill. The attempt of the opposition, however, to exempt the income from the public funds did not prevail although, as we shall see, the foreign holders of government securities were not made liable to the tax. To the objections raised by the opponents on account of the lack of discrimination, Addington replied that "equality of taxation was a thing not to be brought about by human wisdom."[4] The

[1] *Observations upon the present state of the Finances of Great Britain: suggested by Mr. Morgan's Supplement to his "Comparative View," and by Mr. Addington's Financial Measures.* By Thomas Peregrine Courtenay. London, 1803, p. 5.

[2] *Parliamentary History*, vol. xxxvi, p. 1596.

[3] *Op. cit., Session of 1802*, iii, pp. 740, 749.

[4] *Op. cit.*, vol. xxxvi, p. 1662.

bill as amended became law on August 11, 1803, under the significant title of "An Act for Granting to his Majesty until the sixth day of May next after the ratification of a definitive treaty of peace, a contribution of the profits arising from property, professions, trades and offices." [1]

The law of 1803 introduced a fundamental change in the method of assessment. As this new method is virtually identical with the one followed at the present time, it deserves a somewhat more elaborate description. The alteration consisted in the fact that the taxpayer was no longer assessed directly on his total income regarded as a lump sum, but that his income was now divided into a convenient number of categories or schedules, and that in each schedule the tax was imposed as far as possible upon the source of the income; that is, upon the person who paid the sum which became the income of the party in question. In other words, the tax was stopped at the source. Thus the tax on the owner of the land or of the house was paid by the tenant, who deducted it from the rent; the tax on persons in the employ of the government or of public corporations was paid by the latter, and was deducted from the amounts payable. The exact nature of the alteration and the reasons why the change was made are set forth in an interesting publication which was issued under official auspices.[2] The old income tax, we are told, "called upon the ultimate proprietor to account for that portion of his property, from all and whatever sources it was derived." [3] Unfortunately, however, as we are told, this method

[1] 43 George III, 122.

[2] *An Exposition of the Act for a Contribution on Property, Professions, Trades, and Offices; in which the Principles and Provisions of the Act are fully considered, with a View to facilitate its Execution, both with respect to Persons chargeable, as Persons liable, to the Tax by way of Deduction, and the Officers chosen to carry it into Effect.* London, 1803.

[3] "Comprehending all, without distinguishing any of the sources, it laid an equal contribution on the mass of annual acquirement. . . . It involved the whole, however intricate or extensive, in one account, to be furnished by the party. The produce of trade and commercial adventures, the laborious and industrious avocations, was mixed with the produce of property, requiring neither the skill nor industry of the proprietor to attain or preserve. It was imposed, not

did not work successfully. "It has so happened that this wise and judicious measure, in its operation on the interest of individuals, was found to depend too much on the imperfection of human nature. It became unequal in the execution, and thereby defeated its own principle." In order to obviate these difficulties, and "to preserve and protect the principle of equality," the new method was devised. "As the former was imposed on the general account of income derived from all the sources; the present duty is imposed on each source by itself, in the hand of the first possessor, at the same time permitting and authorizing its diffusion through every natural channel in its course to the hand of the ultimate proprietor. The present measure, then, must be considered as a tax on the first produce, gradually subsiding itself into a tax upon the income of the ultimate proprietor; affecting in its immediate object the hand that acquires, but extending by direct motion to the hand which converts the income so acquired. . . . By these means its object is attained with more facility and certainty, and with less intricacy and disclosure, diminishing the occasions of evasion by the means of execution."[1]

After explaining more in detail the operations of this principle of stoppage at source, the exposition concludes: "Thus the charge is gradually diffused from the first possessor to the ultimate proprietor; and one of the greatest causes of defalcation, arising from the necessity of protecting private transactions from exposure, experienced under the Income Act, is avoided; at the same time protecting the private transactions of life from the public eye, whilst the revenue is more effectually guarded."[2]

In order to distinguish the new tax as much as possible from its predecessor, another name was given to it. Addington, as we have seen, called it in turn a tax upon property, a tax on land and property, or a tax on rents and funds. The law

on its first acquirement, but after its separation into all the channels to which it was destined, on the ultimate possessor." — *Op. cit.*, p. 2.

[1] *Op. cit.*, pp. 3, 4.

[2] *Op. cit.*, p. 5.

itself called it a "contribution of the profits arising from property, professions, trades and offices";[1] while the official exposition called it a "tax on property and productive industry," contrasting it continually with the old "income tax." Others called it a tax on produce. Courtenay, who discussed the subject at some length after the enactment of the law, took exception to all these clumsy attempts at a new nomenclature. "If I may be allowed I will call it a tax upon income. Ministers have shewn a very unworthy desire that this tax should not be so called, but they have not yet hit upon any other name which can be properly applied to it."[2] The criticism of Courtenay, however, shows that he did not appreciate the real character of the change.

As a matter of fact, the law really provided for a series of taxes rather than for a single income tax. As the official exposition correctly puts it: "The act comprehends four different sources of profit, applicable to four principal classes of individuals, under different modes of taxation, each of which must receive a distinct consideration, as if they had formed the subject of four distinct acts of Parliament."[3] These were landed property, funded property, produce of industry, and offices held under government. "Landed property" was reached in two ways, by what was known respectively as the "landlord's duty" and the "tenant's duty." The landlord's duty was dealt with in Schedule A. It was levied on the annual value of all lands, tenements, and hereditaments, that is, the rack rent, less certain deductions for repairs (not to exceed two per cent of the rent for farm-houses, or five

[1] The law of 1803, like that in force at present, speaks in several places of "profits and gains." These words have repeatedly been held to be synonymous and to signify income. "Profits" thus include "interest," from which they are to be distinguished in both the popular and the strict economic sense.

[2] "I must allow," he adds, "that his Majesty's ministers took all the pains they could to depart from the principle of such a tax, so as to get rid of the odium supposed to attach to the name. . . . Unfortunately they abandoned one principle, before they had adopted another in its room." — Courtenay, *Observations*, p. 61. For full title, see *supra*, p. 89.

[3] *An Exposition of the Act*, etc., p. 5.

per cent for other buildings), for land taxes, and for sewers, fencing, embankment, and drainage rates. A few cases of property of a so-called "uncertain annual value," like mines, when carried on as a trade by the owner or a lessee, were to be assessed, as will be seen below, in Schedule D. These subsequently came to be called "concerns about lands," or "concerns arising out of land."

Schedule B dealt with the tenant's duty. It applied to the same property as Schedule A, except that dwelling-houses from which the tenant expected no income were chargeable only when they were connected with farms. Whereas, however, the duty in Schedule A was at the normal rate of five per cent (1*s.* in the £), the rate in Schedule B was 9*d.* in England, and 6*d.* in Scotland. Furthermore, one-eighth was deducted for all tithe-free lands. The tenant's duty was based on the theory that the tenant, after paying his rent, his expenses of cultivation, and his local taxes, would ordinarily acquire for his own purposes a sum equal to three-fourths of the rack rent. Since, however, the local rates in Scotland were paid by the landowner instead of by the occupier, as in England, the net profits of the Scotch tenant were fixed at a sum equal to only one-half of the rent. These figures were selected as affording an approximate standard of accuracy; but, as the exposition tells us, the taxes, in this way, "approximate to that equality which is so desirable without the intricacy of a complicated account, which under the income tax was found so difficult in the execution."[1] The endeavor to ascertain the exact income by the method prescribed in the original law of 1799 had led to such gross evasions and such glaring evils that it became necessary to substitute a new method, and "the certainty, the convenience, and the favourable result to the party, must be taken to be the principle of the alteration, and must be set against the defects which may appear in the inaccuracy, whatever that may be."[2] As we are told in another passage: "A criterion is admitted by all to be necessary, where it is impossible to arrive at the actual

[1] *Op cit.*, p. 13.

[2] *Op. cit.*, p. 14.

profits. Whatever criterion is fixed must necessarily introduce some inequality: the most simple is the most convenient; the most general is the easiest to be understood and pursued. The simplicity and convenience will be admitted in its favour."[1]

As opposed to "landed property," "funded property" was taxable in Schedule C, which applied to all "profits arising from annuities, dividends[2] and shares of annuities" payable out of any public revenue. The Bank of England, the South Sea Company, and the Exchequer, to whom the payment of such dividends was intrusted, were required to furnish an annual account, although the tax itself was to be paid by the stockholders or their agents. This provision, as well as the similar one that foreigners not residing in England should be exempted from this part of the tax, was due to the suggestion of Pitt, in order that the tax might not be interpreted as contravening the guaranteed exemption of government securities from taxation.

Passing over for a moment Schedule D, we come to Schedule E, which comprised income from public office or employment of profit, and from salaries, annuities, pensions, or stipends payable by the Crown or out of the public revenue. A wide interpretation was given to the term "public office or employment" so that it was made to include the income from any corporation, company or society, and from any institution under a public foundation. Here, again, as in Schedules A and B, the tax was assessed to those who paid the income, and who thereupon deducted it from the sums receivable by those entitled to the income. As the law puts it: "The duties shall be detained or stopped and deducted out of the sums in respect whereof they shall be charged."[3] The

[1] *Op. cit.*, p. 17.

[2] The term "dividends" is used in a technical sense. In 1752 the "consols" were created, *i.e.*, certain bank annuities for which the government was responsible were "consolidated into one joint stock of annuities," and were payable in half-yearly *dividends*. "Dividends" thus meant these shares of annuities. It gradually came to mean interest in general on moneys invested in the government fund or securities.

[3] Sec. 192.

management of this schedule was entrusted to a separate set of commissioners.

Finally, Schedule D, which contained the so-called sweeping clause, comprised the profits arising from all property not taxed in Schedules A, B, and C, as well as "the annual profits or gains from any profession, trade, employment, or vocation" not chargeable under Schedule E. In the case of persons residing in Great Britain, it applied to all property, whether situated in or out of Great Britain, as well as to any professions or trades carried on in Great Britain or elsewhere. In the case of persons not residing in Great Britain, it applied only to property or vocations exercised in Great Britain.

The schedule was divided into six so-called cases, a name taken over from the law of 1799. These six cases were as follows: The first case included income from any trade or manufacture. Here the tax was computed on an average of three years' profits. No deductions were allowed for repairs of business premises, and the deductions for repairs and for tools or articles used in carrying on the trade or manufacture was limited to the average of three years. An important point in which the act of 1803 differed from that of 1799 was that in computing the business income, no deductions were permitted for interest and debt except in the case of debts to foreigners not resident in Great Britain. In the old law, where the entire income of the individual was taxed, debts were naturally deducted; in this law, where the object was attained in another way, by the application of the principle of stoppage at source in the other schedules, no deduction for debt was allowed. This was due to the expectation that the debtor would pay the tax, and deduct it from the sums due to the creditor. The object of this regulation, which is still in force to-day, was to avoid both the necessity of disclosure and the fraud which had proved to be inseparable from the older methods.[1] Apart from this, how-

[1] We are told that under the old law "it was thought necessary not to compel the debtor, who was allowed to deduct the interest of debts from the income. to disclose the name of the creditor. This indulgence was the occasion of a

ever, the principle of stoppage at source was thought to be inapplicable in this schedule, although the inquisitorial powers conferred upon the commissioners were supposed to be reduced to a minimum, and the commissioners were "subject to the strictest obligation of secrecy."

The second case included professions, employments, or vocations, and the tax was assessed on the "profits, gains and emoluments within the preceding year," without any deductions. The third case comprised property of an uncertain annual value not charged in Schedule A. It included profits arising from canals, docks, water-works, mines, iron-works, and salt-works, when not let at a certain rent.[1] The tax was assessed on the annual profits or gains, except that in the case of mines a five years' average was taken, unless the mine was "failing," that is, decreasing annually in output, or in case it stopped working altogether. The fourth case included the interest of securities in Ireland, in any of the British possessions, and in any foreign countries. The fifth case comprised income from Irish, colonial, or foreign possessions computed on a three years' average. The sixth case included the "sweeping" clause, that is, annual profits or gains not charged anywhere else. In the whole of Schedule D temporary residents were to be charged only after six months' residence.

The system of exemptions and abatements was altered

great defalcation in the revenue. The debtor was allowed to make the deduction. He, of course, in every instance took advantage of that indulgence. If he also indulged a fraudulent intention he might overstate the amount of his debt, inasmuch as the act, for want of a knowledge of the creditor, afforded no check. If the creditor was inclined to suppress his income arising from interest of money, he might do so without detection, the source of his income not being known. Under the present measure, no inquiry into the amount of debts is necessary; no investigation is required which can affect the debtor's credit. His duty will coincide with his interest. The transaction, as to the duty payable on those debts, will pass wholly between the debtor and the creditor. No greater sum can be deducted, whilst the amount is insured, than the proportion of the duty to the sum actually paid. No disclosure will take place, whilst the revenue is protected." — *An Exposition*, etc., 1803, pp. 46–47.

[1] Secs. 101–103.

in some particulars. Incomes under £60 were entirely exempted, while from £60 to £150 a gradually diminishing abatement was permitted. The normal rate of tax applicable to incomes of £150 and over was five per cent, that is, a shilling in the pound. On incomes from £60 to £70 the rate was only 3*d*; from £70 to £80, 4*d*, and so on, until incomes from £140 to £150 paid 11*d*. The allowances for children, which were made applicable whenever the number of children exceeded two, were now fixed as follows: —

On incomes from £60 to £400, 4 % for each additional child.
On incomes from £400 to £1000, 3 % for each additional child.
On incomes from £1000 to £5000, 2 % for each additional child.
Over £5000, 1 % for each additional child.

The administrative features of the act of 1803 were copied from that of 1799, with a few significant exceptions. The General Commissioners were, as before, selected by the Commissioners for the Land Tax; but provision was now made for the appointment of a new class of commissioners known as the Additional Commissioners, who still exist to-day. These commissioners were to be selected by the General Commissioners, with qualifications fixed at one-half of the property necessary for the latter.[1] Not more than seven nor less than three of these were to act in any district, and they might divide themselves into committees, if necessary.

The Additional Commissioners were now to assess the duty in Schedule C, which, as before, did not apply to government stock held by foreigners.[2] In Schedule D the assessors were to be summoned by the Additional Commissioners, and all returns were to be made to them.[3] If the surveyors or inspectors, however, were dissatisfied at the decision of the Additional Commissioners, they might require them to "state a case" for the General Commissioners. The Additional Commissioners, moreover, might, of their own volition, in general refer any statements to the General Commissioners.

In Schedules A and B, the surveyors or inspectors, who

[1] Secs. 18–20. [2] Sec. 71. [3] Secs. 105 *et seq.*

were to be the same as those appointed to enforce the duties on houses and windows, and the assessed taxes, might amend or surcharge the returns of individuals as brought in by the assessors. The surcharge was to be treble duty; but the officials were subjected to a severe penalty in case they made "a false or vexatious surcharge."[1] A new provision was also inserted for the business assessments. If the taxpayer preferred, he might nominate two referees who, when satisfactory to the commissioners, were to estimate the profits from such certificates or other documents as might be submitted to them by the taxpayer. If the referees could not agree, a third referee might be appointed, the decision of the majority to be binding.[2] The referee might also serve in cases where appeals were made against any assessment by the Additional Commissioners, or against any objection made by the surveyors or inspectors.[3] The general penalty, where assessments were increased or where persons were convicted of fraud, was now fixed at double the duty,[4] while the penalty for neglecting to deliver a schedule or to attend the summons of the commissioners was £50. It was also provided that the tax should be payable in quarterly instalments.[5] Finally, a curious survival of the triple assessment consisted in the provision made for the acceptance of voluntary contributions from citizens.[6]

Thus was introduced into England the principle of stoppage at source in the income tax. As compared with the old method of the direct, lump-sum assessment of incomes, the effects were immediately noticeable. Although the rate of the new tax was only one-half of the old one, — five per cent instead of ten per cent, — the yield was almost the same, — £5,350,000 in 1803 as compared to £5,600,000 in 1801. In other words, the alteration in the principle of assessment at one blow doubled the efficiency of the tax. No more signal proof could be afforded of the vital importance of good administrative methods in fiscal practice.

[1] Secs. 63–64.
[2] Secs. 111 *et seq.*
[3] Sec. 157.
[4] Secs. 155–156.
[5] Sec. 210.
[6] Sec. 218.

The old opponents of the system could not reconcile themselves to the law, however. Travers, for instance, sent out a circular letter calling for a mass meeting to agitate for a repeal of at least that part of the tax which applied to business profits. In a letter addressed "to the Citizens of London engaged in commerce and profession," he stated: "The tax on property, so-called, is, in fact, a revival of that most hateful tax — the tax on income, under more severe and objectionable restrictions."[1] The letter was sent to the mayors of the various towns. Some officials, like the town clerk of Northampton, applauded his "laudable and patriotic exertions for procuring a repeal of that odious and degrading part of the Property Tax Act, which relates to trade and commerce." Others, on the contrary, like the mayor of Totnes, considered "that the tax, in its present form, is perfectly just and reasonable: it is just, as it affects property of every description; and it is reasonable, from its scale of taxation."[2] The City of London, which had prided itself on contributing to the repeal of the tax in 1802, held a public meeting in July, 1803, to consider the matter. Some extremists declared that if the income tax were necessary to save the country, it would be better to have the country go than to endure the tax. But others said that it would be wiser to declare part of one's profits to the income tax commissioners than to give up all to Napoleon. As a consequence, no resolution was adopted. The most vociferous opponent of the measure was Frend, who poured out the vials of his wrath on "the present falsely called Property Act, . . . which, though less oppressive on income, is far more inquisitorial than the last."[3] In forming

[1] He added: "When the odious, degrading, and injurious nature of the tax is considered, the vexatious and tyrannical inquisition it will give rise to, and more especially the immorality of its tendency, by reason of the utter impossibility of ascertaining income of this kind . . . it is earnestly hoped that the citizens of London will show their unqualified abhorrence of a tax which, if persisted in, cannot fail to excite the most general discontent." This letter is printed in full in Frend, *The Principles of Taxation*, 1804, p. 16. For full title, see *supra*, p. 88.

[2] Frend, *op. cit.*, pp. 18, 20.

[3] Frend, *op. cit.*, pp. iii, iv.

our estimate of a tax we must consider, said Frend, "not only the sum raised, but the frauds, the perjuries, the prevarications, the imprisonments, the ruin of families, the destruction of morals." [1] The new law, moreover, he thought, was so complicated as to be unintelligible.[2] The government, however, went its way undeterred and undismayed, and the murmurings gradually subsided.

In 1805 the exigencies of the war caused Pitt, who was now again in office, to propose and to carry through an addition of one-fourth to the income tax, the rate now being increased from five to six and one-quarter per cent.[3] Fox objected that the tax "was taking little by little from the property of the subject till the reduction was tantamount to the risk of the whole," but Pitt held that it would be "most desirable to levy direct rather than indirect taxes as far as possible." [4] A subsequent act of the same year[5] provided for several changes in the regulations. Among the important ones were the following: the transference of the assessment of "concerns about lands,"[6] from Schedule D to Schedule A, where they still remain to-day; the provision that the profits of a married woman living with her husband be considered a part of his profits;[7] a further allowance of deductions for repairs in Schedule A;[8] the extension of exemption to charitable institutions in general in Schedule A; the deduction of the tax paid on business premises in Schedule B from the tax due on business profits in Schedule D; and the adoption of a new rule in the third case of Schedule D, relating to "profits on exchequer bills and other securities bearing interest out of the public revenues and on all discounts and on all interest of money not being annual interest." [9]

[1] Frend, *The Principles of Taxation*, p. 9.

[2] Referring to the act itself in 114 folio pages and the *Exposition* in 66 8vo pages, Frend said: "*Obscurum per obscurius*. If there is a single man in the kingdom who understands either the one or the other, I congratulate him on his patience and attention." — *Op. cit.*, p. 29.

[3] 45 George III, c. 15.

[4] Hansard, vol iii, pp. 552 *et seq.*

[5] 45 George III, c. 49.

[6] See *supra*, p. 93.

[7] Sec. 101.

[8] Sec. 37.

[9] Sec. 93.

In 1806, after the battle of Austerlitz and the death of Pitt, the coalition ministry of Grenville and Fox came into power, and the rate was further increased by the new Chancellor of the Exchequer, Lord Henry Petty, to ten per cent. Petty defended the increase on the ground that "a gradual rise would have led to the supposition that this was a fund to be drawn upon to an indefinite extent; but, being raised at once to its natural limit, there would be less suspicion of future augmentation." Fox now stated that this explanation satisfied him, although Francis pertinently asked "Why is ten per cent a more natural limit than eleven per cent?"[1] The experience with the law, however, had disclosed several defects, so that advantage was taken of the opportunity to make some notable changes in the system. As the law now in force is, with slight alterations, a virtual reprint of the Act of 1806, it merits special attention.

§ 7. *The Act of 1806*

As early as 1805, Heslop had published a pamphlet in which he pointed out some of the shortcomings of the tax with special reference to the abatements, which he thought had been carried too far.[2] Relying chiefly on the advice of the administrative officials, Lord Henry Petty, in introducing the bill and in alluding to the frauds which had been committed by persons claiming total exemption, proposed that these exemptions should be materially restricted. In the debate of May 20, 1806, Vansittart declared that "for three years exemptions had been tried and were uniformly found to defeat themselves and the operation of the tax." The government, therefore, had no difficulty in carrying through its proposals.

[1] Hansard, vol. vi, p. 577.

[2] *Observations on the Duty on Property, Professions, etc., to render its Assessment simple and to Improve it.* [By Luke Heslop] London, n. d. [1805]. Heslop also advocated the principle of discrimination, with higher rates on what he called permanent property. *Cf.* pp. 13 *et seq.*

The new "property and income tax act," as it was now called, which was especially limited to the April following a definitive treaty of peace,[1] contained three important classes of modifications, most of which have remained to the present day. The first was the extension of the stoppage-at-source idea originally applied in Addington's act of 1803. It will be remembered that in Schedule C, while the Bank of England was required to make certain returns as to the dividends from the public funds, the tax itself was assessed on the owner or his agent.[2] Henceforth, however, the Bank of England itself was required to make the assessment and to deduct the tax. Foreigners not resident in the British dominions were exempt upon proof of their claims. Thus was Schedule C assimilated to Schedules A, B, and E. Moreover, Schedule C was now enlarged by taking over from the third case of Schedule D the duty on all securities issued at any governmental office.

The second class of alterations involved the abatements and deductions. In the first place, the right of total exemption was declared inapplicable to incomes derived from property, such as real estate, securities, and moneyed capital in general, with a few minor exceptions.[3] The total exemption, hence, was restricted substantially to incomes from trades, professions, and personal exertions.[4]

Secondly, the limit of total exemption, in the cases where it still remained, was reduced from £60 to £50. The reasons for this change are well put in the official Guide Book. "So

[1] 46 George III, c. 65. "An Act for granting to his Majesty during the present war, and until the sixth day of April next after the ratification of a definitive treaty of peace, further additional rates and duties in Great Britain on the rates and duties on profits arising from property and professions, trades and offices."

[2] The last provision as to agents had been repealed by 44 George III, c. 37.

[3] These were cottages not exceeding forty shillings a year, occupied by the owners; property not exceeding the annual value of £5, belonging to laborers whose wages did not exceed thirty shillings a week; ecclesiastical profits; profits of mines and quarries, and annuities under £50 a year.

[4] Dowell, *History of Taxation*, 2d ed., iii, p. 103, is characteristically inaccurate in stating that it applied only to wage-earners. Buxton, *Finance and Politics*, i, p. 309, who evidently copied from Dowell, makes the same mistake.

baneful is indulgence on weak minds that this regulation, intended to have a strict and limited operation, has been introductive of the greatest fraud on the public," many people in easy circumstances having returned their income as just under £60.[1] In the third place, the system of abatements was so changed that with every pound of income below £150, 1 shilling tax was deducted; thus, at

£50 the charge was 100*s*.	The abatement was 100*s*.	The tax was 0*s*.
£51 the charge was 102*s*.	The abatement was 99*s*.	The tax was 3*s*.
£52 the charge was 104*s*.	The abatement was 98*s*.	The tax was 6*s*.
	and so on, until at	
£149 the charge was 298*s*.	The abatement was 1*s*.	The tax was 297*s*.
£150 the charge was 300*s*.	The abatement was 0*s*.	The tax was 300*s*.

Fourthly, as the deduction for children under the old law had led to an astounding official increase of large families, this was now discontinued. Fifthly, the allowance for repairs to houses in Schedule A was abandoned, for the reason, as stated in the Guide Book, that it had been found "so inadequate and to operate so inequally, and to be demanded in many cases where repairs were done by tenants."[2] Finally, the allowance for life-insurance premiums was restricted to persons with an income under £150.

Several changes were also made in the details of the different schedules. In Schedule A, where the ordinary rule was the assessment on the profits for the year, tithes in kind were assessed on an average of three years, manors and other royalties on an average of seven years, and mines on an average of five years. In Schedule B, warehouses and other business premises were exempted from taxation. In Schedule D, in the third case applying to profits of "an uncertain annual value" a new provision was inserted applicable to dealers in cattle and sellers of milk. Where the lands occupied by such dealers were not sufficient for the sustenance of the cattle, so that the rent of the lands did not afford a just estimate of the profits of the dealer, the commissioners were authorized to increase the charge.

[1] *Guide to the Property Tax Act*, 1806, p. 13.

[2] *Op. cit.*, p. 14.

The important changes in administrative procedure were as follows: In the first place, the whole system of referees, as provided in the law of 1803, which had not worked well, was now dropped. The system of Additional Commissioners was, on the contrary, retained. In the next place, provision was made for a new set of commissioners known as commissioners for the "special purposes of this Act," or, for short, Special Commissioners. These were invested with the function of granting allowances in Schedule A, of supervising the exemptions in Schedule C, and of taking charge of the assessment of foreign dividends. These Special Commissioners were not selected by the General Commissioners, as were the Additional Commissioners, but were appointed by the Commissioners for the Affairs of Taxes, representing the central government.

The provision as to the liability to the tax after six months' residence was altered so as to make the residence cumulative; that is, if a person resided in England for a short time, then departed, and again returned, he was liable, if during the year he had resided altogether for a period of six months.[1] The provisions with reference to assessors, notices, lists, etc., which had previously been confined to Schedule D, were now made applicable to all schedules. The abatement in Schedule D which was permitted to taxpayers when they could prove that their actual profits were less than the amount assessed upon them and which, under the law of 1803, had been allowed only where the taxpayer was not assessed on the average system, was now extended to all cases, irrespective of whether the taxpayer had been assessed on his year's profits, or on the three years' average system.[2] In all other respects, however, the administrative provisions of the earlier laws were continued.

The improvements effected in the operation of the law through the extension of the stoppage-at-source principle, and through the alterations mentioned above, were at once reflected in the yield. The rate, as we have seen, was raised

[1] Sec. 52.

[2] Sec. 139.

from six and one-fourth to ten per cent; yet the produce of the tax jumped from £6,429,599 in 1805 to £12,822,056 in 1806. In other words, roughly speaking, an increase in the rate of the tax by only one-half doubled the yield; a fifty per cent augmentation resulted in one hundred per cent increase in the produce. This, again, affords a striking illustration of the significance to be attached to administrative methods.

During the continuance of the war, that is, for just a decade, the tax remained in force at the same rate of ten per cent. Owing in part to the growth of population and industry, but in still larger measure to the increasing efficiency of the administrative methods, the yield of the tax gradually rose, until toward the end of the period its produce amounted to almost £16,000,000 — well-nigh eighty million dollars — a prodigious sum for those days. As a fiscal device, there could be no doubt as to its success.

The fame of the income tax spread to the Continent.[1] The literary critics were gradually silenced, and were limited either to well-meaning and somewhat crack-brained enthusiasts, like Coad, who included well-nigh all existing taxes in his denunciations,[2] or to writers like Grey, who demanded a reduction of the burdens on particular classes, as, for instance, the military and naval officers.[3] Several efforts were made by the

[1] *Cf. Das Britische Besteuerungs-System, insbesondere die Einkommensteuer, dargestellt mit Hinsicht auf die in der Preussischen Monarchie zu treffenden Einrichtungen.* Von Friedrich von Raumer. Berlin, 1810. Raumer, however, is much opposed to the whole scheme. See esp. p. 233.

[2] Coad speaks of the income tax as being "in its nature the most perplexing, in its effects the most ruinous, and in its opperations (*sic*) the most partial." — *A New Plan of Taxation. This Plan will render the Custom and Excise Duties useless, abolish the Income Tax, take off all the Assessed Taxes, and reduce Provisions more than Seventy per cent, etc.* By Joseph Coad. London, 1807, p. 10. He uses almost equally violent language, however, as to all other taxes, except the land tax and the poll tax, which constitute his "new plan of finance."

[3] Grey grows very eloquent in his metaphors. "The tax has no passover; the destroying angel visits every door, allows of the validity of no mark of blood on the lintel and side-posts, to induce him to pause in his destructive course; for the destroyer comes, with ferocious swoop, into our houses, to smite us and our first-born; no door is exempt from his dire visitations." — *A Letter Addressed by Col.*

opposition, but to no avail, in 1806, 1808 and 1809, to abolish the exemption for foreign holders of government stock.[1] The Scotch farmers also complained, in 1808 and 1810, of the method of assessing profits on the basis of rentals, holding that farmers' profits were often as fluctuating as those of business men.[2] In 1811, Turton protested against the lack of what would now be called both differentiation and graduation, but the Chancellor of the Exchequer objected to both schemes, stating as to the latter that "as for laying a higher income tax upon the richer classes, it would be a complete subversion of all the principles of justice, by which the property of all men should be equally protected by the law."[3] In the main, however, all discussion of the tax was silenced in the face of the gigantic struggle against Napoleon.

§ 8. *The Repeal of the Income Tax*

As the war drew to a close, however, a movement was set on foot to compel the government to redeem its pledge and to drop the tax. The City of London, as usual, led in the agitation, and drew up a petition in December, 1814. Other towns followed during the next few months. When parliament opened, in February, 1815, Vansittart, Chancellor of the Exchequer, declared that he did not intend to renew the tax. He stated that it ought to be held "as a great and powerful resource which, in times of public emergency, might and ought to be resorted to," but he thought that the great fluctuations in prices then going on would "render it peculiarly vexatious and disagreeable to large classes."[4] So great was the joy occasioned by the announcement that Tierney made a celebrated speech with a peroration in which "he begged

John Grey to a Member of the House of Commons on the Subject of the Liability of the Pay of the Officers of the Navy and Army to the Tax upon Property. London, 1810, pp. 28, 29.

[1] See Hansard, vol. vii, p. 407; vol. xi, p. 898; vol. xiv, p. 1018.

[2] See the *Farmer's Magazine* for 1808, *passim*, and for 1810, p. 519.

[3] Hansard, vol. xx, p. 747.

[4] Hansard, vol. xxix, p. 853.

pardon of God and of the public for the part he had taken in imposing the property tax in 1806." "The greatest merit of the tax," said he, "was the dislike so generally felt to it, and if it could be held out to the people *in terrorem* against entering into war, it had done great service indeed." [1]

There were not wanting, indeed, able and far-sighted men, both in and out of parliament, who contended that it would be a serious mistake to destroy the system that had been so laboriously built up. Thus the anonymous author of an excellent monograph called attention, at the close of 1814, to the "considerable pains that have been or are about to be taken to prejudice the public mind on the subject of the property tax." He ascribed to the income tax much of the existing prosperity, and in discussing the great productiveness of the tax, he asked whether anyone would claim that "the (so-called) inquisitorial power attached to its assessment and collection has been more actively and vexatiously exerted. This assertion," he thought, "no one will be found bold enough to make, for it is self-evident that the inconveniences of this nature have rather diminished than increased." [2] In another place he tells us that "its inquisitorial powers have in a great measure, as to practice, gone to the 'Tomb of all the Capulets.' Those who recollect the impost in the earliest stages, will all join in this opinion." [3] After adverting to the unexpected augmentation of the yield, he asked: "To what cause, then, is the increase of its produce to be ascribed?" "To nothing," he replied, "but the efficacy and excellence of its principle." "Why, then," he asked, "destroy in its infancy a system calculated to call forth the wealth of the nation, to enable it to expand its powers, to increase its energies, and in a great measure relieve it from the horrible burthen of debt under which it now groans." [4] Referring to the opposition to

[1] Hansard, *ibid.*, p. 875.

[2] *Strong Reasons for the Continuance of the Property Tax. To which is added an Estimate of the National Income recently made by Patrick Colquhoun.* By a Friend to his Country. London, 1814, p. 12.

[3] *Op. cit.*, pp. 34, 35.

[4] *Op. cit.*, pp. 12–14.

the tax, he pointed out that "its character is curious. It partakes of those symptoms always indicating a mind tinctured with prejudice, and prejudice of the grossest and most ignorant kind. It seems to be a species of mania."[1] The author closed his refutation of the objections by stating: "I contend that so far from the tax bearing the features ascribed to it, that there are no proofs of their existence."[2]

Another writer, although nominally opposed to the "present income or property tax," suggested what he called "the general substitute," which on close analysis turned out to be nothing but a general income tax. For individuals, he thought, ought to pay according to their abilities, and "the means to be employed as a criterion of their abilities which is the best that can be procured of all criterions, is the income of the parties."[3] A third writer, who described himself as "a considerable landed proprietor," said that he was "one of those who certainly think that an income tax has some advantages that make it very proper to be retained."[4] The author, nevertheless, inclined to the opinion that taxes on commercial and trade profits were inadvisable, because of their tendency to be shifted to the consumer.

The most weighty defence of the tax, however, was made by Rose in a speech in parliament. Baring had maintained that "the property tax is the most unjustifiable and oppressive measure of finance that has ever been resorted to in any country on earth. . . ."[5] All the opprobrious epithets that had been heaped upon it appeared to him not to come up to its deserts. Rose, in his reply, did not deny that the tax

[1] *Strong Reasons*, etc., p. 73.

[2] *Op. cit.*, p. 74.

[3] *Three most Important Objects Proposed.* By the author of *The Income and Property Tax.* York, 1815, p. 26.

[4] *Two Letters to the Right Honourable Viscount Castlereagh, on the Present Situation of the Landed Interest, and the intended Partial Repeal of the Income Tax.* London, 1816, p. 16. *Cf. A Defense of the Landowners and Farmers of Great Britain and an Exposition of the Heavy Parliamentary and Parochial Taxation under which they labour.* By an Agricultural Gentleman. London, 1814. See also *A Pat from the Lion's Paw inflicted in the Name of Common Sense, upon the Railers against the Property Tax.* By Leo Britannicus. London, 1815.

"has been felt as a most severe pressure by many,"[1] but after recounting the history of the tax and the enormous services which it had rendered to the country, he contended that its abolition would necessitate the laying of fresh taxes which would "not only be more oppressive than the one so strongly objected to," but would result in shifting the burden of supporting the state from those better able to pay to those of less ability. If the income tax is abolished, he warns us, "those who can best bear the burden can be relieved only at the expense of persons less opulent and in inferior situations in life."[2] In conclusion, Rose expressed himself as "satisfied to conviction on very long experience and deep reflection, that the ingenuity of man cannot devise so wise and provident a mode of raising the money immediately wanted, as by the Property Tax amended and modified."

The escape of Napoleon from Elba a few days later, on February 26, 1815, created the greatest consternation, and led the government to reconsider its determination. On April 17, Vansittart proposed to continue the tax for another year, and, after considerable opposition, carried his point. Whitford warned the House that if again imposed it would be saddled on the country forever, and Ponsonby stated that "few persons in the House or out of it would live to see it taken off." The Marquis of Douglas concluded that the tax was unjust and unconstitutional, and frankly stated

[1] The speech was reprinted in a pamphlet entitled *The Speech of the Right Honourable George Rose in the House of Commons on the 20th of February, 1815, on the Subject of the Property Tax.* London, 1815. *Cf.* p. 8.

[2] *Op. cit.*, p. 21. "It is not in the smallest degree to be wondered at," said Rose, in another passage, "that when a numerous assembly of persons of all descriptions were asked whether they desired to be relieved from a heavy contribution, without a substitute for it being mentioned, every hand should be held up in the affirmative; but it may reasonably be doubted whether a very different sensation might not have prevailed at such meetings, if the parties present had been aware that an immensely productive tax could not in the present state of the country be given up, without some other heavy impositions to a very great amount being substituted to supply its place." — *Op. cit.*, p. 7. *Cf. Considerations addressed to the People of Great Britain on the Expediency of continuing the Property Tax a certain number of Years.* London, 1815.

that the proper objects of taxation were articles of luxury and "matters of that kind because they limited themselves."[1]

When the battle of Waterloo finally assured peace, every one supposed that the government would now abandon the tax. Vansittart, however, had been much influenced by the arguments of Rose, and at the opening of the next parliament in February, 1816, proposed the retention of the tax for a few years at least, although at half rates.[2] This gave the signal for a storm of opposition. It seemed a golden opportunity to the business classes, and petition upon petition poured in on parliament, praying for the repeal of the tax. At one of the county meetings a supporter of the petition for repeal characterized the duty as a "pistol tax."[3] The merchants of London, as usual, took the lead in the opposition, the Court of Common Council unanimously adopting resolutions that "it was not necessary to enumerate the grievances resulting from it, and that the taxes had become altogether insupportable." They added that "the manner in which the tax is carried into execution (by means of an odious, arbitrary, and detestable inquisition into the most private concerns and circumstances of individuals) is still more vexatious, unjust, and oppressive; hostile to every sense of freedom, revolting to the feelings of Englishmen, and repugnant to the principles of the British Constitution." They declared "their abhorrence of the measure," and resolved that "to adopt the tax, upon a reduced scale, would be to make a fatal inroad upon the Constitution and would lead to the subversion of the Rights and Liberties of the People."[4] The Court was followed by a Common Hall of the Livery which resolved "that to attempt a renewal of a tax so oppressive and unconstitutional" would be "highly irritating to a loyal and generous People, and calculated to

[1] Hansard, vol. xxxi, p. 242.

[2] Hansard, vol. xxxii, pp. 376 *et seq.*

[3] *Taxes on Beer and Wine.* By William Cobbett. London, n. d. [1863], p. 23.

[4] The Resolutions are printed in full on p. 20 of the pamphlet entitled *Resist or be Ruined*, mentioned on the next page.

produce consequences of the most alarming nature."[1] One of the members of parliament, by the name of Grant, stated that the bare introduction of its name was "insulting to the sense and feelings of the nation." The general sentiments of the opposition are illustrated in a violent essay of Glover, a clergyman, who put the ordinary objections in grandiloquent terms,[2] and who, after declaring that "we have no superfluity of property, whether public or private, to be idly sported with," concluded that it is "inconsistent with all our best notions of the principles of legislation, and deficient in every essential property of a tax suited to a free government; that it is arbitrary and unlimited in principle, partial and unjust in operation, destructive of agriculture, and ruinous to commerce; that it saps the foundation of public virtue, and commits the most horrible havoc upon public morals."[3] A widely circulated pamphlet bore a title beginning with the words, "Resist or be Ruined," and was filled with the most extreme statements.[4]

The agitation throughout the country was fomented by the opposition in every conceivable way. The Ministry regarded it as a mere political manœuvre, and endeavored

[1] *Ibid.*, p. 30.

[2] "Credit and mutual confidence are the great bases of commercial intercourse. . . . With unceremonious intrusion, the income tax violates and invades every one of these stamina, and, while it tempts on one hand the ruined bankrupt to make a show of profits and of income which he does not possess, and affords him a friendly screen for his frauds and his imposture, it pries with inquisitorial eye into the concerns of the honest and substantial trader, and exposes the channels of his trade."—*Thoughts on the Character and Tendency of the Property Tax, as adapted to a Permanent System of Taxation.* By the Rev. George Glover. London, 1816, 2d ed., p. 564. The first edition appeared in the *Pamphleteer.*

[3] *Op. cit.*, p. 566. The author's erudition may be seen from his statement that "Florence was a free republic, and I remember no traces of an income tax." *Cf.* also *The Property Tax considered with reference to its Renewal.* London, 1816.

[4] The full title of this pamphlet is *Resist or be Ruined! The Property Tax must be abolished now, or a State Inquisition will be established in England for ever. The immediate Resistance of the whole Nation shewn to be the only Means of averting an Inquisitorial and Perpetual Income Tax, from which Mr. Vansittart has declared no Class of Society will be exempted. With a full Account of the Proceedings in London.* London, 1816.

to expedite the decision of the matter. On March 5 Vansittart explained in detail the various modifications which he proposed to introduce in order to render the bill more palatable.[1] The opposition, however, saw their opportunity in delay; for the longer the decision could be postponed, the greater the chances of their fanning the flames of discontent. Accordingly, the speeches in parliament became interminable, Brougham calling it the "most tormenting of all taxes." Lord John Russell said that "there could be no more dreadful calamity for this country than its continuance." Tierney maintained that, "if the people of England would submit to bear half of it, they were fully entitled to be saddled with the whole." One speaker characterized it as "that detestable and shameful tax"; another as an "abominable measure." Meetings of protest throughout the country were multiplied. Petitions to parliament poured in by the thousands, and it is said that it took six weeks simply to receive and classify them. So fierce was the clamor of opposition that the newspapers discussed what might be done to prevent the further execution of the law in case the government should succeed in continuing the tax. Some even proposed an outright refusal to pay, on the ground that if this refusal became universal, the government would be rendered impotent. The Ministry, on the other hand, contended that all this agitation was being artificially engendered by the opposition; that in reality the country was not opposed to the tax; that they were not guilty of betrayal of promise, since every parliament had a perfect right to continue any tax it saw fit. Above all, they maintained that the excitement was due to the machinations of a few wealthy individuals who desired to escape their fair share of taxation.

Up to the last moment the fate of the bill remained in doubt. The government had counted upon a majority, and the opposition had hoped at best for only a bare victory. When the bill finally came to a vote in parliament on March 18, 1816, after a most exciting debate, Lord Brougham, the

[1] Hansard, xxxii, p. 809.

leader of the opposition, contented himself with reading in impressive tones the wording of the law: "Be it enacted that this act shall continue in force during the present war and until April 6th next and after the definite signing of a treaty of peace, *and no longer.*" "The shouts which these three words raised," says Lord Brougham, in his autobiography, "I shall never forget. We divided immediately and threw out the bill." The motion to retain the tax was defeated by the comparatively narrow majority of thirty-seven, and the result, we are told, "was declared amidst the greatest cheering and the loudest exultation ever witnessed within the halls of the English Senate."[1] Brougham thereupon moved that all the records of the tax be destroyed, and the motion was adopted by an overwhelming majority.

Thus came to an end England's first attempt to introduce the income tax, and thus by a slight majority and by dint of a most skilfully conducted political campaign did parliament set its seal of disapproval on the project of making the tax a permanent part of the fiscal system.

When we reflect that the agitation both in parliament and throughout the country had been carried on with the utmost adroitness, and even unscrupulousness; when we remember that every effort had been made to fan the flames of prejudice and of discontent; when, finally, we note the disadvantages under which every government necessarily labors when it proposes to continue, in time of peace, a tax that is expressly granted only for a period of war, — when we bear in mind all these considerations, it is only a fair inference to conclude that so slight a majority, attained in such a way, in favor of the repeal of the tax, did not really represent the well-considered opinion of the great mass of the public. It

[1] *The History of the Taxation of England.* By William Tayler. London, 1853, p. 71. Even the staid Hansard says: "As soon as the numbers were announced in the House, a loud cheering took place which lasted for several minutes. Similar exultation was manifested by the crowd of strangers in the lobby and the avenues of the House."

was in reality only a victory of parliamentary strategy. But after all it was a victory.

Those, however, who hoped that a final quietus had been put on what they affected to consider a hateful impost were doomed to disappointment. The sentiment in favor of an income tax, in fact, never completely died out, and scarcely more than a quarter of a century was to elapse before the tax was to be reimposed, and that, too, as history was to show, in a permanent form.

APPENDIX

The Produce of the Income Tax, 1798–1815[1]

1798	£1,855,996
1799	6,046,624
1800	6,244,438
1801	5,628,903
1802	——
1803	5,341,907
1804	4,111,924
1805	6,429,599
1806	12,822,056
1807	11,905,588
1808	13,482,294
1809	13,631,922
1810	14,453,320
1811	14,462,776
1812	15,488,546
1813	15,795,691
1814	14,188,037
1815	15,642,338

[1] *Cf. Report of the Commissioners of the Inland Revenue*, 1870, vol. ii, Appendix, p. 184.

CHAPTER II

THE INCOME TAX ON TRIAL, 1842–1862

§ 1. *The Interval, 1816–1832*

NOTWITHSTANDING the reduction of expenditure to a peace footing, the repeal of the income tax left a gap in the revenues which it became necessary to make good by imposing new taxes. As Rose had predicted, the great mass of these new revenues consisted in burdensome indirect taxes, and before long England was groaning under a heavy load. The situation as it existed in the year 1820 is well portrayed in the familiar description by Sydney Smith, in an article in the *Edinburgh Review* of that year. "We can inform Brother Jonathan what is the inevitable consequence of being too fond of glory. Taxes upon every article which enters into the mouth or covers the back or is placed under the foot. Taxes upon everything which it is pleasant to see, hear, feel, smell or taste. Taxes upon warmth, light and locomotion. Taxes on everything on earth or under the earth, on everything that comes from abroad or is grown at home. Taxes on the raw material, taxes on every fresh value that is added to it by the industry of man. Taxes on the sauces which pamper man's appetite and the drug which restores him to health; on the ermine which decorates the judge, and the rope which hangs the criminal; on the poor man's salt and the rich man's spice; on the brass nails of the coffin and the ribbons of the bride; at bed or board, couchant or levant, we must pay. The schoolboy whips his taxed top; the beardless youth manages his taxed horse with a taxed bridle, on a taxed road, and the dying Englishman, pouring his medicine, which has paid seven per cent, into a spoon which has paid fifteen per cent, flings himself back upon a chintz bed, which has paid twenty-two per cent, and expires in the arms of an apothecary who has paid a license of one hundred pounds for the privilege of putting him to death. His whole property is then immediately taxed from two to ten per cent, besides the probate judge's fees demanded for burying him in the chancel; his virtues are handed down to posterity on taxed marble, and he will then be gathered to his fathers to be taxed no more."

Few, however, ventured to suggest a return to the old system. Wilkinson, it is true, wrote in 1820 a work designed to prove that "the present fiscal system compels the labourer, a dwarf in wealth, to carry the load of the lord, who is a giant in affluence"; and he implored the government to "express the taxes out of the accumulated wealth of the country, and not out of the blood and sinews and bones of a devoted and indefatigable people."[1] Wilkinson laid down the general principle that "however prejudice, interest, and sophistry may decide, it is contended that property is the only legitimate source of taxation: all the subterfuges of chicane and jesuitism ought never to cloud over this important fact."[2] His was, however, a voice in the wilderness. It was not until about a decade later that any real interest was manifested in the subject.

Toward the end of the twenties and the beginning of the thirties the agitation for a change in the system of taxation became more marked, and reflected itself not only in parliamentary discussion, but in a considerable literature. At first

[1] *The Principle of an Equitable and Efficient System of Finance: Founded upon self-evident, universal and invariable Principles, capable of diminishing Taxes and Poor-Rates; reviving and permanently supporting Agriculture, Trade, Commerce, Wealth, and Happiness. Demonstrating that the existing System of Finance is Capricious, Impolitic and Improvident; Injurious to Liberty, Property, and Legislation; Proving the Necessity of repealing all existing Taxes, both General and Local; and adopting One, Simple, Equitable, and Efficient, grounded upon a Scale Just, Wise and Unchangeable. By the Adoption of this Plan the Dread of the Rich would be removed, the Distress of the Poor relieved, and the Confidence of All restored; etc., etc.* By Harrison Wilkinson. London, 1820, pp. x, xi.

[2] *Op. cit.*, p. xii.

the reformers cast about for some other substitute. Thus the author of an interesting publication, who was bitterly opposed to the whole existing system of indirect taxes, suggested that it be replaced by a general tax on houses. This, he thought, would be an inestimable boon to the public, while as a consequence of its great yield, even the "poor rates would tumble down like an ill-built and unseemly edifice; and all would slide on with tranquillity and ease into increasing prosperity."[1] Gradually, however, the reversion to the original idea became more pronounced, and some writers proposed an income tax, others suggested a property tax, and some even advocated a graduated property or income tax.

In Parliament, Huskisson, speaking on March 18, 1830, on the subject of the general distress, recommended a repeal of the most grievous indirect taxes, and suggested in their stead "a direct tax upon property, limited to capital not directly employed in the pursuits of industry."[2] A few days later, a general debate was precipitated by Poulett Thomson who, in making an unsuccessful motion for a committee on taxation a week later, declared himself in principle at least in favor of a property tax. Referring to Huskisson's speech, he announced his entire agreement with the proposal,[3] although, to use the words of an eminent successor, he was "cautious and even timid in suggesting the idea"; and while "avowing his own disposition to adopt it," took "care to disclaim it as

[1] *Thoughts on Taxation. Dedicated with the most profound Respect to the Right Honorable the Speaker and Gentlemen of the Commons House of Parliament.* London, 1827, pp. 9, 23.

[2] Hansard, vol. xxiii, pp. 604–606.

[3] "On the question of a great mutation of taxation, and the substitution of a direct tax upon income for a large portion of our indirect taxes, I think it but just to myself, and but fair to the House to declare my concurrence in the view he takes upon the subject. I agree with him in thinking that under proper regulations and with sufficient securities, such a change would be beneficial in the highest degree to the industry and improvement of the country." He added, however, "that as a consideration of this question did not form a part of the motion for a committee he would not discuss it any further at this time." —Speech of March 25, 1830, in Hansard, vol. xxiii, p. 876.

an essential part of his plan."[1] Even Lord Althorp, who admitted his inconsistency, declared that, in his opinion, to reduce taxes and to "impose a property tax to meet the deficiency thus occasioned, would be a very good measure."[2] The strongest advocate of the scheme, however, was Sir Henry Parnell. Parnell had hoped to bring the whole matter before the Finance Committee appointed at his instance in 1828. But the committee was discontinued, and Parnell, as a consequence, published his views in a weighty and influential volume. In the debate in 1830 he contented himself with saying that "he should have no objection to a modified property tax."[3] In his book on the general subject of fiscal reform, he took far stronger ground. Maintaining that bad taxes could not be repealed without a suitable substitute being found, he pointed out that in the choice of this substitute there was no doubt in his own mind. "In selecting a new tax," he tells us, "there seems to be but one opinion with respect to what tax that ought to be. Persons who hold the most opposite doctrines on the subject of our financial, commercial and agricultural difficulties, in suggesting remedies, make an income tax a part of them."[4] Parnell did not go into detail, but contented himself with suggesting a rate of one and one-half or two per cent, which he thought would probably yield three millions sterling a year, as opposed to the ten per cent tax which in 1815 yielded fifteen millions.

Parliament, however, was not ready for such a step and as the proposition was vigorously opposed by Lord Palmerston and Baring, nothing came of it. Much interest, nevertheless, was aroused in the public mind, and the discussion of the subject became quite general. Even before the parliamentary episode, Matson had maintained that the substitution of a general income tax, in lieu of all the existing indirect taxes,

[1] *Twenty Years of Financial Policy. A Summary of the Chief Financial Measures passed between 1842 and 1861, with a Table of Budgets.* By Sir Stafford H. Northcote. London, 1862, p. 24.

[2] Hansard, vol. xxiii, p. 908.

[3] *Ibid.*, p. 911.

[4] *On Financial Reform.* By Sir Henry Parnell. London, 1830, p. 267.

would be of the greatest advantage to the public.[1] After Parnell's statement the advocacy of the scheme became more pronounced. The author of a work which ran through several editions laid down his general principles in the following words: "This is my panacea — and for it I claim no originality, except, perhaps, in the details — to relieve from every description of impost, all creating means of wealth, and to supply the deficiency by levying taxes on created wealth alone."[2] He called his scheme one for an "income and property tax," in order to mark the necessity of taxing incomes from labor at a lower rate than those from property.[3] Entering rather fully into the alleged shortcomings of the tax, he said: "If I be told that the property or income tax has been scouted by the people of England as 'inquisitorial,' 'oppressive,' and 'unconstitutional,' I should like to ask what tax, amounting to fifteen millions a year, would not have had as many hard names levelled against it, if their mere utterance would remove the grievance."[4] In conclusion the author maintained that the real opposition to the tax came from the "leviathans of wealth."[5]

Another writer, who called attention to the moral evils of the excise and the customs, stated that he preferred on the whole a property tax, holding to the naïve belief that perjury would be less likely than in the income tax.[6] He

[1] *Repeal of all Taxes with security to the Fund Holder, in a Letter, shewing also the great Advantages by the Land-Owner and all other Classes of his Majesty's Subjects. Addressed to the Duke of Wellington.* By John Matson. London, n. d. [1829]. See esp. pp. 3, 10, 11.

[2] *A Letter to the Earl of Wilton on the Commutation of existing Taxes for a Graduated Property and Income Tax; connecting therewith a Plan of Parliamentary Reform.* By an Englishman. London, 1830, 2d ed., p. 5. The author tells us that after writing these words he ascertained that the same idea had been propounded by Badnal in his *Letter to the Lords and Commons*, 1830, p. 177.

[3] *Op. cit.*, p. 17. [4] *Op. cit.*, p. 16. [5] *Op. cit.*, p. 28.

[6] "Without entertaining the highest opinion of the moral or religious feeling of the present date, it really were difficult to believe it so wholly lost that a man would sit down coolly and deliberately, and call on the Almighty to aid him in such fraud." — *Property (not Income) the only Just Ground of Taxation.* n. d. [1831], p. 4.

was, however, bitterly opposed to the idea of progressive taxation.[1]

Buckingham, on the contrary, advocated a graduated property tax on the general principle of "making wealth to contribute largely of its wealth; permitting moderate competency to contribute moderate support; and leaving poverty entirely free."[2] In order, however, to avoid the chief difficulty of assessment, Buckingham suggested a graduation by rank, carrying out his rather absurd scheme to the minutest detail.[3] Another writer of the following year suggested a graduation directly by property rather than by rank.[4] Still another author, who waxed indignant at the existing system by means of which "a vast number of the people, who exist in comparatively easy circumstances, are allowed to escape from the obligation of bearing a just share of the public burthens; and the helpless indigent, who ought to be wholly removed from the reach of taxation, are, injuriously for the general interests, absurdly comprehended in the class of tax-contributors," suggested what he called a population tax, which, as he proceeded to explain, turned out to be really a combination of a poll and an income tax.[5] A writer who signed himself "A Capitalist," disclosed his sympathies by suggesting a tax on all lands and professional profits, leaving trade and industry free.[6] Finally, an author who dis-

[1] *Cf.* also the two pamphlets *An Equitable Property Tax: a Financial Speculation and a Fair Rate of Wages to the Labouring Poor.* By a Loyal Briton. London, 1831; and *The Expediency of a Property Tax considered in relation to the Objections of Earl Grey and Lord Brougham.* London, 1831.

[2] *Outlines of a new Budget, for raising Eighty Millions, by means of a justly Graduated Property Tax, With Suggestions on the representative System, the National Debt, etc. Prepared for the consideration of the Reformed Parliament of England.* By J. S. Buckingham. London, 1831, p. 5.

[3] See the table on p. 8 of his work.

[4] *A Scheme for a Graduated Property Tax.* London, 1832.

[5] *Suggestions for Combining an improved System of Taxation, with a wide Division of the Elective Franchise.* London, 1831, pp. 3, 6–9.

[6] *A Practical Plan for the Immediate Annihilation of Taxes, and Equitable Liquidation of the National Debt.* By a Capitalist. London, 1832, 2d ed., p. 9.

cussed the causes of "the unusual and generally prevalent depression and distress," found the secret to consist in the system of taxation, of which "the consequences are such as might be fairly calculated upon—the impoverishment of the lower classes, and the accumulation of wealth, in masses, amongst the aristocracy."[1] He maintained that "the antidote to this glaring injustice is the substitution of an equal property tax sufficient for the exigencies of the State, in lieu of all existing taxes." In reality, his scheme was a combination of a property and an income tax, and when he came to discuss the objection on account of its "inquisitorial tendency," he concluded that "the good effect resulting from every individual examining the real state of his affairs annually, would overbalance the obnoxious nature of the enquiry, and would prove a most salutary measure to the commercial interest."[2]

§ 2. *The Unrest, 1832–1842*

The political revolution of 1832 could not fail to turn public attention to the fiscal question. In this discussion the income tax at first played a considerable rôle. In the year 1833, the question of a graduated property tax was brought up in parliament by Robinson, who moved on March 26 for a Select Committee "to consider and revise our existing taxation, with a view to the repeal of those burthens which prey most heavily on productive industry, and a substitution of an equitable property tax in lieu thereof." This led to a warm debate, in the course of which Joseph Hume made the rather startling statement that "all taxes are confiscation, and the only question is, which is the least oppressive mode of confiscation." Lord Althorp, who, as we know, had manifested no particular repugnance to the income tax three years before, now opposed the motion, which, nevertheless, received 155 votes in favor, compared to 221 against. As a result, a veritable flood of

[1] *The Property Tax the only effectual Remedy for the present Embarrassment of the Country.* Birmingham, 1832, 2d ed., p. 4.

[2] *Op. cit.*, p. 7.

pamphlets now appeared. Richardson boldly advocated what he called "equalizing taxation, — *i.e.*, throwing off from the shoulders of the poor, the weight of taxation on to the shoulders of the rich, who ought to bear it."[1] A fiery appeal to the working classes favored a similar plan, declaring that "an equitable property tax means a property tax, the percentage of which shall increase with the amount of property taxed."[2] A more important disputant thought that the new popular control of parliament would render it possible to levy, at all events, a tax on permanent income, or what he calls "realized capital," in lieu of the corn laws.[3] He objected, however, to a graduated tax on the ground that "any distinction between different classes would cause much confusion and jealousy."[4] Heathfield, in a temperate essay, discussed the arguments of Poulett Thomson and Lord Althorp, who were now opposed to Robinson's motion, declaring himself also in favor of an income tax, although demurring to the principle of graduation.[5] Pebrer, a Spaniard, who wrote a bulky work on English finance, contented himself with advocating a tax of nine and one-fourth per cent on all incomes except the

[1] *Unequal Taxation, the chief Cause of the Misery now suffered by the industrious and middle Classes of Society; and its Remedy, a Graduated Tax upon Property. 3rd ed., considerably enlarged, with a Table showing the Inequality of Taxation.* By James Richardson. London, 1833, p. 9.

[2] *British Taxes Dissected. Being a Plain Letter addressed to the Workingmen of Great Britain and Ireland; explaining how fifty Millions are yearly raised, who pay these fifty Millions; how they ought to be raised, and who ought to pay them.* By One of the Council of the National Political Union. London, 1833, p. 13.

[3] "So long as the House of Commons did not truly represent the feelings of the people, and men of property and rank alone had the control of Parliament, it was needless to hope for a tax on property. . . . So obnoxious, indeed, was the very term 'property tax,' that it was never even alluded to but in the most delicate manner." — *Tax on Capital and Fixed Duty on Corn.* London, 1833, pp. 3, 4.

[4] *Op. cit.*, p. 9. *Cf.* the pamphlet *Reflections on a Graduated Property and Income Tax to raise the sum of £17,822,000.* By Edward Jones. London, 1833.

[5] *Observations occasioned by the Motion in the House of Commons on the 26th of March, 1833, by George R. Robinson, Esquire, for a Select Committee, etc. Addressed to the Landed Proprietors of the United Kingdom.* By Richard Heathfield, Accountant. London, 1833, pp. 9, 12.

wages of labor;[1] while Vaux preferred a property tax on all land and personal property. "The fund-holders," Vaux sagely remarks, "cannot bear to hear a property tax mentioned; but at this no man can be surprised, who reflects that it is the only tax whatever, that can make them contribute as much as others to the necessities of the state."[2] Another writer who was especially interested in repealing the indirect taxes, advocated either a property or an income tax, leaning, however, on the whole, to the latter, "incomes being more easily estimated than property, and the difference between a property tax and an income tax being more in name than in reality."[3] Some authors, however, like Easton, who still had their doubts as to the advisability of an income tax, were content to renew the old recommendation for a house tax.[4]

The most elaborate attempt to advocate the income tax was made in a large volume written by Benjamin Sayer, an official connected with the original income tax.[5] Sayer begins by stating that he "is anxious to be understood throughout his attempt in the comparative sense only, not as denying that the income or property tax is attended with evils such as arise from other taxes in general, but as attributing

[1] *Taxation, Revenue, Expenditure, Power, Statistics and Debt of the whole British Empire. Their Origin, Progress and Present State, etc.* By Pablo Pebrer. London, 1833, p. 506.

[2] *Relative Taxation; or Observations on the Impolicy of taxing Malt, Hops, Beer, Soap, Candles, and Leather; with a view of the Manner in which the Duties imposed upon them affect the different Kinds of Land, whether in Grass or Tillage, and their constant Tendency to increase Pauperism; with Reasons for Substituting a Tax on Property, etc.* By Thomas Vaux. London, 1833, p. 228.

[3] *Outline of a Plan for amending the System of Taxation.* Birmingham, 1833, p. 8.

[4] *A Plan for Commuting and Abolishing Taxes on the Necessaries of Life, and All the assessed Taxes, to the Amount of £25,000,000 per Annum, etc.* By Josiah Easton. Taunton, 1833, p. 5.

[5] *An Attempt to shew the Justice and Expediency of substituting an Income or Property Tax for the present Taxes, or a part of them; as affording the most Equitable, the least Injurious, and (under the modified Procedure suggested therein) the least Obnoxious Mode of Taxation: also, the most Fair, Advantageous, and Effectual Plans of reducing the National Debt.* [By Benjamin Sayer.] London, 1833.

to it a less degree only." He contrasts the existing system of taxation — both the indirect taxes on expenditure and the direct taxes on "use," like the land taxes and the assessed taxes — with the income tax, from the point of view of abstract theory, of administrative procedure, and of what he calls "excess of taxation" — a threefold phenomenon, according as it involves the individual giving up more than the treasury receives, or more than his industry can replace, or more than it is just or necessary for the government to take. In all of these respects Sayer gives unqualified preference to the income tax.

Discussing the chief objection attributed to it, namely, the exposure of private affairs, he maintains "that persons who do not carry on trade speculatively, but prudently, do not dread an exposure of the state of them." [1] And he sagely adds, "It might be doubted whether the feeling against publicity of income did not in some cases proceed from the apprehension that when taxation was to be taken from income, publicity would prevent or disclose that evasion which there was a disposition in those cases to commit." [2] Sayer is fully aware of the general feeling against the tax, due largely to the preference of old over new taxes. But he takes occasion to point out that "the excise, at its first institution and long afterwards, was as much reprobated as the income tax has been; and considered even more odious, although now people have become quite accustomed to it." [3] He thinks that those who will suffer by a change to an income tax are chiefly misers, absentees, and smugglers.[4] Sayer takes up in detail the various possible modifications of the old income tax which experience might suggest, and he discusses with considerable fulness all manner of possible projects. Among the topics treated are such points as graduation, differentiation, taxation of realized property only, taxation of capital instead of income, taxation of trades and professions, the capitalization of income, and a composition of the tax. Sayer's

[1] *Op. cit.*, p. 32.

[2] *Op. cit.*, p. 32.

[3] *Op. cit.*, p. 101.

[4] *Op. cit.*, p. 103.

volume, in fact, is a veritable arsenal of arguments on both sides of almost every scheme that has ever been advanced in connection with the income tax. A full description would require a chapter by itself. We must content ourselves with his general conclusion "that whatever degree of evil there be in taxation is less to be obviated or mitigated by reducing the amount of it, than by changing the system or raising it, that is, by adopting that more equal, more certain, and less injurious mode of transferring the exact amount of income due from the payers to the receivers of it, which the direct tax on income most palpably presents." [1]

Shortly afterwards Buckingham, who was now in parliament, again brought the matter up, and introduced on July 2, 1837, a motion for a committee to consider the advisability of creating a graduated property or income tax, with which to liquidate the national debt. Buckingham stated "that a property or income tax was the fairest as well as the easiest of all taxes." [2] He confessed that "when speaking of this subject in private he had been conjured not to let the words 'income tax' escape from his lips in Parliament, as it would drive a large majority from even listening to him afterwards." [3] Buckingham devoted most of his speech to the attempt to prove the justice of graduation. Lord Althorp in reply again stated that it "was fair debatable ground whether some portion of the tax of this country might not be commuted for an income tax, but he should be very sorry to see Parliament sanction the principle of a graduated property tax." [4] After a short discussion, Buckingham's motion was negatived. In the following year, however, Buckingham put his ideas into writing. He now proposed that the rate should differ according to the

[1] *An attempt to shew the Justice*, etc., p. 356.

[2] Buckingham's speech, in which he makes plentiful quotations from Sayer's book, was republished by him after the lapse of sixteen years under the title, *Debate in the House of Commons on the Gradual Extinction of the National Debt, and on the true Principle of a Property and Income Tax. Republished for comparison with Mr. Gladstone's Financial Proposition.* London, 1853. See esp. p. 15.

[3] *Op. cit.*, p. 19.

[4] *Op. cit.*, p. 29.

kind, as well as according to the size, of income.[1] Referring to the claim that the income tax is inquisitorial, he stated that "this objection would be entitled to some weight if the present system of taxation for which that on income is proposed as a substitute were entirely free from any inquisitorial examinations into men's property operations and affairs;" but this he vigorously denied.

In opposition to all these writers, the prevalent feeling of the political leaders is well reflected in a leading article, which, after reviewing in some detail the various schemes, concluded that "taxes on income, though theoretically equal, are, in their actual operations, the most unequal and vexatious of any that it is possible to imagine."[2] The very idea was indignantly repelled by Wells, a barrister-at-law, who declared it as his belief that "a tax which will convert every collector into a spy, which will compel the gentleman of estate and the merchant of capital, and the professional man, even of limited practice, to disclose the actual net amount of income to the state, will never again be tolerated in England."[3]

The discussion of the early thirties proved to be only a flash in the pan. The old system continued with but slight changes until an entirely different situation was brought about by the growing movement to repeal the corn laws. This movement, as is well known, before long became a formidable one, and led to a reconsideration of the whole fiscal problem. The agitation, in fact, began shortly before 1840.

The advantages of a direct tax over the excise and the customs were set forth in a well-written pamphlet, in which the author suggested "an assessment on all property, including the public debt itself, in substitution for the present

[1] "The Superiority of an Income and Property Tax to every Other Source of Revenue," *The Parliamentary Review*, vol. v (1834), p. 363. *Cf. Thirty Years Observations on the Effects of taxing Provisions instead of Income, with a just Scale to tax Income.* By a Farmer. London, 1836.

[2] "The Proposed Tax on Property and Income," *Edinburgh Review*, vol. lvii (1833), pp. 143–168.

[3] *The Revenue and the Expenditure of the United Kingdom.* By Samuel Wells London, 1834, p. 187.

system of taxation."[1] Another writer made an earnest plea for a property tax, by which, he explained, is meant "a tax upon income derived from real and realized property; but not upon the profits of professions and business."[2] He thought that "a graduated scale according to the amount of income would probably be the most just principle."[3] The production, however, which perhaps carried the most weight, because of the reputation of its author, was that of Wilson, who advocated an income tax not only because of its "honesty and fairness," but also because of "the probability of receiving it without materially pressing on the ability of those interests from which it is derived."[4] Wilson confessed that if the Chancellor of the Exchequer, instead of suggesting more taxes on consumption, had proposed a tax on property and income, "there can be little doubt but the proposal would have been in the first instance received with great surprise and alarm. But," he adds, "very little consideration will show that it could have been justified by every consideration of justice, policy, and necessity."[5]

§ 3. *Peel's Act of 1842*

By the beginning of 1842 Sir Robert Peel was finally won over. Peel had never been a friend of the income tax. In 1830, in discussing Huskisson's motion, he manifested his disbelief in it. In 1833, when in opposition, he praised Lord Althorp for not proposing an income tax, and declared that in his opinion nothing but a case of extreme necessity could justify parliament in imposing an income tax in time of

[1] *Argument for the General Relief of the Country from Taxation, and eventually from the Corn Laws, by an Assessment on Property.* London, 1839, p. 4.

[2] *A Property Tax. The Justice and Utility of a Property Tax as a Means of Restoring the Revenue, placing it upon a permanent Basis, and affording Facilities for the Development of the Commercial and Manufacturing Resources of the Country.* By a True Conservative. London, n. d. [1839], p. 5.

[3] *Op. cit.*, p. 15.

[4] *The Revenue: or, What should the Chancellor do?* By James Wilson. London, 1841, p. 19.

[5] *Op. cit.*, p. 18.

peace. In 1835, when in office, and opposing the reduction of the malt tax, he warned the landed interest to beware how they exchange "the light pressure of a malt duty for the scourge of a property tax." In 1839 he opposed the government's proposal to introduce penny postage, and stated that this would virtually commit the House to a property tax, although he now added that possibly it might be wise to resort to it. But even in 1840 he approved of Baring's plan to meet the deficiency in the revenue by additional indirect taxes. As Buckingham correctly states, Peel and Althorp "manifested the most cordial unanimity on this subject, and to judge from the speeches of both, one could hardly have thought it possible that either would ever have consented to be a party to such a tax, by whomsoever it should be proposed."[1]

In 1842, however, matters had come to a crisis. The panic of 1837 had left behind it a wake of long-continued distress; the new poor law was unpopular; the Chartist agitation was acquiring momentum; and the Corn Laws were becoming increasingly unpopular. For the last five years there had been a repeated deficit in the budget. In 1840 the Chancellor of the Exchequer, Baring, had attempted to make both ends meet by a general increase of duties; in 1841 he endeavored to produce the same result by reducing the duties in order to augment the revenues. All these experiments failed. As a consequence, Peel finally decided, as the most likely method of escaping from the difficult situation, to propose a revival of the income tax.

In his great budget speech of March 11, 1842,[2] Peel pointed out that the deficit for the coming year would again be over two and one-quarter millions sterling, bringing the deficit for the six years from 1837 to over ten millions. He declared that a reduction of expenditure was out of the question, and

[1] *Plan of an Improved Income Tax.* By J. S. Buckingham. London, 1845, p. ix.

[2] Hansard, vol. lxi, pp. 431 *et seq.* A good summary of this is found in Northcote's *Twenty Years of Financial Policy*, pp. 12–32.

thus addressed himself to a consideration of the best methods of increasing the revenue. To augment the indirect taxes he dismissed as impracticable; for, quite apart from his reluctance to add to the burdens of the laboring classes, he stated that Baring's experience was decisive on this point. "I cannot consent to any proposal for increasing taxation on the great articles of consumption by the labouring classes of society. Moreover, I can give you conclusive proof that you have arrived at the limits of taxation on articles of consumption." One by one he took up the other possible alternatives, only to reject each in turn. Finally, after adverting to the dangers of a continued deficit, he made "an earnest appeal to the possessors of property, for the purpose of repairing this mighty evil." "I propose," he said, "for a time at least — (and I never had occasion to make a proposition with a more thorough conviction of its being one which the public interest of the country required) — I propose that, for a time to be limited, the income of this country should be called upon to contribute a certain sum for the purpose of remedying this mighty and growing evil. I propose that the income of this country should bear a charge not exceeding *7d.* in the pound, which will not amount to £3 per cent, but speaking accurately £2 18*s.* 4*d.* per cent, for the purpose of not only supplying the deficiency in the revenue, but of enabling me with confidence and satisfaction to propose great commercial reforms, which will afford a hope of reviving commerce and such an improvement in the manufacturing interests as will react on every other interest in the country; and, by diminishing the prices of the articles of consumption, and the cost of living, will, in a pecuniary point of view, compensate you for your present sacrifices; whilst you will be relieved from the contemplation of a great public evil."

Peel had hoped that parliament might be willing to vote the tax for five years, but he finally decided to content himself with asking for its imposition for only three years. He did not demand that it should be applied to Ireland, but as a partial compensation he proposed the raising of the duty on

Irish spirits to the Scotch level, as well as the raising of most of the Irish stamp duties to the English level. With these new sources of revenue, Peel counted on a surplus of almost two millions, which he proposed to devote to a reduction of the most burdensome import duties.

The introduction of Peel's income tax bill precipitated a long and exciting debate. The opposition objected to the whole fiscal scheme in general, and to the income tax in particular. Baring declared that there was no real necessity for "a recurrence to that odious impost." In the House of Lords Brougham introduced a whole series of resolutions in opposition, calling forth a reply from Lord Ripon, which, in the light of future events, is exceedingly interesting. "Entirely concurring," said Ripon, "in the noble and learned Lord's declaration that the proposed tax was a resource to which Parliament ought not to have recourse except under the pressure of dire necessity, still, unless the noble and learned Lord thought he had reason to believe . . . that there existed a design on the part of the government to entrap Parliament into the passing of this act on the plea of absolute necessity, and for a limited period only . . . unless the noble and learned Lord thought them mean and shabby enough to direct Parliament in order to get the measure passed, and then afterwards to continue it as a permanent tax . . . he did not see why, as a preliminary step, their lordships should be called upon to declare by resolution their opposition to it."[1]

During the discussion Peel reverted to the subject from many different points of view. In his speech of March 18 he referred to "the great objection to the income tax, that which arose from its necessarily inquisitorial character," and he called attention to the measures suggested by him for reducing the evil to a minimum.[2] Alluding again to the

[1] Speech of March 17, 1842.

[2] This was reprinted in a large penny edition as *The Income Tax. Sir R. Peel's Speech, in the House of Commons, on Friday Evening, March 18, 1842.* See esp. p. 8.

demand, voiced especially by Attwood,[1] that holders of terminable annuities be taxed at a lower rate, Peel asserted that "if he once began to make distinctions of this kind there would be no end to applications from particular interests to be exempted from the operation of the measure, and he would be obliged to abandon the original ground of the project altogether. If a distinction of this kind was to be made in behalf of a class who were notoriously powerful, wealthy, and affluent, it would be very easy to show that there were many other classes who were much more justly entitled to the exemptions which they claim."[2] He made a fervid appeal to the property owners, expressing a hope "that the high and low were prepared, in a crisis of commercial difficulty, to pay a fair portion of the expense rendered necessary by the circumstances of the country."

The long debate was so heated that it involved not less than sixteen divisions, but the bill was finally passed by the House on May 31, by a majority of 106. The Act of 1842[3] which was popularly called the Property and Income Tax Act, was a reprint of the law of 1806, with a few notable alterations. In the first place, the deduction of £150, which in 1806 was restricted to incomes from trade, professions, and personal exertions, was again made applicable to all incomes. Secondly, the conditions of agriculture had so changed that the net profits of the tenant were now computed as amounting in England to only one-half the annual value and in Scotland to about one-third, instead of the old figures of two-thirds

[1] Attwood's speech was reprinted and widely circulated under the title of *The Speech of M. Attwood, Esq., M.P., on the Income Tax, Committee of Ways and Means in the House of Commons, on Wednesday, March 23rd, 1842.* London, 1842. See esp. pp. 3, 4.

[2] *Ibid.*, p. 10.

[3] 5 and 6 Vict., c. 35. "An Act for Granting to her Majesty Duties on Profits arising from Property, Professions, Trades and Offices." June 22, 1842. A summary of the act was issued by one of the officials and distributed by thousands under the title of *The Income Tax Act, Epitomized and Simplified.* By William Nicholson. London, 1842. A more comprehensive account was published in 178 pp. as *The Income Tax Act, 5 and 6 Victoria, c. 35, with an Explanatory Introduction and Index.* By John Paget. London, 1842.

and one-half respectively. In other words, in Schedule B the rate of the tax, in lieu of being *7d.* in the pound, or about three per cent, was fixed at 3½*d.* for England and 2½*d.* for Scotland. The other alterations were of somewhat minor importance. In Schedule A, in the case of the so-called "concerns about lands," gas-works and railroads, which were of course unknown at the period of the previous income tax, were now included. In Schedule C, savings banks were now exempted, while, on the other hand, the exemption to foreign holders of the public debt, which, as we remember, had been introduced at the solicitation of Pitt, and which had remained throughout the entire period of the old war income tax, was now withdrawn. In Schedule D, the income of charitable institutions was exempted, while, on the contrary, the privilege of deduction for life insurance premiums was abolished. Finally, the old section permitting the acceptance of voluntary contributions was dropped.

In the administrative provisions only slight changes were made from the law of 1806. The most important, perhaps, was the provision affecting the Special Commissioners. The Special Commissioners appointed by the central authority (now known as the Commissioners of Stamps and Taxes) had their functions notably extended in the case of Schedule D. All persons liable under that schedule might, if they preferred, ask to be assessed by the Special Commissioners in lieu of making their returns to, or being assessed by, either the General or the Additional Commissioners. Both the General and the Additional Commissioners, it will be remembered, were supposed to live in the locality. If the taxpayer was averse to having his business affairs in any way known to neighborhood officials, he would naturally select the Special Commissioners appointed by the central government, and not coming from the neighborhood. These Special Commissioners were to have the ordinary powers of the General or Additional Commissioners. Furthermore, in case of an assessment by the Additional Commissioners, where the inspector or surveyor objected, appeals might also be taken to the Special Commissioners. The final appeal in all such cases was to be to the Commissioners of Stamps and Taxes.

The other administrative changes were as follows: In Schedule A, the first assessment was to stand for three years, and not for two years, as in the old law. The penalties for erroneous returns, as well as the surcharges, were henceforth to be three times the amount of tax, and not, as before, twice the amount. Finally, the taxpayer was permitted in the case of assessment by the Special Commissioners in Schedule D to compound at once for a period of three years, the composition rendering any subsequent statements on his part unnecessary during that term. In all other respects, the provisions of the old income tax law were continued, with the ingenious combination of local self-government through the Commissioners of the Land Tax, and of control by the central government through the inspectors and surveyors. All these provisions, with a few changes that will be subsequently noted, are still in force to-day.

The reimposition of the income tax naturally gave rise to a discussion which swept over the country, and which lasted for a considerable period. Some writers were bitterly opposed. Whitock, for instance, declared that "the only thing original in the scheme is its introduction during a time of peace. It is most inquisitorial in its nature, and unequal in its application."[1] Hilditch poured out a volume of protests in no less than three separate productions.[2] He tells us

[1] *An Inquiry into the Cause of the present Depression of Trade, and a Remedy proposed, in a Measure calculated at the same time to obviate the Necessity of an Income Tax.* By Richard Whitock. Edinburgh, 1842, p. 62. Whitock suggested as an alternative the enactment of a new usury law.

[2] These were: (*a*) *Aristocratic Taxation: Its present State, Origin, and Progress, with Proposals for Reform.* [By R. Hilditch.] London, 1842, 52 pp. This was written while the discussion was still on. (*b*) *Aristocratic Taxation, its present State, Origin and Progress, with Proposals for Reform: comprising Proofs of the Justice and Expediency of a Land Tax for Redemption of National Debt: Strictures on the Income Tax and the Idea of a System of Taxation not only without Burthen, but absolutely in itself Beneficial.* By Richard Hilditch. London,

that "nothing enlarged or great-minded—nothing in fact beyond the most rickety accommodation and joinery of discrepant interests and parties was to be expected from Sir Robert Peel";[1] and he concludes that "no other tax is so objectionable as the income tax. No other is at the same nominal rate so really unequal; no other so imperiously felt; no other involves such odious, though ineffectual inquisition into private affairs; no other puts upright men of the productive classes to so much expense and inconvenience, or offers to the fraudulent such easy and successful evasion; finally, no other is collected by such bungling and dangerous arrangements, establishing secret and irresponsible tribunals, fomenting private cabals, using most harshly the best subjects, and unnecessarily inconveniencing all."[2] Buchanan, the author of a large work on taxation, bitterly complained of "these inquisitorial proceedings, arbitrary as they are,—a practical inroad on the rights of freemen, to which there is no parallel, even under the most absolute governments in Europe, and truly an anomaly in a country long famous for its love of liberty."[3] Others maintained that a property tax was preferable to an income tax, and that if an income tax was unavoidable, it should be levied only on the income from permanent property. Russell, for instance, declared an income tax to be "an awkward and cumbrous, unequal, inquisitorial way of raising the revenue." Defining permanent property as consisting only of land, he demanded that no tax be imposed on "fluctuating property, such as stock in trade."[4]

1842, 70 pp. This appeared originally in the *North of England Magazine*. (*c*) *The Income Tax criticised and epitomized, containing some Plain Statements on the Income and Property Tax, showing that it falls most heavily on the industrious Classes; with full Instructions for filling up the Tax Papers.* By R. Hilditch. London, 1843.

[1] *The Income Tax criticised*, p. 15; and *Aristocratic Taxation*, p. 60.

[2] *The Income Tax criticised*, p. 7; *Aristocratic Taxation*, p. 54.

[3] *Inquiry into the Taxation and Commercial Policy of Great Britain; with Observations on the Principles of Currency and of Exchangeable Value.* By David Buchanan. Edinburgh, 1844, p. 102.

[4] *Financial Reform. A Digest of the Reasons for and against a Tax upon*

The tax, however, did not lack ardent defenders.[1] The author of a Chartist work thought that "property has been in masquerade long enough, and the sooner the mask is removed from false pretences the better."[2] "Whatever obloquy," he adds, "may belong to the income tax, the solvent and the honest will thank the Minister, who repudiates the odium unfairly cast on what is termed the inquisitorial, but really efficient, machinery, which can alone ensure its working."[3] Another radical who declared that the income tax "is a tax upon the rich and upon those persons who being idle and comparatively useless members of the commonwealth, live upon small incomes" referred to "the talk of those radicals who oppose the income tax, about their 'love for the people, the masses,' etc., as just so much insincere blarney and balderdash."[4] Makepeace, finally, defended the law, although he desired several amendments, stating "that parts thereof are good, and parts thereof are new; but those parts which are good are not new, and those which are new are not good."[5] After refuting the ordinary current objections, he stated that he desired graduation, higher taxation for absentees, and exemption for children.[6]

§ 4. *The Development to 1851*

The income tax turned out to be more productive than had been anticipated. Instead of yielding three and

Permanent Property, in lieu of some of the Present Taxes, especially those on Commodities. By R. W. Russell. London, 1842, pp. 20–21.

[1] *Cf. Three Letters to the Rt. Hon. Sir Robert Peel on the Repeal of the present System of Revenue and Protection Imports, Excise, Stamps, and the Adoption of a great System of Income Taxation.* By W. Morris. Exeter, 1843.

[2] *Tory Taxes.* London, 1842, p. 9.

[3] *Op. cit.*, p. 10.

[4] *Income Tax. A few Words to the Operative and Lower Classes of the People of England, upon Sir R. Peel's proposed Income Tax. By One of Themselves.* London, 1842, pp. 6, 8.

[5] *Taxation, in its Operation by means of the Income and Assessed Taxes considered; together with Suggestions for its Alteration and Amendment.* By William Makepeace. London, n. d. [1843], p. 5.

[6] *Op. cit.*, pp. 11–14.

three-quarter millions annually, it yielded over five millions. But by the time that the tax was to expire in 1845, expenditure had increased to such an extent that Peel foresaw another deficit for 1845. In his budget speech of 1845 he asked: "Will you run the risk of entailing a deficiency in future years by making no provision for the time; and seeing that in 1846 the revenue will be sufficient to meet increased expenditure, will you postpone the consideration of what will be fitting to do until that year shall have expired?" The answer he gave was that such a course would not be a prudent one. The real cause of the continuance of the tax, however, was different. So convinced had Peel now become that greater progress must be made in reducing the protective tariff and in diminishing the most burdensome of the excises, that after a frank acknowledgment of the fact that there was no absolute financial necessity for his course, he suggested a continuation of the income tax for another three years, "not for the purpose of providing the supplies for the year, but distinctly for the purpose of enabling us to make this great experiment of reducing the taxes." He, however, still declared that he did not recommend the income tax as a permanent substitute for the more onerous burdens. In his opinion it was to be only a mere temporary resource, to be utilized while the ordinary revenue was recovering itself. "I have been asked what assurance I could give that this tax should expire at the end of three years: if I could have been perfectly sure of success I would have proposed it for five years; at the same time I do think that there are good grounds for hoping that at the end of three years you may be at liberty to discontinue it."[1] As Sir Stafford Northcote points out: "When we compare the language of Peel in 1845 with his words in 1842 it is impossible not to feel that there is a difference of tone, indicating a perhaps unconscious change of sentiment. Not that in 1845 any more than in 1842 Sir Robert Peel intended to impose the income tax as a permanent tax, or contemplated its

[1] Speech of February 17, 1845.

becoming such in time of peace; but he had become a little blinder to its faults, a little kinder to its merits, and, above all, a little more alive to the magnitude of the work that might be done by its aid."[1] Lord John Russell, the leader of the opposition, although characterizing the tax as one in which "inequality, vexation and fraud were inherent," nevertheless stated that "if the question be between a perpetual income tax and the continuous monopoly and restriction, I declare for the income tax and a diminution and final abolition of all monopoly."

The country as a whole also supported the scheme, not because it loved the income tax more but because it loved the indirect taxes less. The prevalent view is rather vigorously expressed in a widely circulated pamphlet which declared that the existing system of indirect taxation was "bad in principle, mischievous in operation, interruptive in prosperity in every department of active life, disadvantageous to the rich, and oppressing and destructive to the poor."[2] As Buckingham pointed out in reprinting his article referred to above,[3] "Time, that great innovator, has wrought marvelous changes. Sir Robert Peel proposes an income tax and his followers support him. It was at first meant to be only temporary. It is now spoken of as probably to be made permanent. Lord John Russell objects to this in theory, but votes for it in practice."[4] Even McCulloch, who published in 1845 his comprehensive treatise on taxation in which he vigorously opposed the income tax, conceded the strength of Peel's argument, and added: "It was, also, we admit, no easy matter, in the present state of the country, to point out any tax or taxes, fitted to produce four or five millions a year against which several formidable objections might not be

[1] *Twenty Years of Financial Policy*, pp. 70, 71.

[2] *Reasons for a Tax on Property, in Substitution for Duties of Excise and Customs.* London, 1846, p. 8.

[3] *Supra*, page 121.

[4] *Plan of an Improved Income Tax and Real Free Trade. With an Equitable Mode of redeeming the National Debt.* By James S. Buckingham. London, 1845, p. ix.

urged."[1] McCulloch thought, however, that even the worst of the taxes on expenditure "are less objectionable than the most carefully devised income tax."[2]

Although the government proceeded rapidly with its programme of reducing and abolishing the protective duties, it did not go fast enough with the repeal of the excise taxes to suit some of the radicals. Furnivall, for instance, objected vehemently to the high excise on malt and hops, and suggested as a substitute the extension of the income tax to incomes below £150.[3] The same idea was elaborated with somewhat different arguments by Smee, who proposed an addition to an income tax by "a tax per head" on all day laborers.[4] On the other hand, Miller, who was also a heated opponent of the malt excise and who suggested in its stead an expansion of the death duties, inveighed bitterly against the income tax and went so far as to ascribe the crisis of 1847 very largely to its influence. "In any other free country besides Great Britain," he added, "the imposition of a perpetual income tax, with all its inquisitorial accompaniments, would be the germ of a revolution."[5] The climax, however, was reached by Gibbon, who, after recounting every possible objection, stated: "If human ingenuity had been racked to invent a tax, the imposition of which should be the greatest possible departure from, and the greatest violation of, the principle of making every member of society contributory to it, in due proportion to . . . his means . . . a tax more effective of that purpose than the tax upon income could not perhaps

[1] *A Treatise on the Principles and practical Influence of Taxation, and the Funding System.* By J. R. McCulloch. London, 1845, p. 133.

[2] *Ibid.*, p. 134.

[3] *Taxation Revised and National Progress.* By Thomas Furnivall. London, 1847, p. 5.

[4] *The Income Tax; Its Extension at the present Rate proposed to all Classes; abolishing the Malt Tax, Window Tax, and other Taxes, with some Observations on the Tea Duties.* By William Ray Smee. London, n. d. [1846], 2d ed., p. 9.

[5] *Suggestions for a General Equalization of the Land Tax and the Abolition of the Income and Real Property Taxes, and the Malt Duty.* By Samuel Miller. London, 1848, pp. 5, 6.

have been devised."[1] Extreme statements of this kind were counterbalanced by almost equally extravagant panegyrics, of which that of Cobham may serve as a type. Cobham confessed that "perfection cannot be attained in anything," but added, "Let those who disapprove of the income tax only try to propose a better system; they will then discover the difficulty — the impossibility, indeed, of doing so."[2] He went so far as to demand the abolition of all other taxes, and their replacement by a single income tax.

When the three years expired, in 1848, Great Britain was in the throes of the distress caused by the railway crisis of 1847–1848. John Stuart Mill, in his great work published in that year, had lent the weight of his authority to the opponents of the tax. Although he conceded its theoretic justice, he found the real objection to be "in the present low state of public morality, the impossibility of ascertaining the real incomes." The supposed hardship of compelling people to disclose the amount of their incomes ought not, Mill held, to count for much. But as flagrant fraud is unavoidable, "the tax, on whatever principles of equality it may be imposed, is in practice unequal in one of the worst ways, falling heaviest on the most conscientious. . . . The unscrupulous succeed in evading a great proportion of what they should

[1] *A Familiar Treatise on Taxation, Free Trade, etc. Comprising Facts usually unnoticed or unconsidered in Theories of those Subjects. With Notes on Subjects arising incidentally.* [By Alexander Gibbon.] London, 1846, p. 223.

A somewhat reduced version of this work was published a few years later under the title, *Taxation: its Nature and Properties, with Remarks on the Incidence and the Expediency of the Repeal of the Income Tax.* By Alexander Gibbon, London, 1851. The passage quoted above is found here on p. 74. Gibbon now adds: "The tax is more offensive in its collection than any other tax, being an inquisitorial infringement of the liberty of the subject — violating the sacred reserve and modesty of private life — lowering the dignity of honourable poverty by exposure of it — causing disgust and mortification, and exciting evil passions, at the subjection of the most private affairs to the scrutiny (often the vexatious or malicious scrutiny) of equals or inferiors, by an enforced disclosure to them of such affairs." — *Ibid.*, p. 76.

[2] *Direct Taxation. The Income Tax, the Property Tax, and Free Trade. Peace, Retrenchment, and Captain Warner's awful Engines of War.* By Samuel Cobham. 1848, p. 19.

pay; even persons of integrity in their ordinary transactions are tempted to palter with their consciences: while the strictly veracious may be made to pay more than the state intended, by the powers of arbitrary assessment necessarily entrusted to the commissioners. . . . It is to be feared, therefore, that the fairness which belongs to the principle of an income tax cannot be made to attach to it in practice: and that this tax, while apparently the most just of all modes of raising a revenue, is in effect more unjust than many others which are *prima facie* more objectionable. This consideration would lead us to concur in the opinion which, until of late, has usually prevailed — that direct taxes on income should be reserved as extraordinary resources for great national emergencies."[1] With a large deficit staring him in the face, however, Lord John Russell had no thought of abandoning the income tax; on the contrary, in introducing the budget on November 18, he went so far as to recommend its renewal for five years, at the rate of five per cent, *i.e.*, one shilling in the pound.

This proposition aroused so great an uproar that on February 28 Sir Charles Wood, the Chancellor of the Exchequer, dropped the suggestion and asked only for a continuance of the tax at the old rate, and for another three years. "I do not think it would be wise," he said, "to attempt to force upon an unwilling House an addition to an unpopular tax." With this modification the government proposition was accepted. On the other hand, Hume's motion to limit the tax to one year, as well as Horsman's motion to introduce the principle of discrimination, were both defeated by overwhelming majorities. As has been well said, "the income tax, instead of being a temporary staff which might be thrown aside when it had served its turn, had become a permanent and necessary support upon which it was evident that we should have still to lean, and to lean more strongly than ever. . . . A triennial

[1] *Principles of Political Economy, with some of their Applications to Social Philosophy.* By John Stuart Mill. London, 1848, ii, pp. 376, 377. Book v, ch. iii, § 5.

income tax of seven shillings in the pound upon every kind of income alike, seemed to have taken its place among the recognized institutions of the country, and to be equally impregnable by ministers and by amateurs."[1] The only change in the administration of the tax during the next few years was that by the law of 1849 the Commissioners of Stamps and Taxes, to whom was intrusted the supervision of the income tax as well as of the other internal taxes in general, were now converted into the Board of Inland Revenue which has ever since administered the income tax.[2]

In 1851 the income tax was for the third time expiring. While the fiscal situation was more favorable than in 1848, Sir Charles Wood maintained that it was preferable to drop some of the remaining taxes on consumption rather than to abandon the income tax. In his budget speech of February 17, 1851, he accordingly recommended the renewal of the income tax at its old rate for another three years. This was now combated by Lord Stanley, later the Earl of Derby, in his speech of February 28. "I hold it to be an object not only of vital importance but one to which the faith of successive ministers has been pledged, that the income tax should not be permitted to degenerate into a permanent tax."[3] Although the government carried its point, Hume introduced a motion that the tax be limited to one year instead of three years, in order to enable a committee to be appointed to consider the general character of the tax and the desirability of differentiation. On May 2 his motion prevailed, and a few weeks later the Select Committee was appointed. The act of 1851 made only a slight change in the tax, providing that when

[1] Stafford Northcote, *op. cit.*, p. 107.

[2] 12 and 13 Vict., c. 1.

[3] "Without that pledge," he added, "there is not a man living who believes that the House of Commons in 1842 would have consented to the imposition for an hour, of a tax which has always been held to be a resource in time of war, which has always been deprecated in time of peace, and which, take it as you will, leave it as you please, must be full of anomalies and inconveniences, pressing variously upon different classes of the community with a complicated injustice that no modification can altogether remove."

actual profits fell short of the assessment under Schedule B, an abatement should be allowed in the case of tenant farmers.[1]

The agitation which culminated in Hume's successful motion is well reflected in the pamphlet literature. Shortly after the parliamentary debate of 1848 an anonymous author advocated a tax not simply on "realized property," but on "all property" or "capital," defining this as "everything having a money value."[2] "A man's nominal income," he thought, "is very far indeed from being a test of his ability to bear taxation." He held that incomes from professional earnings and trade should be reduced to an equitable value by the process of capitalization at a varying number of years' purchase.[3] Heathfield advanced a slightly different scheme in which he suggested a tax on property combined with a succession duty. "The proposal to charge property and not income," said Heathfield, "proceeds, in part, from a strong sense of the inexpedience, especially in a commercial country, of an annual inquiry into the affairs of individuals. There is a natural and reasonable repugnance to such a system."[4] MacGregor, who was convinced of the impracticability of the scheme of differentiation, as proposed by Horsman, preferred a "duty upon the rents and profits of all realized property," which he was quite willing to have arranged according to a progressive schedule.[5] Phipps strongly criticised MacGregor's scheme, maintaining that "profits of trade, so far as they represent the interest of the fixed and floating capital invested in it, are just as legitimately taxable, under the denomination of profits of realised

[1] 14 and 15 Vict., c. 12, sec. 3.

[2] *Two Letters to a Member of Parliament; containing Suggestions for a Property Tax upon an Improved Basis; with Remarks upon the principal Speeches in defense of the present Income Tax, during the late Debates.* By R. S. B. London, 1848, p. 9.

[3] *Ibid.*, pp. 6, 25.

[4] *Means of Extensive Relief from the Pressure of Taxation, on the Basis of a Charge of Five per cent on all Property in the United Kingdom, Real and Personal.* By Richard Heathfield. London, 1849, p. 20.

[5] *Financial Reform: A Letter to the Citizens of Glasgow, from John MacGregor, M. P., with an Introduction and Supplementary Notes.* London, 1849.

property, as is the interest of money in the funds."[1] Phipps thought that the alleged inequality of the income tax could be easily removed by joining to it a general inheritance tax.[2] Babbage, on the other hand, based his defence of the income tax on the theory "that taxation ought to be proportional to the cost of maintaining those institutions without which no property or industry can be protected, or even exist.".[3] Babbage drew the conclusion that, as all kinds of income occasion a similar cost to the government, they should be taxed equally and, furthermore, that all exemptions should be done away with. "Abolish all exemptions—or else reduce the exemption to the lowest possible point, and disqualify from voting all electors who claim the exemption."[4] In a second edition of his work,[5] published three years later, he went so far as to state that exemptions lead "directly towards true socialism." Professor Heron, who defended the income tax as certainly not "nearly so inquisitorial in its nature as the excise,"[6] objected to differentiation on the "scientific" ground that "all should pay to the government at the same rate for the security which enables them to enjoy a unit of income during a unit of time."[7] But he maintained that since "income is literally all that comes in to a man in the year," it "must include property coming in by way of gift, inheritance, etc." Thus he thinks that "it is self-evident that this solves the suggested difficulty as to the inequality of taxation upon incomes of the same amount, arising from sources essentially different in their nature."[8] MacLeod took a somewhat similar position in an able and well-written production, in which he stated as

[1] *A few Words on the three Amateur Budgets of Cobden, MacGregor and Watson.* By the Honourable Edmund Phipps. London, 1849, p. 12.

[2] *Op. cit.*, pp. 18-19.

[3] *Thoughts on the Principles of Taxation, with reference to a Property Tax, and its Exceptions.* By Charles Babbage. London, 1848, p. 7. For the general theory of cost of service, see Seligman, *Progressive Taxation*, 2d ed., 1908, part ii., chap. ii.

[4] *Op cit.*, p. 18.

[5] London, 1851, p. iii.

[6] *Three Lectures on the Principles of Taxation, delivered at Queen's College, Galway, in Hilary term, 1850.* By Denis Caulfield Heron. Dublin, 1850, p. 80.

[7] *Op. cit.*, p. 89.

[8] *Op cit.*, p. 90.

his conclusion that "the popular objections to a uniform income tax have all been examined and found invalid, in the case of a temporary, as well as in that of a perpetual, tax."[1]

§ 5. *The Select Committee of 1851*

Hume met with considerable difficulty in getting his committee together; but after it was once formed, the committee listened to so many witnesses that it was unable to make any report during the session of 1851. It was accordingly reappointed. The testimony covers two stout volumes and is almost entirely confined to the question of the desirability of differentiating the rate of the tax according to the kind of income.[2] Among the most important witnesses were actuaries like Hill, Williams, Scott, Brown, Jellicoe, Edmonds, Hardy, and Neison. Some of these maintained that the trouble arose from calling the tax a "property and income" tax. But virtually all agreed that there should be a distinction in the rates between what was variously called professional, or industrial, or temporary, or perishable, or terminable, or life, or labor, or variable, or fleeting income on the one hand, as over against what was called permanent, or imperishable, or perpetual, or certain, or spontaneous, or property income on the other. And almost all agreed that the way to accomplish this was to reduce all incomes to a capital basis

[1] *Remarks on some Popular Objections to the present Income Tax.* By John MacPherson MacLeod. London, 1849, p. 22.

[2] *First Report from the Select Committee on the Income and Property Tax; together with the Minutes of Evidence and Index*, 1852. London, 458 pp. *Second Report from the Select Committee on the Income and Property tax; together with the Proceedings of the Committee, Minutes of Evidence, Appendix, and Index.* London, 1852, xxxiv, 520 pp.

A good summary of the evidence is found in *Elements of Taxation; to which are added a Summary of the Evidence adduced before the Parliamentary Committee on the Property and Income Tax. And also a complete Analysis of the Finance Accounts of the United Kingdom, for the year 1851.* By X + Y. Authors of the Prize Essay on Direct Taxation. London, n.d. [1853]. An extended criticism of most of the witnesses is found in *The People's Blue Book: Taxation as it is, and as it ought to be.* By Chas. Tennant. London, 1853. This went through several editions. *Cf.* esp. the 4th ed., 1872, pp. 628–650.

by capitalizing the various incomes at different rates. In agreement with the actuaries, we find Farr, the expert on life statistics, and Jeffery, who represented the Liverpool Financial Reform Association. On the other hand, the principle of differentiation was opposed by Babbage and Warburton, the latter endeavoring to fortify his position by recondite algebraical reasoning. John Stuart Mill, also one of the witnesses, thought that there ought to be a differentiation, but considered the plan of capitalizing incomes fallacious. He objected to graduation as strongly as he supported differentiation. Mill advanced the theory that savings ought to be exempt from the income tax, so that a tax would really be one on expenditure. He confessed, however, that such a scheme would be quite impracticable. Three Americans, Messrs. Dudley Selden, Ashbel Smith, and Colonel Johnson, described the system of the general property tax as it existed in New York and Texas, and seemed to make a decided impression on the chairman, although their testimony as to the operation of the law was not universally favorable. The most valuable evidence, however, was given by the English income tax officials, like Pressly and Welsh, who, after showing the immense superiority of the stoppage-at-source system over the earlier method of assessment, stated that it would be extremely hazardous to tamper with the existing administrative arrangements, and declared that all the various schemes that had been propounded were utterly impracticable.[1]

The Chairman, Mr. Hume, proposed an elaborate draft report, suggesting and explaining certain changes.[2] He desired that the tax be adjusted in accordance with the value

[1] Referring to the proposition to introduce a general property tax, for instance, Pressly stated: "Instead of being an Act to impose a tax on property, I fear it would only be an Act for collecting voluntary contributions in aid of the support of the State." — *Op. cit.*, vol. ii, p. 252. Referring to the actuaries, he stated: "I am satisfied that you will never get a return of the capital, and that you will make the tax much more inquisitorial and odious than it is at present." — *Ibid.*, p. 255.

[2] The report was republished by the Liverpool Financial Reform Association as New Series, no. 4, of the *Financial Reform Tracts* under the title, *The Draft Report proposed by Joseph Hume, Esq., the chairman of the Select Committee on the Income and Property Tax.* Liverpool, n. d. [1852].

of the property, as well as with the tenure and the age of the owner. The members of the committee, however, were not convinced by his arguments, and failed to agree. As a consequence, the evidence was transmitted to Parliament without any recommendation at all.

The failure of the committee to agree was the signal for an outpouring of periodical and pamphlet literature on both sides of the question. Hemming, in reviewing the evidence, opposed what he called Babbage's "bargain and sale theory" of taxation, and declared himself in favor of a discrimination between "certain and precarious income."[1] Farr expanded his testimony in favor of capitalization, in a lengthy article.[2] Willich, who declared that the evidence showed the impossibility "of arriving at any mode of levying the tax which will be theoretically just and practically possible,"[3] contented himself with recommending a rate of two per cent on temporary incomes and of four per cent on permanent incomes. An anonymous writer suggested six and a half per cent on professional incomes, seven per cent on life incomes, and eight per cent on incomes from realized property.[4] The manager of a life insurance company, Scott, advocated a somewhat analogous scheme.[5] Major Court desired that the inequalities between the two chief sources of income be removed by making the distinction in the abatements rather than in the rate of tax.[6] Hubbard, who shortly afterward became Gov-

[1] *A Just Income Tax, how possible. Being a Review of the Evidence reported by the Income Tax Committee, and an Inquiry into the True Principle of Taxation.* By G. W. Hemming. London, 1852, p. 21.

[2] William Farr, "The Income and Property Tax," *Journal of the Statistical Society of London*, vol. xvi (1853), pp. 1–44.

[3] *Letters on the Income Tax; Conversion of Consols; Savings Banks and Friendly Societies.* By Charles M. Willich. London, 1852, p. 5.

[4] *Equitable Taxation and Representation on a fixed, general and clearly defined Principle.* London, 1852, p. 6.

[5] *The Property and Income Tax the best Tax for the Community.* By E. Erskine Scott. London, 1852.

[6] *A Review of the Income Tax in its Relations to the National Debt; with Suggestions for Removal of its present Inequalities, by a more Uniform Mode of Assessment.* By Major M. H. Court. London, 1853. *Cf.* p. 29 of the 2d. ed., 1855.

ernor of the Bank of England, took up in detail the arguments in favor of what he calls the "indiscriminating tax on incomes,"[1] and paid his respects to both Babbage and Warburton, while he chided Mill for advocating a progressive inheritance tax. "Mr. Mill disclaims the impolicy of a graduated tax on the property of the *living*, but would apply one to the property, not of the *dead* (for the dead have *none*), but of the living who gain it by an inheritance. Surely, in either case, graduation arraigns the dispositions of Providence, subverts individual rights, and shows itself to be in principle but a step towards Socialism."[2] In the following year Hubbard considered more at length the objectors to the scheme, especially Maitland and Warburton, and endeavored to refute their arguments.[3] The Liverpool Reform Association, through its president, Robertson Gladstone, issued a letter to Babbage taking exception to his views on exemption, and objecting strongly to the fact that owners of unproductive property were not liable to income tax.[4] An enthusiastic argument in favor of a property tax was made by Gisborne who, in commenting on the excellent administration of the income tax as disclosed in the evidence before the committee, said: "We only regret that so much industry and ingenuity, and good machinery should have been applied to a tax which is so outrageous in principle, that the wisest man could not

[1] *How Should an Income Tax be levied? Considered in a Letter to the Right Honourable Benjamin Disraeli, Chancellor of the Exchequer.* By John Gellibrand Hubbard. London, 1852, p. 26.

[2] *Op. cit.*, p. 31.

[3] *Reform or Reject the Income Tax. Objections to a Reform of the Income Tax considered, in two Letters to the Editor of the Times, with additional Notes.* By John Gellibrand Hubbard. London, 1853, pp. 24 *et seq.* Hubbard's book is reviewed rather adversely in an article in the *Edinburgh Review*, vol. xcvii (1853), p. 240. A number of other works on the same subject are reviewed, *ibid.*, p. 531.

[4] *A Letter to Charles Babbage, Esq., in Reply to his "Thoughts on the Principles of Taxation, with reference to a Property Tax and its Exceptions."* By the Liverpool Financial Reform Association. Liverpool, 1852, p. 18. In an Appendix to this tract is printed a strong letter from Lord Jeffrey, in favor of discrimination.

say anything in its defence which any ordinary man could not refute."[1] Gisborne was enamored of the system of the general property tax as he found it described as existing in the United States. In the light of our modern experience it is not a little amusing to read that "we cannot but admire the easy and simple machinery by which the tax works both in New York and Texas."[2] He closes with the naïve remark that "no one can avoid a property tax, and this I think one of its main recommendations."[3]

The chief opponent of differentiation was Maitland. In an anonymous pamphlet he stated that the tax had now undoubtedly become permanent. "I cannot help concluding that the tax will, with or without modification, be a permanent national burden."[4] This, in itself, he thought, robbed the argument for "discrimination" of much of its weight. Even apart from this, however, he opposed discrimination on the ground of the diffusion theory of taxation, holding that, in the long run, matters would right themselves.[5] He maintained, further, that "although graduation and discrimination are different things, yet I believe it will be found that they are closely related. Both depend upon the feeling that any deduction from a small or precarious income will press more heavily than a large deduction from a large and secure income."[6] Accordingly, while he applauded Mill for opposing graduation, he declared him illogical in at the same time upholding discrimination. In a production published in the following year, Maitland returned to the charge and sought to show that the arguments of his opponents defeated each other.[7]

[1] *Thoughts on an Income Tax and on a Property Tax; principally founded on the Evidence taken by the House of Commons Committee in the session 1851.* By Thomas Gisborne. London, 1852, p. 14.

[2] *Op. cit.*, p. 41.

[3] *Op. cit.*, p. 61.

[4] *Property and Income Tax, Schedule A and Schedule D.* [By J. G. Maitland.] London, 1852, p. 2.

[5] *Op. cit.*, pp. 3–11.

[6] *Op. cit.*, pp. 56, 57.

[7] *Property and Income Tax. The Present State of the Question.* By J. G. Maitland. London, 1853. See esp. p. 38.

Disraeli, however, was won over by the arguments of the discriminationists. When he became Chancellor of the Exchequer in the new cabinet of Lord Derby, he had time, in making his financial statement in April, 1852, only to propose the continuance of the income tax for another year. In December, however, when he presented his budget for the following year, he proposed to renew the income tax for three years, and to reduce the rate of Schedules D and E from *7d.* to 5¼*d.* He also suggested that farmers should be assessed hereafter on one-third instead of one-half of their rent, and that the limit of exemptions be reduced to £50 for industrial incomes and £100 for property incomes. As he combined with these suggestions the scheme of a great increase in the house tax, this practically meant a decided relief to the agricultural community at the expense of the towns. Disraeli's proposals, however, led to vehement opposition. They were denounced by Duncombe as "preposterous," by Osborne as "based upon tyranny and injustice," and by Gladstone as "most regardless of those general rules of prudence which it is most absolutely necessary we should preserve."[1] The government was defeated on the house tax proposition, and Disraeli was replaced by Gladstone as Chancellor of the Exchequer.

§ 6. *Gladstone's Budget of 1853*

Gladstone's financial statement of April 18, 1853, is rightly considered one of his masterpieces.[2] He began by asking whether an effort should be made to part with the income

[1] *Cf.* the discussion in *Fiscal Legislation, 1842–1865. A Review of the Financial Changes of that period, and their effects upon Revenue, Trade, Manufactures and Employments.* By John Noble. London, 1867, p. 53.

[2] Nicholson, *Principles of Political Economy*, iii, 1901, p. 339, declares it to be "probably the finest oration on finance ever delivered, and certainly the strongest in argument." In addition to the passage in Hansard, it is found in full in *The Financial Statements of 1853, 1860–1863. To which are added a Speech on Tax-Bills, 1861, and on Charities, 1863.* By the Rt. Hon. W. E. Gladstone. London, 1863. It is discussed in Northcote, *Twenty Years of Financial Policy*, pp. 185–199.

tax at once. "I do not say that such an alternative is impossible," he replied; but he did not recommend it, because in his opinion the new taxes which it would be necessary to impose "would, upon the whole, be far more unequal, and would cause greater dissatisfaction than the income tax," and furthermore, because "it would arrest other beneficial reforms of taxation." He went on to emphasize the fact that the House "should fully appreciate the power of this colossal engine of finance," and, referring to the imposition of the income tax by Pitt in 1799, he maintained that "if there had been resolution enough to submit to the income tax at an earlier period, our debt need not at this moment have existed."

Referring to Peel, "who called forth from repose this giant, who had once shielded us in war, to come and assist our industrious toils in peace," he said: "The second income tax has been the instrument by which you have introduced, and by which I hope ere long you may perfect, the effective reform of your commercial and fiscal system." This he thought would finally spread to other countries as well; "If we rightly use the income tax, we shall be entitled, when we part with it, to look back upon it with some satisfaction, and to console ourselves for the annoyance it may have entailed by the recollection that it has been the means of achieving a great good immediately to England, and ultimately to mankind." He did not, however, for a moment conceal his opinion that the tax "is not well adapted for a permanent portion of your fiscal system, unless you can by a reconstruction remove what are called its inequalities. Even, however, if you could remove its inequalities," he added, "there would still remain, in my mind at least, objections to it of the gravest character."

With some of the objections he did not agree. The matter of discrimination, for instance, he declared was virtually a question of the distinction between land and trade. As to this, after a careful analysis of the facts he concluded that land and houses actually paid a higher rate than trade. He held, therefore, that so far as these are concerned, there was no sufficient ground to attempt a reconstruction of the income tax. Taking up next the other phase of discrimination, namely, the difference between precarious and realized incomes, or what he preferred to call "industrious" and "lazy" incomes, Gladstone held that there was practically no income which was "perfectly and entirely a lazy income, except the income of the fund-holder"; and there were in his mind insuperable objections to levying a higher tax on the funds. The scheme of the actuaries for a capitalization of the income tax he brushed aside as a "mere mathematical speculation," which "of all the plans of income tax reform is placed the furthest beyond the reach even of imagination, as a possible, or as a feasible measure." Finally, coming to the case of professional incomes, Gladstone confessed that it "appeals to our sympathies." But he held that here also "you cannot exempt professional incomes without breaking up the whole scheme of the tax." "The real tendency of all these exemptions," said Gladstone, "is the breaking up and destruction of the tax. I do not say the 'relinquishment,' because relinquishment is one thing and breaking up is another. To relinquish it is altogether safe because it is altogether honourable; but to break it up is to encourage the House of Commons to venture upon schemes which may look well upon paper and may serve the purpose of the moment, yet which will end in the destruction of the tax by the absurdities and by the iniquities which they involve."

Gladstone closed this part of his speech by stating: "One thing I hope this House will never do, and that is to nibble at this great question of state policy. . . . Depend upon it, when you come to close quarters with this subject, when you come to measure and test the respective relations of intelligence and labour and property in all their myriad complex forms, and when you come to represent these relations in arithmetical results, you are undertaking an operation of which I should say that it is beyond the power of man to conduct it with satisfaction. . . . Whatever you do in regard to the income tax, you must be bold, you must be intelligible, you must be decisive. You must not palter with it. . . . I believe it to be of vital importance, whether you keep this tax or whether you part with it, that you either should keep it or should leave it, in a state in which it will be fit for service on an emergency; and this it will be impossible to do, if you break up the basis of your income tax."

Passing on to the question of the permanence of the tax, Gladstone pointed out that, while it is an engine of gigantic power for great national purposes, "there are circumstances attending its operation which make it difficult, perhaps impossible, at any rate, in our opinion not desirable, to maintain it as a portion of the permanent and ordinary finances of the country. The public feeling of its inequality is a fact most important in itself. The inquisition it entails is a most serious disadvantage, and the frauds to which it leads are an evil such as it is not possible to characterize in terms too strong." It is essential, he thought, to allay the feeling "that the country is about to be entrapped unawares into its perpetuation." He proceeded to unfold his plans "to lay the ground for placing Parliament in such a position that at a given period it may, if it shall think fit, part with the tax." Here, however, he put fairly and squarely before the House the alternative: "If you determine to renew the income tax, will you make its early extinction your first and sole object, or will you, in order to bring to completion the noble work of commercial reform which is so far advanced, once more associate the income tax with a remission of duties, extensive in itself and beneficial to the community? We have considered fully these two alternatives," added Gladstone, "and we have decided deliberately in favour of the second." In other words, Gladstone proposed that the tax be renewed for two years at *7d.* in the pound, for two more years at *6d.* in the pound, and for three more years at *5d.* in the pound; so that at the end of seven years, or in 1860, the tax would expire.

Such was Gladstone's argument on the income tax. The income tax has been of incalculable assistance, but it is an inherently bad tax. It must therefore serve only as a temporary measure. The alleged inequality of the tax, especially from the point of view of differentiation, is perfectly true; but the remedy is impracticable. The only way to get rid of the inequality is to abolish the tax itself; and since the tax is to be kept only as a temporary tax it is better to continue it with these inequalities rather than to disrupt it as an engine of finance. The objection that property as such pays but little as compared with industry is met by the proposal to extend and to generalize the Death Duties.

Gladstone's suggestions led to a heated debate, in which Cobden, Disraeli, Henley, and Bulwer-Lytton took part; but Gladstone carried all his points by a large majority. Not only did he succeed at the time in turning the tide of public opinion, but so commanding was his mastery over parliament and the country, that as long as he remained in power he was able successfully to resist any attempt to alter the essential character of the tax.

The new law of 1853[1] included some important changes. The tax was extended to Ireland, which was now treated like Scotland, except that the assessment in Schedules A and B, instead of being on the full annual value, was upon the valuation for the poor rate; *i.e.*, generally twenty per cent below the full annual value. In arguing for the cessation of the exemption of Ireland from the taxation, Gladstone had said: "Let me remind the Committee what exemption means; it does not mean that we have got a bottomless purse, that we can dispense exemptions to one man without injuring another. No, sir. The exemption of one man means the extra taxation of another, and the exemption of one country means the extra taxation of another." It was this consideration that carried the day.

Professional incomes (Schedule D, second case) were now charged on the average profits of the last three years, like the profits of trade. Investors in life-insurance policies were allowed to deduct the amount of their premiums. In the act of 1806, it will be remembered, the allowance for life-insurance premiums was restricted to persons with an income of

[1] 16 and 17 Vict., c. 34.

£150 or less. In 1842 this allowance was not granted. Now it was reintroduced, but made applicable to incomes of all amounts. So far as abatements and exemptions were concerned, the total exemption was now reduced from £150 to £100, while incomes between £100 and £150 were charged only 5*d.* instead of the regular 7*d.* Some changes were also made in the administration of the tax. The concession granted in 1850 to tenant farmers to have the assessments in Schedule D reduced to the actual profits, if they fell short of the assessment, was now extended to all tenants. Furthermore, an important alteration was made in Schedule D. Under the Act of 1842, it will be remembered that the income from foreign government securities in Schedule C was to be assessed by Special Commissioners, and that the bankers, or other individuals charged with the payment of the interest were required to make returns of such payments. This provision was now extended to the securities of all foreign companies under Schedule D, thus making the bankers, or agents, virtually responsible for the tax on all foreign securities whether public or private.

§ 7. *A Decade of Quiet*

The expectations aroused by Gladstone as to the early extinction of the tax were doomed to be disappointed. Instead of the tax being reduced according to his forecast, the preparations for the Crimean War in 1854 and 1855 entailed the necessity of increasing the rate until it reached the figure of 1*s.* 2*d.* — a rate higher than any time since 1842. In 1857 Sir G. Lewis reduced the rate to 7*d.*, and in 1858 Disraeli, in the hope of carrying out the proposals of 1853, reduced it still further to 5*d.* In 1859, however, when Gladstone again became Chancellor of the Exchequer, he raised the rate from 5*d.* to 9*d.*, simply because he needed the money. Now, for the first time, the tax was utilized, in time of profound peace, as the elastic element in the budget, and was increased for the year in order to make good a deficiency in the ordinary revenue. When 1860 arrived, Disraeli pointed out that the income tax "is unfortunately still alive; nay, more, it is a child which has gradually grown." As has been well said: "Alas, at the end of seven years, the long-suffering nation found itself in possession not of the much-desired Rachel, but of the ill-favored Leah."[1]

Mr. Gladstone now made his second great budget speech, in which he carried through the commercial treaty with France and did away with all the remaining survivals of the protective tariff. But in order to make up the deficiency, in part at all events, he was compelled to increase the income tax to 10*d.*, the highest point it had yet reached in time of peace; "and this, cruel fate, in the very year in which it was to have disappeared."[2] The question of the repeal of the tax was not even discussed.

The administrative and other changes that were made in 1861 and the two previous years were as follows: In 1859 the allowance for life-insurance premiums was extended to contracts for deferred annuities issued by the government.[3] In 1860 it was provided that railway profits should henceforth be assessed by the Commissioners for Special Purposes,[4] and that the tax on salaries of railway officials and employees under Schedule E, likewise to be assessed by the Special Commissioners, should be paid by the company.[5] In 1861 the provisions of the act of 1853 applicable to the securities of foreign companies were still further extended to those of colonial companies, the banker or agent being made responsible for the tax.[6]

So convinced, however, were many members of parliament that the tax was now in a fair way of becoming permanent, that Hubbard was able, despite the opposition of Gladstone, to carry, on February 19 1861, his motion for the appoint-

[1] *Mr. Gladstone: A Study.* By Sidney Buxton. London, 1901, p. 124.

[2] *Ibid.*, p. 44. For exact figures as to the annual rate and yield of the income tax see Appendix to chap. iii, *infra.*

[3] 22 and 23 Vict., c. 18, sec. 6.

[4] 23 and 24 Vict., c. 14, sec. 5.

[5] *Ibid.*, sec. 6.

[6] 24 and 25 Vict., c. 91, sec. 36.

ment of a Select Committee "to inquire into the present mode of authorizing and collecting the income and property tax, and whether any mode of levying the same, so as to render the tax more equitable, can be adopted." An interesting glimpse into Mr. Gladstone's attitude on the question of permanence is afforded by his speech of that date. "Necessity," said Gladstone, "drove us to it in 1842, and necessity has attached us to the use of it." And when he was interrupted by cries of "no! no!" he added: "When I used the word 'attached' I meant not as a bridegroom is attached to his bride, but as a captive is attached to the car of his conqueror."

The spell of Gladstone's eloquence in 1853 had not only converted parliament, but had silenced for a time all discussion. The only exception was the republication, with a new preface, of the speech [1] for a graduated income tax which Buckingham had delivered in 1833.[2] Toward the end of the fifties, however, the discussion was resumed, and the movement for reform soon acquired considerable momentum. In 1858 the Birmingham Income Tax Reform Association was formed, for the purpose of "removing the injustice and oppression which are goading the tax-paying classes into a state of discontent and disaffection." [3] They objected to the tax as "a violation of the principles of free trade," [4] and demanded not only the adoption of the system of capitalization, but also the acceptance of that of self-assessment. "As to industrial incomes, let every man make his return, which shall be final, under the sanction of an oath or solemn declaration. Thus inquisitorial powers, and the secret tribunal, would be got rid of." [5]

[1] *Debate in the House of Commons on the Gradual Extinction of the National Debt, and of the true Principles of a Property and Income Tax. Republished for comparison with Gladstone's Financial Proposition.* [By J. S. Buckingham.] London, 1853. *Cf.* also *Some Observations on Direct Taxation in reference to Commercial Reform.* By S. Coleman. London, 1853.

[2] *Supra*, p. 121.

[3] *Address of the Income Tax Reform Association.* Birmingham, 1855, p. 3.

[4] *Op. cit.*, p. 6.

[5] *Op. cit.*, p. 12.

Two years later the Committee issued a forcible address, declaring themselves "uncompromising opponents of the present income tax laws because those laws are unjust in principle, inequitable in application, and oppressive in operation."[1] Schedule D was naturally the chief subject of their objurgations, and they concluded that "a tax that outrages justice alike in principle and in operation, will be abolished by your fiat in spite of any ministry."[2] A similar association formed in London issued an address in the same year, protesting against the continuance and increase of the tax and complaining of the "stealthy" proceedings of the government.[3] An amusing dialogue on the income tax which appeared at about the same time states that "an income tax, levied as at present, is a graduated property tax, the graduation of taxation being so contrived as to fall with crushing weight on the shoulders of industry, to the relief of accumulated wealth."[4] The author of a diffuse treatise on taxation known as *The People's Blue Book*,[5] was invincibly opposed to the continuance of the tax. "It is manifestly an impossibility," he tells us, "ever to impose a tax on incomes, necessarily uncertain in amount and precarious in termination, which will not be unequal and unjust, and in direct violation of every rule and maxim which should govern taxation."[6] His remedy was a tax on realized property combined with a "tax on persons" through the medium of a house tax. The same plan was approved, with a few modifications, by the author of a tract, who signed himself a mill-owner.[7] Stans-

[1] *Address of the Birmingham Income Tax Reform Association to the Electors of Great Britain and Ireland, Feb. 1857.* Birmingham, n. d. [1857], p. 3.

[2] *Op. cit.*, p. 10.

[3] *The Property and Income Tax Association to the Taxpayers of the United Kingdom.* London, n. d. [1857], p. 5.

[4] *The Shade of Cocker and the Chancellor of the Exchequer. A Dialogue on the Income Tax.* London, n. d. [*c.* 1858], p. 8.

[5] For the full title see above, page 145.

[6] *Op. cit.*, p. 346 of the ed. of 1872.

[7] *Taxation: Gross Injustice of the present System. Direct Taxation the true Remedy. By a Mill Owner.* Edinburgh, 1859, p. 17.

feld preferred a property tax to an income tax on the ground that "money may be considered as the honey of a society, and from its accumulated stores and deposits, and not from the working bees returning to their hives with laden limbs against the adverse winds should the chief contributions for the support of the State be taken: To starve the bees and spare the drones is bad policy, even for the drones themselves."[1] Gibbon repeated his uncompromising opposition to the income tax, and declared his preference for taxation on expenditure, basing his opinion on an old and long exploded fallacy. "Taxes upon income, however modified in the imposition of them, can never be incident so fairly and impartially as taxes upon expenditure or consumption. Taxes upon income are compulsory contributions — while taxes upon expenditure or consumption are, in a very great measure, optional contributions."[2]

Other writers were willing to accept the income tax, provided the principle of discrimination might be adopted. Thus the Liverpool Financial Reform Association confessed that there were defects in the tax, but contended that with all its faults it was preferable to indirect taxation. Referring to the anti-income-tax agitation, they said: "Fully endorsing your catalogue of grievances, and having reminded you of others which seem to have been very generally forgotten, we are not at all surprised that you should be indignant and disgusted at and with the income and property tax, as it is at present assessed and levied; but we think, nevertheless, that a little

[1] *Outline of a System of Direct Taxation for superseding Customs and Excise Duties, and establishing perfect Freedom of Trade.* By Hamer Stansfeld. London, n. d. [1859], p. 9. The metaphor, it will be seen, is the same as that used in 1907 by Andrew Carnegie in opposing the federal income tax in the United States. *Cf.* his speech before the *National Civic Federation* at the annual meeting in December, 1907.

[2] *The Income Tax; its Causes and Incidence: showing by Analysis that it is a Land Tax, a House Tax, a Tax upon Commodities and a Repudiation of Public Debt.* By Alexander Gibbon. London, 1860, p. 21. Gibbon declares, in an explanatory note, that this tract is only a reprint of a part of his book of 1851.

serious reflection will suffice to convince you that the remedy you seek will be very much worse than the diseases of which you complain."[1] Browning stated that "judging from the readiness with which it has been received by the nation, it may be assumed that, although much clamour was made for the repeal of the war portion of it, generally speaking, a tax on income is favourably viewed by a large majority."[2] He thought that discrimination would remove whatever objections remained. Hubbard, who lost no opportunity of harping on his own idea, delivered a lecture in which he claimed that "a property tax, as it is now levied, is an odious thing."[3] Professor Levi wrote a treatise in which he stated that "the injustice of taxing all kinds of income at equal rates will be best appreciated when we consider the saleable value of different kinds of property."[4]

[1] *Address on the Present Anti-Income Tax Agitation: showing how and why Direct Taxation is preferable to Customs and Excise Duties.* By the Liverpool Financial Reform Association. New Series, no. 19. Liverpool, 1856, p. 5. Numerous essays were published either by, or under the auspices of, the Association, all emphasizing the same point. *Cf.* the following: *Direct and Indirect Taxation contrasted; or the immeasurably Preferable Policy of an Income Tax to Customs and Excise Duties, elucidated.* By Lawrence Heyworth. n. d. [1861]; *Taxation: Direct or Indirect. An Essay intended to be read to the Economic Section of the British Association.* By Francis Boult. Liverpool, 1861; *The Rights of Rich and Poor: Just Taxation: Abolition of all Duties on the Necessaries of Life, etc.* By George Henry Smith. Liverpool, n. d. [1861]; *Essay on Taxation, Direct and Indirect, with Suggestions for its Revision.* By Thomas Clarke. Liverpool, 1851. *Cf.* also the Scotch pamphlet, *Indirect Taxation: Its Wasteful and Burdensome Nature, as compared with Direct Taxation, in necessarily causing the Public to pay much more than the Amount imposed by Parliament; and the most Equitable Mode of imposing Direct Taxes on Property.* By Duncan M'Laren. Edinburgh, 1860. For a later pamphlet by the same author see *infra*, page 164.

[2] *The Finances of Great Britain considered. Comprising an Examination of the Property and Income Tax, and Succession Duty Act of 1853.* By Reuben Browning. Part I, London, 1859, p. 11.

[3] *A Lecture on Currency, Taxation, and Finance, delivered at the Town Hall, Buckingham, on the 21st of April.* By John Gellibrand Hubbard. n. d. [1859] p. 22.

[4] *On Taxation: How it is Raised, and how it is Expended.* By Leone Levi, London, 1860, p. 153. The substance of this was published in a paper, "On the Distribution and Productiveness of Taxes with reference to the Prospective

Professor Neate contended that the principle of differentiation flowed naturally from the theory of benefits in taxation, although he conceded that "it may not be easy, and may possibly be impracticable, to estimate in money the value of that difference."[1] On the other hand, Dr. Booth in an address before the British Association opposed discrimination chiefly on the ground that if the tax were perpetual, perpetual incomes would pay their share.[2] This was in effect the argument of Warburton before the committee of 1852, and an attempt to refute it was made by Sargant, in an address in which he declared himself strongly in favor of the principle of differentiation.[3] It is evident, therefore, that there was a widespread interest in the matter which formed the subject of Hubbard's committee.

§ 8. *The Committee of 1861*

The Committee comprised, in addition to the chairman, Mr. Hubbard, such men as the Chancellor of the Exchequer, Mr. Lowe and Sir Stafford Northcote.[4] Among the chief witnesses were Hubbard himself, Newmarch, Farr, and Mill, all of whom agreed with the chairman. Hubbard presented a memorandum in which he made a classification of "property-incomes" as compared to "industrial incomes."[5] Inciden-

Ameliorations in the Public Revenue of the United Kingdom," in the *Journal of the Statistical Society*, vol. xxiii (1860), pp. 37–65, and separately reprinted.

[1] *Three Lectures on Taxation, especially that of Land, delivered at Oxford in the year 1860.* By Charles Neate. Oxford, 1861, p. 19.

[2] "On the Principles of an Income Tax." in *Journal of the Statistical Society*, vol. xxiii (1860), p. 456. Booth also opposed the scheme of the Liverpool Financial Reform Association. *Ibid.*, p. 461.

[3] William Lucas Sargant, "Some Observations on the Fallacy of the Warburton Argument in favor of an indiscriminating Income Tax," in *Journal of the Statistical Society*, vol. xxiv (1861), p. 213.

[4] *Report from the Select Committee on Income and Property Tax; together with the Proceedings of the Committee, Minutes of Evidence, and Appendix.* 1861, 302 + 51 pp.

[5] In the first class he included all of Schedule A (lands, houses, rent-charges, mines, quarries, manors, fisheries, and public companies like railroads, canal, gas, and dock companies), except incomes from mining adventures; all of Schedule C

tally he referred, in an interesting passage, to the nomenclature of the tax. "The existing tax is called the property and income tax. Why it is so called is not apparent. It does truly, in many instances, tax both property and the income arising from that property, but it is not probable that to declare the special vice of the tax was the intention of its double name. Obviously, however, the same tax should not be a property and an income tax; and, while a tax on the transfer of property may rightly be a property tax, occurring as it would at intervals of many years, so an annual tax, necessarily payable out of income, should be an income tax."[1]

Hubbard submitted a report, the principal features of which were as follows: First, a proposal to make net, instead of gross, income the basis of assessment of the tax; not ascertaining the net income by an account of actual outgoings, but assuming it by a deduction, founded on an average, from certain classes of gross incomes. Second, a proposal to divide all incomes into two classes, of which the one should comprise incomes called spontaneous, and the other incomes called industrial; and to tax the former upon the full amount of the net income, and the latter upon two-thirds of that amount. Third, a proposal to distinguish in certain cases between the interest of invested capital and the repayment by instalments of the invested capital itself, and to levy the tax upon the interest entirely, and not upon the paid portions of capital.[2]

Mr. Lowe submitted a contrary report in which he took exception to the theory advocated by Mill and accepted by Hubbard, that savings ought to be exempted from taxation. "It is no part of the duty of the State," said Lowe, "to give bounties to saving, or to lay penalties on expenditure. The

(public securities); Schedule D, so far as it comprised banking, trading, and manufacturing property, foreign property and securities; and Schedule E, so far as it included pensions. Industrial incomes would thus comprise virtually the whole of Schedule D (profits of business and professions), together with profits from mining adventures (Schedule A), farms (Schedule B), and stipends (Schedule E). — See *Report*, etc., p. 282.

[1] *Report*, p. 283.

[2] *Report*, p. iii.

State cannot put itself in the position of individuals, to judge for them; and, as it cannot judge whether it is better for a man to save or to spend, it ought not to interfere. . . . There is a vice of saving, as well as of spending. Avarice is as odious as prodigality. It is not every man that has an opportunity of saving. Saving implies something to spare, after satisfying the wants of the year. To give a remission to savings is, therefore, to give a remission to wealth."[1] Northcote proposed a draft report which finally, after some slight changes, was adopted by a narrow majority as the report of the committee.

The report mentions the three complaints popularly directed against the income tax, namely "that it taxes the owners of property in respect of income which they do not get; that it presses too hardly upon skill and industry, as compared with property; and that it deals with capital in certain cases as if it were income, and taxes it accordingly." It then proceeds: "Your committee, however, after full consideration, have arrived at the conclusion that the plan proposed by their chairman does not afford a basis for a practicable and equitable readjustment of the income tax; and they feel so strongly the dangers and ill consequences to be apprehended from an attempt to unsettle the present basis of the tax, without a clear perception of the mode in which it is to be reconstructed, that they are not prepared to offer any suggestions for its amendment." They add finally: "This tax having now been made the subject of investigation before two Committees, and no proposal for its amendment having been found satisfactory, your Committee are brought to the conclusion that the objections which are urged against it are objections to its nature and essence, rather than to the particular shape which has been given to it."

Many years later Hubbard stated that the committee's report had been prearranged by the government.[2] However

[1] *Report*, p. xxi.

[2] "In the formation of the committee I had great difficulties: the selection of names was, as usual, arranged between the respective whips; and as both

that may be, Hubbard was ingloriously defeated, and thus the second attempt to reform the tax came to an end.

Notwithstanding this defeat, the echoes of the controversy were some time in dying away. A writer in a leading review accepted most of Hubbard's arguments and declared that "the income tax must be reformed before it becomes permanent."[1] M'Laren, a prominent Scotch merchant, issued a report, containing the same idea, to the Edinburgh Chamber of Commerce, which adopted it in February, 1862.[2] On the other hand, Sargant was won over to the side of the opponents, and in an article, the theory of which was still based on the cost-of-service principle, retracted his former admissions, and demanded only a uniform abatement of £100 on all assessments.[3] Not a few, however, grasped at the final sentence in the report of the Committee, and demanded a repeal of the tax. Thus a writer in the *Quarterly Review* stated that "experience must have convinced the House that the farce of calling the income tax provisional cannot go on much longer. The decision must soon be taken whether the income tax is to be exceptional or permanent. They must not trust that its mere odiousness will destroy it, and that Chancellors of the Exchequer will ever spontaneously dispense with so convenient a substitute for statesmanship. It is demoralizing, inquisitorial, intolerable. . . . But in spite of this, unless a blow be struck at it right early, this generation will not see its end."[4] Beal, in an address to the London Financial Reform Association, suggested, as a substitute, a

political parties were opposed to me, names I had proposed were struck out, and replaced by those of men unfavourably affected to the enquiry." — *Gladstone on the Income Tax*, etc. London, 1885, p. 26. For full title see *infra*, page 175.

[1] "Income Tax Reform," *The Westminster Review*, vol. lxxvii. (1862), pp. 97–127. See esp. p. 111.

[2] *Report to the Edinburgh Chamber of Commerce, proposing a Just and Simple Mode of laying on the Income and Property Tax.* By Duncan M'Laren. Edinburgh, 1862.

[3] William Lucas Sargant. "An Undiscriminating Income Tax Reconsidered," *Journal of the Statistical Society*, vol. xxv (1862), p. 339.

[4] "The Income Tax and its Rivals," *The Quarterly Review*, vol. 109 (1861), p. 247.

land tax.[1] Hankey declared that he considered it "an odious tax."[2] Cobbett, who characterized it as "a highwayman's tax," desired to substitute a tax on patents.[3] In parliament, however, the idea of abandoning the income tax was gradually disappearing.

In his budget speech of 1861, Gladstone again referred to the subject. It was here that he made his famous comparison between direct and indirect taxes, in which he voiced, in a statesmanlike way, the relative advantages of the latter.[4]

"To many people both, as is natural, appear sufficiently repulsive. As for myself, I confess that, owing to the accident of my official position, rather than to any more profound cause of discrepancy, I entertain quite a different opinion. I never can think of direct or indirect taxation except as I should think of two attractive sisters, who have been introduced into the gay world of London; each with an ample fortune; both having the same parentage (for the parents of both I believe to be necessity and invention), differing only as sisters may differ, as where one is of lighter and one of darker complexion, or where there is some agreeable variety of manner, the one being more free and open, and the other somewhat more shy, retiring, and insinuating. I cannot conceive any reason why there should be unfriendly rivalry between the admirers of these two damsels; and I frankly own, whether it be due to a lax sense of moral obligation or not, that as Chancellor of the Exchequer, if not as a member of this House, I have always thought it not only allowable, but even an act of duty, to pay my addresses to them both.

[1] *Direct Taxation. London Financial Reform Association. Observations addressed to the Members of the Westminster Reform Union.* By James Beal. London, 1862, p. 16.

[2] *Taxes and Expenditures; or How the Money comes in and how the Money goes out.* By Thomson Hankey. London, 1864, p. 28.

[3] *A Letter to the Chancellor of the Exchequer on the relative Political Merits of Beer, Wine, and Tea; shewing the Effects of Taxes on those Articles, and Substitutes for those Taxes and also for the Income Tax.* By William Cobbett. London, 1863, p. 26.

[4] Gladstone, *Financial Statements*, pp. 241, 242.

I am therefore, as between direct and indirect taxation, perfectly impartial."

Going on, however, to discuss the remission of the income tax, Gladstone took no uncertain position. "I should like very much," said he,[1] "to be the man who could abolish the income tax. I do not abandon altogether the hope that the time may come. ['Hear.'] I can assure the honorable gentlemen that I am not about to be too sanguine, for, in finishing the sentence, I should have proceeded to quote Mr. Sidney Smith, who, in his admirable pamphlet upon the ballot, speaking, I think, of its establishment, or of something else, as of a very remote result, says he thinks we had better leave the care of this subject to those little legislators, who are now receiving a plum or a cake after dinner. I am afraid that some such amount of self-restraint may be necessary with regard to the income tax. . . . I think that it would be a most enviable lot for any Chancellor of the Exchequer — I certainly do not entertain any hope that it will be mine — but I think that some better Chancellor of the Exchequer, in some happier time, may achieve that great consummation; and that some future poet may be able to sing of him, as Tennyson has sung of Godiva, although I do not suppose the means employed will be the same,

"'He took away the tax,
And built himself an everlasting name.'"

Thus came to an end, for a time at least, all thought of abandoning the income tax.

[1] Gladstone, *Financial Statements*, pp. 244, 245.

CHAPTER III

THE MODERN INCOME TAX: A HALF CENTURY OF ACHIEVEMENT, 1862–1911

§ 1. *The Uneventful Decade, 1862–1872*

As we have seen in the last chapter, it had proved to be impossible to abolish the income tax at the beginning of the sixties. The only result of the discussion was that Gladstone contented himself knocking 1*d.* off the rate. During the next few years the same policy was followed. The tax continued, but the increasing prosperity of the country made possible a progressive diminution in the rate. In 1863 Gladstone reduced the tax to 7*a.*, and in 1864 to 6*d.*, basing his action on the ground that the country might soon be able to decide fairly and squarely whether it desired to retain the tax permanently. "For it is very undesirable," declared he in 1864, "that the income tax should creep unawares into perpetuity." In 1865 the rate was reduced to 4*d.*, a reduction which in Gladstone's opinion made the reduction of the tax easy, or its extinction practicable. The succeeding years, however, with their frequent changes in ministry, were not uniformly prosperous, and Gladstone's second attempt to prepare for the extinction of the tax proved a failure. Under both the Conservative and the Liberal ministries up to 1874 the income tax was continued, now at a higher and now at a lower rate.

In the interval from 1862 to 1874 several minor changes were made in the law. In 1863 the abatement which in the case of incomes between £100 and £150 had been allowed on so much of any duty as might exceed the rate of 5*d.*, was fixed at the definite figure of £60, and was now made applicable to incomes of from £100 to £200. Incomes below £100 were as before totally exempted. In 1865 a modification was made in the system of permitting deductions in

Schedule D in cases where the actual profits for the year fell short of the profits computed on the average system. Section 133 of the act of 1842, following a similar section in the old law of 1806, had made general provision for such deduction. Taxpayers were permitted to avail themselves of this privilege when the actual profits for the year turned out to be less than the average profits for the three years; but the government was not permitted to charge more in the reverse case. The provision, therefore, was so one-sided, and had worked so unfairly in practice,[1] that the taxpayer was now required to prove not only that his profits for the year were less than the sum assessed, but that they were less than the average of three years, including the year of assessment. In other words, the taxpayer was compelled to show that his profits for the year were abnormally low. Moreover, the reduction was limited to the difference between an average based on the profits of the three preceding years and an average based on the profits of the year of assessment and two preceding years.[2] In 1866 permission was given to the concerns mentioned in No. III of Schedule A — mines, quarries, iron-works, and the like — to be assessed, if they preferred, according to the rules of Schedule D.[3] Practically, this was a concession to mine owners, enabling them to return their profits in one sum to the Special Commissioners, instead of having them assessed by the General Commissioners.[4] In 1869 the Valuation (Metropolis) Act placed the assessment of Schedules A and B in London in the hands of surveyors, and provided for a quinquennial valuation — a custom that was subsequently extended to the rest of the

[1] *Cf. Report of the Departmental Committee on the Income Tax*, 1905, p. xvii.

[2] 28 and 29 Vict., c. 30, sec. 6.

[3] 29 and 30 Vict., c. 36, sec. 8.

[4] See *Twenty-fourth Report of the Commissioners of Inland Revenue* (1881), p. 78. This provision was at first held to transfer these concerns from Schedule A to Schedule D; but in 1881 the House of Lords reversed the decision on the ground that mines would be reduced from a five-year to a three-year period, and quarries increased from a single year to a three-year period, — which had evidently not been contemplated. See Dowell, *The Acts Relating to the Income Tax*, 6th ed., by Piper. London, 1908, p. 81.

country.[1] Another act of the same year abolished the quarterly payment of income tax in Schedules A and B, as fixed by the law of 1842, and converted it into an annual payment, except in the case of railways.[2] In 1872 poundage — remuneration of so much per pound on the assessment — was abolished so far as it applied to civil service departments, and replaced by fixed salaries.[3] In the same year an important change in abatements was made. The limit was now extended from £200 to £300, and the amount of abatement was increased from £60 to £80, so that incomes below £100 were wholly exempt, while incomes from £100 to £300 enjoyed an abatement of £80. In 1874 the privilege granted to taxpayers under Schedule D, who were assessed according to a three-year average, to compound for a term of three years, was withdrawn.[4]

The feeling of opposition to the tax was now gradually diminishing, although it had indeed by no means disappeared. McCulloch, for instance, in a new edition of his general treatise, declared his repugnance to the tax to be unshaken.[5] Scarcely less antagonism was shown by Peto, who, after a long consideration of its defects, arrived at the conclusion that "the tax must be put upon a footing which will permit of fair assessment, and which will make it properly productive to the revenue at a moderate rate of duty. If this cannot be done, the tax must be abandoned. It is too oppressive, too obnoxious, too unequal, too immoral in its character to permit of its continuance."[6] In the same way Professor Thorold Rogers[7]

[1] 32 and 33 Vict., c. 67.

[2] 32 and 33 Vict., c. 14, sec. 8.

[3] 35 and 36 Vict., c. 82.

[4] 37 and 38 Vict., c. 96.

[5] *A Treatise on the Principles and Practical Influence of Taxation and the Funding System.* By J. R. McCulloch, 3d ed., Edinburgh, 1863. See esp. pp. 105–107, 115, 135. But see *Proposed Reform in the Income Tax and Extension of the Franchise to the Payers of the Same.* By J. O. Y. London, 1863.

[6] *Taxation: Its Levy and Expenditure, Past and Future; being an Enquiry into our Financial Policy.* By Sir S. Morton Peto. London, 1863, p. 82.

[7] J. E. Thorold Rogers, "On the Statistical and Fiscal Definitions of the Word Income," *Journal of the Statistical Society*, vol. xxviii (1865), p. 257.

declared his preference for a property tax. Urquhart, also, desired the abolition of the tax, suggesting that it be replaced by a land tax coupled with a house tax;[1] and Baxter held that the feeling against the income tax was held in check only by the public attachment to a theory. "The income tax is an excellent example of the love of the British nation for abstract principles. It is founded upon two — the great principle of Direct Taxation, so strongly advocated by financial reformers; and the still greater principle of Equality of Taxation, so dear to political economists. Yet, if the income tax should be the test, it will be difficult to decide which of the twain is the most cordially hated by a discerning public."[2] The opposition reached its climax, perhaps, in a violent pamphlet published in 1872, and written in the interests of an Anti-Income Tax Association. In this it is declared that "the income tax is unequal in its incidence, is vexatious in its operation, and is immoral in its mode of assessments and in its influence on those taxed."[3]

Notwithstanding all these utterances, however, the general sentiment, which was slowly gaining ground, was expressed not only by Sir Stafford Northcote in 1862, when he stated that "the income tax is generally regarded as the financial reserve of the country, which should be kept available for emergencies,"[4] but especially by Noble in 1867. Noble, after showing how the administration of the income tax was being improved from decade to decade, declared that "the income tax may be regarded by the unreflecting with aversion; it may be more agreeable to be deceived into the payment of taxes, than to meet the open demand of the tax gatherer; yet unless the facts narrated in this volume are imaginary and our prosperity

[1] *Dialogues on Taxation, Local and Imperial.* By W. Pollard Urquhart. Aberdeen, 1867, pp. 102, 103.

[2] *The Taxation of the United Kingdom.* By R. Dudley Baxter. London, 1869, p. 92.

[3] *The Income Tax. A Review of its History, and Reasons for its Repeal. To which is added a Reprint of a Pamphlet, "Resist or Be Ruined," originally published in 1816.* London, 1872, p. 13.

[4] *Twenty Years of Financial Policy*, p. 367.

a delusion, the question naturally arises, whether the limits of improvement have been reached, or whether it would not, on every consideration, be a wise and statesmanlike policy to seek fresh triumphs in a field in which such laurels have been won. Shall we dismiss the mighty engine of such undoubted advantages from the public service; or shall we endeavour, by its aid, still further to advance the prosperity and happiness of the community?"[1] The same idea is elaborated in a second work, where Noble now also demanded differentiation.[2] Perhaps the strongest defence is made in a third work by Noble, published in 1875, in which he tells us that "it should, moreover, never be forgotten that the income tax is the great instrument by means of which our recent national prosperity has been accomplished." He adds that "this tax has one great and transcendent merit in comparison with the taxes that it has replaced; it does not hinder the creation of wealth, the expansion of trade, nor the development of manufacturing industry." He refers scornfully to the action of the Chambers of Commerce in "demanding the repeal of the income tax which, with all its faults, has been the main source of the great prosperity which has accrued to British commerce during the last twenty years."[3] There were even not wanting writers like Burt who were so enthusiastically favorable to the tax as to declare the distress of England between 1816 and 1842 to be due largely to the abolition of the income tax.[4] Referring to the fact that it was being denounced as an inquisitorial tax, Burt added: "As a matter of fact, I

[1] *Fiscal Legislation, 1842–1865. A Review of the Financial Changes of that Period and their Effects upon Revenue, Trade, Manufactures, and Employment.* By John Noble. London, 1867, p. 179.

[2] *The Queen's Taxes: An Inquiry into the Amount, Incidence, and Economic Results of the Taxation of the United Kingdom, Direct and Indirect.* By John Noble. London, 1870, chap. 17–22.

[3] *National Finance: a Review of the Policy of the last two Parliaments, and of the Results of Modern Fiscal Legislation.* By John Noble. London, 1875, pp. 226–228. *Cf.* also pp. 328–329.

[4] *The Incidence of Taxation and Debt on Industry.* By J. Gurney Burt. London, n. d. [1871], p. 4.

believe our neighbors are seldom any the wiser; but if they were, I hold that so long as in every centre of population there exist such masses of abject misery, no minister of a great country would be justified in regarding such an argument as any more than dust in the balance."[1]

§ 2. *The Growing Permanence of the Tax, 1874–1894*

Notwithstanding the diminution of the opposition, however, a final effort was made by Gladstone in 1874 to abolish the tax. After five years of office he was in possession of a large surplus and he now suddenly dissolved parliament, going to the country on January 24 with an appeal in which he promised, if returned to power, to abrogate the income tax once and for all. The tax, he thought, had been borne with "exemplary patience," but this was because of its temporary character, "the country cherishing, together with the desire, the expectation, the hope of its extinction." And its extinction Gladstone now declared to be possible: "According to the older financial tradition, the income tax was a war tax. For such a purpose it is invaluable: . . . At a sacrifice for the financial year of something less than four and one half million pounds, the country may enjoy the advantage and relief of its total repeal. I do not hesitate to affirm that an effort should now be made to attain this advantage, nor to declare that according to my judgment it is in the present circumstances practicable."

The election, however, turned only partly on fiscal questions. Moreover, it must not be forgotten that the Tories also held out some prospect of repealing the tax. In Disraeli's election address he referred to "the diminution of local taxation, and the abolition of the income tax—measures which the Conservative party have always favored, and which the Prime Minister and his friends have always opposed." In fact, the general expectation was now widespread that no matter how the election might turn out, the end of the income tax had come. The *Times*, in its issue of January 26,

[1] *Op. cit.*, p. 6.

1874, stated: "It is now evident that whoever is Chancellor of the Exchequer when the budget is produced, the income tax will be abolished."

The Liberals were overwhelmingly defeated, and Gladstone regarded the defeat as the definitive end of the movement to repeal the tax. Many years later he sought to explain his action at this time, and to defend himself against the charge of political bribery which had been preferred against him by Lecky.[1] "Those who gave the promise (in 1853)," wrote Gladstone, "believed the thing they promised to be politic and right. . . . They bound themselves to get rid of the principal direct tax, and none but the nation could absolve them from the attempt to fulfil their effort. Public exigencies postponed for fourteen years the practical acknowledgment of the obligation, but it has never been forgotten. The way had been carefully prepared by the ministry of 1868–1874, through successive reductions of the tax from 8*d.* to 3*d.* In 1874, for the first time since 1845, the opportunity arrived. The nation had its opportunity to take its choice; it may have been wise or unwise, but it was made by competent authority. The result is told in our present expenditure of ninety millions. What, in Mr. Lecky's mind, is a basis of unequalled political profligacy was, in prospect, and is in retrospection, according to my conviction, the payment of a debt of honour and the fulfilment of a solemn duty."[2] Lecky replied that he did not impugn Mr. Gladstone's motives, but that bribery, nevertheless, was the nature of the act. "He must excuse me," Lecky went on to say, "if I add my opinion that the decisive and somewhat indignant rejection of his offer by the constituencies was an encouraging sign of the sound political morality of the nation."[3]

[1] Lecky, *History of England*, vol. 6, p. 300, had said: "No modern statesman would attempt to bribe individuals or purchase boroughs, like Walpole or like North, but we have ourselves seen a minister going to the country on the promise that, if he was returned to office, he would abolish the principal direct tax paid by the class which was then predominant in the constituencies."

[2] *The Nineteenth Century*, xxi (1887), p. 935.

[3] Lecky, "Mr. Gladstone and the Income Tax," *ibid.*, vol. xxii, p. 54.

The new Chancellor of the Exchequer under the Tory ministry, Sir Stafford Northcote, in introducing his budget, proposed that the income tax be continued at the nominal rate of *2d.* "Such a mighty structure," said he, "as that of the income tax was not to be allowed to be thrown down at six weeks' notice." He did, indeed, intimate that the tax would expire entirely as the surplus continued, although he stated that it ought to be kept "ready only for some great emergency, and not to be called upon for trivial occasions." As a matter of fact, however, the surpluses were soon dissipated, and not only was there no thought of abrogating the tax, but the government and the country virtually abandoned the idea of retaining it at a simply nominal rate. The consequence was that the income tax was now utilized from year to year as the exigencies of the budget demanded, and became an acknowledged part of the permanent fiscal system.

The belief in the temporary character of the tax, however, died hard. In 1874, after the election, Professor Levi stated: "Its unpopularity, its uncertainty, and its injustice are a sufficient barrier to the general acceptance of the tax as a permanent branch of the revenue, and it is wise to accept the irrevocable judgment formed of the tax long ago on this subject, by the public at large, and the dicta more recently pronounced against it by the Rt. Hon. W. E. Gladstone."[1] Three years later an anonymous author, who was now becoming somewhat fearful of the outlook, placed all the responsibility on Gladstone. "No one more than he had committed himself to the extinction of the tax. No one had done so much to prevent that extinction."[2] Quoting the petition of the Hull and East Riding Anti-Income-Tax Association, that "the income tax ought to be entirely excluded from the ordinary revenue, and kept as the fiscal reserve for which it was designed," he closed his appeal by

[1] Leone Levi, "On the Reconstruction of the Income and Property Tax," in *Journal of the Statistical Society*, vol. xxxvii (1874), p. 169.

[2] *Shall the Tax be Permanent?* By the author of *Our Deficient Revenue and the Income Tax.* London, n. d. [1877], p. 9.

saying: "to prolong the policy of the last dozen years is little less than political lunacy; it is trifling with loyalty and an abuse of patience."[1]

In 1880 Gladstone returned to power, but the question of the abolition of the income tax was touched upon by him only once. In a speech of April 25, 1884, he alluded to the action of the country ten years before. "The matter was referred to the country at a general election. They declined the offer of abolishing the tax that was given them, and I can promise that a sufficient number of years will pass over the heads of Englishmen before they will have another opportunity of abolishing it." Hubbard, however, gave a more adequate explanation: "Mr. Gladstone has not explained why he did not abrogate the income tax when he resumed office in 1880. The reason is obvious: neither in 1874, nor in 1880, nor in any later year, could an income tax be dispensed with, for it is now, as a substitute for indirect taxation, the only means of taxing classes of persons who would otherwise escape scot free, or nearly so."[2] Thus we can thoroughly agree with the opinion of his biographer that "in all these divers ways, then, while Mr. Gladstone's dream was to repeal the income tax, his fiscal reforms and his financial work have tended to make it permanent."[3]

While Gladstone, however, found it impossible to repeal the tax, his influence sufficed to prevent any important change in its constitution. Hubbard, despite his failure in 1861, had never abandoned his cherished hope of accomplishing its differentiation. In 1875 he attempted to bring the matter up again in parliament, but found no opportunity to deliver his speech, which was thereupon printed separately.[4] In this

[1] *Op. cit.*, p. 18.

[2] *Gladstone on the Income Tax. Discussion of the Income Tax in the House of Commons on 25th April, 1884. With Preface and Historical Sketch, including a Proposed Bill.* By the Rt. Hon. J. G. Hubbard. London, 1885, p. 14.

[3] *Mr. Gladstone*, etc. By Sydney Buxton. London, 1901, p. 135.

[4] *Local and Imperial Taxation. A speech of the Right Hon. John Gellibrand Hubbard, M.P., the Delivery of which on Tuesday the 20th of July, was precluded by the Counting out of the House at 9 P.M.* London, 1875.

speech Hubbard stated that the official returns "furnish a distressing series of details of fraudulent returns." After citing these *in extenso*, he lamented that "the records of the Inland Revenue exhibit so frightful a picture of habitual untruthfulness and fraud."[1] He ascribed this situation, as usual, almost entirely to the lack of differentiation. Others agreed with him. In 1883 Haywood, of the Council of the Liverpool Financial Reform Association, read a paper at the Social Science Congress at Huddersfield, reverting to the old idea that the tax should be levied on property alone.[2] Shortly afterwards, the former Financial Secretary of the Treasury, Laing, enunciated "the broad, simple principle of observing a distinction between earned and unearned income, and making the latter pay at a higher rate."[3] Finally, in 1884, Hubbard returned to the fray. In February he published an article reviewing the entire history of the subject.[4] "Peel's property and income tax," he tells us, "survives the lapse of forty-two years. Detested, denounced, and doomed again and again to extinction, it has crept on by stages of three years, of seven years, but mostly by yearly renewals, and its continuance now stands more firmly rooted than ever as a permanent instrument of revenue." In April he found an opportunity in the House to repeat in substance his motion of over twenty years before. But Gladstone replied:[5] "The Right Honourable Gentleman has devoted himself to this matter with a chivalrous loyalty. He began upon it shortly after his entrance into Parliament, now more than twenty years ago; and I believe that he will pursue it to the death. It reminds me of the Crusades. They began somewhere about the year 1100, and they continued, at intervals, for

[1] *Op. cit.*, pp. 13–17, 24.

[2] *Direct Taxation, and how it may be applied.* By G. R. Haywood. Liverpool, 1883. See esp. p. 11.

[3] *Taxation and Finance.* By S. Laing, Chairman of the London and South Coast Railway Company. London, n. d. [1883], p. 14.

[4] J. G. Hubbard, "Forty Years of Income Tax," *National Review*, February, 1884.

[5] Hansard, vol. cclxxxvii, p. 677.

about two and one-half centuries; and if the condition of human life permitted the Right Honourable Gentleman to extend his parliamentary career to a period as lengthened as that embraced by the Crusades, I am sure that at the end of two centuries and a half he would still be found arguing with undeniable force, and all his clearness of demonstration in favour of his plan for the reconstruction of the income tax."

Gladstone, indeed, did not deny the inequalities of the tax. "I do not contest one of them," he said. "I make a whole armful of concessions to him. I will not accuse him of exaggerating those inequalities; it is hardly possible to exaggerate them." But he stood by his speech of 1853, and stated that he agreed with every important official of the department in regarding the scheme "as a wholly visionary project, though no doubt philanthropic and benevolent in intention, and as absolutely impossible of practical application." Hubbard discussed the entire episode in a pamphlet the following year,[1] in which he accused Gladstone of "cynical injustice to the demoralizing influence of an unequal and oppressive impost," and in which he put upon Gladstone the responsibility of "intensifying every one of its crying anomalies." He concluded with the statement that "the futile pretexts on which finance ministers have resisted the adjustment of the tax have vanished."[2] Yet such was the glamour of Gladstone's name that it took another two decades before the force of these "futile pretexts" was overcome.

In the twenty years following the change in the law of 1874 mentioned above,[3] a few important alterations were made. In 1876 the limit of absolute exemption was again raised, this time to £150, and an abatement of £120 was granted on all incomes between £150 and £400.[4] In 1878 incomes under Schedule D were allowed such deductions for depreciation and for the wear and tear of machinery and plant

[1] For full title, see *supra*, page 175, note 2.

[2] *Op. cit.*, p. 16.

[3] *Supra*, page 169.

[4] 39 and 40 Vict., c. 16.

as the Commissioners might think "just and reasonable."[1] In 1880 the Taxes Management Act summarized and re-enacted the administrative provisions of the laws of 1874 and 1878 as to instances of appeal. In all cases of appeal by the General or Special Commissioners, either appellant or the surveyor might henceforth require the Commissioners to state a case for the opinion of the High Court on questions of law. Further appeal might then be taken to the Court of Appeals, and finally to the House of Lords.[2] The same law renewed the authority given to the Board of Inland Revenue in 1865 to increase the number of General Commissioners from seven to fourteen.[3] In 1885 the control over incomes from foreign and colonial securities was rendered more effective by including in the list of persons intrusted with the payment of such dividends or interest, and required to make returns to the government, dealers in bills of exchange and dealers in coupons who purchase foreign coupons from any one excepting a banker.[4] In 1887 it was provided that farmers, *i.e.*, persons occupying land for purposes of husbandry only, might henceforth elect to be assessed under Schedule D instead of Schedule B, that is, on actual profits, instead of on an assumed income.[5] This, it will be remembered, had been a source of complaint as far back as 1808.[6] In 1889 the exemption accorded to friendly societies for dividends and interest under Schedule C was extended to their income from real estate under Schedule A.[7]

In 1890 an important alteration as to losses was introduced. In the act of 1842, as in its predecessors, losses could be deducted if they were particular losses whereby the profits of the business were diminished, or the loss in one business could be set off against the profits of another distinct business, under the same proprietor. Now, however, they might have such a loss set off against their other taxable income in general, if they applied within six months after the year's assess-

[1] 41 and 42 Vict., c. 15, sec. 1.
[2] 43 and 44 Vict., c. 19, sec. 59.
[3] 28 Vict., c. 30, sec. 5.
[4] 48 and 49 Vict., c. 51, sec. 26.
[5] 50 and 51 Vict., c. 15, sec. 18.
[6] *Cf. supra*, page 106.
[7] 52 and 53 Vict., c. 42, sec. 12.

ment.[1] In 1891 the poundage which had been abolished in 1866 to some extent so far as Civil Service officials were concerned was now completely done away with.[2] It was hoped in this way to diminish the suspicion on the part of the public that the more the officials could extort from the taxpayer, the more they would be paid. In 1893 so much of the income of trade-unions as was employed for benefits was exempted in Schedules A, C, and D, provided the amount of benefit did not exceed £200 or the amount of annuity did not exceed £30.[3] All these changes tended to smooth away some of the existing inequalities, and to render the machinery of the tax more efficient and more productive.

§ 3. *The Emergence of the Newer Problems, 1894–1904*

With the beginning of the nineties we enter upon a new and modern epoch of the income tax. The income tax in an improved form had been adopted in Italy; it had been practically reformed, and was becoming a vast fiscal resource in Germany; and it was being discussed in many other countries as an engine of social progress. In England its administration had been so perfected that not only was it now generally accepted as a permanent and necessary part of the revenue system, but the complaints against it were fast disappearing. In 1891, indeed, we still find a suggestion that permission be given to the taxpayers to buy themselves free of the income tax by a method of composition.[4] Such expressions of opinion, however, were now becoming rare. Sir John Lubbock, who at one time had vigorously opposed the tax, now stated that "we must recognize it as a permanent portion of our fiscal system."[5] Blunden, who had called attention to

[1] 53 and 54 Vict., c. 8, sec. 23.

[2] 54 and 55 Vict., c. 13; and 55 and 56 Vict., c. 25.

[3] 56 and 57 Vict., c. 2.

[4] *Redemption of the National Debt by Composition of Income Tax.* By R. Printed for private circulation. London, 1891, pp. 18–21.

[5] Sir John Lubbock, "The Income Tax in England," *North American Review*, vol. 158 (1894), p. 150.

the undeniable fact that the income tax was not a product of theoretical economic science [in England],[1] and who was by no means blind to the difficulties involved in Schedule D, explained the continued existence of the tax as due to its "merits which distinguish the income tax above the other taxes, as a fiscal resource for great emergencies." Blunden was still so much impressed by the old arguments of Sir Stafford Northcote that he defended the tax chiefly on the ground that "its potentialities for the hour of need are so great, so valuable, and so unique, as to justify its permanent retention in the British tax list, and to insure perfect readiness and efficiency for the emergency, its constant use at a minimum rate is indispensable."[2] Public opinion, however, as we now know, had by this time advanced beyond this position.

The real problem that now attracted attention was not only the old one of differentiation, but the new one of graduation. Although the principle of progressive or graduated taxation had occasionally been advanced in England by radicals, as the preceding pages have shown, it had been uniformly reprobated not only by all English statesmen, but by the great mass of important British thinkers.[3] In the early eighties Mr. Labouchere had hinted at the probability of a progressive income tax,[4] only to have it criticised by a commentator as "a preposterous and impossible system of finance."[5] Another writer maintained that such a scheme "would be indeed fatal to the whole spirit of our commerce and manufacturing energy."[6] A gradual change was, however, coming over the public mind, and by 1894 the Chancellor of the Exchequer, Sir William Vernon Harcourt, de-

[1] G. H. Blunden, "The Position and Function of the Income Tax in the British Fiscal System," *The Economic Journal*, vol. ii (1892), p. 642.

[2] *Op. cit.*, pp. 650, 651.

[3] For a general review of the arguments, see Seligman, *Progressive Taxation*. 2d ed., 1908, Historical Appendices.

[4] "A Democrat on the Coming Democracy," *Fortnightly Review*, March, 1883.

[5] *The Economist*, March 10, 1883, p. 284.

[6] *On the Incidence of Taxation, as affecting Different Classes in the United Kingdom at the Present Time.* By Investigator. London, 1883, p. 23.

clared himself a convert to the new doctrine. Although he applied it to the new death duties, he refrained from extending the principle to the income tax, simply on the ground that he did not yet see his way to perfect the practical details. In his budget speech of April 16, 1894, he conceded that "in principle there is nothing to be said against such a system; indeed, there is every argument in its favor. The difficulties which lie in its way are of an administrative and a practical nature, which as yet I have not been able to find means to overcome."[1] He sought, however, as far as possible, to effect a part of the scheme by an elaborate change in the system of abatements and exemptions. He proposed to fix the limit of total exemption at £160; to have incomes between £160 and £400 receive an abatement of £160; and to have incomes between £400 and £500 enjoy an abatement of £100.

The act of 1894 carried out these recommendations,[2] and also adopted two other changes, one of minor and one of major importance. The minor alteration was the exemption of the income of savings banks, chargeable under Schedules C or D, so far as this is applied to payments of interest not exceeding five pounds for each depositor. The important change affected Schedule A. It had long been complained that real estate had been assessed in Schedule A at its gross, instead of its net, income. Under the new act it was provided that the assessment might be reduced by one-eighth in the case of farm lands with buildings thereon, and by one-sixth in the case of other buildings, so as to permit deductions for repairs. This was recognized as at once a substantial concession to the landowners and a decided improvement in the theory of the tax itself. Finally, in Schedule B the charge was now equalized in the whole of Great Britain. Up to this time, it will be remembered, the rate of duty in Schedule B was in England one-half of the rate in Schedule A, and in Scotland and Ireland about one-third. Now the rate was made uniform, being fixed for the year at 3*d.* in all three countries, as against 8*d.* in Schedule A.

[1] Hansard, 1894, p. 502.

[2] 57 and 58 Vict., c. 30, secs. 34–38.

The statement of the Chancellor that he had been converted to a belief in the abstract principle of graduation could not fail to start a notable discussion. Most of the disputants were inclined to agree with the Treasury officials, who had summed up the situation in 1885 as follows: "With regard to the inquisitorial character of the income tax, we may observe that under the present system the evil is reduced to a minimum. At the present time it is not too much to say that under Schedules A, B, and E fraudulent evasion is very difficult, and that under Schedules C and D, in a large number of instances, no temptation to fraud exists. . . . It is probably owing to these considerations that proposals which have been made from time to time for a graduated income tax have never been received with favour by any one who has had a practical experience of the working of the case. A graduated income tax could only be made dependent on personal returns of incomes, and the doors would thus be widely reopened to fraud."[1] About a decade later Blunden, one of the most accomplished of the British officials, took a similarly conservative view of the situation, and summarized his arguments as follows:—

1. "That the British income tax is at present constructed on lines peculiarly ill-adapted for conversion to the progressive model, owing to the very large extent to which incomes are taxed at their sources.

2. "That its conversion would involve the reconstruction of the tax on the discarded and unscientific lines of direct assessment on general returns of the total income.

3. "That evasion would then be easy, and would speedily become general. The tax would be an effective instrument of national demoralization.

4. "That the yield of the tax would be very little, if at all, enlarged by the change.

5. "That the suggestions made for attaining (in part) the desired ends, by a considerable extension of the system of degressive rates are impracticable."[2]

[1] *Twenty-eighth Report of the Commissioners of Her Majesty's Inland Revenue.* London, 1885, p. 85.

[2] G. H. Blunden, "A Progressive Income Tax," *The Economic Journal*, vol. v (1895), p. 531. Blunden repeated virtually the same argument six years later in the article entitled, "The Future of the Income Tax," *The Economic Journal*, vol. xi (1901), esp. p. 161.

Goddard, who thought that the chief object of progressive taxation was to secure the additional revenues needed for putting into effect the new scheme of old-age pensions, suggested in preference to a graduated income tax a very high tax on income from investments and a somewhat lower tax on incomes from business.[1] And Blunden later on proposed that the income tax be supplemented by a tax on rent and interest.[2] It was reserved, however, for James Burns to publish the suggestion which, after the lapse of another decade, was to bear fruit. In an article written in 1896, in which he stated that "the machinery for assessing and collecting the income tax is much more effective to-day than fifty years ago," he advocated what he called "a graduated and differential scheme," and he here advanced the idea of what he called a super-tax. "The solution of the difficulty can be found in the retention of the present scheme (of stoppage at source) as a means of obtaining the first quota of taxation, and by the direct super-imposition of a graduated tax on incomes exceeding a certain sum — in other words, by a combination of the direct and indirect schemes."[3]

During the ensuing decade, however, foreign affairs, and especially the South African War, prevented the giving of much attention to the problem, and the government contented itself with making various minor changes in the system. In 1896 assessments in Schedule B were arranged according to a relative scale. It will be remembered that in 1894 the rates in Schedules A and B were fixed at 8*d.* and 3*d.* respec-

[1] J. G. Goddard, "Graduated Taxation," *Economic Review*, vol. v (1895), p. 37 *et seq.*

[2] "A New Property Tax," *The Economic Journal*, vol. vii (1897), p. 610.

[3] James Burns, "A Graduated Income Tax," *Westminster Review*, vol. cxlvi (1896), p. 563. Whether this was really the first suggestion of a super-tax is a little doubtful. In Sir Charles Dilke's report to the Select Committee of 1906 we are told that the Board of Inland Revenue had in 1893–1894 advised Sir William Harcourt against graduation, "after examining a proposal for a super-tax by direct assessment on all persons having more than £5000 a year." He does not tell us, however, by whom the proposal was made and whether the word "super-tax" was used. *Cf. Select Committee on the Income Tax*, 1906, p. xix.

tively. Now it was provided that henceforth the annual rate of taxation should be charged upon one-third of the annual value of lands chargeable in Schedule B; that is, the assessable net income in Schedule B, on which the annual normal rate of tax was imposed, was deemed equivalent to one-third of the rent or annual value.[1] In the same year a notable change was introduced into the practice by executive order. The concession made by the law of 1878 with respect to the wear and tear of plant and machinery in Schedule D[2] was extended by a letter of the Chancellor of the Exchequer to the Association of the Chambers of Commerce, in which it was laid down that "where a claim is made in respect of the introduction of more modern machinery into a factory, no objection is to be taken to the allowance, as a deduction from the assessable profits of the year, of so much of the cost of replacement as is represented by the existing value of the machinery replaced."[3] In 1898 Sir Michael Hicks-Beach introduced several improvements. In the first place, he enlarged the system of abatements. The limit of complete exemption still remained at £160, and the abatements on assessments from £160 to £400 remained at £160. But a further abatement of £150 was now granted on incomes from £400 to £500, an abatement of £120 on incomes from £500 to £600, and an abatement of £70 on incomes from £600 to £700, the full rate to be levied only on incomes of over £700. Furthermore, it was provided that the deductions in Schedule D for the annual value of business premises should not exceed the amount for which the premises are assessed under Schedule A, as reduced according to the law of 1894. Finally, permission was given to either party to an appeal to employ a barrister or solicitor. In 1899 the last "Names" Act (designating by name the Land Tax Commissioners who select the General Commissioners) was

[1] 59 and 60 Vict., c. 28, sec. 26.

[2] *Supra*, page 178.

[3] This letter is printed in full in the *Report of the Departmental Committee on Income Tax*, London, 1905, Appendix V.

enacted;[1] and after 1906 the custom arose of appointing the Commissioners by reference to a schedule of names signed by, and deposited with, the clerk of the House of Commons, in lieu of inserting the names in the act itself.[2] The same law of 1906 also abolished the property qualifications for the Land Tax Commissioners, thus extending still further the gradual democratization of the tax.

§ 4. *The Departmental Committee of 1904*

With the return of peace and the growing insistence upon the social as well as the fiscal aspects of taxation, the government was finally induced to take up afresh the whole matter of differentiation and graduation. In 1903 the Chancellor of the Exchequer, Mr. Ritchie, announced his intention of appointing a committee to consider the question in all its bearings; but in 1904, when the committee was actually appointed, provision was made only for a Departmental Committee. The special matters referred to the committee were the following: The prevention of fraud and evasion; the estimation of income derived from copyrights, patent rights, and terminable annuities; the allowance made in respect to the depreciation of estates charged to capital account; the system of computing profits on the three-year average; the rules governing the recovery of overpayments; and finally, the exemption of coöperative societies.

The committee was composed of six leading officials connected with the income tax administration: Messrs. Ritchie, Primrose, Buxton, Bonsor, Murray, and Gayler, with Mr. Llewelyn Davies as secretary. It heard a large number of witnesses, among them important officials like Sir Thomas Hewitt, Mr. Stoodley, Sir Francis Gore, and Mr. Walter Gyles; eminent actuaries like Messrs. Cockburn, Carter, and Blandford; prominent bankers like Mr. (now Sir) Felix Schuster, and various representatives of mercantile associations.

[1] 62 and 63 Vict., c. 24. *Cf. supra*, page 58. [2] 6 Edward VII, c. 52.

The committee began its sittings on June 7, 1904, and made its report in June, 1905, publishing in a portly volume the report proper, the minutes of evidence, and fifteen valuable memoranda and statements, in the form of appendices.[1]

The report, which sums up the testimony in these respects, begins with a short account of the methods then in force for assessments in Schedule D. At the commencement of each year the legal assessor for the parish — who is appointed by the General Commissioners of the district — prepares a list of all persons whom he considers properly liable to assessment under Schedule D, and issues to each a form of return. Persons coming into the parish, even though they have no ostensible income under Schedule D, also receive a form; and if no liability is disclosed, the process is repeated every three or five years. Employers are required to furnish a list of persons in their employ, and a return is then issued to each of these. General notices are also posted on the church doors. If the return form is not sent back in due course, another notice is sent. The assessor makes out the list of all persons to whom the forms have been sent, stating whether they have been returned to him, and giving his estimate of the assessable income, where the return has not been made. From this list, submitted about July 20, the clerk to the General Commissioners prepares the assessment, adding, for purposes of comparison, the particulars for each of the past three years. This takes considerable time, as the commissioners' books in the City of London alone are no less than two hundred and twenty in number. The assessment is then delivered to the surveyor of taxes, who checks the returns, sends a further application to those who have made no returns, institutes inquiries as to the returns in doubtful cases, and adds whatever details may have come to his knowledge for the information of the Additional Commissioners. The Additional Commissioners, who are appointed

[1] *Report of the Departmental Committee on Income Tax.* London, 1905. (Cd. 2575.) *Appendix to the Report of the Departmental Committee on Income Tax with Minutes of Evidence taken before the Committee*, 1905.

by the General Commissioners, then hold meetings, beginning about the end of August, which are attended by the surveyor, and settle upon an assessment which they consider correct. The Additional Commissioners are selected as possessing expert knowledge of separate classes of trade and commerce. Their character may be inferred from the fact that Sir Felix Schuster is one of the Additional Commissioners for the City of London. The work of the Additional Commissioners in London is most elaborate, and they form themselves into committees, sitting three times a week during the whole of the latter part of the year, with all the surveyors present, giving the benefit of their knowledge and experience. They then deliver these assessments to the General Commissioners who, after fourteen days, cause notices to be issued to the persons assessed, giving the date of the meeting fixed to hear appeals, with instructions as to the course to be followed. The notices of appeal must be given to the surveyor ten days before the date fixed for hearing, and accounts or other evidence in support of any objections made by the taxpayer must be furnished to him before the meeting. The evidence is examined by the surveyor, who in a large number of cases interviews the appellant and settles the matter, the settlement being submitted to the General Commissioners for their approval. Where, however, the appeal meeting takes place, the surveyor attends and supports the assessment made by the Additional Commissioners. The General Commissioners, after hearing the evidence, fix the liability. From this determination there is no appeal on questions of fact, although an appeal is allowed to the high court on questions of law.

There are some complicated cases which cannot be settled in time, and accordingly belated assessments, or first additional assessments, are presented by the Additional Commissioners as late as the 5th of April in the following year. In order to provide for still further omissions which may be ascertained, a second additional assessment may be made not later than the 5th of August of the second year. At that time the power of the commissioners to make any assessment of their own initiative expires. Nevertheless, under a special provision,[1] the surveyors of taxes still have power for a period up to the 5th of April of the following year, of surcharging or making a supplementary charge in respect to all cases that have not been brought into charge in the commissioners' assessments.[2] It must also be remembered that anybody who is assessed in Schedule D may, if he so desires, be assessed by Special Commissioners, instead of the local commissioners of the district. Considerable advantage is taken of this provision, but the procedure is virtually in all other respects the same. We are told, however, that the surveyors make no "vexatious demands,"[3] and it is not entirely settled whether the commissioners have the power of inspecting the books. The officials inform us that, since a recent decision in which the question was indirectly involved, they have no difficulty in getting at the books in case of necessity. The law, however, does not explicitly give the power to call for books, and the point has never been directly decided by the courts.[4] In the case of appeals, the commissioners can insist upon the submission of schedules of particulars, which practically amount to profit and loss accounts; and if the appellant desires to make good his claim for a reduction, he must produce his books. The accounts of business firms are now usually prepared by professional accountants.

Before taking up the question of fraud, which was the chief concern of the committee, we shall devote a few words to the other points. As regards the treatment of income derived from copyrights, patent rights, and terminable annuities, the committee substantially held that the existing methods were unexceptionable. They also decided that there was no

[1] Taxes Management Act, 1880, sec. 63.

[2] *Report*, pp. iv, v; *Appendix*, pp. xxx, xxxi, and pp. lxxix *et seq.*

[3] *Evidence*, p. 101.

[4] *Evidence*, pp. 23, 24, and 109. In the *Income Tax Report* of 1906, quoted below, this matter is further explained on p. 25.

reason for changing the law with reference to the exemption of coöperative societies. Finally, they declared themselves as in the main satisfied with the system in vogue as to repayments for exemptions and abatements. Counselling only some slight changes in the forms for this purpose, they made one important recommendation, namely, that the grant of exemptions and abatements should be abolished in the case of persons residing outside of the United Kingdom; for this, as we shall see, had led to considerable fraud.

The question of allowance for depreciation gave them a little more difficulty. It will be remembered that the acts of 1842 and 1853 allowed the actual cost of repairs, but made no provision for depreciation. The practice, however, gradually became more liberal than the letter of the law, which was interpreted to include renewals; and in certain cases, especially in regard to ships, allowances were made which to some extent admitted of the writing off from profits of certain amounts toward replacement. In 1878 this practice was specifically recognized by law. But the interpretation of the new law was never very clear, although it gradually became more liberal. Thus, in the case of ships, a fixed allowance of four per cent on the prime cost of the vessel was permitted as a deduction from annual profits. In the case of printing machinery, no precise scale of allowance was laid down, but we are told that "considerable progress has been made in establishing typical rights of allowances on different classes of machinery."[1] The amount of income exempted on account of wear and tear thus grew from a little more than four millions sterling in 1893–1894 to almost twelve and three-quarter millions in 1902–1903. The concession in the act of 1878 was still further developed by administrative action in 1897, when, by order of the Chancellor of the Exchequer, it was decided that "where a claim is made in respect of the introduction of more modern machinery into a factory, no objection is to be taken to the allowance, as a deduction from the assessable profits of the year, of so much of the cost of

[1] See *Report*, Appendix 4.

replacement as is represented by the existing value of the machinery replaced."[1] The committee pointed out that no very definite steps had been taken by any one to make this matter public, and that most people seemed to be ignorant of it. They concluded, however, that, with due publicity, the existing law and practice would suffice. Finally, it will be remembered that, in 1894, a deduction of one-sixth from the rack-rent value of buildings had been authorized as an allowance to cover maintenance and repairs. It was supposed that this allowance was intended to include the eventual replacement of buildings. The act of 1898, however, had directed that in estimating the amount of profits for the purposes of Schedule D only the net amount assessed under Schedule A, instead of the full annual value, should be allowed as a deduction. The allowance for wear and tear of buildings was thus limited to actual expenditure for repairs. The committee now decided that, in view of the fact that the amount of wear and tear of mills, factories, etc., greatly exceeds that of buildings, the full annual value of the premises so occupied should be allowed as a set-off in computing the liability under Schedule D, instead of being restricted to five-sixths.[2]

The next point discussed was the question of the three-year average system. This, it will be remembered, applied in general to incomes under Schedule D, and also to the so-called variable and uncertain incomes in Schedules A and E. The income thus ascertained by average is termed the statutory income, as opposed to the actual income. Statutory income is, as a rule, computed on a three-year average, but the profits of mines are computed on a five-year average, while railways, iron-works, gas-works, quarries, and a few other concerns are charged on the amount of profits in the preceding year. The average system, as we know, was first applied to Schedule D in the case of trade in 1842. It was extended to provisions, employments, and vocations under

[1] *Cf. supra*, page 184.

[2] *Cf.* on this whole subject, *Report*, pp. xiii–xv, and *Appendix*, p. xxxviii.

Schedule D by the act of 1853,[1] and it was thereafter allowed by practice in the case of subordinate officers under Schedule E. It might, however, happen that when profits were falling off, the actual profits in the year of assessment would be less than those which would be worked out on the average system. Accordingly, section 133 of the law of 1842 provided that when the actual profits fell short of the sum assessed, they might be substituted for any estimate, whether based on the preceding year or on an average of years. This section, however, proved to be so one-sided that it was amended in 1865. The taxpayer was now required to prove, as a condition precedent to any relief, not only that his profits for the year were less than the sum assessed, but that they were less than the average of three years, including the year of assessment. It also restricted the amount of relief to the difference between an average based on the profits of three preceding years, and an average based on the profits of the year of assessment and two preceding years.[2] This system gave rise to many anomalies, and led to a serious loss of revenue to the government. The shortcomings are fully set forth in a memorandum by Sir F. Gore.[3] He took five cases, assuming that the firms originally paid taxes for the same year upon the same average, namely, £10,000; that the total profits for the three years were in each case £30,000; and that the actual profits of each firm during the year of assessment were £5000. Yet according to the law one firm would receive back nothing, while the others would receive back respectively the tax on £333, £833, £1666, and £3333. It is no wonder that section 133 is characterized as producing "the most capriciously unequal and unfair results among individual taxpayers." He also emphasized the fact that it afforded temptations to make untruthful returns, and that it placed additional difficulties in the way of detecting false returns. Following his advice, therefore, the committee recommended

[1] *Cf. supra*, page 154.
[2] *Cf. supra*, page 168.
[3] *Appendix* 7, pp. 22–30.

that section 133 of the act of 1842, as well as the section in question of the act of 1865, be repealed.

The committee, furthermore, went into the general question of the average system and summed up the arguments for and against. They stated that if the country were starting *de novo*, they would, on the whole, counsel the rejection of the average system, largely for the reason that when his profits are diminishing, the taxpayer is each year paying the tax on more than the profits then earned, and this at a time when he can least well afford it. Other reasons were also advanced against the system. The committee decided, however, inasmuch as the three-year average system had been in force for over sixty years and had on the whole given rise to but little complaint and since any change would necessarily lead to some temporary confusion and distress and might be unpopular, that unless a very decided public sentiment to the contrary should be manifested, they would recommend no further change. Thus the average system was substantially upheld. This brings us, then, to the chief discussion of the whole investigation, namely, that of fraud. This point, however, is so important that it merits a separate section.

§ 5. *The Question of Fraud*

As an introduction to this discussion, the committee called attention to the fact that "the feeling formerly entertained against the income tax system as inquisitorial and oppressive has, we believe, largely died away. The impartiality and secrecy of the local Commissioners deserve and obtain public confidence in a high degree." But the committee made no attempt to deny the fact that there was still "a substantial amount of fraud and evasion." In their opinion, however, this was true of only a small part of the operation of the act. They estimated, on the basis of the Inland Revenue memorandum, that something like four-fifths of the income tax is either assessed at the source, or subjected to other special methods of verification; and they stated that the sphere within which evasion can take place has been still further circumscribed by the rapid conversion of private business into public companies and by the operation of the act of 1885, which provided for the deduction and payment of income taxes from foreign investments by bankers or dealers. There is still left, however, a sphere in which self-assessment is requisite, and it is in this sphere that the committee state that while they cannot attempt a quantitative estimate, they have no doubt that the loss of the revenue is serious enough to demand some change in the law.[1] In the evidence we find somewhat conflicting statements. Thus Mr. Stoodley maintained that "the department is in possession of evidence showing that grossly insufficient returns, or no returns at all, are made over long periods of years, with impunity," and he contended that the powers of the department to cope with fraud were inadequate.[2] In another place, however, he stated that he did not think there was as much fraud and evasion as was generally believed. He considered that at worst, out of a total gross income in 1901–1902 of eight hundred and sixty-seven millions sterling, there was appreciable room for evasion in only one hundred and fifty millions.[3] Sir Thomas Hewitt stated in his memorandum that in his opinion "the number of cases of actual fraud (excluding cases of mere evasion and mistaken views of accounts) are not very extensive, but there are certain cases. These cases have sometimes run to very large amounts."[4] The Right Honorable C. T. Ritchie stated that "it is a matter of common knowledge that evasions of income tax, payable under Schedule D, are of very frequent occurrence."[5] Mr. (now Sir) Felix Schuster, one of the Additional Commissioners and a prominent banker, thought that "speaking for the City of London, it may be said that on the whole the returns are very fairly and honestly made." But he thereupon proceeded to give an experience of his own, which deserves to be quoted in full: "One of the surveyors

[1] *Report*, p. v. [2] *Appendix*, no. 1. [3] *Evidence*, pp. 82–83.

[4] *Appendix*, no. 8, pp. 32–33; with interesting examples.

[5] *Evidence*, p. 113.

came to the commissioners and said: 'Here is Mr. So-and-So, who never sends in a return. We have assessed him at £300 a year for the last two or three years, and he has always paid on his £300. Don't you think that we might put him up now?' The Chairman said, 'Yes, I do.' He said, 'Well, what shall we call it? What would you put it at—£4,000 or £5,000?' The Chairman said, 'No; make it £50,000.' He happened to know something about the man, who paid without a murmur."[1]

One official witness divided the chief examples of fraud into four classes: First, the deliberate evasions, chiefly in the professional classes. Secondly, the practice of those who think that everybody else is in the habit of under-declaring, and that they are only doing themselves justice if they also under-declare. Thirdly, where it is a question of ignorance, and where no books are kept, as in the case mainly of little traders and lodging-house keepers. And fourthly, those who evade because they do not make any declaration at all.[2] With reference to the last point, one of the Special Commissioners said: "I am astonished to find the peculiar code of honor which is to be found all over the country. A man who would cut his arm off before he would deliberately write a false statement, will wait until he is assessed, in the hope that the assessment will be wrong. And he will deliberately abstain from giving information which, according to the return, he is bound to give, and yet consider that he is not doing anything dishonourable or illegal."[3]

Another witness, on being asked what objection there could be to requiring every man to make a return, stated: "There is really no reason why they should object, except that persons do not seem to deal so rationally with questions of income tax as with other subjects."[4] A little later, and subsequent to the report of the committee, the secretary of the

[1] *Evidence*, pp. 172–173.

[2] Testimony of Commissioner Debenham, *Evidence*, p. 176.

[3] Walter Gyles, *Evidence*, p. 119.

[4] *Evidence*, p. 83.

Income Tax Reform League, Mr. Hallet Fry, asserted that the chief frauds were to be found in the following classes: "foreigners residing in England, money-lenders, journalists, theatrical people, recipients of large professional incomes, people without a definite residence, like bachelors, speculators, and recipients of large incomes living in very modest houses."[1] In the evidence before the committee, however, every one agreed that the frauds which had been chiefly growing in recent years were to be found in the case of corporations which declared themselves foreign companies, with only a branch office in London. Mr. Simpson stated that within the last three or four years the claims for abatements from so-called foreigners had increased enormously, and that special income-tax-repayment agencies had even been formed for this purpose alone.[2] Sir Thomas Hewitt asserted, "I know that the evasion under the provisions of the Act extends, and is daily more widely extending, to Belgian iron, to silks from France and elsewhere, to wines from Germany, France, and Italy; to a very great extent to velvets, mantles and other goods peculiar to foreign trade from various foreign countries, and secondly to trade from India and the Colonies."[3]

After carefully considering all these points, the committee concluded that an adequate remedy would be attained by the adoption of the following measures: First, that every person should be compelled to make a return, whether he is liable to income tax or not. "We recognize," said the committee, "that no steps should be taken that can possibly be avoided, which would tend to make the income tax more unpopular, and therefore more difficult of collection." But they did not think that this compulsion would impose any hardship on the taxpayer. They recommended, furthermore, that the penalty for failure to make a return be limited to five pounds, where the individual is not liable to pay any tax. Where the indi-

[1] Hallet Fry, "The Income Tax Problem," in *Magazine of Commerce*, September, 1907, p. 33.

[2] *Evidence*, p. 103.

[3] *Appendix* no. viii, p. 36.

vidual is liable, however, and makes no return, or an incorrect return, a change in the law is also recommended. Under the existing system the penalty was twenty pounds and treble the duty, and the law allowed only one year in which to rectify the omission by a surcharge. These provisions the committee thought entirely inadequate, and recommended not alone that the surcharge or supplementary assessment might be made at any time within three years from the end of the year of assessment, but furthermore, that the maximum penalty should be treble duty for the entire period. Finally, the committee recommended that the most effectual and appropriate penalty for fraud would be publicity, and that the government should be empowered to publish names and details in case of gross fraud, whenever they considered it advisable. As a minor point, the committee also recommended that employers who were now required to send in lists of their employees, should henceforth be compelled to include also the amounts of their salaries.

§ 6. *The Select Committee of 1906*

Such was the famous report of the departmental committee. It was several years before any of the recommendations were put into force. In the meantime, and especially after the return of the Liberal party to power in 1906, the interest in the more fundamental questions of differentiation and graduation of the tax had become so widespread that the government of Sir H. Campbell-Bannerman decided to appoint a parliamentary committee to consider these particular questions.

On May 4, 1906, a Select Committee of seventeen members was authorized "to inquire into and report upon the practicability of graduating the income tax, and of differentiating, for the purpose of the tax, between permanent and precarious incomes." The committee was composed of Sir Charles W. Dilke, as chairman, and of prominent members like Mr. Keir Hardie, Sir Thomas Whittaker, Messrs. McKenna, Redmond, Trevelyan, Cavendish, and others. The witnesses were comparatively few in number, but were all of them distinguished men, including officials like Sir Henry Primrose, who had been a member of the departmental committee of 1904, Sir Thomas Hewitt, and Mr. Gyles; prominent merchants and bankers like Sir Felix Schuster; economists and statisticians like Messrs. Bowley, Coghlan, Chiozza Money, and Bernard Mallet; and socialists like Philip Snowden. The committee sat during the remainder of the session of 1906, and brought in their report on November 29, 1906.[1]

The report had practically been a foregone conclusion in view of the existing sentiment in parliament and the particular complexion of the committee. The officials of the inland revenue department, especially Sir Henry Primrose and Mr. Gyles, were indeed opposed to the scheme of the committee, but the evidence of the other witnesses was so overwhelming that the committee found no difficulty in arriving at its conclusion. A draft report prepared by Sir Charles Dilke, which was voluminous and interesting,[2] was not accepted, but the important conclusions were virtually the same as those to which the committee as a whole gave its adherence.

Taking up first the question of graduation,[3] the committee pointed out that the tax was already graduated by abatement in the case of incomes of not over £700. They proceeded to consider whether the graduation could be extended or made universal, with due regard to economical administration. Graduation, as the committee pointed out, might be effected in various ways. First, they might follow what we have called in this volume the "lump-sum" scheme, or, as the committee put it, "the method of collecting the whole of the tax directly from each person, upon his own declaration." This, however, would involve an abandonment of the principle of stoppage at source. To such a course the committee were unalterably opposed. "The importance of retaining a principle which is mainly responsible for the present development of the tax and the ease with which it is collected, and

[1] *Report from the Select Committee on Income Tax; together with the Proceedings of the Committee, Minutes of Evidence, and an Appendix.* London, 1906.

[2] *Report*, pp. xv–xxxvi.

[3] *Report*, secs. 4–17.

the extreme undesirability of doing anything which would reduce its efficiency, can scarcely be over-estimated." Accordingly, the committee declared their conviction that "direct personal assessment for the whole tax is not practicable in this country in the sense of being an expedient or desirable means of collecting revenue."

A second method of graduating the tax would be that of the so-called "super-tax"; that is, a second tax distinct from, and supplementary to, the existing tax, to be levied on individuals by direct personal assessment. The chief suggestion of this nature that had been made was that all persons with incomes over £5,000 should be required to make a separate return showing the total amount of the income. Graduation might then be applied to this part of the tax. The committee conceded that this new portion of the tax would be directly personal in its nature, and that some of the objections just urged would apply to the proposal. They considered, however, that these objections "are modified to the extent that the tax which is now collected at the source would continue to be so collected, consequently there would be no loss of revenue there as the result of failure to obtain full disclosure for the direct personal tax."

The committee adverted to the difficulty of discovering individuals who have an income of £5000 a year, and referred especially to the objections on the part of the official witnesses. They contended, however, that the difficulties had been exaggerated, although they conceded that time would be required to make the tax work smoothly. They indorsed the recommendations of the departmental committee of 1904 that every individual be required to make a return, whether he is liable or not. The committee therefore concluded that "the super-tax upon the larger incomes is practicable, but it offers some disadvantages and difficulties which have been pointed out."

The third method of graduation which the committee discussed was that of graduation by degression, which might take the form of extending the existing system of abatements, or of charging a lower rate of tax on the smaller incomes. The committee assumed that whatever changes might be made in the rates, it was not desirable to diminish the total yield of the tax. Since, therefore, graduation was advocated by some, not only for the sake of securing greater equality as between individuals, but also for the purpose of securing additional revenue, it would be necessary to raise the rates on the higher incomes in proportion as the abatements were extended, as well as to enlarge decidedly the costly process of repayment. On the one hand the very much higher rates on the larger incomes "would arouse a feeling of resentment against the tax which it is very desirable to avoid"; and secondly, the collection of immense sums, which would afterwards have to be returned, "would be a serious inconvenience, and a genuine ground of grievance" to individuals, and "could not fail to interfere injuriously with the ordinary operations of commerce." Out of 1,100,000 people, with an income of nearly £700,000,000, abatements were already allowed on incomes of some 700,000 people, with a total income of £250,000,000, the amount collected and returned being about £1,600,000. While this gave rise to no particular difficulties, the committee held that "there are limits beyond which it cannot conveniently and usefully be extended." They concluded that it would be perfectly feasible to increase the abatements to £1000, or even more; but they maintained that they did not possess sufficient information to fix the precise figure at which the extension of the present system would cease to be prudent and convenient.

Coming, then, to the question of differentiation[1] between permanent and precarious incomes, the committee stated that they had found it desirable to define clearly the meaning of the terms. Other terms that have been used are "industrial and spontaneous, earned and unearned, incomes from investment and personal effort." A great many more terms, which were customary half a century ago, might have been mentioned.[2] The committee stated that probably the words

[1] *Report*, secs. 18–24.

[2] *Cf. supra*, p. 145.

"earned" and "unearned" most accurately represented the distinctions which they had in mind. They confessed that they were unable to provide a completely logical and satisfactory definition, and they called attention to some of the difficulties. "A rough working distinction which would probably meet with general acceptance," they thought, "would be to regard the profits of private traders as earned and those of public companies and similar undertakings as arising from investment"; that in the same way "the owner of land who cultivates it himself would be regarded as earning his income," but that "the owner of an estate who let it to others to cultivate would not be regarded as earning the net income which he derived from the lands of that estate, although he might act as his own steward and devote much time to its supervision." Having settled that point, the committee stated that "the existing feeling in favor of some differentiation in the amount of the tax levied upon earned incomes does not require that all incomes, irrespective of size, should receive privileged treatment"; for, in general, "the smaller the business and the smaller the profits derived from it, the larger will be the proportion of that profit which has in the strictest sense of the term been 'earned.'" These and other difficulties and objections would be avoided, in the opinion of the committee, by limiting the differentiation between earned and unearned incomes to incomes not exceeding, say £3000 a year. "Your Committee," we are told, "are of opinion that such differentiation is practicable and can most conveniently be carried into effect by charging on such incomes a rate of tax lower than the normal or foundation rate."

It may be remarked that Sir Charles Dilke had referred with approval in his draft report to the German system, which, as we shall learn, attains differentiation through a separate property tax. But he recognized the difficulty of introducing a new property tax and declared his preference for the scheme which was ultimately adopted by the committee. Another point deserving of special mention is the opinion expressed by Sir Felix Schuster, in discussing the advisability of asking the recipients of larger incomes to make a declaration of their total income. Sir Felix, while recognizing the immense advantages of the English over the German system, nevertheless held that it might be possible to exaggerate the method of stoppage at source. "I think the collection of a tax at the source might be carried to an extreme, and I do not think it is desirable to carry it to an extreme. I think the effect now of the collection at the source on the minds of many people is that the revenue gets the tax wherever it can, and that there is no more duty imposed on people to make a correct return. I would not like to strengthen that feeling. Personally I think that there are limits."[1]

Finally, the committee proceeded to consider the bearing of death duties on graduation and differentiation.[2] They referred especially to the calculations submitted by Sir Henry Primrose and Mr. Mallet, showing that if, as is perfectly legitimate, the death duties be regarded as partaking to some extent of the nature of a deferred income tax, the combined operation of the two taxes does in practice effect a very considerable graduation and differentiation. Despite this fact, the committee concluded that further graduation was desirable.

The conclusions are summarized as follows:[3]—

(1) "Graduation of the income tax by an extension of the existing system of abatements is practicable. But it could not be applied to all incomes from the highest to the lowest, with satisfactory results. The limits of prudent extension would be reached when a larger increase in the rate of tax to be collected at the source was necessitated, and the total amount which was collected in excess of what was ultimately retained, became so large as to cause serious inconvenience to trade and commerce, and to individual taxpayers. Those limits would not be exceeded by raising the amount of income on which an abatement would be allowed to £1000 or even more.

[1] *Evidence*, question 3013, p. 174.

[2] *Report*, secs. 25 to 29.

[3] *Ibid.*, sec. 30.

(2) Graduation by a super-tax is practicable. If it be desired to levy a much higher rate of tax upon large incomes (say of £5000 and upwards) than has heretofore been charged, a super-tax based on personal declaration would be a practicable method.

(3) Abandonment of the system of 'collection at the source,' and adoption of the principle of direct personal assessment of the whole of each person's income would be inexpedient.

(4) Differentiation between earned and unearned income is practicable, especially if it be limited to earned incomes not exceeding £3000 a year, and effect be given to it by charging a lower rate of tax upon them.

(5) A compulsory personal declaration from each individual of total net income in respect of which tax is payable is expedient; and would do much to prevent the evasion and avoidance of income tax which at present prevail."

Such were the two celebrated reports on the income tax. It was not long before most of the proposals of the two committees were substantially put into practice; but with characteristic English conservatism it was decided to take only one step at a time. Thus it was that some of the reforms were accomplished in the year 1907, and some more in the year 1910. The law of 1907 dealt primarily with the subjects of differentiation and fraud and with certain administrative features; while the law of 1910 took up the topic of graduation and made further attempts to prevent fraud.

§ 7. *The Adoption of Differentiation in 1907*

In his budget speech of April 18, 1907, H. H. Asquith, the Chancellor of the Exchequer, took up the matter of differentiation. "The income tax," he tells us, "as it is one of the most productive, so it is one of the most delicate parts of our fiscal machinery. There is nothing like it to be found anywhere else in the world."[1] Starting with the important

[1] *The Parliamentary Debates*, 1907, vol. 172, p. 1198.

statement that "it must now be regarded as an integral and permanent part of our financial system," he discussed the theory of the question. Comparing two individuals, one "who derives, we will say, £1000 a year from a perfectly safe investment in the funds, perhaps accumulated and left to him by his father," and, on the other hand, "a man making the same nominal sum by personal labour in the pursuit of some arduous and perhaps precarious profession, or some form of business," he maintained that "to say that those two people are, from the point of view of the state, to be taxed in the same way is, to my mind, flying in the face of justice and common sense." He referred to the unanimous decision of the committee as to the necessity of making a difference between earned and unearned incomes.

"What is an earned income?" asked the Chancellor. "It is not easy to draw a distinction," he answered, "but we can but do our best." He declared that earned incomes included incomes of all officers and employees paid by salaries, including clergymen; of every class of professional men; and of all traders whose income is derived substantially from their own personal labor. He conceded that to distinguish in this third class between incomes which are either wholly earned or partly earned and partly unearned, "means a degree of logical precision where there will be the greatest possible difficulty in hindering overlapping in dubious cases." The most practical way of dealing with the problem, therefore, he held, was to confine the differential treatment to earned incomes which do not exceed £2000 — not, as the select committee had recommended, £3000. That is to say, the lower rate on earned incomes was to be limited to persons whose total income from all sources does not exceed £2000. The Chancellor suggested for the coming year the full rate of one shilling in the pound as the normal tax on unearned incomes, and the lower rate of 9*d.* for earned incomes. The benefit of the lower rate was to be granted by abatement, and the abatement in the case of mixed incomes was always to be made from the earned, and not from the unearned, portion.

Taking up next the question of graduation, the Chancellor declared that he was not yet ready for it. "Quite apart from other reasons, it would not be possible, for administrative reasons, to introduce any change in graduation simultaneously with the already sufficiently complicated alterations of a differentiated tax. The machinery would break down under the strain."[1] He stated, however, that he did not desire to announce at that moment any final opinion on the question of graduation.

The law of 1907[2] adopted the Chancellor's proposals. The rate of income tax in general for the coming year was put at 1s., but it was provided that if any individual claimed and proved that his total income from all sources did not exceed £2000, and that any part of that income was earned income, he should be entitled to such relief from income tax as would reduce the amount payable to 9*d.* A statutory definition of earned income was given,[3] and the usual methods followed in the proving of all claims to exemption, relief, or abatement were to apply to this new form of relief.[4] Two points are here to be noted: First, that earned income includes partners' salaries and interest on capital, while profits of a limited or sleeping partner are deemed to be unearned income. Secondly, as soon as a private business becomes a

[1] *The Parliamentary Debates*, 1907, vol. 172, p. 1206.

[2] The Finance Act, 1907, 7 Edw. VII, c. 13, part v, secs. 18–28.

[3] Earned income is stated to be: (*a*) Any income arising in respect of any remuneration from any office or employment of profit held by the individual, or in respect of any pension, superannuation, or other allowance, deferred pay, or compensation for loss of office given in respect of the past services of the individual, or of the husband or parent of the individual, in any office or employment of profit, whether the individual or husband or parent of the individual shall have contributed to such pension, superannuation, allowance, or deferred pay or not;

(*b*) Any income from any property which is attached to or forms part of the emoluments of any office or employment of profit held by the individual; and

(*c*) Any income which is charged under Schedules B or D in the Income Tax Act, 1853, or the rules prescribed by Schedule D in the Income Tax Act, 1842, and is immediately derived by the individual from the carrying on or exercise by him of his profession, trade, or vocation either as an individual, or, in the case of a partnership, as a partner, personally acting therein. — Sec. 19, par. 7.

[4] Sec. 19, pars. 1 and 6. The claim must be made by Sept. 30.

corporation, the profits change from earned to unearned income. The test whether a given income is earned or unearned may be described as follows: If it is derived from personal labor or from pensions, or from property forming part of the emoluments of office, or from carrying on a business or profession, and the recipient is actively engaged therein and is not protected by limited liability, then such income is earned, otherwise it is unearned.[1]

The law, furthermore, provided for the carrying out of some of the recommendations of the departmental committee. In the first place, employers are henceforth required to make a return not only of the names and places of residence of their employees, but also of the salaries paid to them.[2] Thus was adopted a scheme which, as we shall see later, had long been in vogue in Italy. In the second place, every person is required to make a return of his income, whether or not he is liable to income tax, the penalty for failure so to do being fixed at £5. This provision also follows some of the continental laws. In the case of corporations, etc., the secretary is to make such returns.[3] In the third place the time for making a surcharge or additional assessment is extended to three years.[4] Fourthly, section 133 of the law of 1842 and section 6 of the act of 1865, which deal with the three-year average system in Schedule D, are repealed, and it is provided that when any one who is charged upon the three-year average system proves that his actual profits fall short of the profits as computed according to that system, he shall be entitled to be charged on the former, instead of the latter, basis. If any business is discontinued during the year, the taxpayer shall be entitled to a repayment of the excess, in case he can prove that the total tax paid during the three previous years exceeds the total amount which would have been paid if he had been assessed in each of these years on the actual profits.[5] Finally, specific provision is made for

[1] E. E. Spicer and E. C. Pegler, *Income Tax in Relation to Accounts.* 2d ed., London, 1910, p. 19.

[2] Sec. 21. [3] Sec. 22. [4] Sec. 23. [5] Sec. 24.

such allowance as the commissioners may think just and reasonable for wear and tear of machinery or plant; and if the deductions for this purpose happen to be greater than the profits for that year, they may be carried on to subsequent years. In no case, however, will such deductions be allowed if they exceed the actual cost of the machinery or plant, including in cost any capital expenditure by way of renewal, improvement or reinstatement.[1]

Thus, finally, was introduced in 1907 the principle which, almost from the very introduction of the tax at the close of the eighteenth century, had been demanded by numberless critics and reformers. The great change which, as we remember, had been so persistently and successfully opposed by Gladstone, was now definitively accomplished. But it was after all only the entering wedge. As compared with the more highly developed system in the Italian tax, for instance, the distinction between earned and unearned incomes must be considered simply as a first and halting step in the process of differentiation.

Some of the opponents of the change had based their opposition on the old idea of Gladstone that it would obviously interfere with the revenue. These fears, however, proved to be unfounded. The fiscal results, in part, were unexpectedly favorable. Asquith had estimated in his budget speech that the loss due to the introduction of the principle of differentiation would be about two million pounds — one and one-fourth millions due to the effect of differentiation itself, and three-fourths of a million due to delays in collection, in consequence of the change in the law. It turned out, however, that there was virtually no loss at all. In the budget statement of May 7, 1908, which was delivered by Asquith (who had in the meantime become Prime Minister), in lieu of the new Chancellor of the Exchequer, D. Lloyd

[1] Sec. 26. This provision was inserted to overrule a court decision to the contrary, in a case that was won by a lawyer, who now, as Chancellor of the Exchequer, was instrumental in undoing his own work. See Spicer and Pegler, *Income Tax in Relation to Accounts*. 2d ed., London, 1910, p. 72.

George, he stated that "the cause of this remarkable increase in the revenue is to be found in the differentiation clause itself. The mere offer of the lower rate of tax has sufficed to increase the amount of income submitted. Thus I may say that differentiation has worked not only a financial, but a moral reform."[1] Asquith went on to give his judgment of the matter in a passage which deserves to be quoted in full: "I hope I may say without undue self-complacency, that differentiation, always deemed to be just and fair, was for sixty years strongly denied by almost every great authority to be workable in practice. Differentiation has been proved by experience to be not only practicable, but smooth and easy in its operation; and it has in fact paid for itself, and it has removed, once and for all, the most obvious and crying grievances and inequalities, — I do not say all of them, by any means, — but the most crying grievances and inequalities which have marred the equity and clogged the efficiency of the income tax as a permanent instrument of revenue."

§ 8. *The Adoption of Graduation in 1910*

Now that the principle of differentiation had been definitely adopted, the government was ready to proceed to the consideration of the other great principle — that of progression. It is doubtful how soon this would have become a practical matter, however, were it not for the exigencies of the treasury and the need of securing additional revenue for the purpose of financing the great scheme of social reform known as the Old Age Pensions. The hope was that the adoption of the scheme of progressive taxation as applied to the income tax would thus accomplish two results; first, it would yield considerably increased revenue, and second, it would make the wealthier classes feel that they were directly interested in the programme of social reform, the benefits of which were to apply to the less fortunate members of the community.

[1] *The Parliamentary Debates*, vol. 188, p. 451.

On April 29, 1909, Lloyd George introduced his now historic budget. After reviewing the history of the income tax, he pointed out that it was feasible to keep the tax at the permanent figure of five per cent, and at the same time render it possible to rely upon the tax for additional large sums in case of emergency. "A careful consideration of these figures ought to convince the most sceptical that the maximum rate of the tax may be retained at 1*s*., or even increased, without seriously encroaching upon our available reserves for national emergencies."[1] Lloyd George called attention to the fact that "the income tax, imposed originally as a temporary expedient, is now in reality the centre and sheet anchor of our financial system," and he proceeded to discuss the question of securing additional revenue from it. The time, he thought, had gone by "when a simple addition of pence to the poundage of the tax, attractive as the simplicity of that expedient is, can be regarded as a satisfactory solution of a financial difficulty." He pointed out that "the principles of graduation and differentiation, the apportionment of the burden as between different classes of taxpayers, according, on the one hand, to the extent, and, on the other hand, to the nature of their resources, are in the lower stages of the income tax scale already recognized by abatements and allowances." He added that "it remains to complete the system by extending the application of these principles, and in regard to differentiation by taking account to some extent, at any rate, not only of the source from which income is derived, but also of the liabilities which the taxpayer has contracted in the discharge of his duties as a citizen, and of the other burdens of taxation borne by him by virtue of those responsibilities."[2] Notwithstanding the changes effected by the law of 1907, Lloyd George held that the burden of the tax upon earnings was still disproportionately heavy. He therefore proposed that while the general rate of the tax should be raised to 1*s*. 2*d*., the rate upon earned incomes in the case of persons whose total income did not exceed £3000 should remain as it

[1] *The Parliamentary Debates*, Session 1909, vol. iv, p. 506. [2] *Ibid.*, p. 507.

then stood, namely at 9*d.* up to £2000 and at 1*s.* between £2000 and £3000. He also suggested that in case of incomes not exceeding £500 there be an abatement of £10 for every child under the age of sixteen.

Proceeding to the question of progression, the Chancellor took a conservative position. "The introduction of a complete scheme of graduation, applicable to all incomes, besides raising questions of general principle, which it is not necessary now to discuss, would require an entire reconstruction of the administrative machinery of the tax, including in all probability the abandonment to a very large extent of the principle of collection at the source, upon which the productivity of the tax so largely depends."[1] He therefore stated that he would accept in principle the scheme suggested by the Committee of 1906, namely, the idea of a super-tax. After considering various methods of accomplishing this result, he proposed to limit this additional tax to incomes exceeding £5000, and to levy a super-tax at the rate of 6*d.* upon the amount by which such incomes exceed £3000. He pointed out that the machinery of the tax would in the main be independent of that of the existing income tax, but that the assessments would be made by Special Commissioners appointed under the general code. In the case of real property in Schedule A he also proposed that a special five per cent allowance be made for cost of management, in addition to the existing allowance of one-sixth and one-eighth for repairs. The Chancellor estimated that the super-tax proper, when in full working order, would yield an additional £2,300,000.

The proposals of the government with reference to the income tax met with remarkably little opposition, largely perhaps for the reason that the main fight was concentrated upon some of the other features of the budget, more especially the land-tax provisions.[2] The super-tax proposition was

[1] *The Parliamentary Debates*, Session 1909, vol. iv, p. 509.

[2] For a general statement of the real meaning of the now historic budget, see the article by the present writer entitled "The English Budget Proposals" in *The Survey*, vol. xxiii (1910), pp. 575 *et seq.*

indeed opposed by some speakers; but even Balfour, the leader of the opposition, confessed that he had "never been able to take that clear abstract view of John Mill," and said that he was not prepared to deny "that some graduation is fair, convenient and expedient." Balfour contented himself with remarking that if the effect of the death duties be considered, it would be found that they, in connection with the proposed super-tax, led to a perilously high degree of progression. "I think the Chancellor of the Exchequer will find that the rise is almost dangerously steep."[1] The overwhelming majority, however, expressed an approval of the views of the Chancellor of the Exchequer.

In a later speech Lloyd George definitively extinguished the lingering idea that even the super-tax might be considered simply as a reserve for special exigencies. "Why should the tax be treated as a reserve," he asked, "as something which is of a temporary character, while other taxes are regarded as permanent? Why should not the other taxes have their turn as temporary taxes, the taxes on the food of people, for instance? Why should taxes on the necessaries of life be regarded as permanent and the taxes on high incomes as purely temporary? If any taxes are to be treated as a reserve, I should say that the taxes which ought to be so treated are those which would press heaviest on the people who can least afford them."[2] And somewhat further on he discussed the administrative features of the proposed super-tax. "In this country," he said, "you have got taxation at the source. In Germany the whole of the income is submitted; there is a system of investigation which probably we would not stand in this country; it is a very severe one. We do not propose anything of the kind here. We have done everything in our power to make the conditions as little oppressive as possible to those whom we are obliged to submit to this process. I do not see that there is any

[1] Speech of May 3, 1909; *The Parliamentary Debates*, Twenty-eighth Parliament, 4th session, pp. 755-757.

[2] Speech of May 12, *ibid.*, p. 1959.

real protest against it. . . . I think the general feeling among the rich people is that they can afford to give more and they are prepared to give more; I honestly do not think that this proposed income tax has created protests. . . . Certainly there is no real resentment against this proposal. We have not made it oppressive. We have made it perfectly fair. The graduations are quite gentle."[1]

The budget of 1909, after first being thrown out by the Lords, was, as is well known, adopted in 1910.[2] The income tax for the year 1909–10 was levied at the rate of 1*s.* 2*d.*, but it was provided that whenever the total income of any individual exceeds £5000, there shall be "an additional duty of income tax (in this act referred to as a super-tax) at the rate of sixpence for every pound on the amount by which the total income exceeds three thousand pounds."[3] The super-tax was to be assessed by the Special Commissioners. The law states it to be the "duty of every person chargeable with a super-tax to give notice that he is chargeable"; but provision is also made for the serving of notice upon such persons by the Special Commissioners. If any one without reasonable excuse fails to make return or to give the notice, he shall be liable to a penalty of fifty pounds for every day during which the failure continues, and if he fails to make any return, the Special Commissioners may make an assessment of the super-tax according to the best of their judgment. The rest of the procedure is similar to that in force for the ordinary income tax, although it is again specifically provided that the Additional Commissioners may amend any assessment, or make a new or an additional assessment during any time within three years of the expiration of the original year of assessment.[4]

With reference to the differentiation, it was now provided

[1] Speech of May 12, 1909; *The Parliamentary Debates*, Twenty-eighth Parliament, 4th session, p. 1963.

[2] *The Finance (1909–1910) Act, 1910*, April 29, 1910, 10 Edw. VII, c. 8. The income tax provisions are found in part IV, secs. 65–72.

[3] Sec. 66.

[4] Sec. 72.

that on all earned incomes, when the total income exceeds £2000 and does not exceed £3000, the tax should be 1*s.* instead of 1*s.* 2*d.* Another new feature in the law was the granting of relief in the case of children. Where the total income is not over £500, a relief from income tax equal to the amount of the tax upon £10 is permitted for each child under the age of sixteen.[1] An important change was also made in Schedule A. It was now provided that if the owner of any land including farm-houses and buildings or any house, the annual value of which does not exceed £8, shows that the cost of maintenance, repairs, insurance, and management, on the average of the preceding five years, has exceeded in the case of land one-eighth part of the annual value, and in the case of houses one-sixth part of that value, he shall be entitled to a repayment of the tax on the excess, not exceeding in the case of land one-eighth part, and in the case of houses, one-twelfth part of the tax on the annual value.[2] This brings the maximum total allowance for repairs and maintenance up to twenty-five per cent of the annual value of the property in both cases.[3] If a person occupies his own house, the net annual value is still considered as income. Furthermore, the exemption accorded to friendly societies and trades unions is enlarged so as to apply in all cases where the amount does not exceed £300 gross insurance, or £52 by way of annuity.[4] Finally, the law contains an important provision, withdrawing the right of exemption and abatement or relief from any person who is not resident in the United Kingdom, with the exception of officials of the government, missionaries, and individuals who remain abroad because of their health. It provides, however, that the tax on interest or dividends of any securities of a foreign state or a British possession which are payable in Great Britain shall not be assessed

[1] Sec. 68.

[2] Sec. 69.

[3] In the case of farm property the old allowance of one-eighth plus the new allowance of one-eighth equals one-quarter or twenty-five per cent; in the case of houses the old allowance of one-sixth plus the new allowance of one-twelfth equals one-quarter or twenty-five per cent.

[4] Sec. 70.

when the owner of the securities does not reside in Great Britain.

Thus was accomplished the second great reform of the income tax. Henceforth not only differentiation, but graduation, is to be an avowed feature of the English system. Moreover, virtually all the important suggestions offered by the departmental committee for the reduction of fraud have now been enacted into law. It is worthy of especial note that a system of allowances for children, which, as we remember, was a part of the original income tax of 1799, and which worked so badly that it was soon abolished, has now again been introduced. It is a striking testimony not only to the recognition of the more modern ideas as to the social functions of an income tax, but also to the increased confidence that is felt by the British government in the administrative features of the tax. What was utterly impossible a century ago has now become entirely feasible.

§ 9. *Conclusion*

The English income tax has lasted in its present shape for well-nigh three-quarters of a century. The most striking fact in its history is the great change that has taken place in public sentiment. Slowly and very gradually the original and inveterate repugnance to the tax has been overcome, and has given way to a recognition of its inevitableness and to an appreciation of the great function that it has to perform in English fiscal and social life. This change in sentiment is due in part to the evolution that has occurred in England, as elsewhere in Europe, in the general attitude with regard to the social functions of taxation. But it is also in perhaps even greater degree due to the improvements that have been made in the underlying principle, as well as in the administrative machinery, of the tax; so that what was originally considered insupportable has now come to be regarded as not only endurable but proper.

That the income tax is administratively ideal is indeed far

from the truth. We still find occasional complaints. Fry, for instance, has called attention to several matters, some of which subsequently formed the subject of consideration by the departmental committee.[1] Stamp maintains that the system, with its wholesale survivals of the verbiage of the eighteenth century acts, its maze of averages and bases of calculation, its quaint references to alum and mundic, forms one of the most difficult branches of the law, constituting a sealed book to all but experts, and an exasperation to the lay mind.[2] Another writer characterizes it as the "most dishonourable and humiliating tax that has ever been put upon a willing and generous nation."[3] A recent anonymous writer speaks of "methods about which there is infrequently anything that is creditable and often much that is tyrannical," and thinks that "the ingenuity of the collectors in gaining advantage over the taxpayers is really most wonderful. Their guile is superb."[4] No tax, however, is really popular, and as against these magazine writers we may on the whole take as more typical the judgment of Armitage-Smith, the author of a recent British treatise, "that the method of collection is simple and economic, that the tax is highly productive, and that it satisfies fairly all the canons of Adam Smith. It has now become an established element in the British tax system, and democratic tendencies strengthen its position."[5]

If we attempt to summarize the features of the English income tax which are responsible for its undoubted success, we might state them as follows:—

First, the happy blending of regard for local interests and for

[1] T. Hallett Fry, *Income Tax Anomalies*. London, 1903; and the same author's *The Income Tax Burden*. London, 1904.

[2] J. C. Stamp, "Economic Aspects of Income Tax Change," in *The Economic Review*, vol. xix (1909), p. 420.

[3] "The Tyranny of the Income Tax," *Blackwood's Magazine*, vol. 178 (1905), pp. 279–284.

[4] "Anomalies of Income Tax Collection," in *Chambers's Journal*, 1907, pp. 321, 324.

[5] *Principles and Methods of Taxation*. By G. Armitage-Smith. London, 1906, pp. 64, 65.

fiscal productiveness. The original assessment of the tax, it will be remembered, is placed in the hands of appointees of the Land Tax Commissioners, and these Land Tax Commissioners are non-salaried representatives of the local gentry. It was rather by accident that England stumbled into this method at the very outset of the income tax, at the close of the eighteenth century;[1] but with the characteristic British fondness for old customs, it has survived to the present day. The taxpayers feel that their interests are in a sense looked after by their own representatives, and yet the interests of the revenue are guarded by careful supervision on the part of representatives of the central government. On the one hand the danger of too much bureaucracy is eliminated; on the other hand the risk of inadequate yield is averted.

Second, the ingenious system of the utilization of experts through the medium of the Additional Commissioners. The weak point in every income tax is in the assessment of business incomes. If this be left to ordinary administrative underlings, there is great danger either of ineffectiveness or of inquisition. Great Britain has been able to avoid both of these perils in large measure, by the system of Additional Commissioners, who, as we know, are frequently drawn from the ranks of the most prominent business men in the community, and who consider the service both a duty and a privilege. The public spirit which animates this part of the administration, and which attracts to the service the aid of what may be called outside experts, cannot be too highly commended. It is in no small degree responsible for the comparatively smooth working of the law.

Third, the absence of inquisitorial procedure. One of the most difficult things in fiscal matters is to avoid on the one hand the Charybdis of lax administrative methods, which must everywhere result in a travesty of the law, and on the other hand the Scylla of drastic methods, the very rigidity of which is apt to defeat itself. A long experience has enabled the English administrators to steer their course skilfully between

[1] *Cf. supra*, page 58.

these two perils. The early complaints against the inquisitorial character of the tax have long since well-nigh completely disappeared; and yet the effectiveness of the administration and its success in minimizing fraud have, as we know, grown more and more pronounced from decade to decade.

Fourth, the system of stoppage at source. This is perhaps the chief cause of the great success of the English income tax. The original lump-sum income tax was, as we know, abandoned as unworkable, and it has been the universal testimony of all English officials that any attempt to return to this early and discredited system would be fraught with disaster. If there is any one point to which the British authorities tenaciously cling, it is this system of dividing the tax into schedules, and of seeking, as far as possible, to secure the revenue by stoppage at source.

Fifth, the studied moderation of the rate. England has always sedulously refrained from incurring the risk which, as we shall see, has actually befallen some other states, of so straining the possibilities of the system as to imperil the revenues. For several decades, while the permanence of the tax was not yet assured, it is perhaps easily explicable that the rate should have hovered around three to four per cent. But even in recent decades, where the tax has become an acknowledged permanent part of the system, the normal rate has been kept down to five or six per cent. To take away six per cent of a man's income by what has become almost the sole example of general direct taxation cannot be considered in any way excessive. It is this moderation of the rate that has contributed not a little to the success of the tax.

Sixth, the introduction of differentiation. We have seen that almost from the inception of the tax the policy of assessing all the different kinds of income at the same rate gave rise to strenuous objections. For many weary decades the eloquence of Gladstone, in opposition to what have since turned out to be the imaginary dangers of a change, was sufficient to prevent all serious attempts at reform. But with the weakening of the individualistic tendencies for which Gladstone stood, and with the coming to the front of a new generation of statesmen, the seemingly impossible has been accomplished, and what has always been the greatest single objection to the English income tax has now been removed.

Seventh, the adoption of the system of progression. Here again a noticeable change has taken place in the public mind. At the beginning of the eighteenth century any system of graduation was looked upon by reputable thinkers and by prominent statesmen as a species of confiscation. All through the middle of the nineteenth century the proposition to introduce progressive taxation seemed to smack of socialism. But here again a new generation has brought with it new ideas, and what was long since taught by the scientists of the Continent was reënforced by the conclusions drawn from actual life, until the way was prepared for the definite acceptance by the statesmen of a principle that had come to approve itself to the public mind. Yet the essential conservatism of the English people made them shrink from adopting the principle in all its baldness. With that wisdom so characteristic of all political and economic advance in Great Britain, the new was built on the old, and the ingenious scheme of a super-tax, which retained all the advantages of the original system of stoppage at source, has succeeded in accomplishing everything that is really needed for the realization of the system of progressive taxation, without incurring the dangers which sometimes attend its introduction.

The English income tax has thus become a mighty fiscal and social engine. Nearly two hundred million dollars a year are now raised in a way that gives perhaps as little trouble as any form of taxation. No tax can ever be popular, for at bottom individuals are never sufficiently public-spirited to prefer the interests of others to their own. Under the necessary limitations of human nature, however, it may be confidently affirmed that the British income tax is a signal example of how sound theory and admirable administration may combine to overcome long-continued prejudice and opposition, and may succeed in rendering acceptable a system at first considered obnoxious and undeserving of support.

Taking it all in all, the British income tax has become a phenomenal success, because it is recognized by the public as a loyal and well-considered effort to accomplish that which the people desire, and in a way which commands their sympathetic approval.

APPENDIX 1

NET PRODUCE OF THE INCOME TAX FOR THE YEARS 1886–1913

YEAR ENDING APRIL	NET PRODUCE	RATE OF TAX	YEAR ENDING APRIL	NET PRODUCE	RATE OF TAX
1886	£15,843,065	8*d.*	1900	£18,828,958	8*d.*
1887	15,723,555	8*d.*	1901	29,705,312	1*s.*
1888	13,948,844	7*d.*	1902	35,440,070	1*s.* 2*d.*
1889	12,273,521	6*d.*	1903	38,037,931	1*s.* 3*d.*
1890	12,849,349	6*d.*	1904	28,188,067	11*d.*
1891	13,295,136	6*d.*	1905	30,966,404	1*s.*
1892	13,428,780	6*d.*	1906	31,601,237	1*s.*
1893	13,439,135	6*d.*	1907	32,002,412	1*s.*
1894	15,337,000	7*d.*	1908	32,380,000	1*s.*
1895	15,856,000	8*d.*	1909	33,408,754	1*s.*
1896	16,265,296	8*d.*	1910	37,679,902	1*s.* 2*d.*
1897	16,788,821	8*d.*	1911	38,344,767	1*s.* 2*d.*
1898	17,507,040	8*d.*	1912	39,631,630	1*s.* 2*d.*
1899	18,274,315	8*d.*	1913	40,600,000[1]	1*s.* 2*d.*

[1] Budget estimate.

APPENDIX 2

RECEIPT BY SCHEDULES, 1911–1912

		% OF WHOLE
Schedule A:	£9,307,700	23.5
Schedule B:	194,000	.5
Schedule C:	2,557,673	6.5
Schedule D:	24,661,301	62.2
Schedule E:	2,910,956	7.3

APPENDIX 3

1908–1909

GROSS INCOME BROUGHT UNDER REVIEW FOR INCOME TAX PURPOSES

Schedule A:	Lands	£51,894,826	
	Houses	216,664,907	
	Other property	1,329,041	£269,888,774
Schedule B:	Occupation of lands . . .		17,386,798
Schedule C:	Government securities . .		47,470,976
Schedule D:	Business and professions .	408,703,827	
	Railways in Kingdom . .	43,360,126	
	Mines	16,614,322	
	Gas works	7,834,291	
	Iron works	5,101,350	
	Waterworks	6,168,669	
	Canals	4,242,526	
	Quarries	1,356,076	
	Markets, tolls, etc. . . .	854,269	
	Fishing and sporting rights	222,264	
	Cemeteries	190,625	
	Salt springs and alum works	99,075	
	Foreign securities . . .	18,475,404	
	Coupons	15,105,979	
	Railways out of Kingdom .	23,014,330	
	Loans secured on rates . .	6,539,275	
	Other interest	5,769,524	
	Profits from land	18,710	
	Other profits	1,900,679	565,601,321
Schedule E:	Salaries of government and corporation officials . .		109,588,057
			£1,009,935,926

APPENDIX 4

SUPER-TAX

	TOTAL INCOME ASSESSED	INCOME CHARGED WITH SUPER-TAX	AMOUNT OF SUPER-TAX	NUMBER OF PERSONS LIABLE
1909–1910	£140,120,492	£105,980,492	£2,649,512	11,380
1910–1911 [1]	141,300,000	——	2,670,000	11,500
1911–1912 [1]	145,950,000	——	2,775,000	11,650
1912–1913 [1]	149,400,000	——	2,850,000	11,800

[1] Estimated, because assessments may continue for three years.

BOOK II

THE INCOME TAX IN OTHER EUROPEAN COUNTRIES

CHAPTER I

The Income Tax in Germany

§1. *The Taxes on Product and the Prussian Class Tax of 1820*

The characteristic feature of the German fiscal system during the first half of the nineteenth century was the taxation of product. The mediæval system of the general property tax had long since broken down and disappeared in Germany as everywhere else. The general property tax had gradually split up, and instead of being levied on the individual himself who was responsible for his entire property, had come to be assessed on the things or the particular constituent elements of property. With the gradual slipping of personal property out of the assessment list, and with the disinclination of the large land-owners to subject themselves to high taxation on real estate, the direct taxes were now in the eighteenth century supplemented by a system of taxes on expenditure, which ordinarily took the form of a general excise. In the meantime, the custom had arisen of assessing property on the basis of the yield or product, rather than of the selling value.[1] Thus the old general property tax was replaced by a system which attempted to reach the various elements of product. In almost all the German states the system comprised taxes on land and on buildings and in some instances taxes on business also. At the beginning of the nineteenth century an effort was made to round out the system by adding other taxes on product, such as the tax on wages and the tax on interest or funded capital; and in proportion as the taxes on produce were developed, it became possible to reduce the general excise.

[1] *Cf.* A. Kölle, "Zur Entstehung der Ertrags- und Katastersteuern in den deutschen Staaten," *Finanz Archiv*, vol. 16 (1899), pp. 477–496.

Before long, however, and in fact in some cases almost from the very outset, unofficial opinion came to the conclusion that neither a system of taxes on product, — despite certain advantages of its own, — nor a system of taxes on expenditure availed to respond in all respects to the newer ideas of ability to pay, which under the influence of the modern industrial and political system were gradually permeating the public mind. Accordingly, we now find an effort both to diminish the burden of the exaggerated excises and to modify the taxes on product by a return to some method of personal taxation which should be able to reach the wealthier taxpayers. The form which this personal taxation ultimately assumed was the income tax. Hence the fiscal history of the nineteenth century in the German states is a record of the gradual disappearance of the general excise, the elaboration in some places of a complete, well-rounded system of taxation on product, and the gradual introduction of a system of taxation of personal income, at first supplementing, and finally replacing, the older methods. By the end of the nineteenth century this process had been fairly well worked out, although it was not entirely completed everywhere. The tempo of the development, however, has naturally varied in the different states.[1]

In Prussia, which we shall naturally discuss first as the most important of the German states, the tax on product had been only partially developed, and the consumption tax played the greater rôle.[2] The Prussian system, in the form which

[1] For a general account of this development during the nineteenth century, see von Heckel, *Die Fortschritte der Directen Besteuerung in den Deutschen Staaten.* Leipzig, 1904. *Cf.* also, for a more succinct account, the same author's *Lehrbuch der Finanzwissenschaft*, vol. i, 1907, pp. 217–338. See also in general Wagner, *Finanzwissenschaft, Vierter Theil. Die Deutsche Besteuerung des 19. Jahrhunderts.* Leipzig, 1899. For brief surveys, see Conrad's *Handwörterbuch der Staatswissenschaften.* 3d ed., Jena, 1909. *Cf.* esp. *sub verbo Einkommensteuer.* For the last few decades numerous articles on various phases of the subject will be found in Schanz, *Finanz Archiv.*

[2] For the fullest account of the early period of Prussian taxation, see K. Mamroth, *Geschichte der Preussischen Staats-Besteuerung, 1806–1816.* Leipzig, 1890. *Cf.* C. Dieterici, *Zur Geschichte der Steuer-Reform in Preussen von 1810–1820.* Berlin, 1875; J. G. Hoffman, *Die Lehre von den Steuern.* Leipzig, 1840; and

had been given to it especially by the Great Elector, consisted of two chief parts; the so-called direct contribution, which was a land tax levied only in the rural districts, and the general excise, or so-called universal excise, which consisted of a system of taxes on consumption applicable to the towns. There was also a small general tax on salt. In the land taxes there were all kinds of exemptions, especially for the nobility, and all manner of variations in local administrative methods. In the towns the burden was felt especially by the poor and by the lower commercial class.

The period which opened after the peace of Tilsit was marked by efforts at reform. The introduction of the modern system of freedom of commerce, which led to the gradual breakdown of the guild system, not only destroyed, in part at least, the opposition of town and country, but created a demand for the liberation of industry from oppressive taxation; and at the same time the growing movement toward greater fiscal equality brought into prominence the idea, voiced by the French Revolution, of taxation according to ability or means. Thus a double tendency disclosed itself: on the one hand the attempt to abolish the existing privileges and exemptions in the land tax as well as to make it uniform throughout the state, and in the second place, the effort to reform the excises by reducing the number of articles liable to taxation, and by supplementing them by some form of direct taxation. It was, however, only by slow degrees that these reforms were accomplished.

In 1810 the movement was initiated by Hardenberg through two enactments. One of these attempted to concentrate the excises upon a smaller number of commodities. But the

R. Grätzer, *Zur Geschichte der Preussischen Einkommen-und Klassensteuer, 1812–1851.* Berlin, 1884. For the later period an excellent work is that of Fuisting, *Geschichtliche Entwickelung der Preussischen Steuersysteme und Systematische Darstellung der Einkommensteuer.* Berlin, 1894. Many details will also be found in Adolf Held, *Die Einkommensteuer. Finanzwissenschaftliche Studien zur Reform der Directen Steuern in Deutschland.* Bonn, 1872. A good survey for the earlier period will be found in J. A. Hill, "The Prussian Income Tax," *Quarterly Journal of Economics*, vol. vi (1892), pp. 207 *et seq.*

necessities of a large revenue compelled a corresponding increase in the rate of the excises which were retained. Moreover, some of the old taxes on consumption, as well as some new ones like the grist or meal tax (*Mahlsteuer*), the meat or slaughter tax (*Schlacht- und Fleischsteuer*), and the taxes on beer and brandy, were now extended to the rural districts. In the second place, a general business tax (*Gewerbesteuer*) was introduced and made applicable throughout the entire state. This endeavor to put town and country on an equality led to so much opposition to the grist tax, especially on the part of the farmers, that in the following year, 1811, the old distinction was reintroduced in a modified form. The reformed excise and the new consumption taxes were now limited to the larger towns, while the rural districts as well as the smaller towns were freed from the unpopular grist tax, and were made liable to the slaughter, beer, and brandy taxes, at a much reduced rate. As a compensation for the loss of revenue, however, the rural districts and the smaller towns were now subjected to a so-called direct personal tax, which was in effect an annual poll tax of one-half a thaler (37 cents), for every one over sixteen years of age. Thus was introduced the entering wedge of personal taxation.

The troubles of 1811 and 1812 led, both in Prussia and elsewhere, to some merely temporary expedients. In 1811 a class tax was imposed, which was replaced in 1812 by a so-called income and property tax. The income tax was levied at the rate of five per cent on all incomes over 300 thalers, while the property tax, which was in part a forced loan, like that of France during the Revolution, amounted to three per cent. These war measures lasted only a short time and were repealed in 1814. The income tax was never considered a part of the regular system; and its great unpopularity was to produce unfortunate consequences later on.

The conclusion of peace brought with it substantial additions to the Prussian territory, each with its own system of taxation. As a consequence, a not altogether successful attempt was made to bring about greater uniformity in taxation. In 1816 most of the tolls or internal customs duties which had been so widespread in the Middle Ages were abolished, and in 1818 a general customs tariff for the entire state was adopted, with practically free trade as between the separate provinces — a great step forward in political development.[1] In 1819 the old general excise was definitely abandoned, and the excise duties which were now made applicable to the entire state were limited to taxes on tobacco, beer, wine and brandy. Prussia thus reached in this respect a position which England did not attain until several decades later, with the important exception, however, that the salt monopoly (*Salzverkaufsregal*) still continued, even though the old and vexatious obligation of purchasing a certain quantity of salt (*Salzconscription*) was abolished in 1816.

In 1820 the business tax, which was now uniform throughout Prussia, was remodelled. The various kinds of business were divided into a number of classes, some of which were taxed according to external criteria, as in France. In other cases, however, the interesting expedient was devised of assessing a lump sum upon the particular trade as a whole in each locality and then providing for a repartition of a tax to each individual through the medium of tax associations (*Steuergesellschaften*) — one in each trade. As a matter of fact, although it is not commonly known, this was an old scheme, which can be traced back to mediæval Spain.[2] Thus was attained a kind of personal tax in indirect fashion; but the tax was light and the yield very small. In 1822 a new and uniform stamp tax was imposed, which replaced all the local and provincial stamp taxes. In the case of the chief source of revenue, however, — the so-called land tax, which was actually a tax on all real estate, — it proved to be impossible to bring

[1] This aspect of the law is well elucidated in G. Schmoller, *Rectoratsrede über das Preussische Handels- und Zollgezetz von 1818*. Berlin, 1898. *Cf.* also the same author's "Die Epochen der Preussichen Finanzpolitik" in Holtzendorff-Brentano's *Jahrbuch für Gesetzgebung*, etc., vol. i (1877), pp. 31 *et seq.*

[2] The same is true, as we have seen above, p. 52, of the French *vingtièmes d'industrie*. Wagner was evidently ignorant of both these facts when he spoke of the Prussian system as a "Singularität." *Finanzwissenschaft, op. cit.*, p. 20.

about the desired uniformity, the only general regulation which it was practicable to enact being to the effect that wherever the tax had been introduced or increased since 1789 it should not exceed one-fifth of the net produce.

The chief feature of the legislation of 1820, however, consisted in the introduction of the class tax. The government was not favorable to an expansion of direct taxation, but the growing fiscal needs, combined with the unalterable opposition of the rural districts to the grist tax, left the government no alternative. As a consequence a law was now enacted whereby the whole country, with the exception of the larger towns, 132 in number, was compelled to pay in addition to the land tax a so-called class tax. According to this law the population was divided into a small number of categories or classes, differentiated according to simple external criteria like social standing, occupation, general estimate of wealth, and ordinary mode of life. The same sum was payable by each household in the class. In the original bill provision had been made for four classes, but the law as enacted increased these to six, and in 1822 a final arrangement was made providing for a still further classification into four chief sections, with three sub-classes in each; that is, in reality, twelve classes. The rates varied from a minimum of one-half a thaler, in the lowest sub-class, to 144 thalers in the highest class.[1] Liability to taxation began at the age of 14 (changed in 1828 to 16), and ended at the age of 60 (as changed by the law of 1827). In the 132 larger towns, however, the class tax was not levied. They were liable, in addition to the light business and stamp taxes, only to a combined grist and slaughter tax, the administration of which rendered necessary a continuation of the octroi or local customs duty. It was provided, however, that if the city so chose, it might, with the consent of the general government, vote itself liable to the class tax instead of the grist tax, and the privilege of an inverse choice was conferred on the rural districts and

[1] The exact rates were half a thaler, 2, 3–4, 6, 8–12, 18, 24–48, 96, 144 thalers respectively. A thaler is about 75 cents.

towns. A number of cities exercised this right, so that by 1851 only 83 were left in the category of grist-tax cities. The relative importance of the three direct taxes in 1821 may be inferred from the fact that in that year the land tax yielded 9,878,752 thalers; the class tax, 6,285,874 thalers; and the business tax, 1,706,234 thalers.

The class tax seemed to many to be the proper solution of the problem. The ministerial ordinance of 1820 tells us that it "is entitled to be the happy medium between an income tax, which is always odious because it cannot be enforced without an inquisitorial inspection into the conditions of the taxpayer's wealth, and a poll tax levied at the same rate on the whole population, without any differentiation. It is intended to reach the various classes of taxpayers according to a gradation resting on a few easily visible criteria." And it adds: "In order not to let the tax degenerate into an income tax we must be careful to avoid putting into the figures any definite amount of the property or income of the members of the various classes. . . . The notorious mode of life and the taxpayer's own view of the situation will thus take the place of the very odious inquisition which is moreover least of all suitable for a tax that endeavors to reach so small a part of a man's income."[1]

The general principles underlying the class tax were perhaps most emphatically defended by Hoffmann, the author of the weightiest German book on taxation in the first half of the century.[2] Hoffmann calls attention to the fact that in the existing structure of German society there were in reality four sharply differentiated classes. In the country one could easily distinguish between the large landowners, the smaller farmers, the peasants and the agricultural laborers. In the towns, also, a similar distinction was to be drawn between the

[1] The ordinance will be found in Held, *op. cit.*, p. 275.

[2] *Die Lehre von den Steuern als Anleitung zu gründlichen Urtheilen über das Steuerwesen mit besonderer Beziehung auf den preussischen Staat vorgetragen.* Von J. G. Hoffmann. Berlin, 1840. *Cf.* also F. G. Schimmelpfennig, *Die preussischen direkten Steuern*, 2 vols. Potsdam, 1843; and especially Sinnhold, *Die Klassensteuerverfassung des Preussischen Staats.* Liegnitz, 1831.

large capitalists, the higher middle classes, the small tradesmen and the day laborers. Hoffmann therefore considered the class tax far superior to any practicable income tax.

From our point of view it may be conceded that the class tax was perhaps as great a step in advance as was possible at the time. As Gneist, the distinguished jurist, forcibly expressed it many years later: "The founders of the class tax and especially Hoffmann, with that practical insight which characterized them, recognized that an income tax could not be forthwith introduced among a people where more than nine-tenths of the families were not accustomed, nor even able, to calculate their revenues and expenditure in money, and to strike a balance of income. It was also recognized that even for the privileged and exempted classes of the population, an assessment of income, without reference to any personal distinctions, would seem to them as unfamiliar as it was in contradiction to their conceptions of rank."[1] Entirely apart, however, from the fact that the class tax did not apply at all to the large cities, it carried out only to a very slight degree the principle of ability to pay, and possessed no machinery calculated to make the enrolment in the various classes conform to the real wealth of the taxpayers. In fact, even by 1846 there were only 346 persons enrolled in the highest class paying 144 thalers annually.[2] The overwhelmingly large part of the yield was derived from the lower and the lowest classes. It was therefore inevitable that after a time the demand for putting a greater share of the burden on those better able to pay should make itself heard. This demand took the form of a recommendation of the income tax.

§ 2. *The Movement toward the Income Tax*

The general opinion as to the desirability of an income tax was considerably divided. Among the public at large and in government circles the judgment was undoubtedly adverse,

[1] *Die Preussische Finanz Reform durch Regulirung der Gemeindesteuern.* Von Rudolf Gneist. Berlin, 1881.

[2] Held, *op. cit.*, p. 284.

for very much the same reasons that had made the old income tax so unpopular in England. Among the scientists the matter was slightly different. The old writers on finance during the first half of the nineteenth century were for the most part content to adopt Adam Smith's first rule (which, it will be remembered, declared that the norm of taxation was the revenue that the individual enjoyed under the protection of the state), without, however, taking up in any detail the question as to whether this general ideal was to be reached by an income tax.[1] When they began to discuss the income tax as such, most of the authoritative writers, like Rau, preferred a continuance of the system of taxes on product as it existed or was being developed.[2] On the other hand, so prominent an author as Murhard was a warm advocate not only of an

[1] The most important of these writers were :—

C. Kröncke, *Das Steuerwesen nach seiner Natur und Wirkungen untersucht.* Darmstadt, 1804; and *Ausführliche Anleitung zur Regulirung der Steuern.* Giessen, 1810; Christian von Schlözer, *Anfangsgründe der Staatswirthschaft.* Riga, 1805; Stockar von Neuforn, *Finanzwissenschaft.* Rothenburg, 1808; D. H. Eschenmayer, *Vorschlag zu einem einfachen Steuersysteme.* Heidelberg, 1808 [E. was opposed to the excise]; J. P. Harl, *Vollständiges Theoretisch-praktisches Handbuch der gesammten Steuerregulirungen oder der Steuerwissenschaft.* Erlangen, 1816; E. Kröncke, *Ueber die Grundsätze einer gerechten Besteuerung.* Heidelberg, 1819; D. Krehl, *Das Steuersystem nach den Grundsätzen des Staatsrechts und der Staatswirthschaft.* Erlangen, 1816; Georg F. v. Sartorius, *Ueber die gleiche Besteuerung des Königreichs Hannover.* Göttingen, 1815; W. J. Behr, *Die Lehre von der Wirthschaft des Staats, oder Pragmatische Theorie der Finanzgesetzgebung und Finanzverwaltung.* Leipzig, 1822; J. F. E. Lotz, *Handbuch der Staatswirthschaftlehre.* Erlangen, 1822; L. H. von Jakob. *Die Staatsfinanzwissenchaft theoretisch und praktisch dargestellt.* Halle, 1823; A. S. von Kremer, *Darstellung des Steuerwesens.* Wien, 1825; C. A. von Malchus, *Handbuch der Finanzwissenschaft und Finanzverwaltung.* Stuttgart, 1830; F. C. Fulda, *Handbuch der Finanzwissenschaft.* Tübingen, 1827; and *Ueber die Wirkung der verschiedenen Arten der Steuern auf die Moralität, den Fleiss, und die Industrie des Volks.* Stuttgart, 1837; J. Schön, *Die Grundsätze der Finanz. Eine kritische Entwickelung.* Breslau, 1832; A. L. V. Seutter, *Die Besteuerung der Völker, rechts- und geldwissenschaftlich untersucht.* Speyer, 1828; K. V. Rotteck, *Lehrbuch der ökonomischen Politik.* 1835. A fuller treatment of some of these authors will be found in Seligman, *Progressive Taxation*, 2d. ed., 1908, pp. 176 *et seq.*; 187 *et seq.*

[2] Karl H. Rau, *Grundsätze der Finanzwissenschaft.* 1832–1837. Held, *op. cit.*, p. 248, attempts rather unsuccessfully to explain away Rau's objections.

income tax, but of a single income tax to replace all the existing taxes on product.[1]

This discussion of the single tax in Germany, of which we have only sporadic examples in the earlier period,[2] came into the foreground as a result of the fiscal reform in Saxony. The Saxon system was a survival of earlier conditions, consisting of an old land tax and a combination of business and poll tax known as the *Quatembersteuern*. The latter had become of minor importance since the introduction, at the beginning of the eighteenth century, of the general excise supplemented by a grist tax. When the constitution of 1831 was adopted, and especially after Saxony joined the customs union (*Zollverein*), thus instituting a reform of existing tax methods, preparation was made to introduce a more equitable system. A number of pamphlets now appeared containing the suggestion of a single income tax. Among these the most important was by Lucius, who was an enthusiastic advocate of the scheme.[3] An attempt to refute the views of Lucius was made by an anonymous writer.[4] In this work, which contains good arguments designed to show that the fiscal difficulties would be aggravated by any kind of a single

[1] Karl Murhard, *Theorie und Politik der Besteuerung*. Göttingen, 1834.

[2] *Cf.*, for instance, A. Lips, *Ueber die allein Wahre und Einzige Steuer, die Einkommentaxe und ihre Ausführbarkeit.* Erlangen, 1812. The same idea was repeated in his *Deutschland's National-Oeconomie.* Giessen, 1830, pp. 210 *et seq.* See also Breitenstein, *Nur Eine Steuer und deren Catastrirung, Erhebung und Verrechnung, mit vorausgeschickter praktischer Betrachtung aller bisherigen directen und indirecten Auflagen.* Gotha, 1826. The essay of Lips was sharply criticised by Strelin, *Revision der Lehre von den Auflagen.* Erlangen, 1821, pp. 113 *et seq.* *Cf.* also Seeger, *Ueber das vorzüglichste Abgabensystem.* 3d. ed., 1815. A somewhat later discussion may be found in the anonymous *Ueber verhältnissmässige Besteuerung oder wie jeder Staatsangehörige nach der Grösse seiner finanziellen Kraft zu den Allgemeinlasten beitragen würde.* Leipzig 1834.

[3] *Plan zur Einführung einer Steuer im Königreiche Sachsen.* Vom Gerichtsdirector und Advocat Lucius in Borna. Leipzig, 1833. A similar pamphlet was issued by Cunow which, however, simply repeats the arguments of Lucius.

[4] *Die Einkommenssteuer als Einzige Abgabe, aus staatsrechtlichem, nationalökonomischem und finanziellem Gesichtspuncte und mit besonderer Beziehung auf den vom Gerichts-Director Lucius herausgegebenen Planentwurf beleuchtet.* Von W. R. Leipzig, 1833.

tax, the author inveighed against the use of the income tax at all, and gave a peculiar interpretation of the English income tax in order to bolster up his theories.[1] He concluded with quoting from a nameless writer whom he characterized as "one of our greatest and most experienced fiscal experts," as follows: "I consider the income tax an instructive and horrible example of the radical unsuitability of all direct taxes designed to produce great results, and as a striking proof of the error of all the delusive theories which attempt to show that this tax is bound up with the liberty and prosperity of nations."[2]

The Saxon government, while not inclined to the scheme of Lucius, was, nevertheless, induced to adopt a part of his project and succeeded in 1834 in enacting a law for a new business and personal tax (*Gewerbe und Personalsteuer*). The business part of the tax was, like its Prussian predecessor, based on external criteria. The personal part of the tax likewise endeavored to reach by indirect methods all other incomes except those from land, which were supposed to be hit by the land tax. The administrative methods of both parts of the tax were so arranged as to avoid as completely as possible all inquisitorial procedure.[3]

The Saxon development exerted at the time no further influence either in Prussia or in the other German states. With the enactment of Peel's income tax in England, however, and especially with the democratic upheaval of 1848, the inadequacy of the Prussian class tax forced itself upon popular notice and led to a determined effort at reform.

The ball was set rolling in 1842 by Benda, who was a violent opponent of the modern system of public debts, and especially of what he called the "stock-exchange swindles."

[1] He maintained, for instance, that the entire burden of the English income tax had fallen on the landowners and the salaried classes, and that the tax had been abolished for this reason. — See p. 36.

[2] *Op. cit.*, p. 48.

[3] *Cf.*, for a summary of the details of the law, *Zeitschrift des Königlichen Sächsichen Statistischen Bureaus.* Leipzig, 1858, pp. 55 *et seq.*

Benda emphasized, in a somewhat exaggerated fashion, the social aspects of the income tax, and especially its efficacy, when levied at a high rate on the wealthy, in cutting down the public debt.[1] A far weightier production was that of Sparre, an official who, as we are told, had occupied himself for twenty-three years with the Prussian class tax. He called attention to the fact that while at the time the income tax was everywhere so warmly desired, most people did not know what was really meant by it, or how it ought to be arranged.[2] Sparre held that a direct income tax was far preferable to what he called indirect income taxes, based on mere presumptive evidence. He worked out in detail the administrative methods of his suggested impost, taking up among others the moot questions of differentiation and progression. He freely admitted that the country was not yet quite ready for the income tax, but he predicted for it a "great, even if a distant, future," and maintained that it would gradually take the place not only of the most burdensome existing indirect taxes, but also of the most important direct taxes, so that ultimately the fiscal system would, in his opinion, be composed primarily of an income tax and of a few great indirect taxes on expenditure. "The income tax," said he, "is a tax on the new citizenship (*Bürgerthum*) which is still in the making." Sparre disposed of the chief objection, namely that the administration of the income tax would cause a prying into people's affairs, by asserting that self-assessment without inquisitorial methods could be made to suffice, but that even if some compulsion were needed, too narrow a view must not be taken, for in reality "the state is mankind's great educative institution."[3]

In a second edition published six years later, Sparre con-

[1] Benda, *Peel's Finanz System.* Leipzig, 1842.

[2] *Die allgemeine Einkommensteuer als einzige gerechte directe Abgabe, aus Theorie und Erfahrung nachgewiesen.* Von Karl v. Sparre. Giessen, 1848, p. vii. Sparre also published a separate work on the Prussian system entitled *Die Preussiche Classensteuer und Mahl- und Schlachtsteuer.*

[3] "Der Staat ist eine Erziehungs-anstalt für das Menschengeschlecht." See p. 89 of the 2d ed.

ceded that his original scheme was premature, and that for a long time to come only a partial income tax was possible. He therefore changed the title of his book[1] and discussed primarily the eventuality of such a tax. He was, however, still firm in his conviction that that would be only a half-measure, and he deplored the government's "lack of courage in not throwing overboard all the old direct taxes." "Only shyly," he tells us, "is our government grasping at the partial income tax, leaving it unsuitably enough as a subsidiary and supplementary impost to be added to old taxes which have long since been condemned by science and sentenced by experience. Let us hope that the future will show the inadequacy of all such makeshifts."[2]

Other writers did not fail to take the cue and even to exaggerate the scheme. Freiherr von Gross, a member of the National Assembly, suggested in 1848 an income tax with progressive rates running up to thirty-three and one-half per cent;[3] and Ziegler, the mayor of Brandenburg, proposed in 1850 to replace all the existing direct taxes by a progressive income tax, having succeeded, as he tells us, temporarily at least, in introducing the system in his native town.[4] Perhaps the extreme glorification of this single tax idea is found in a production of von Graffenried, who deduced his scheme from the old theory of taxation as an insurance premium.[5] These enthusiastic projects, however, soon engendered a host of objections. Baumstark, a weighty disputant, declared that "the income tax is a growth cultivated, although by no means discovered, by the German Revolution, as well as a product

[1] *Die allgemeine und die partielle Einkommensteuer, verglichen mit der bisherigen Steuertheorie und Praxis.* Zweite Auflage, Frankfurt a/M, 1854.

[2] "Nur schüchtern greift man zu der partiellen und läszt sie als ein subsidiäres und supplementares Wesen neben alten Steuern unpassend genug hergeben, die längst von der Wissenschaft gerichtet und von der Erfahrung verurtheilt sind. Hoffen wir aber, dass die Zukunft die Unzulänglichkeit aller solcher Nothbehelfe aufdringen werde." — *Op. cit.*, p. 99.

[3] Freiherr von Gross, *Allgemeine Progressive Grund- und Einkommensteuer. Gleiches Maas und Gewicht für Deutschland.* 1848.

[4] Held, *op. cit.*, p. 260.

[5] Von Graffenried, *Über die Einkommensteuer.* Zürich, 1855.

of bitter sentiments and unclear ideas."[1] He preferred taxes on special kinds of income to a general income tax. A less important writer, Quarizius, entered the lists against Sparre and stated that "it would be a relatively simple matter, scientifically to refute the sanguine admirers of the income tax."[2] His own refutation, however, was far from scientific, for he based his criticism chiefly on a general opposition to the increase of any direct tax, for the reason that it would prevent the rich from employing the poor, and would thus directly increase pauperism.

§ 3. *From the Revolution of 1848 to the Franco-Prussian War*

On the whole, however, it may be said that the democratic movement at the end of the forties was distinctly favorable to some kind of an income tax, designed to alleviate the existing burdens of the poor. In Baden, for instance, there had been since 1820 a class tax. But this tax, which was intended to supplement the land, building, and business taxes, applied only to incomes from wages, salaries, and pensions. A remarkable feature of the tax was the application of a progressive scale, the rate rising from one and two-thirds per cent in the lowest class (1 kr. per gulden up to fl. 1000) to sixteen and two-thirds per cent on the highest class (10 kr. per gulden, above fl. 80,000). The revolutionary movement of 1848 accordingly brought with it a demand for some tax to reach the revenue of the wealthier classes in general. While the project of an income tax failed, the agitation resulted in the imposition, in 1848, of a so-called capital tax — or what we in America should call a tax on all intangible personalty.[3]

[1] "Ein von der Deutschen Revolution gepflegtes wenn auch keineswegs entdecktes Gewächs, ein Product bitterer Empfindungen und unklarer Vorstellungen." — Baumstark, *Zur Einkommensteuer*. Greifswald, 1850, p. 27.

[2] Quarizius, *Die Einkommensteuer*. Weimar, 1853.

[3] *Cf.* in general, for the fiscal history of Baden, Lewald, "Die Direkten Steuern in Baden," *Finanz Archiv*, vol. iii (1881), pp. 764 *et seq.;* and Philippovich, *Der Badische Haushalt von 1868–1889*. Freiburg, 1889. A shorter

An interesting innovation of the same year was the introduction of a so-called Council of Assessment (*Schätzungsrath*), a small body elected by, and directly representing, the taxpayers and designed to assist the official commissioners in assessing the new capital tax as well as the old class and business tax.

The movement found its most extreme expression in Bavaria, where the law of 1848 actually introduced not only a capital tax but also an income tax. These two taxes were combined in 1850 into a general income tax, with a normal rate of two per cent and with abatements for lower incomes. The law, however, was defective in that the tax was superadded to the existing taxes on product. Above all, the administrative machinery was woefully inadequate. It worked so badly and gave rise to so many complaints that, with the subsidence of the revolutionary enthusiasm, the tax was virtually abolished in 1856. The name indeed remained, but it now applied only to incomes which were supposed not to be reached in some way by the remaining taxes. Practically it became a tax on wages and salaries only.[1] In Hesse also an income tax was introduced in 1848, applicable to all incomes not subject to the land and business taxes. This likewise proved to be a failure.[2] Finally, in the city republic of Bremen, an income tax was introduced in 1848, resting on a system of self-assessment which had long been practiced there in connection with the old property tax and which for that reason worked fairly well.[3]

The Prussian government also was influenced by the same

account will be found in A. Wagner, *Finanzwissenschaft, Vierter Theil, Zweiter Halbband.* 1901, pp. 245 *et seq.* For the laws themselves, see Philippovich, *Gesetze über die Direkten Steuern in Baden.* Freiburg, 1888, 2 vols.

[1] *Cf.* S. Gerstner, *Das Bayrische Einkommen- und Kapitalrentensteuergesetz.* Erlangen, 1858. See also L. Hoffmann, *Geschichte der direkten Steuern in Baiern vom 13–19 Jahrhundert.* Leipzig, 1883; and Vocke, "Beitrage zur Geschichte der Einkommensteuer in Baiern," *Tübinger Zeitschrift*, vols. 20 and 21. *Cf.* also Schanz, "Das Bayrische Ertragssteuersystem und seine Entwickelung," *Finanz Archiv*, vol. xvii (1900), pp. 551–772.

[2] *Cf.* the article by Schanz, "Die direkten Steuern Hessens und deren neueste Reform," *Finanz Archiv*, vol. 2 (1885), pp. 235–381.

[3] For a good account of this see Wagner, *op cit.*, pp. 622–629.

tendency, and in 1847 introduced a bill to abolish the grist tax and to make all persons with an income of over 400 thalers liable to an income tax at the rate of three per cent for funded incomes, and two per cent for unfunded incomes. Those with incomes below 400 thalers were still to be subjected to the class tax. Minister Camphausen defended the measure in an eloquent speech in which he pronounced himself as indeed opposed to a single income tax, as being entirely impracticable and for that matter unjustifiable. But he upheld his scheme of an income tax primarily on grounds of social reform. The bill, he tells us, "aims to secure a recognition of the fact that the 'haves' are in duty bound to do much for the 'have-nots'; it aims at a greater recognition on the part of the latter that the former are ready to make sacrifices for them. It is the function of our modern legislation to recognize the hardships of life, and to alleviate them."[1] Camphausen, however, appealed to deaf ears. There proved to be no such readiness on the part of the wealthy to make sacrifices for the poor, and the very mention of self-assessment was sufficient to kill the bill. Nothing was accomplished except that in 1848 the state now abandoned one-third of the grist tax to the towns, in order to lighten the burden resting on the working classes.

In 1849 the government returned to the fray with a slightly altered scheme. The tax was now to begin only at 1000 thalers. The distinction between funded and unfunded incomes was dropped, and the question of self-assessment was relegated to the pleasure of the taxpayer. Nearly every one agreed in the discussion that something must be done to make the wealthier classes pay their proper share, but no effective majority could be secured for any particular method of accomplishing this result. Perhaps the best speech was made by an old tax official, Kühne, who, in referring to the necessity of abandoning the old taxes, conceded that this would involve "a painful operation on the body politic." But, he added: "When one finally concludes to undergo an operation and

[1] Quoted in Held, *op. cit.*, p. 286.

then demands that it be made by a dull knife, I can only call him a fool. We all confess that we want an income tax, but we are not willing to grant the means whereby it can become an income tax. We are ready to have people pay according to their income, but we refuse to let any one ascertain what the income is."[1]

Nothing came of this second project. But the need of more revenue had now become so imperious that the government resolved to take what it could get. Consequently in 1851 it introduced a third bill, which endeavored to accomplish only a partial realization of the income-tax idea, and which included a retention of the grist and slaughter taxes. This finally went through both houses, and became law.

The act of 1851 provided for a so-called "class- and classified income tax."[2] The old class tax was, with a few modifications, limited to taxpayers with an income up to 1000 thalers, and was levied throughout the state except in the 83 largest cities, which in lieu of this were to be subjected to the old grist and slaughter tax. On the other hand, the new classified income tax was payable by all individuals having an income of 1000 thalers, whether they lived in town or country. The class tax was divided into three main and twelve subclasses; the classified income tax was divided into thirty classes, with fixed monthly payments varying from 2½ to 600 thalers, *i.e.*, 30 to 7200 thalers annually. This was, however, subject to the provision that the annual tax should never exceed three per cent of the income in each class. Accordingly, the highest income taxable was 240,000 thalers. Incomes above this amount were entirely exempt, and even the wealthier individuals, nominally subject to the tax, could escape their modest contribution by remaining in a large city for one day more than a half year. Moreover, as the limitation of three per cent applied only to the minimum income in each class, the higher incomes in each class paid considerably less than three per cent. The characteristic

[1] Quoted in Held, *op. cit.*, p. 292.

[2] *Die Klassen- und klassifizierte Einkommensteuer.*

part of the system, however, consisted in the fact that while the incomes were to be assessed by officials, these were strictly forbidden to make any "vexatious inquiry into the income or property conditions of the taxpayer."[1]

Thus a step in advance, although a very small one, was taken, and with this the tax reformers had to be content for two decades. With every year, however, not only the administrative shortcomings, but the essential inequalities, of the tax, were more and more realized, and the growing prosperity of the kingdom brought into continually stronger relief the virtual exemption of the wealthier taxpayers. The successful experience of the English income tax, which had already been touched upon in the fifties, especially by Kries,[2] was made known to the German public toward the close of the sixties in a comprehensive work by Vocke,[3] and the scientific writers now began a discussion of the problem from the newer standpoint of social reform. Professor Nasse in 1861, like Hoffmann in 1840, had indeed declared himself as on the whole favorable to the retention of the tax on product, side by side with a developed income tax.[4] But he was almost the last of the important publicists to take this attitude. Not only did secondary writers like Emminghaus, Rössler, Walcker, Eisenhart, and Maurus,[5] in the sixties show themselves in favor of the income tax, but prominent men like

[1] "Jedes lästige Eindringen in die Vermögen-und Einkommen-Verhältnisse des einzelnen Steuerpflichtigen."

[2] See Kries, "Grundzüge und Ergebnisse der Englischen Einkommensteuer," in *Zeitschrift für die Gesammte Staatswissenschaft*, vol. x (1854). Kries followed this by two studies of the Prussian system. "Ergebnisse der Preussischen Einkommensteuer," *ibid.*, vol. xi (1855); and "Die Preussische Einkommensteuer und die Mahl- und Schlachtsteuer," *ibid.*, vol. xii (1856).

[3] *Geschichte der Steuern des Britischen Reichs. Ein Finanzgeschichtlicher Versuch.* Von W. Vocke. Leipzig, 1866. See esp. pp. 505–590.

[4] W. Nasse, *Bemerkungen über das Preussische Steuersystem.* Bonn, 1861.

[5] K. B. A. Emminghaus, *Ueber die Steuerfrage.* Bremen, 1862; C. Rössler, *Die Gesichtspunkte der Steuerpolitik.* Berlin, 1868; K. Walcker, *Die Selbstverwaltung des Steuerwesens.* Berlin, 1869; H. Eisenhart, *Die Kunst der Besteuerung.* Berlin, 1868; Maurus, *Die Moderne Besteuerung und die Besteuerungsreform.* Heidelberg, 1870.

Stein affirmed that "the taxation of income in whatever form it may appear is the fiscal field of our present and future; just as surely as it was impossible in former centuries, so surely will it more and more become the chief tax of the future."[1] Above all, at the beginning of the seventies, men of the first rank, like Held, Knapp, and Conrad, now took the matter up vigorously.[2]

The happy termination of the war with France, with its immense indemnity, had removed all concern of a purely fiscal nature not only from the new empire, but from the separate states, and the way was now clear for a discussion of tax reform from the point of view of equality and social justice. In this movement the young and brilliant Professor Adolf Held took a leading part, and his book on the income tax, published in 1872, was a thoroughgoing study of the fundamental principles of taxation, from the new standpoint, with special reference to the German conditions.[3] Held dissected the existing situation with a merciless knife, and showed conclusively that there was imperative need not only for the abandonment of the Prussian grist and slaughter tax in the towns, but also for the repeal of the taxes on product, and the substitution of a general income tax in place of the class tax. This income tax, together with carefully chosen indirect taxes, form in his opinion the model revenue system. For Held, like all modern writers, was unalterably opposed to a single income tax, or for that matter, to a single tax of any kind. A similar programme was sketched for the other German states, especially Saxony and Bavaria. His conclusion is worth

[1] "Die Einkommensbesteuerung, möge sie nun in welcher Form immer auftreten, ist das Steuergebiet unserer Gegenwart und Zukunft; so gewiss sie in allen früheren Jahrhunderten ummöglich war, so gewiss wird sie mehr und mehr die Hauptsteuer der Zukunft werden." — *Lehrbuch der Finanzwissenschaft.* Von L. von Stein. Leipzig, 1861, p. 303.

[2] See an article by J. Conrad, in Hildebrand's *Jahrbücher*, 1871, p. 6; and the book of F. Knapp, *Ertragssteuer oder Einkommensteuer.* Leipzig, 1872.

[3] *Die Einkommensteuer. Finanzwissenschaftliche Studien zur Reform der directen Steuern in Deutschland.* Von Dr. Adolf Held. Bonn, 1872.

giving. "In this development and shape we consider the income tax to be the relatively best direct tax. Even though Thiers has recently called the income tax the socialism of taxation, — a dangerously concealed socialism, — we are not disturbed by the objections of this old protectionist and bourgeois economist; for there is a kind of socialism, *i.e.*, the emphasis on the social and political duties of the upper and wealthier classes, which is decidedly necessary if we desire to avoid the really dangerous socialism, that of the Paris Commune."[1]

The newly formed Association for Social Politics (*Verein für Sozialpolitik*) also took up the matter and published in 1873 a series of expert opinions on the subject.[2] Professor Birnbaum, of the university of Leipzig, followed with an interesting work on the applicability of the income tax, especially to Saxon conditions.[3] In this he made a thorough study of the English methods, and of the income tax, which had for some time been in existence in the free states of Hamburg and Bremen. Birnbaum concluded that the tax on product must give way to the income tax. A study even more favorable to the direct income tax in contrast to what he called the semi-produce tax system of the English income tax (*ertragsteuerähnliche Einkommensteuer*) was made by Dr. Glattstern.[4] Finally, Professor Neumann, of Freiburg, wrote two masterly works on the income tax, one of which dealt especially with the situation in Baden, where conditions were not quite so favorable as in Prussia to a conversion of the taxes on product into an income tax.[5]

[1] Held, *op. cit.*, p. 329.

[2] *Die Personalbesteuerung. Schriften des Vereins für Sozialpolitik. Gutachten* von E. Nasse, A. Held, J. Gensel, von Wintzingerode, und C. Rössler. Leipzig, 1873. An independent work was that of Weygold, *Zur Steuerreformfrage in Preussen mit besonderer Rücksicht auf die Ausführbarkeit einer allgemeinen Einkommensteuer*, Leipzig, 1872.

[3] *Ueber die Anwendbarkeit der Einkommensteuer und Steuerreformen überhaupt.* Von Dr. R. Birnbaum. Leipzig, 1873.

[4] *Die Steuer vom Einkommen. Eine finanzwissenschaftliche Studie.* Von Dr. S. Glattstern. Leipzig, 1876.

[5] Fr. J. Neumann, *Die Progressive Einkommensteuer im Staats- und Gemeinde-Haushalt.* Leipzig, 1874; and the same author's *Ertragsteuern oder Persönliche*

§ 4. *The Reforms in the Seventies and Eighties*

As usual, however, the statesmen lagged behind scientific opinion. The efforts of Von der Heydt in 1869 and of Camphausen in 1871 to reform the Prussian system, met with failure; but in 1873, after a very lively discussion, a decided step in advance was taken. The grist and slaughter tax was abolished as a state impost, and the class tax was now applied to the towns as well as the country. The class tax, although still so called, really became an income tax,[1] because of the provision in the new law that the tax was to be levied "on the basis of the assessed value of the annual income."[2] As a matter of fact, however, this practice had been followed since 1867. For at that date instructions had been issued to take the "presumed income" as "not indeed the only factor in the assessment, but nevertheless the principal one." The line of division between the class- and the classified-income tax in the law of 1873 remained as before, at 1000 thalers — or now, according to the new German monetary unit, 3000 marks ($750); but a complete exemption was introduced for the so-called minimum of subsistence, which was fixed at 420 marks. With this exception the old twelve classes were still retained, with taxes varying from three to seventy-two marks, so that the rate in the lowest income in each class ranged from five-sevenths of one per cent to two and two-thirds per cent, thus providing for a system of degressive taxation.

The income tax was still so calculated that the rate rose to three per cent on the smallest income in each grade, and the intervals were reduced, thus increasing the number of grades. The upper limit, moreover, was entirely

Steuern vom Einkommen und Vermögen? Ein Wort zur Steuerreform. Freiburg i. Br., 1876.

[1] Law of May 25, 1873. The law itself will be found in Hirth's *Annalen des Deutschen Reichs*, 1874, as well as in the *Zeitschrift des Preussischen Statistischen Bureaus*, vol. xv (1875). *Cf.* A. Held, "Die neuen Preussischen Steuergesetze," in Conrad's *Jahrbücher für National-Oekonomie und Statistik*, vol. xx (1873), pp. 369 *et seq.*

[2] Sec. 7.

abolished. Incomes were arranged in forty grades, up to 780,000 marks; beyond this point the tax increased 1800 marks for every 60,000 marks additional income. Moreover, the two lower classes — *i.e.*, incomes up to 420 marks — were abolished, and the next two lower classes were now to enjoy the old system of abatements and exemptions, which had hitherto been applied only to the class tax.[1]

In the main, however, the old system of official assessment, with its injunctions against any "more searching inquiry" (*tieferes Eindringen*) or inquisitorial procedure continued, so that the tax was only slightly more effective than before. The exemption of the minimum of subsistence was indeed a welcome boon, and the removal of the maximum limit brought the wealthier within the meshes of the law. In 1873, for instance, out of 9,300,000 taxpayers, 5,000,000 paid the lowest, or half-thaler, tax; in 1874, after the new law went into effect, 6,400,000 persons were exempted.[2] But the combination still remained one of disparate taxes, with a more rigorous assessment in the class tax than in the income tax, and with such great frauds in the latter that, according to the calculations of some writers, from one-half to two-thirds of the real income was not reached at all. So unsatisfactory, in fact, was the combination — which had been predicted by Held in 1872, when he said that "easy-going methods of assessment will not be cured by any such half reforms"[3] — that even Wagner, the great admirer of everything Prussian, later on declared that during this period, which was so favorable to tax reform, "unfortunately nothing of any great consequence was attained."[4] Things remained in very much the same state as before, and the only important alterations that were effected during the next two decades were the law of 1881, which reduced the rates in the class tax

[1] *Cf. supra*, pp. 228, 239.

[2] See *Zeitschrift des Preussischen Statistischen Bureaus*, vol. xv (1875).

[3] "Die Gemüthlichkeit der Schätzung wird in allgemeinen durch solche halbe Reformen nicht aufhören." — Held, *op. cit.*, pp. 299–300.

[4] "Leider nichts sehr Erhebliches geleistet worden." Wagner, *Finanzwissenschaft, op. cit.*, 1899, p. 27.

as well as in the five lowest grades of the income tax by one-quarter, and the law of 1883, which abolished the two lowest grades of the class tax (thus bringing the total exemption up to 900 marks), and which slightly reduced the rate, not only in the class tax, but in the two lowest grades of the classified income tax.

The movement, however, which on the whole made such slight progress in Prussia, was more successful elsewhere. The income tax was seriously discussed in the early seventies in Baden, and a bill embodying that principle actually passed the lower house in 1874. Neither there, however, nor in Würtemberg or Bavaria, which had worked out an entirely developed system of taxes on product, were there any immediate results of consequence. The so-called Bavarian income tax imposed in 1856 was, we remember, nothing but a tax on wages and salaries.[1] In a few of the minor states, indeed, the income tax had actually been introduced during the sixties, as in Oldenburg in 1864 and Hesse in 1867, as well as in the free cities of Hamburg in 1866 and Lübeck in 1869. In only one of the important states, however, was a real step in advance taken during the seventies. This was the kingdom of Saxony.

The old Saxon law of 1834, imposing a personal tax,[2] had been amended several times—as in 1845, 1850, and 1858. But this was, we remember, in reality nothing but a part of a conglomerate system of taxes on product, as in the other states.[3] Beginning at the close of the sixties, the discussion became more active, and in 1871 the Saxon government introduced a project for a unification of the taxes on product. This, however, did not satisfy the growing public sentiment, and finally in 1874 the legislature enacted an income tax, to go into force in 1878.[4] The law of 1874, as slightly

[1] *Cf. supra*, page 237.

[2] *Cf. supra*, page 233.

[3] *Cf.* especially Kretschmer, *Die directen Steuern in Sachsen*, 1858, and A. Judeich, *Die Rentensteuer im Königreiche Sachsen*. Dresden, n. d. [1857.]

[4] The text of the law may be found in the volume entitled *Königliche Sächsische Steuergesetze*, 1880, republished every few years. For an account of the dis-

amended in 1878, provided for an income tax as a supplement to the existing land and business taxes. Almost from the beginning, however, a more important place was assigned to the income tax, so that before long it became the principal source of revenue, and the other taxes became supplementary. In 1878, for instance, it was provided that any additional revenue that might be needed, over and above that secured by the nominal rate of the existing direct taxes, should come from the income tax; and in 1886 the important step was taken of relegating half of the land tax to the localities.[1] The consequence was that by 1888 the income tax yielded 17,917,000 marks out of a total of 20,860,000 derived from all direct taxes.

Among the important features of the Saxon law, were the liability to taxation of corporations as well as of individuals, and the fact that the tax applied to individuals instead of households, the wife and the children being separately assessed. The taxpayers were divided into a large number of classes, beginning at 300 marks (below which figure incomes were totally exempt), and were liable to a fixed tax in each class. Beginning with a tax of one-half mark for the lowest classes (300-400 marks), or 0.143 per cent of the minimum income, the rate rose to three per cent when the income attained 5400 marks. These were, however, to be only the normal rates, which could be raised or lowered annually by adding or subtracting a certain percentage, as in England.

The administrative features, however, were the most significant part of the Saxon law. For the first time in any important German state, the principle of obligatory self-valuation was introduced, although indeed revised and controlled

cussion see the articles of Gensel in Hirth's *Annalen des deutschen Reichs*, vols. vii and viii (1874, 1875). The statistics from 1875 to 1894 may be found in an article by Böhmert in the *Zeitschrift des Sächsischen Statistischen Bureaus* for 1894.

[1] Cf. the article entitled "Die Ueberweisung der halben Grundsteuer an die Schulgemeinden im Königreiche Sachsen," *Finanz Archiv*, vol. iv (1887), pp. 1123 *et seq.*

by an assessment of officials with adequate powers.[1] All employers were required to hand in a list of the salaries paid to their employees and officials, and penalties for fraud rose as high as ten times the amount of the tax. These more adequate administrative methods at first aroused much complaint; but the tax proved to be so valuable a fiscal engine, and the administration was gradually so greatly improved, that the complaints diminished in both volume and frequency. Competent investigators showed that there was a progressive movement, and one unbiased writer tells us that "whereas at the beginning the law seemed to work in a demoralizing fashion, it gradually, after a longer application, came, on the contrary, to exert an ethical and educational influence."[2] Thus, while all the difficulties of administration were by no means done away with, the experience of the Saxon income tax law pointed out the path of reform to the other German states.

The Saxon experiment, joined to the growing dissatisfaction with existing methods, as well as the more thorough treatment of the subject by scientific writers, could not fail to produce its results elsewhere. The decade from 1880 to 1890 witnessed a phenomenal activity on the part of the scientific writers. It was during this period that there appeared the elaborate treatises by Schäffle, Wagner, Meyer, Roscher, Vocke, Neumann, and Cohn,[3] as well as numberless

[1] The improvement effected by the law in inducing the landowners and farmers to keep better accounts is adverted to in *Wie hat sich der Landwirt zur progressiven Einkommensteuer zu verhalten*. Von Dr. Hermann Howard (professor of agricultural accounting at the University of Leipzig). Leipzig, 1889.

[2] "Während anfangs das Gesetz demoralisirend zu wirken schien übt es bei längerer practischen Handhabung im Gegentheil einen sittlich erzieherischen Einfluss." Von Bosse, *Die Gemeindebesteuerung in Sachsen*. Leipzig, 1890, p. 42.

[3] Adolph Wagner, *Finanzwissenschaft*. Leipzig, vol. i, 3d ed., 1883; vol. ii, 1880; A. G. F. Schäffle, *Die Grundsätze der Steuerpolitik und die schwebenden Finanzfragen Deutschlands und Oesterreichs*. Tübingen, 1880; R. Meyer, *Die Principien der gerechten Besteuerung*. Berlin, 1884; W. Roscher, *System der Finanzwissenschaft*. Stuttgart, 1886; F. J. Neumann, *Die Steuer und das öffentliche Interesse*. Leipzig, 1887; G. Cohn, *System der Finanzwissenschaft*. Stuttgart, 1889.

smaller contributions, among which are especially to be signalized the monographs of Gneist and Frantz.[1] All of these laid a deep and firm foundation for the income tax, as against the old system of taxes on product. Some less balanced writers reverted to the old idea of a single tax on property, but made no headway against the income-tax movement.[2]

As a consequence of this movement Baden was the next important state to take up the matter. It has been explained[3] how Baden, in 1848, sought to round out her system of taxes on product by a tax on capital. This tax was subjected to various minor changes in 1850 and 1860. As a result of the discussion after the Franco-Prussian War, however, an income tax scheme was introduced and, as mentioned above, even passed the lower house,[4] but failed to become law. In lieu of this, the old capital tax was converted into a tax on the income of capital (*Kapitalrentensteuer*) in 1874, the tax now being measured by the actual yield instead of by the par value of the securities and the yield being capitalized at the rate of five per cent. This was followed by a law of 1876, which combined the old class tax and the business tax into a new impost, known as the tax on earnings or on acquisitions (*Erwerbsteuer*). This tax endeavored to reach the presumed business profits a little more directly, and with less reliance on the system of external signs or indicia than the ordinary business tax; but it also was not very successful. Consequently, after a long and interesting discussion,[5] the final step was taken in 1884 by the enactment of an income tax.

The Baden income tax law of 1884,[6] like that of Saxony of

[1] R. Gneist, *Die preussische Finanzreform.* Berlin, 1881; Constantin Frantz, *Die soziale Steuerreform als die Conditio sine qua non wenn der socialen Revolution vorgebeugt werden soll.* Mainz, 1881.

[2] *Cf.* J. G. Kellermann, *Das Besitzsteuersystem, die künftige, einzige, direkte Steuerquelle aller Rechtsstaaten.* 1889.

[3] *Supra*, page 236.

[4] *Supra*, page 245.

[5] A most valuable part in this discussion was taken by Professor Neumann, in various works, some of which have been mentioned above, page 242.

[6] For the text of the law see Philippovich, *op. cit.*

the preceding decade, applied to associations and corporations as well as to individuals;[1] but unlike that of Saxony it provided for an avoidance of double taxation by making corporations liable only on their incomes over three per cent, that amount of income being presumed to be reached in the hands of the individual security holder. The tax was assessed on the individual except that the head of the family was liable for the entire family income whenever he had the right to dispose of it. Incomes under 500 marks were exempt. In order to retain the same nominal rate of taxation —2½ per cent —with an actual degressive tax (a lower rate on the small incomes), a complicated system, known as taxable valuations (*Steueranschläge*) was introduced, whereby various grades of income were taken up in the tax list at different figures; *e.g.*, 500 marks at 125, 2000 marks at 750, and so on, until incomes were assessed at their full value when they reached the figure of 30,000 marks. The administrative machinery rested, as in Saxony, on the principle of declaration or self-valuation, combined with a careful supervisory official assessment.

The old taxes on product, like the land and building tax and the capital tax, were retained, but the earnings tax (*Erwerbsteuer*) of 1874 was now limited to profits derived from capital actually invested in business. The consequence was that although the income tax was nominally put side by side with the old produce taxes, in practice the system meant a general income tax, with a differentiation between funded and unfunded incomes. For incomes in general were now reached by the income tax, while additional taxes at various rates were imposed on incomes derived from property, whether consisting of land, of business capital, or of securities.

The adoption of the income tax in Saxony and Baden was followed by its introduction in a few of the smaller states, like Saxe-Weimar in 1883 and Anhalt in 1886. The general discussion which ensued did not fail to affect public sentiment in Prussia, which was now lagging far behind some of her

[1] In 1892 corporations and associations were exempted from the tax.

sister commonwealths. The Prussian government finally took up the matter with great energy, and in the early nineties, under the ministry of Dr. Miquel, succeeded in enacting a series of laws which put Prussia as far in the lead as she had hitherto been in the rear.

§ 5. *The Prussian Income Tax of 1891*

The great Prussian reforms of the nineties consisted of four parts: the reconstruction of the business tax, the introduction of a general income tax, the enactment of a supplementary property tax, and the remodelling of local taxation.[1]

The income tax law of 1891 abolished the class tax but retained the dividing line of 3000 marks as the one beyond which the taxpayers were required to declare their income. Several other features of the class tax, primarily of an administrative nature, were likewise retained, as we shall see. The income tax was now made a general tax.[2] The chief provisions may be discussed under four heads: first, to whom does the tax apply? second, what is taxable? third, what are the rates? and fourth, how is the tax assessed and collected? As the law of 1891 is, with a few modifications, still in force we shall speak of its provisions in the present tense.

The law applies to certain specially designated associations, including ordinary corporations, as well as to individuals and it follows the Baden principle in that corporate

[1] For a general account, especially of the last two phases of the reform, see Seligman, *Essays in Taxation*, chap. 10, part iv.

[2] *Einkommensteuergesetz v. 24 Juni, 1891.* The law has been frequently reprinted with annotations. A good commentary is that of Kolisch, 1893. The best and fullest work is the *Commentar zum Einkommensteuergesetz*, by B. Fuisting, which forms the first volume of his *Die Preussischen Direkten Steuern*. The 7th edition (1907) is a volume of 993 pages and gives the text of the law of 1891 together with the amendments of 1906 followed in each section by explanations, judicial decisions, and comments. A pocket edition is also published every few years, the most recent being that of 1910. An English translation of the law will be found in the Blue Book *Reports respecting Graduated Income Taxes in Foreign States*. Misc., no. 2, 1905. Cd. 2587.

incomes are taxed only on the excess over three and one-half per cent. All Prussians are subject to the tax except those who, without having any domicile at home, have lived abroad for more than two years, as well as those who are exempt according to the imperial law regulating the subject of double taxation, to which reference will be made later. The law also applies to other Germans residing in Prussia as well as to foreigners who reside in Prussia for business purposes or, if there for other reasons, who are resident for more than one year. Finally, the law applies to any one who derives an income from Prussian real estate, industry, or trade or from Prussian salaries or pensions. Members of the royal family and of the former royal families of Hanover, Kurhessen, and Nassau are exempt.

Coming next to a consideration of what is taxable, income is declared to consist of the annual net receipts from the four categories of capital, real estate, trade and industry, and lucrative occupations. Extraordinary receipts from inheritance, gifts, life-insurance policies, the sale of real estate (if not carried on as a business or for purposes of speculation), and similar receipts (*ähnliche Erwerbungen*) are not regarded as income, but are treated as accessions to capital. Detailed provisions are laid down as to what deductions are to be made from gross receipts in order to arrive at the net receipts or taxable income. Revenues and expenses are divided into fixed and uncertain (*feststehende und unbestimmte*); in the former case the income for the year is taken, in the latter the average for the last three years. The taxable income is still the family income, *i.e.*, it includes the income of the wife (except when she lives apart from her husband), and of the children, unless they have an independent income which is not at the disposal of the father.

In the third place, considerable changes were made in the classification and rates. Incomes below 900 marks are, as before, exempt, but they are then arranged in different stages, with a fixed tax in each. Incomes from 900 to 1050 marks pay 6 marks (0.66 to 0.57 %), and the scale rises in twenty-six classes until incomes from 9500 to 10,500 marks pay 300 marks (3.15 % to 2.85 %, or 3 % of the mean income). Then the grades rise by 1000 marks to 30,500 marks, by 1500 marks to 32,000 marks, and by 2000 marks to 100,000 marks, at which figure the normal rate of four per cent is applied. Altogether there are now seventy-five grades, whereas in the old classified income tax there were only twenty-seven. Moreover, the normal rate of the higher incomes is now four per cent as against the old three per cent.[1] The rates for limited-liability companies were made slightly higher in the lower grades.

The system of abatements was now also extended. The general provisions of the old laws of 1851 and 1873 were retained, permitting abatements for children and for special reasons which diminish the taxpayer's ability to pay, like illness, accident, indebtedness, and extraordinary outlays for the education or living expenses of the family. But in the case of children the abatements from the taxable income in all cases where the income did not exceed 3000 marks was now definitely fixed at fifty marks for every child under fourteen. In case this should not result in an actually lower tax, it is provided that if there are three or more children the taxpayer should be moved down one grade. Finally, in the case of the special reasons mentioned above, diminishing the ability of the taxpayer, the permissible abatement now consists of a reduction of three grades provided the income does not exceed 9500 marks. This was a substantial enlargement of the system.

Most important, however, are the new administrative provisions regulating the assessment and collection of the tax. In the first place the local officials are required to make a careful annual list of all persons presumably subject to the law. In the next place is to be noted the introduction of the principle of compulsory declaration of income

[1] For a complete table of these income-tax rates, see Seligman, *Progressive Taxation*, 2d ed., 1908, p. 48; and Kennan, *Income Taxation*, Milwaukee, 1910, p. 94.

by the taxpayer. The old free and easy system which, as we know, had by express legislation and administrative provision sedulously avoided any minute inquiry into the conditions of the individual's position, had made the tax, especially in the upper grades, very much of a farce. As a high Prussian official himself tells us: "The laws in the German states were in the highest degree defective. Where, as in Prussia, the assessment was made under the legal prohibition of any 'more searching' or 'intrusive inquiry' into the income or property conditions, the ascertainment of the real income was entirely out of the question. The complete break-up of the income tax was the necessary result. The tax was in the highest degree arbitrary and unequal."[1] Practically no one was correctly assessed except the recipients of fixed wages or salaries, and in particular the owners of intangible property were scarcely reached at all. Another author, who wrote just before the reform of the early nineties, went so far as to pronounce the income tax a "lie and cheat system,"[2] and to confirm the prediction of Kühne in 1851 on the floor of the house, that the tax would become a very caricature of an income tax.[3]

It was but natural, therefore, that the question of compulsory declaration should be in the forefront of the discussion. It was, in fact, the point around which most of the objections to the bill crystallized. The way, however, had been prepared by scientific writers who, like Neumann, had stated that "in such matters nothing can be accomplished by kid gloves,"[4] and by special works devoted to this single topic, one of which, by Henrich, appeared at the close of the eighties, and ran through several editions.[5] The controlling

[1] *Die Einkommensbesteuerung der Zukunft in Anknüpfung an das Preussische Einkommensteuer-Gesetz.* Von B. Fuisting. Berlin, 1903, p. 1.

[2] "Ein Lug- und Trug-system" — *Die Reform der Directen Steuern, insbesondere die Einführung der Selbsteinschätzung in Preussen. Ein Mahnwort an die Preussischen Landtagswähler.* Von L. Henrich, 2d ed., Berlin, 1889, p. 58.

[3] *Ibid.*, p. 49.

[4] Neumann, *Die Progressive Einkommensteuer.* 1874, p. 191.

[5] See *op. cit.*, above.

consideration, however, was the virtual breakdown of the old system. If any success at all was to be achieved by the new law, entirely different administrative methods were universally conceded to be necessary. These new methods were secured by a series of elaborate provisions.

Every one with an income of over 3000 marks is now compelled to hand in, within two weeks, a declaration in writing of his income, classified into the four categories mentioned above. The declaration is to be made "to the best of his ability,"[1] but without the use of oaths. In the case of delay the taxpayer loses his right of appeal and is, moreover, subject to a penalty of five per cent. In case of further delay — after a second notice — an additional penalty of twenty-five per cent is imposed. Refusal to make a return entails a fine, and in case of false returns the penalty rises to ten times the amount of the tax. The declaration is then submitted to the scrutiny of an assessment commission (*Veranlagungs-kommission*), which replaces the valuation commission (*Einschätzungs-kommission*) of the old law. The majority of the assessment commission are elected, while the minority (including, however, the chairman) are appointed by the government. The commission is directed to subject the taxpayer's declaration to a precise (*genauen*) and careful (*sorgfältigen*) examination. In case of any doubt the commission may summon the taxpayer and other witnesses and question them. If still dissatisfied, it may proceed to make its own assessment, using the taxpayer's declaration, if any, as a help. Appeal is permitted to a special commission (*Berufungs-kommission*), one of which exists in every governmental district (*Regierungsbezirk*). This appeal commission is composed of members partly appointed by the government, partly elected. A second and final appeal is permitted in certain cases, to the Supreme Administrative Court (*Oberverwaltungsgericht*). All officials connected with the law are pledged to secrecy, and a disclosure of any detail that has come to their notice

[1] "Nach bestem Wissen und Gewissen."

is punishable with fifteen hundred marks' fine and three months' imprisonment.

In the case of the smaller taxpayers — those up to 3000 marks — no declaration is nominally required, and an additional administrative body known as the "Preliminary Valuation Commission" (*Voreinschätzungs-kommission*) is interposed. This commission, also composed partly of appointed and partly of elected members, is presided over by the village head or appointed official. It examines and amends the list of taxables prepared by the local officials, and transmits it, with corrections, to the head of the ordinary assessment commission for review and decision. The procedure in this case is the same as in the other. The new measure thus represents a genuine income tax, with administrative machinery that must be characterized as entirely adequate.

In the discussion of the income tax bill the propriety of differentiating the tax was recognized on all sides. But it was not thought wise to attempt this through a direct variation of the rate. In the government project it was proposed to do precisely what Gladstone did in 1853, namely, to leave the rate of the income tax uniform, and to supplement it by a direct inheritance tax. In this way funded income would be reached twice, once by the income tax, and again by the inheritance tax. This project, however, failed of adoption. In lieu thereof Dr. Miquel two years later introduced and secured the passage of a bill embodying a scheme up to that time entirely unknown in Germany, but which had been applied the year before by Pierson, in Holland.[1] This consisted of an additional direct property tax. The scheme was approved by the legislature, which in 1893 passed a law providing for a property tax, under the name of the supplementary tax, at the rate of one-half of one per mill on all property.[2]

[1] For a full description of the Dutch scheme see Seligman, *Essays in Taxation.* 5th ed., 1905, pp. 322–330.

[2] *Ergänzungs-Steuergesetz* of July 14, 1893. A good account of this will be found in J. Jastrow, "Die Vermögenssteuer und ihre Einfügung in das Preussische Steuersystem." Conrad's *Jahrbücher*, Dritte Folge, vol. 59 (1892), pp. 161–218.

Estimating ordinary interest rates at five per cent, a tax of one-half mill on property is equivalent to a tax of one per cent on income. The practical result, therefore, is to tax incomes derived from property one per cent more than incomes derived from labor; thus securing the differentiation between earned and unearned incomes. The supplementary property tax is applicable only to individuals and not, like the income tax, to corporations. It is arranged in grades, so that the one-half per mill rate applies only to the lowest figure in each class.[1] Exemption is accorded to all property of less than 6000 marks; to all persons whose income does not exceed 900 marks, provided their property does not exceed 20,000 marks; and to women wage earners and minor orphans, whose income does not exceed 1200 marks and whose property does not exceed 20,000 marks. The administrative procedure is very much the same in the income tax, except that no declarations are required, the income tax returns in general sufficing for the purpose. Although the rate is fixed at one-half a mill, the tax is known as a contingent tax (*Contingentirungssteuer*), *i.e.*, one where the expected yield is estimated at a definite figure, and where, in case the actual yield exceeds or falls short of the estimate, a slight change in the rate is permitted. The "contingent" was fixed at thirty-five million marks, but the actual yield in 1895–1896 was only about thirty-one millions, so that the rate was raised to 5.2 per mill.

The new income tax proved unexpectedly successful. The yield, irrespective of the tax on corporations, jumped the very first year from seventy-nine and one-half million marks to

	Property			Tax	
[1] Thus	6000 to 8000	marks	pay	3	marks
	10,000 to 12,000	"	pay	5	"
	20,000 to 22,000	"	pay	10	"
	40,000 to 44,000	"	pay	20	"
	60,000 to 70,000	"	pay	30	"

From 70,000 to 200,000 marks the tax increases 5 marks for each 10,000. Above 200,000 marks the tax increases 10 marks for each 20,000.

almost one hundred and fifteen millions. This fact, coupled with the additional revenue from the new property tax and with the great and growing surplus of the state railway system, made possible the final reform of the finances.

The income tax of 1891 was designed, in the first instance, to round out the existing taxes on product, that is, the land tax, the buildings tax, and the business tax, as well as the old tax on mines. The business tax, moreover, had been reformed in the same year, 1891,[1] and use was made of the new income tax returns to check up the estimated business profits. It could not be denied, however, that this combination of produce and of income taxes was illogical, and that it resulted in different kinds of double taxation. Miquel, in the discussion of 1891, had already expressed the hope that it might be possible for the general state government to secure enough revenues from other sources to enable it to do away with the entire system of taxes on product or, at all events, to relegate them to the local divisions. In 1893, after the unexpectedly great yield of the income tax, the realization of this hope became possible and, as a consequence, all the existing taxes on produce were discontinued as state taxes. At the same time the entire system of local revenues was reformed. Both laws[2] were to go into effect in 1895.

The local finance law contained an important feature affecting the income tax, which needs special mention. The local revenues, so far as direct taxes are concerned, were henceforth to be raised from the three chief taxes on product — land, buildings, and business taxes — together with supplements to the state income tax. The three produce taxes, although no longer utilized for state purposes, were still to be assessed by state officials, and it was directed that for every increase in the rate of the income tax, there must

[1] For a good account in English of this law, see Hill, "The Prussian Business Tax," *Quarterly Journal of Economics*, vol. viii (1893), pp. 71 *et seq.*

[2] *Preussisches Kommunalabgabengesetz* and *Gesetz wegen Aufhebung der Direkten Staatssteuern.* These two laws will be found in the *Finanz Archiv*, vol. x (1893), pp. 318 *et seq.*, and pp. 795 *et seq.*

be at least a similar increase (but at most not more than one-half as much again) in the rate of the taxes on product. If the taxes on product, however, are augmented so as to reach one hundred and fifty per cent of the old rates, further increases are permitted at the rate of two per cent in the income tax for each one per cent in the taxes on product, until the latter reach two hundred per cent of the old rate. Any further increase of the rate of the taxes on product, and any increase of the income tax rate beyond double the original rate can be permitted only in exceptional instances by governmental sanction. As this has sometimes been permitted, however, it means that the state income tax of four per cent is supplemented by a local tax which varies all the way from nothing to over eight per cent, making the total income tax payable by individuals reach, in some cases, twelve per cent. If we add the supplementary property tax (which can not be increased by local additions), we have an income tax which in some cases may amount to over thirteen per cent. Finally, it must be noted that for local purposes the income tax may be assessed on corporations without deducting the three and one-half per cent income, and that the minimum of subsistence, fixed at 900 marks in the general law, may be reduced to 450 marks. In 1895–1896, there were no towns of over 10,000 population which made no addition at all to the income tax, while 60 added from 1 to 100 per cent, 82 from 100 to 150 per cent, 38 from 150 to 200 per cent, and 22 over 200 per cent.

§ 6. *The Spread of the Movement to the Other German States*

The adoption of the Prussian reforms gave the signal for a great movement throughout Germany. Even though Saxony, Baden, and a few minor states, as we have seen, had preceded Prussia in the introduction of an income tax proper, the administrative features had nowhere been worked out so carefully; and neither in these states nor anywhere else, had the other features of the Prussian system, namely the supplementary property tax, the abolition of the state produce taxes, and the reform of the local tax system been introduced. But now, toward the end of the nineteenth century and especially during the first decade of the twentieth century, the phenomenal success of the Prussian system produced its effect upon one after another of the German states.

In Saxony, where, as we know, the income tax had become the chief tax in 1878 and where half the yield of the only remaining tax on product, the land tax, had been relegated to the rural districts, the income tax was modified in 1900 on Prussian lines, and in 1902 a supplementary property tax was added.[1] At first, however, this did not include landed property, for all efforts to abolish the remainder of the land tax as a source of state revenue proved unsuccessful. In 1906, however, the property tax was extended so as to include all property, and the land tax — the only existing survivor of the earlier taxes on produce — now became of entirely subordinate importance.

In Baden, after some minor alterations in 1892, 1894, and 1900, all the taxes on produce were definitely abolished in 1906, and converted into a supplementary property tax.[2] In Hesse, where the income tax, as we know, dates from 1869, the reform of 1899 followed the Prussian lines very closely, in that it developed the income tax and added to it a supplementary tax, while at the same time relegating the tax on product to the localities.[3] In Würtemburg, where Professor

[1] See, in general, Von Nostitz, *Grundzüge der Staatssteuern im Königreich Sachsen*. Jena, 1903; Hoffmann, *Die direkten Staatssteuern im Königreich Sachsen*. Leipzig, 1906.

[2] See Buchenberger, *Finanzpolitik und Staatshaushalt im Grossherzogtum Baden*, 1850–1900. Heidelberg, 1902; Voigtel, *Die direkten Staats- und Gemeindesteuern im Groszherzogtum Baden*. Jena, 1903; and von Zwiedineck-Südenhorst, "Der Abschluss der badischen Steuerreform durch das Vermögenssteueuergesetz vom 28 September, 1906," in *Finanz Archiv*, vol. xxiv (1907), pp. 531–595.

[3] Glässing, "Die Neugestaltung der direkten Staatsbesteuerung im Grossherzogtum Hessen," *Finanz Archiv*, vol. xvii (1900), pp. 178–360.

Neumann was the great protagonist of the newer system,[1] the reform was not effected until 1903, when the income tax was introduced. It was supplemented, not by a property tax as in Prussia, but by a combination of the old although reformed taxes on product, namely, the land, house, business, and capital taxes. These were all reduced in rate and were henceforth to serve the purpose of taxing funded incomes higher than labor incomes.[2]

Of all the states which until recently proved themselves recalcitrant in the introduction of the income tax, the most important is Bavaria. In that state, where, as explained above,[3] the so-called special income tax had been, since 1856, nothing but a tax on wages, the reforms of 1899 were limited to an improvement of the old taxes on product, especially the business tax and the capital tax. A renewed agitation looking toward the introduction of a true income tax was, however, initiated in 1908, and came to a successful culmination in 1910.[4] An income tax is still lacking in the two Mecklenburgs, where the semi-mediæval conditions are so strong in the political as well as in the economic sphere, and in Alsace-Lorraine, where the example of the French tax system was naturally of great weight. In Alsace-Lorraine, however, important changes were effected toward the close of the century, consisting of a modification of the old French methods in the direction of the German system of taxes on product. Thus in 1895 there was established a new house tax; in 1896, an improved business tax; and in 1901 a more modern land tax, as well as a tax on the earnings of capital

[1] See esp. Neumann, *Die persönlichen Steuern vom Einkommen*, etc. Tübingen, 1896. Neumann attempts in this work, not however with complete success, to explain the fact that personal taxes seem to succeed better in the northern German states, and taxes on produce in the southern. *Cf.* pp. 3–8.

[2] See Eichmann, "Die Württembergische Steuerreform" in *Hirth's Annalen des Deutschen Reichs*, 1904; and Pistorius, "Die Württembergische Steuerreform," *Finanz Archiv*, vol. xxi (1904), pp. 1–114.

[3] *Supra*, page 237.

[4] *Cf.* E. Steinitzer, *Die Entwickelung zur Einkommensteuer in Bayern.* Munich, 1909; and *Finanz Archiv*, vol. xxix (1912), pp. 341–370.

and on wages and salaries. This is as far as the government dared go.[1]

In all the smaller German states, with the exceptions noted, the Prussian system has either been adopted, or is in process of being adopted.[2] The general income tax is found in all the twenty-five states except the two Mecklenburgs (and Alsace-Lorraine), while the supplementary property tax is found in Prussia, Saxony, Hesse, Oldenburg, Brunswick, Sachsen-Weimar, Sachsen-Meiningen, Sachsen-Coburg-Gotha, Reuss (old line), and Schaumburg-Lippe. The scheme of the income tax is everywhere similar. The exemptions range from 300 to 900 marks; the rate of the tax is degressive,[3] reaching the normal figure of four or, in some states, five per cent, on the higher incomes, and with abatements and administrative procedure akin to those in Prussia.

§ 7. *Criticisms and Amendments, 1900–1909*

Although the Prussian tax proved to be so remarkable a success from the treasury point of view, several not unimportant defects disclosed themselves in the course of the next decade, not only in the administrative, but in the substantive, part of the law. There existed, from the very beginning in

1 An excellent account in French of the reform of the system in Alsace-Lorraine is *L'Impôt sur le Revenu en Alsace-Lorraine. Histoire d'une Réforme des Contributions Directes.* Par Marcel Rouffie et Fernand Mommeja. Paris, 1910. A good account in German is that of J. Kloos, *Die Entwickelung der direkten Steuern in Elsass-Lothringen.* Leipzig, 1908. *Cf.* also the article by Ludwig Gieseke, "Die Entwickelung der direkten Steuern in Elsass-Lothringen von 1872 bis 1905," *Finanz Archiv*, vol. 23 (1906), pp. 558 *et seq.*

2 A detailed account — legislative and statistical — of the tax system of each of the German states will be found in the *Denkschriftenband zur Begründung des Entwurfs eines Gesetzes betreffend Äenderungen im Finanzwesen*, published by the German Imperial Treasury (*Reichsschatzamt*). Berlin, 1908. See especially the highly useful comparative tables on pp. 358–431. In the *Appendix* to this chapter will be found some of the important statistics as to the income tax.

3 The detailed scale for the larger states will be found in Seligman, *Progressive Taxation.* 2d ed., 1908, pp. 48–51; and Kennan, *Income Taxation*, 1910, chap. vii.

1892, in wide circles of the taxpayers, a discontent which manifested itself in numerous attacks in the public press, heated discussions in the legislature, and an inordinate mass of appeals against the assessments. One of the foremost German experts tells us that the earlier years were marked by veritable "enormities" in the execution of the law.[1] While this was no doubt in part due to the newness of the law, the fact remains that even after the lapse of a decade the dissatisfaction continued and was expressed in similar terms. The conclusion is inevitable that the causes are to be sought, in part at least, in the law itself as well as in the manner of its execution. In the fifteen years that elapsed from the passage of the law to its amendment in 1906, the yield of the income tax rose from one hundred and twenty-five million to two hundred and ten million marks, whereas the population increased only from thirty to thirty-seven and one-quarter millions. This was of course due primarily to the fact that wealth was increasing faster than population. But it was also in part due to more efficient administrative methods. The success from the fiscal point of view, however, was accompanied by an undue pressure on the taxpayer, of which we have abundant testimony.

The Prussian law has been sharply criticised by foreign observers, especially by the French investigators. Thus Paul Deschanel is never weary of speaking of the "inquisitorial processes of this country which has been hierarchised and militarized to the extreme, and in which, to adopt Bismarck's term, every one is born in a uniform."[2] Reinach, in a discussion in the French chamber of deputies in 1908, stated that in Prussia "they have been obliged to resort to an intolerable espionage, and a degrading system of informers; they interrogate caterers, neighbors, servants, children; they keep account of the dinners that are given and of the cigars

[1] See p. 272 of the work of Fuisting, quoted below.

[2] "Les procédés inquisitoriaux de ce pays hiérarchisé et militarisé à outrance, dans lequel suivant le mot de M. de Bismarck chacun naît avec un uniforme." — Quoted in Gaston-Gros, *L'Impôt sur le Revenu*. Paris, 1907, p. 291.

that are offered to the guests."[1] The French Minister of Finance, M. Caillaux, used some rather hard words about the German methods.[2] In Belgium, a recent author has presented in great detail samples of the questions that are put to different kinds of taxpayers, when they have to submit to their oral examination. These are shown to enter into the very minutiæ of daily existence.[3] Some of them are worthy of repetition.

A tradesman was asked, "Don't you use a telephone for your private use — that is, apart from business purposes?" He answered "No." But when it was discovered that he had ordered a box at the theatre by telephone, he was punished by an additional assessment. A financial magnate was asked about his securities: "How many did you sell last year? On what day and at what exchange did you sell them? What is the price of each? What is the name of each company in which you own securities? Who are your associates? How much do you save every year? What do you do with it? How do you explain the increase of income this year? Is it derived from capital? If so, where did the capital come from? Was it a gift? Who gave it to you? Is it the result of a profitable sale? If so, tell us all about it." A house owner was asked: "Do you intend to raise the rents of the tenants? Have you invested the money which you got from selling some furniture last year?" A farmer was asked: "How many cows have you got? How much milk and butter does each one give? How many chickens? How much hay was consumed by your own cattle, and how much did you sell? What is the value of the fruit, vegetables, and other farm produce that you and your family consumed last year? Did the owner from whom you rent your lands really pay a mortgage on his property last

[1] "En Prusse il a fallu en venir à un espionnage intolérable et à une délation dégradante; on interroge les fournisseurs, les voisins, les domestiques, les enfants; on tient compte des diners donnés, des cigares offerts aux invités." — Speech of Feb. 2, 1909, in the *chambre des députés*.

[2] See *infra*, chap. ii, § 9.

[3] Ingenbleek, *L'Impôt sur le Revenu*. Bruxelles, 1908, pp. 224–232.

year? Have you not put the wear and tear of your agricultural machinery too high?" A commercial traveller was asked: "How much do you ordinarily spend in your trips? How much do you spend for amusement? What are your other expenses?"

It is questions like these that led one of the liberal members of the Reichstag, von Eynern, to say that "the country is covered with a perfect system of espionage."[1]

Such comments, however, are not confined to foreigners or to German liberals, from whom it would be easy to multiply criticisms of the law. We shall content ourselves with the published animadversions of a most competent and unbiassed observer, the President of the Royal Administrative Supreme Court of Prussia — Herr Fuisting. In a large volume devoted entirely to this subject,[2] Fuisting discusses in detail the chief defects of the Prussian law.

Among the defects in the substantive part of the law Fuisting mentions: (1) the taxation of corporations in a personal income tax, side by side with the business tax; (2) the inclusion of speculative profits; (3) the failure to define with precision the permissible deductions from gross receipts, in order to reach the real income, more especially with reference to taxes, interest on debts and amortization quotas; (4) the inadequate abatements for the lower classes; (5) the incorrect determination of the income period, which is fixed in some cases at the previous year, in others at the coming year, and in still others at an average of several years; (6) the taxation according to households instead of individuals. Among the defects in administrative procedure are mentioned a great number of details, all of which may be summed up in the accusation that while the interests of the treasury are admira-

[1] "Eine vollständige Spionage über das ganze land verbreitet wird."

[2] *Die Einkommensbesteuerung der Zukunft in Anknüpfung an das Preussische Einkommensteuer-Gesetz.* Von B. Fuisting, Senats-Präsidenten des Königlichen Oberverwaltungsgerichts. Berlin, 1903. The principles underlying his strictures are discussed in a separate volume entitled *Grundzüge der Steuerlehre.* Berlin, 1902.

bly safeguarded, the rights of the taxpayers are sadly neglected, leading to a "one-sided fiscal development," to an "overzealousness of officialdom," to "an exaggerated consideration of purely fiscal interests," and to a "riotous and luxuriant growth of petty bureaucracy."[1] This is seen in the facts that in 1900 over 71 per mill of the assessments were appealed from (in some towns as high as 134 per mill), and that the court of appeals upheld forty-seven per cent of the complaints. This situation, we are told, argues most unhealthy conditions,[2] which have been only partly cured by decisions of the supreme court. In other respects, also, we are informed that "abuses of the worst kind" have developed.[3] So the commission, which was supposed in some measure to protect the taxpayer, has become a mere ornamental addition to the presiding officer, who conducts all the inquisitional examinations himself.[4] The most deplorable fact is, in our critic's opinion, that the officials themselves seem unable to recognize the disadvantages and dangers of the system.[5] They appear to be still impressed with their own capacity to set an exact valuation on everything, and to regard this as a panacea according to the old rule: —

> "Was sich nicht anders finden lässt,
> Das stellt man leicht durch Schätzen fest."[6]

As an actual fact, however, the result is a "complete confusion in the matter of valuation, with a checkered variety and inadequacy of the methods employed."[7] It is true that wil-

[1] The words used are "eine einseitig fiskalische Richtung." — *Op. cit.*, p. 4; "Uebereifer des Beamtenthums," p. 5; "eine übermäszige Berücksichtigung der fiskalischen Interessen," p. 149; "Ueberwuchern des Subaltern-beamtenthums," p. 162. *Cf.* also p. 190.

[2] "Ein höchst ungesunder Zustand." — *Op. cit.*, p. 153.

[3] "Es haben sich Miszstände der schlimmsten Art herausgebildet." — *Op. cit.*, p. 184.

[4] "Blosses Ornament des fiscalischen Vorsitzenden. Eine Form ohne Inhalt." — *Op. cit.*, p. 176.

[5] *Op. cit.*, p. 189.

[6] *Op. cit.*, p. 211.

[7] "Der ganze Wirrwarr im Schätzungswesen mit der Buntscheckigkeit und Unvollkommenheit der angewandten Methoden sowie der Unrichtigkeit und Ungleichmäszigkeit ihrer Ergebnisse." — *Op. cit.*, p. 247.

ful opposition to the law has gradually diminished. We are told that "the cases of actual fraud are certainly not sporadic, but still they are not frequent."[1] This result is purchased at a great cost, however. The distinguished jurist concludes that if, after more than a decade, despite the determined efforts of the courts, the procedure still suffers from so many and such important defects, nothing can be hoped for from the bureaucracy itself, and it becomes necessary to define by law the rights as well as the duties of the taxpayers.

So serious an indictment of the system, coming from such a source, could not well be ignored. Consequently, after a discussion which was resumed again and again, some at least of the weaknesses of the law were removed by the amendatory act of 1906.[2]

The first amendment in the law of 1906 concerned the inclusion of limited-liability companies. In the original act, the so-called "open commercial associations" (*offene Handelsgesellschaften*), i.e., the small semi-private associations, had been exempt from taxation (although the individual owners naturally remained taxable), while ordinary stock corporations were taxed on the surplus income over three and one-half per cent. In the interval, however, these new limited-liability companies had undergone a great development, so that their capital now represented over one and one-half billions of marks, as compared with six billions invested in stock corporations. After much discussion, these new limited-liability companies were, as a compromise, declared subject to taxation at the full rate (not simply on the surplus over three and one-half per cent), but the shareholders were exempted. As a compensation for this, a slightly increased scale of taxation was adopted for the limited-liability companies.[3] Scientific,

[1] *Op. cit.*, p. 138.

[2] Law of June 19, 1906. This is discussed by Maatz, "Die Novelle zum preussischen Einkommensteuer- und Ergänzungs-steuergesetz" in *Finanz Archiv*, vol. xxiii (1906), pp. 556 *et seq.*

[3] For this scale, see Seligman, *Progressive Taxation*. 2d ed., 1908, p. 49.

educational, philanthropic, and artistic associations were also exempted, but coöperative consumers' associations were now made liable to the tax, largely because of the prodigious success of the Breslau coöperative, with fourteen million marks turnover and two millions of profit.

In the second place, the ascertainment of actual income through deductions from gross receipts was made more precise by including among the permissible deductions the following items: (1) not only any direct state tax, as in the law of 1891, but also the local taxes on product, at least up to a certain amount, as well as various special assessments; (2) contributions to the compulsory labor-insurance funds; (3) insurance premiums for children; (4) additions to a sinking fund for mortgages. In all these cases except the first, the deductions applied only up to 600 marks; and in the last case only up to one per cent of the indebtedness.

In the third place, the old distinction between fixed and uncertain incomes[1] which had given a great deal of trouble, was abolished. The income for the year just closing is taken as the taxable income in all cases, except in that of associations as well as of individuals engaged in trade, industry, or agriculture where careful bookkeeping is practised. In such cases the average of three years is taken, and the losses of one year may be deducted from the profits of another.

In the fourth place, the character of the tax as one on household income was considerably changed in that only the wife's income is henceforth included with that of the husband. Finally, so far as abatements are concerned, an important innovation was introduced, making the abatement for children applicable to any member of the family (except the wife), dependent on the head of the household — thus including parents and other relatives. Furthermore, the privilege was expanded from 3000 to 6500 marks (the attempt to extend it still further to 9500 marks failed). Finally, not only were fifty marks deducted for each child or other dependent, but the taxpayer is henceforth entitled to a reduction of one grade

[1] See *supra*, p. 251.

in the case of three children and of two grades in the case of five children.

The second part of the amendment related to the administrative procedure. Here several changes were introduced. The scheme requiring employers to submit lists of wages and salaries paid to their employees was adopted, following the custom in Saxony and Austria. The punishment for failure of the individual to hand in his declaration betimes was converted from a loss of his right to appeal into a money penalty of five per cent. The far-reaching privileges of the presiding officers of the assessment commission were materially reduced, and various minor changes were made in the interests of the taxpayer. On the other hand, the right of appeal to the supreme court was entirely taken away from taxpayers with incomes of 3000 marks or less, and the powers of the commission itself in general were, if anything, augmented, so that the practice of detailed inquisitorial questioning and of inspection of the books and papers now received legal sanction. The commission may, as a consequence, now examine the taxpayer and any witnesses that it chooses to summon, and may require him to show his "business books, contracts, receipts, or any other papers which may be of use."[1] If the papers are not deemed satisfactory, the commission may take whatever action it likes.[2] Thus the most far-reaching and arbitrary powers are given to the commission. It is significant of the temper of the German people that in the discussion which preceded the enactment of the law, no one rose to oppose these particular provisions. It cannot be said, therefore, that the real objections of Fuisting have been adequately met.

The most recent change in the Prussian income tax is the general increase of rates effected by the law of 1909. For some years an effort had been made to augment the exceed-

[1] Par. 40. *Cf.* Fuisting, *op. cit.*, p. 367.

[2] The discussion of the legal decisions up to 1909, as to the provisions which led to the amendment, may be found in the article of L. Buck in the *Finanz Archiv*, vol. xxvi (1909), pp. 813 *et seq.*

ingly exiguous salaries of the Prussian officials, and in 1909 provision was made to procure a revenue for this purpose. The final disposition of the matter was to be effected by a general revision of the tax laws, but in the meantime the rates of the income tax were increased for what purported to be only a three-year period. Because of the temporary character of the arrangement, the alterations were inserted not into the income tax law itself, but in the so-called "Cloak" or "Garment" Law (*Mantelgesetz*).[1] The rates were increased for individuals by from five to twenty-five per cent; for limited-liability companies by from seven and a half per cent to forty-five per cent; for stock companies by from ten per cent to fifty per cent. The local additions to income tax, however, were to be made on the old basis.

Advantage was taken of the discussion to effect one important change in the income tax itself. This concerned the subject of abatements. The changes of 1906 which have been mentioned above were found to be inadequate, and accordingly a new law was passed in 1909.[2] This not only extended the privilege of abatements from incomes of 6500 to those of 9500 marks, but increased the abatements themselves. In the case of incomes not exceeding 6500 marks, a reduction of one grade was permitted for two children, or other dependents; of two grades for three or four children or dependents; of three grades for five or six children or dependents; and of an additional grade for every two additional children or dependents. In the case of incomes between 6500 and 9500 marks there was permitted a reduction of one grade for three children or dependents, of two grades for five or six children, and of one additional grade for every two children or dependent members of the family. The other important part of the amendment was the extension of abatements for

[1] Gesetz v. 26. Mai, 1909. For the exact figures, *cf.* the *Finanz Archiv*, vol. xxvi (1909), p. 809. The annual figures as to the yield of the Prussian income tax may be found in *Mittheilungen aus der Verwaltung der direkten Steuern im preussischen Staate. Statistik der preussischen Einkommensteuern.*

[2] Printed in *Finanz Archiv*, vol. xxvi (1909), p. 807.

"exceptional causes" affecting the taxpayer's ability to pay from 9500 to 12,500 marks.

The minor changes in the law were the permission to estimate incomes according to the business rather than the calendar year, and the provision making the income tax law conform to the new and revised imperial act of 1909 regulating the entire subject of double taxation.[1] This law provides that when the trade or industry is carried on in several states, only a proportionate part of the income can be taxed in any one state. The commonwealth laws must all conform to the imperial law.

§ 8. *Conclusion*

If we try to form a conclusion as to the German, and especially the Prussian, income tax, it is evident in the first place that it has become an effective fiscal engine. Step by step, as we have seen, the theory of the law was bettered and the administration was improved; while the opposition of the people, which was at first quite as keen and determined as in England, was slowly overcome, until they became satisfied with the drastic methods introduced toward the end of the nineties. The German administration is admirably efficient, and the public has a well-merited confidence in the officials. Two considerations, however, force themselves upon our mind.

In the first place, the German system of direct assessment does not seem, even from the fiscal point of view, to be as satisfactory as the English system of stoppage at source. As will be seen from the table in the appendix, the income tax yielded in all Germany in 1908, 407 million marks (about 102 million dollars) for state purposes. To this ought be added the proceeds of the supplementary property tax, 62 million marks, making a total of about 117 million dollars. To this might further be added the sums raised for local purposes, which amounted to 301 million marks in localities of over

[1] *Deutsches Doppelsteuergesetz* v. 22 März, 1909. Printed in *Finanz Archiv*, vol. xxvi (1909), p. 369.

10,000 people alone. The total yield of the income tax in all divisions for the whole of Germany was 768 million marks or, including the supplementary property tax, over 830 millions—about 208 million dollars. In view of the fact that the tax does not exist in Bavaria as well as in two of the smaller states, it might be claimed that the German system compares not unfavorably with the English and that, in fact, more revenue is raised by the income tax in Germany than in England. It must be remembered, however, that in the above computation the income tax in Germany includes both local and state taxes, and that the total rate, accordingly, is much higher, rising to as much as twelve or fifteen per cent on the income in some cases; whereas in England the rate is only five or six per cent.[1] Moreover, the exemptions and abatements are very much more limited than in England, so that the yield ought to be proportionately greater. As a matter of fact, however, the yield for state purposes is far smaller than in Great Britain, notwithstanding the population of Great Britain is only about two-thirds that of Germany. The relatively unfavorable results of the German tax are, of course, in part due to the fact that Germany, although it has made such immense strides of recent years, is nevertheless not so wealthy as England, and that the whole scale of incomes is lower. Even allowing for these facts, however, it is impossible to avoid the conclusion that the administrative methods are both more costly and less effective in Germany than in England. As a mere fiscal engine, the German income taxes are inferior to the English.

In the second place, the administrative methods employed in Germany, and especially in Prussia, would be impracticable almost anywhere else. In no other place is the bureaucracy so powerful. Nowhere else are the people so meek in the face of officialdom. In no other country of the world would it be possible to enforce so inquisitorial a procedure as we have

[1] In the *Denkschriftenband*, vol. 1, pp. 788 *et seq.*, will be found a number of elaborate tables calculating the total rate of the income tax in the local divisions of the nine chief states of Germany, arranged according to scales of income.

learned to be customary in Prussia. And even with all these rigorous and stringent methods, it is questionable, to judge from the fiscal results, whether the frauds and evasions are appreciably less than in England.

Taking it all in all, however, the German income tax, which, as in England, has been the slow product of a long evolution, must be pronounced a decided success. It is accepted by the people; it has become indispensable to the government. Its methods of assessment are, on the whole, in conformity with public opinion, the honest taxpayer has but little to fear from even the most rigorous officials, and the tax now constitutes not only an important, but an increasingly important, part of the general tax system.

Note to 2d ed. — An imperial income tax was levied for the first time at the end of 1913 by a law of the same year. The defense-contribution (Wehrbeitrag) is a tax levied once and for all on all property and income. The property tax is levied on all property at a rate which varies from 0.15 % for the first 50,000 marks to 1½ % for sums over 5,000,000 marks. Property of 10,000 marks is exempt; if the income does not exceed 2000 marks, 50,000 marks of property are exempt; if the income does not exceed 4000 marks, 30,000 marks of property are free. When the property does not exceed 100,000 marks, or the income 10,000 marks, the tax is reduced 5 % for the third and every additional minor child. When the property does not exceed 200,000 marks or the income 20,000 marks, the tax is reduced 10 % for the third and every additional son that has performed military duty.

The income tax is levied at a rate which rises from 1 % on incomes to 10,000 marks to 8 % on incomes over 500,000 marks. If the income tax payer has any property, a sum equal to 5 % on the taxable property is deducted from the income. The tax is assessed by the separate states.

In addition to the defense-contribution, which is levied only once, an imperial so-called tax on possessions (Besitzsteuer) is to be levied in 1917 and every three years thereafter. This is a tax on the increment of property, *i.e.*, on the amount by which the value of the property of individuals (not of corporations) at the expiration of the three-year term exceeds its value at the beginning. The discussion of this interesting innovation, however, does not fall within the scope of the present study. See for details *Die Reichsfinanzgesetze vom 3 Juli, 1913*. Von Karl Theodor von Eheberg. Leipzig, 1913.

APPENDIX

Arranged from pp. 38, 572, 575, 576, 724, of the *Denkschriftenband* referred to *supra*, p. 261.

	STATE REVENUES, BUDGET OF 1908						REVENUES OF LOCALITIES OF 10,000 POPULATION, 1907 [1]		
	1	2	3	4	5	6	7	8	9
In marks, 000 omitted except in column 5.	Total Revenue	Total Direct Taxes	Income Tax	Supplementary Property Tax	Income Tax per Head	Per Cent of Total Taxes	Population in 1905, 000 omitted	Total Direct Taxes	Income Tax
Prussia	3,319,535	287,369	240,000	44,000	6.44	70.22	15,148	423,312	244,766
Bavaria	632,191	46,058					1,816	37,584	288
Saxony	387,419	60,595	51,575	4,005	11.44	73.31	2,073	34,595	29,278
Würtemburg	219,224	26,928	18,000		7.82	43.56	571	16,240	5,044
Baden	240,439	24,994	15,600	9,215	7.76	35.90	594	14,467	4,217
Hesse	114,925	14,298	10,860	3,355	8.98	54.37	306	9,644	5,421
Mecklenburg-Schwerin	41,868	3,700					151	1,327	471
Grandduchy Saxony	12,719	3,544	3,104		8.	80.96	125	1,815	1,807
Mecklenburg-Strelitz	4,497	553					23	230	34
Oldenburg	43,942	4,892	2,630	855	5.99	45.	83	1,125	775
Brunswick	27,799	4,743	3,219		6.36	59.08	182	3,890	2,924
Sachsen-Meiningen	9,405	1,982	1,330		4.95	65.44	56	1,238	1,027
Sachsen-Altenburg	5,393	1,766	1,278		6.19	61.78	49	773	649
Sachsen-Coburg-Gotha	6,777	2,045	1,645	205	6 79	71.30	59	1,079	921
Anhalt	14,461	3,226	2,415		7.36	63.93	142	2,272	2,153
Schwarzburg-Sondershausen	3,345	709	534		5.93	70.59	16	303	240
Schwarzburg-Rudolstadt	2,853	707	561		4.76	62.52	12	201	190
Waldeck	1,389	396	252		4.27	61.62			
Reuss, old line	1,253	639	548		7 77	80.96	23	525	
Reuss, new line	2,638	1,260	1,100		7.61	84.11	46	946	
Schaumburg-Lippe	974	292	235	54	5.22	72.62			
Lippe	3,467	1,139	720		4.95	60.14	13	169	157
Lubeck	12,857	3,749	2,910		27.49	60.96			
Bremen	43,224	15,267	10,677		40.53	59.65	23	542	106
Hamburg	162,902	57,690	38,480		43.98	57.56	23	272	164
Alsace-Lorraine	66,267	15,690					472	4,649	59
Total	5,381,773	584,090	407,586	62,425	6.72	52.91	22,017	557,200	300,711, or 53.98% of the direct taxes

[1] About three-fourths of the entire local revenue. Out of a total revenue of all local divisions in the empire of 3138 millions of marks, the localities of over 10,000 population had a revenue of 2393 millions.

CHAPTER II

The Income Tax in France

Preliminary

The fiscal work of the Revolution consisted in substituting for the personal taxes of the *ancien régime* a system of so-called real taxes, or taxes on product. The abuses, inequalities, and privileges connected with the old methods had been so potent a cause of the Revolution that the very first step was to make a clean sweep of the entire existing system. It was hoped at first, somewhat under the influence of the Physiocratic doctrines, to defray all the public expenditures by a new system of direct taxes alone; but this proved to be impossible, and one by one the indirect taxes, in a modified and improved form indeed and largely denuded of their old abuses, were gradually reintroduced. So far, however, as the direct taxes were concerned, it was universally conceded that all excuse for inquisition and for arbitrariness must be avoided; and as a consequence a system of taxation was elaborated, based primarily on the thing to be taxed and not on the person of the taxpayer.

The system of direct taxation which was created in the last decade of the eighteenth century exists with slight modification to-day. It comprises four principal imposts: the real estate tax (*contribution foncière*), including both land and buildings; the business tax (*patentes*); the door and window tax (*contribution des portes et fenêtres*); and the personal and personal property tax (*contribution personnelle et mobilière*).[1]

[1] The fullest account of the details of the French system at present is found in *Traité de l'Impôt Direct*, by Marcel Trélat, in collaboration with Corneille Berget and Dessart. 2 vols., Paris, 1902. A shorter account will be found in *Cours Elémentaire de Science des Finances et de Législation Financière Française*, by Gaston Jèze. Paris, new ed., 1909.

The real estate tax is divided into two parts, the land and the building tax. The land tax is levied on the assumed net produce of the land as determined by a periodical survey and valuation (*cadastre*). Since it is a tax on the produce of the land and not on the income of the owner, mortgage debts are not deducted. The other part of the real estate tax which falls upon buildings is assessed according to their rental value. The business tax is designed to hit the profits of the business, but it is levied only according to outward signs or presumptions, such as the rent paid for the business premises, the number of clerks, the size of the town, *etc.* The door and window tax is imposed on all openings for doors or windows, and is presumed to reach the ability of the individual indirectly in three ways: hitting in some cases the owner of the house, in others the occupant of the dwelling, and in still others the proprietors of the business conducted on the premises. The personal and personal property tax consists of two elements: The first (*contribution personnelle*) is a kind of poll tax, fixed originally at a sum equivalent to three days' wages, and varying since 1830 in different parts of the country, from one and a half to four and a half francs. The other portion of the tax, on movables or personal property (*contribution mobilière*), is a tax on house rent (*loyer d'habitation* according to the *valeur locative*).

These were the original four taxes, all of them, as is seen, being imposed on the thing rather than on the person. With the growth of corporate wealth, and especially with the increased fiscal needs of the government after the reverses of 1870, the system of taxes on product was rounded out by a tax on securities or on corporations (*impôt sur les valeurs mobilières*). This tax was originally imposed in 1872 at the rate of three per cent on the interest, dividends, and other income of corporations and associations, and is advanced by them, being deducted from the sums payable to the security holders. In 1890 the rate was raised to four per cent. The local revenues in France, finally, are raised chiefly by additions (*centimes additionels*) to the four taxes on product.

The French system has been remarkably successful from several points of view. It has yielded immense revenues, and it has been attended by a minimum of annoyance. With the lapse of time, however, the defects of the system have made themselves more and more apparent. Above all, the recent growth of large fortunes and the development of democracy have conspired to set the inevitable shortcomings of a system of taxes on product into greater relief. The land tax was from the very beginning an apportioned, not a percentage, tax, and the methods of assessment were so imperfect that the proportionate amounts paid by landholders in different parts of the country bore less and less relation to the actual yield of the land. Attempts at the equalization (*péréquation*) of the land tax were frequently made, but failed in France, as they have usually failed in the United States. So glaring did the inequality become, that in 1890 the building part of the real estate tax was separated from the land tax proper and was made a personal tax at the rate of 3.2 per cent on the annual rental value. But all efforts to introduce the same system into the land tax have thus far failed, and the land tax, with the *centimes additionels,* has been a crushing burden to the peasant and the small farmer. The business tax has become honeycombed with the grossest kind of inequalities, the presumed profits of many classes of occupation and enterprise standing in very slight relation to the actual income. The door and window tax has been universally recognized to be a tax on light and health, inimical to the best interests of the whole population. The personal tax is open to all the objections of a poll tax, and the tax on movables or house rent presses with special severity on the poorer classes. Taking it all in all, the French system of taxes on product which responded so admirably to the needs of the early nineteenth century, has been outgrown through the development of the last hundred years.

In recent years the pressure to consider, in part at least, the personal conditions of the taxpayer has been so strong as to lead to minor changes in the system. Thus, in the land tax, the law of 1897 exempts the taxpayers where the tax does not amount to more than ten francs, deducts three quarters of the tax when it is from ten to fifteen francs, one-half of the tax when it is from fifteen to twenty francs, and one-quarter of the tax when it is from twenty to twenty-five francs. These abatements are made only to Frenchmen, and under the double condition that this is their total land tax, and that their liability to the personal property tax does not exceed twenty francs. In 1906 there were 5,165,977 such abatements amounting to 14,854,167 francs.[1] In the business tax the very smallest traders and the petty employers are now exempt, while, on the contrary, the law of 1905 subjects the large department stores to a special additional scale of taxation.[2] In the door and window tax, the existence of large tenements in the great cities led, as early as 1852--1855, to the permission, in the case of Paris, Lyons, and Bordeaux, to grade the tax according to the rent paid rather than according to the number of doors and windows. Paris and Bordeaux have availed themselves of this privilege. Moreover, since 1894, model workingmen's tenements are exempted both from the door and window tax and from the house tax.[3] In the case of the personal tax, towns having an *octroi* or municipal customs duty, are permitted to substitute the latter for the former. Finally, in the case of the personal property tax, abatements are now made in the case of large families. Thus the law of 1890 entirely exempts parents of seven children when they are subject to a tax of not more than ten francs; and by the laws of 1900–1904 special abatements are made for large families in the case of taxpayers who pay very small house rents.[4]

These concessions to a growing sentiment have not been adequate, however, and with the growth of the democratic movement there has been a strongly marked tendency toward

[1] Jèze, *Cours Elémentaire de Science des Finances*, p. 752.

[2] Jèze, *op. cit.*, pp. 795, 800.

[3] Jèze, *op. cit.*, p. 820.

[4] For details of this system, see Seligman, *Progressive Taxation*, 2d ed., 1908, p. 88. *Cf.* also Jèze, *op. cit.*, p. 826.

the abolition of the entire system of taxes on product, and its replacement in whole or in part by the taxation of income. Beginning with the revolution of 1848 and resumed after the creation of the Third Republic, these efforts have become more and more insistent, until they culminated, in 1909, in the passage by the Chamber of Deputies of an income tax bill. A review of this half century of struggle will be found instructive from many points of view.[1]

[1] In Heuschling, *L'Impôt sur le Revenu*, Brussels, 1873 (a later edition of a book originally published in 1848), will be found a short account of the income tax projects up to that date. Joseph Chailley, *L'Impôt sur le Revenu. Législation Comparée et Économie Politique*. Paris, 1884, pp. 483–619, contains a full and interesting account of the period from 1848 to 1883 inclusive. In *L'Impôt sur le Revenu*, by Yves Guyot, Paris, 1887, which is a reprint of an official report, will be found a short treatment of the projects from 1871 to 1887. A complete enumeration of all the bills introduced from 1871 to 1896 is contained in the *Rapport fait au nom de la Commission du Budget* (*Impôt Général sur le Revenu*), by M. Paul Delombre, Chambre des Députés, Session de 1896, no. 1831, pp. 53–64. A chronological list of all the income tax projects from 1848 to 1907, with a summary of each and an analysis of the more important, will be found in *L'Impôt sur le Revenu, Essai d'Économie Financière*, by Gaston-Gros. Paris, 1907, pp. 423–472 and 511–530. A somewhat shorter list and a description of all the income tax projects from 1848 to 1910 will be found in *L'Impôt sur le Revenu*, by Just Haristoy. Paris, 1910, annexes ii, pp. 802–835. The fullest account of all the bills and projects is contained in the official *Rapport fait au nom de la Commission de la Législation Fiscale chargée d'examiner le Projet et les Propositions de Loi tendant à l'Établissement d'un Impôt Général sur le Revenu*. Par M. Réné Renoult, Chambre des Députés, Session de 1907, no. 1053, vol. ii, annexe i, pp. 5–87. An elaborate description of the discussion on each of the projects up to 1898 will be found in *Le Problème Fiscal — de L'Impôt sur le Revenu*, by Charles Philippe, 6th ed., 1898 (the first edition was published in 1894), pp. 37–311. For the period subsequent to 1903, full details of all the schemes are published in the current numbers of the *Revue de Science et de Législation Financière*. A short analysis of the most important later projects will be found in *Eléments de Science Financière*, by Boucard et Jèze, vol. ii (1906), pp. 911 *et seq.* — All these books will hereafter be referred to simply by quoting the name of the author.

A German treatment of the subject is *Die Einkommensteuerprojecte in Frankreich bis 1887*, by Hermann Meyer, Berlin, 1905, and a later study by the same author, "Ein Ueberblick über die französischen Einkommensteuer-projecte in Frankreich bis 1887, nach Annahme der Resolution vom 10 Febr. 1887," in *Finanz Archiv*, vol. 32 (1906), pp. 13–41. A very short account in English will be found in an article by H. Parker Willis, "Income Taxation in France," *Journal of Political Economy*, vol. 4 (1896), pp. 37–53.

§ 2. *The Revolution of 1848*

The earlier history of the income tax projects in France is well summed up by a French writer in the statement that "The Revolution did not want to establish it, and the governments which succeeded either would not or could not."[1] It was the Revolution of 1848 that brought the income tax scheme to the front. As a result of the financial crisis of 1847–1848 the provisional government, confronted by the necessity of extraordinary expenditure, found itself face to face with a large deficit. M. Garnier Pagès, the Minister of Finance, proposed to make good the deficit by selling the crown jewels, by disposing of some of the national forests, by increasing the rate of the existing taxes, and by a patriotic loan. But at the last moment his courage failed him, and the plan was not carried through. It was then that he suggested the possibility of an income tax, pointing to the experience of England. On March 16 he stated: "I should have liked to submit to your approval the plan of an income tax. Just in principle, more just than all the others, the income tax possesses, in addition, the advantage that it can be easily collected."[2] But he confessed that it would take too long to prepare such a measure, and abandoned the project for the moment. On May 8, however, he came back to the subject and said: "Of all taxes the most just, the most efficacious, the one which I shall endeavor with all the power of a deep-seated conviction to have you accept, is the progressive income tax. You citizens will have in the eyes of posterity the eternal glory of having established it definitively in a France that has become republican and democratic."[3]

The radicals in the Assembly could not let such a suggestion pass. The country was being flooded with a mass of pamphlets and more serious projects, suggesting more or less

[1] "La Revolution n'a pas voulu l'établir, les Gouvernements qui l'ont suivie ne l'ont pas voulu ou ne l'ont pas pu." — Chailley, p. 483.

[2] Philippe, p. 50; and Chailley, p. 485.

[3] *Le Moniteur Universel*, no. 130, May 9, 1848, p. 981. *Cf.* Philippe, p. 51.

extreme methods of taxing the rich. Passing over the merely socialistic pamphlets, it may suffice to call attention to the works of Hébert, Lefebvre, Guigard, and Nabos, the last writer advocating a single tax on incomes.[1] On the other hand, a single tax on property rather than on income was enthusiastically supported by Girardin, who based his project on the insurance theory of the state.[2]

The radical party was represented in the legislature by Barbès and Proudhon. Barbès proposed, amid almost universal stupefaction, as we are told, a tax of one thousand million francs to be assessed exclusively on the rich. Proudhon, in order to secure the large funds required for his scheme of People's Banks, suggested an income tax, going as high as $33\frac{1}{3}$ per cent on some incomes and even reaching 50 per cent on others.[3] Such propositions, however, were entirely too extreme, and after a report by Thiers,[4] they were incontinently turned down by the legislature, which declared that they savored of revolution. The same fate befell the project of Joseph Lempereur, who had suggested a ten-per-cent income tax.[5]

That the sentiment of the time was not wholly unfavorable

[1] *De l'Impôt sur les Créances Hypothécaires de l'Income Tax ou Impôt Progressif admis en Principe par le Citoyen Garnier Pagès, Ministre des Finances,* etc. Par J. B. Hébert, Notaire Honoraire. Paris, 1848; *De l'Impôt sur le Revenu Mobilier,* etc. Par Thibault Lefebvre, Avocat. Paris, 1849; *De l'Impôt sur le Revenu, le Capital, la Propriété, l'Industrie, le Commerce,* etc. Par J.-A. Guigard. Paris, 1850; *Impôt Unique et Proportionnel sur le Revenu. A Messieurs les Membres de l'Assemblée Nationale.* Par Henri Nabos, Maire de la Ville de Marciac. Auch, 1851.

[2] *Le Socialisme et l'Impôt.* Par Émile de Girardin. Paris, 1849. The scheme is repeated in the same author's *L'Impôt,* Paris, 1852, and was reprinted two decades later, in 1872, under the title, *L'Impôt Inique et l'Impôt Unique.*

[3] *Proposition relative à l'Impôt sur le Revenu présentée le 11 Juillet 1848, par le Citoyen Proudhon.* By Pierre Joseph Proudhon. Paris, 1848.

[4] "Rapport du Citoyen Thiers, fait au nom du Comité des Finances sur la Proposition du Cit. Proudhon, le 26 Juillet, 1848." — *Le Moniteur,* p. 1831. This report, together with the scheme and the speech of Proudhon, was published in a volume entitled *Rapport du Citoyen Thiers, précédé de la Proposition du Citoyen Proudhon relative à l'Impôt sur le Revenu et suivi de son Discours prononcé à l'Assemblée Nationale le 31 Juillet, 1848.* Paris, 1848.

[5] *Cf.* Renault, p. 7.

to the income tax scheme is shown by the fact that Thiers himself, who was subsequently to prove so implacable an enemy to the project, now declared himself as by no means indisposed to accept the principle. When the government a little later presented a plan for a tax on mortgages, Thiers, who had been named head of the committee to which the proposition was referred, counselled its rejection, saying, on August 2: "If the project had been one for an income tax, we should have examined it, without, indeed, binding ourselves. . . . Among all the taxes that have been suggested the income tax is the one which deserves to be the most seriously examined, and even tried. When the government brings in such a plan I shall discuss it in good faith, for it merits serious consideration."[1] He went on to state that the income tax was not an arbitrary thing (*une chose arbitraire*), but that although the English tax had been received with disfavor and had been frowned upon, yet the good sense of England had finally accepted it as necessary.[2]

Following the good advice here given to the government, the new Minister of Finance, Goudchaux, submitted on August 23 the draft of an income tax, which was, however, to be levied only on the income from personal property, and which was designed to raise sixty million francs. The scheme was referred to a committee of which Parieu was chairman, and which brought in an adverse report, basing its opposition chiefly on the ground of the inquisitorial character of the tax.[3] Every one, said the committee, approved

[1] "Si c'était un impôt sur le revenu qu'on eût la prétention de nous apporter, nous l'examinerions sans toutefois nous engager. Car sous un gouvernement nouveau tout impôt nouveau a de grandes difficultés et celui-là en présente de singulièrement grandes. Cependant j'ai déclaré devant le comité des finances que parmi tous les impôts nouveaux, c'était celui que méritait d'être le plus sérieusement examiné et même essayé. Lorsqu'il sera apporté ici, pour ma part je le discuterai en toute bonne foi, car je reconnais que c'est un impôt qui mérite d'être pris en sérieuse considération." — Philippe, p. 52; Chailley, pp. 487–488.

[2] Cf. the notes on this speech by Wolowski in 1872, on pp. xxxv–xxxvi of the book mentioned below on page 285.

[3] The draft will be found in Chailley, pp. 489–490. It is also discussed in Guyot, pp. 19 *et seq.*; in Gaston-Gros, p. 511; and in Philippe, pp. 53–55.

of the principle of the tax; but in Parieu's words: "What a frightful inquisition is that of which the result will be to compel a rich man to reveal a fortune which it perhaps pleases him to surround with mystery, and to condemn the financially unfortunate citizen to choose between the hard alternative of throwing on his situation a light fatal to his credit, or of purchasing by a mendacious tax the preservation of the prestige of comfort by which he is still surrounded."[1] Goudchaux's project was also savagely attacked by the noted economist and former Minister of the Interior, Léon Faucher, who declared that the income tax would necessarily lead to a progressive tax, which was to him the climax of absurdity. "Blind is he who does not see it; bereft of sense is he who dissembles it."[2]

As a result of this unfavorable report, Goudchaux resigned and was succeeded by the well-known economist and statesman, Hippolyte Passy. Passy, however, made another attempt, on slightly different lines, with a scheme resting on a self-declaration of income.[3] But scarcely had the project been introduced when Passy was for other reasons forced to resign, and was succeeded by M. Fould, an inveterate opponent of the tax. Fould stated, on November 14, 1849, in withdrawing Passy's project, that "this tax, the last resource of hard-pressed governments, is in its nature arbitrary and inquisitorial. The general discontent which would result from its application would soon lead to a lamentable loss

[1] "Quelle inquisition redoutable que celle dont le résultat sera d'obliger le riche à révéler une fortune qu'il se platt peut-être à entourer de mystère, et de condamner le citoyen pecuniairement malheureux à cette dure alternative de répandre sur sa situation une lumière fatale à son credit, ou d'acheter par un impôt mensonger la conservation du prestige d'aisance dont il est encore environné." — Chailley, p. 492.

[2] "Oui, l'impôt progressif est au bout de l'impôt sur le revenu. Il en represente la fatalité. Aveugle qui ne la voit pas, et insensé qui la dissimule." — *De l'Impôt sur le Revenu.* Par M. Léon Faucher. Paris, 1849, p. 35. This was a reprint with some additions of an article that appeared in the *Revue des Deux Mondes* for October, 1849. See also a similar article by A. Cochut in the same volume.

[3] Passy's draft will be found in Chailley, pp. 496–497.

through the concealment and emigration of capital, and through a reduction of individual expenses which would soon reach the public revenues." [1]

Nothing daunted, however, the partisans of the tax continued their efforts. Passy declared on the floor of the House: "Sooner or later you will be compelled to do in France what has been done in England." Various bills were introduced by deputies Febvrel, Adelswaerd, Lamarque, Laurent, and De Veauce; [2] but they all met the unrelenting opposition of Minister Fould, and although there was a lively discussion of the projects in the chief economic journals,[3] it was, as one of the French writers puts it, "the swan song. The ignorance, the bad faith, the preoccupations of a government whose very origin compelled it to handle gingerly certain classes of taxpayers, finally the awkward exaggerations of the partisans of the tax, all contributed to lead public opinion astray, and to bring about for a long time a policy of silence on this delicate question." [4]

With the advent of the Second Empire the movement for reform died out, and the policy of silence to which we have just referred was inaugurated. Even in scientific circles, with the gradual dominance of the so-called liberal school, devoted to *laissez faire* and free trade, whatever prepossessions may have existed in favor of the income tax gradually disappeared. Only one important writer, Parieu, the opponent of the scheme under the republican govern-

[1] "Cet impôt, ressource extrême des gouvernements obérés, est, de sa nature, arbitraire et inquisitorial. . . . L'inquiétude générale, résultant de sa mise en pratique, amènerait bientôt une facheuse compensation par la dissimulation et l'émigration des capitaux, et par une réduction des dépenses des particuliers qui atteindrait les revenus publics." — Chailley, p. 498.

[2] For these proposals, see Gaston-Gros, p. 312; Renault, pp. 8–9.

[3] See esp. the article by Joseph Garnier, in the *Journal des Économistes*, June, 1851. Also the article by Passy in the same journal, June, 1852.

[4] "Ce fut le chant de cygne. L'ignorance, la mauvaise foi, les préoccupations d'un Gouvernement à qui son origine imposait le menagement de certains contribuables, enfin les exagérations maladroites des partisans de cet impôt, tout contribua à égarer l'opinion publique et à organiser pendant longtemps le silence sur cette question délicate." — Chailley, p. 500.

ment, devoted any attention at all to the subject, and he returned to it repeatedly.[1] The entire project of fiscal reform slumbered.

§ 3. *The Franco-Prussian War*

The next outbreak of reformatory activity was due to the Franco-Prussian War. In fact, even shortly before the downfall of the Empire the unfavorable fiscal outlook in 1870 had led two deputies, Larouche-Joubert and Haentjen, to propose income-tax bills. The first one was a rather fantastic scheme recommending a general income tax and calling upon all the citizens to declare their income, without any supervision on the part of the administration. The only control, we are told, was the conscience of the individual and the only sanction, his remorse. The other proposition was a little more serious; but both, although leading to some discussion, met with the opposition of the Minister of Finance, Segris, and came to naught.[2]

The unfortunate outcome of the war, however, and the imperious necessity of raising the five milliards, necessarily brought up the entire question of tax reform. Numerous pamphlets appeared on the subject, and when the national assembly met at Bordeaux at the opening of 1871 it was at once flooded with all sorts of projects. Some, like Tellier,[3]

[1] Esquirou de Parieu, "Examen des Avantages et des Inconvénients des Impôts Généraux sur la Propriété ou le Revenu" in the *Journal des Économistes*, June, 1857, and in his great work, *Traité des Impôts considérés sous le Rapport Historique, Économique et Politique*. Paris, 1862. 2d ed., 1866, 4 vols.

Cf. also the articles by De Gourgas, "De l'Impôt sur le Revenu" in *Journal des Economistes* for 1858; and by H. Baudrillart, "L'Impôt sur le Capital et l'Impôt sur le Revenu." — *Ibid.*, 1866.

[2] For the two propositions, see Gaston-Gros, p. 512; Philippe, p. 58; Chailley, pp. 503–504.

[3] Tellier had suggested this scheme even before the disaster, and now repeated it. *Cf.* his three monographs: *L'Impôt Unique et ses Conséquences*. Paris, 1868; *L'Impôt Unique et l'Invasion de 1870; La Libération par l'Impôt Proportionnel sur les Factures. Avec Projet de Loi et Commentaires à l'Appui*. Paris, 1872. Fifteen years later the same scheme was reintroduced by Alfred Lechopié in a work entitled, *L'Impôt Unique et Indirect sur le Revenu par la Taxe Proportionnelle sur les Quittances*. Paris, 1886.

suggested a single tax on receipts. Others like Count Branięki proposed a single tax on property.[1] But the great bulk of the projects were in favor of an income tax, some with a purely fiscal motive, some designed to introduce more equity into the revenue system, and some inspired by a radical opposition to wealth in general.[2] Perhaps the most weighty production was that of Jules Siegfried, who was subsequently to play a leading part in the French government, and who now made a well-balanced and strong defence of the income tax based on English models. "We now have an opportunity," said he, "of introducing into our customs an income tax. Let us not let it escape."[3] The early bills of Flotard,[4] Hèvre, and Bamberger had primarily a fiscal object in view. But the government showed itself ill-disposed to the scheme, and proposed to raise the necessary revenue from the customs duties. M. Larcy, the Minister of Public Works, said in his speech of June 20, 1871, "The income tax — it is the glory of the budget that we have none." And Thiers now arose, declaring in brief terms his opposition to "this deplorable tax, this tax of discord, which is nothing but the *taille* of the ancient régime."[5] He conceded that the tax was popular, but he warned the Assembly that he would not flatter popular passions, and that he would resign from the government rather than consent to the tax.

[1] *L'Impôt sur le Capital Libérateur de la Contribution de Guerre. Moyens pratiques de l'appliquer.* Par le Count Zavier Branięki. Paris, 1871.

[2] *Cf. L'Impôt Unique représentatif et possessif appliqué et contrôlé par le Suffrage Universel.* [Par Adelante.] Havre, 1870; *L'Impôt sur le Revenu. Delivérance du Territoire.* 1871; Crotard, *L'Impôt sur le Revenu, son Objet et sa Législation dans les Pays qui l'ont adopté.* 1871; *Un Système Pratique d'Impôt sur le Revenu.* 1872; *De L'Impôt et de la Production. Lettre à Messieurs les Députés à l'Assemblé Nationale.* Par un Industriel, 1871.

[3] *L'Impôt sur le Revenu et les Droits de Douane.* Par Jules Siegfried. [Havre, 1871], p. 28. The same idea is broached, although not so fully elaborated, in his earlier work of the same year, entitled, *Situation Financière de la France.*

[4] For these, see Gaston-Gros, p. 513, and Chailley, pp. 508–509.

[5] "Cet impôt déplorable, cet impôt de discorde, qui était tout simplement la taille de l'ancien régime, et la taille en temps de Révolution."

His opposition, however, only served to fan the flames, and new income tax bills were now introduced almost by the score. Among them were the projects of Louis Passy and Houssard, Rouveure, Flotard, Amât, Langlois, and Folliet,[1] all of them except the first being propositions which, as Chailley remarks, "while the product of a generous patriotism, clearly showed either their lack of experience, economic ignorance, or dangerous tendencies toward the employment of strictly revolutionary methods." All the bills were referred to the Budget Commission which, under the presidency of Casimir Perier, worked out a carefully elaborated scheme largely on English models, and by a vote of sixteen to eight decided to report the bill to the Assembly.[2]

In the interval, however, two other bills had been introduced, one by the socialist Langlois, and another, based even more largely on the English scheme, by the well-known bimetallist Wolowski. A general discussion [3] now ensued, in December, marked on the part of most of the opposition speeches by all kinds of errors and misstatements, resting evidently upon ignorance of facts.[4] The temper of the Assembly seemed,

[1] The project of Passy and Houssard was for a tax only on non-commercial incomes from personal property; that of Rouveure was based upon the English income tax; that of Amât was for a tax on capital; that of Langlois was a war tax of twenty-five per cent on all incomes for three years; that of Folliet was similar to Passy's. See Gaston-Gros, pp. 513–514, and Chailley, pp. 511–515.

[2] *Rapport fait au nom de la Commission sur le Budget rectifié de l'exercise 1871.* Présenté par Casimir Perier. *Cf.* Philippe, pp. 63–64; Chailley, pp. 518–521.

[3] *Cf.* Philippe, pp. 64–69.

[4] Wolowski called attention to some of these, especially with reference to the experience of the income tax in the United States. His treatment of the American income tax occupies no less than twenty-two pages in the book which contains a reprint of his speech and of the ensuing discussion. See *L'Impôt sur le Revenu. Discours de M. Wolowski (Séances des 22 et 27 Décembre, 1871) avec des Observations et des Annexes sur l'Impôt du Revenu aux États-Unis et en Angleterre.* Paris, 1872, pp. viii–xxx. Wolowski quotes an interesting personal letter from the American economist, Amasa Walker, reading as follows: "I hope that your government will adopt the income tax as a permanent part of the fiscal system. No tax could be more rational or more just. With us, it is to be feared that the tax will be abolished because the great capitalists are waging a bitter war

however, to be not unfavorable to the project, and even the leading Chambers of Commerce throughout the country stated that they preferred an income tax to the import duties on raw materials, which had been suggested as a substitute by the government.[1] On December 26, 1871, however, Thiers, the head of the provisional government, arose and in a memorable speech completely changed the temper of the Assembly and crushed his adversaries.

Thiers had by this time entirely altered his views. It will be remembered that in 1848 he was not unfavorable to the income tax, and in his book published at about that time he took very much the same attitude.[2] So well known were his opinions that in 1862 he was even cited, by a member of the Assembly, Granier de Cassagnac, as an avowed partisan of the income tax. His attitude, now, however, was very different. He called the tax a tax of discord and of disguised socialism, and a weapon of tyranny in the hands of political parties. He attempted to show that the conditions of France were very different from those of England, where the income tax might be to a certain extent endurable, and he did not tire of emphasizing the immediate dangers of arbitrariness and inquisitorial conduct on the part of the faction in power in France. In an eloquent peroration he conjured the Assembly not to imitate the despotic power which flatters the masses by deceiving them.[3]

Perhaps in the conditions of the time Thiers' opposition was not out of place. The political situation was unstable, a

on it, and they exercise a powerful influence in the legislative counsels. If they should succeed, it would be a great injustice to the laboring classes." — *Op. cit.*, p. xxxiii.

[1] These views are well-represented in *De l'Impôt et de la Production, Lettre à Messieurs les Députés à l'Assemblée Nationale.* Par un Industriel. The author advocates a property tax in preference to taxes on production.

[2] Thiers, *De la Propriété.* Paris, 1848, pp. 348–365.

[3] *Discours contre l'Établissement d'un Impôt sur le Revenu. Prononcé par M. Thiers le 26 Decembre, 1871, à l'Assemblée Nationale.* This was reprinted several times, the latest reprint being in 1896. The speech will also be found in full in Philippe, pp. 68–90.

bitter contest between the various factions was already in sight, and the country needed the full sympathy of the commercial and financial classes in order to extricate itself from its unfortunate plight. However that may be, Thiers succeeded quite as completely as did Gladstone in 1853 in winning over a hostile parliament. After his great speech, the income tax had no further chance. It is true that even after Wolowski's bill was defeated, new projects were presented in January, 1872, one by Hèvre and Bamberger,[1] who reintroduced their old scheme of a progressive tax on all incomes, and one by Wolowski, who now proposed a simple house-rental tax of fifteen per cent.[2] But the matter had been settled and the attempt of several writers to turn the discussion in the direction of an income tax based on house rents met with no success.[3]

The movement, however, could not be entirely stifled. In 1874 two more projects were introduced, one by Messrs. Aubry, Jozon, Defournelle, and Courcelle, based on a system of outward signs, chiefly house rents,[4] and one by Rouvier, of whom we shall hear a few decades later. Rouvier advocated a low tax on the whole of the taxpayer's income, and sounded the keynote of a future movement by stating in his speech: "You have several times proposed an income tax. You have always condemned it, but it is like a convict who has faith in the justice of his cause, and who has confidence even in his most prejudiced judges, and who for that reason appeals. The income tax will be established in France; no one can doubt it, and if it is not established by you, it will be by your successors."[5]

[1] See Philippe, pp. 105–106; Chailley, p. 541; and Gaston-Gros, p. 515.

[2] Chailley, p. 542.

[3] *Cf.* M. Aubry, *L'Impôt sur le Revenu sans Déclaration ni Inquisition, basé sur le Rapport de la Valeur Locative du Foyer Domestique de chaque Contribuable avec l'Ensemble de son Revenu.* Paris, 1873.

[4] Chailley, p. 543.

[5] "Vous avez plusieurs fois déjà statué sur l'impôt sur le revenu, vous l'avez toujours condamné, mais c'est un condamne qui a la foi dans la justice de sa cause et qui a confiance dans ses juges même les plus prévenus contre lui, c'est pourquoi

The general judgment on this whole period has been summed up by a recent French writer. He tells us that the bourgeoisie which had attained power and replaced the nobility and the clergy in the government of the country, reintroduced, to a great extent, although indeed in a somewhat less brutal form, the privileges which the Revolution had desired to destroy. On one pretext or another, they opposed all the plans which from 1848 on were submitted to remodel the fiscal system, and to give to direct taxation a just and equitable preponderance over the indirect taxes supported chiefly by the less fortunate classes.[1]

§ 4. *From Gambetta to the Périn Amendment. 1876–1887.*

After the setback of 1871, perhaps the most notable attempt to reintroduce the idea of the income tax was that of the famous statesman Gambetta. In 1876, after the adoption of the new constitution, Gambetta was chosen chairman of the budget commission, and in his report outlined a general programme rather than a definite bill embodying an income tax scheme. The way had been prepared, in a measure, by several monographs on the income tax, of which the most important were those of Staehling and Rochard.[2] Gambetta, however, went his own way. He tells us in his report that, so far as direct taxes are concerned, it is necessary boldly to

il en appelle de vôtre première décision à vôtre barre même." — Philippe, p. 109. See also Yves Guyot, p. 195.

[1] "La bourgeoisie qui avait conquis le pouvoir et remplacé, dans le gouvernement du pays, la noblesse et le clergé, fit donc, sous une forme moins brutale il est vrai, revivre en grande partie les privilèges que la Révolution avait voulu anéantir. Sous divers prétextes, elle repoussa tous les projets qui, surtout à partir de 1848, furent déposés pour, au moyen de la refonte de nôtre système fiscal et par l'établissement d'un impôt sur le revenu, donner à l'impôt direct une juste et équitable préponderance sur l'impôt indirect supporté, surtout, par les classes peu fortunées." — Geraud-Bastet, *Une Transformation Sociale. M. Caillaux et l'Impôt sur le Revenu expliqués.* Paris, n. d. [1910], pp. 142–143.

[2] Charles Staehling, *L'Impôt sur les Revenus.* Paris, 1876; and *De l'Impôt sur le Revenu.* Paris, 1877; M. Rochard, *De l'Impôt Direct sur le Revenu.* 2 parts, n. d. [1877].

undertake the consideration of an income-tax project. "We have investigated how such a tax could be established here with due regard to our actual organization and our financial habits, while dealing delicately with the transition and preserving in our actual system all that is not opposed to it. We do not wish to upset anything, nor to compromise the credit of France. We desire only to eliminate from our legislation the other bases which have been introduced into it, and which are opposed to the higher principle of proportionality, as found in the income tax."[1] The only part of the old system that Gambetta desired to retain was the land tax; all the other existing taxes he expanded into the various schedules of a comprehensive income tax. He was, however, not in favor of the abolition of the existing direct taxes and their replacement by a single income tax resting on the declaration of the taxpayer. This, he thought, would involve entirely too great a risk. It would lead to immense frauds and evasions, and would thus necessitate a rate so high as to be burdensome to the honest taxpayer. Moreover, it would involve too much inquisition.[2]

Gambetta's scheme was opposed in committee by Léon Say who, from now on, became one of the leading opponents of the income tax.[3] Notwithstanding Say's heated opposition, however, the project was adopted by the commission and was submitted to the Chamber. But although the report led to a general discussion, the great political crisis of 1877 prevented any serious attention being paid to it, and nothing was accomplished.[4]

In the following year, 1878, Laroche-Joubert repeated his old proposition for a general property tax, which had been originally advanced in 1870 and again in 1876. This bill

[1] This part of the report is reprinted in Chailley, pp. 545–546.

[2] For this part of Gambetta's report, see J. Caillaux, *L'Impôt sur le Revenu*. Paris, 1910, pp. 133–134. For Gambetta's speech, see also Guyot, pp. 196–200.

[3] For Say's objections, see Chailley, pp. 554–555.

[4] For a discussion of Gambetta's project, see an article by Léon Say, entitled, "Les Reformes projetés dans la Système d'Impôts en France. La Proposition de M. Gambetta. L'Impôt sur le Revenu," *Journal des Économistes*, May, 1877.

purported to "transform the entire tax system in order to serve more equitably the interests of the most numerous parts of the population."[1] This scheme for a general property tax or a tax on capital had been advocated in France for several years by quite a number of writers, of whom Menier was the most prominent.[2] Menier's enthusiasm for a single property tax was, however, based largely on mistaken information as to the workings of the system in America, and found but scant favor with Parliament. In 1880 it was succeeded by the project of Marion for a low general income tax[3] and in 1882 by that of Silhol, who followed rather closely the scheme which had been adopted a few years previously in Italy.[4] In 1883 several bills were submitted to the consideration of the Chamber, that of Leydet[5] for a progressive income tax, that of Sourignes[6] for a combined property tax and income tax, and that of Ballue for a compensatory income tax on movable property, with high rates and differentiation. Ballue's proposition attracted wide attention and was referred to a committee. Between 1883 and 1886 Ballue varied these

[1] *Proposition de Loi ayant pour Objet de transformer tout nôtre Système d'Impôts, de façon à ce que l'Intérêt des Populations les plus nombreuses se trouvent plus équitablement observés.* Présentée par M. Laroche-Joubert, Chambre des Députés, Session de 1878, no. 305.

[2] See especially his books entitled, *Du Relatif et de l'Absolu en matière d'Impôts ou Étude Comparative du Principe des Impôts Directs et des Impôts Indirects,* 1872; *Réponse aux Objections faites contre l'Impôt sur le Capital à la Séance de la Société d'Économie Politique,* 1872; *La Réforme Fiscale,* 1873; *L'Impôt sur le Capital,* 1874; *La Société d'Économie Politique et l'Impôt sur le Capital,* 1875; *Mémoire à MM. les Membres de la Commission du Budget,* 1876. Other contemporary advocates of the single tax on capital or a general property tax were Chardon, *Projet d'un Impôt Unique établi en raison du Capital.* Paris, 1875; Amedée Lasseau, *Sur diverses Questions relatives à l'Impôt.* Paris, 1876; and the anonymous work *De la Transformation de l'Impôt. L'Unitaxe. Impôt sur le Capital et sur les Éléments Constitutifs des Bénéfices et du Revenu.* Saint Quentin, 1877.

[3] Printed in Guyot, pp. 202–203.

[4] *Cf.* Chailley, pp. 557–570.

[5] *Proposition de Loi ayant pour Objet d'établir un Impôt sur le Revenu, proportionnel et progressif.* Presentée par M. Leydet. Chambre des Députés, Session de 1883, no. 2224.

[6] For the schemes of Leydet and Sourignes, see Guyot, pp. 204–206.

propositions so as to introduce them in reality four times. The introductions to these bills, together with the report of the commission to which they were referred, contained long descriptions of the existing situation in France and abroad, as well as an interesting discussion of the various methods of income taxation. In a detailed history of the French reform, the propositions of Ballue would merit a careful analysis.[1] Nothing came of all these efforts, however. In the meantime, analogous schemes had been presented by Paul Bert in 1885, calling for a seven-per-cent general income tax,[2] and by Wilson, by Bourgeois, and by Camille Dreyfus in 1886.[3]

By 1886, however, the movement in favor of a reform of the tax system had become so pronounced that the entire subject of the income tax was referred for careful consideration to the budget commission. The report, which was written by the well-known economist and subsequent Minister of Commerce, Yves Guyot, was presented in October, 1886. It was a notable production, and was published separately in book form.[4] Guyot gave a short account of the principal systems in existence throughout the world, and added a summary of all the projects which had been advocated up to that time in France. Although he was a confirmed free trader and a determined opponent of all indirect taxes, he concluded

[1] These bills and reports are as follows: *Proposition de Loi ayant pour Objet la Réforme de l'Assiette de l'Impôt.* Presentée par M. Ballue. Chambre des Députés, Session de 1883, no. 1610, 80 pp.; *Proposition de Loi ayant pour Objet la Réforme de l'Assiette sur l'Impôt.* Presentée par M. Ballue, et plusieurs de ses Collègues. Chambre des Députés, Session Extraordinaire de 1885, no. 65, 209 pp.; *Rapport fait au nom de la Commission chargée d'examiner . . . la Réforme de l'Assiette de l'Impôt.* Presentée par M. A. Ballue. Chambre des Députés, Session Extraordinaire de 1886, no. 1314, 273 pp.; *Rapport Sommaire fait au nom de la Première Commission d'Initiative Parlementaire chargée d'examiner la Proposition de Loi de M. Ballue et plusieurs de ses Collègues, ayant pour Objet la Réforme de l'Assiette de l'Impôt.* Par M. Francis Laur. Chambre des Députés, Session 1886, no. 360, 65 pp.

[2] *Cf.* Gaston-Gros, p. 519.

[3] *Cf.* Philippe, p. 121.

[4] Yves Guyot, *L'Impôt sur le Revenu, Rapport fait au nom de la Commission du Budget sur les Questions soulevées par diverses Propositions relatives à l'Impôt sur le Revenu.* Paris, 1886.

that the path of reform lay rather in the improvement of the existing system of "real" taxes than in the adoption of any form of income tax. A discussion ensued in November. Andrieux declared himself in favor of the principle, but stated that the great question to be determined was: What kind of an income tax are we prepared to accept? Camille Dreyfus attempted to answer in full the objections to an income tax which had been raised by some other speakers. The discussion was cut short by Carnot, the Minister of Finance, who declared that in his opinion the time had not yet come for the introduction of an income tax.[1]

The growing feeling in favor of some kind of an income tax could not be checked, however. Tax reform was fast coming to the front as a political question, and the Ministers, Sarrien and Jules Ferry as well as Freycinet himself, were led to emphasize the point which had been made a decade before by Rouvier, namely, the need of reform on democratic lines. When Freycinet was succeeded by Goblet in 1886, he put the plank of democratic tax reform in the very forefront of his programme. The feeling had now become so pronounced that on February 18, 1887, Deputy Périn and a number of his colleagues moved an amendment to the annual finance law in the words: "The government is invited to present the project of a single and progressive income tax." After an elaborate speech by Périn the motion was adopted by the House, by the substantial majority of 257 against 228 votes, although the words "single and progressive" were eliminated.[2]

It is true that the Senate expunged this addition to the law, but the important point had been gained; since the Chamber of Deputies had now, for the first time, put itself on record as in favor of some kind of an income tax. What was henceforth known as the Périn amendment thus came to play a great rôle in the movement, and from now on the government itself began to take the matter energetically in hand.

[1] The discussion will be found in Philippe, pp. 122–138.

[2] For Périn's speech see Philippe, pp. 139–150.

§ 5. *From Dauphin's Bill to the Extra-parliamentary Commission, 1887–1894*

From 1887 on, at intervals of every year or two, government after government introduced an income tax project, each of which differed more or less from that of its predecessors, in the vain hope of winning the assent of the House to some particular scheme. It needed, however, a quarter of a century to bring about the desired result. The opposition was loud and energetic, and the natural repugnance of the propertied classes to any such innovation was heightened by the attitude of the economists. The liberal school was now at the zenith of its influence, and the introduction of the study of economics into the law schools, which was after a decade or two to bear fruit in a younger and more progressive set of economists, was still too recent to produce any effect.

Leroy-Beaulieu, in his classic work on the *Science of Finance*, originally published in 1877, and reissued in new editions every few years, vigorously opposed the income tax. In this he was ably seconded by Léon Say, who now in the eighties and early nineties did not tire of making speech after speech against it, and who gave a special course of lectures in the school of political science, devoted to the attempt to show the dangers and iniquities of the system.[1] The monotonous uniformity of the literary opposition to the income tax was broken in the eighties by only two books. One of these was written by Professor Denis at the instigation of the common council of Brussels, and consisted of an admirable report on local income taxes in Belgium, and national income taxes abroad.[2] As this was, however, meant primarily for Belgian consumption, it exerted but little influence in France. The other was by a French lawyer, Chailley, who wrote what is still to-day one of the best books on the subject, — accurate,

[1] These lectures were published in book form under the title, *Les Solutions Démocratiques de la Question des Impôts. Conférences faites à l'École des Sciences Politiques.* Par M. Léon Say. 2 vols., Paris, 1886.

[2] H. Denis, *L'Impôt sur le Revenu. Rapport et Documents présentés* [*au*] *Conseil Communal de Bruxelles.* Brussels, 1881.

sober in judgment, and progressive.[1] Chailley sought to explain how it was that so necessary a measure, feared by some, ridiculed by others, submerged under the general indifference, should nevertheless always return to the surface. He explained it by the fact that it is extremely difficult to convince a country, where old habits are so powerful, of the necessity of reform. But he asserted that in France a question is never completely buried; and he predicted that the time would come when the income tax would have its day.[2] Although Chailley was a member of the Society of Political Economy, he was really outside the charmed circle, so that he also made but a slight impression. Other books were published at about this time, by men like Besson, Jenot, Boucher, and Martinet, but they did not really represent scientific opinion.[3] The general attitude of the economists may be inferred from the action taken by a committee which awarded a prize offered for the best suggestion as to a reform of taxation. In 1877 a society was founded to consider the whole subject of fiscal reform.[4] It was created by a manufacturer, A. Raynaud, and on the advisory council were the most prominent economists of the day, like Chevalier, Passy, Leroy-Beaulieu, and Garnier. The founder offered a large prize for the best essay, and no less than sixty competitors handed in their papers in 1879. The committee of award agreed that the actual system was in urgent need of reform, but decided that the income tax was inquisitorial and that the prize should consequently go to M. Lorrain, who advocated a stamp tax on government securities.[5]

The government was now, however, alive to the exigencies

[1] Chailley, *L'Impôt sur le Revenu.* Paris, 1884. [2] *Op. cit.*, pp. 573–575.

[3] Besson, *L'Impôt sur le Revenu.* Paris, 1884; Jenot, *de l'Impôt sur le Revenu*, Paris, 1885; Boucher, *Réforme de l'Impôt.* Amiens, 1887; Martinet, *Les Différentes Formes de l'Impôt sur le Revenu.* Paris, 1888. Compare also the book of Deputy Ballue mentioned above, *Observations sur la Loi de l'Impôt sur le Revenu.*

[4] Under the name of *Société d'Études Économiques pour les Réformes Fiscales.*

[5] An account of the deliberations of the Committee and a reprint of the prize essay will be found in the book entitled, *Les Réformes Fiscales. Révolution Pacifique par l'Impôt sur les Revenus. Système de M. Jacques Lorrain premier Lauréat du Concours ouvert par la Société d'Études Économiques, fondée en 1878.* Par A. Raynaud. Avec une Préface d'Augustin Galopin. Paris, 1888.

of the situation, and after the favorable vote of the House on the Périn amendment in 1887 decided to persist. In February of that year the Minister of Finance, Dauphin, introduced an elaborate scheme which was in effect an attempt to measure individual incomes by legal presumptions or outward signs, and to utilize for this purpose primarily the amount paid for house rent.[1] Dauphin's project was almost entirely based on a memoir by Dr. G. Koenig, an Austrian writer, which was published shortly after in book form.[2] It was opposed primarily by M. Jules Roche, who from now on became second only to Léon Say as the most vigorous opponent of any income tax scheme. As a consequence, Dauphin's bill was withdrawn.

After the failure of this attempt the new Minister of Finance, Peytral, submitted a somewhat different project in the following year. Peytral tells us that "it is superfluous to remind Parliament of the fact that the income tax has for a long time been a plank in the republican platform."[3] In contradistinction to Dauphin's scheme, he suggested a general income tax based somewhat on English lines, but containing the principle of differentiation. He concluded his *Exposé de Motifs* in the following words: "Far from inciting to a class war, we regard the income tax as the surest method of reestablishing peace between interests which often think themselves in opposition, because they are called upon in our society to play different rôles, interests which will be the better able to comprehend the advantages of union when the government ceases to burden them unequally."[4] Peytral's bill, how-

[1] For Dauphin's *Exposé des Motifs*, see Philippe, pp. 150–155.

[2] G. Koenig, *Un Nouvel Impôt sur le Revenu. Mémoire qui a inspiré le Projet du Gouvernement relatif à la Réforme de la Contribution Personnelle-Mobilière.* Déposé sur le Bureau de la Chambre, par M. Dauphin, Ministre des Finances, le 26 Fevrier, 1867. Paris, 1887.

[3] *Projet de Loi portant Établissement d'un Impôt Général sur le Revenu.* Présenté par M. Peytral. Chambre des Députés. Session Extraordinaire de 1888, no. 3123, 82 pp. See p. 2.

[4] "Bien loin de pousser à la guerre des classes, nous envisageons l'impôt sur le revenu comme le plus sur moyen de rétablir la concorde entre des interêts qui

ever, did not fare any better than that of Dauphin. It was referred to a committee, but did not meet with a favorable public reception [1] and was not reported out. As a consequence, the income tax now for a short time disappeared from the government programme.

But tax reform was none the less energetically discussed in the Chamber of Deputies. Outside the income tax the most prominent plans that were from time to time submitted to the country were the general property tax and the graduated inheritance tax. The earlier schemes of Menier and Laroche-Joubert, for a general property tax, have been referred to above.[2] From time to time similar bills were introduced and even discussed during the eighties, but Menier found continually fewer adherents. Among these perhaps the most prominent was Catalan, an old tax official who now published his scheme for a single tax which had been originally submitted to the universal scientific congress in 1883.[3] In 1888, however, Planteau submitted a bill embodying a rather elaborate combination of a progressive property tax and a progressive inheritance tax. His explanation of the scheme affords an interesting and instructive account of the French situation, from the radical point of view.[4] The committee to which the plan was referred reported it as on the whole somewhat chimerical, and could not see its way to approve the

souvent se croient opposés parce qu'ils sont appelés à jouer dans nôtre société un rôle différent, et qui pourront mieux comprendre l'utilité de s'unir lorsque le fisc cessera de les frapper inégalement." — *Ibid.*, p. 18.

[1] Cf. the series of letters in the *Messager de Paris*, in November, 1888, by Henri Duguies, which were reprinted in book form under the title, *Le Projet d'Impôt sur le Revenu.* Paris, 1888.

[2] *Supra*, pp. 289–290.

[3] *De la Transformation de l'Impôt. L'Unitaxe. Impôt sur l'Avoir de Chacun et sur les Eléments Constitutifs des Bénéfices et du Revenu.* Par A. de Catalan. Paris, 1890.

[4] *Proposition de Loi ayant pour Objet la Réforme des Impôts.* Presentée par M. Planteau. Chambre des Députés. Session de 1888, no. 2568, 147 pp. Compare Gaston-Gros, p. 519. Two years later Planteau expanded his proposition into a considerable book with the title, *La Réforme des Impôts.* Par F. E. Planteau, ancien député. Paris, 1890.

scheme.[1] Similar projects for some kind of a general property tax were introduced in 1890, by Locroy and colleagues, by Rabier and colleagues, and by Leconte, but met with no success.[2] The same fate befell a somewhat similar proposition of Maujan in 1891. Maujan's scheme is especially interesting, not so much because of its advocacy of a graduated inheritance tax, but because he joined to this the proposition for a combined property and income tax. He divided property into four categories and income into four additional schedules, with separate rates on each, calculated according to the net income and with a progressive scale. It was virtually a combination of the Italian and German systems, with some new features of his own. The plan attracted so much interest that it was referred to a commission and separately published.[3] The commission brought in two separate reports in 1892. One report, devoted to the progressive inheritance tax, was written by Dupuy-Dutemps, and was unfavorable to the scheme.[4] The other, by Pierre Merlou, accepted Maujan's proposition for a property and income tax, but elaborated it considerably.[5] Nothing, however, came of the report. Accordingly Maujan reintroduced his scheme with some modifications in 1893, and again almost a decade later. During the nineties he found a few followers in the somewhat similar projects of Guillemet and Terrier, in February, 1894 (repeated in 1896),[6] and of Pierre Merlou and Pelletan in March, 1894.[7]

[1] *Rapport Sommaire fait au nom de la 21e Commission d'Initiative Parlementaire chargée d'examiner la Proposition de Loi de M. Planteau.* Par M. Charles Chevalier. Chambre des Députés, Session Extraordinaire, 1888, no. 3064.

[2] For these, see Gaston-Gros, pp. 520, 521.

[3] *La Réforme Générale de l'Impôt.* Par M. Maujan, Député, et un grand nombre de ses Collègues. Paris, 1891.

[4] *Rapport fait au nom de la Commission chargée d'examiner la Proposition de Loi de M. Maujan et un grand nombre de ses Collègues ayant pour Objet la Réforme Générale de l'Impôt.* Par M. Dupuy-Dutemps. Chambre des Députés, Session de 1892, no. 2289, 34 pp.

[5] A summary of this report will be found in Gaston-Gros, pp. 521–523.

[6] See Philippe, pp. 178–185.

[7] *Ibid.*, pp. 186–191.

As a consequence of these miscarriages of reform, the legislators reverted to the scheme of the income tax. Occasional monographs had appeared on the subject, like Chaix's enthusiastic plan for a single tax on incomes.[1] In 1891 three deputies, MM. Laur, Le Veillé, and Goussot reintroduced Peytral's bill of 1888. In their *Exposé des Motifs*, they ask: "How is it possible that a project of this nature, embodying so lofty a principle, and emanating from the government, has not had the success which democracy had the right to expect?" "We do not know," they answered; "parliamentarism has mysteries even for those who watch it at work from day to day."[2] They also succumbed to the same mysterious influence.

Beginning in 1893, however, there was ushered in with the new Chamber a period of scientific discussion of the income tax which was now again taken up by the ministry. The partisans of the income tax gradually crystallized into three groups, each with a separate plan which now received a different nomenclature. The first group was in favor of what Ribot shortly afterwards called "the French form of the income tax," namely, a tax resting on outward signs or presumptions, and based largely on some modification of the existing *contribution personnelle et mobilière*. This, as we know, was at the bottom of Dauphin's scheme in 1877. It became known as the *impôt indiciaire sur le revenu*, that is, the "presumptive income tax," and found a literary advocate in Catalan.[3] The second group was in favor of a lump-sum income tax, largely on the Prussian model, resting on declaration, and with severe

[1] *Étude sur l'Organisation d'un Impôt Unique et de Répartition.* [Par E. Chaix, Percepteur.] Marseilles, 1890.

[2] "Par suite de quelles considérations un projet de cette nature, engageant un principe aussi supérieur, émanant du Gouvernement, n'a-t-il pas eu la suite que la démocratie était en droit d'espérer? Nous ne la savons. Le parlementarisme a des mystères, même pour ceux qui le voient à l'œuvre tous les jours." — *Proposition de Loi portant Établissement d'un Impôt Général sur le Revenu.* Presentée par MM. Laur, Le Veillé, et Goussot. Exposé des Motifs, Chambre des Députés, Session de 1891, no. 1382, 27 pp. See p. 7.

[3] Étienne Catalan, *L'impôt et la famille. Projet de Réforme de l'Impôt Mobilier.* Argenteuil, 1892; and *L'Impôt Direct.* Argenteuil, 1894. Catalan based his scheme on house rentals, modified by the number of children.

administrative control. This gradually became known as the *impôt global*, or simply as the *impôt sur le revenu*. The third group was in favor of a stoppage-at-source income tax, divided into schedules, largely on the English model. This became known as the *impôt cédulaire*, or the *impôt sur les revenus*. These new names were finally accepted by all disputants.

In March, 1894, the Minister of Finance, Burdeau, introduced an income-tax bill of the first kind, somewhat akin to that of Dauphin in 1887, in that it also rested, in part at least, on the legal presumption of income, as measured by house rent. After the failure of this scheme and of similar attempts emanating from the floor of the Chamber to effect a reform on the basis of a house-rentals tax, the discussion for a time narrowed down to a choice between the Prussian and the English systems. Moderates like Cochéry and Poincaré were in favor of the English system, or *impôt sur les revenus;* radicals like Cavaignac leaned to the Prussian system, or *impôt sur le revenu*. Many bills were introduced and reports of commissions made.

Among the bills of 1894 leaning toward the *impôt global*, or lump-sum tax, were those of Cavaignac and Doumer, of Rameau and of the socialists Jaurès and Millerand.[1] On the other hand, the English stoppage-at-source scheme was favored by Réné Goblet. Finally Gendre took middle ground, and adopted what he considered the best elements of each.[2] In the summer of 1894 discussion ensued, and the vote was taken. Jaurès' radical scheme was tabled by a large majority, Cavaignac's by a smaller one. Codet thereupon moved that the government be requested to frame some sort of an income-tax bill, and this important motion was adopted by a vote of 380 to 369. Pelletan furthermore moved that a parliamentary committee be appointed to study the whole problem and to bring in a report. In the meantime, on the motion of Minister Poincaré, an extra-parliamentary commission had

[1] See Philippe, pp. 196–201.

[2] For Goblet, see Gaston-Gros, p. 523; and Philippe, pp. 191–196.

been constituted in June by the President of the Republic. This was perhaps the most interesting event of the period, and deserves fuller mention.

§ 6. *From the Extra-parliamentary Commission to the End of the Century, 1894–1899*

The extra-parliamentary commission of 1894 was formed primarily to consider the projects of Goblet, mentioned above, and of Pierre Merlou, to whose views allusion has been made several times. The commission was invited, however, to consider the whole problem. Its membership was composed of the most eminent economists, financiers, legislators and officials. In order to provide a basis for their deliberations, the Minister of Finance caused to be collected a great compilation of documents,[1] illustrating the systems of income taxation in force throughout the world. The committee deliberated for a whole year and made its report in the summer of 1895, publishing the testimony in full, as well as the report, which was written by Coste.[2]

The report was an exceedingly thorough discussion of the whole problem, but it suffered from several weaknesses. From the very beginning of their deliberations it was seen, as Coste himself tells us, that they were concerned primarily with the effort to avoid two dangers — a declaration which

[1] *L'Impôt sur le Revenu et l'Impôt sur les Revenus dans les Pays Étrangers. Notes réunies par la Direction Générale des Contributions Directes.* Paris, Imprimerie Nationale, 1894, 915 pp. This compilation not only contains the full text (in French translation) of every income-tax law in force at the time, but also comprises summaries, explanatory descriptions, and statistics. It is by all odds the fullest document of the kind in existence.

[2] The testimony was published in two huge volumes, under the title of *Commission Extraparlementaire de l'Impôt sur les Revenus instituée au Ministère des Finances.* (*Décret du* 16 *Juin,* 1894.) *Procès-Verbaux.* Paris, Imprimerie Nationale, 1895, 2 vols. The report of Coste was also published separately under the title, *Rapport Général présenté au nom de la Commission Extraparlementaire de l'Impôt sur les Revenus.* Par M. Adolphe Coste. Paris, Imprimerie Nationale, 1895. The resolutions of the Commission will be found in Gaston-Gros, Appendix iii, pp. 531–536, and the report itself is discussed, *ibid.*, pp. 424–431.

might engender fraud, and an official control which might degenerate into inquisition. This attitude is well represented by Senator Trarieux, one of the more important members of the commission, who disclosed a heated opposition to the lump-sum method, maintaining its incontestable inferiority to the English system from the point of view of the liberty of the taxpayer, of the certainty of yield, and of justice and social peace. The report itself, in referring to the Prussian system, says: "It is difficult to imagine that we should ever be reduced to submitting ourselves to so formal an administrative discipline: in comparison with such a system, our old régime of direct taxes, all of them so easy-going and routine-like, would seem like a fiscal oasis."[1] The commission, however, was not especially favorable to the English system, and drew up a scheme which was a curious mixture of the stoppage-at-source and the presumption systems, divided into schedules indeed, but virtually retaining the land tax and the house tax, and making only slight changes in the other existing direct taxes. The report had an imposing appearance on paper, but on closer inspection it turned out to be really the old system in a somewhat new dress. As one of its critics said of the commission: "In the soul of these economists, statistics had dried up their enthusiasm; they fulfilled their task conscientiously, but without the faith which triumphs over obstacles; their scepticism froze them. Philosophers around a green table, they almost all lacked that stimulus which enlivens parliamentary debates — the identity of personal and general interest; scholars accustomed to universal criticism, they criticised their own opinions; theorists of doubt, they doubted their own judgment; the desire to be circumspect made them timorous; the fear of something new paralyzed them; what they lacked was precisely that which

[1] "Il est difficile de concevoir que nous parvenions jamais à nous plier à une discipline administrative aussi formaliste; et en comparaison d'un tel système, nôtre vieux régime de contributions directes, indolentes et routinières, nous apparaîtrait comme une oasis financière. *Rapport Général présenté au nom de la Commission Extraparlementaire de l'Impôt sur les Revenus.* Par M. Adolphe Coste. Paris, Imprimerie Nationale, 1895.

they most despised — politics."[1] Ribot, who had become Minister of Finance when their report was submitted, pronounced what is no doubt the correct verdict: "Such a conception as theirs," said he, "is evidently inspired by an idea of justice; but we must judge a reform by results rather than by intentions. From this point of view we do not think that the putting into practice of the system elaborated by the extra-parliamentary commission would respond to the hopes engendered by the promises of a general tax reform."[2]

At about the same time as the report of the extra-parliamentary commission, the parliamentary committee referred to above, which had also been at work for a year, made its report, written by Cavaignac. This report came out strongly in favor of a progressive lump-sum tax.[3] Cavaignac's project, however, was opposed by Cochéry, as well as by Ribot, and was tabled by a rather close vote. Ribot then decided to try his luck and introduced, in October, 1895, a scheme which in reality did not differ greatly from that of one of his predecessors, Burdeau. Ribot's *Exposé des Motifs* contains an interesting discussion of the three different types of

[1] "Dans l'âme de ces économistes, la statistique avait desséché l'enthousiasme; ils remplirent leur tâche en conscience, mais sans le foi qui triomphe des obstacles; leur scepticisme les glaça. Philosophes réunis autour d'un tapis vert, presque tous manquèrent de ce stimulant qui vivifie les débats parlémentaires: l'identité de l'interêt personnel et de l'interêt général; savants habitués à la critique universelle, ils critiquèrent leurs propres opinions; théoriciens du doute, ils doutèrent de leur propre jugement; le désir de circonspection les rendit timores; la crainte de l'aventure les immobilisa. Ce qui leur fît le plus defaut fut ce qu'ils méprisaient le plus: la politique." — Gaston-Gros, p. 424.

[2] "Une pareille conception s'inspire évidemment d'une idée de justice; mais c'est d'après ses résultats, bien plus que d'après l'intention qui l'a inspirée, qu'une réforme doit être jugée, et à ce point de vue nous ne pensons pas que la mise en pratique du système élaboré par la commission extraparlementaire répondrait aux espérances qu'ont fait naître les promesses de réforme générale de l'impôt." — *Projet de Loi portant Suppression de la Contribution des Portes et Fenêtres et Transformation de la Contribution Personnelle-Mobilière.* Chambre des Députés, Session Extraordinaire de 1895, no. 1560. Paris, Imprimerie Nationale, 1895, 53 pp. See pp. 3–4.

[3] For a description of this report, see Philippe, pp. 241–244; Gaston-Gros, pp. 523–524; and Renoult, p. 59.

income tax, as well as a treatment of the question whether a new income tax should be added to, or should be a substitute for, the existing taxes (*impôt de superposition*, as compared with *impôt de remplacement*). The single income tax he characterized as an entirely unrealizable conception in a great modern state. A stoppage-at-source or schedule tax he opposed because he maintained that under it public charges could not be distributed with the justice that modern democratic society demands. The lump-sum income tax he considered impracticable because "perfect fiscal honesty is an exceptional virtue." Accordingly he based his project largely on a modification of the *contribution personnelle-mobilière*, which he characterized as the true French form of the tax on income.[1] Ribot's scheme, however, met with scant favor from Parliament, and the deputies, after the long vacation in which they had a chance to consult the temper of their constituents, incontinently voted it down and thus brought about the resignation of Ribot.

The new Minister of Finance, Doumer, was enthusiastically greeted when in February, 1896, he introduced his bill for a general lump-sum income tax, embodying both progression and differentiation. His *exposé des motifs* is a long, well-considered treatise on the topic.[2] The project was referred to the budget commission presided over by Cochéry. The valuable and interesting report, however, was written by Delombre, and proved to be adverse to the scheme.[3] The

[1] *Projet de loi*, etc. [for full title see *supra*, p. 303]. *Cf.* esp. pp. 3, 4, 5, and 15.

[2] *Projet de Loi relatif aux Contributions Directes et aux Taxes y assimilées de l'Excice, 1897. L'Impôt sur le Revenu.* Paris, Imprimerie Nationale, 1896. A comparative study of five projects, those of the extra-parliamentary commission, of Ribot in 1895, of Doumer in 1896, of Maujan in 1903, and of Rouvier in 1903, will be found in P. Duclos, *L'Impôt sur le Revenu.* Paris, 1904, pp. 174–254.

[3] *Rapport au nom de la Commission du Budget chargée d'examiner le Projet de Loi portant Fixation du Budget Général des Dépenses et des Recettes de l'Excice, 1897.* (*L'Impôt sur le Revenu.*) Par M. Paul Delombre. Chambre des Députés, Session de 1896, no. 1831, p. 64. This report of Delombre contains at the close a full list of all the income-tax projects which had been presented up to date.

report, which was followed by the introduction of several independent income-tax bills such as those by Chenavaz and by Berteaux and some companions,[1] led to what promised to be an interesting discussion in the Chamber.[2] This was, however, cut short by the fall of the Bourgeois government and its replacement by the Méline ministry, with far less radical ideas.

The new Minister of Finance, Cochéry, accordingly introduced, in June, 1896, an income-tax bill resting largely on the conclusions of the extra-parliamentary commission, based primarily on English rather than German models, and introducing in the lowest schedule or category of income a *taxe d'habitation*, or improved rentals tax.[3] Cochéry's bill was referred to the budget commission which brought in a full and valuable report written by Camille Krantz, and which was adverse to the scheme.[4] In February of the following year, 1897, Cochéry introduced a similar bill,[5] and when Peytral returned, after a ten years' absence, to the ministry of finance, he in turn submitted, in October, 1898, a scheme which differed entirely from his original plan of 1888, and which now was based entirely on external criteria, very much like Pitt's Triple Assessment in 1798.

These waverings of the government between the legal-presumption, the lump-sum, and the stoppage-at-source income tax, were reflected in the legislation. Almost every year similar bills were introduced, and many of them sent to committee, only to be rejected one after another. These schemes, based more or less on external criteria, were proposed by Ducos in 1896, by Malzac and Gellé in 1897, and

[1] For these bills, together with *Exposés des Motifs*, see the Publications of the Chambre des Députés, Session de 1896, nos. 1850 and 1860.

[2] For the discussion see Philippe, pp. 255–290.

[3] For Cochéry's scheme see Renoult, pp. 64–68, and Philippe, pp. 290–301.

[4] *Rapport fait au nom de la Commission du Budget chargée d'examiner le Projet de Loi relatif aux Impôts Directs sur les Revenus et aux Taxes y assimilées de l'Exercice, 1897.* Par M. Camille Krantz. Chambre des Députés, Session de 1896, no. 1951, 110 pp.

[5] For this see Renoult; pp. 72–73.

by Massabuau in 1899.[1] The lump-sum-income-tax idea was represented by the bills of Cavaignac in 1897 (but with the partial use of the legal-presumption idea), of Klotz in 1898, and of Magniaudé in 1899. The schedule-income-tax projects were submitted in bills of Doumergue and of Guillemet in 1896. Finally the old idea of a general property tax was represented by bills of Linard and Mahy in 1896, of Rose in 1899, and of Menier in 1899.[2]

The public was gradually being educated to the urgency of the question. During the nineties not only did official publications, like that of 1895, give the facts, but some of the parliamentary reports were republished for general circulation. Writers, like De Swarte in 1893, Philippe in 1894, Luçay in 1896, and Muller in 1901, went more or less fully into the history of the subject.[3] The general literary discussion also waxed warm. Passing over the articles in the periodicals,[4] we now find books devoted to the subject by Kergall, Doumer, Trouille and Philippe,[5] as well as numerous pamphlets.[6] But the economists as such were still opposed,

[1] For these see Gaston-Gros, pp. 524–528.

[2] For these various schemes see Renoult, pp. 72–75.

[3] *Cf.* De Swarte, *L'Impôt sur le Revenu: Historique et Législation Comparée.* Paris, 1893; Philippe, *L'Impôt sur le Revenu.* Paris, 1894; Luçay, *L'Impôt Général sur le Revenu, dans le Passé et le Présent.* Paris, 1896; Miller, *L'Impôt sur le Revenu et sa Législation dans les Divers Pays.* Paris, 1901.

[4] Among the most important articles may be noted: Gide, "La Psychologie et l'Impôt sur le Revenu," *Revue d'Économie Politique*, 1889; D. Davidson, "L'Impôt sur le Revenu," *ibid.*, 1891; E. De Worms, "De l'Impôt sur le Revenu," *Revue Politique et Parliamentaire*, 1895; L. Arnaud, "L'Impôt sur le Revenu appliqué à Verviers," *ibid.*, 1896; Abbé Ferret, "L'Impôt sur le Revenu," *L'Association Catholique*, 1895; N. Frederiksen, "Les Principes et la Pratique de l'Impôt Général sur le Revenu et la Propriété," *Le Monde Économique*, 1896; A. Liesse, "L'Impôt sur le Revenu et les Socialistes," *ibid.*, 1896; H. Barbaux, "De l'Impôt sur le Revenu à Florence au XVe Siècle," *Revue Politique et Parlémentaire*, 1898.

[5] Kergall, *L'Impôt Démocratique sur le Revenu.* Paris, 1896; P. Doumer, *L'Impôt sur le Revenu.* Paris, 1896; E. Trouille, *L'Impôt sur le Revenu.* Paris, 1897; Ch. Philippe, *L'Impôt sur le Revenu.* Paris, 1898.

[6] *Cf. Le Projet d'Impôt sur le Revenu devant la Presse Économique et Financière*, 1903; Rochard, *Réforme Radical de l'Impôt par l'Adoption de l'Impôt sur le Revenu*, 1894; Dupont, *Le Projet d'Impôt sur le Revenu*, 1896; Fouquet,

as can be seen from the title that Leroy-Beaulieu chose for his chief fulmination;[1] while M. Jules Roche, then, as now, one of the uncompromising opponents of the system, published in 1896 a book in which he collected a large number of articles written originally for the *Figaro*, and in which he attempted to draw a warning lesson from the experiences of the *ancien régime* and the Revolution.[2] The country was gradually waking up.

§ 7. *From Caillaux's First Ministry to his Second, 1899–1907*

With the new century the interest in the discussion grew in importance. Although the advocates of the income tax were still in the minority, their numbers augmented from year to year. In 1899, under the ministry Waldeck-Rousseau, M. Joseph Caillaux, who was destined in a second ministry ten years later to carry to successful completion an income-tax scheme, became minister of finance. A few months before his appointment, and while still a deputy, Caillaux had submitted, in March, 1899, in a committee report a project for an income tax very similar to that of Peytral, but combining declaration, official assessment, and the use of legal presumption.[3] When he became minister, Caillaux introduced a bill for an income tax designed to replace the existing door and window tax, as well as the *personnelle-mobilière*. It was a combination of a direct income tax with one resting on outward presumptions.[4] The bill,

L'Impôt sur le Revenu Global ou la Taille ressuscitée, 1897; Sarrault, *L'Impôt Progressif sur le Revenu*, 1898; Couron, *L'Impôt sur le Revenu*, 1899; Manchez, *L'Impôt Général sur le Revenu*, 1899.

[1] "La Mystification du Projet d'Impôt Général sur le Revenu," *L'Économiste Français*, 1896.

[2] *Contre l'Impôt sur le Revenu.* Par Jules Roche. Paris, 1896.

[3] Gaston-Gros, p. 527.

[4] *Projet de Loi portant Réforme des Contributions Directes presenté au nom de M. Émile Loubet, Président de la République Française.* Par M. J. Caillaux, Ministre des Finances, Chambre des Députés, Session de 1900, no. 1634, 106 pp.

however, did not find favor with the special commission charged to consider the scheme together with several of the other projects mentioned above. The commission was presided over by Rouvier, but the excellent report was written by Pierre Merlou, and leaned rather to the lump-sum idea.[1] The budget commission of 1901 recommended, however, that some income-tax scheme be included in the budget of 1902, and a sub-committee was intrusted with the duty of working out a project for a progressive lump-sum income tax. But Caillaux was not ready for the scheme, and because of his opposition it was dropped.

After Caillaux's retirement from office the disinclination to anything looking like inquisitorial procedure became so strong that in 1903 Rouvier, who was then minister of finance, advanced an income-tax proposition based very largely on rentals.[2] Rouvier, as minister, had changed considerably from Rouvier the deputy, who, it will be remembered, had introduced in 1874, and again in 1877, projects for a lump-sum income tax. He now found much to admire in the old system which he then so strongly opposed. The essential shortcomings of this entire theory, however, were emphasized by Poincaré, a little later, when he called attention to the fact that every such scheme that had ever been submitted to Parliament had suffered shipwreck because all the attempts had moved in the same vicious circle;[3] and Caillaux declared that there was no formula more false than that of legal presumption. It was precisely because the outward signs were

[1] *Rapport fait au nom de la Commission de l'Impôt sur le Revenu chargée d'examiner les Projets et Propositions de Loi portant Établissement d'un Impôt Général sur le Revenu.* Par M. Pierre Merlou, Chambre des Députés, Session de 1901, no. 2365, 48 pp.

[2] *Projet de Loi portant Suppression des Contributions Personnelle-Mobilière et des Portes et Fenêtres et Établissement d'un Impôt Général sur le Revenu (renvoyé à la Commission de Législation Fiscale), presenté au nom de M. Emil Loubet, president de la République Française.* Par M. Rouvier, Ministre des Finances. Chambre des Députés, Huitième Législature, Session ordinaire de 1903. Paris, Imprimerie Nationale, 1904, 36 pp.; and *Annexe* to the above, *ibid.*, 1904, 157 pp.

[3] Chambre des Députés, Seánce of July 12, 1906.

so deceptive that the whole question of French taxation was so unsatisfactory.[1] The more radical members of Parliament, however, were ready to go further, and introduced bill after bill for a direct income tax. Thus, apart from the committee report of Merlou in 1901, special attention must be called to the schemes of Magniaudé and of Lacombe in 1902, and of Brun in 1903, while Maujan, with whom we have become acquainted above, came back to his favorite combination of a property and income tax in 1903, and again in 1904.[2] All these bills were referred to a committee presided over by Merlou, which brought in a voluminous report, as well as a supplementary report, both written by Renoult.[3] Nothing daunted, however, both Maujan and Magniaudé submitted new bills with still more vigorous *exposés des motifs* in July, 1906, and Malvy also added a new bill.

So pronounced, however, was the general trend toward radicalism by this time, that the government considered the time to have come for a determined forward step. In the election of 1906, 263 successful candidates had declared

[1] "Je n'hésite pas à dire qu'il n'y a pas de formule plus fausse que celle de l'impôt sur le revenu fondé sur les signes extérieurs. Ce dont on se plaint, ce qui fait condamner, par tous ceux qui savent ces questions, nôtre système d'impôts, c'est précisément qu'il repose sur des presomptions, sur les indices les plus decevants. Taxer les réalités directement mésurées, c'est la substance de la réforme. On ne fait rien, on propose de se traîner dans la même ornière quand on suggère de remplacer des impôts sur les signes extérieurs par d'autres impôts sur d'autres signes extérieures." See Gaston-Gros, p. 137.

[2] Lacombe's scheme contains an interesting *exposé des motifs*. See *Proposition de Loi ayant pour Objet d'établir un Impôt Général sur le Revenu.* Presentée par M. Louis Lacombe, Chambre des Députés. Huitième Législature, Session de 1902, no. 13. *Cf.* also Gaston-Gros, p. 529.

[3] *Rapport fait au nom de la Commission de la Législation Fiscale chargée d'examiner le Projet de Loi et les diverses Propositions de Loi ayant pour objet d'établir un Impôt Général sur le Revenu.* Par M. Réné Renoult. Chambre de Députés, Session de 1904 no. 1799, 161 pp.; and *Rapport Supplémentaire fait au nom de la Commission de Législation Fiscale chargée d'examiner:* 1° *Les Projets de Loi portant Suppression des Contributions Personnelle-Mobilière et des Portes et Fenêtres et Établissement d'un Impôt Général sur le Revenu;* 2° *Les diverses Propositions de Loi . . . ayant pour Objet d'établir un Impôt sur le Revenu.* Par M. Réné Renoult, Chambre des Députés, Session Extraordinaire de 1904, no. 2097, 16 pp.

themselves in their election platform for a direct income tax; 150 had stated that they believed in a radical reform of the existing system, and only 166 remained silent. In the new ministry formed by Clemenceau in October, 1906, the portfolio of finance was offered to Caillaux, who, it will be remembered, had occupied a similar position under the Waldeck-Rousseau ministry from 1899 to 1902. His immediate predecessor, Poincaré, had not been able to effect any agreement with the Budget Commission, and the new government was now called upon to fulfil its election promises. Caillaux had gradually solidified his opinions on the subject. Although originally in favor of an *impôt indiciaire*, he took strong ground, in criticising Rouvier's plan several years later, against the system of legal presumptions, and expressed his preference for the British system.[1] As early as 1899 he had manifested his repugnance to the German system. "Let us hasten to state," said he, "that in theory the German income tax is almost perfect. Unfortunately, the weak spot is precisely this ideal mode of assessment — the declaration — which in practice leads to the most unsatisfactory results." [2]

In a public speech of April, 1906, while still a deputy, Caillaux clearly explained his present views, and this speech led Clemenceau to offer him the portfolio. "We must not think," said Caillaux, "of replacing the direct taxes only in part. If we were to touch one or two, all would crumble. What is necessary is their entire renovation. We must understand that taxes founded on external signs of wealth, on the system of presumptions, have had their day; that their injustice condemns them, and that we must replace them by taxes on actual income or on capital, in part on one, in part

[1] *Une Transformation Sociale. Mr. Caillaux et L'Impôt sur le Revenu expliqués.* Par Geraud-Bastet, Paris, n. d. [1909], p. 103. This book, which contains a schedule of Caillaux's career leading up to the passage of the income-tax law, will hereafter be quoted as *Géraud-Bastet.*

[2] "Empressons-nous de constater que, en théorie, l'impôt sur le revenu allemand est presque parfait. . . . Malheureusement la pierre d'achoppement, c'est precisément ce mode d'assiette idéal (la déclaration) qui, dans la pratique, conduit à des résultats les plus mediocres." — Quoted in Gaston-Gros, p. 286.

on the other. In order to be at once equitable and productive, and in order not to allow too large a place for fraud, these taxes must be organized by schedules, and must reach incomes at their source." [1]

§ 8. *Caillaux's Income Tax Bill of 1907*

Clemenceau, in accepting office, outlined the general plan of his ministry and made the statement that the government would soon submit the project of a law providing for an entire reform of the existing tax system, which was no longer adapted to the conditions and the new forms of private wealth.[2] Accordingly Caillaux set to work at once to elaborate his scheme, and on February 7, 1907, the now famous bill for an income tax was introduced.

Caillaux's *exposé des motifs* was an admirable one,[3] and may, in some respects, be compared with Gladstone's famous pronouncement of 1853. The essential difference, however, is that whereas Gladstone had the task of dispelling the prejudices and changing the convictions of his hearers, Caillaux was reasonably sure that almost any income-tax scheme that might be formulated by the government would secure the suffrages of the majority of the House.

Starting out with a theoretical discussion of the general basis of taxation, Caillaux contrasted the benefit with the faculty theory. Although he declared his individual adhesion to the latter, he pointed out that it makes little dif-

[1] "On ne peut songer à partiellement remplacer les impôts directs, en touchant à un ou deux on ferait tout croûler ; c'est leur renovation totale qui s'impose. Il faut comprendre que les impôts fondés sur les signes extérieurs de la richesse, sur le système des indices, ont fait leur temps, que leur injustice les fait condamner, qu'on doit leur substituer des impôts sur le revenu réel ou sur le capital, parfois sur l'un et sur l'autre. Pour être à la fois équitables et productives pour ne pas faire la place trop large à la fraude ces impôts devront être organisés par cédules ; ils devront atteindre les revenus à leur source."

[2] See his pronouncement in Géraud-Bastet, p. 87.

[3] It will be found in full in Géraud-Bastet, pp. 158–203. *Cf.* also *Revue de Science et de Législation Financières*, 1907, pp. 78 *et seq.*

ference which doctrine one espouses, in the face of the existing system of indirect taxation. For all fiscal theorists agree, he thought, in demanding that the old system of indirect taxes be modified and that more stress be laid on the wealth of the opulent than on the expenditure of the poor. All great nations, with the exception of France, have taken part in this development, and the French system of direct taxes, a product of forgotten theories or of abandoned traditions, is to-day, he contended, an antiquated and disparate organism, utterly out of touch with modern institutions.[1] Taking up, one by one, the French direct taxes, he subjected them to a withering criticism. The land tax falls with crushing severity on the peasant and small farmer. The *patentes* or business taxes give rise in practice to the most shocking inequalities. The door and window tax is a tax on air and light. The *personnelle-mobilière* has practically become a tax on expenditure, like the indirect taxes on sugar and coffee. The tax on securities, which constituted the first serious attempt to improve the general system, has in reality created unjust privileges, and has sensibly checked industrial progress. Every one, concluded Caillaux, confesses that the system is in need of a complete renovation.

The solution found in other countries is the income tax. Brushing aside the *impôt indiciaire* as unworthy of consideration, Caillaux pointed out that there are two chief types of income tax, which he called the *impôt réel sur les revenus* and the *impôt personnel et global sur le revenu*. Of these two systems the former is represented by the British income tax, which Caillaux considered a marvellous fiscal instrument, at once potent and supple.[2] "It is exceptionally productive, and yet it avoids as far as possible contacts, that is, conflicts between the Treasury and the citizen." The chief objection to the English income tax he found in the fact that it does not admit of discrimination and progression. For it must be remembered that when Caillaux wrote these words those principles had not yet been adopted in England. "The German

[1] Géraud-Bastet, p. 161.

[2] Géraud-Bastet, pp. 165–166.

system," on the other hand, "may seem to be equitable, because the tax is exactly proportioned to every one's wealth. It may suit a highly centralized and hierarchic country, and a subservient and docile people. But it allows room for much arbitrariness and inequality — arbitrariness because the administration does not hesitate to make official assessments, and to cut to the quick when it suspects fraud; much inequality, because, despite all, it permits many incomes, and especially many large incomes, to escape, with the consequence that the mass of the taxpayers are relatively overburdened. Above all, the Prussian system is so little productive, because it is so little scientific."[1]

Proceeding next to the question which of the two systems to adopt, Caillaux stated that in arriving at a decision he was actuated by two general principles; the necessity of taxing actual rather than presumed income, which implies the exclusion of all systems of external signs or presumptions; and the necessity of suppressing all privileges. These principles once granted, the choice between the English and the Prussian system becomes easy. "My fellow-citizens are too fond of independence to subject themselves to the rigors of the Germanic system; nor would they find it entirely easy to accommodate themselves in all its details to the British system."[2] The ideal, Caillaux held, is a combination of the two systems suited to French conditions.

He proceeded thereupon to elaborate his scheme. First he urged the adoption of the English stoppage-at-source system arranged in schedules, or what the French call the *système de stoppage*. Owing, however, to the lower standard of life and the conditions of the distribution of wealth in France, it would be necessary to have the exemptions fixed at a much lower figure than in England. Furthermore, Caillaux advocated the system of discrimination, that is, of having the various schedules taxed at different rates, instead of at the same rates, as was then the case in England. Above all, the scheduled income tax is to be supplemented by

[1] Géraud-Bastet, pp. 167–168. [2] Géraud-Bastet, p. 169.

a "complementary tax," or additional tax on large incomes. In this way, provision will be made for both differentiation and progression. Compulsory declaration of incomes will be needed only in the case of professional incomes and of the income from securities. Finally, in the administration of the system, every care is to be taken to avoid inquisitorial and arbitrary procedure. It is for this reason, said Caillaux, that "we refuse to give the administration the exorbitant powers which it enjoys in Prussia."[1] In his eloquent peroration Caillaux appealed to the French sense of justice, and closed with the words: "When we begin to make reforms we must always expect to encounter the many embarrassments caused by the manœuvres and the outcry of men of all kinds, who are interested in maintaining existing abuses; for there is no abuse on which some one does not live."[2]

Caillaux's scheme made a profound impression, and was referred to the commission of fiscal legislation, which was deputed to consider not only this project, but also the bills of Maujan, Magniaudé, and Malvy, mentioned above. The commission, presided over by Camille Pelletan, studied the project carefully and made its report, written by Renoult, on June 13, 1907.[3] The commission declared its adhesion to Caillaux's project in almost every particular, making only a few important changes. Of these the most significant were the application of the principle of stoppage at source to the income from securities also, and a lowering of the tax rate on agricultural profits.[4]

[1] Géraud-Bastet, p. 200.

[2] "On doit toujours s'attendre quand on entreprend des réformes, aux embarras multipliés que feront naître les manœuvres et les cris des hommes de toute espèce intéressés à maintenir les abus, car il n'en est point dont quelqu'un ne vive." — Géraud-Bastet, p. 203.

[3] *Rapport fait au nom de la Commission Fiscale chargée d'examiner le Projet et les Propositions de Loi tendant a l'Établissement d'un Impôt sur le Revenu.* Par M. Réné Renoult. Chambre des Députés. Session de 1907, no. 1053, 2 vols., 304, 418 pp.

[4] Many minor changes were made. A complete list of these changes will be found in Gaston-Gros, pp. 537–539. The tax, as modified by the commission, will be found, *ibid.*, pp. 547–582.

In the meantime, the ministry started to make preliminary investigations or soundings (*sondages*) as to the probable practical result of the scheme in different parts of the country. On June 25 the Chamber voted by a majority of 309 to 111 to take up the commission's report on July 1, and accordingly on that date the general discussion began. It lasted to July 11 and was then adjourned during the extra session of 1907. Renewed at the opening of the 1908 session on January 20, it lasted continuously until February 18. The house then decided, by the overwhelming majority of 487 to 56 votes, to proceed to a discussion of the separate articles of the bill, and on March 7, 1908, this was initiated. It occupied the remainder of both the ordinary and the extraordinary sessions of 1908, and was resumed at the opening of the 1909 session in January, continuing until March. Each of the one hundred and one sections was subjected to a fierce discussion and to a separate vote. In the course of this discussion not a few of the provisions were changed, and some alterations, as in the case of the taxation of business profits, were made.[1] Finally, after further discussion of the bill as a whole, and the presentation of seven supplementary reports by the commission of fiscal legislation, each of them taking up some of the mooted questions,[2] the project

[1] The discussion will be found in the *Annuaire du Parlement* for 1907, 1908, 1909. This annual volume, which has appeared since 1900, is edited by Réné Samuel and Georges Bonnet. An admirable summary of the general discussion, as well as of the discussion of each article, is found in the volume entitled *L'Impôt sur le Revenu, Le Projet Caillaux devant la Chambre. Textes, Discussions, Commentaires.* Paris, 1910, 680 pp. This volume was published by the *Association de Défense des Classes Moyennes* formed to oppose the income tax; but the summary and the notes are perfectly impartial. *Cf.* also, for a still more abbreviated summary of the discussion, the *Revue de Science et de Législation Financières* 1907, pp. 407, 645; 1908, pp. 236, 415; 1909, pp. 85, 321.

[2] In addition to the seven supplementary reports there were seven annexed reports, making fourteen in all. The official numbers of these *Rapports Supplémentaires* were as follows: Session of 1908, first report, no. 1445, 38 pp., with a separate *Annexe* entitled *Comptes Rendus des Expériences d'Application de l'Impôt Général sur les Revenus*, 135 pp.; second report, no. 1565, 4 pp.; third report, no. 1591, 4 pp.; fourth report, no. 1730, 6 pp.; with six separate *Annexes*, 3 pp., 4 pp., 22 pp., 3 pp., 2 pp., 3 pp.; extraordinary session of 1908,

was adopted by the Chamber on March 9, 1909, by the decisive vote of 388 to 129 present, or 406 to 166 revised. Thus, after a most careful discussion which lasted more than two years, the French Chamber of Deputies finally adopted a general income tax scheme.

§ 9. *The Discussion of 1907–1909*

The minority put up a very strong fight against the bill. Among the most prominent opponents were Ribot, Reinach, Aynard, Benoist, and Pierre Leroy-Beaulieu. The chief antagonist, however, was Jules Roche, who had been an implacable enemy of the income tax for several decades. He maintained that the tax would become an instrument of social warfare and of economic destruction, that the bill virtually overturned the work of the Revolution, and that it would reestablish the very worst fiscal methods of the *ancien régime*. The majority had, however, no difficulty in answering the various points. Not only the leading liberal and radical Republicans, but also the prominent socialists, like Jaurès, warmly espoused the bill. The president of the commission, Pelletan, and the reporter, Renoult, spoke several times with great effect in ardent defence of the project; but the lion's share in upholding the measure naturally fell to Caillaux.

Caillaux made no less than seven great speeches in the course of the two years' discussion.[1] In his introductory speech of July 11, 1907, he elaborated the points that he had made in the *exposé des motifs*. He declared that there had always been two shortcomings in the French system — the privileges in favor of certain classes or of certain sections, and the undue extension of indirect taxation.[2] He contended that a system which worked fairly well at the beginning of

fifth report, no. 2127, 28 pp.; session of 1909, sixth report, no. 2232, 43 pp.; seventh report, no. 2291, 60 pp.

[1] These speeches are printed in full in the volume entitled *J. Caillaux, L'Impôt sur le Revenu*, Paris, 1910, 538 pp.

[2] *Op. cit.*, p. 9.

the nineteenth century was utterly unsuitable for the twentieth. Confessing that his earlier views on the subject had not been thoroughly thought out and that in 1900 he had been much tempted to follow the Prussian idea of relegating the real tax to the localities and of furnishing the resources of the general treasury by a single income tax, he now stated that further study had shown him the impracticability of that scheme.[1] So again he declared that while he had been at first seduced by the system of the British income tax, he found, on going to the bottom of the subject, that that also was unsatisfactory, and for three reasons: first, that if there were to be nothing but a scheduled tax, certain classes would escape, especially the owners of foreign securities; secondly, that if all the existing taxes were to be replaced by a scheduled income tax, the rate in each schedule would have to be put so high as to make it virtually unendurable; and finally, that without a knowledge of the entire income of the individual, it would under French conditions at least be impracticable to introduce the scheme of progression. Amid much applause he declared that the privilege of a gradual evolution in one's ideas was perhaps allowed to those who work hard and who do not content themselves simply with reading the *Journal Officiel*.[2] He took up the objection that his estimated figures as to the yield of the tax were not exact, because the country's income was not accurately known. "If, on the pretext that I do not know with absolute certainty the revenues of every Frenchman, you desire to prevent me from making this reform, you will never succeed in causing the actual inequalities of the tax system to disappear."[3] In reply to the objection that the owners of securities would transfer them or themselves abroad, Caillaux said, "I am not in the habit of proclaiming my intentions nor the government negotiations from the house tops; but I should advise my compatriots who are thinking of departing with a light heart and of taking their securities under their arm to Switzerland or to Belgium, not to be astonished if, in a short time, they were to

[1] *J. Caillaux, op. cit.*, p. 23. [2] *Op. cit.*, p. 55. [3] *Op. cit.*, pp. 58–59.

have a little surprise."[1] Referring again to the obligation imposed on the bankers to keep a registry or list of their various payments to others, he pointed out that such a list was already provided for in the stock-exchange tax, and had aroused no opposition at the time.[2] Finally, he considered the objection that the scheme was socialistic. This charge he characterized as at once puerile and miserable. "Do you think, gentlemen, that it is wise to state to the country that the Socialist party alone can advocate measures of justice? Do you not see that it would be the surest way of recommending socialism to a progressive democracy?"[3] He concluded with an eloquent appeal to the Chamber to collaborate with him, through the medium of a careful discussion, in erecting on a scientific foundation a new fiscal régime, a "régime of progress and of justice, a régime which will lighten the burden of the small man and which will put a moderate, although by no means exaggérated, charge on the richer classes."[4]

Half a year later, on February 11, 1908, Caillaux delivered another great speech, in which he replied to the general objections to the scheme. He again pointed out the undue preponderance of indirect taxes. In the existing budget of thirty-six hundred million francs, his most recent calculations had brought him to the conclusion that indirect taxes yielded from fifteen to sixteen hundred millions, direct taxes only nine hundred millions, while the remaining two to three hundred millions came from taxes which it was hard to classify. Under these conditions it would be universally confessed, he thought, that a larger share of the revenue must be secured from direct taxes.[5] In an effective passage he deplored the action of those uncompromising opponents whose objections to

[1] *J. Caillaux, op. cit.*, p. 62. [2] *Op. cit.*, p. 85. [3] *Op. cit.*, p. 98.

[4] "Ce que le gouvernement demande c'est que la Chambre veuille bien travailler, collaborer avec lui, à édifier scientifiquement un nouveau régime fiscal, un régime de progrès, de justice, un régime qui exonère les petits, qui charge un peu plus les riches, sans nulle exagération cependant." — *Op. cit.*, p. 103.

[5] *Op. cit.*, p. 116.

this scheme were just as great as to those of any other income-tax scheme. "Judge our system for itself. If you are not satisfied, propose something else; but do not continually wrap yourselves up in a perpetual negation which takes the shape of an attempt to defeat every project that is ever brought into this house, in order to retard the coming of the reform which you so much fear." [1] The adoption of a lump-sum income tax, to replace all the existing taxes, was advocated by some. "I declare flatly," said Caillaux, "that a thorough study of the question has convinced me that such a solution would be a most dangerous and deplorable leap in the dark." [2] To those who demanded a servile copying of the British income tax, he made an effective answer by calling attention to the recent report of the English commission, which had just recommended a supertax comparable to his own complementary tax.[3]

Passing on to the opposition's defence of the existing systems, he maintained that the business tax (*patentes*), far from being the best of the French taxes, was the most unequal and most lacking in proportion.[4] Again, answering the advocates of the system of taxation by legal presumptions, he said: "You may rack your mind as much as you like. You may invent all the possible external signs in the world; you may combine them and intertwine them as you please — the day after you have worked out a law of two or three hundred paragraphs on such a basis, the only result will be the discovery that you have committed the maximum of injustice." [5] In another place he said: "For a hundred and fifteen years we have been moving in the same circle of attempting to reach actual income by outward signs. Are

[1] *J. Caillaux, op. cit.*, p. 129.

[2] "Un saut dans l'inconnu, des plus redoutables et des plus dangéreux." — *Op. cit.*, p. 133. [3] *Op. cit.*, p. 135. [4] *Op. cit*, p. 163.

[5] "Vous aurez beau vous mettre l'esprit à la torture, vous aurez beau inventer tous les signes extérieurs du monde, les combiner, les enchevêtrer à votre guise; le lendemain du jour où vous aurez établi une loi en 200 ou 300 articles sur une telle base, vous arriverez tout simplement à découvrir que vous avez fait le summum d'injustices." *Op. cit.*, p. 215.

you not a bit tired of this little sport?"[1] Taking up in some detail the question of declaration, Caillaux pointed out that compulsory declaration was employed only when it was absolutely necessary, and that it was confined to the narrowest limits.[2] "I am perfectly well aware," he stated, "that in fiscal affairs we must regard the traditions, the customs, and even to a certain extent the prejudices of the people; but," he added, "you may be sure that when the new system shall once have been put into operation, the same thing will happen here that has happened in every country where a compulsory declaration was not required at first: there will be a general change of public sentiment in the direction of declaration which is, in reality, the only logical system, the only really admissible method in such matters."[3] With regard to the complementary tax, the objection had been made that it would reach only half a million taxpayers. "That, in my opinion," said Caillaux, "is precisely its great advantage." He concluded by alluding to the three reasons in favor of his scheme. In the first place, France was about coming to the end of its resources under the existing system of taxation, and more money was needed, especially for social reforms. Secondly, the system in vogue imposed an intolerable burden on the general economic and industrial development of the country; the new system would lighten the burden. Thirdly, the great majority of the deputies had made solemn promises to their electors to introduce the new system; they must now keep their promises.

In his other speeches Caillaux took up some of the remaining important problems. Thus one entire speech was devoted to the question of the desirability of taxing government bonds, a question which Caillaux answered in the affirmative.[4] Again, in considering the problem of progressive taxation, he stated that without taking any position on the general question of the desirability of progression as a whole, the graduated features of his scheme could easily be

[1] *J. Caillaux, op. cit.*, p. 273. Cf. also a similar passage on p. 491.
[2] *Op. cit.*, p. 213. [3] *Op. cit.*, p. 192. [4] *Op. cit.*, pp. 317–431.

defended on the ground of a makeweight to the upside-down progressive indirect taxes, which would still remain. In other words, Caillaux contented himself with what we have elsewhere called the compensatory theory of progressive taxation.[1] The objection that if we once insert the entering wedge of progression there would be no stopping, Caillaux characterized as an outworn schoolboy's thesis. In his final speech of March, 1909,[2] he took up again in turn all the principal objections that had been advanced in the course of the two years' discussion, namely, the stock arguments of inquisitorial procedure, of fraud, of the threatened flight of capital, of socialism, and of reaction on the poorer classes. Particularly effective was his reply to the last contention that in levying a higher tax on the rich, the bill was really imposing burdens on the poor. Amid enthusiastic applause Caillaux quoted from authorities to show that precisely the same arguments had been urged at the time of the Revolution against the suppression of the *corvées* and against the abolition of the privileges of the nobility and the clergy. So admirable was his succinct presentation that the Chamber ordered it to be printed and placarded throughout France.

As soon as the bill was introduced, it was at once recognized that a majority of the house was practically pledged to its enactment into law, and a heated discussion throughout the country kept pace with that in the Chamber. The old guard, like Leroy-Beaulieu, Stourm, and Neymarck, as well as deputy Roche, poured forth their broadsides against the income tax in the dailies, weeklies, and quarterlies.[3] But a new generation of economists had arisen, who took a different attitude. These now began to contribute most effectively to the discussion. Among them were men like Jèze, Allix, Gaston-Gros, and Ingenbleek,[4] ably seconded by statesmen like

[1] *Supra*, page 31.

[2] *Op. cit.*, pp. 465–535.

[3] *Cf.* the numerous articles in the *Économiste Français, Le Monde Économique, Journal des Économistes, Revue des deux Mondes.*

[4] Jèze, *Science des Finances*, 1909; Allix, *Traité Élémentaire de Science des Finances*, 1907; Gaston-Gros, *L'Impôt sur le Revenu*, 1907; Ingenbleek, *Impôts*

Senator Gauthier.[1] Some of these writers, like Gaston-Gros, did indeed not approve of the details of Caillaux's bill, but they all approached the problem from a new and progressive point of view, and contributed in no small measure to the passage of the bill.

§ 10. *The Provisions of the Income-Tax Bill as adopted*

The chief provisions of the bill as it was passed by the Chamber of Deputies are as follows:[2] —

The revenues or incomes are divided into seven schedules, namely, incomes from houses, from land, from movable capital, from business profits, from agricultural profits, from wages and salaries, and finally from professional earnings and all other sources not otherwise charged.[3] The rates are fixed at four per cent in the first three schedules, three and one half per cent in the fourth schedule, and three per cent in the remaining schedules.

Directs et Indirects sur le Revenu, 1908. *Cf.* also Michel *Impôts sur les Revenus* 1907; Canon, *L'Impôt sur le Revenu, son Passé, ses Modes d'Application, ses Effets sur la Rente et les Valeurs Étrangères*, 1906; Faure, *Le nouveau Projet d'Impôt sur le Revenu*, 1907; Eybert, *L'Impôt sur les Revenus Commerciaux et Industriels*, 1907; Pelletan, *L'Impôt sur le Revenu*, 1907; *L'Impôt sur le Revenu: où en sommes-nous?* 1908; Aimond, *La Réforme Fiscale et le Projet Caillaux*, 1908; and for the earlier period Vigne, *L'Impôt Général sur le Revenu. Rapport présenté au Conseil Communal de Gand*, 1903; Duclos, *L'Impôt sur le Revenu*, 1904.

[1] *La Réforme Fiscale par l'Impôt sur le Revenu.* Par A. E. Gauthier, Paris, 1908.

[2] The bill as passed will be found in Géraud-Bastet, *op. cit.* pp. 204–254. It is reprinted with the date of adoption of each section, and with the names of the participants in the discussion, in the bulky volume entitled *Impôt sur le Revenu et Impôt Complémentaire sur l'Ensemble du Revenu. Texte complet du Projet de Loi, voté par la Chambre des Députés le 9 Mars, 1909. Notice Historique du Projet de Loi et Table par Article des Débats de la Chambre.* Paris, 1910. It is also found in *L'Impôt sur Le Revenu* referred to above on p. 314. The bill is entitled *Law embodying the Suppression of the Direct Taxes and establishing a General Tax on Incomes and a Complementary Tax on the whole income.* "Loi portant Suppression des Contributions Directes et établissant un Impôt Général sur les Revenus et un Impôt Complémentaire sur l'Ensemble du Revenu."

[3] Art. 3.

The house-tax schedule is virtually a continuation of the existing house tax according to which, by the law of 1900, the assessable income is fixed at the net revenue *i.e.* the rental value, less twenty-five per cent in the case of dwellings, and forty per cent in that of factories.[1] In the land-tax schedule the assessable income is the rental value of the land, less a deduction of one-fifth. Fresh valuations are to be made every ten years.[2] In this second schedule abatements are made for smaller incomes. Where the total income does not exceed 1250 francs, 625 francs are completely exempt; where the income is between 1250 and 5000 francs there is an abatement of three-fourths on the first 625 francs, an abatement of one-half of the income between 626 and 1000 francs, and an abatement of one-fourth on incomes from 1001 to 1250 francs.

The third schedule comprises the revenue from personal property (*capitaux mobiliers*) including government securities, with some exceptions of a public nature.[3] This tax is assessed, as far as possible, on the corporations and associations that pay the interest or dividends. In the case of mortgages and the like, the tax is levied by means of a stamp. In the case of all securities, foreign or otherwise, the interest or dividends of which are paid through the medium of bankers or other agents, the tax is assessed upon these agents, who must keep two lists or registers of the transactions to be preserved for at least two years, and always open to the inspection of the government officials.[4]

The fourth schedule deals with business profits, or so-called profits of industrial and commercial enterprises. The tax is here assessed on the average of three years' income, and the taxpayers are invited to make a declaration of their revenue. This declaration is compulsory, however, only in the case of incomes over 5000 francs. The declaration is presented to the comptroller cf taxes (*contrôleur*). In case he is dissatisfied, he may ask the taxpayer to modify the declaration within twenty days. If this is not done, he may proceed to

[1] Art. 7. [2] Arts. 8–10. [3] Arts. 16–17. [4] Arts. 20–26.

make an official assessment, which is subject to an appeal to the administrative courts. In this appeal the comptroller may defend his assessment by any information at his disposal, and the taxpayer may in turn present what documents he chooses. In no case, however, can the taxpayer be required to show his books. In case of false declaration, the penalty is double the tax.[1] In this fourth schedule, certain deductions or abatements are made. In every case incomes of less than 1250 francs are exempt. In incomes under 20,000 francs the abatements are as follows: so much of the income as is under 1500 francs enjoys an abatement of six-sevenths; in the fraction of income from 1500 to 2500 francs two-thirds are deducted; in the fraction of income from 2500 to 5000 francs, one-fourth is deducted. The residue is taxed in full.[2]

The fifth schedule comprises agricultural profits, that is, the income from the actual operations of agriculture, rather than from the ownership of land. The income is here deemed to be equal to one-half of the actual rental value of the property for the fraction of the rental value under 500 francs and two-thirds of this value for the fraction over 5000 francs. Where the rental value does not exceed 12,000 francs, 1250 francs are exempt in every case, while abatements are made for two-thirds between 1251 and 2000 francs, and for one-third between 2001 and 3000 francs. In the case of private parks and pleasure grounds, the income is deemed equal to the total rental value, without any exemptions or deductions.[3]

The sixth schedule includes wages, salaries, and pensions. Here the tax is advanced by the individuals, associations, or governments, which pay the respective incomes. Every business man or company is required to hand in a list of employees with special details. In the case of salaries under 5000 francs two-thirds of the income is exempt, and abatements are made calculated partly according to the size of the income, and partly according to the number of inhabitants.[4]

The seventh and final schedule concerns itself with the

[1] Art. 30. [2] Arts. 32–34. [3] Arts. 37, 38. [4] Arts. 39–46.

incomes from the liberal professions. Here also abatements and deductions are made, calculated on the same principle as in the preceding schedule. Every taxpayer is required to file a declaration of his income from this source. It will be observed that this is the only schedule to which compulsory declaration applies; and even here provision is made that no professional secrets shall be divulged.[1]

The scheduled income tax, in which the principle of stoppage at source is observed as far as possible, is supplemented by what is called the complementary tax on the entire income. This is imposed only upon individuals, and not, as the preceding part of the tax, upon corporations as well. The tax is assessed upon the head of the family, who is responsible for his own income as well as that of his wife and children, except when the wife lives apart, and when the children have an independent income. It is levied only on individuals whose income exceeds 5000 francs, and applies to all individuals who have their domicile in France. In the case of those who reside in France, without having their domicile there, the income is deemed to be seven times the amount of their house rent.[2] The rate of the complementary tax is progressive, and is graduated as follows: The first 5000 francs income are deducted; the next 5000 francs are counted at one-fifth of their real amount; the next 5000 francs at two-fifths; the next 5000 francs at three-fifths; the next 5000 francs at four-fifths. It is only after 25,000 francs have been reached that the full rate of five per cent is imposed. In other words, each successive fraction of 5000 francs pays one per cent additional tax until the full rate of five per cent is reached at 25,000 francs.[3]

As to the administrative provisions of the supplementary tax, the comptroller of direct taxes makes up a list of all those subject to taxation. Each of these must file a declaration which, however, need contain only the name of the taxpayer, his residence, the abatements which he claims, and the amount of income from foreign property or business. It is only in the case of the revenue from personal property that he is

[1] Arts. 47–51. [2] Arts. 62–65. [3] Art. 66.

compelled to hand in the amount of his income. These declarations are submitted to a cantonal commission composed of the comptroller of taxes, the receiver of the stamp taxes (*receveur d'enregistrement*), and a collector (*percepteur*), all of them appointed by the prefect. This commission may ask the taxpayer to explain the situation, and if he does not do so the commission may assess the tax. He can appeal from the commission, but only on bearing the expense of the appeal, and submitting documentary proof of his contention. In case of false declaration the taxpayer or his heirs suffer a penalty equal to one-half of the income that has been concealed, and furthermore, every one who fails to make his declaration, or who makes an inadequate declaration, is penalized in a sum equal to triple the amount of tax.[1] Finally, it may be mentioned that in the case of all incomes under 12,000 francs, a tax to the amount of eight francs is deducted in favor of every member of the family, young or old, that is supported by the taxpayer.[2]

§ 11. *Conclusion*

The French scheme, it will be observed, is an ingenious combination of the English and the Prussian systems. It is based primarily on the English system of schedules, but it carries out, in far greater detail than the English system, the principle of differentiation, and it extends the exemption and abatements to a considerably lower amount of income. It adopts from the Prussian system the idea of the taxation of the entire income, but applies it only to the higher incomes, through a complementary tax which is akin to the present English super-tax, although the rate of progression is somewhat higher. It differs from the Prussian system in the great solicitude that is shown to avoid inquisitorial procedure. Direct declarations of income are, it will be remembered, required of individuals only in the case of professional incomes under the scheduled stoppage-at-source part of the tax, and in the case of incomes from personal property in

[1] Arts. 67–75.

[2] Art. 94.

the case of the complementary tax. The system is anxiously calculated to afford the maximum of revenue with the minimum of annoyance.

During the discussion of the income-tax project, much difficulty was experienced from the fact that M. Caillaux had not yet definitely made up his mind as to what disposition to make of the whole subject of local finance. He was able to overcome the difficulties only by promising to dispose of this subject in a separate bill, to be submitted later, and which would be so arranged as not to interfere in any way with the principle of the income tax itself. Accordingly on March 3, 1909, M. Caillaux presented his scheme for the reform of local taxation.[1] As this bill has not yet been discussed, however, it may suffice to state in general that it replaces all the existing *centimes additionnels* with a supplement to the state income tax. But several modifications are made in this local supplement. In the first place, there is no local tax on the income from movable capital. In the second place, since the progressive rate was introduced only as a makeweight against the indirect taxes, and inasmuch as indirect taxes play a slight rôle in local finance, the local income tax is made proportional. In the third place, the *impôt global* is permitted on incomes below 5000 francs, but is then to be calculated for local purposes in some relation to house rentals. Certain additional exemptions and abatements are also permitted.

Shortly after the adoption of the income-tax bill by the chamber of deputies, it was submitted, on March 16, 1909, to the Senate. M. Caillaux prefaced it with a short *exposé des motifs*,[2] in which he expounds the reasons which had

[1] *Projet de Loi portant Suppression des Centimes Departementaux et Communaux.* Chambre des Députés, Session de 1909, no. 2351. *Cf.* as to this the *Revue de Science et de Législation Financières*, 1909, pp. 342, *et seq.*

[2] *Exposé des Motifs. Projet de Loi adopté par le Chambre des Députés, portant Suppression des Contributions Directes et Établissement d'un Impôt Général sur les Revenus et d'un Impôt Complémentaire sur l'Ensemble du Revenu. Présenté au nom de M. Armand Fallières, Président de la République Française.* Par M. J. Caillaux, Ministre des Finances. Sénat, Année 1909, no. 66, 54 pp.

actuated the lower house. "Taking account of the distribution of wealth in France, of the existing state of affairs, and of the customs and traditions of the French taxpayers, the Chamber and the Government have succeeded in avoiding everything that might compromise the success of the work that had been undertaken. We have, however, not been willing to content ourselves with a mere semblance of reform; and inasmuch as the predominance of indirect taxes in our actual system involves a decided disadvantage to the small taxpayer, and an upside-down progression of individual payments, we have endeavored to reëstablish, as far as possible, the principle of proportioning every one's sacrifices to his income, and thus to restore an equilibrium that has for a long time been disturbed."[1] A few months later, with the overthrow of the Ministry on an entirely different matter, Caillaux resigned in June, 1909. He did not re-enter the cabinet until 1913.

The Senate, however, is proverbially conservative, and the commission to which the bill was referred brought in an unfavorable report early in 1910. In the meantime, the various interests in the country that were opposed to the enactment of the law, rallied to the defence, and an active campaign was augurated. Two important associations were formed. One entitled "The League against the Income Tax and Fiscal Inquisition" (*Ligue contre l'Impôt sur le revenu et l'Inquisition fiscale*) is presided over by M. Paul Fournier, a prominent Paris business man. The other association is called the "Association for the Defence of the Middle Classes" (*Association de Defence des Classes Moyennes*), of which the president is M. Maurice Colrat. Both of these associations have been pursuing an active campaign, holding meetings and publishing large volumes and small pamphlets designed to influence public opinion.[2]

[1] *Exposé des Motifs*, p. 2.

[2] *Cf.* esp. *Protestations de 1500 Syndicats contre le Projet Caillaux.* Paris, 1908; *Questionnaire sur l'Imposition des Valeurs Mobilières.* Paris, 1910. The middle-class-defence association also has published since 1908 a quarterly

What the result will be is uncertain. That the large legislative majority in favor of the income-tax scheme will be reversed is unlikely; but on the other hand, the conservative Senate gives way to the radical movement only after the most unmistakable expressions of popular opinion. Thus the Senate finally deferred to the judgment of the lower house on the question of the purchase of the Western Railway, and it came to a similar conclusion, despite its own original opinion, on the subject of the workman's insurance bill. It is entirely probable, therefore, that unless these new defence associations should succeed in changing the present temper of the French people, the Senate will sooner or later adopt the Caillaux project. That this will take place within the next two or three years is not to be expected, but that it will come before long is scarcely open to question.

bulletin entitled *Les Études Fiscales et Sociales*. A recent doctor's dissertation inspired by the same ideas is a rather elaborate study of R. Moreau, *L'Impôt Global et Progressif sur le Revenu*. Poitiers, 1910.

CHAPTER III

The Income Tax in Other Countries

The income tax is found in many other countries.[1] But with a few exceptions it is a fact either that these countries are themselves small and unimportant, or on the other hand that the income tax plays a most insignificant rôle in the fiscal system. As this work is an attempt not to compile statistics or legislative provisions, but to explain the important developments, we shall pass over all the other foreign countries with exception of Austria, Italy, and Switzerland. These we shall now proceed to examine, for each of them has a decided lesson to teach us.

§ 1. *Austria*

In the eighteenth century Austria, as a part of the German Empire, had very much the same system of taxes as the other German states, — namely a system of property and produce taxes combined with an excise.[2] Austria differed,

[1] The income tax is found for either state or local purposes, or both, in almost all the European countries, like Austria, Italy, Spain, Belgium, Sweden, Norway, Denmark, Switzerland, Holland, Greece, Luxemburg, and Finland; in Australia and New Zealand; in Japan and India; and in the Cape of Good Hope and Hawaii. The statistics as to these will be found in Kennan, *Income Taxation*, 1910. A large amount of detail on these countries will also be found in Seligman, *Progressive Taxation*, 2d ed., 1908, part 1, and the literature there mentioned. An appreciation of the Australian system will be found in the evidence of Mr. Coghlan before the *Select Committee on the Income Tax*, 1906, pp. 88–105.

[2] For an account of the earlier Austrian experiments with the income tax, see M. Heckel, *Lehrbuch der Finanzwissenschaft*, vol. 1, 1907, pp. 371 *et seq.* For the more recent developments, see the articles by M. Lesigang, "Die bisherigen Versuche zur Reform der Direkten Steuern in Oesterreich," *Finanz Archiv*, vol. vi (1889), pp. 538 *et seq.*; Sieghart, "Die Steuerreform in Oesterreich," *ibid.*, vol. xiv (1897), pp. 1 *et seq.*; Freiherr von Myrbach, "Die Reform der Direkten Steuern in Oesterreich," Schmoller's *Jahrbuch*, vol. xxii (1898), pp. 93 *et seq.*; Von Fürth,

however, from some of her sister states in that she made experiments with a personal tax during the eighteenth century. These took the form of class taxes under the name of *Personal-, Rang-, und Standessteuern.* We find even sporadic attempts at an income tax, as, for instance, in 1743, and again in the war taxes of 1778, 1789, and 1790. All these taxes were, however, entirely of an ephemeral nature, and we hear nothing more of them during the first half of the nineteenth century.

The revolution of 1848, however, brought about the same movement in Austria as in the other German states, with the exception that in Austria it was financial necessity rather than democratic tendency which led to the introduction of the income tax. At that time the direct taxes consisted of the land tax, the buildings tax, and the earnings tax (*Erwerbsteuer*), and the idea was to add to these taxes on product another tax of a similar nature which should reach the earnings of capital as well as of wages. Accordingly, in 1849, the so-called income tax was introduced as a temporary measure. The law was confessedly defective, but was excused on the ground both of its pressing urgency and of its temporary character; but instead of being abolished at the end of the term, as had been anticipated, it was continued from year to year with occasional amendments. Moreover, the wars of 1859 and 1866 necessitated not only a continuance of the law, but an increase of the rates. The original act of 1849, with its amendments during the fifties and the sixties, provided for three schedules. The first included incomes from business already subject to

Die Einkommensteuer in Oesterreich und Ihre Reform. Vienna, 1892. For the latest reforms see F. von Wieser, *Die Ergebnisse und Aussichten der Personal-Einkommensteuer in Oesterreich.* Leipzig, 1901; Freiherr von Myrbach, *Grundriss des Finanzrechts.* Vienna, 1906; O. Mann and H. Jedlicka, *Das Oesterreichische Personalsteuergesetz nach dem derzeitigen Stande der Praxis.* Vienna, 1904; Meyer, Pensch, et al., *Die direkten Personalsteuern.* Vienna, 1907 [with a full bibliography]; E. Bundsmann, *Die österreichische Personal-Einkommensteuer.* Innsbruck, 1909; V. Marcé, *L'Impôt sur le Revenu en Autriche.* Paris, 1907. An account of the Austrian system will also be found in the English *Blue Book* quoted on p. 339. *Cf.* also R. Sieghart, "Reform of Direct Taxation in Austria," *Economic Journal*, vol. viii (1898), pp. 173 *et seq.*

the earnings tax. It also comprised mining profits and agricultural profits. Originally levied at the rate of five per cent, it became, in the course of time, a progressive tax. In the case of certain associations and corporations falling within the schedule, a rather extreme progressive rate was adopted, ranging from two and one-half to almost ten per cent.[1] The second schedule comprised incomes from personal exertions, including professional incomes not subject to the earnings tax. This was also arranged according to a progressive scale. The third schedule included incomes from capital and what we should call intangible personalty. The rate was not progressive, but different kinds of income were taxed at different rates. Corporations were taxable in the first schedule, and had the right to deduct the tax from the dividends and interest. But in practice they made no use of this right.

The income tax of 1849, with its amendments, suffered from several defects. In the first place, the construction of the law was clumsy in that no real attempt was made to adjust the income tax to the already existing taxes on product, thus leading to much double taxation. Secondly, the administrative features were not worked out in harmony with the customs of the country, and in the third place, the rate of the tax was entirely too high. Not only had the normal rate become ten per cent, but additions for local purposes were permitted, ranging in some cases up to double the state tax. A tax of twenty per cent on income in time of peace was, of course, entirely unendurable, and just as is the case with the local property tax in the United States which, strictly enforced, would take from thirty to fifty per cent of a man's income, the ordinary taxpayer considered it perfectly justifiable to evade the tax as far as possible. The struggle which ensued between the administration and the government resulted in Austria, as it has resulted very largely in the United States, in a system of exceedingly lax administration, whereby

[1] The exact graduation of this and of the other schedules in the Austrian income tax will be found in Seligman, *Progressive Taxation*, 2d ed., 1908, pp. 58, *et seq.*

the officials made a practice of permitting individuals to return only a small part of their income. The vice of such a system, there as here, is of course the inequality and the resulting injustice of the arrangement in particular cases.

The dissatisfaction with these immense frauds and evasions on the one hand, and with the lax administration of the law on the other, prompted the Austrian government, during the seventies, to attempt a general reform of the whole system. So deep-rooted, however, had the old customs become that such a general reform proved to be entirely impracticable. It was only toward the end of the eighties, when the government finally decided to content itself with attempts at partial reform, that any progress at all was made, and even here it took several years of hard work until various ministers of finance, like von Plener, Bilinski, and the well-known economist Boehm-Bawerk, took part before the law of 1896 was enacted.

The new act is entitled "The law affecting the direct personal taxes,"[1] and as the title indicates, no attempt was made to deal with the existing taxes on product, and especially the taxes on land and buildings. The law is divided into five parts. In the first place, it deals with the so-called general earnings tax (*Allgemeine Erwerbsteuer*), which is modelled largely on the Prussian tax. Secondly, it includes a so-called "corporation" tax, applying to all associations, at the rate of ten per cent. The third element is the so-called *Rentensteuer*, which takes the place of the old third schedule of the original tax. The rates, however, are from one and one and one-half to ten per cent. The remaining two schedules of the original income tax were consolidated into what is known as a general income and salary tax (*Personaleinkommen- und Besoldungssteuer*). These are arranged according to a graduated scale, rising to five per cent on general incomes, and reaching six per cent on salaries over 15,000 florins [or, to use the recently introduced money unit, 30,000 crowns].[2]

[1] *Das Gesetz über die Direkten Personal Steuern, v. 25 Oct. 1896.*

[2] For details, see Seligman, *op. cit.*, p. 60.

The income tax is assessed on all resident Austrians, so far as their income is concerned. Non-resident Austrians are taxable on their income derived in Austria. Foreigners, including Hungarians, who have resided for more than a year in Austria, are taxable on their income derived in Austria. The income from foreign sources is exempt if it is already subject to a lump-sum income tax. The higher courts, however, have decided that this exemption does not apply in the case of the English, the Italian, or the Hungarian income tax. The law authorizes the government to conclude treaties with foreign countries, on the principle of reciprocity, and by an act of 1899 such a reciprocal arrangement was made with Germany, whereby the income from real estate is to be taxed only where it is situated, and the income from personal property only in the land of actual domicile.

The exemptions and abatements are similar to those in Germany. A minimum of 1200 crowns is entirely exempt. In the case of incomes under 4000 crowns an abatement of one-twentieth of the income is permitted for each dependent beyond two; in the case of incomes under 10,000 crowns an abatement of not to exceed three classes is permitted for any circumstances which diminish the ability to pay, such as illness, assistance of parents, education of children, or military service. Finally, peasant proprietors with an income up to 500 crowns (which may be increased by the Minister of Finance to 600 crowns) are freed from taxation.

Taxable income is defined as the sum of all revenues in money or in money's worth to the individual, including the rental value of his house and the value of his produce consumed for family purposes, after deducting interest on indebtedness, as well as all expenses incurred in securing the revenues. Extraordinary receipts, such as those from gifts, inheritances, and the like are not considered taxable income. Profits from sales are included only if they are the result of regular business or of speculative transactions. Life insurance premiums are deducted up to 200 crowns a year for a single life, and 400 crowns for the family. The items that may be deducted for expenses are carefully enumerated. They do not include the payment of debts, the investment of capital, or improvements which exceed the customary allowance for such purposes. Ordinary and periodical profits are reckoned for the preceding year, while profits of an uncertain annual value are computed at the average of three years. This, it will be observed, is just the reverse of the English practice.

Every recipient of income of more than 2000 crowns must make a declaration of his income; those with incomes between 200 and 2000 crowns need do so only when the declaration is especially asked for. The declarations are made on a large sheet, and one of the higher officials advises the taxpayer "to consecrate to this purpose a leisure hour, a moment when he has entire tranquillity of mind, for the matter is not so simple, and is of considerable importance to him."[1] It is, indeed, not a simple matter. Taxpayers are asked to fill out, in two separate columns, headed fixed and uncertain incomes, the revenues from six possible sources: land, houses, business, personal exertion, personal property, and sources not otherwise mentioned. The difficulties in making the declaration arise partly from the definition of income, and partly from the provision as to expenses. What should be considered "money's worth" is very uncertain. Technically, for instance, the value of the official dinners given by a higher to a lower official is required to be included in income. Much difficulty again arises from the fact that a careful account must be kept by the peasants of what they buy and of what they raise for home consumption. In the case of deductions for expenses, again, the wages of the farm laborer may be deducted, while those of the cook may not be deducted.[2] Similar complications, which might be multiplied, show how

[1] *Wie das Personaleinkommensteuer-Bekenntniss verfasst werden soll.* Von Dr. Rudolph Pensch. Vienna, 1908. For a somewhat earlier work on the same subject, see *Steuererklärung und Steuerauflage auf dem Gebiete der direkten Personalsteuern in Oesterreich.* Von H. Rauchberg. Vienna, 1907.

[2] *Die Oesterreichischen Steuerträger.* Von Leopold Berg. Vienna, 1898, p. 38.

difficult it is even for the honest taxpayer to make up his return. Moreover, in the declaration he must state the sums due to all creditors, and also the name and address of his employer if he is an employee, or the name, address, and wages of his employees if he is an employer. Finally, two pages are left for further details. In view of all these complexities, it does not surprise us to learn that "when the Mayor of Carlsbad pointed out the facts to a gentleman and asked him: 'Would you like to own some property here?' he turned tail and ran, and has been running ever since."[1]

After the declarations are made, they are turned over to the so-called "trusty individuals" (*Vertrauensmänner*). These trusty individuals existed under the old law; but according to the law of 1896 they now represent the taxpayers, being elected by the local districts. According to the Austrian voting system, however, they represent primarily the larger, rather than the smaller, taxpayers. These trusty individuals are supposed to correct the lists in case of doubt, and then to hand them over to the assessment commissioners. As a matter of fact, however, the trusty individuals have become very largely a paper organization. The assessment commission (*Schätzungs-Commission*) is composed of a president named by the Minister of Finance and of members half of whom are elected by the taxpayers and half appointed by the government. Their powers are rather wide, although not so wide as in Italy. In case of doubt they may demand further explanation from the taxpayer and may summon experts, but they cannot require the books, nor enter upon the business premises. If still dissatisfied after the examination of the taxpayer, they may estimate his income according to outward signs. Appeals are permitted to the Appeal Commission (*Berufungs-Commission*) and to the higher courts.

There is no injunction of secrecy, as in a great many other countries. When the law was passed there was a heated contest between those who advocated publicity of returns and those who were in favor of secrecy. The compromise

[1] Quoted in Marcé, *op. cit.*, p. 36.

which was adopted provided for making accessible to every taxpayer for two weeks, not the returns of income, but the registers of orders of payment, which contain the names and assessment of taxpayers; but any invidious publication of details was made punishable with fine. The penalties for fraud and evasion are very severe. Evasion (*Steuerhinterziehung*) is punishable by a fine varying from three to nine times the amount of tax. Evasion (*Steuerheimlichung*)—which consists in the omission of certain of the returns demanded—is punishable by a fine varying from twice to six times the amount of income.

Such are the chief administrative provisions of the law. They seem to be comprehensive enough and, barring some rather difficult complications, quite up to the level of modern requirements. When we come to inquire how the law works in practice, however, the picture is a different and by no means a rosy one. That the situation is considerably better than it was before the reform of 1896 is undoubted. Nor can it be said that the tax is very unpopular. This absence of discontent is due to several causes. In the first place, the taxpayers themselves participate to a certain extent in the administration of the law, partly through the "trusty individuals," and partly through the assessment commissions. Secondly, the not very high progressive rates are counterbalanced by the preponderance given to the wealthier classes in their official representatives. Thirdly, the income tax is not supplemented by a progressive inheritance tax as in England, or by a property tax as in Germany. Fourthly, and chiefly, the income tax is only a supplementary tax of comparatively slight importance. Not only is the yield of the income tax insignificant, when compared with the other direct taxes, but the produce of all the direct taxes together is small, in comparison to that of the indirect ones. The yield of the income tax indeed increased from forty-four million crowns in 1898 to fifty-nine millions in 1905, and to seventy-eight millions in 1909. But in 1903 the income tax yielded only one-sixth of the income from direct taxes, and only one thirty-fifth of the total government revenue; and among these indirect taxes must be mentioned not only the taxes on spirits and tobacco, but also those on sugar, on meat, and on salt. The tax on salt alone yielded almost as much as the entire income tax.

Notwithstanding the progressive improvement of the administration, the law is honeycombed with fraud. Those who anticipated that Austria would repeat the unexpectedly good results of the enactment of the Prussian law in 1893 were wofully disappointed. Despite a rather wide latitude given to the officials, and a procedure which, although not comparable to the Prussian, may nevertheless be considered inquisitorial, the officials seem to be unable to ascertain the income of the taxpayers with any approach to accuracy, and the returns are notoriously defective. Writing five years after the enactment of the law, Professor Wieser called attention to the notorious undervaluations, not only in the country districts, but in general among the wealthiest, as well as among the poorest classes of the population. He sadly confessed that there was no general disposition on the part of the public to make even half-way satisfactory returns. Owing to this lack of public sentiment Professor Wieser called the income tax a torso,[1] and after adverting to what he termed "the deplorable (*klägliche*) results of the new law," he maintained that "all merely legislative changes and any additional powers that might be conferred upon the administrative authorities would be useless without a change in the inner spirit of the law, which could be attained only when the irresistible force of public opinion was gained in favor of the law."[2] But only exceedingly slight progress has been made in winning over public opinion in support of the law,[3] and Dr. Meyer, one of the high government officials, concedes that frauds and evasions have become "epidemic." While it is undeniable that the frauds are slowly diminishing, they still attain immense figures. It is estimated that not more than a third or a half of the actual income is really reached.

So unsatisfactory, indeed, are the results of the efforts to

[1] Wieser, *op. cit.*, p. 139. [2] *Op. cit.*, p. 134. [3] Marce, p. 60.

reach the real income that recourse has been taken, to a very large extent, to that section of the law[1] which permits the officials to estimate a man's income according to outward signs, and especially his house rent. There has been much litigation as to the exact meaning of this paragraph.[2] In actual practice, however, a man's income is computed at about five times the amount of his house rent. Thus what was designed to be an accurate income tax turns out to be, in large measure, nothing but a very rough sort of a house-rentals tax.

The Austrian income tax, therefore, is far from being a success. Insignificant in yield, it is inadequate in administrative practice. According to the letter of the law, the tax is in many respects admirable; but in the working out of the system there is a sad gap between the intention of the legislator and the actual results. The Austrian income tax is a striking example of the impossibility of making purely paper reforms, and it shows us that no matter how excellent the law or the administrative provisions may be, if they do not respond to the deep-seated convictions of the people, and if they are out of harmony with the business, political, and economic conditions of the country, they cannot possibly succeed. A successful income tax depends in most instances upon the readiness of the people to support the administration, and if this support is lacking, the tax is bound to be a failure. Austria has not yet reached the stage where the public has come to the support of the government, and consequently, despite the undeniable progress that has been made during the past fifteen years, the Austrian income tax must still be pronounced a relative failure.

§ 2. *Italy: The Historical Development*

The Italian income tax was one of the first products of united Italy.[3] In the separate states which united to form

[1] Par. 214. [2] *Cf.* esp. Mann and Jedlicka, *op. cit.*, pp. 292 *et seq.*

[3] The best accounts of the Italian income tax are, for the earlier period, A. Vesselowsky, *L'Impôt sur le Revenu Mobilier en Italie.* St. Petersburg, 1879:

the new kingdom there was to be found a system of taxation on product, which differed, however, from state to state, supplemented in a very few cases by so-called "personal taxes." Thus, for instance, we find in Venice a business tax as well as a capital tax, and in Lombardy both these taxes, together with a poll tax; while a so-called income tax, which was of a very partial character, and which rested largely on outward presumptions, had been introduced in both of these states in the early fifties. In Parma we find a business tax and a so-called personal tax; in Modena, a poll tax with a rather complicated system of property taxes; in Piedmont a personal and movable property tax; in Tuscany a so-called family tax; in the Papal states a business tax and a class tax; in the Neapolitan monarchy a tax on wages and pensions; and in Sardinia a rather complicated system of taxes on industry and business.[1] It was, however, not so much a desire to bring order into this fiscal chaos as the imperious need of securing an adequate revenue for the new monarchy that led to a movement for the introduction of an income tax.

and for the more recent period, Le Vicomte Olivier de Spoelberch, *L'Impôt sur le Revenu en Italie.* Brussels, 1908. A French doctor's dissertation on the subject is that by A. Papin Labazordière Ruillier Beaufond, *L'Impôt sur les Revenus de la Richesse Mobilière en Italie.* Paris, 1906. A good account for the earlier period is found in Chailley, *L'Impôt sur le Revenu.* Paris, 1884, pp. 219–345.

In Italian, the best publication is O. Quarta, *Commento alla Legge sull'Imposta di Richezza Mobile.* 3 vols., Milan, 1902. This contains the laws themselves, with full accounts of judicial decisions and administrative practice. Other Italian discussions of the law are Giuseppe Vinci, *L'Imposta di Richezza Mobile in Italia nel suo Funzionamento.* Palermo, 1893; Enrico Bruni, *L'Imposta sui Redditi di Richezza Mobile.* Milano, 1894; F. Flora, *L'Imposta sui Redditi di Richezza Mobile.* Milan, 1898; Tivaroni, *Le Imposte Dirette sulla Richezza Mobiliare e sul Reddito.* Rome, 1904; and A. Lia, *L'Imposta Mobiliare e la Riforma dei Tributi Diretti in Italia. Ordinamento, Funzione, Proposte.* Turin, 1906. The official returns are published annually by the *Direzione Generale delle Imposte Dirette e del Catasto.* The most important of these figures are reproduced in the annal of statistics known as *Annuario Statistico Italiano.*

A summary account in English will be found in the Blue Book entitled: *Reports from his Majesty's Representative abroad respecting Graduated Income Taxes in Foreign States.* London, 1905 (Cd. 2587). *Cf.* also Kennan, *op. cit.*, p. 150.

[1] *Cf.* Bruni, *op. cit.*, pp. 2, 3.

Cavour, with his wise prevision, had already sent his friend Broglio to England a few years before, in order to study the British system, and the results of Broglio's studies were made available to the Italian public in 1857.[1]

Scarcely had the new government been inaugurated when Bortogi, in 1861, suggested a general tax on the income from personal property. The time was not yet ripe, however, and in 1862 Minister Sella presented a similar project, with an introduction in which he gave a clear exposition of the advantages of the scheme.[2] It was, however, only when the scheme had been presented for a third time, and now by the new Minister Minghetti, that it was finally adopted by Parliament and became law by the act of July 14, 1864.

In the discussion of the law the chief differences of opinion showed themselves in the choice between the old Italian systems of taxation according to presumptions, or outward signs, and the system of direct assessment. The advocates of the second method won the day, and as the English tax was the only successful one then in operation, the English model was followed rather closely, with its system of stoppage at source. The Italian tax, however, differed from its English prototype in several particulars. In the first place, whereas the English tax applied to all incomes, the Italian tax did not include incomes from the ownership of land. The reason for this distinction is not far to seek. When the British tax was imposed, it will be remembered that the land tax had virtually become a redeemable rent charge, and that as a consequence in a large part of the country no burden was imposed for state purposes on land rents. In Italy, on the other hand, the real-estate tax was the most important part of the entire system of taxation on product. It worked fairly well, and no one desired to change it. The income tax was therefore applied only to incomes not reached by the real estate tax. In the second place, the English tax was

[1] Emilio Broglio, *Lettere sull' Imposta del Reddito al Conte Camillo di Cavour*. 2 vols., Turin, 1856–1857.

[2] *Cf.* the *Relazione* of Sella, printed in Bruni, *op. cit.*, p. 19.

levied at a uniform rate. All the attempts to secure a differentiation of the tax, as we know, had thus far failed. In Italy, however, the arguments of the two committees of 1851 and 1861 on the English tax had made a great impression, and there was little objection to a differentiation of the tax. As a matter of fact, not only was the principle of differentiation introduced, but it was carried much further than had even been suggested in England. In the third place, the government was in such immediate need of a definite revenue, and so much doubt was felt as to the yield of the tax, that it was made not a percentage tax, as in England, — *i.e.* a tax of so much per cent on income — but an apportioned tax. That is, it was determined that there should be raised by the tax a sum of thirty million lire which was to be apportioned among the different provinces.[1] The provincial quotas were apportioned in the same way among the communes, and the amounts were then levied upon individuals according to their income. In no case, however, could the rate of the individual income exceed ten per cent.

The law was officially called "the tax on the income of movable wealth," but was popularly termed, "the tax on personal property."[2] Subject to the tax were corporations and most associations, as well as individuals. The tax was imposed upon all incomes except those subject to the real-estate tax, and excepting also the income from government securities. This last exception was due to the desire of the

[1] The law of 1864 decreed that the tax should be apportioned to each province according to the following criteria: —

One-fifth in proportion to the land tax;

One-fifth in proportion to population;

One-fifth in proportion to the pensions and salaries paid by the city, and the dividends of corporations;

One-tenth according to the customs duties;

One-tenth according to postal and telegraph charges;

One-tenth according to the stamp tax;

One-tenth in proportion to the mileage of the railways and the national and provincial highways.

[2] *Imposta sui Redditi della Richezza Mobile;* or, for short, *Imposta sulla Richezza Mobile.*

government not to depress the credit of the new-born state. The principle of differentiation, or, as it was called, diversification (*diversificazione*) was applied so as to result in the classification of incomes into three categories: (*a*) the so-called permanent and spontaneous incomes, which were those derived chiefly from property; (*b*) mixed temporary incomes, which were those derived from business in which capital was invested; and (*c*) temporary incomes which were derived from personal exertion. The nominal rate of tax was the same in each class, but the proportion of the assessable income varied. In class A incomes were assessed at the full valuation; in class B they were taken up at six-eighths of the real income; and in class C at five-eighths. Abatements were made for the smaller incomes as follows: Incomes under 250 lire were subject only to a fixed tax of 2 lire — reduced to 1 lira where the apportionment of the tax resulted in a rate of less than four per cent. These revenues were also not subject to the additions for local purposes. Incomes from 250 to 500 lire were taxed on a rising scale beginning with a tax of 2 lire for an income of 250 lire until the normal rate, which could not exceed ten per cent, was reached at 500 lire. Everybody was compelled to make a declaration of all his income except from land. Lists of taxables were made out by the municipal government, and were ultimately submitted to certain commissions in order to fix the assessments. As far as possible the revenues were stopped at the source.

During the next decade, changes in the law were made every few years. In 1866 the income from land was included, but in the following year, 1867, under Depretis, the original scheme was reintroduced, and has since remained in effect, except that in 1870 the income from agricultural industry, that is, from the working of land as opposed to the income from the ownership of land, was included. In 1866 also the tax was changed to a percentage tax, the rate being made 8 per cent or, with one-tenth added for expenses of collection, really 8.8. In 1870 the rate was increased to 12 per cent (or with the one-tenth added, really 13.2). But this increase was only nominal, because the additional centimes which had been levied for local purposes were now abolished in 1870. Government securities were subjected to the tax by the law of 1868, and in 1870 the principle of differentiation was extended by the introduction of a fourth category (Schedule D), for the income from pensions and the salaries of public employees. In this schedule taxable income was assessed at only four-eighths of the real income. As the salaries of private individuals were taxable under Schedule C at a higher rate, this would seem to be a rather unjust exemption; but in reality it is to be explained by the fact that public officials had never been subject to the additional centimes for local purposes, and that now, when that system was abolished in 1870, it was thought wise not to increase the burden on them. Various changes also were made from time to time in the exemptions. In 1867 the minimum of subsistence was raised from 250 to 400 lire, while incomes from 400 to 500 lire enjoyed an abatement of 100 lire. The declaration was still made by schedules.

The rate of the tax had now become so high that the whole system was honeycombed with frauds, and abuses of various kinds set in. In 1873 high penalties for fraudulent returns were enacted, and in 1874 the important provision was introduced — a provision which has since been followed in other countries including England — that all employers were required to hand in the names of their employees and of the wages paid. The law, in fact, even went a step further, and required the employers to pay the tax for the employees.

The income tax as a whole, however, worked rather poorly, and led to so much dissatisfaction that commissions of enquiry were appointed from time to time and attempts at reform were made. Among the important commissions were the Corbetta commission of 1872, whose report led to a few minor reforms in 1874, and the Torrigiani commission appointed in 1876 by Depretis. This latter commission devoted full consideration to two propositions: on the one hand to introduce the principle of graduation, and on the other hand to convert the tax into a general income tax, with the corollary that all other direct taxes be repealed. Both of these propositions were negatived, and the commission contented itself with a number of reforms, all of which are embodied in the law of 1877.[1]

The law of 1877 made comparatively slight changes in the substantive provisions. The rate of the tax remained the same, namely 12 per cent, to which, however, were to be added the one-tenth of 1866 (or 1.2 per cent) and a further addition calculated at 2 per cent of the tax for expenses of administration, as well as a further local duty, varying from place to place, to be applied to the collectors to whom the tax was farmed out. The total rate therefore was slightly under 13½ per cent, *i.e.*, 13.2 plus the further additions. The abatements were slightly changed so as to be as follows: —

250 lire on incomes from 400 to 500 lire;
200 lire on incomes from 500 to 600 lire;
150 lire on incomes from 600 to 700 lire;
100 lire on incomes from 700 to 800 lire.

These figures, however, applied only to Schedules B and C. In Schedule D the old system still continued. As the other provisions of the law of 1877 are virtually in force to-day, they will be considered below, and we shall limit ourselves here to calling attention to the changes introduced by the laws of 1894 and 1907.

In 1894 the rate of the tax was increased from 13.2 per cent (with the slight additions) to 20 per cent. The reason of this was an effort to reduce the interest on the public debt. As the fiscal situation at the time would not admit of a direct conversion of the public debt, the government thought it would secure the same result indirectly by increasing the rate of the tax. But in order not to augment the burden on the other taxpayers, the proportions in the other schedules were reduced. Consequently, in Schedule B the incomes were no longer assessed at six-eighths of the real amount, but only at twenty-fortieths, that is, one-half; and in Schedule C incomes were

[1] Law of August 24, 1877.

assessed not at five-eighths, but at only eighteen-fortieths. In Schedule D, incomes were assessed not at four-eighths, as before, but at fifteen-fortieths. This would practically mean the same rate of tax as before. Finally, in order that the government securities might not appear to be singled out for higher taxation, Schedule A was divided into two parts: A-1 was now made to include not only government securities, but also those of corporations guaranteed or aided by the government, and state lottery premiums. All the incomes in this sub-class were to be assessed at their full amount. On the other hand, a new sub-class A-2 was introduced, consisting of other incomes derived from capital of any nature, and these were now assessed at only thirty-fortieths of their full income. The net result was that with a normal rate of 20 per cent the actual rates paid by the different schedules would be as follows: A-1 20 per cent; A-2 15 per cent; B 10 per cent; C 9 per cent; D 7½ per cent. The law of 1894 also further complicated the abatements, which, with the additional change introduced in 1907, will be explained below.

§ 3. *The Actual Conditions*

Coming, then, to a consideration of the tax as it exists at present, it may be said that the income tax applies to all incomes save those from real estate. It includes, however, income from agricultural industry — that is, from the tilling of the land, but only in case these agricultural profits are made by individuals who do not own the soil. This distinction between agricultural profits made by owners and by non-owners is of course as illogical as it is unjustifiable. The tax also applies to certain revenues like tithes, etc., which are not liable to land tax. Moreover, the farmers who work the land on shares, on the *metayer* system, are subject to a tax of five per cent on the amount of land tax paid by the land-owner when it is over fifty lire. Otherwise they are exempt.

The tax is payable by Italians and foreigners alike, by individuals as well as by corporations, but only on incomes received in Italy. Quite a discussion took place on this point when the tax was first imposed in 1864; but at that time the theory of taxation was still that of reciprocity, and since the government was not supposed to protect property outside of the country, it was decided not to tax incomes therefrom.[1] The more modern view considers this position mistaken, not only because it puts citizens and foreigners on the same plane, but because there is no reason why a citizen who happens to invest his money abroad should be free of all obligation to the state.[2]

The tax is imposed on the head of the family, including the income of the wife and of the minor children. The legal exemptions include the actuarial reserve of life insurance companies, the income of mutual aid societies (with some slight exceptions), and the income of the royal family. Charitable institutions are not exempt. In addition to the legal exemptions, however, it has become the custom virtually to exempt all day laborers. According to Garelli, the law actually reaches only about 12,000 workmen.[3] In 1897 the Minister of Finance, Branca, desired to enforce the law in the case of private laborers as it is already enforced with the public employees, and he suggested that only those with an income under three and a half lire should be exempted. But the law failed of adoption, and when the same principle was sought to be enforced by ministerial ordinance in 1899, the decree soon became a dead letter.[4]

The incomes subject to the law are declared to comprise not only the certain and fixed incomes (*certi*), but also the uncertain and variable incomes coming from business or individual exertion (*incerti* and *variabili*), and the tax is stated to be applicable on the basis of the assured or presumed

[1] Bruni, *op. cit.*, pp. 23, 24.

[2] *Cf.* the discussion on these points in Chailley, *op. cit.*, p. 223, and Spoelberch, *op. cit.*, pp. 37–39.

[3] A. Garelli, *Le Imposte nello Stato Moderno.* Milan, 1903, p. 158.

[4] *Cf.* Magrini, *Le Imposte di Richezza Mobile nei Rapporti con le Societa Commerciale obbligate alla Presentazione dei Bilanci.* Milan, 1903, p. 189.

(*presunti*) incomes of the individual. The tax is paid in three different ways. The first method is what is called that of holding back, or retention (*ritenuta*). For instance, the tax on salaries of public officials, as well as on the interest of public securities, is withheld or retained by the government. A sub-class under this method is the system of so-called direct payments (*versamenti*). The income tax due from savings banks, the Red Cross fund, the Sardinian War securities, the fund from which the clergy are paid, etc., is also withheld or paid directly by the state. The second method is that of register or rolls (*ruoli nominativi*), that is, payments made directly by individuals who are put on the tax rolls. Finally, in the case of corporations, of employers, and of all debts in general, the tax is inscribed on the register not in the name of the person who receives the income, but in the name of the person who pays it out. Although the names appear on the register, it is the names of the persons who pay the income and not of those who receive the income. This method may therefore be put into a third class, and is sometimes called the method of *ritenuta di rivalsa*. Strictly speaking, this method, it will be seen, includes some of the characteristics of each of the preceding methods. Taking the first and the third methods together, it will be seen that the principle of stoppage at source is applied at all events in part to the Italian tax.

The taxpayers are all required to make their declarations. After the amount of gross revenue has been determined, they are reduced to the amounts of assessable incomes as fixed by the law. The incomes are divided into what is practically five schedules. Schedule A-1 includes the income from capital and so-called perpetual revenues, which are derived from state or provincial securities or loans, including government mortgages, ground rents, and fixed annuities, as well as income from securities issued by corporations that are guaranteed or subsidized by the state, and the income from lottery prizes. In this schedule the incomes are assessed at their full amount, and the rate is therefore twenty per cent.

Schedule A-2 embraces all other income derived from capital, and all other perpetual revenues which are not included in Schedule A-1. Here the assessable income is fixed at thirty-fortieths of the real income; the rate, therefore, is really fifteen per cent. Schedule B includes the so-called temporary mixed revenues, — that is, incomes derived from the coöperation of capital and labor. Practically it means the income derived from industry and trade. Here the assessable income is fixed at twenty-fortieths of the real income, — that is, the rate is ten per cent. Schedule C comprises the temporary incomes derived exclusively from individual exertion, such as wages or professional earnings. Here the assessable income is fixed at eighteen-fortieths of the real income, the rate consequently being nine per cent. Schedule D includes the incomes from pensions and salaries paid by government and the wages of public employees. Here the assessable income is fixed at fifteen-fortieths, that is, the rate is seven and one-half per cent. All these rates are increased by two centesimi per cent to cover the expense of verification and collection.

The abatements are fixed differently in Schedule D from those in Schedules B and C, and are arranged according to the list mentioned above.[1] But a complication is introduced by the fact that in the case of incomes subject to abatement, the reduction of the general income to the assessable income follows the old figures of the law of 1877, and not the new figures of the law of 1894. That is to say, the "net reduced" incomes are arrived at by reducing the incomes in schedules B, C, and D not to twenty-fortieths, eighteen-fortieths, and fifteen-fortieths of their actual amount respectively, but to six-eighths, five-eighths, and four-eighths respectively. The consequence is that in Schedules B and C the old abatements of 250, 200, 150, and 100 lire, respectively, became new abatements of 166.66, 133.33, 100, and 66.66 lire. For instance, the recipient of an income of 600 lire in category B, who would, according to the calculation of 1894 be exempt as not having the minimum of subsistence of 400 lire, is actually

[1] *Supra*, page 344.

taxable because according to the law of 1877 his assessable income would be 600 times six-eighths or 450 lire. When, however, the question arises as to what the abatements should be in such a case, there are still further complications. According to the new law he would be assessable, if there were no abatement, at 300 lire; but instead of deducting the old abatement of 250 lire from these 300 lire, there is now abated only the sum of 166.66 lire. He would therefore pay a tax of 20 per cent on 133.34 lire (300–166.66), that is, he would pay about 27 lire. The same would be true of other abatements.[1]

When we come to the administrative features of the tax, we are confronted by several interesting facts. The list of persons subject to the tax in each commune is supposed to be prepared annually by the municipal council (*giunta municipale*). If prepared with care this would, of course, be of very great value; but as a matter of fact, the lists are scarcely ever revised, and are of little use. The chambers of commerce in the different towns are legally required to notify the authorities of the formation of any new corporations or the opening of any new business, and the notaries, as well as the registers or managers, etc., are supposed to send to the tax office a list of all documents. Moreover, the court officials are prohibited, under severe penalties, from taking note of any document which is not shown to have paid the tax. As a matter of fact, however, this penalty has never been applied.[2] Every taxpayer is also compelled to make a declaration of his income, under heavy penalty; but in practice the penalty is not enforced, and he therefore never does so. As a result, the officials (*agenti delle imposte*) have either to depend upon the indirect payment of the tax, that is, in those cases where the tax is stopped at the source, or they have to make their own assessment in all cases of the direct taxation of the individual. The tax agents, therefore, almost universally make the assessment of the income themselves. The assess-

[1] *Cf.* for other calculations Spoelberch, *op. cit.*, pp. 88–92.

[2] Spoelberch, *op. cit.*, p. 137.

ment was only recently made on the average of the two preceding years, in the case of private business or unlimited-liability companies; on the income of the current year, in the case of incomes from securities, pensions, and fixed allowances; and on the basis of the business year ending in the preceding July, in the case of banks and limited-liability companies. In 1907, however, the biennial valuation was changed to a quadriennial valuation, to the extent, at all events, that the government itself cannot change the valuations for four years, while the taxpayer still has the right of altering the valuation at the end of two years.

Originally, when the income tax was an apportioned tax, the assessment of the shares payable by individuals was confided to a commission of citizens elected by the local council. When the tax became a personal tax, the government entrusted the matter of assessment to the fiscal agent, although a little later the local commission, to which references will be made in a moment, was also given the right of aiding the fiscal agent to fix the assessments. As a matter of fact, however, the commission never utilized this right, so that the matter rests in the hands of the tax officials.[1]

Owing to the enormous rate of taxation, the fiscal agent is very moderate in his demands. He scarcely ever thinks of assessing the so-called actual income at the real figures, and he generally comes to some amicable understanding with the taxpayer. If, however, the taxpayer objects to the assessment levied by the fiscal officer, he may appeal. There are two kinds of appeal — administrative and judicial appeal. The bodies to which is entrusted the administrative appeal consist of three kinds of commissions. The commission of first instance, or communal commission, is composed of a presiding officer appointed by the prefect, and of four members elected by the communal council. This commission often divides itself into sub-commissions and, being generally favorable to the taxpayer, ordinarily reduces the assessment as fixed by the fiscal agent. Either party may then appeal

[1] Spoelberch, *op. cit.*, p. 136.

within twenty days to the provincial commission, consisting of five members, one of whom is nominated by the provincial council, one appointed by the chamber of commerce of the province, two appointed by the department of direct taxes, and one, who presides, by the prefect. As the majority of this commission represent the government rather than the taxpayer, they generally take the opposite attitude, and ordinarily uphold the fiscal agent as over against the communal commission. A third and final appeal is possible to a central commission of twelve members, appointed by the government. This central commission not only acts as a court of appeal, but also takes up in the first instance other questions like that of double taxation. This exhausts the possibility of appeal on questions of fact, but on questions of law a further appeal is possible to the courts, and in Italy there are no less than five such instances of appeal.

In making their assessments the fiscal agents have broad powers. They are permitted to do seven things: (1) they may demand from the public officers an extract of any document which they need; (2) they may summon any taxpayer to appear before them for examination; (3) they are allowed access to any industrial or commercial establishment; (4) they may summon to their office anybody who they think can give them information; (5) they may examine the ledgers or registers of certain companies known as anonymous societies (the French *compagnies en commandite*); (6) they may demand inspection of securities; and (7) they may consider the house rent paid by the individual.

While they have these rather considerable powers, as a matter of fact they very rarely make use of any except the last; and accordingly they guess at the individual income very largely on the basis of the house rent and the mode of living. In other words, what was meant to be a system of direct taxation of income has become in practice a method of assessment based upon presumptions or outward signs.

Finally, it may be stated that the tax is collected not by the government officials themselves, but by contractors to whom the collection of the revenue is farmed out, in return for a proportion of the tax collected, which must not exceed six per cent. The contract usually lasts for ten years, and is put up for public auction in the communes.

§ 4. *The Question of Fraud*

When we consider the actual working of the Italian law, we find that notwithstanding the many admirable provisions which it contains, the tax rates are so enormously high that evasion and fraud are almost universal. Almost from the very beginning of the high rates complaints of fraud were heard, and these have not been diminishing in recent years. In 1893, for instance, we are told, "a large part of incomes, perhaps, in fact, the greater part, completely escapes taxation."[1] So notorious have these frauds become that a special study of this subject has recently been made by a Frenchman, Perdrieux, in a most interesting volume, to which the present prime minister of Italy, Sig. Luzzatti, contributes a preface.[2] We are told that the officials are at least honest. Luzzatti emphasizes the fact that the government has succeeded in eliminating the "fraud of frauds," — that is, the favoritism due to political or religious reasons. "In Italy," says Luzzatti, "if we have not attained the ideal, which belongs to heaven and not to earth, every taxpayer at least has the assurance that such stormy passions do not enter in the least into the assessment of taxes."[3] More than that is not claimed, even by Luzzatti. He speaks of Minister Sella as the real author of this "code of financial torture." While he maintains that the taxpayer in Italy is "the most peripatetic, the most admirable, and the most patient human animal known in fiscal history," he also finds a limit to the sacrifices that can be made, and agrees that "the tendency

[1] Vinci, *op. cit.*, p. 20.

[2] *Les Fraudes dans l'Impôt Italien sur les Revenus de la Richesse Mobilière, Avec une Lettre-Préface de M. Luigi Luzzatti.* Par Pierre Perdrieux. Paris, 1910.

[3] *Op. cit.*, p. 8.

to fraud develops in proportion to the fiscal greediness (*l'âpreté fiscale*) with which the taxpayer is afflicted." Luzzatti refers to the attempts made by the government to change the law or the customs, and points out that they all failed in the presence of the outcry on the part of the taxpayer. As he wittily remarks: "We officials carry on art for art's sake, but the taxpayers carry on art in order to live."[1] In Italy only about four-tenths of the tax is collected by stoppage-at-source, so that in the greater part of the tax the door is wide open to fraud. We are told that perhaps the worst frauds are found in the professional classes, where, as Luzzatti again so well puts it: "the diversities and the 'undulations' of conscience attain a degree of refinement of which the higher talents alone are capable. The common people are always more frank."[2]

Where declarations are made by the ordinary business man, they are notoriously inadequate. Obviously an income tax running up to twenty per cent, to which all manner of other kinds of local taxes are to be added, would indeed be unendurable if enforced to the hilt. Satisfactory arrangements are therefore usually made between the individual and the fiscal agent. But for a great mass of income from personal property the agent has no means at all of estimating the real income. He does not dare, as we have seen, to use his powers, for such an attempt would lead to a revolution — and so far as the owners of securities are concerned, they either have to put their money into foreign securities, which as we have seen, by a great defect in the law, are not taxable at all, or they can deposit their securities in private banks or in the particular kind of companies which are not in any way subject to inspection by the officials. The consequence is that the ad-

[1] "C'est que nous autres financiers, nous faisons de l'art pour l'art, et que les contribuables font de l'art pour la vie." — *Op. cit.*, p. 7.

[2] The professional classes "où les 'diversités' et les 'ondoiements' des consciences atteignent des degrés de finesse dont seulement les talents supérieurs sont capables. Le peuple dans sa rudesse est toujours plus ingénu et plus franc." *Cf.* also Spoelberch, *op. cit.*, p. 139 and in general Lia, *op. cit.*, pp. 109–121.

ministration, disarmed not only by law but also by the force of public opinion, is practically unable to control the assessments, and contents itself with making a rough guess based very largely on house rents. Scarcely any one thinks of making an honest return of his income, and no one believes that the tax represents any real approximation to the actual capacity of the individual. This results in shocking inequalities as between individuals and a complete disorganization of the revenue. And yet, such as it is, the government is unable to dispense with the income tax, which forms, with all its shortcomings, a relatively important part of the revenue system. In 1907, for instance, the income tax yielded, in rough figures, 275,000,000 lire, out of 458,000,000 derived from direct taxes in general, and as against 1,187,000,000 derived from indirect taxes, and 308,000,000 from other sources.[1]

But when we compare the Italian income tax with either the English or the Prussian, these figures are insignificant. It is true that income from real estate is not included, and it is of course true that Italy has less wealth than England or Germany. But with a tax rate four to five times as high as in England or Germany, the total yield is less than half of what it is in Germany and less than a third of what it is in England.

It was thought at one time that these immense frauds might be stopped by publishing the lists of the taxpayers, but so ingrained has the habit of under-assessment become in

[1] The yield of the Italian income tax at different periods has been as follows:

1864 (6 months)	14,799,697 lire
1866	61,078,160 lire
1870	89,707,238 lire
1877	184,839,641 lire
1890	230,690,000 lire
1895	287,310,000 lire
1900	289,060,000 lire
1906	305,000,000 lire
1907	275,000,000 lire
1910 (estimated)	267,000,000 lire

The falling off in 1907 was due to the conversion of the Italian debt at a lower rate of interest.

Italy that the publicity of the returns has made virtually no difference. The only thing that would surprise an Italian would be to ascertain that his neighbor had either declared his real income, or had been assessed in any degree comparable to his real income.

Our general conclusion, therefore, must be that while the Italian income-tax law possesses some admirable features, such as the stoppage-at-source provisions and the principle of differentiation of revenues, the tax rates have become so enormous that the administration has broken down under the weight, and that the public conscience has given way to an equal extent. The Italian income tax is a signal proof of the folly of the attempt to tax incomes at anything more than a very modest figure.

§ 5. *Switzerland*

The Swiss cantons rely to a very large extent on the general property tax as the chief source of revenue. This was the mediæval system, and disappeared only gradually with the dominance of the aristocratic *Geschlechter* in the seventeenth and eighteenth centuries. When the Swiss democracy again came to its own in the nineteenth century, the old general property taxes were everywhere reintroduced, with this difference, however, that they were now gradually supplemented in some cases by cantonal income taxes, and that the system of progression was applied.[1]

[1] An account of the development of the property taxes and a detailed table of the rates of the existing property and income taxes in every canton in Switzerland will be found in Seligman, *Progressive Taxation*, 2d ed., pp. 62–77. The three best books on the general subject of Swiss property and income taxes are Schanz, *Die Steuern der Schweiz in ihrer Entwickelung seit Beginn des 18 Jahrhunderts.* Stuttgart, 1890. 5 vols.; M. de Cérenville, *Les Impôts en Suisse.* Lausanne, 1898; and J. Steiger, *Grundzüge des Finanzhaushaltes der Kantone und Gemeinden.* 2 vols. Bern, 1903. Of studies on the separate cantons the best for the earlier period is Karl Bücher, *Basel's Staatseinnahmen und Steuervertheilung.* Basel, 1888; and for the more recent period H. Ernst, *Die direkten Staatssteuern des Kantons Zürich im neunzehnten Jahrhundert.* Winterthur, 1903; and Esslen, *Die direkten Steuern im Kanton Zürich.* Zurich, 1910.

The introduction of the income tax as a supplement to the general property tax was due to the experience of the larger cities and to the recognition of the fact that the system of property taxation fails to reach professional and other earnings from personal exertion which bulk so large in modern times. In one locality, in fact, Baselstadt, the income tax was introduced first, namely in 1840, and was supplemented by a property tax only at a later period. Everywhere else, however, the income tax, where it exists at all, was introduced to round out the property tax.

At the present time there are several systems in vogue. In the first place, we find the general property tax, supplemented by a tax on the income from property as well as from labor. This is the system in vogue in Baselland, in Solothurn and in Ticino. The second group of cantons is composed of those that have a general property tax, but only a labor income tax. These include a majority of the Swiss cantons, or precisely thirteen out of twenty-five; all, in fact, except those specifically mentioned in the other categories. In these cantons the income tax plays an entirely secondary rôle, and is levied for the most part only on labor incomes and pensions. This is true more especially of Aargau, Appenzell-a.-Rh., Graubünden, Obwalden, St. Gallen, and Schaffhausen. In a few cantons there is a slight deviation from the general rule. Neuchâtel includes the revenue from real estate outside of the canton. Freiburg, which exempts from the property tax securities of corporations engaged in commerce and industry, includes in the local income tax business incomes as well as labor incomes. (3) The third class of cantons have only the general property tax and no income tax at all. These are Nidwalden, Glarus, Appenzell-a.-Rh., Geneva, and Vaud. Vaud, however, has a business tax (*Gewerbesteuer*) instead of the income tax. Schwyz stands midway between the second and the third class, in that it possesses, in addition to the property tax, a tax levied on incomes from pensions and from dividends on capital. Finally, a fourth class is represented by Bern, which has a general income tax but no general property tax, with the exception, however, that in the case of real estate and of the mortgages thereon, the property and not the income is assessed.

The prevalent Swiss system, therefore, may be said to consist of a property tax together with a tax on labor incomes. The two taxes together thus reach the entire income, the one the income from property, the other the income from labor. This principle is, however, not carried out everywhere with precision; for in Lucerne real estate is subject not only to the property tax, but also to an income tax under the name of *Katastersteuer*, which is the survival of a tax that can be traced back to 1699. Moreover, in Thürgau and Uri, whenever the interest on capital exceeds four or four and one-half per cent respectively, the surplus income beyond that figure is taxable by the income tax also. In the four cantons of the first category, however, including Basel, the supplementary income tax is added to the property tax, so that the owner of property pays both property and income tax. This results, of course, in the fact that incomes from property are taxed at a higher rate than incomes from labor, thus effecting a differentiation like that recently introduced into England.

The rate of the income tax, where it exists, is on the whole a very moderate one, being in most cases only two per cent. This is due to the fact that it serves as a tax supplementary to the property tax, the rates of which are, in some of the cantons, very high.[1] In Bern, however, where it will be remembered the income tax is the chief tax, and where there is no general property tax, but only a tax on land, the rate on the income tax is much higher, rising in the various grades to about six and one-half per cent. The custom of progression is found in most of the cantons that levy the income tax, except

[1] The details for both the property tax and the income tax for each of the separate cantons will be found in Seligman, *Progressive Taxation*, 2d ed., pp. 67–73. Attention ought to be called to the misprints whereby the rate of the property tax in Appenzell-a.-Rh., Baselstadt, Lucerne, Solothurn, and Vaud, is printed as % instead of o/oo, *i.e.* the rates on property are so much per mill, not so much per cent. The figures for the income tax are correctly printed %, *i.e.* so much per cent.

in Bern and in Neuchâtel; but even where it exists, the maximum rate is comparatively low. The system of impositions and abatements for lower incomes is widespread. Finally, the income tax applies generally to corporations as well as individuals; but the taxation of corporate incomes is exceedingly varied. In some cantons corporate incomes are taxable and the shareholders are exempt; in others both corporations and stockholders are taxable on the same income; in still others the system in vogue is that of taxing corporations on incomes above a certain normal figure, which is supposed to represent the income of the security holders. The latter system, it will be remembered, is the one that has been adopted in Prussia and some other German states.

The point of chief interest to us is the administration of the law. As to this, it may be said that on the whole the income tax, especially in the industrial centres, works just about as badly as the general property tax, or in fact is still more unsuccessful than the general property tax.

With reference to the general property tax, the system is almost as notorious as in the United States. In Switzerland, as in the United States, the greater the population and the industrial development, the more defective is the administration of the general property tax. In the smaller towns and in the agricultural districts, where more primitive economic conditions still continue, the property tax works fairly well. In the larger cantons the reverse is true. There are in Switzerland only four cantons with a population of over 250,000 people, — in their order, Bern, Zurich, Vaud, and St. Gallen.[1] In most of these places the growing needs of the communities and the reliance to a very great extent on the general property tax as the chief source of revenue have brought about a nominal rate of taxation comparable to that of the United States, where, if honestly assessed, the property tax would take from one-third to one-half of the entire income. Under such conditions, of course, failure is inevitable. In

[1] According to the census of 1904 the population was as follows: Bern, 606,000; Zurich, 451,000; Vaud, 290,000; St. Gallen, 256,000.

the report of the canton of Zurich, for instance, where it became possible to check up the returns from the general property tax by means of the inheritance tax, it was stated that in 1897 only fifty-four per cent of the property was reached.[1] In an address on the question of fraud, that was given by one of the officials in 1895, a careful analysis was made of the situation, with the conclusion that the frauds increase four times as fast as the wealth increases.[2] A few years later Professor Wolf, who declared the property tax the "child of sorrow" (*Schmerzenskind*) of all tax reformers, stated that where the tax rates were felt to be too high, the taxpayers found the natural corrective in under-assessment.[3] The situation has not improved at the present day.[4] In Bern, the conditions are not much better, and we are told that in Appenzell and St. Gallen there is no thought at all of an honest assessment.[5] In other cantons the inhabitants look upon it as something that goes without saying, that they should declare not more than one-third of their income; and in still other places it has become the custom for the assessors to ask the taxpayers directly as to how much they care to pay. This is especially true where the rate of the property tax is so high that it is virtually impossible to pay it.

Even where the rates are not so very high, the situation is not much better. Everywhere in Switzerland, we are told, the people are tired of taxes.[6] Moreover, the use of the general property tax both for local and for cantonal purposes has brought about the same result as in the United States,

[1] *Cf.* Steiger, *op. cit.*, p. 70.

[2] "Hieraus wird der Schluss abgeleitet, das die Verheimlichung mit zunehmendem Reichtum nicht nur proportional sondern fast in quadratischem Verhältniss anwachse." — J. Walder, *Referat vor der Versammlung der Kantonalen gemeinnützigen Gesellschaft zu Bülach*, quoted in Ernst, *Die Direkten Staatssteuern des Kanton Zürich.* Winterthur, 1903, p. 209.

[3] *Die Steuerreform im Kanton Zurich*, von Dr. Julius Wolf. Zurich, 1897. Quoted in Ernst, *op. cit.*, p. 210.

[4] Esslen, *Die direkten Steuern im Kanton Zürich.* Zurich, 1910, pp. 33 *et seq.*

[5] "Von einer ehrlichen Versteuerung gar keine Rede sein kann." — Steiger, *op. cit.*, p. 72.

[6] "Überall in der Schweiz ist mann steuersatt." — *Op. cit.*, p. 232.

namely, the endeavor of each locality to keep the assessments down as low as possible, in order to escape their share of general taxation. As we are told, "it is an old story."[1]

Other writers tell the same tale. In Zurich the declarations are notoriously inexact. Nobody is astounded nor is any one scandalized by these under-assessments. In Appenzell they go still further. It has become good form (*de bon ton*), to use an official expression, to return as small a fraction of one's property as possible. Not only does the public not think of blaming the taxpayer who conceals the greater part of his property, but people are actually esteemed in proportion to the skill with which they can evade the payment of the tax.[2] In many of the towns regular contracts are entered into between the taxpayer and the assessor, whereby the individual agrees, in consideration of the small assessment, not to transfer his residence to some other town.

In only two of the towns of fair size are conditions at all better. One of these is Geneva, with a population of 145,000, where, we are told in a government report, almost "one-half of the proceeds of the tax is paid by a little more than one hundred taxpayers, who, it must be conceded, have always acquitted themselves of their obligations with absolute correctness and loyalty. It is not there that the evasions are to be found; they must be sought elsewhere."[3] This, however, is due to the fact that the *taxe mobilière* is very low, amounting, if reduced to terms of income at four per cent on the capital, to a tax of less than eight per cent on the income. The entire proceeds, moreover, are insignificant, being less than one-quarter of a million dollars. The other exception to the general rule is Baselstadt, a town of about 120,000 inhabitants, where we are also told that "the taxpayers, at least according to government reports, acquit themselves of their fiscal obligations with the greatest loyalty."[4] But in Basel, also, it will be remembered that the rate is exceedingly

[1] "Es ist alles schon dargewesen." — Steiger, *op. cit.*, p. 232.

[2] Cérenville, *op. cit.*, p. 139.

[3] *Ibid.*, p. 134.

[4] *Ibid.*, p. 80.

low, running up from one to three per mill on the property. This is a very different situation from the other cantons, where the rates become "unreasonable and absurd" (*unsinnig*)[1] and reach the figure of one and a half or two per cent on the property.

Careful students of the problem have therefore been forced to the conclusion that it is only where the rates are exceedingly low and the tax itself insignificant that it meets with any measure of success, and that in proportion as the rates are raised and the property tax plays a more important rôle, it fails. "If the rate is moderate," we are told, "the tax is paid regularly; if it is exaggerated, frauds, which are more or less avowed, are employed in order to reduce the tax rate to a reasonable sum."[2] In the larger towns the situation is like that of which we are told in St. Gallen and Rorschach, where official documents inform us that "so far as concerns our deplorable tax situation, we must at the very outset reckon with the presumption of a more or less considerable system of fraud. Every taxpayer who is even half-way honest is the victim of a hundred others who snap their fingers at the law and who, in doing so, are to a very great extent not interfered with in the least by the officials."[3] All this has a familiar sound to us in the United States. It shows that where conditions are similar the results must be the same. The general property tax accordingly is almost as much of a failure in Switzerland as in the United States, and succeeds fairly well

[1] *Cf.* Steiger, *op. cit.*, p. 73.

[2] Cérenville, *op. cit.*, pp. 134–135, where he sums up his investigations of each of the separate cantons. The same conclusion is reached by Professor Bullock in his address on "The General Property Tax in Switzerland" in *State and Local Taxation, Fourth International Conference under the Auspices of the International Tax Conference.* Columbus, 1911. As Esslen, *op. cit.*, p. 39, points out, however, a mere reduction of the rate will in itself not help, unless there is a decided change in administrative methods.

[3] "Angesichts unserer Steuermisere ist zum vornherein mit der Präsumption einer mehr oder weniger erheblichen Steuerhinterziehung zu rechnen. . . . Jeder auch nur halbwegs ehrlich Versteuernde ist eben bei uns das Opfer von hundert andern, die dem Gesetz eine Nase drehen und darin vielfach von den Steuerbehörden nicht gestört werden." — Steiger, *op. cit.*, p. 117.

only in agricultural districts, and in places where the tax is so insignificant that it plays but a slight rôle in the budget.

The experience with the income tax is not a whit more favorable than with the general property tax. The methods of assessment are practically the same, and we have all degrees of variation, from complete local autonomy in assessment to more or less centralized control by the cantonal authorities. Although the rate of the income tax in general is, as we have seen, lower than that of the property tax, the results are about the same, because the assessment is imposed upon the same individuals. Those who escape or avoid the property tax do not pay the income tax. Moreover, the difficulties in the assessment of income are greater than those in the assessment of property, because some property, at all events, is visible and tangible, while income cannot be put into that category. If any comparison is to be drawn between the income and the property taxes in Switzerland, it is in favor of the property tax. In the one important canton, Bern, where, as we have learned, the income tax is of a more general character, and where it is levied on all incomes except that from real estate, it has been proved by experience that the income tax works less well than the analogous property tax in other cantons. We are told that the frauds are far more numerous in Bern, where the personal tax is levied on incomes, than in the other cantons, where the tax is levied on property; and this is true even of those cantons where the property tax is not checked up by the system of inventory after death.[1] Moreover, it is conceded that on general principles the income tax in Switzerland is inferior to the property tax. For the business man it makes very little difference whether the tax is assessed on income or on capital. For the workman who spends his money daily, without keeping

[1] "D'après les expériences faites dans le canton de Berne qui, seul de son espèce, prélève un impôt exclusif sur le revenu des capitaux mobiliers, les fraudes paraissent y être beaucoup plus nombreuses que dans les cantons se ralliant à l'impôt sur le capital, même dans ceux qui de ne connaissent pas l'inventaire au décès." — Cérenville, *op. cit.*, p. 100.

accounts, the calculation of income is considerably more difficult than that of capital, if he has any. For the peasant, a large part of whose income is derived from the produce of the land which he and his family consume, a satisfactory estimate of income becomes impossible. In the canton of Vaud, for instance, it was pointed out that the introduction of an income tax would result in the whole agricultural population paying not a single cent. It is for this and similar reasons that the students of Swiss taxation consider it absurd to hope for an escape from the evils of the cantonal general property tax through the substitution of a cantonal general income tax. If the property tax works badly, the income tax works still more badly.[1]

The Swiss experiences are especially instructive because of the political analogies with the United States. Everything in the way of the patching up of the general property tax that well-intentioned but misdirected zeal has attempted in the United States, has been tried in Switzerland and with similar lack of success. Not only has the general property tax broken down as the chief source of revenue, especially in the industrial centres, but the income tax, where it exists, is even more unsuccessful than the property tax. If any one lesson is to be learned from Swiss experience, it is that a system of state income taxes, resting, as do the general property taxes, upon methods of local assessment, even when modified by a central state control, is bound to fail. It is a conclusive proof of the fact that the way out of American difficulties is not to be sought in the direction of any kind of local or state income tax.

[1] Cérenville, *op. cit.*, pp. 93–103; *cf.* Esslen, *op. cit.*, p. 38.

PART II

THE INCOME TAX AT HOME

CHAPTER I

THE INCOME TAX IN THE AMERICAN COLONIES

IN taking up the discussion of the income tax in the United States, it is doubly important to treat it from the historical point of view. For in the first place, not only is it true that one generation is prone easily to forget the experiences of its predecessor, but in the second place the correct interpretation of certain important clauses in the American constitution which have a vital bearing upon our topic depends in very large measure upon the historical setting, and upon the mental attitude of the fathers of the constitution to the actual conditions of the time. It is for both of these reasons that a discussion of colonial conditions becomes more than ordinarily important. Our endeavor in this initial chapter will be to compare the colonial taxes with their analogues past and present in the American commonwealths, and to attempt to ascertain how far these colonial imposts deserve the name of income tax.[1]

§ 1. *The Beginnings*

The first general tax law in the American colonies, with the exception of the early poll tax in Virginia,[2] was the law of 1634

[1] This chapter was published fifteen years ago in the *Political Science Quarterly*, vol. x, no. 2 (June, 1895). It was originally written, with the exception of a few paragraphs, in 1893, and was intended to form a part of a general work on the income tax, the appearance of which has been delayed until now. At the request of Mr. Clarence A. Seward, one of the counsel in the income-tax cases of 1895, a portion of this essay was submitted to him in manuscript form, and was utilized in the preparation of the monograph presented by him in the original hearing as a supplementary brief. The majority of the quotations in that monograph are taken from the manuscript essay.

[2] For the early Virginian legislation, see Ripley, *Financial History of Virginia*, pp. 17–24 (Columbia University *Studies in History, Economics and Public Law*, vol. iv, no. 1).

in Massachusetts Bay.[1] This provided for the assessment of each man "according to his estate and with consideration of all other his abilityes whatsoever." It is probable that the measure of this ability was to be found in property; for, although the law itself does not further explain the term, the matter is elucidated in a provision of the next year, that "all men shall be rated for their whole abilitie, wheresoever it lies."[2] This seems to imply only visible property; for such property alone is susceptible of a *situs*.

It was not until seven years later that "ability" was defined to include something more than mere property. This, however, occurred not in Massachusetts Bay, but in the colony of New Plymouth. In 1643 assessors were appointed to rate all the inhabitants of that colony "according to their estates or faculties, that is, according to goods lands improoued faculties and ᵖsonall abillities."[3] This law is noteworthy for a double reason. It is the first to use the term "faculty," and it distinguishes faculty and personal ability from visible property. But although it provides for a faculty tax, it does not tell us exactly how to measure this faculty. This was reserved for the more comprehensive law enacted three years later by the Court of Assistants of the Massachusetts Bay Company. The court order of 1646 provides not only for the assessment of personal and real estates, but distinctly mentions "laborers, artificers and handicraftsmen" as subject to taxation, and then goes on to say: "And for all such persons as by advantage of their arts and trades are more enabled to help bear the public charges than the common laborers and workmen, as butchers, bakers, brewers, victuallers, smiths, carpenters, taylors, shoemakers, joyners, barbers, millers and masons, with all other manual persons and artists, such are to be rated for returns and gains, proportionable unto other men for the produce of their estates."[4]

[1] *Colonial Records of Massachusetts Bay* (Shurtleff's ed., 1853), i, p. 120.

[2] *Ibid.*, p. 166.

[3] *Records of the Colony of New Plymouth:* Laws 1623–1682 (Pulsifer's ed.), xi, p. 42.

[4] *Colonial Records of Massachusetts Bay*, ii, p. 173. *Cf.* ii, p. 213, and iii, p. 88.

Here for the first time we have the definition of faculty or ability. Just as the faculty of the property owner is seen in the produce of his estate, so that of "artists" and "tradesmen" is to be found in their "returns and gains." Of course, since the property value of an estate is approximately equal to the capitalized value of the annual produce, the faculty of the property owner can be measured by the value of the property, that is, by the value of his "estate"; but when there is no property, the assessors are compelled to fall back on the "returns and gains."

The principle thus laid down in the records of Massachusetts Bay was soon adopted by other colonies. The colony of New Haven, for instance, at first levied a land tax. As early as 1640, however, personal property was assessed, by the provision that a new rate should be "estreeted, halfe upon estates, halfe upon lands." [1] In 1645 it was seen that even this was not adequate, and a proposal was made to tax others besides property owners; but no decision was reached at that time.[2] As the dissatisfaction grew, a committee was appointed in 1648 to inquire into the feasibility of the Massachusetts system of taxing all property in general, and also of levying a tax on the profits of those who possessed no property.[3] The committee reported that they were in doubt as to the advisability of taxing houses and personal property,

[1] *Records of the Colony and Plantation of New Haven*, i, p. 40.

[2] The court considered "how heavy the publique chardges grew, that most of them have bin expended for the publique safty and about things of common public vse, wherein all that live in the plantation have a like benefit in their proportions and yet many live in the plantation and have manny priveledges in it have hitherto borne noe part of these publickque chardges, wherevppon it was debated whether or noe in equety such should not be rated some way or other for time to come, so as those that have borne the whole burden hitherto may be eased; but because it was not ripe for an issue, the court referred to . . . a committee."—*Ibid.*, p. 181.

[3] Lieutenant Seely propounded that the court would "consider of some other waye of rateing men than is settled by lands for divers men wch had good estates at first and land answerable, whose estates are sunke and they not able to paye as they did, and divers ᵖsons whoe had land for their heads, whose estates are smalle, yett paye great rates, and others whose estates are increased, haveing but little land, paye but a small matter to publique charges," *etc., etc.*—*Ibid.*, p. 448.

but that "for tradesmen they thinke something should be done that may be equall in waye of rateing them for their trades." As a result the law of 1649 was enacted, which introduced the taxation of profits of laborers, tradespeople, and others.[1]

In Connecticut the early laws were patterned on the Massachusetts Bay legislation. It was provided in 1650 that "every inhabitant who doth not voluntarily contribute proportionably to his abillity to all common charges shall be compelled thereunto by assessments and distress"; and it was further provided that the lands and estates should be rated "where the lands & estates shall lye," but "theire persons where they dwell."[2] Then follow detailed instructions how to assess various kinds of property. The final clauses in these instructions provide for the faculty tax on all "manuall persons and artists," *etc.*, following word for word the Massachusetts Bay law of 1646, as quoted above. These provisions are frequently repeated in the laws of the seventeenth century.

In Plymouth Colony the practice inaugurated by the law of 1643 continued, although we find only two more instances where it is expressly mentioned, namely, in 1665, when "visible estates and faculties" are spoken of,[3] and in 1689, when a court order fixed the valuation for different kinds of visible estate, but left the valuation of "faculties and personall abillities" to be determined "at will and doome."[4]

In Rhode Island the faculty tax was introduced a little later. In 1673 the Assembly laid down the rule that taxes

[1] The reason given was: "Seeing that labourers and handycrafe trades & seamen are of divers sorts & conditions, some live more comfortably, some less, some follow ther trades more and some less, ther time being taken vp more aboute husbandry wch payes another way, that therefor a due consideration be had, and every man justly rated as neere as the comittee can judge, and that other men whoe trade in way of merchandizing bee duely rated according to their trades and stockes they improve, as neere as they can judge." — *Ibid.*, i, p. 494.

[2] *Colonial Records of Connecticut*, i, p. 548.

[3] *Records of the Colony of New Plymouth* (Pulsifer's ed.), xi, p. 211; Shurtleff's ed., iv, p. 102.

[4] *Ibid.*, p. 221.

ought to be assessed according to "equety in estate and strength," *i.e.*, not only according to the property, but also in proportion to what was elsewhere called the "faculty," or "profits and gains."[1] In Rhode Island we find, moreover, the curious survival of the mediæval practice that every man should assess his neighbor as well as himself.[2] Later on "three able and honest men" were chosen in each town to "take the view of each of their inhabitants," and as to "the merchants and tradesmen to make this part of the rate according to the yearly profit."[3]

Outside of New England this early taxation of profits by the side of the general property tax is found also in New Jersey, where it was provided by the law of 1684 that not only property owners, but also "all other persons within this province who are free men and are artificers or follow any trade or merchandizing, and also all innholders, ordinary keepers and other persons in places of profit within this province, shall be lyable to be assessed for the same according to the discretion of the assessors."[4]

This completes the list of examples of the faculty tax during the seventeenth century. Subsequently, as we shall see, the tax appeared in some of the Southern colonies. In New York it never secured a foothold. During the Dutch domination the tax system of this latter colony was composed almost entirely of excises and duties; when the English obtained control, the general property tax was introduced, but with-

[1] "This assembly, taking into consideration the great dissatisfaction and irregularity that hath been by makeinge rates or raisinge a common stock for public charges in this Collony in general or for any perticular towne, and the great faileableness to accomplish it and great delaies in performance, what was done, and the necessity there is for publick charge to be borne, and the justice it should be done according to equety in estate and strength," *etc., etc.* — *Colonial Records of Rhode Island*, ii, p. 510.

[2] The individual shall be required to "give in writeinge what proportion of estate and strength in pertickelar he guesseth tenn of his neighbours, nameinge them in pertickular, hath in estate and strength to his estate and strength." — *Ibid.*, ii, p. 512.

[3] *Ibid.*, iii, p. 300 (1695).

[4] *Laws of New Jersey*, 1664–1701 (Leaming and Spicer), p. 494.

out any additional "faculty" tax as in the New England colonies.[1]

§ 2. *The Development in New England*

During the eighteenth century the custom of assessing profits continued and extended to other colonies. In Massachusetts more earnest and repeated efforts to explain and to enforce the law were made than anywhere else. This will be our excuse for tracing the legislation in more detail.

Upon the union of the Plymouth and Massachusetts Bay colonies into the Province of Massachusetts, under the charter of 1692, a law was immediately enacted providing that all estates whatsoever, real and personal, should be taxed at "a quarter part of one year's value or income thereof." But this was not very clear. Nor was the doubt removed by another law of the same year, to the effect that "every handicraftsman" be valued "for his income."[2] In 1697, however, we find the old terms used as of general application. The assessors are now again cautioned to rate the taxpayers, "having due regard to persons' faculties and personal abilities." In 1698 the clause "not excluding faculties" is inserted. And in the following year the assessors are instructed to tax "incomes by any trade or faculty which any persons do or shall exercise."[3] A few years later fuller instructions are given. Thus in 1706 the assessors are admonished to rate "income by any trade or faculty, which any person or persons (except

[1] Ely, in his *Taxation in American States and Cities* (New York, n. d. [1888]), p. 110, says that "the estimated incomes of certain classes were taxed." The context is not clear, but Professor Ely could only have meant that this was the case in New England, whose tax system is described in the New Netherland document to which allusion is made. Yet this passage was quoted in the brief submitted by Mr. Seward to the Supreme Court as showing that the system was to be found in New Netherland. This is a complete mistake. No such system ever existed in New Netherland. Mr. Seward's mistake is not wholly inexcusable, because it is not easy to ascertain from Dr. Ely's text whether he is referring to New England or to New Netherland.

[2] *Acts and Resolves of the Province of Massachusetts Bay, 1692 to 1780* (5 vols.), i, pp. 29, 92.

[3] *Ibid.*, i, pp. 302, 413.

as before excepted) do or shall exercise in gaining by money, or other estate not particularly otherwise assest, or commissions of profit in their improvement, according to their understanding and cunning, at one penny on the pound, and to abate or multiply the same, if need be, so as to make up the sum hereby set and ordered for such town or district to pay."[1] The law of 1738 adds the words "business or employment," commanding the assessment of "the income or profit which any person or persons (except as before excepted) do or shall receive from any trade, faculty, business or employment whatsoever, and all profits which may or shall arise by money or other estate not particularly otherwise assessed, or commissions of profit in their improvement. . . ."[2]

Except as to the rates, this form of law continued unchanged till 1777. The law enacted in this year gives a fuller interpretation of income than any hitherto. Taxpayers are assessed "on the amount of their income from any profession, faculty, handicraft, trade, or employment; and also on the amount of all incomes and profits gained by trading by sea and on shore, and by means of advantages arising from the war and the necessities of the community."[3] Again, the law of 1779 provides that, "in considering the incomes and profits last mentioned, the assessors are to have special regard to the way and manner in which the same have been made, as well as the quantum thereof, and to assess them at such rate, as they on their oaths shall judge to be just and reasonable; provided, they do not in any case assess such incomes and profits at more than five times" [increased in the next year to "ten times"] "the sum of the same amount in other kind of estate."[4] In 1780 a constitution was adopted which commanded, among other things, that the public charges of government should be assessed "on polls and estates in the manner that has hitherto been practised." The same methods, therefore, continued to the end of the century.

[1] *Acts and Resolves of the Province of Massachusetts Bay, 1692 to 1780*, i, p. 592.

[2] *Ibid.*, ii, p. 934.

[3] *Ibid.*, v, p. 756.

[4] *Ibid.*, v, pp. 1110, 1163.

In none of the other colonies do we find so full or so frequent indications of the legislative intent as in Massachusetts. Occasional references, however, are found to the practice of assessing income. And although it is probable that the custom was gradually dying out, the storm and stress of the Revolutionary period again brought it to the front in several places.

In Connecticut we have seen that the early laws followed almost word for word the Massachusetts legislation. Later acts provided that "all such persons who by their acts and trades are advantaged shall be rated in the list . . . proportionable to their gains and returns, — butchers, bakers . . . and all other artists and tradesmen and shopkeepers."[1] As the assessors might find it difficult to rate them justly, the law sometimes gave more explicit directions as to fixing the income. Thus the following was enacted in 1725: "For the future every one of the allowed attorneys at the law shall be set in the annual list for their faculty, *i.e.*, those that be the least practitioners fifty pounds, and the others in proportion to their practice."[2] It may be doubted whether even this settled the matter definitely.

Later enactments prove, however, that instead of directly estimating the profits of the taxpayers liable to the tax, the assessors used different criteria to compute the amount. For instance, it had several times been provided that "all traders, tradesmen and artificers shall be rated in the list proportionable to their gains and returns." But as there seems to have been no uniformity in the methods employed, the following important act[3] was passed in 1771: —

"All traders or shopkeepers in this Colony shall be rated in the list after the rate of ten *per cent* on the prime cost of all goods, wares, and merchandizes which they purchase for sale by retail (except the produce and manufactures of this Colony). And all traders by wholesale, tradesmen, artificers,

[1] *Acts and Laws of Connecticut.* New London, 1715, p. 100.
[2] *Colonial Records of Connecticut, 1717–1725*, vi, p. 525.
[3] *Ibid., 1768–1772*, xiii, p. 513.

tavern-keepers, and others by law rateable on account of their faculty or business, shall be rated in the list to the amount of their annual gains, incomes or clear profits by means of their business, according to the best estimate that can be made thereof by the listers, who shall assess such traders, tradesmen, Sc. by their best discretion, agreeable to the rules aforesaid. But when it appears that any persons have been unsuccessful or sustained considerable losses in their trade, in such cases the listers may make proper abatement for the same. And if any person shall be assessed by the listers for any of the matters aforesaid more than at the rates aforesaid, upon proof thereof, by oath or otherwise, to the satisfaction of the listers, or authority and selectmen, who have right by law to grant relief, such overcharge may be abated."

The faculty tax continued in Connecticut to the close of the century substantially unchanged, with the exception that ordinary artisans were subsequently exempted. Secretary Wolcott, in his famous report on direct taxes in 1796, described the tax system as embracing first, a tax on various kinds of property, real and personal, and second, "assessments proportioned to the estimated gains or profits arising from any and all lucrative professions, trades and occupations, excepting compensations to public officers, the profits of husbandry and common labor for hire." This second element was included in the annual lists of taxable property as "assessments on lawyers, shopkeepers, surgeons, physicians, merchants," *etc.*[1]

In Rhode Island, where the faculty tax was originally levied as in the neighboring colonies, it seems to have fallen into disuse somewhat earlier. In 1744 the tax law still provides "that the assessors in all and every rate shall consider all persons who make profit by their faculties, and shall rate them accordingly."[2] This is the last direct mention of the

[1] *American State Papers, Finance*, i, pp. 423, 454.

[2] *Acts and Laws of His Majesty's Colony of Rhode Island and Providence Plantations.* Newport, 1745, p. 295.

faculty tax. In 1754 and 1755 the only taxes named are those on "estates and polls."[1] This expression might possibly still be considered to include faculties. But in the revision of 1766, which served as a basis of valuation during the remainder of the century, we search in vain for any mention of the faculty tax.[2] And when Wolcott drew up his report in 1796, he described the system of taxation simply as one "on polls and the collective mass of property."[3] It may safely be said, therefore, that the faculty tax had disappeared in Rhode Island by the middle of the century.

In New Hampshire the faculty tax came into use somewhat later. The first detailed assessment law passed in the province, in 1719, instructed the selectmen to assess the residents "in just and equal proportion, each particular person according to his known ability and estate." Later on, in 1739, "an act for the more easy and speedy assessing" of taxes was passed, which authorized the selectmen to assess "the poles and estates of the inhabitants, each one according to his known ability."[4] In 1772 greater definiteness was attained by the provision that a person's "faculty" should be estimated at the discretion of the assessor, although not at a sum over twenty pounds.[5] Before the close of the century, however, the tax had disappeared. For the law of 1794, which fixed all the details of the state's system, while taxing tradesmen, storekeepers, and others, assessed them merely on their stock in trade as a part of their personal property.[6]

In New York, as we know, there never was any faculty

[1] *Records of the Colony of Rhode Island*, v, pp. 309, 465. A curious protest against the arbitrariness in the assessment of the general taxes is to be found in 1766. *Ibid.*, vi, 518 pp.

[2] *Acts and Laws of the English Colonies of Rhode Island and Providence Plantations*, p. 219.

[3] *American State Papers, Finance*, i. p. 422.

[4] *Acts and Laws of His Majesty's Province of New Hampshire*, 1761, pp. 30, 180.

[5] Law of January 2, 1772.

[6] Law of February 22, 1794; *New Hampshire Laws of 1793*, p. 472.

tax. But Vermont, when it split off from New York, followed the example of Connecticut in taxation as in much other legislation. The first law on the subject, that of 1778, is very explicit in its provisions, and repeats the Connecticut law in some places word for word.[1] The part of interest to us is as follows: —

"Be it further enacted by the authority aforesaid, that all allowed attorneys at law in this commonwealth, shall be set in the annual list for their faculty, — the least practitioner fifty pounds, and the others in proportion according to their practice; to be assessed at the discretion of the listers of the respective towns where said attorneys live during their practice as such. All tradesmen, traders, artificers, shall be rated in the lists proportionable to their gains and returns; in like manner, all warehouses, shops, workhouses and mills where the owners have particular improvement or advantage thereof, according to the best judgment and discretion of the listers." In 1791 attorneys also were assessed "proportionable to their gains according to the best judgment and discretion of the listers."[2] And in 1797 the general provision was inserted that "all licensed attorneys, practitioners of physic or surgery, merchants, traders, owners of mills, mechanics, and all other persons who gain their livelihood by buying, selling, or exchanging, or by other traffic not in the regular channel of mercantile life," be listed in proportion to their returns.[3]

§ 3. *The Middle and Southern Colonies*

Outside of New England, the faculty tax was to be found also in Pennsylvania, though not until after the Revolution had commenced. In 1782 a law was enacted which imposed

[1] An Act directing Listers in their Office and Duty. Printed in *Laws of Vermont, 1779* (295 of Slade's *State Papers*). No copy of the laws of 1778 is known to be in existence. The laws of that year were embodied in the volume for 1779. See Wood, *History of Taxation in Vermont*, pp. 32 and 36 (Columbia University *Studies in History, Economics, and Public Law*, vol. iv, no. 3).

[2] *Laws of Vermont, 1791*, p. 266.

[3] *Compilation of Laws* of 1797, p. 565. See Wood, *op. cit.*, p. 39.

a poll tax on all freemen. But the law went on to say that "all offices and posts of profit, trades, occupations and professions (that of ministers of the gospel of all denominations and schoolmasters only excepted) shall be rated at the discretion of the township, ward or district assessors, and two assistant freeholders of the proper township, ward or district, having due regard to the profits arising from them."[1] In 1785 mechanics and manufactures were added to the list of exempted classes. The discretion which this act left to the assessors was very slight, as the lower and higher limits of the tax were definitely fixed. In distinction from the faculty tax proper, this might rather be termed a classified poll tax with a very low maximum. For instance, freemen of no profession or calling might be assessed from fifty cents to ten dollars; mechanics and tradesmen, thirty cents to two dollars; tavern-keepers, shop-keepers, and other retailers, fifty cents to five dollars; brokers, bankers, merchants, lawyers and physicians, one to ten dollars; persons of professions or occupations not before described, twenty-five cents to eight dollars. These rates applied only when the tax on real property amounted to one per cent. When the rate fell below this, the "taxes on occupations and professions," as they were called, were to be proportionately reduced.[2]

In Delaware, also, we find the faculty tax. The law of 1752, indeed, simply provided that all persons should be assessed on their estates. But that this included more than mere visible property is apparent from the section which states that single men who have no visible estates shall be assessed at not less than £12 nor more than £24, and that in all cases the assessors shall pay "due regard to such as are poor and have a charge of children."[3] When Wolcott described the system, he spoke of it as based on the assessment of profits. But in 1796, when a new law was passed, provision was made for

[1] *Laws of the Commonwealth of Pennsylvania* (Dallas), ii, p. 8.

[2] *American State Papers, Finance*, i, p. 428.

[3] *Laws of the Government of New-castle, Kent and Sussex upon Delaware*, Philadelphia, 1752, p. 234.

"ascertaining the stock of merchants, tradesmen, mechanics and manufacturers, for the purpose of regulating assessments upon such persons, proportioned to their gains and profits."[1] In other words, stock in trade was now assessed as personal property.

Even in the more southern states the faculty tax was not unknown. In Maryland, during the colonial period, the tax system was very primitive; as its historian states, taxes were levied "by even and equal assessment, without reference to ability to pay, revenue enjoyed or property worth."[2] But when the state constitution was adopted in 1777 and the poll tax was abolished, not only was a property tax inaugurated, but provision was made for the faculty tax by imposing an assessment of one-quarter of one per cent on the "amount received yearly" by "every person having any public office of profit, or an annuity or stipend," and on the "clear yearly profit" of "every person practising law or physic, every hired clerk acting without commission, every factor, agent or manager trading or using commerce in this state."[3] In 1779 the tax was raised to two and a half per cent.[4] In the next year, however, the whole system was abolished.

In South Carolina the faculty tax began earlier. We find that in 1701 a law was enacted which imposed a tax on the citizens according to their "estates, stocks and abilities, or the profits that any of them do make off or from any public office or employment." And two years later it was provided that individuals should be assessed on their "estates, goods, merchandizes, stocks, abilities, offices and places of profits of whatever kind or nature soever." This system continued throughout the century. The law of 1777, which was the first under the state constitution, phrased it a little differently by providing for a tax on "the profits of all faculties and pro-

[1] *American State Papers, Finance*, i, p. 429.

[2] "Sketch of Tax Legislation in Maryland." Printed as an appendix to the *Report of the Maryland Tax Commission.* Baltimore, 1888, p. cxxix.

[3] Maryland *Laws of 1777*, c. 22, secs. 5, 6.

[4] *Laws of 1779*, c. 35, sec. 48.

fessions, the clergy excepted, factorage, employments, handicrafts and trades throughout this state."[1] Wolcott, in his report of 1796, describes the system as "founded on conjectural estimates, according to the best judgment of the collectors." These estimates were "understood to be very moderate." In Charleston, for instance, they were graduated according to the circumstances of individuals, from $100 to $5000.[2]

Finally, it may be said that in Virginia an attempt was made in 1786 to introduce the faculty tax, by assessing attorneys, merchants, physicians, surgeons, and apothecaries. But the experiment lasted only four years. In 1790 the whole system was abolished.[3]

In addition to these cases of the taxation of profits as such, there were many cases in which, while the tax was imposed on property, the assessment was made on the basis of product. That is, it was deemed easier to ascertain the profits than the value of the property: the property was gauged by the revenue. Thus in Massachusetts in 1692 all estates real and personal were to be rated "at a quarter part of one year's value or income thereof." To make this clearer, it was provided in the following year that "all houses, warehouses, tanyards, orchards, pastures, meadows and lands, mills, cranes and wharffs be estimated at seven years' income as they are or may be let for; which seven years' income is to be esteemed and reputed the value of craftman, for his income." From this time on until the Revolutionary period the valuation of real estate was computed on the income derived from it, but the number of years varied. From 1698 to 1700 the valuation was one year's income, but during most of the eighteenth century it was six years' income.[4]

In Rhode Island the ratemakers were to "take a narrow inspection of the lands and meadows and so to judge of the

[1] Cooper, *Statutes at Large of South Carolina*, ii, pp. 36, 183; iv, p. 366.

[2] *American State Papers, Finance*, i, p. 435.

[3] Hening's *Statutes*, xii, p. 283; xiii, p. 114.

[4] *Acts and Resolves of the Province of Massachusetts Bay*, i, pp. 29, 92, 413.

yearly profit at their wisdom and discretion."[1] In New Hampshire the assessors were directed to take the estimated produce of the land as a basis; while houses, mills, wharves, and ferries were valued at one-tenth or one-twelfth of their yearly net income, after deducting repairs.[2] In New York it was customary to assess land according to its annual yield, even when other property was valued at a fixed sum. We find this as early as 1693, and frequently thereafter.[3] Even as late as the middle of the eighteenth century the New York assessors for the general property tax took an oath to estimate the property by the product — a pound for every shilling.[4] In Delaware, even after 1796, real estate was still valued according to the rents arising therefrom.[5] Finally, in Virginia, although land was generally estimated at the presumed capital value, the yearly rent or income was sometimes utilized, especially in the towns, as a basis for estimating the value.[6] Toward the close of the century we are told that the usual tax on city property was "five-sixths of one per cent of the ascertained or estimated yearly rent or income."[7]

§ 4. *Conclusion*

After this somewhat tedious review of the facts, let us attempt to ascertain exactly what they mean.

At the very outset the distinction between real and personal taxes must be borne in mind. A real tax is a tax on things; a personal tax is a tax on persons. A land tax, for instance,

1 *Colonial Records of Rhode Island*, iii, p. 300.

2 Acts of January 2, 1772, and February 22, 1794. *Laws of the State of New Hampshire, passed at the General Court, 1793*, p. 471.

3 *Journal of New York*, March 9, 1693. *Cf.* Act of September 29, 1709.

4 *Cf.* the assessor's oath in New York, law of 1743, sec. 13: "I do swear . . . that I shall carefully . . . compute the yearly value of the income of such estate, and for each shilling which I shall so value each person's estate at yearly, I shall rate such person a pound," in Van Schaack's *Laws of New York from 1691 to 1773*.

5 *American State Papers, Finance*, i, p. 429.

6 Act of 1793. Shepherd's *Statutes at Large of Virginia, 1792–1806*, i, p. 224.

7 *American State Papers, Finance*, i, p. 431.

whether it be levied on property or on produce, is a tax on the land — on the thing itself, a real tax. No attention is paid to the personal condition of the landowner; the government looks to the land itself, as in the case of a tax on houses or a tax on tangible personalty. The objective point is the thing rather than the person. Of course it is always the person, the individual, who is under obligation to pay taxes to the state. But the endeavor to assess the individual as such has always met with great difficulty, and many governments have therefore had recourse to the various pieces of property rather than to the person.

As we have learned in an earlier chapter,[1] when the conception of taxable capacity first forced itself through, in the early mediæval towns, we find the general property tax. In all early communities, and especially under the feudal system, land is very rarely sold. We accordingly find the earliest land taxes to be taxes on gross produce. The ability of the farmer is measured by the produce of the land, the ability of the landowner by the rental from the land. Thus the land taxes in early mediæval Europe were taxes on produce or rents. In more democratic communities, like those of Switzerland, the land tax soon became a tax on the selling value. In the other European countries this transformation was effected a little later. Only in relatively recent times has it been deemed possible in most of the European states to get more closely at the taxable capacity of the land by a careful estimate of its actual yield. On the greater part of the continent of Europe to-day the land taxes are assessed on the basis of the yield, but now on net yield, and detailed surveys and valuations are made in order to determine this with accuracy.

In America the development was very much the same. At the outset, when land was not bought and sold readily, the tax was assessed more or less arbitrarily, either according to the quality of the land or according to its assumed produce. In only a few cases was the still more primitive method pur-

[1] *Supra*, pp. 6, 43.

sued of taxing land simply by quantity. But all these taxes were real taxes; they were taxes on the thing itself, on the land, not on the income of the landowner. When in the course of time transfers of land began to be more frequent, these produce taxes turned into taxes on the actual or selling value, as is the case everywhere to-day throughout the United States. This plan, with the democratic methods of assessment, is supposed to furnish a sufficiently close approach to the truth. We make no attempt, as a rule, to ascertain the exact produce of each parcel of land as a basis for the tax. But whether we assess land upon its produce or upon its value, is immaterial; the tax is on the thing itself.

In addition to this land tax, we find in all partly developed communities a tax upon personalty also. In so far as most of the personalty is visible and tangible, the natural basis of assessment is its actual or selling value. This basis was used in all the mediæval states as well as in the American colonies. But it was very soon recognized that property alone, whether in land or in personalty, was not an adequate measure of taxable capacity. Revenue is derived from other sources than property. Hence it was that an attempt was made to supplement the property tax by a faculty tax upon persons that derived revenue from these other sources. The tax on earnings was supposed to correspond to the property or produce tax on special pieces of personalty or realty. It was not an income tax in the modern sense. By an income tax we mean a tax upon the personal income of the individual. It is a personal tax, not a tax on things, not a real tax. Allowance is made for indebtedness and for other elements affecting the personal situation of the taxpayer. But this faculty tax, as it was called in mediæval Europe as well as in colonial America, was not levied on the total income of the individual. It was a tax not on actual profits, but on assumed profits. Just as articles of personal property were put down on the lists at fixed rates; just as plots of land were set down at sums supposed to represent their capitalized annual produce, — so the individuals subject to the faculty tax were not required to make returns of their earnings, but were assessed by the listers at fixed amounts. As we have seen more specifically in the cases of Connecticut and South Carolina, — and the same was true in the other colonies, — the faculty tax was nothing but a classified product tax, in which different employments and different classes within each employment were rated at fixed amounts. It was precisely for this reason that the faculty tax, which at the outset gave satisfaction, soon became antiquated and unjust. Instead of being a tax on actual profits or gains as a part of a general tax on incomes, in which attention might be paid to the individual situation of the taxpayer, it was nothing but an arbitrarily levied class tax on certain assumed earnings. It bore very little relation to the actual income; it became grievous and unequal; and it was therefore allowed to fall into disuse. It never was an income tax in the modern sense.

On the other hand, as we shall see in the next chapter, most of the state income taxes of the nineteenth century, with the exception chiefly of that of Massachusetts, which is simply a survival of the old faculty tax, have been true income taxes. They have not been confined to the assumed gross profits of certain particular classes, but have been levied on the actual total income of the taxpayer. The difference between the colonial taxes on profits and the state income taxes is very much like that between the European taxes on product and the income taxes. In Germany, in France, and in many other countries, after the general property tax had been abandoned, and after it had been recognized that net product was in some respects a better index of taxable capacity than property, the whole tax system was changed into one on product: that is, first we had the land tax, which was levied on net produce; then came the buildings tax, levied on the rental value of buildings; then came the tax on capital, according to the yield of capital; then came the tax on business, in which the assumed profits were calculated according to the outward signs. All these were taxes on things — on the land, on the house, on the business, on the capital; and finally, to round out the system, there was sometimes imposed a tax on the remaining source of profit, that is, the professions and employments which yield a produce in the shape of a salary or compensation. These taxes are still to-day known as real taxes (*impôts réels*), or produce taxes (*Ertragssteuern*). It is only within a comparatively recent period that product has come to be recognized as a less satisfactory theoretical basis of taxation than income. Product looks at the thing that produces; income looks at the person that receives. In the first case, no allowance is made for debts or other qualifying circumstances; in the second, such allowance is possible. As a consequence, modern income taxes have been imposed partly in place of, and partly in addition to, these produce taxes.[1] The system of real taxes is being supplanted by that of personal taxes. Or, if we persist in using the term "income," the first class of taxes may be called indirect or partial income taxes, because the income of the individual is only indirectly reached and only partially assessed; while the new and more general taxes are income taxes in the proper sense of the term, and have the characteristics of a personal tax.

In a subsequent chapter we shall endeavor to ascertain what was meant by the term "direct tax" in the constitution of the United States, and whether it included this faculty tax — the only form of profits taxation then known in America. If there is any value in the above exposition, however, it is plain that the profits taxes of the American colonies were not direct income taxes, and that in so far as they are called income taxes at all, they must be classed as indirect income taxes. It is remarkable that in all the legal briefs and arguments presented to the Supreme Court in connection with the first income tax case in 1895 no reference was made to the statement of Oliver Wolcott, the Secretary of the Treasury, who in 1796 drew up the celebrated report on direct taxes in the states. Wolcott was thoroughly familiar with all the details of the laws, and in his enumeration of the various taxes imposed he described the faculty tax in the following words: —

[1] *Cf.* the discussion, *supra*, pages 12 *et seq.*

"4th. *Taxes on the profits resulting from certain employments.* This head will comprise a variety of taxes collected in certain of the states upon lawyers, physicians and other professions, upon merchants, traders and mechanics, and upon mills, furnaces and other manufactories. In some states these taxes are attempted to be proportioned to the gains and profits of individuals, in which cases they are both arbitrary and unequal; in other states the taxes are uniform, in which cases they are only unequal.

"It is presumed that taxes of this nature cannot be considered as of that description which the Constitution requires to be apportioned among the states. . . . It is impossible to render them exactly equal; that they are easy of collection, that their operation is indirect, and that they are capable of being rendered perfectly certain, are recommendations in their favor."[1]

Oliver Wolcott clearly saw, as he expressed it, that the operation of these taxes was indirect, and, with a full knowledge of everything that had been said on the subject in every state, he came to the conclusion that they were not direct taxes in the contemplation of the constitution. The points which it is desired to emphasize here are that these faculty taxes were not income taxes at all; that they were simply an addendum to the early land taxes, originally levied on product; and that with the change of the taxes on product into taxes on property, these faculty taxes gradually fell into disuse. To call them income taxes is a misnomer.[2] Income taxes in the modern sense were levied for the first time in England in 1799, and it was at a considerably later period that they spread to other countries. To claim, then, that our colonial taxes on faculty were income taxes, betrays a confusion of thought and

[1] *American State Papers, Finance*, i, p. 439.

[2] Wolcott, in referring to the somewhat peculiar system in Delaware, described above, said, "taxes have been hitherto collected on the estimated annual income of the inhabitants." This naturally led the counsel in the income taxes of 1895 to speak of the Delaware system as the "income tax." But the same system is virtually in vogue to-day, and no one thinks of calling it an income tax.

an ignorance of economic distinctions. The faculty tax had its origin in the same motives that have led to the introduction of modern income taxes, but it was not an income tax; just as the French land and business taxes of to-day, levied on the produce of land and of industry respectively, are not income taxes. In fact, the entire modern movement on the continent can be understood, as we have learned in earlier chapters, only if interpreted as an attempt to levy income taxes in place of the produce taxes, among which are to be found imposts precisely analogous to the American colonial "faculty tax." The European movement is one to replace the "faculty taxes" by income taxes. If the faculty tax were an income tax, this movement would be unmeaning.

The distinction between taxes on product, on the one hand, and taxes on income, on the other, is one of fundamental importance in the science of finance. To disregard it can only produce confusion. To observe it will enable us to explain what is otherwise inexplicable in American economic history.

CHAPTER II

State Income Taxes

The history of the taxation of incomes by the separate commonwealths of the American Union[1] may be divided into four periods: first, the survival and development of the old faculty tax of colonial times; second, the partial resort to income taxes as a result of the fiscal difficulties of the early forties; third, the utilization of the income tax especially by the southern commonwealths during the period of the Civil War; and fourth, the newer movement of the last two decades.

Let us study first the survival of the colonial faculty tax.

§ 1. *The Survival of the Colonial Faculty Tax*

During the early decades of the nineteenth century not only did the faculty tax gradually fall into disuse, but with the increasing mobility of landed property, assessment according to selling instead of annual value or product, became universal. In Vermont the old custom continued for several decades. In the consolidated act of 1825 certain classes liable to the faculty tax were to be assessed according to their gains, but with both a minimum and a maximum limit. For instance, attorneys, physicians, and surgeons were listed at not less than ten dollars nor more than three hundred dollars,

[1] The greater part of this chapter was printed as an article in the *Political Science Quarterly*, vol. x (1895), pp. 235 *et seq.* Eight years later a more detailed study was made by Delos O. Kinsman, *The Income Tax in the Commonwealths of the United States*, in the *Publications of the American Economic Association*, 3d series, vol. iv, no. 4, New York, 1903. Five years later the study was brought up to date, so far as graduated income taxes were concerned, in Seligman, *Progressive Taxation*, part i, sec. 15; and in the following year Kinsman completed his study in an article, "The Present Period of Income Tax Activity in the American States," in *Quarterly Journal of Economics*, vol. xxiii (1909), pp. 296 *et seq.*

"according to their respective gains." Merchants and traders were taxed at figures varying from fifteen dollars to six hundred dollars "in proportion to their several gains, taking into consideration the capital employed in said business." Mechanics and manufacturers were assessed up to one hundred dollars, "according to the best discretion and judgment of the listers." This survival of the old custom, however, worked very badly and produced much dissatisfaction. The act of 1841 dropped all reference to the faculty tax, and although by an act of the following year the tax was revived as to attorneys, physicians, and surgeons, it was finally abolished in 1850 amid general jubilation.[1]

In Connecticut the old custom continued, nominally at least, until the adoption of the new constitution in 1819. The revenue commission of 1887 described the old system as follows:[2] —

"Connecticut from her earliest history had followed the plan of taxing incomes rather than property. Those pursuing any trade or profession were assessed on an estimate of their annual gains. Real estate was rated not according to its value, but in proportion to the annual income which, on the average, it was deemed likely to produce. Land . . . was put in the list at a fixed rate for each kind . . . not because these sums were deemed to be the value of the land, but because they were thought to represent the average income they would produce." This "ancient system of income taxes," as it was called by the commission, came to an end in 1819, and was replaced by the plan of taxing property according to the modern methods.[3]

In Rhode Island and New Hampshire, as we know, the old custom did not survive the eighteenth century. Massachusetts enjoys the distinction of being the only state in the

[1] *Laws of Vermont, 1825*, c. ix; 1841, c. xvi; *1842*, c. i; *1850*, c. xxxix, p. 28.

[2] *Report of the Special Commission of Connecticut on the Subject of Taxation*, New Haven, 1887, pp. 9–10.

[3] *Connecticut Session Laws of 1819*, p. 338.

Union in which the faculty tax has continued down to the present day, and for that reason deserves a somewhat fuller treatment.

In the last chapter we traced the history of the faculty tax in Massachusetts to the law of 1777, which, as we saw, was virtually continued by the new constitution of 1780. We noticed the gradual process by which the term "faculty tax" was displaced both in popular usage and in legal parlance by "income tax." No change was made in the wording of the provisions until 1821, when an act was passed which included among the sums to be returned to the assessor "the amount of the income of such inhabitants from any profession, handicraft, trade or employment, or gained by trading at sea or on land, and also all other property of the several kinds returned in the last valuation, or liable to taxation by any law."[1] This wording is repeated in the act of 1830;[2] but in this act the term "faculty" is omitted, and it never reappears in later legislation. In the revised statutes of 1836 another change was made through the omission of the word "handicraft." The section reads as follows: "Personal property shall, for the purpose of taxation, be construed to include . . . income from any profession, trade or employment, or from an annuity, unless the capital of such annuity shall be taxed in this state."[3]

The next change came in the law of 1849,[4] providing that "income from any profession, trade or employment, shall not be construed to be personal estate for the purpose of taxation, except such portion of said income as shall exceed the sum of six hundred dollars per annum; provided, however, that no income shall be taxed which is derived from any property or estate which is the subject of taxation." In 1866 the exemption was increased to one thousand dollars, and in 1873, as a result of a compromise with those who were at-

[1] *General Laws of Massachusetts from the Adoption of the Constitution to 1831* (3 vols.), vol. ii, *Laws of 1821*, c. 107, sec. 2.

[2] *Session Laws of 1830*, c. 86.

[3] *Revised Statutes*, c. 7, sec. 4.

[4] *Laws of 1849*, c. 149.

tempting to have the law entirely repealed, to two thousand dollars.[1] This is still the law to-day.

In fixing the meaning of the law of 1849, two decisions of importance were handed down by the Supreme Court. In 1856 it was decided that the tax did not apply to the income derived by citizens of Massachusetts from stocks of foreign corporations held by trustees.[2] In 1870, however, the more important decision was made that the clause exempting incomes derived from property already taxed did not apply to the profits of merchants and others who employed such property in their business.[3] The result was that although the stock in trade of a merchant was already taxable as personal property, the income which was derived from his business was again liable to the income tax. It was this decision which led in the early seventies to the counter-movement to repeal the tax, and which resulted in a compromise whereby, as stated above, the limit of exemption was raised to two thousand dollars.

In 1875 a comprehensive report on taxation was made by a special commission.[4] The commission stated that "no one of our taxes reveals so great a lack of uniformity in its construction and enforcement, and such a wide difference of opinion as to its worth, as is found with reference to the income tax."[5] They called attention to the fact that although the law "has plainly and explicitly required the taxation of income, as a matter of fact, income is taxed in but very few places of the state; and the revenue derived from its assessment, either by municipalities or the state, is very inconsiderable." Out of a total of 340 towns on the valuation list of 1873 only 41 reported returns of incomes, while only five additional towns reported

[1] *Laws of 1866*, c. 48; *Laws of 1873*, c. 354.

[2] Susan Dorr *vs.* City of Boston, 6 Gray, p. 131.

[3] Wilcox *vs.* County Commissioners of Middlesex, 103 Mass., p. 544. *Cf.* Collector *vs.* Day, 11 Wall., p. 113.

[4] *Report of the Commissioners appointed to inquire into the Expediency of revising and amending the Laws relating to Taxation and Exemption therefrom.* Boston, 1875.

[5] *Op. cit.*, pp. 48, 49.

income and personal property, and only three reported income from salaries and learned professions. As a matter of fact, in the overwhelming mass of cases where the income tax was levied at all, it was imposed only upon people who already paid a personal property tax. The commissioners quoted the case of one town of 14,000 inhabitants, with a valuation of over $8,400,000 and containing many prosperous merchants and manufacturers, where only thirteen persons — consisting of cashiers, lawyers, clergymen, physicians, a mill agent, and an actuary — were assessed for income on a total valuation of $15,121. The commission went on to state that "in view of the great discrepancy existing in the construction and application of the law in the few places where any attempt even is made to enforce it, of the small amount of revenue obtained from it, and of its entire disregard in so great a portion of the commonwealth, much doubt has been felt as to the expediency of retaining it on the statute book. Construed differently in different, and perhaps adjoining, places, — enforced here, and allowed there to remain a dead letter, — it no doubt works hardship, inequality and injustice."[1]

Several memoranda were submitted arguing on each side of the question of repeal. Mr. Beard presented a strong paper in which he concluded that the "tax is oppressive and unjust to individuals, and of very little benefit to the community."[2] Mr. Pendergast objected strongly to what he considered the undue exemption of two thousand dollars.[3] On the other hand, one of the principal assessors of Cambridge declared himself in favor of the tax. Calling attention to the fact that in one of the wards of Cambridge the assessment to the income tax amounted to about twenty-five per cent of the total value of personal estate and income, and that twenty-seven persons paid a tax on income that was

[1] *Report of the Commissioners, op. cit.*, pp. 50–51.

[2] "The Massachusetts Income Tax." By Alanson W. Beard. *Op. cit.*, pp. 433–437.

[3] "Income from an Annuity, and Income from Profession, Trade or Employment." By George S. Pendergast. *Op. cit.*, pp. 437–440.

valued at $519,400,[1] he concluded, as a result of his experience that "individuals are just as ready and interested in rendering an account of their income as they are of any taxable property they may possess." He did not, however, expatiate upon their readiness to declare their personal property.

As a concession to public sentiment, as revealed by this testimony of Mr. Brown, the commission declared itself unable to recommend its repeal, chiefly on the ground of the admitted defects of the general property tax. The general property tax was working so badly that in the opinion of the commissioners even the slight help given by the income tax in reaching the ability of those who otherwise would not be hit at all was worth preserving. They found, however, that the exemption was entirely too high, and recommended its reduction to one thousand dollars. They also realized that one great defect in the law was the undue decentralization of the system, and they suggested a "central supervising department of taxes."[2] Finally they called attention to the double taxation that was imposed under the decision in Wilcox *vs.* Middlesex, and recommended a change in the law so as "to allow a deduction from the gross income of a sum equal to six per cent of the assessed value of the property employed in the business from which the income is derived."

None of the recommendations of the commission was followed. As a result the administration of the tax became more and more lax from year to year. In 1889 a special committee of the business association of Boston voiced its protest against what was left of the income tax. "The business men of this city," said the report, "are now living under an income tax than which nothing more irritating, indefensible and unjust can be well imagined."[3] The report dealt espe-

1 "The Income Tax, Why it should be Retained, and the Importance of Equally Enforcing It." By Dr. A. Z. Brown. *Op. cit.*, pp. 441–450.

2 *Op. cit.*, p. 55.

3 *Report of Special Committee on Taxation. Boston Executive Business Association.* Boston, 1889, p. 11. The report was signed by a committee of five prominent business men, headed by Mr. Jonathan A. Lane.

cially with the injustice of the double taxation imposed upon the business men in taxing the stock in trade as well as the income derived from the business. Referring to the concession on the part of the assessors that the tax should be levied only on the surplus over six per cent of the capital, the committee said: "We repudiate this concession as by no means meeting the facts or justice in the case, especially when what a man spends out of his business is reckoned as profits, whether or not; and the gains or profits of business can rarely be determined until the same is sold out or wound up." Largely because of this confusion of the income tax with the personal tax, they concluded: "The more your Committee consider the whole subject, the more they are impressed with the needlessness, as well as the weakness in all our dealings with personal estate." [1]

Two years later a special commission was appointed by the city of Boston to consider the question. This commission came to the same conclusion, stating that "in the taxation of income derived from personal property there is also in this state an extraordinary injustice and inequality." [2] They called attention to the fact that the only part of the income tax which was ever assessed was that upon business men who already paid a tax on stock in trade, and they naturally adverted to the essential injustice of this scheme. "There is no reason why the income derived from taxed personal property should be taxed which does not apply to the income derived from taxed real estate. No attempt is made to violate common sense and common justice by taxing income from real property, and yet that income depends upon care and skill." [3]

This effort of the business men to free themselves from the survival of the faculty tax was continued during the next

[1] *Report of Special Committee, op. cit.*, p. 121.

[2] *Message of the Mayor transmitting Report of the Special Commission on Taxation.* Boston, 1891, p. 19. The commission consisted of Messrs. George G. Crocker, Jonathan A. Lane, and William Minot.

[3] *Op. cit.*, pp. 21–22.

few years. In 1893 a joint special committee of the legislature was appointed to consider the whole problem of taxation, and some interesting testimony was given on the subject of the income tax. Mr. Jonathan A. Lane effectively quoted the reports of tax commissions in other commonwealths, and characterized the effort to tax the property and also the income arising from its employment as intolerable double taxation. Referring to the attempted division of a business man's gains, ascribing a portion of it to his capital and the remainder to his faculty, and charging a tax upon the latter, Mr. Lane stated: "Such a division is as impracticable as it is absurd. It violates common sense, every aspect of it, and it is impossible to conceive of such a thing as income derived from capital without some power, force, or effort to get that income out of capital."[1] He referred to the fact that in Boston the assessors usually deducted six per cent of the profits of capital before assessing the tax, and he quoted the reply of the corporation counsel, who had been asked for an opinion by the Boston board of assessors: "There is no reason, so far as I can see, why you should deduct the amount of six per cent of such value, any more than the amount of four, or five, or seven per cent, or an amount arrived at in any other way."[2] Mr. Endicott, one of the tax commissioners, reported that the assessment of the tax "is confined chiefly to the larger places, where a large, an immense business is done."[3]

The committee, after considering this subject, reported against the proposition to repeal the tax. Their reason, however, is rather remarkable: "If income was a mere offshoot or natural product of property already taxed, the taxation of such income might indeed be double taxation. But no reasoning has been adduced tending to make such a proposition entirely clear. To obtain an income, whether based upon professional ability, business capacity, or mechanical skill, requires the use of application of ability, shrewdness, talent,

[1] *Hearing before the Joint Special Committee appointed to consolidate, arrange and revise the Statutes of this Commonwealth relating to Taxation*, p. 96. Boston, 1893.

[2] *Op. cit.*, p. 97.

[3] *Op. cit.*, p. 102.

and adroitness. These qualities and forces combined fix and determine the *faculty* of the individual and it is this *faculty*, or actual ability, which we tax."[1] The learning and good judgment of the commission may be inferred from the following quotation: "The taxation of incomes in England, Germany and France is not only popular, but the condition of the people is such in those countries that any attempt to abolish this form of taxation would probably result in a revolution." In view of the fact that the income tax had just been introduced after a hard fight in Prussia, that it did not exist at this time in most of the other German states, and that it had no chance at all in France, this piece of information is delicious. Believing, therefore, that "the faculty possessed by an individual is rendered especially valuable by the protection afforded by the state," the committee concluded that "to allow such individual to escape from his just obligation would be in entire opposition to the practice long in force in this commonwealth."[2] A strong dissenting opinion, however, was submitted by Mr. Charles F. Brown.[3]

Three years later a commission of entirely different calibre was appointed to consider anew the entire question of taxation. After making a careful investigation of the whole situation, the commission found that in all the cities of the state, except Boston and Somerville, the assessed income on which the tax was imposed amounted to $3,880,220 out of a total personal property of $194,783,718; and that in Boston, according to the last returns, — those of 1894, — the assessed income was returned at $742,100 out of a total personal property of over $38,000,000.[4] In the state as a whole the assessment

[1] *A Full Report of the Joint Special Committee on Taxation, Recommendations and Codifications relating to the Laws of Taxation.* Boston, 1894, p. 33.

[2] *Op. cit.*, p. 34.

[3] "Report of the Minority relative to the Taxation of Incomes derived from Property subject to a Tax." *Op. cit.*, pp. 50–52.

[4] *Report of the Commission appointed to inquire into the Expediency of revising and amending the Laws of the Commonwealth relating to Taxation*, pp. 46–48, Boston, 1897. The report was signed by James R. Dunbar, Alvan Barrows, T. Jefferson Coolidge and F. W. Taussig.

of income in all the towns amounted to $1,529,705 out of a total personal estate of $147,800,703.[1] These figures are sufficiently enlightening, and show what an absolute shadow of its former self the faculty tax had become. The commission, aware of the failure of the general property tax, considered carefully the advisability of replacing it by a general state income tax. They concede that such a tax "would avoid at least one great hardship of constant occurrence under the present system; for unlucky investments yielding no income at all would not be taxed, as they now are." But they conclude that "it suffices to say that, in the present situation of this country, with our political traditions and business habits, we are of the opinion that an income tax would prove exceedingly difficult to administer with certainty and with equality of treatment as between different taxpayers. . . . We fear that no effective public opinion would be present to aid the administration of a state income tax, and that evasion and concealment would take place to so great an extent as to render it ineffective and deservedly unpopular."[2]

Since 1897 no further attention has been paid to the income tax. None of the recent reports of the tax commissions of Massachusetts, such as those of 1903, 1907, and 1908, has even dignified the subject by a reference. The larger questions connected with the taxation of business and of corporate property have completely overshadowed the problem of what to do with the remnants of the faculty tax. The assessment of salaries and personal incomes has virtually disappeared, except in an occasional instance of a college professor or of a state official, and in the few cases where business incomes are assessed at all, the assessment is added to the personal property tax and does not figure separately on the tax books. What is therefore still called the income tax in Massachusetts is nothing but an unequal and entirely arbitrary additional assessment upon a few members of the professional classes and a few large business men selected at haphazard in Boston and one or two other towns. Instead of being an

[1] *Op. cit.*, p. 263.

[2] *Op. cit.*, pp. 86–87.

income tax, it is nothing but a simulacrum of an income tax; instead even of being a faculty tax such as existed during colonial days, it has become nothing but the torso of a faculty tax.

The only other state in which the faculty tax lasted during the nineteenth century is South Carolina. In Delaware and Maryland, as we have seen, the tax disappeared before the close of the eighteenth century; but in South Carolina the first tax law under the new constitution which taxed "the profits of all faculties and professions, the clergy excepted, factorage employments, handicrafts and trades," [1] remained, with a few slight changes, in force up to the Civil War. In 1813 a special tax of four and one-half mills was imposed on the salaries of all state officials; [2] and was increased in the following year to sixty-two and one-half cents on every hundred dollars. In 1838 the system was slightly changed so as to provide for a tax of six per mill on income derived from employments, faculties, and professions, and from commissions received by vendors, factors, and commission merchants. Exemptions were allowed to clergymen, school-teachers and mechanics, and it was specially provided that attorneys should pay upon their entire professional income.[3] The yield remained as before, however, quite insignificant. The later history will be touched on hereafter.

The faculty tax was also employed in South Carolina for local purposes for a time. In 1809 an ordinance of the city of Charleston declared subject to taxation "all profit or increase arising from the pursuit of any faculty or profession, occupation, trade or employment." Clergymen, judges and schoolmasters or other teachers were exempt, and the rate was one-third of one per cent.[4] In 1844 the same words were used in a Charleston ordinance, except that "gross profit

[1] *Supra*, p. 379.

[2] McCord, *Statutes of South Carolina*, vol. v, p. 712.

[3] *Ibid.*, vol. vi, p. 605.

[4] This ordinance is quoted in City Council *vs.* Lee, 3 Brevard, p. 226, decided in 1812, which held that public salaries were not included.

or gross income" took the place of "all profit or increase." Exemption was also extended to mechanics so as to conform to the state system.[1]

In a few other states we find sporadic instances of survivals of the faculty tax. Thus, in Pennsylvania the law of 1782, which was discussed in the last chapter,[2] survived for a time. In 1799 mechanics and manufacturers were again included in the tax,[3] and in 1817 ministers and schoolmasters were also made taxable.[4] The tax, however, was rarely enforced, and afforded virtually no revenue. Of its temporary resuscitation in the forties we shall speak on the next page.

Except in the two states of Massachusetts and South Carolina, thus, the old custom of assessing profits as an adjunct to the property tax had totally disappeared by the middle of the century. Moreover, the assessment of real estate according to profits had almost everywhere been supplanted by assessment on selling value. The only exception was Delaware. In that state it is still provided that when houses or lands yield an annual rent, the owner shall be assessed for every twelve dollars of rent as for one hundred dollars capital; while in the case of ground rents eight dollars of rent are to be assessed as one hundred dollars of capital.[5] In practice, however, this method is now confined to assessments for school purposes only, while for county and municipal purposes real estate is assessed, as elsewhere, on selling value.

§ 2. *The Period of the Forties*

The second phase of income taxation in the American commonwealths began in the early forties. It is well known how the withdrawal of the federal government from the field of internal improvements and the distribution of the surplus

[1] Quoted in State Amendment, Elfe, 3 Strobhart, p. 318.

[2] *Supra*, p. 378.

[3] *Laws of the Commonwealth of Pennsylvania* (Dallas), vol. vi, p. 397.

[4] Henning's *Statutes at Large*, vol. ix, p. 353.

[5] *Revised Statutes of Delaware*, 1839, c. x, secs. 3 and 5, pp. 107–108.

revenue in 1836 started the commonwealths on that wild career of extravagance which soon resulted in disaster. Many of the states found themselves involved in serious financial difficulties at the close of the thirties, and the matter of the assumption of the large state debts by Congress became a burning political question in the early forties. When this project came to naught, and the states found that they had to rely upon their own efforts in order to meet the interest charges on their swollen indebtedness, several of them were confronted by the necessity of increasing their revenues, and a few turned to the project of some form of income taxation.

The first state to resort to this expedient was Pennsylvania. We have seen in the last paragraph that the colonial faculty tax had lingered along, but that it had become virtually a dead letter. Now in 1840 it was partly resuscitated. The law of that year imposed a tax of one per cent upon all salaries, and of one mill upon each dollar received from every trade, occupation, or profession not already taxed by the commonwealth.[1] The law of the following year increased the tax upon salaries to two per cent, and upon the profits from trade, occupation, or professions to one per cent, but also provided for an exemption of two hundred dollars on all incomes.[2] In 1844 a slight change was made in the law,[3] and in this form the tax lingered along for a few decades. In 1854 it was provided that the tax on trades, professions, and occupations, when levied for school purposes, should not be less than fifty cents,[4] a figure increased in 1857 to one dollar.[5] What the real proceeds of the tax were, it is impossible to state, as no separate accounts were kept. An indication is, however, afforded by a statement in the governor's message that in 1843, out of a total revenue from taxation of $910,000, the amount received from offices was $1386.[6] So insignificant,

[1] *Laws of 1840*, act no. 232, sec. 2.

[2] *Laws of 1841*, no. 117, sec. 9.

[3] *Laws of 1844*, no. 318, sec. 24.

[4] *Laws of 1854*, no. 610, sec. 30.

[5] *Laws of 1857*, no. 667, sec. 2.

[6] *Governor's Message* of January 1, 1844.

in fact, had the tax become that it was allowed to disappear in 1871, when the law was repealed.

What had been done in Pennsylvania was now attempted in some of the other states, especially in the South. In Maryland, where for many decades there had been no direct taxes at all upon property, a general assessment was imposed in 1841, in order to raise the required revenue.[1] In the following year a law imposed a tax of two and one-half per cent upon salaries and emoluments, and all incomes and profits from professions, faculties, and employments.[2] The law was like that of Pennsylvania in that it exempted salaries of judges and clergymen; but it differed in that it also exempted incomes derived from taxed property, as well as incomes under five hundred dollars. A progressive tax was imposed by another law on all ground rents, so arranged as to be equivalent to a tax of two and one-half per cent upon an annuity amounting to ten per cent.[3] Later on, however, the rate of the tax on ground rents was made the same as that on other incomes, except that five hundred dollars was not exempt. An interesting feature of this law was the provision requiring taxes upon official and other salaries to be paid by the employer or by the state respectively. It is not worth while, however, to go into the administrative features of the law, because the whole system worked most unsatisfactorily. The governor, in his message of 1844, stated that there was a deplorable remissness in the execution of the tax laws; "some of the counties have utterly, and others partially, disregarded them." He stated that the revenues could "not be materially increased by the income tax heretofore partially collected." [4] A few years later, according to the state treasurer's report of 1849, no income tax at all seems to have been collected, and in 1850 the law was virtually repealed by an act which provided that "the collectors should not be held liable for the recovery of the tax if they proved it not to have

[1] *Report of the Maryland Tax Commission to the General Assembly.* Baltimore, 1888, pp. cxxxviii, cxliii.

[2] *Laws of 1841–1842*, c. 325.

[3] *Laws of 1841–1842*, c. 329.

[4] Quoted in Kinsman, *op. cit.*, p. 34.

been collected."[1] We are told in the proceedings of the state constitutional convention that the law was repealed "because of its inquisitorial character, its impertinent scrutiny into the affairs of private life, and of other difficulties which it had to encounter, and the frauds and impositions it caused, and above all, its utter failure to produce a sufficient sum."[2]

While the resuscitation of the income tax in Pennsylvania and its introduction in Maryland in the early forties were due primarily to fiscal needs, there was a group of southern states where we find at this time a development of some form of income taxation, partly indeed as a result of fiscal exigencies, but partly also as a concession to the demand for more equal taxation. As is well known, the southern states, not only in colonial times, but in the early part of the nineteenth century, had a system of taxation which differed materially from that found in the rest of the country.[3] At first, it will be remembered, poll taxes and customs played a much larger rôle than in the middle or northern colonies. Then, when a system of land taxes developed, they were of a rather primitive kind; and although we occasionally find faculty taxes in some of the southern states,[4] there was as a rule no development of the general property tax as in the remainder of the country. When, now, in the early forties, the cotton factors, the merchants, and the professional classes began to assume a distinct importance side by side with the large plantation owners, the movement set in to draw them into the meshes of the taxgatherer. In some places this assumed the form of a system of license taxes, which has continued in most of the southern states down to the present day. In a few cases it took the form of the attempt to introduce an income tax. This was the case in Virginia, in North Carolina, and in Alabama.

In Virginia the taxation of incomes began in 1843. In

[1] *Laws of 1849*, c. 294.

[2] *Debates and Proceedings of the Maryland Reform Convention, to revise the State Constitution*, vol. iii, p. 227.

[3] Seligman, *Essays in Taxation*, chapter 1.

[4] *Supra*, p. 379.

that year a law was enacted imposing what were technically known as a "tax on incomes," a "tax on fees," and a "tax on interest." The tax on incomes was a tax of one per cent on all incomes over four hundred dollars "in consideration of the discharge of any office or employment in the service of the state, or of any corporation, company, firm or person." The income of ministers of the gospel and incomes from labor in mechanic arts, trades, handicrafts or manufactures were exempt. The "tax on fees," at the same rate, was imposed on attorneys, physicians, dentists, and "all other persons in respect to their fees above four hundred dollars, derived from any office, calling or profession." The "tax on interest" was at the rate of two and one-half per cent on all "interest or profit, whether arising from money loaned, or from bonds, notes or other securities for money or from bonds or certificates of debt of states or public corporations."[1] In other words, this was a tax on salaries and professional income, and a partial tax on funded income, with separate rates for temporary and for permanent income. In 1846 the "tax on interest" was reduced and made applicable only to profits over six hundred dollars.[2] In 1853 that part of the tax which applied to income from public securities was raised to three and one-half per cent. But by this law the tax on "incomes" and "fees" was graduated. Incomes below two hundred dollars were exempt; on incomes from two hundred dollars to two hundred and fifty dollars the rate was one-quarter of one per cent; and it rose by regular increments to one per cent on incomes of over one thousand dollars.[3] In 1856 and 1859 some minor changes were made in the law, but it was not until the Civil War period that it was converted into a general income tax. That period will be treated in the next section.

In North Carolina the income tax dates from 1849. In that year a law was passed with the following preamble: "Whereas there are many wealthy citizens of this state who

[1] Law of March 27, 1843; *Acts 1842–1843*, pp. 6–8.

[2] Law of February 28, 1846; *Acts 1845–1846*, p. 7.

[3] Law of April 7, 1853; *Acts of 1852–1853*, c. 8.

derive very considerable revenues from moneys which produce interest, dividends and profits, and who do not contribute a due proportion to the public exigencies of the same, be it resolved," etc. The dissatisfaction here manifested led to a three-per-cent tax on all moneys at interest, and on all profits from moneys invested in shares or in trade. Profits to the extent of sixty dollars were exempt. The law also provided that after the first five years of their practice all professional classes except ministers and judges should pay an annual tax of three dollars, provided their income exceeded five hundred dollars.[1] The tax was popularly known as the "tax on salaries and fees," but it was in reality a kind of license tax levied on all commercial and precarious incomes. In 1851 the exemption was reduced from sixty to thirty dollars, and other slight alterations were made.[2] In 1855 the exemption was still further reduced to six dollars, and various minor changes were introduced.[3] In 1857 the rate was increased to four per cent,[4] and in 1859 the tax was further extended and slightly changed so that, while the rate of income from interest remained at four per cent, the tax upon salaries and fees was now applied to all individuals at the rate of one per cent.[5] Soon afterward, however, the Civil War broke out, which led to a notable change in the system.

In Alabama the movement toward the taxation of income dates from 1843. The new tax began there, as in the other southern states that have been noticed, as a tax on certain business incomes, at the rate of twenty-five cents on every hundred dollars of the income of auctioneers, factors, cotton brokers, and commission brokers.[6] In 1844 it was reduced to twenty cents, and there was added a tax of one-half of one per cent on the income of lawyers, physicians, surgeons,

[1] North Carolina, *Acts of 1848–1849*, c. 77, p. 129. Law of January 29, 1849.

[2] *Laws of 1850–1851*, c. 120, sec. 2.

[3] *Laws of 1854–1855*, c. 37, secs. 19–21.

[4] *Laws of 1856–1857*, c. 34, secs. 19–21.

[5] *Laws of 1858–1859*, c. 25, sec. 27.

[6] Alabama, *Laws of 1842–1843*, act 1, sec. 5.

and dentists, and of all persons receiving salaries from the state government, or from any bank, mercantile house, or educational institution.[1] If any one refused to hand in a return, he was to be assessed at three thousand dollars. In 1848 the tax on professions was extended to the income of "every person of whatever craft, employment or profession except artisans and manual laborers."[2] The law also provided that the tax upon commissions and brokers should not apply when the capital invested in the business was taxable. In 1850 it was enacted that surgeons, physicians, and dentists who had practised three years might pay either a specific tax of ten dollars or a one and one-half per cent tax upon their annual income. Thus the professional income tax was again partly changed into a license tax, and after a few years it became entirely a license tax. In the case of public officials, clerks, and the officers of corporations, the tax was now to be levied only on the income above five hundred dollars. Cotton pickeries and warehouses for the storage of cotton and other products were made taxable at the rate of one per cent of the income.[3] The tax continued in this shape until the Civil War.

Finally, it may be stated that in Florida the system was also initiated in 1845, when a tax of twenty cents was levied upon every hundred dollars of income received by lawyers, doctors, public weighers of cotton and other products, public inspectors, and pilots.[4] In 1850, after the state comptroller had recommended an extension of this tax to business incomes in general, commission merchants and factors were made subject to a tax of two per cent on their commissions.[5] In Florida, however, the law seems to have worked even less successfully than in the other southern states, and in 1855 the whole system was abolished.[6]

[1] Alabama, *Laws of 1843–1844*, act 106, secs. 5, 7, 8.

[2] *Laws of 1847–1848*, act 1, sec. 1.

[3] *Laws of 1849–1850*, act 1, sec. 1.

[4] *Laws of Florida, 1845*, c. 10, sec. 7, and c. 28, sec. 9.

[5] *Laws of Florida, 1850*, c. 3, 5, 7.

[6] *Laws of Florida, 1855*, c. 715, sec. 4.

It will be seen, therefore, that all these early attempts at income taxation were exceedingly crude, and that in the southern states they amounted to very little more than a system of license taxes. In no case was the revenue at all significant, and in only one case — that of Virginia — was it even appreciable. In Virginia, in 1844, the income tax yielded about $16,000 out of a total state tax of $432,000. But of that amount almost $12,000 came from the tax on interest.[1] During the fifties the yield slowly increased. In 1853, out of a state tax of over a million, the income tax yielded only $36,000. In 1856, after the tax rate had been doubled, the revenue amounted to over $99,000, and in 1858 it increased to $104,000. In the other states, however, these figures were never approached, although North Carolina did fairly well. In 1849, the first year of the operation of the law in that state, the yield was slightly over $28,000, most of it being derived from the tax on interest. In 1851 the yield was about $30,000, but it then began to diminish. Virginia was virtually the only state in which the tax can be taken at all seriously.

§ 3. *The Period of the Civil War*

When the Civil War broke out, the southern states found themselves in a grave predicament. Practically none of them had developed the system of the general property tax as it was found in the North, and it was felt to be entirely out of the question to expect that the burdens of the impending conflict should be borne entirely by the owners of real estate and slaves. What, therefore, was done in a comparatively easy way in the North, through a simple increase in the rate of the general property tax, it was necessary to accomplish in a different way in the non-industrial South, where the capital invested in industry was exceedingly small. The South, therefore, was compelled to turn primarily to the commercial and professional classes, and had to make use of an income

[1] *Auditor's Report*, November 20, 1845.

tax rather than a property tax. This movement soon became well-nigh universal throughout the South.

In Virginia, where, as we remember, there had been since the forties a kind of partial income tax, the real change took place in 1862. In 1861, indeed, the old progressive salaries tax was replaced by a low proportional tax of one per cent on the amount in excess of five hundred dollars;[1] but in 1862, after the war had broken out, comprehensive changes were made, chiefly in the rates of the existing tax.[2] In 1863, however, not alone were the rates still further increased, so that salaries and fees paid two and one-half per cent, and interest of bonds and income from toll-bridges and ferries paid seventeen per cent, but a tax of ten per cent was now levied upon the income received from any licensed trade, business, or occupation, from the use of money by others, from the exchange of any kind of property, and from any other trade or speculation.[3] The amount of three thousand dollars was exempt in all cases; and there were additional exemptions in the case of certain profits from property to be used by the purchaser and from the sale of cattle or farm produce on the part of the farmer.

This system continued until 1866, when a new system was introduced, including a general property tax as well as license taxes and a tax on incomes. Incomes were now subjected to an elaborate classification in six categories, and salaries were separately assessed in a distinct schedule. The rates varied from one and one-half to three per cent, according to the different classes of income.[4] In 1867 the rates were changed so as to vary from one to five per cent.[5] In 1870, however, all the schedules and classes were abolished, and a general tax of two and one-half per cent was imposed on the amount

[1] Virginia, *Acts of General Assembly, 1861*, c. 1, sec. 10.

[2] The rate upon salaries and fees was increased one and one-half per cent; the rate upon interest from bonds and from purchases to ten per cent. — *Laws of General Assembly, 1861–1862*, c. 1, sec. 9.

[3] *Acts of General Assembly, 1863*, p. 1.

[4] *Acts of General Assembly, 1865–1866*, c. 3, secs. 8 *et seq.*

[5] *Acts of General Assembly, 1866–1867*, c. 298, secs. 18 *et seq.*

of incomes in excess of fifteen hundred dollars, while the combined license and income tax upon professional classes was converted into a pure license tax.[1] Incomes were defined so as to comprise certain specified items, together with "all other gains and profits derived from any other source whatever," and deductions were granted for losses by fraud or shipwreck, losses incurred in trade, sums paid for fertilizers, labor, or service, except the outlay for improvements, new buildings, and betterments. In 1871 the exemption was reduced to one thousand dollars, and the rate to one and one-half per cent.[2] In 1872 some minor changes were made, and in 1874 the exemption was lowered to six hundred dollars and the definition of income was somewhat altered.[3] In this form the Civil War income tax has continued to exist, with only slight modifications, to the present time.

During the war the tax yielded substantial revenues. In 1863 the proceeds amounted to $178,945, of which $92,780 was due to the ten-per-cent tax on profits. As soon, however, as the war was over, and the law was changed in 1866, the yield decreased greatly, amounting in 1866 to only about $23,000. The revenue thereafter remained at an insignificant figure. In 1873, for instance, the income tax yielded only $33,140 out of a state tax of $2,268,000.[4]

In North Carolina, where, as we remember, the old tax, dating from the forties, was in existence at the outbreak of the Civil War at the rate of four per cent, the law of 1861 modified the system to some extent by repealing the exemption of judges from the tax, and by increasing the rate of tax upon toll roads, bridges, and ferries to two and one-half per cent.[5] In 1863, however, when the general exemption in the case of salaries and fees was raised to one thousand dollars, the tax on profits was extended and modified, and various

[1] Virginia, *Acts of General Assembly, 1860–1870*, c. 226.
[2] *Acts of General Assembly, 1870–1871*, c. 193, sec. 7.
[3] *Acts of General Assembly, 1874*, c. 240, sec. 109.
[4] *Cf.* the figures quoted in Kinsman, *op. cit.*, p. 56.
[5] North Carolina, *Laws of 1861, Second Extra Session*, c. 31.

classes of incomes were taxed at different rates. Thus ten per cent was levied on the income of all brokers and bankers; ten to twenty per cent on the profits of liquor dealers; two per cent on the profits of money or capital invested in certain manufactures and commodities; and five per cent on the profits derived from the purchase and sale of articles imported into the state from neutral ports.[1] In 1864 certain specified professions and occupations were taxed at the rate of two and one-half per cent, "and all other persons whose fees, wages, perquisites, salaries and emoluments" exceeded one thousand dollars were taxed one per cent.[2] The tax on the profits of certain manufacturers was now made progressive, the rate ranging from five to fifteen per cent.[3] In 1865 certain minor changes were made. In 1866, however, all incomes except those from salaries and fees were taxed according to a progressive scale from one to three and one-half per cent. In 1867 the progression was materially reduced, and in 1869 the income tax was again made proportional, at the rate of two and one-half per cent.[4] Finally, in 1870, the rate was reduced to one and one-half per cent, and in that shape it continued for a number of years.

The income tax in North Carolina never worked well. While it was of some help during the Civil War, the total yield of the tax in 1867 was only $3839, and by 1877 it had fallen to $1685, out of a total state tax of $495,542, only 28 out of 94 counties in the state making any returns at all.[5]

In South Carolina, where it will be remembered that the old faculty tax had continued virtually unchanged from the eighteenth century, the law of 1861 provided a tax of one per cent upon all incomes from "factorage, employment, faculties and professions," as well as upon commissions from all com-

[1] North Carolina, *Laws of 1863, Regular Session*, c. 55.

[2] *Laws of 1864*, c. 27, schedule A, sec. 70.

[3] For details, see Seligman, *Progressive Taxation*, 2d ed., p. 106.

[4] For details, see *ibid.*, p. 107, and Kinsman, *op. cit.*, p. 69.

[5] *Auditor's Report for 1878.*

mission merchants and commercial agents, and upon all salaries over five hundred dollars.[1] In 1865 the tax upon salaries and wages was dropped, and the tax on profits extended to "persons engaged in inland navigation or operating steam saw-mills, hotel and boarding-house keepers, bar-rooms and lime and charcoal burners."[2] In 1866 the tax was extended to all incomes, including rents.[3] But when the new constitution was adopted in 1868, the dissatisfaction was such that the taxation of incomes was completely abandoned.

In addition to Virginia, North Carolina, and South Carolina, Alabama was the only state to continue, with some modifications, its existing taxation of incomes. In 1862 a tax of five per cent was levied upon the net profits received from certain specified businesses which included virtually all the occupations in the state,[4] and the few classes which had not been enumerated were now taxed by a law of the following year.[5] In both cases it was provided, however, that the capital invested in any business whose profits were taxed should be exempt. After various changes in rates, the law of 1866 was made in terms a general income tax, by a provision that a tax of one per cent should be imposed on "the annual gains, profits, salaries and income in excess of five hundred dollars received by any person within the state."[6] In 1867 the exemption was raised to one thousand dollars, and in 1868 the rate was made three-fourths of one per cent.

After the war was over, the tax continued with certain minor changes; but its administration went from bad to worse. The revenue accordingly became ludicrously small. In 1870 it amounted to about $11,000 out of a total state tax of $1,122,000. The proceeds then gradually diminished until, in 1879, it yielded only $8100. During the next four or five years the revenue was a little larger, but the prejudice against the tax grew considerably. The tax, although only sporadi-

[1] South Carolina, *Laws of 1861*, p. 837.

[2] *Laws of 1864–1865*, p. 231.

[3] *Laws of 1866*, p. 395.

[4] Alabama, *Laws of 1862*, act 1, sec. 10.

[5] *Laws of 1863*, act 83, sec. 2.

[6] *Laws of 1865–1866*, act 1, c. 1.

cally levied, had become exceedingly unpopular, and in 1883 the auditor reported as follows: "Taxes upon salaries, gains, incomes and profits are regarded with disfavor by almost every taxpayer. . . . They are in the very nature of things attained by processes inquisitorial in character, and therefore to most persons exceedingly obnoxious. In addition to this the law has never been and probably never will be properly executed, and consequently does not bear equally alike upon all. . . . I do not hesitate therefore to give it as my opinion that it should be repealed."[1] As a result of this recommendation the provisions for the levying of the income tax were dropped from the statutes, so that the tax came to an end in 1884.

In addition to the four southern states which utilized their old income tax during the Civil War, a number of other states now introduced it for the first time. The most remarkable example, perhaps, is that of Georgia, for that state not only levied an income tax in 1863, but introduced the progressive principle. It was indeed not a general income tax, in that it was limited to profits, but the rate on large profits was absurdly high. According to the law of 1863,[2] if the income was twenty per cent of the capital, the tax was one-half of one per cent; if the income was twenty to thirty per cent of the capital, the tax was one and one-half per cent; and for every increase of ten per cent in the percentage of profits to capital, the rate increased one-half of one per cent *ad infinitum*. The result was that when the profits equalled the capital invested, the rate would be five per cent, and if the profits were ten times the capital, the entire profits would go as taxes. It actually happened that with the depreciation of paper money several people made nominal profits on a

[1] *Auditor's Report, 1883*, p. 17.

[2] *Georgia Laws of 1863, Extra Session*, title 18, sec. 156. *Cf.*, for the experience of Georgia, Seligman, *Progressive Taxation*, pp. 105 *et seq.*; Kinsman, *op. cit.*, pp. 93 *et seq.*; and a special article by William A. Shelton, "The Income Tax in Georgia," in the *Journal of Political Economy*, vol. xviii (1910), pp. 610–627.

small capital at these higher rates, and were thus assessed at practically all of their profits.[1] In 1863 the law was changed, making the tax rate proportional to the amount, instead of to the percentage, of the income, and several minor changes were made in the next few years. The act yielded some revenue during the war, although not to any appreciable extent.[2] Far from being a success, as we are sometimes told,[3] the law was both unsuccessful and exceedingly unpopular. The Comptroller General, in 1864, for instance, stated: "I am free to confess that . . . I have felt satisfied that there has been so much fraud and hard swearing, or to say the least of it, so many different opinions relative to income tax returns, I have but little partiality for the system. So far as my observation extends, only a few whose business was such that they could not hide, if they would, have paid most of this tax. . . . The real sharper, or monopolizer, and speculator who does no regular business, but buys up produce, etc., and holds it up for high prices, gets off by dodging the receiver, or by claiming to have made no profits above eight per cent."[4] As soon as the war was over, protests poured in upon the legislature, and the tax was soon dropped. Instead, therefore, of being an unprecedented success, the Georgia income tax may be declared to have been an almost unqualified failure.

In addition to Georgia, experiments were made with the income tax also in a few other southern and border states. Missouri introduced a partial income tax in 1861, the law

[1] See the amusing instance of the brewer, mentioned in Seligman, *op. cit.*, p. 105, note 17.

[2] Kinsman, *op. cit.*, p. 96, gives the yield of the tax in 1863 as $683,235. As Shelton, however, points out, *op. cit.*, p. 626, this is doubly erroneous. In the first place, the figures given are those of returns, not of receipts; in the second place, Kinsman failed to notice the point that the figures were calculated in the depreciated Confederate money. The actual yield of the tax in gold was only $33,190.

[3] As, for instance, by Kinsman, who speaks (*op. cit.*, p. 654) of the "unprecedented success of the law." Kinsman was led astray by the mistake referred to in the last note.

[4] *Report of the Comptroller General of Georgia*, 1864, p. 36.

providing for a tax of thirty-two cents on each hundred dollars of income from all salaries over eight hundred dollars and from stocks and other property not taxed in the state.[1] In 1864 both the exemption and the rate were lowered, and in 1865 the old exemption was repealed. With the close of the war, however, Missouri's experiment came to an end.

Texas levied a tax in 1860 on salaries of over five hundred dollars,[2] and also imposed a license tax, which in a certain sense included incomes. In 1866, however, following a recommendation from the governor, who declared that the tax upon professions operated very oppressively and unequally, the legislature imposed a general income tax upon every person doing business within the state, the tax being graduated from one to three per cent, according to the amount of income. The tax on business incomes, however, included incomes from securities. There was joined to this general tax on business incomes a tax on salaries. The law worked so badly that in 1870 the income tax was confined to the interest from bonds,[3] and even that was allowed to lapse the following year.

In Louisiana the income tax was not introduced until 1864, when a law was enacted providing for a tax of one-quarter of one per cent on all incomes in excess of two thousand dollars from any "trade, profession or occupation."[4] With some modifications,[5] the Louisiana law continued to the end of the century; but its efficiency was quite negligible. In 1868, for instance, the tax yielded $2476 out of a total state tax of over $508,000;[6] and in 1899 the proceeds were exactly $104.[7] Since then it appears not to have been levied.

Two of the border states also experimented with the income tax. In West Virginia, which, as is well known,

1 Missouri, *Laws of 1860–1861, Regular Session*, p. 62.

2 Texas, *Laws of 1863*, c. 33, sec. 3.

3 *Laws of 1870*, c. 84, sec. 32.

4 Louisiana, *Laws of 1864*, act 55, sec. 3.

5 These are described in Kinsman, *op. cit.*, p. 101.

6 *Auditor's Report for 1868.*

7 *Auditor's Report for 1899.*

adopted most of the existing laws of the parent state, an act of 1863 introduced the Virginia income tax law,[1] but it seems never to have been enforced. Finally, in Kentucky, a law of 1867 imposed a partial income tax, confining it to the income from United States bonds, and for a few years yielded considerable revenue.[2] In 1872, however, the law was declared unconstitutional.[3]

If we sum up the history of the Civil War period, we may say that in only a few cases was a general income tax imposed, and that in all cases, with the possible exception of Virginia, the tax, after the first ardor of war enthusiasm had subsided, worked exceedingly badly. The administration was inefficient, the revenue was ludicrously small, and the tax in most cases became a farce. As a consequence, it was, with a few exceptions, allowed to lapse after the close of the war.

§ 4. *The Recent History of State Income Taxes*

The fourth movement in the direction of the state taxation of income dates from the period of the early nineties, and especially after the federal income tax of 1894 had been declared unconstitutional. It was during these years that an attempt was made to revive the old Civil War income tax in Virginia and North Carolina, and that an income tax was reintroduced on newer lines in South Carolina. In these three states, as well as in Massachusetts, with its survival of the old faculty tax, the income tax accordingly is still found to-day; and to these four states there must now be added Oklahoma and Wisconsin.

In Virginia the income tax of the Civil War period continued, as we have learned,[4] during the seventies and eighties, with slight modifications, and with the same poor success. In 1898, however, the law now in force was enacted.[5] The tax

[1] *Laws of West Virginia, 1862–1863*, c. 64, sec. 8.

[2] *Laws of Kentucky, 1867*, vol. i, ch. 1832.

[3] 9 Bush, p. 46.

[4] *Supra*, p. 407.

[5] *Acts of General Assembly, 1897–1898*, c. 496.

is imposed upon all incomes in excess of $600 (changed in 1909 to $1000), and income is defined as "all rents, salaries, interest upon notes, bonds or other evidences of debt, . . . the amount of all premiums on gold, silver or coupons, the amount of sales of live-stock and meats less the value assessed thereon the previous year, the amount of sales of wool, butter, cheese, hay, tobacco, grain, vegetable or other production grown or produced by said person during the preceding year, . . . less all sums paid for taxes and for labor, fences, fertilizers, clover or other seed purchased or used upon the land . . .; all other gains and profits . . . ," with a deduction for losses. The assessor is required to list all such incomes, except that the tax on the salaries of state officials is to be collected at the time of payment by the state. The rate of taxation is one per cent. The care taken in the enactment of this law may be inferred from the retention of the now unmeaning words "the amount of premiums on gold," etc.

For a long time the yield of the income tax in Virginia varied between thirty and fifty thousand dollars as over against a state revenue of about two millions. During the last few years the yield has only slightly increased.[1] The special tax commission attributed this result "to the lax administration of the law, to the confused and conflicting computation of losses chargeable against income and to the absence of central supervisory authority."[2] In over thirty per cent

[1] The yield has been as follows: —

1901	$46,023
1902	59,252
1903	60,357
1904	64,781
1905	70,954
1906	77,414
1907	94,291
1908	122,058
1909	102,810
1910	106,909
1911	134,562

[2] *Report to the General Assembly of Virginia by the Tax Commission, etc.* Richmond, 1911, p. xxxvii.

of the counties of the state the income tax is never collected at all.

Virginia is the only state in which any appreciable income is derived from the income tax. In North Carolina, where, as we know, the Civil War income tax also continued, the principle of differentiation was introduced in 1887, with a rate of one-half of one per cent on salaries and one per cent on income from property.[1] In 1893, however, the principle of progression was reintroduced, and that of differentiation was extended.[2] In 1895 and 1897 the rates were slightly changed, and remained in force until 1907. According to the system at that time the income from salaries and fees was taxed at the rate of one-half of one per cent on the excess over one thousand dollars. All profits on incomes derived from property not taxed paid five per cent, while all other incomes were taxed according to the following schedule: —

Incomes from $1,000 to $5,000 paid ¼ of one per cent.
Incomes from 5,000 to 10,000 paid ½ of one per cent.
Incomes from 10,000 to 20,000 paid 1 per cent.
Incomes in excess of 20,000 paid 2 per cent.

In 1901, however, the rate was again made proportional. In 1905 the law was changed in several respects, and secrecy was now imposed on the officials. The law of 1905 was virtually reënacted in 1907 and 1909, and at present the tax is imposed at the rate of one per cent on all gross incomes over $1000, excluding incomes from property already taxed.[3]

The yield during the nineties was ludicrous in the extreme, ranging from about $2000 to $4500 annually. During the first decade of the twentieth century a slight improvement has taken place, owing largely to an effort of the new state tax commission, so that in the year 1911 the income tax produced $39,638 as over against a revenue of more than

[1] North Carolina, *Laws of 1887*, c. 135, sec. 5.
[2] *Laws of 1895*, c. 116, schedule A, sec. 5.
[3] *Revenue Act of 1909*, secs. 22–25.

$1,038,000 from the general property tax.[1] But even thus the income tax is little more than a farce.

In South Carolina, where, as we remember, the Civil War income tax had been allowed to lapse, the income tax was reintroduced in 1897, but now with a progressive scale. The tax was a general income tax, at the following rates:—

Incomes from	$2,500 to $5,000	paid 1 per cent.
Incomes from	5,000 to 7,500	paid 1½ per cent.
Incomes from	7,500 to 15,000	paid 2 per cent.
Incomes of	15,000 and over	paid 3 per cent.

This law also has, until recently, been a complete failure. The yield for the years 1900, 1901 and 1902 was respectively $975, $609, and $292. Beginning in 1905, however, a more energetic attempt has been made to enforce the law, with the result that the revenue has slowly increased, although with the most remarkable variations from year to year.[2] The Comptroller General, in one of his recent reports, tells us that he has "made earnest efforts to enforce the provisions of the law." But he adds, "the enforcement of the law has, as a matter of fact, been incomplete. Much dissatisfaction and opposition is shown to it by many who are liable for the tax, because they see others escape from its payment. In a later report he concurs in an assessor's statement: "I very much hope the law will be repealed, as I find it practically impossible to get accurate or satisfactory results."[4]

[1] The figures for recent years, as given in the *Report of the State Auditor of North Carolina*, are as follows:—

1901	$19,030.79	1906	$31,292.82
1902	19,022.48	1907	36,829.44
1903	23,509.77	1908	36,383.25
1904	24,589.04	1909	37,490.18
1905	27,844.13	1911	39,638.15

[2] The yield of the income tax since 1905 has been as follows:—

1905	$2,130	1909	$16,236
1906	12,201	1911	14,387
1907	10,687	1913	17,449

[3] *Report of the Comptroller General for the Fiscal Year 1909.* Columbia, 1910, p. 24.

[4] *Ibid., 1911.* Columbia, 1912, p. 18.

Outside of the three southern states, into the administrative features of whose system it is not worth while to enter, the income tax was found until very recently only in Massachusetts and Oklahoma. The situation in Massachusetts has been portrayed above. In Oklahoma a so-called professional income tax was imposed in 1908[1] on all incomes from salaries, fees, professions, and property, in excess of $3500, upon which a gross-receipts or excise tax[2] has not been paid. The rates are as follows: —

5 mills	(½ of 1 %)	on the excess over	$3,500 up to	$5,000.
7½ mills	(¾ of 1 %)	on the excess over	$5,000 up to	$10,000.
12 mills	(1.2 %)	on the excess over	$10,000 up to	$20,000.
15 mills	(1.5 %)	on the excess over	$20,000 up to	$50,000.
20 mills	(2 %)	on the excess over	$50,000 up to	$100,000.
33⅓ mills	(3⅓ %)	on all amounts over	$100,000.	

Every taxpayer is required to sign a certificate of his income. The assessor in the township is to send to the state auditor lists of income recipients who have not filled out the blanks. The auditor may then take such steps as he deems necessary to require any such person to make proper returns of his income, and he may also summon witnesses. The efficacy of all these provisions seems to be doubtful, for in 1909 the returns made by the county clerks amounted to only $2816 and in 1910 to $4914.[3] In the succeeding years the law continued to work just as badly, and public opinion refused to support it. It is not surprising then to find that the Attorney-General writes in 1914: "The income tax law adopted in 1908 is a farce. It is not workable or practicable for lack of machinery to make it work." Oklahoma is no more fortunate than the other states.

[1] Oklahoma, *Session Laws, 1907–1908*, c. 81, art. 10.

[2] The gross-receipts tax referred to is the so-called "Gross Revenue Tax" of 1908, imposed on the gross-receipts of all public-service corporations, mining corporations, and petroleum and natural gas companies, with rates varying from one-quarter of one per cent to three per cent. Oklahoma, *Session Laws of 1907–1908*, c. 71, art. 2.

[3] *Second Biennial Report of the State Auditor of Oklahoma, 1910*, p. 162.

§ 5. *The Wisconsin Income Tax*

From the preceding survey it will be seen how utterly insignificant and unsuccessful had been the experiments with state income taxation up to the year 1911. Under the stress of modern conditions the old faculty tax of the eighteenth century died away everywhere except in Massachusetts, where it still lingers as a shadow of its former self. In the northern and middle states no serious attempt was ever made to impose an income tax, as sufficient difficulty was experienced in enforcing the property tax. In the southern states the absence of a property tax led, as we have seen, in the forties, to an unsuccessful endeavor to introduce income taxes. The only experiment which deserves to be called even a halfway notable one was made by the southern states during the Civil War.

In most of the states the current from 1890 to 1900 set strongly against the income tax. As far back as 1889 the special tax commission of Maine reported against the advisability of a state income tax.[1] A few years later a New York report took a similar position.[2] In Massachusetts, as we have seen above,[3] the commission of 1897 came to a like conclusion as to the inadvisability of any attempt to revive or to generalize the income tax.

No further efforts, outside of a few southern states, were made for some years to suggest an income tax for state purposes. In 1907, however, the revenue commission of Colorado discussed the subject, but reported against a state income tax,[4] stating that "as a federal tax, . . . much can be said in favor of an income tax; as a state tax it is utterly indefensible." In 1906 the tax commission of California took up the matter and reported strongly against any attempt to introduce

[1] *Report of the Special Tax Commission of Maine, 1899.* Augusta, 1890, p. 36.

[2] *Report of Counsel to revise the Tax Laws of the State of New York, 1893.* Albany, 1893, p. 7.

[3] *Supra*, p. 397.

[4] *Report of the Revenue Commission of Colorado.* Denver, 1907, p. 18.

an income tax.[1] A fuller discussion of the subject is found in the report of the special tax commission of New York of the following year. In New York, where the fifteen members of the commission agreed upon certain general recommendations, two members brought in a supplemental report in favor of a graduated lump-sum state income tax. This proposition was voted down in general committee, and the argument against it was presented as a supplemental report by a few members.[2]

After presenting the various arguments in opposition, the report closed as follows: "In short, we incline to the opinion that even if the income tax is advisable at all, it is advisable at present only as a federal tax. As long as New York is surrounded by commonwealths which seek to attract to themselves much of the wealth of their rival, it is unreasonable to expect a development of interstate comity in taxation which would redound to their disadvantage. Such an interstate comity can probably be forced upon the American commonwealths only from above; and it is a debatable question whether the national government has the constitutional power to do this. At all events, for New York State to act independently in this matter would be, in our opinion, highly inexpedient.

"Whatever may be the situation in future years, your Commissioners are convinced that to advance the project of a direct state income tax at the present time is an iridescent dream. The scheme might succeed in bringing in some revenue, but it would, in our opinion, be sure to bring in its train inequality, fraud and corruption. Far from being a remedy for our present evils it would only accentuate those evils.

"It is for these reasons that we consider the imposition at the present time of a direct state income tax inexpedient and inadvisable."

[1] *Report of the Commission on Revenue and Taxation of the State of California, 1906.* Sacramento, 1906, p. 14.

[2] *Report of the Special Tax Commission of the State of New York.* Albany, 1907, pp. 46 *et seq.*

While states at the opposite ends of the country, like California and New York, were taking this attitude of dissent, an entirely different movement was in progress in Wisconsin. Wisconsin, as is well known, has been among the leaders in the American states in the reform of its fiscal administration; and since the beginning of the century the state tax commission, which was given considerable powers over local assessments, has done admirable work. As early as 1903 the dissatisfaction with the general property tax led Mr. Nils P. Haugen, a member of the state tax commission, to propose an income tax; and a general resolution authorizing a constitutional amendment for a graduated income tax passed the legislature in 1903. Through a technical defect the amendment could not be submitted to the people, and in 1905 the resolution was again passed. In 1907 it passed the second time and in 1908 it was finally adopted by the people by a large majority.

From now on Professor Thomas S. Adams became one of the leading advocates of the new scheme.[1] In 1909 an income tax bill was introduced and referred to a recess committee to investigate the subject. At the next session of the legislature in 1911 the committee reported favorably and the law was adopted on July 15, 1911.[2]

The fundamental point in the law was a revolution in administrative methods. The administration of the law, instead of being left to local officials, as is the case with all other state income taxes of the United States and as is the general rule with the general property tax, was now centralized in the state

[1] *Cf.* his address on "The Place of the Income Tax in the Reform of State Taxation," in *Papers and Discussions of the 23d Annual Meeting of the American Economic Association*. Princeton, 1911, pp. 302–321. See also his paper in *State and Local Taxation. Fourth International Conference under the Auspices of the International Tax Association. Addresses and Proceedings*, Columbus, 1911, pp. 87 *et seq.*

[2] The best discussion of the Wisconsin income tax will be found in the Report of the Wisconsin Tax Commission for 1910, Chapter II; in the Report for 1912, Chapters III and IV; and two articles by Professor T. S. Adams, the one entitled "The Wisconsin Income Tax," in the *American Economic Review* for December, 1911, the other entitled "The Significance of the Wisconsin Income Tax," in the *Political Science Quarterly* for December, 1913 (volume xxviii, pp. 569 *et seq.*).

tax commission. The assessors charged with the duty of levying the income tax were to be appointed after civil service examinations and were thus made entirely independent of local influences. This was the first great achievement of the law.

The tax itself was not conceived of as a tax over and above the general property tax, as is the case in the other states, but was intended to be a substitute, in part at least, for the unworkable tax on personal property. In the original bill the income tax was declared to be a substitute for the personal property tax. In the bill as finally enacted it was felt very doubtful as to whether it would raise as much money as the old personal property tax, and therefore only a few classes of personal property, like moneys and credits, farm machinery, household furniture and personal ornaments, were exempted from the property tax. It was provided, however, that any tax paid on personal property might be subtracted by the taxpayer from his income tax. Moreover 70% of the proceeds go to the locality where the tax is collected, 20% to the county, and only 10% to the state. The state is expected to spend this 10% in administering the tax, so that it will derive no net income from the tax.

Finally, it may be pointed out that the income tax does not apply to those corporations which pay taxes directly to the state government. These are the railroads, street railways, gas and power companies associated with street railways, and insurance companies. By an amendment of 1913 banks and trust companies have also been exempted from the income tax for the same reason that they are subject to an *ad valorem* tax imposed by the state.

The Wisconsin income tax is applicable to persons living in Wisconsin, to the business transacted there, and to income derived from property within the state. The tax is a graduated one. The exemptions are $800 for an individual, $1200 for a husband and wife, and $200 additional for each child entirely dependent upon the taxpayer for support. Only the surplus income above these exemptions is taxable. The rate is 1% on the first thousand dollars and rises to 6% on the taxable income over $12,000.[1] In the case of corporations the rate is different. The original law was rather complicated, the rate being determined by the relation between the taxable income and the assessed value of the property used in the acquisition of the income, and amounting to practically one-half of the earnings as calculated on the assessed value of the property.[2] This was found, however, to be a very cumbrous method, and in 1913 the system was changed so as to tax corporations on net incomes according to the same principle as individuals, with the exception that the rates are different. In the case of corporations the rate rises from 2% on the first thousand dollars' income (without any exemptions or deductions) up to 6% on income over $6000.[3]

[1] The exact figures are as follows: —

Income	Rate per $1000	Income	Rate per $1000
1st $1000	1 %	8th $1000	3½%
2d $1000	1¼%	9th $1000	4 %
3d $1000	1½%	10th $1000	4½%
4th $1000	1¾%	11th $1000	5 %
5th $1000	2 %	12th $1000	5½%
6th $1000	2½%	13th $1000	6 %
7th $1000	3 %		

[2] The original scale of the income tax on corporations was as follows: —

Per Cent of Taxable Income to Assessed Value of Property Employed in its Acquisition	Rate on Entire Taxable Income	Per Cent of Taxable Income to Assessed Value of Property Employed in its Acquisition	Rate on Entire Taxable Income
1 per cent or less	½%	From 6 to 7 per cent	3½%
From 1 to 2 per cent	1 %	From 7 to 8 per cent	4 %
From 2 to 3 per cent	1½%	From 8 to 9 per cent	4½%
From 3 to 4 per cent	2 %	From 9 to 10 per cent	5 %
From 4 to 5 per cent	2½%	From 10 to 11 per cent	5½%
From 5 to 6 per cent	3 %	From 11 to 12 per cent	6 %

[3] The exact figures are as follows: —

Income	Rate Per Cent	Income	Rate Per Cent
1st $1000	2 %	5th $1000	4%
2d $1000	2½%	6th $1000	5%
3d $1000	3 %	7th $1000	6%
4th $1000	3½%	Over $7000	6%

The principle of collection at source has been applied only to incomes derived from corporations. As the corporation pays an income tax, the individual stockholder is not taxable on his dividend; and since corporations also include the interest on bonds, the individual bondholders are likewise exempt.

The constitutionality of the income tax law was attacked soon after its passage, but the Wisconsin court upheld the law in every detail.[1] In the first year, 1912, the income assessed amounted to $100,845,863 and the total tax was $3,501,161, of which corporations paid $2,392,454. This remarkable result was due very largely to the non-partisan administrative methods introduced by the State Tax Commission.

The first year's operation of the law shows how much better results can be obtained by a system of centralized administration than by the ordinary local methods to which we have been accustomed in the United States. At the same time, while the Wisconsin income tax has been for this reason far more satisfactory than any of the other existing state income taxes, it is still open to doubt whether a state income tax works much better than a state property tax.

It is difficult to compare a property tax to an income tax, because of the lack of correlation. If we knew with accuracy how much property there was in a given community and if all the income in that community were derived from that property, a more or less exact computation could be made. But there are three difficulties in the comparison: First, not all income is derived from property, and especially in modern times there are large professional and even business incomes more or less independent of property; secondly, not all property incomes received within the state are derived from property within the state, and *vice versâ*; thirdly, not all incomes derived from property are taxed, because of the exemptions which, especially in the United States, include a great majority of the citizens and which in part affect the incomes that are derived from property. It is for these reasons that

[1] Income Tax Cases, 148 Wis. 456.

only a vague comparison can be made between the two forms of taxation. We accordingly relegate to a footnote what we conceive to be the best available proof of the actual inferiority of the income tax.[1]

While exact comparison is therefore impossible, it is largely for the last of the three reasons just stated that on general principles we should expect an income tax to be less lucrative

[1] During the period from 1900–10, when virtually all property was nominally taxable in Wisconsin, the State Tax Commission made an annual computation of the true value of the property that was assessed by the local officers. During this decade the per cent of the local assessment to true values, as ascertained by the state, varied from about 52% to 78%; that is, the local assessors were able to find from one-half to four-fifths, or, roughly speaking, about two-thirds of actual property values.

What now is the situation in the case of income assessments? We are informed by the State Tax Commission that the true value of assessed property in Wisconsin for 1913 is $2,998,187,705, or, in round numbers, three billions. This does not include the property of the railroads and other public utilities which are, however, not subject to the income tax; nor does this figure include the personal property which was exempted when the income tax was introduced and which was estimated by the state board in 1911 at 234 millions (moneys and credits, 151 millions; farm machinery, etc., 74 millions; watches, bicycles, etc., 10 millions). In the two years that have elapsed the figures would naturally be greater. On the other hand, some allowance must be made for indebtedness. If we conservatively estimate the true value of exempt personal property as, say, 200 millions, we would have a total true value of net taxable property of a little less than three and a quarter billions. At 6% the income from this would be over 190 millions. Yet the assessed income as reported by the State Commission as being liable to the income tax was, as we have seen, only 100 millions. The conclusion would be that while the general property tax succeeded in reaching two-thirds of the actual property, the general income tax succeeds in reaching only slightly more than one-half of the actual income.

Of course there are two possible criticisms to be made in the above computation. In the first place, we have assumed the income from property to be 6%. If the real income is somewhat less than that, the figures would need corresponding revision; but 6% does not seem to be too high. Secondly, and more important, we have no means of ascertaining how much is the total amount of income which is exempted from taxation and a part of which, at all events, represents income from property. It must be remembered, however, that there are many incomes, such as all labor incomes above the low exempt minimum, as well as all professional incomes, that are included in the list of taxable income, although they do not represent property at all. It is, therefore, not wholly illicit to estimate that the deductions on one hand will be balanced, in part at least, by the additions on the other.

than a property tax. If property yields 6 %, a tax of one-half of one per cent would be equivalent to an income tax of about 8 %. A property tax would probably yield far more than a corresponding income tax, if both were assessed according to the same administrative principles, chiefly for the reason that in a property tax there are in general no exemptions to speak of, while in an income tax there are ordinarily large exemptions, designed primarily to free the small incomes from personal exertion but affecting also the smaller incomes from property. In the one case all property is taxed; in the other case the income from only a part of the property is taxed.

It is for this reason that the Wisconsin income tax, although imposed on incomes from all sources, was designed as a substitute for the tax on certain classes of personalty only. In fact the Wisconsin income tax, far from raising as much revenue as did the general property tax at a corresponding rate, has not been able, even with its admirable administration, to raise in many counties as much as the former discredited personal property tax. In not a few of the country districts the falling off is marked; while it is only in the larger towns where the tax on intangible personalty has been more or less farcical that the income tax yields as much. It is this consideration which has led the State Tax Commission to stand sponsor for a scheme of modified home rule in taxation, whereby it will be left to the localities themselves to elect between the income tax or the personal property tax.

This discloses also the unsatisfactory nature, even in theory and apart from administrative considerations, of an attempt by a state to levy a general income tax as a substitute for a personal property tax. We do not wish to deny — we have even emphasized the fact[1] — that income is often to be preferred to property as a basis of taxation. In so far as corporations in general are concerned we were perhaps the first to call attention to the advantages of net receipts over property as a basis of taxation.[2] Nor do we wish to deny that in dealing with a particular class or classes of enterprise, like mines,

[1] *Cf. supra*, p. 15. [2] Seligman, *Essays in Taxation*, 8 ed., 1913, p. 245.

forests, and certain businesses exposed to sudden mutations of business life, a state tax on yield or produce is preferable to a state tax on property. What may be fairly criticized in the Wisconsin scheme is the idea that a general income tax to include personal as well as corporate income is to be preferred either to a general property tax or to a tax on particular classes of property. In Wisconsin, for instance, if A has invested $100,000 in land, he has to pay both a property tax and an income tax, while if B has invested a like sum in certain classes of personalty, he pays only the income tax.

While a general income tax is, for the reasons mentioned above, not apt to work better than a general property tax, there are additional reasons which militate against the success of a state income tax. These reasons are connected with the impossibility of localizing income and the difficulty of ascertaining business income derived from interstate commerce or business. It may be contended that the difficulties are not greater than in the property tax; but in this there is small comfort, for it is in no small measure due to precisely this reason that the property tax is in general such a failure. It must, moreover, be remembered that Wisconsin has greatly simplified the matter. In the first place, the law excludes from the income tax all railroads and other public utilities, where the difficulties of interstate taxation are apt to be the greatest. In the second place the law abandons the attempt to tax the income of any business except that which is actually transacted within the state or derived from property located within the state. Is it not clear that in the more industrial and commercial states, the homes of large business ventures doing a great business outside of the state, such a method would be sadly lacking? So that even at the very best a state income tax would not be apt to succeed unless it was controlled and regulated by the federal government, either in the formulation of the principles to be adopted or in the choice of the administrative methods to be employed; for in no other way can the incomes derived from interstate business be reached.

If there is any lesson to be drawn from the short experience of Wisconsin with the income tax it is, that while much can be accomplished by improved and centralized administrative methods, some form of federal regulation is necessary to secure the best results.

§ 6. *Conclusion*

In the face of the contentions reproduced in the previous sections, the prospects for a state income tax in general seem rather doubtful. In only one state of the union — Wisconsin — has the uniformly disheartening experience of the American commonwealths with an income tax been interrupted, and as to Wisconsin it must be remembered not only that the conditions are exceptional but that the results are only in part successful. The conditions in Wisconsin are exceptional, first, because the prevalence of "the Wisconsin idea" made it comparatively easy to bring about a thoroughly centralized and expert administration; secondly, because Wisconsin is not a predominantly industrial state; and thirdly, because the law excludes those corporations where the greatest difficulty would ordinarily be encountered in administering a state income tax. The results, again, are even then only partly successful, in that a general income tax in Wisconsin has thus far proven itself unable to take the place, not of a general property tax, but, in not a few counties, even of a tax on special classes of personal property.

The history of Great Britain has shown us the fatuity of a local income tax; the experience of Switzerland has shown us [1] the difficulties connected with a state income tax and has disclosed the fact that in certain respects at least a personal income tax is more difficult of administration than a personal property tax. Furthermore, to quote the example of the German state income taxes in support of an American state income tax is, as we have pointed out above,[2] beside the mark, for in Germany there exists an imperial law governing the whole subject of interstate double taxation which it is not very likely

[1] *Cf. supra*, p. 362. [2] *Supra*, p. 270.

that we shall soon see here. In a country like the United States, where the basis of economic life has become national and where the income of taxpayers has almost universally transcended state lines, the attempt to levy a really successful state income tax is fraught with difficulties. Whatever may be the future of tax reform in the American commonwealths, it is not likely that a general income tax will be one of its permanent features. In special classes of property it may well be that the taxation of property will be replaced by the taxation of yield or of income; and under special favorable conditions, administrative and economic, it is possible that here and there a general income tax may do fairly well. But in the purely agricultural states a general income tax is not apt to succeed, because farmers' incomes are proverbially refractory; and in the developed industrial states a general income tax is not apt to succeed because of the national scope of great business incomes. Consequently, if an income tax is to be utilized on a large scale in the United States, it must be primarily as a national income tax. To a consideration of the national taxation of income we shall accordingly now address ourselves.

CHAPTER III

The Civil War Income Tax

§ 1. *The Origin of the Tax*

The first suggestion of a federal income tax[1] was made in January, 1815, by Secretary Dallas.[2] As a so-called direct tax on lands and slaves was already in existence, Dallas, like virtually everybody else at the time,[3] assumed that this suggested income tax would not be one of the direct taxes contemplated by the constitution. Had the war lasted a few months longer there is every probability that an income tax would have been imposed, but the conclusion of peace made any further resort to internal taxes unnecessary, and two years later the whole system of internal revenue was abolished.

It was not until the outbreak of the Civil War that the government again resorted to the system. On July 4, 1861, Secretary Chase made a report in which he suggested that a

[1] A short account of the Civil War income tax will be found in F. C. Howe, "Federal Revenues and the Income Tax," in *Annals of the American Academy of Political and Social Science*, vol. iv (1894), pp. 64 *et seq.*, and in the same author's *Taxation in the United States under the Internal Revenue System*, New York, n. d. [1896]; and in an official return entitled *Income Tax*, prepared by Henry H. Smith, the Assistant Register of the United States, and published in November, 1893. A somewhat longer account will be found in an article by J. A. Hill, in the *Quarterly Journal of Economics*, vol. viii (1894), pp. 416 *et seq.* Among the contemporary works mention may be made of G. S. Boutwell, *Manual of Direct and Excise Tax System in the United States*, 1863; the works of Bump and of Estee mentioned *infra*, p. 469; and manuals like *The Taxpayer's Manual, The Taxpayers' and Assessors' Guide*, published from 1862 to 1872.

[2] "Special Report on the State of the Finances, January 17, 1815," in *American State Papers*, vol. vi (1832), pp. 885–887. Dallas, after suggesting a tax on inheritances, a tax on wheat flour, and a tax on bank dividends, added that "an income tax may be easily made to produce three millions."

[3] The committee on ways and means, in reporting adversely a bill to tax certain incomes, in Dec. 1814, assumed that it was not a direct tax. See *op. cit.*, p. 873.

small part — not to exceed twenty millions — of the required revenue be raised by direct taxes or internal duties or excises, or both. Following his suggestion, Stevens, the chairman of the committee of ways and means, introduced, on July 24, a bill providing for a direct tax and certain internal duties.[1] The direct tax suggested was modelled upon that of 1813. It was to amount to thirty millions, the quotas expected from the loyal states being put at twenty millions. The introduction of the bill led to a heated discussion. Conkling spoke of the obnoxious features of the law, and proposed in its stead a system of requisitions on the states. Stevens conceded that the bill was a most unpleasant one, but contended that Congress must choose "between these disagreeable duties," since "the annihilation of this government is the alternative."[2]

As the discussion in the House proceeded, it was manifest that the chief objections to the scheme consisted in the fact that it was confined to real estate, and that the constitutional method of levying the tax by apportionment would result in crass inequality, bearing with especial rigor upon the western states. Colfax, for instance, stated that "the most odious tax of all we can levy is going to be the tax upon the land of the country."[3] And in reply to the plea of urgent necessity he said: "There is no stress of weather which can induce me to vote for the bill as it now stands. I cannot go home and tell my constitutents that I voted for a bill that would allow a man, a millionnaire, who has put his entire property into stock, to be exempt from taxation, while a farmer who lives by his side must pay a tax." McClerland pointed out that it would fall "with very heavy, if not ruinous, effect upon the great agricultural states of the West and Southwest," and Arnold called attention to the inequality that would ensue as between Massachusetts and Illinois.[4] Stevens, however, replied that a direct tax under the constitution is necessarily a tax upon real estate, and Bingham agreed that

[1] *The Congressional Globe, 37th Congress, First Session.* Washington, 1861, p 246.

[2] *Op. cit.*, p. 247.

[3] *Op cit.*, p. 248.

[4] *Op. cit.*, p. 325.

the uniform construction of the constitutional provision had been "that the power to levy and apportion direct taxes could be rightfully applied only to lands and slaves."[1] As a consequence of this position, Colfax now proposed that the direct tax clause be stricken out, and that a provision be made for a tax on stocks, bonds, mortgages, money, and interest, as well as for an income tax. Pike supported this motion in a strong speech. Referring to the disproportion of population and wealth as between Rhode Island and Kansas, he said: "It is unfair to levy such a tax when we have the ready and fair way of raising that sum by an income tax upon real and personal estate."[2] The bill was accordingly recommitted, with instructions to arrange for taxing something else besides lands. On the next day the chairman of the committee reported they were "unable to devise any provision that will be constitutional which would carry into effect the instructions of the house."[3] This led to another important discussion in which the old arguments were repeated. Bingham pointed out that while incomes could indeed not be taxed under the direct-tax clause of the constitution, they could be taxed as duties or excises.[4]

On the following day after Edgerton had stated that "a more odious bill cannot be devised" than this tax on farmers,[5] Edwards made a strong plea for the income tax. Speaking of the scheme to tax all property rather than lands, he said: "We can tax it in some mode if we cannot impose on it what is technically called a 'direct tax.' If so, why should we not do it? Why should we stickle about terms? Why should we not impose the burdens which are to fall upon the people of this country equally, in proportion to their ability to bear

[1] He added: "I undertake to say that the uniform construction of that clause of the constitution is this: that under the head of direct taxation, as provided for in the constitution, to be apportioned among the several states, according to the ratio of representation, there is nothing to be taxed except land, tenements, and slaves as appurtenant to land, unless it be a direct capitation tax on the person, without respect to his property or to his income." — *Op. cit.*, p. 249.

[2] *Op. cit.*, p. 252.

[3] *Op. cit.*, p. 268.

[4] *Op. cit.*, p. 272.

[5] *Op. cit.*, p. 282.

them?"[1] Wyckliffe contended that the direct-tax bill was "unjust in its main principles" because it proposed "to impose a tax upon a great interest of the country least able to bear it at this time,"[2] and moved an amendment that personal property should be included. After some discussion, this amendment was adopted by a majority of over two-thirds.[3] Accordingly, the committee reported the bill back with a substitute reducing the amount to be raised by the direct tax from thirty to twenty millions, and providing for a tax of three per cent on all incomes over six hundred dollars a year.[4] Morrill stated that the income tax was to be distinguished from the direct or land tax, and pointed out that personal property could not be constitutionally reached by the methods of the direct tax. "The indirect or income tax which is to be raised by this bill will be, in my judgment, at least twice as much as what we shall raise by direct taxation."[5] With these explanations the bill was passed on July 29 by a vote of 77 to 60.

In the meantime the matter had been taken up in the Senate. Simmons, the chairman of the finance committee, introduced on July 25 the tariff bill which had passed the House a few days earlier.[6] He moved to strike out all after the enacting clause and insert a substitute which he now proceeded to explain. Instead of proposing a direct tax, he held that the new import duties had better be supplemented by an income tax. "Let us tax property in the last resort, when we have to reach the poor as well as the rich, people of small means as well as those who have large; but I do not believe this country has come to a pass to be driven to a resource of such extreme measures. I think, with what we can collect by a moderate duty on importations and a moderate tax on incomes exceeding one thousand dollars, we can meet all the exigencies of the public service, loaded down as it will be by this wicked rebellion!"[7] Fessenden agreed, stating: "I am inclined

[1] *Op. cit.*, p. 283.
[2] *Op. cit.*, p. 301.
[3] *Op. cit.*, p. 308.
[4] *Op. cit.*, p. 323.
[5] *Op. cit.*, p. 330.
[6] *Op. cit.*, p. 205.
[7] *Op. cit.*, p. 254.

very much to favor the idea of a tax upon incomes for the reason that, taking both measures together, I believe the burdens will be more equalized on all classes of the community, more especially on those who are able to bear them."[1] On July 29 Simmons reverted to the matter. Referring to the rule of the British Parliament, formed under some "mysterious" and "inexplicable" influence to lay "first imposts, then excises, then land taxes, and then income taxes," he declared: "I am perfectly satisfied, that there is no propriety in our putting a land tax on. The very reasons that induced England to put a land tax on should induce us to put on an income tax."[2] The committee accordingly suggested a five-per-cent tax on all incomes over one thousand dollars, with a lower rate upon incomes from government securities and a higher rate on the income of citizens residing abroad.

Senator Clark referred to the ambiguity in the amendment because of the failure to explain whether income meant gross or net income; and when objection was taken to certain other defects, Simmons stated that the desire of the committee was simply to give the government the power to levy the tax, but that all the details should be worked out by the Secretary of the Treasury.[3] The Senate accordingly adopted the committee's amendment, and after the appointment of a committee of conference, the law was enacted. The direct-tax section was included as it had been passed by the House, and the income tax sections provided for a tax of three per cent on the excess over eight hundred dollars of the "annual income of every person residing in the United States, whether such income is derived from any kind of property or from any profession, trade, employment or vocation carried on in the United States or elsewhere, or from any source whatever." In the case of citizens residing abroad the rate was five per cent, and in the case of income from securities one and one-half per cent.[4]

From the above survey two conclusions stand out clearly.

[1] *Op. cit.*, p. 255.

[2] *Op. cit.*, p. 314.

[3] *Op. cit.*, p. 321.

[4] Act of August 5, 1861, c. xlv, sec. 49.

In the first place, the income tax was due to the dissatisfaction expressed with the scheme for a tax on real estate only; and in the second place, every one agreed that a direct tax in the constitutional sense denoted only a tax on real estate and slaves and a poll tax, and that the income tax was to be put in the category of indirect taxes. It was for this reason that both houses refused to insert in the direct-tax law any provision taxing personalty; and that a separate paragraph was introduced in order to include the income tax among the duties and excises levied by the internal revenue law. In fact, it now became the custom to call the tax "the income duty." It was so characterized by Morrill in the House, in 1862,[1] and the successive laws from 1862 on specifically describe the tax as an income duty. The significance of this will appear when we come in a later chapter to discuss its constitutionality.

§ 2. *The Act of 1862*

As a matter of fact, the act of 1861 was never put in force. The law had provided that the tax should be payable on June 30, 1862, but in the meantime Congress was to reassemble. In his annual report in December, 1861, Secretary Chase referred to the "prudent forecast which induced Congress to postpone to another year the necessity of steps for the practical enforcement of the law," and expressed considerable doubt as to the wisdom of so enforcing it. "The Secretary is acquainted with no statistics which afford the means of a satisfactory estimate of the amount likely to be realized from the income tax. Considering, however, how large a proportion of incomes, after the deductions sanctioned by law, will fall within the exemption limit of eight hundred dollars a year; and considering also what numerous questions will certainly perplex its assessment and collection, he respectfully submits whether the probable revenue affords a sufficient reason for putting in operation, at great cost, the machinery of the act,

[1] *The Congressional Globe, 37th Congress, 2d Session.* Washington, 1862, p. 1196.

with a view, should the states assume the direct tax, to the collection of the income tax alone."[1]

With his proverbial timidity he asked for only fifty millions to be raised from internal revenue, and did not include an income tax. But the committee of ways and means, who had a far better comprehension of the necessities of the situation, reported the following March an internal-revenue bill, which was not only to yield three times as much as Secretary Chase had asked for, but which also included an income tax. Morrill, as chairman of the committee, in reporting the income-tax bill, said: "The income duty is one, perhaps, of the least defensible that, on the whole, the Committee concluded to retain or report. The objection to it is that nearly all persons will have been already once taxed upon the sources from which their income has been derived. There are few persons in this country who have any fixed incomes for a term of years. . . . The income tax is an inquisitorial one at best; but, upon looking into the considerable class of state officers, and the many thousands who are employed on a fixed salary, most of whom would not contribute a penny unless called upon through this tax, it has been thought best not to wholly abandon it. Ought not men, too, with large incomes, to pay more in proportion to what they have than those with limited means, who live by the work of their own hands, or that of their families?"[2]

The introduction of this bill led to some discussion, but almost entirely on minor points, for all realized that the need of revenue was imperative. On April 3 the question arose as to whether income meant net income, and whether profits and gains were equivalent to income.[3] After the rejection of amendments to provide for the exemption of bondholders and of real estate, because of the existence of the direct tax, the bill went through without difficulty, and was introduced by

[1] *Report of the Secretary of the Treasury for the year 1861.* Washington, 1861, p. 15.

[2] *Congressional Globe, 37th Congress, 2d Session,* 1862, p. 1196.

[3] *Op. cit.*, pp. 1531–1532.

Fessenden in the Senate on April 10, the discussion beginning there in May. The Senate bill differed from the House bill in that it retained the three-per-cent rate only on incomes not exceeding ten thousand dollars, providing a five-per-cent rate on incomes from ten to fifteen thousand dollars, and a seven-and-one-half-per-cent rate on incomes over fifteen thousand dollars. In all cases the income was to be assessed only on the excess over six hundred dollars. These higher rates were due to the fact that the Senate had voted to strike out the provision imposing a direct tax. Howe objected, but in vain, to the lower rate on government bonds, and a similar fate met his amendment to levy an income tax to yield at least fifty million dollars.[1] When the bill came out of conference, the direct tax was not abandoned, but its assessment was suspended for two years; while the principle of graduation which had been introduced into the Senate bill was retained, although in a modified form.

The law of 1862 imposed a comprehensive code of internal revenue taxes, of which the income duty formed only a part. In addition to a series of taxes on the gross receipts of certain specified corporations, all railroads were required to withhold and to pay over to the government as a tax three per cent on the interest of their bonds and the dividends of their stock; and all banks, trust companies, savings institutions, and insurance companies were to pay a duty of three per cent on dividends, and on assessments added to their surplus or contingent funds.[2] A tax on salaries of government officials was imposed at the rate of three per cent on incomes over six hundred dollars,[3] and the paymasters and disbursing officers of the government were required to withhold the duty at the time of the payment of the salary or pay. The "income duty" proper[4] consisted of a tax of three per cent upon "the annual gains, profits or incomes of any person residing in the United States, whether derived from any kind of property, rents, interest, dividends, salaries or from any profession, trade,

[1] *Op. cit.*, pp. 2449, 2574.

[2] Act of July 1, 1862, chap. cxix, secs. 81–82.

[3] Sec. 86.

[4] Secs. 89–93.

employment or vocation carried on in the United States or elsewhere, or from any source whatever," to the extent that the income exceeded six hundred dollars. If the income exceeded ten thousand dollars, the rate was to be five per cent. In the case of citizens residing abroad, the rate was also five per cent, while in the case of income from government bonds the rate was one and one-half per cent. In estimating the annual gains, profits, or income subject to duty, deductions were allowed for all other national, state, and local taxes assessed upon the property or the source of income, as well as for all incomes taxable under the other sections of the law. The act also provided that there should be deducted "all gains, profits or income derived from advertisements, or on any articles manufactured, upon which specific stamp and ad valorem duties shall have been directly assessed or paid." Strictly speaking, this badly-drawn provision would have meant a complete exemption for all business incomes, for inasmuch as the tax on manufactured articles applied to nearly all commodities, business income might be interpreted as meaning income derived from dealing in such commodities. It does not appear, however, that advantage was taken of this clause, and all danger of its application was removed by an act of the next year, which removed from the list of deductions the words "or on any articles manufactured."[1] The same amendatory act also provided that the amount actually paid by any person for the rent of the dwelling-house, or estate on which he resided, should be deducted from his income.

The tax was to be levied for three years, beginning July, 1863. Every one was required to make a return of his income on a list or schedule, to the assessor or assistant assessor; and in case of neglect or refusal, the latter was to assess the income at his discrètion. If satisfied that the return was understated, he was privileged to increase the amount of the list or return; but if any one declared under oath or affirmation that his income did not amount to six hundred dollars, he was to be exempt.

[1] Act of March 3, 1863, c. lxxiv, sec. 1.

The law was put into force at the period appointed, but it took some time for the machinery to get into working order. During the first two months of the fiscal year of 1863–1864, for instance, the yield amounted to only $172,770 on incomes below $10,000; to $277,461 on incomes above $10,000; to $1872 on incomes from abroad; and to $3637 on interest on bonds.[1] The commissioner of internal revenue, in his report of December, 1863, stated that "the present tax laws on the whole have been not merely endured, but welcomed by the people in a manner it is believed elsewhere unparalleled."[2] He called attention to the difficulties connected with the so-called dividends of life-insurance companies, and recommended that the income tax be not levied upon them. He suggested only a few changes: "This tax," he tells us, "though as fair in theory as any that can be laid, has been found by the experience of other countries to be incumbered with practical difficulties in the assessment which have deprived it of all claims to public favor. The people of this country have accepted it with cheerfulness, to meet a temporary exigency, and it has excited no serious complaint in its administration. In order that it may not be felt to be inquisitorial in its character, the instructions issued by this office required that the returns of income shall not be open to the inspection of others than officers of revenue. Some doubt having been entertained whether a proper construction of the law sustains the instructions, I recommend that the doubt be removed by express enactment."[3] The commissioner also recommended that the provision allowing a deduction for rent paid for dwelling-houses be stricken from the law, and that owners of such houses, residing in them, be charged with their rental value as income. Furthermore, he recommended a decided increase in the scale of graduation, declaring himself in favor of taxing incomes from $5000 to $10,000 at four per cent, from $10,000 to $20,000 at five per

[1] *Report of the Commissioner of Internal Revenue for the Year ending June 30, 1863.* Washington, 1864, pp. 183–184.

[2] *Op. cit.*, p. 3.

[3] *Op. cit.*, p. 11.

cent, and incomes exceeding $20,000 at five and one-half per cent.

§ 3. *The Act of 1864*

As the war progressed, the need of more revenue was apparent, and in the spring of 1864 Congress prepared a far more elaborate and comprehensive code of taxation, which finally became law on June 30. This law included some important changes in the income-tax provisions, which were preceded by an interesting discussion. A large part of this discussion turned on the question of graduation.

The law of 1862, it will be remembered, had imposed two rates, namely, three per cent up to ten thousand dollars, and five per cent above ten thousand dollars. The committee of ways and means, in introducing the bill for a new income tax in April, 1864, had suggested a proportional tax of five per cent. On April 26, Frank, following the recommendations of the commissioner of internal revenue, recommended a progressive scale of five per cent up to ten thousand dollars; seven and one-half per cent up to twenty-five thousand dollars, and ten per cent over twenty-five thousand dollars. He put it on the ground of increased revenue, and claimed that the system of graduation was not repugnant to the uniformity clause of the Constitution.[1] The principle was defended, among others, by Grinnell and Spalding, not so much on the ground of revenue as of justice, It was opposed, however, by Morrill and Stevens. The latter said: "It seems to me that it is a strange way to punish men because they are rich," and declared that the committee "were of the opinion that the principle was a vicious one. I think the principle of taxing a man who is worth twenty thousand dollars more in proportion to his wealth is an unjust one. . . . If he is worth over a million dollars, we might as well provide that the government shall take the surplus."[2] Morrill stated that no one doubted the constitutional power of the government

[1] *Congressional Globe, 38th Congress, 1st Session.* Washington, 1864, p. 1876.
[2] *Op. cit.*, p. 1876.

either to levy an income tax or to provide for a progressive feature. But, he said, "experience shows that people who are taxed unequally on their incomes regard themselves as being unjustly treated, and seek all manner of ways and means to evade it. This inequality is in fact no less than a confiscation of property, because one man happens to have a little more money than another."[1]

The House, however, did not agree with the committee, and adopted a graduated scheme. Two days later Mr. Morrill reverted to the subject in a rather violent diatribe against the "spirit of agrarianism," predicting that the chief result of this "differential system" would be to lead American citizens to expatriate themselves. "On all other subjects we tax every man alike. We do not tax the manufacturer or producer of merchandise a greater percentage because he manufactures or produces more than his neighbor. . . . This provision goes upon the principle of taxing a man more because he is richer than another. The very theory of our institutions is entire equality; that we make no distinction between the rich man and the poor man. The man of moderate means is just as good as the man of more means, but our theory of government does not admit that he is better, and I regard it as an evidence of the spirit of agrarianism to present a law here which shall make any such distinction. It is seizing the property of men for the crime of having too much. . . . We have too few rich men in the country to make a distinction that may induce them to expatriate themselves. . . . Let us be just. . . . In this proposition there seems to me to be something unjust."[2]

When the bill reached the Senate, the finance committee slightly modified the graduated scheme, reducing the upper limit from ten per cent on incomes over twenty-five thousand dollars to seven and one-half per cent on incomes over ten thousand dollars. Fessenden, in reporting the bill, stated that there had been considerable discussion in the committee

[1] *Congressional Globe, 38th Congress, 1st Session.* Washington, 1864, p. 1876.

[2] *Op. cit.*, p. 1940.

and that, "for myself individually, my own opinion is not exceedingly well fixed on this point. The income tax at best is a discrimination. . . . I have been in favor, from the beginning, of making some discrimination as against large incomes." He declared himself to be in accord with "the principle that those having very large incomes can afford, and perhaps better afford than those who have smaller ones, to pay a tax, and a larger tax, the discriminating tax if you please." But he declared that "there is and ought to be a sort of conservative sentiment to protect property," and "that no odious and ungenerous discrimination" should be made.[1] Sumner, although undecided as to whether to prefer the Senate to the House proposition, declared himself not ready to oppose the principle of graduation in general, and read a long quotation from Say in favor of progressive taxation.[2] Sherman also felt doubtful about the whole matter, while Foote and Johnson took strong ground against it. Davis, however, declared that the principle of graduation was nothing but a "recognition of the idea that taxes shall be paid according to the ability of persons to pay."[3] The result was that the amendment was adopted.

A few days later Grimes introduced another amendment, making incomes over fifteen thousand dollars taxable at ten per cent. Referring to Sumner's quotation from Say, he stated that he was simply proposing "to carry the principle out to a little greater extent, and cause those men who have large fortunes and derive therefrom large incomes, to pay a little amount in addition to the rate paid by the small men who exhaust nearly all of this income in the support of their families. If there is any class of men," he continued, "that the distinction ought to be made in favor of and not against, it is the very class of men we have discriminated against, and now we reach a class of men who have a surplus over and above the money that is necessary to meet their family expenses, and it is that class that I propose to reach."[4] The

[1] *Op. cit.*, p. 2513.

[2] *Op. cit.*, p. 2514.

[3] *Op. cit.*, p. 2515.

[4] *Op. cit.*, p. 2760.

Senate again agreed to this proposition. When the bill, however, emerged from conference, the ten per cent rate was made to begin at ten thousand dollars, a fact which shows that the feeling in favor of a higher rate on the larger incomes was constantly growing.

A few other provisions of the bill were also discussed. According to the law of 1863, it will be remembered that the amount paid for house rent was deducted from income. The House bill of 1864 cut down the deduction for house rent to two hundred dollars, but introduced the provision that if a man lived in his own house, the rental value up to the extent of two hundred dollars should also be deducted. In other words, the House bill introduced the principle that income was to include not alone money income, but also benefit or psychic income. When it reached the Senate, however, the committee of finance, as Fessenden explained, "came to the conclusion that it was impossible to carry out that provision without making a very odious discrimination especially between town and country."[1] He thought "the safer and better principle would be to allow every man the rental value of his house, whether he owned it himself or rented it.[2]" Another interesting discussion arose over the question of profits on sales. The commissioner of internal revenue had decided that if a man bought a piece of land and sold it after the expiration of a given period, the difference between the cost and the selling price was to be returned as income within the year of sale. Fessenden pointed out that this was erroneous, because the difference in the selling price was

[1] "Inasmuch," he continued, "as it depended upon the rent, it would have no sort of connection with the cost of men's houses originally, but merely upon the rental value, and the rental value would depend, in a very great degree, upon the place where it happened to be located. Thus it would be impossible to make it equal in any way. It would impose a burden upon certain men who happened to live in a city, from which men living in the country where rents are low, comparatively nothing, would be exempted entirely." — *Op. cit.*, p. 2517.

[2] Senator Fessenden, however, was mistaken in thinking that this was the provision of the old law. As has just been explained, the old law applied only to the actual rent paid, not to the rental value.

really to be considered an accretion to capital rather than as income.[1] He conceded that the matter had given the committee considerable difficulty, but concluded that the easiest way out of the difficulty was to declare that only the net profits realized by sales of property upon investments made within the year should be chargeable as income.

The law of 1864 provided for an income duty at the rate of five per cent on the excess of $600 up to $5000; seven and one-half per cent on the excess over $5000 up to $10,000, and ten per cent on the excess over $10,000.[2] Banks, trust companies, savings institutions, and insurance companies were taxed five per cent on their dividends; and railroads, canals, turnpike, and slack-water companies five per cent on their dividends and the interest on bonds, the amount of tax in all of these cases to be deducted from the sums due to the security holder. Salaries were also taxable at the rate of five per cent on the excess over $600. While the personal income tax was to be levied up to and including the year 1870, no such limitation was put upon the salaries and dividends tax, perhaps through an oversight.

The dividend and interest tax and the salary tax, although separately mentioned, were really a part of the income tax. To this extent, therefore, the principle of stoppage at source was applied. The graduated principle of the income tax could, however, obviously not be applied to the dividends and interest tax, and it was for this reason that the proportional rate of five per cent was imposed. In the case of the salaries tax the same impracticability did not exist, but despite this fact, the only departure from the strict proportional rate was the uniform deduction of $600.

The old distinctions of the law of 1862 with reference to the incomes of citizens residing abroad and the income from government bonds were abandoned, the same rates being now applicable to all kinds of income. A provision was also introduced that "net profits realized by sales of real estate purchased within the year, for which income was estimated,

[1] *Op. cit.*, p. 2516.

[2] Act of June 30, 1864, c. clxxiii, sec. 116.

shall be chargeable as income; and losses on sales of real estate purchased within the year for which income is estimated shall be deducted from the income of such year."[1] In estimating the annual income, deductions were allowed for all taxes, salaries, income from dividends, or interests on securities where the tax was paid by the company, and the amount paid by any person for the rent of the homestead occupied, as well as the rental value of any homestead occupied. A provision was inserted including in the annual income "the income or gains derived from the purchase and sale of stocks or property, and the increased value of live stock, whether sold or on hand, and the amount of sugar, wool, butter, cheese, pork, beef, mutton, or other meats, hay and grain or other vegetable, or other productions of the estate of such persons sold." Allowance was made for "usual or ordinary repairs, not exceeding the average for the preceding five years," but it was provided that "no deduction shall be made for any amount paid out for new buildings, permanent improvements or betterments made to increase the value of any property or estate."[2] A consul of a foreign country, not a citizen of the United States, was exempt from income tax, provided that reciprocal privileges were conferred by the foreign governments.[3]

Finally, the rates of the tax on gross receipts were increased so that steamboat and canal companies paid two and one-half per cent; toll roads, ferries, and bridges, three per cent. But it was expressly provided that the tax might be added to the rate of fare. Express companies paid three per cent; insurance companies one and one-half per cent; telegraph companies five per cent; theatrical and similar enterprises two per cent; lotteries five per cent; advertisements three per cent. All such enterprises were required to return the gross receipts annually. In case of neglect or refusal, ten per cent was to be added, and for any attempt at evasion a penalty of one thousand dollars was to be imposed.

Such was the law of 1864, which served as the model upon

[1] Sec. 116. [2] Sec. 117. [3] Sec. 178.

which all subsequent acts were based. Before the law was put in operation, however, it was amended in several particulars by a law of the following year, which increased the rates to five per cent on the excess over $600 dollars up to $5000, and ten per cent on the excess over $5000.[1] A slight change was also made in section 117 whereby the old clause as to the inclusion in income of the "increased value of live stock," etc., was altered so as to read "the amount of live stock," etc. The administrative sections of the law were improved in several particulars. The assistant assessor was empowered to require every list or return to be verified by the oath or affirmation of the party, and to increase the amount if he had reason to believe it understated. Furthermore, in case of refusal to make a return, or of a false or fraudulent return, the assessor or assistant assessor was to make the return "according to the best information he can obtain by the examination of such person and his books and accounts, or any other evidence." In the case of wilful neglect or refusal, twenty-five per cent was to be added; in the case of false or fraudulent returns one hundred per cent. Any one convicted of fraud, moreover, might be fined $1000 or imprisoned for not more than a year, or be subjected to both punishments. If any return should be increased by the assistant assessor, the individual might "exhibit his books and accounts and be permitted to prove and declare under oath or affirmation the amount of annual income liable to be assessed." Such evidence, however, was not to be "considered as conclusive of the facts." Appeal might be taken to the assessor of the district, and finally to the commissioner of internal revenue.[2] These administrative changes aroused practically no discussion at all, and the same may be said of the joint resolution of July 4, 1864, which imposed an additional special income tax payable in October, 1864, to defray the expenditure for the war bounties, at the rate of five per cent on all incomes over $600 received in 1863.

[1] Act of March 3, 1865, c. lxxviii, sec. 1.

[2] Sec. 118.

In his report of December, 1864, Fessenden, who had now become secretary of the treasury, upheld the doctrine of graduated taxation as contained in the law. He declared himself, however, opposed to the exemption. "The Secretary would further suggest," he said, "whether the income tax should not be collected upon all, without exemption. As the law is, it opens the door to innumerable frauds, and in a young and growing country the vast majority of incomes are small, while all participate alike in the blessings of good government. The adoption of a scale, augmenting the rate of taxation upon incomes as they rise in amount, although unequal in one sense, cannot be considered oppressive or unjust, inasmuch as the ability to pay increases in much more than arithmetical proportion as the amount of income exceeds the limit of reasonable necessity."[1]

The Secretary, however, did not deceive himself as to the practical operation of the law. "From the results of experience, as well as from all the information received, the Secretary is well convinced that much revenue fails to be collected through an imperfect execution of the law, and more through a fraudulent evasion of its provisions." He was, however, not without hope for the future. "Time and effort will, it is hoped, remedy these evils in a great degree, and the confident expectations of those who framed it be realized. In the meantime, no effort should be spared to perfect it, as far as possible, and no experiment to increase its efficiency, of which there is a reasonable hope of success, should be left untried."

In his report of the same period, the commissioner of internal revenue discussed the improvement in the fiscal results. During the year ending July, 1864, the income tax proper yielded over twenty-three millions, or, with the addition of the tax on salaries and on dividends and interest, almost thirty-five millions. The commissioner considered "that the income tax collected during the last fiscal year represents pretty fairly what a levy of three per cent should yield." Referring to the prospects for the coming year, he

[1] *Report of the Secretary of the Treasury for 1864.* Washington, 1864, p. 15.

conceded that "many persons will escape assessment who could not escape payment through banks, railroad corporations and paymasters. But the duties on income will in general be assessed more exactly and collected more closely than heretofore. The assessors are armed with powers for investigation and discovery which have not hitherto been conferred, and they have become more thoroughly acquainted with their obligations under the law than at any prior period." [1] The commissioner called attention, however, to the difficulties connected with the assessment of farmers' incomes. "The best test of the yearly income derived from real estate is its rental value. A rule requiring such income to be assessed on that value would be conveniently practicable, and would obviate the necessity of the vexatious inquisition now required in ascertaining the comparative value of live stock at different periods of the year, the amount of butter, beef, mutton, pork, cheese, wool, hay, grain and other products sold or on hand. Estimates of these must needs be very unequal and returns incomplete, so that the burden of the tax is unequally distributed." Furthermore, he said, "I am unable to see why a man who consumes his income should not be taxed for it as well as one who saves it, nor why one who lives in his own house should not be taxed on its rental value, as much as if he let it to another and put the rent in his purse. If it be deemed right to allow an occupant of his own homestead such a portion of his rental value unassessed as would suffice to pay the rent of a moderate dwelling, the excess of the annual value of such homestead above that sum might, with justice, be taxed." [2] An allowance of three or four hundred dollars, he thought, would suffice for this purpose.

These views of the commissioner were confirmed by the report of the Special Revenue Commission in 1865, which was composed of David A. Wells, Stephen Colwell, and S. S. Hayes. The commission recommended that "in assessing the income tax no allowance whatever be made for house rent, or at

[1] *Report of the Commissioner of Internal Revenue for 1864.* Washington, 1865, p. 5.

[2] *Op. cit.*, p. 13.

least that the income allowed to be deducted for rental should not in any case be allowed to exceed $300. As the law now stands, rentals of an excessive and unreasonable amount are also deducted." The gain to the revenue in the state of New York alone, from the repeal of that part of the act authorizing the deduction of rentals would, in the opinion of the revenue officials, amount to over two millions of dollars per annum.[1] Congress, however, refused to follow their advice.

§ 4. *The Aftermath of the War*

With the close of the war the question arose as to the permanence of the income tax. For the time being, indeed, the revenue was still sorely needed, so that there could be no question of immediate change. On April 25, 1866, Morrill reported a bill from the committee on ways and means, and on May 7 explained the proposal. The committee, he said, "have prepared some modifications of the income law, but have not reached the conclusion, while the industrial employments must remain to a considerable extent heavily burdened, that it can yet be wholly dispensed with."[2] Morrill called attention to the fact that, according to the terms of the original law, the act was to expire in 1870, "and thus a temporary character was put upon its face." That it had been a fiscal success, he thought, could not be doubted. After referring to the large revenues derived from the tax, and to the special income tax levied in 1864, he said: "I point to these facts not only as a broad evidence of their patriotism and wealth, but as a proud evidence of their strict integrity of character. Strong as the temptation might be for evasive returns, sore as they might be in consequence of the swift pursuit and the continuous exactions of the tax gatherer, they even paid more in 1863 upon the second call than on the first. Their country was in need, and even the greed for gain could not tempt

[1] *House Executive Documents, First Session, 39th Congress,* no. 17, vol. vii.

[2] *Congressional Globe, 39th Congress, First Session.* Washington, 1866, p. 2437.

the American people to defraud their government. . . . The law left it almost to the conscience of each man as to how much he should pay, and all seemed to vie with each other as to who should pay the most. I question whether any people ever paid a tax more honestly and accurately, and I question still more whether any free people ever imposed upon themselves, through their chosen representatives, taxes so thick and fast."

If, however, the income tax were to be contemplated as a part of the permanent policy of the country, many changes, he thought, would be needed. He declared the objections to be as follows: First, the law is "inquisitorial of necessity in its character, and Americans, like people elsewhere, though not averse to a knowledge of the secrets of others, are quite unwilling to disclose their own. Among commercial men such disclosures may be disastrous. . . . The temptation to make under-statements, to lend to these statements the sanction of an oath, tends to sap and mine public morals, until men begin to excuse themselves for their own wrong-doing, because, it being so common, that to do otherwise would be to fail in average smartness." Furthermore, "when we take into consideration the sources from which income is derived, the habitudes of the different persons who pay the tax, the difficulty of apportioning it so that each will have paid in just proportion to every other person, leaving each relatively in the same conditions, the perplexities become almost insurmountable." In accordance with these principles, Morrill declared that it was desirable to lessen the weight of the income tax, and he proposed that the exemption be increased to $1000, and that the rate be made uniform at five per cent, for "in a republican form of government the true theory is to make no distinctions as to persons in the rates of taxation. Recognizing no class for special favors, we ought not to create a class for special burdens."[1]

The proposition led to some discussion. Raymond declared his surprise that the chairman of the committee of ways and

[1] *Op. cit.*, p. 2437.

means should have found it necessary to apologize for the continuance of the tax. He stated that "income is the first thing, so far as industry and the products of industry are concerned, which should be taxed."[1] He also objected to the abandonment of the progressive principle. In a passage in which he displayed a slight acquaintance with foreign scientific literature, he stated: "I know that theoretical writers insist that it is unjust and impolitic to impose a graduated income tax; that every man should pay the same percentage on his income, whatever its amount may be." But he nevertheless upheld the principle on the ground of taxing "superfluities instead of luxuries." When the matter was again taken up a few weeks later, on May 23, Pike objected both to the proportional rate and to the proposed increase of exemption, suggesting a continuance of the progressive rate, and stating that "no one of those upon whom the high rate of income tax was charged had asked to be relieved from his burden," while on the other hand "petitions from struggling manufacturers were coming from all quarters of the land, asking for relief from the other taxes."[2]

Ross, of Illinois, suggested a far higher scale of progression, rising to twenty-five per cent on incomes over sixty thousand dollars. Morrill opposed this vehemently, stating that the proposition could "only be defended on the same ground that the highwayman defends his acts." Spalding, however, who proposed a somewhat modified rate, objected to this characterization of the progressive principle by Morrill as "highway robbery," and after an argument which based the defence of graduation on the principle of ability to pay, stated, "I cannot see upon what ground, in morals or in ethics, or in logic, the argument of my learned friend from Vermont has a resting place." Sloane also stated that "if a perfectly just system of taxation could be devised, every man would be taxed just in proportion to his ability to pay the tax; that is, in proportion to the excess which he has left after meeting all the legitimate demands upon him."[3] The House seemed to be

[1] *Op. cit.*, p. 2440. [2] *Op. cit.*, p. 2783. [3] *Op. cit.*, p. 2784.

convinced by the arguments in favor of graduation and accepted Pike's amendment for a duty of five per cent on incomes up to five thousand dollars and ten per cent on the surplus.

Several other points were touched upon in the discussion. Nicholson dwelt upon the injustice of deducting six hundred dollars or one thousand dollars from ordinary incomes, but not where the tax was stopped at its source and paid by the corporations. Morrill, however, pointed out that the difficulties of applying the principle in that case "are almost insuperable." [1] Wilson called attention to the fact that the commissioner of internal revenue had decided that no loss should be deducted from the income which was not incurred in some business out of which the property derived a profit, and where the loss incurred overbalanced the amount of profit. He suggested that all losses actually sustained in any way should be deducted, and his amendment was agreed to.[2] Hale referred to the abuses on the part of the assistant assessors in making their corrected returns of income, and imposing the high penalty whenever they consider the returns fraudulent. He contended that this ought never to be done without a preliminary hearing accorded to the taxpaper.[3] Garfield called attention to one feature of the tax "which has made it very odious in many parts of the country," namely, the publicity of the returns. He suggested that, while the list of incomes should be open to the inspection of the public, it should not be furnished for publication. Morrill defended the amendment, although he conceded that "there is no question that the publication of these lists has a tendency to increase the revenue." [4]

When the bill came up in the Senate on June 21, Fessenden reported for the committee that the changes proposed by the House could not be put into operation until another year, and since Congress would have a later opportunity to consider some of these important criticisms, he proposed that

[1] *Op. cit.*, p. 2786.

[2] *Op. cit.*, p. 2787.

[3] *Op. cit.*, p. 2788.

[4] *Op. cit.*, p. 2789.

no material change be made for the present.[1] The Senate adopted this suggestion, which was concurred in by the House, and thus the new act introduced only a few amendments. The tax which, it will be remembered, had hitherto been applicable only to all persons residing in the United States and to all citizens residing abroad, was now extended so as to include the income from all business, trade, and professions carried on in the United States by persons residing without the United States not citizens thereof.[2] The income tax, moreover, was now declared payable every year "until and including the year 1870 and no longer." The scale of the salaries tax was also altered so as to conform to that of the income tax proper, being made respectively five per cent on the excess over six hundred dollars, and ten per cent on the excess over five thousand dollars.

In December, 1866, the commissioner of internal revenue made a report on the administration of the tax, and for the first time stated the number of taxpayers and the amount of revenue in each class of the progressive tax. He then proceeded to advert to the amendment suggested by the House in the discussion of 1866, calling attention especially to the question of exemption. He declared that the purpose of the law originally had been to exempt so much of one's income as was demanded by his actual necessities; and he pointed out that the raising of the minimum of existence from six hundred to one thousand dollars was advisable on the ground that "since then the internal tax upon commodities, the increase of customs duty, and the depreciation of the currency have wrought an almost universal advance in prices."[3] He characterized the provision governing the profits and losses from real estate as a quite "arbitrary rule," and stated that "there seems to be little reason for its existence." He closed his discussion by calling attention to the fact that the large revenue of the year just ending, including

[1] *Op. cit.*, p. 3221.

[2] Act of July 13, 1866, c. clxxxiv, sec. 9.

[3] *Report of the Commissioner of Internal Revenue for the Year ending June 30, 1866.* Washington, 1866, p. xxiii.

the good returns from the income tax, was "raised with probably less pressure upon the people than that of smaller amounts in previous years. Their enterprise and spirit of accumulation have prevented the depression of business which ordinarily attends heavy taxation." The chief reason, however, which he did not mention in this connection, was the one referred to above, namely, the prosperity connected with the general rise in prices.

In the winter of 1866–1867, the subject was again considered, and after a short discussion most of the amendments suggested in 1866 were adopted. In one respect, however, a change was made. Congress now decided, largely for the reason that the revenue was no longer needed, to abandon the progressive principle. The new law of 1867[1] imposed a tax of five per cent on all incomes over one thousand dollars. Income was declared to include the profits realized from the sales of real estate purchased within the year, or within two years previous. The amount of all premiums on gold and coupons was now also declared to be taxable as income, although the law did not state whether such premium was to be taxed only if realized. A slight change was made in the statement as to the produce of the farmer. Whereas the earlier laws had spoken of the "amount of live stock," etc., as being taxable income, the new law put it as "the amount of sales of live stock," etc. Deductions were allowed for all losses actually sustained during the year, although the provision was inserted that there should not be included in the deduction any "estimated depreciation of values and losses within the year on sales of real estate purchased two years previous."

With reference to the administrative features, the penalty for delay in payment was changed from ten per cent to five per cent, with interest at one per cent a month. The penalty for neglect or refusal to make lists was raised from twenty-five to fifty per cent, that for making fraudulent returns remaining at one hundred per cent. The dates of assessment

[1] Act of March 2, 1867, c. clxix, sec. 13.

and payment were moved closer to the beginning of the year, the date of assessment being changed from May 1 to March 1, and the date when the tax was payable being changed from June 30 to April 30. Finally, the salaries tax was declared inapplicable to mechanics or laborers employed upon public works.

Wells, in his report in January, 1868, called attention to the fact that a "considerable falling off in the revenue to be derived from the income tax, for the present and succeeding fiscal years, may be expected, both from the reduction of the tax under the Act of May 2, 1867; and also from losses recently experienced through the shrinkage in the value of commodities."[1] He estimated that the revenue for the coming year would fall to about thirty-five million dollars. Wells discussed two points of principle in the existing law. The first was the matter of exemption, which was allowed unqualifiedly to all persons returning an income. He thought that "the original object of the exemption would appear to have been entirely lost sight of in making the exemption absolute and unqualified; for what in the one case is an allowance to necessity becomes in the other a mere increase of abundance." He therefore recommended that the English system be followed, and that the law be amended so as to permit the exemption to be applied only to incomes under fifteen hundred or two thousand dollars.

The other point to which he referred was the "curious anomaly which allows, on the one hand, an unqualified deduction from income of the amount paid for rent, and on the other hand does not consider as income in any degree the rental value of property held or enjoyed by its possessor." He pointed out that this was inconsistent, "for while in all other departments of the revenue it is accepted as a fundamental principle that luxuries especially should be taxed, in this they are especially exempted." He held that there was no good reason, "when a sufficient and proper sum is exempted

[1] *Report of the Special Commissioner of the Revenue.* Washington, 1868, p. 62.

in the first instance from an income tax, why this exemption should be further increased by the addition of rentals or rental values." On the contrary, he thought that "all rental in excess of a certain amount should be considered as a luxury and taxed accordingly."[1] Congress, however, refused to take any action.

§ 5. *The Contest over the Retention of the Tax*

The income tax was to expire in 1870. The readiness with which the people had submitted to it during the war diminished with the termination of the conflict, and as each year passed by, the tax became more unpopular and as a consequence less successful. With the approach, however, of the period of its projected disappearance, the discussion as to its continuance became more active. The commissioner of internal revenue, in his annual report of December, 1869, declared himself strongly in favor of its continuance. He queried as to whether "we can part entirely with the receipts from this source of revenue; and if not, whether any substitute can be devised more just and equitable, and less burdensome to tax-payers."[2] "My opinion is," said he, "that, so long as a large internal revenue is required by the official necessities of the government, a portion of that revenue should be collected from incomes. The reasons for this seem apparent and forcible. This tax reaches simply the profits of trade and business, and the increased wealth of the individuals from investments." He thought that many of the complaints would disappear if the tax were "paid as these profits and accumulations accrue," and he proceeded to discuss the chief objection that "it leads to a system of espionage into private affairs that is not only offensive but sometimes injurious to individuals." "I do not see," said he, "why this objection may not with equal force be urged against all taxes upon personal property." And after

[1] *Report of the Special Commissioner, op. cit.*, p. 63.

[2] *Report of the Commissioner of Internal Revenue, for the Year ending June 30, 1869.* Washington, 1869, p. xiii.

some further discussion, he concluded: "After all, it is but a tax upon the increased wealth of the nation. . . . I submit if it will be wise to abolish the income tax as long as the labor, industry and business of the country are directly or indirectly subjected to any considerable taxation."[1]

Wells, in his report of the same year, took similar ground in a passage which, in view of his later opposition to the income tax, is worthy of note. He declared himself in favor of retaining the income tax, although he suggested that the rate be reduced from five to three per cent, not only because it would then be less burdensome to the individual, but because, in his opinion, the lower rate would yield almost as much as the higher. The existing rate he thought too high for revenue purposes, and he held that the tax was "passing through much the same experience as the whiskey tax when at its maximum."[2] Wells also repeated his recommendation that the exemptions for rentals be limited to two hundred dollars. "No claim can be made for the exemption of rent to any extent, which would not be equally valid in support of the exemption of any other expenditure; and certainly high rents are as much a luxury as any form of expenditure, and as little deserving of economical sympathy." If his adoption should be suggested both as to the abolition of this exemption and as to the reduction of the rate, he contended that the revenue from the income tax would be maintained and that but for the depression in business the yield would probably be considerably greater. Referring to the "proposition, seriously advocated in many quarters, that this tax should be wholly removed," he called attention to the fact that during the year 1868 the tax was paid by only two hundred and fifty thousand people, who nevertheless represented an aggregate income of not less than eight hundred millions. "Allowing, then, for the families of these two hundred and fifty

[1] *Op. cit.*, p. xix.

[2] *Report of the Special Commissioner of the Revenue upon the Industry, Trade, Commerce, etc., of the United States, for the Year 1869.* Washington, 1869, p. lxix.

thousand contributors, it is evident that only about a million of the population are interested in having the tax removed, while the remaining thirty-eight and a half millions of the people are interested in having it maintained."[1]

On June 1, 1870, the matter was taken up in Congress. The committee of ways and means had reported a bill to reduce the revenue by nearly thirty-four millions, but did not include the abandonment or reduction of the income tax, preferring to remit the inheritance tax, the tax on sales, the tax on gas, the tax on gross receipts, and many of the special taxes. The committee bill continued the tax, with the one important change of increasing the exemption to fifteen hundred dollars. McCarthy maintained that the revenues might be reduced still further, and that the income tax ought to be included in the list of the taxes to be dropped. "This income tax bears," said he, "what no other tax bears upon its face, the evidence that it was only considered and passed as a war tax, being limited to five years in its duration. The five years are up; the war is over; our revenue will bear the reduction, and we can afford to let it die. I do not hesitate to say there is more dissatisfaction with this tax than any other. Objections to its renewal are long, loud, and general throughout the country. Those who pay are the exception, those who do not pay are millions; and the whole moral force of the law is a dead letter. The honest man makes a true return; the dishonest hides and covers all he can to avoid this obnoxious tax. It has no moral force. This tax is unequal, perjury-provoking and crime-encouraging, because it is at war with the right of a person to keep private and regulate his business affairs and financial matters. Deception, fraud, and falsehood mark its progress everywhere in the process of collection. It creates curiosity, jealousy, and prejudice among the people. It makes the tax-gatherer a spy. . . . The people demand that it shall not be renewed, but left to die a natural death and pass away into the future as pass away all the evils growing out of the Civil War."[2]

[1] *Report of the Special Commissioner, op. cit.*, p. lxx.

[2] *Congressional Globe, 41st Congress, 2d Session.* Washington, 1870, p. 3993.

A heated discussion now ensued. Among those who agreed with McCarthy was Butler, of Massachusetts, who said that 'an income tax levied and collected as ours is, is the most irritating, provocative of opposition, and imperfect of all taxes.' He found the principal defect to consist in the fact that "it mistakes earnings for income. It treats as income the product of honest labor, whether mental or physical, and undertakes by inquisition in collecting it to treat every man in the country as a rogue and rascal most likely to evade the tax, and thereby succeeds only in compelling the conscientious, the honest, and the just men to pay. . . . The difficulty is, we do not tax incomes at all — only the consciences of those who are supposed to have incomes."[1] He suggested, in its stead, "a fair income tax on invested capital to be collected without assessors or inquisition," — virtually on the English model. Davis, referring to the abolition of the English tax in 1816, contended that this government ought also to keep its pledge as "an example of the virtue and value of integrity and fair dealing between a government and its people."[2] On the next day he went into its defects at greater length, and now for the first time intimated that it was of doubtful constitutionality as being a direct tax.[3]

On the other hand, most of the speakers declared themselves in favor of the tax. Blair contended that the revenue could not be spared, and that it must be borne in mind that "every dollar which we take off this income tax, which applies to the rich men of the country, must be laid upon the poorer men."[4] Ela defended the tax on the ground that if it were removed, "the motive of the taxpayers for keeping strict watch upon the expenditures of the government will be wanting;"[5] that all the other internal revenue taxes were war taxes as well as the income tax, and that they ought first to be removed. Finally, as to the question of fraud, he asked whether that was a better reason for removing the income tax than the whiskey and tobacco taxes. Townsend contended

[1] *Op. cit.*, p. 3995.
[2] *Op. cit.*, p. 3996.
[3] *Op. cit.*, p. 4031.
[4] *Op. cit.*, p. 3994.
[5] *Op. cit.*, p. 3997.

that "the clamor in favor of the abolition of the income tax is a local and a manufactured cry. It does not come from the masses of the people. It originated among the men of gigantic capital, among the railroad monopolists, brokers and dealers in stocks, wholesale importers, mostly foreigners, and men of colossal fortunes and extraordinary incomes. It was started by papers in their interest, and is mostly confined to those places and persons. It has not spread to the country."[1] Pomeroy maintained that "the opposition to this tax comes from the men who are fattening on the capital of the country."[2] Roots thought that "the tax is very much like a boil that a man had on his nose. He complained of its being there very much, and his friend asked him, 'Where else would you like to have it?' He thought of the matter for a while, and then answered: 'Well, I swon, I believe I would rather have it on some other man's back.'"[3] Loughridge called attention to the fact that New York state had paid about one-third of the entire tax, and that he easily understood the opposition of the New Yorkers; but he contended that it was nevertheless entirely just, because at least one-third of the entire wealth of the country was to be found in New York. He quoted with telling effect a passage from Amasa Walker, who, in his book on Political Economy, had declared himself strongly in favor of the tax. As a result of these arguments the House voted to continue the tax indefinitely at the rate of three per cent, but with an increase in the exemption to two thousand dollars.

A few weeks later the bill was taken up in the Senate, where it met with determined opposition. Sumner said: "Sir, the income tax must go. It must not be continued. It has already lived too long for the good of the country."[4] Conkling declared that "no exigencies whatever will justify or tolerate the revival of the odious tax misnamed the Income Tax."[5] Corbett, who stated that he had been in favor of the tax as long as it was needed, now said, "I be-

[1] *Op. cit.*, p. 4023.
[2] *Op. cit.*, p. 4033.
[3] *Op. cit.*, p. 4038.
[4] *Op. cit.*, p. 4709.
[5] *Op. cit.*, p. 4711.

lieve that if you want to make this tax so odious so that during another war you can never levy such a tax, you had better renew it; and then I assure you, you will never be able, even in that crisis, to establish or levy it again."[1] And later on he said: "if this tax is re-enacted, the Republican party might as well put on its winding sheet."[2] Buckingham objected to the tax on the ground that owing to the publicity of the returns, people were virtually compelled to pay on more incomes than they possessed in order to bolster up their credit.[3] Thurman found fault with it on the remarkable ground that an income tax is shifted, and is finally paid by the poor. Yates contended that the law, "with its frauds, its inquisitorial character, its cheats, its deceptions by which the honest man paid and the dishonest escaped, should be blotted from the American statute book as you would efface a blot upon the flag of the Nation."[4] Paterson quoted from Gladstone's speech of 1853, in order to elucidate what he considered the inevitable frauds of an income tax.[5]

On the other hand, there were not lacking defenders of the tax. Among the warmest advocates was Sherman, who declared that there was an imperative necessity for retaining the income tax,[6] and who even objected to any increase of the exemption. He contended that on the score of inquisition the income tax was not inferior to the property tax, and he maintained that "property is not a proper test of taxes."[7] Pointing out that in England the income tax had come, in his opinion, to stay, he denied that the country was pledged not to renew the tax, holding that the limitation to the year 1870 was originally inserted "not for the purpose of binding Congress against the reënactment of the income tax, but rather as an introduction of opinion that we should levy it for that time. It was a guarantee to the bondholders that for that time at least they should have the security of the income tax."[8] Morton, referring to the "demoralization" argument,

[1] *Op. cit.*, p. 4717.
[2] *Op. cit.*, p. 4811.
[3] *Op. cit.*, p. 4757.
[4] *Op. cit.*, p. 4897.
[5] *Op. cit.*, p. 5086.
[6] *Op. cit.*, p. 4713.
[7] *Op. cit.*, p. 4714.
[8] *Op. cit.*, p. 4715.

contended that it was equally applicable to all existing property taxes, and stated: "I have no respect for that argument; not a bit." Coming back to the old claim that New York paid one-third of the taxes, he said: "I should be very willing to exchange with New York and agree that we would take her incomes and pay her taxes. . . . They have to pay the income tax simply because the large incomes are there. . . . What kind of an argument is that?"[1] He concluded: "I have not heard an argument against the income tax that had any force in it that was not stronger against every other kind of taxation than the income tax."[2] Cragin, a little later, said, "I know very well that the argument is that this tax is unequal and inquisitorial, etc.; but when all the froth of words, all the wealth of rhetoric is swept away on this subject, the real objection to this is the payment of the money, and nothing more."[3]

The opinion on the whole, however, seemed to be adverse to the continuance of the tax, and the Senate, sitting as a committee of the whole, decided to strike out the house income-tax provision by a vote of 34 to 23. In the meantime, however, the impending deficit turned out to be larger than had been anticipated, and with this additional gap reached an alarming figure. The question how to make good the deficiency was now referred to the committee on finance for further consideration. Sherman, the chairman of the committee, reported that since the income tax had been abandoned, he would suggest the restoration of the tax on gross receipts and on sugar. The committee of the whole was at first not willing to accept these suggestions, but later on decided to adopt them in part, at all events, so far as the duties on sugar were concerned. When the bill came out of committee, Wilson moved to continue the income tax at the reduced rate of two and one-half per cent for two years;[4] but this was rejected, as was a similar motion of Warner that the tax should be continued only as a tax on the income from

[1] *Op. cit.*, p. 4759.
[2] *Op. cit.*, p. 4760.
[3] *Op. cit.*, p. 5085.
[4] *Op. cit.*, p. 5085.

capital.[1] On July 1 the amendment striking out all the provisions relating to income tax was adopted by the Senate, by a vote of 26 to 22. Sherman thereupon moved to restore the tax on gross receipts, stating that he did not believe that "there were many taxes on the tax list worse than the tax on gross receipts," but contending that it was absolutely necessary to prevent a deficit. His motion was lost by a tie vote, and the question now arose what was to be done. Several of the senators who had voted against the retention of the income tax in the expectation that the tax on gross receipts would be restored, found themselves in a quandary. Anthony declared that he, as well as some of his colleagues, was ready to reconsider the vote if the choice should lie between an income tax and a gross receipts tax, as they much preferred the former.[2] Accordingly, the whole matter was reconsidered by a vote of 26 to 25. Wilson now repeated the amendment, which had originally been voted down, and this time it was carried by a vote of 27 to 21.[3]

But the fight was not yet over. Sumner stated that the war and the income taxes were wedded together,[4] while Edmonds declared that the decision was, after all, a choice between evils.[5] Senator Bayard attempted to extend the two-thousand-dollar exemption to the tax on interest and dividends, but did not succeed. The enemies of the tax brought the matter up, through a motion to strike out, and came within an ace of accomplishing their result, the motion being lost by a tie vote of 26 to 26.

During the discussion Sherman really bore the yeoman's part. But for him there is little doubt that the tax would have been repealed at once. In his speech of May 23 he went into the subject at great length.[6] Contending that the income tax "was sustained, by principle, by writers of political

[1] *Op. cit.*, p. 5082.
[2] *Op. cit.*, p. 5098.
[3] *Op. cit.*, p. 5099.
[4] *Op. cit.*, p. 5100.
[5] *Op. cit.*, p. 5101.

[6] The speech is reprinted in *Selected Speeches and Reports on Finance and Taxation from 1859 to 1878*. By John Sherman. New York, 1879, pp. 284 *et seq.*

economy, by the experiences of Great Britain, and that it was the most just and equitable tax levied by the United States," he pointed out that England had been able to diminish the burdens resting upon consumption only through the imposition of the income tax, and he stated that "the only discrimination in our tax laws that will reach wealthy men as against the poorer classes, is the income tax. . . . According to every true theory of taxation, a large part of the taxes ought to fall upon property or income derived from property."[1] He maintained that under the old law "every year the income tax is increasing, although the actual income of the country is diminishing. Every year that the law is enforced, we are getting nearer to an accurate income tax."[2] After quoting a statement from Professor Perry, of Williams College,[3] that "the income law at present in force in the United States has, perhaps, been subject to less complaint than the manufacturers' tax and other forms of indirect taxation, and it has become more and more productive every year, as the forms are perfected," he concluded: "If I had my way, I would retain the income tax at five per cent on all incomes above one thousand dollars, making such modifications as would afford the proper exemptions, and then throw off these taxes upon consumption that oppress the poor and take coppers out of the dollars of the people who earn them by their daily work."[4]

Neither the Senate nor the country at large, however, was ready to accept these advanced views, and although the tax was now continued, it was expressly limited to the years 1870 and 1871, "and no longer."[5] The tax was imposed at the rate of two and one-half per cent on all incomes over two thousand dollars, and the law included several important administrative changes. In the first place, returns were

[1] *Op. cit.*, p. 297.

[2] *Op. cit.*, p. 304

[3] *Political Economy.* By Arthur L. Perry, p. 444. The first edition was published in 1865.

[4] *Op. cit.*, p. 305.

[5] Act of July 14, 1870, c. cclv., sec. 6.

henceforth to be required only of those who had an income of more than two thousand dollars. Second, no official should "permit to be published, in any manner, such income returns or any part thereof, except such general statistics not specifying the names of individuals or firms, as he may make public under such rules and regulations as the commissioner of Internal Revenue shall prescribe."[1] Third, the assessor was not allowed to increase the amount of any one's assessment without due notice to the party. Fourth, no penalties were to be imposed upon any one for neglect or refusal to make returns, or for false or fraudulent returns, except after reasonable notice of the time and place appearing so as to give the person charged an opportunity to be heard.

The above provisions applied to the income tax proper. With reference to the tax on salaries and on government dividends, however, there was a curious confusion. Although all these taxes had been first imposed by the law of 1862, the period covered by the assessment differed. The income tax proper, it will be remembered, was always assessed on the income of the previous year, while the tax on salaries, interest, and dividends, was levied as these were paid or became due. As the law of 1862 went into force on August 1, interest, dividends, and salaries were taxed only from that date, while the tax on incomes in general was assessed on incomes received during the whole of the preceding year. This disparity was pointed out several times during the discussions of 1870.[2] As a consequence, when the Senate originally voted that the income tax proper was to end in 1870, it also voted to prolong the tax on interest, dividends, and salaries until August 1, 1870, in order to bring harmony between the two parts of the law. When, however, it was finally decided to continue the income tax beyond 1870 the original disparity was lost sight of, and it was decided that the tax on interest, dividends, and salaries should be levied only "during the year 1871." The result of this whole situation was that the old five per cent tax on dividends and salaries continued until

[1] Sec. 11.

[2] *Cf. e.g., op. cit.*, p. 5090.

August 1, 1870, and that the new tax, at a rate of two and one-half per cent, was levied only during the year 1871, with an interregnum from August 1 to December 31, 1870. With the close of 1870 the tax on salaries and dividends ceased, while the rest of the income tax was still assessed in 1872, although only on the income of 1871.

The fiscal situation of the country was improving so rapidly, especially during the period of rising prices which preceded the crisis of 1873, that the income tax seemed to be no longer required. No one ventured to propose its continuance after 1872, and in fact, an effort was made during 1871 to repeal it at once. A bill to this effect was introduced into the Senate and led to some discussion. Scott, on January 25, 1871, called attention to the fact that only 94,333 persons in the entire population of the United States paid their income tax and that in one-tenth of all the congressional districts in the county not a single cent was collected. He said that he had inquired of the commissioner of internal revenue as to what diminution could be made in the expenses if the income tax were repealed, and he had received the answer that five hundred assistant assessors, at a salary of five dollars a day, could be dispensed with. "Now," asked he, "is it worth while to keep up an expenditure of $2500 a day for these few thousand taxpayers? Is not the absurdity of the administration of this income tax apparent upon the very system? Does any man believe that if he were to take up the assessments of real and personal estate in the cities of New York and Philadelphia, he would find that there are not 94,000 people in these two cities alone who have an income exceeding $2000?"[1] Sherman, however, came to the defence of the tax in a powerful speech.[2] He claimed that "any modification or repeal of the income tax should be postponed until, by a general revision of our whole revenue system, we can determine what taxes bear most heavily upon the people, and distribute the reduction so as to give them the greatest relief."

[1] *Congressional Globe, 41st Congress, 3d Session*, p. 722.

[2] It is also found in his *Selected Speeches*, p. 317 *et seq.*

He considered the taxes on the necessaries of life, and especially upon sugar, tea, and coffee, to be far inferior to the income tax, and he proceeded to discuss the objections. The first was "that it authorizes espionage into a man's business." "Well, sir, so do all taxes," he answered. No custom house laws can be enforced, for instance, unless this espionage is allowed. Furthermore, he said there was not a state in the Union which through its general property tax did not authorize more espionage in a man's private affairs than did the income tax. He pointed out that "in reframing the law we struck out nearly all its offensive provisions, and perhaps weakened its force by this anxiety to avoid the charge of espionage." What was left, he thought, was mild compared with the practice of the personal property tax in Ohio. In the next place, he stated: "We are told that this is an odious and unpopular tax. I never knew a tax that was not odious and unpopular with the people who paid it." The opinion that the tax was unconstitutional, he brushed aside scornfully, as something that was not entertained by any good lawyer. Finally, referring to the statement that the income tax was expensive to collect, he answered, "Instead of its being an expensive tax, it is the cheapest tax collected by the national government from internal revenue, except the tax on banks."

Sherman, however, was unable to persuade the Senate, which decided by a vote of 26 to 25 to repeal the income tax at once. When, however, the bill reached the House it was returned on the ground that revenue measures could not originate in the Senate.[1] Nothing, therefore, came of the proposition to repeal the income tax at once, although a similar bill that had been introduced in the House by Hooper on February 7 was also defeated by a vote of 105 to 104.[2] The income tax was, however, allowed to die a natural death and expired by limitation in 1872.

In forming a judgment on its disappearance, several points

[1] *Congressional Globe, 41st Congress, 3d Session*, p. 791.

[2] *Op. cit.*, p. 1087.

must be considered. It was too much to expect that a country which did not even have a system of internal revenue at the outbreak of the war should be willing to retain so burdensome an impost after the fiscal exigency had disappeared. The situation at the beginning of the seventies in the United States was, in fact, far more unfavorable to the retention of an income tax than was the English situation in 1816. In England there existed at the time, not only a protective tariff far higher than that in force in the United States at the later period, but the English fiscal system was furthermore characterized by the corn laws which did not exist in the United States, and by a multiplicity of excises or internal revenue taxes which were fast being swept away in America. Neither England in 1816 nor the United States in 1870 was ready for a consideration of the broader social aspects of the income tax which have come to the front in recent years. Since the problem was exclusively fiscal in character, the retention of the income tax at that time in the United States was decidedly less urgent than at the earlier period in England. Even if Sherman's arguments had prevailed, the income tax would have been reasonably sure to disappear as soon as the revenue to be derived from the internal revenue system had shrunk to its normal status of the amount raised from the tobacco, beer, and whiskey taxes as they came to exist during the eighties. One of the great lessons taught by the Civil War was the necessity of having an internal revenue system side by side with the customs duties; but when these internal taxes imposed on a very few commodities supplied all the necessary revenue that was not yielded by the tariff, and when the problem became one, as it did before long, of surplus rather than of deficit financiering, all thought of an income tax would have been vain. Whether, therefore, the income tax was to disappear in 1872 or in some subsequent year, the fact that it was destined to disappear is undoubted. The chief reason why it did not continue is not so much because of the objections raised by its opponents, as the simple fact that it was not needed for revenue purposes.

§ 6. *The Practical Working of the Income Tax*

In considering the actual operations of the income tax during the Civil War period, attention should be directed to three fundamental points: First, what was the interpretation put upon the provisions of the law by the administrative officials? Second, what was the fiscal significance of the tax as compared with the total revenues? And third, what were the shortcomings of the system?

The interpretation of the law was chiefly the work of the commissioner of internal revenue. His decisions were in most cases final, and but little recourse was taken to the courts. Amid the manifold decisions,[1] attention will here be directed only to a few of special importance. So far as concerns the question of what constitutes income, it was decided at an early period that legacies are not income, but that gifts of personal property made *ante mortem* should be so considered.[2] In the same way, amounts received on life-insurance policies were not deemed income,[3] while, on the other hand, the premiums paid on life-insurance policies

[1] The decisions began to be published in 1865, in a volume entitled *The Internal Revenue Recorder and Customs Journal.* With the second volume (July, 1865) the name was changed to the *Internal Revenue Record and Customs Journal.* The most convenient summary of the decisions up to 1870 will be found in the *Internal Revenue Statutes now in force with Notes referring to all Decisions of the Courts and Departmental Rulings, Circulars, and Instructions reported to October 1, 1870.* By Orlando F. Bump, New York, 1870, pp. 283–305. A shorter summary will be found in Foster and Abbot, *A Treatise on the Federal Income Tax under the Act of 1894.* Boston, 1895. For the instructions, forms, regulations, etc., see Charles F. Estee, *The Excise Tax Law, appearing July 1, 1862; and all the Amendments, together with the Instructions and Blank Forms, Decisions, and Regulations of the Commissioner, with full Marginal Notes and References.* The first edition of this was published in 1863. *Cf.* also a similar work of A. A. Redfield, *A Hand-Book of the United States Tax Law, with all the Amendments, comprising the Decisions of the Commissioner of Internal Revenue together with Copious Notes and Explanation.* New York, 1863, and in subsequent years; and Boutwell's work mentioned *supra*, p. 430, which was issued in various editions.

[2] *3 Internal Revenue Record*, p. 133. This will hereafter be referred to as *I. R. R.*

[3] *7 I. R. R.*, p. 59.

were not allowed as deductions. When, however, an individual received an annuity, the payment of the legacy or succession tax on the annuity did not relieve the annuitant from liability to income tax on the annuity.[1] The salaries of state officials were at first declared liable to the income tax,[2] but this decision was later on reversed by the courts, and the salary of a judge of a state court was subsequently declared not liable to income tax.[3]

So far as exemptions were concerned, it was held that husband and wife were to be regarded as members of the same family, although living apart, unless separated by divorce or other operation of the law, so as to break up the family relationship. Minor children and parents were also to be considered members of the same family, whether living together or not.[4] In reference to deductions, the most important questions arose under the head of losses, repairs, and depreciation. Although losses incurred in the prosecution of one kind of business might be deducted from the gains in another, assessors were warned to be especially careful not to allow such deductions when in reality they should be regarded as investments or expenditures;[5] and it was held, furthermore, that no deduction should in any case be allowed for depreciation in the value of stocks or other property unless they were actually disposed of, and a loss realized.[6] Repairs, moreover, were sharply distinguished from permanent improvements. The increased value given to a building by permanent improvements was to be charged to capital, not to income account. Repairs were interpreted to include only those improvements which served merely to prevent the property from becoming useless or depreciating in value, and repairs were not to be confused with betterments.[7] Under these and similar rulings, the laws gradually acquired a more precise meaning, and the number of cases submitted for the

[1] *7 I. R. R.*, p. 60. [2] *4 I. R. R.*, p. 4. [3] *11 I. R. R.*, p. 205.
[4] *7 I. R. R.*, p. 59. [5] *3 I. R. R.*, p. 140.
[6] *3 I. R. R.*, p. 109; *7 I. R. R.*, p. 59.
[7] *2 I. R. R.*, p. 61; *5 I. R. R.*, p. 130; *7 I. R. R.*, p. 758.

decision of the commissioner of internal revenue began to decline.

In the second place let us consider the fiscal results of the tax. The income tax law, as in fact the whole code of internal revenue, was very slow in producing results. An entirely new machinery had to be created, and it took some time before this machinery got into working order. One of the strongest arguments for the permanent retention of the internal revenue system by the federal government was precisely this delay in securing any returns. It is entirely probable that had an internal revenue system existed, even in skeleton, at the outbreak of the war, the financial history of that period would have been very different, and we should have been spared the necessity of using legal tenders with their train of disaster and annoyance until the resumption of specie payments. Because of the absence of any such machinery, it was several years before the income tax yielded its normal revenue. The collections in 1863 were, in round numbers, only about two millions; in 1864, about twenty millions; while they increased in 1865 to thirty-two millions, and reached in 1866 the sum of almost seventy-three millions.[1] The large figures of 1866, however, were due not only to the increased rates, but to the rise of prices which attended the inflation of the currency. In 1867 the revenue fell to sixty-six millions, due in part to the contraction of the currency, but also in part to the fact that after the war was over the payment of the tax did not appeal so strongly to the patriotic motives of the citizens. In 1868 the revenue fell to forty-one millions, owing to the decrease of the rates, while after the law of 1870 went into operation the revenue fell to nineteen millions in 1871 and to fourteen millions in 1872.

To the income tax proper, including the tax on dividends and interest of corporations and the tax on salaries, there ought really to be added the tax on the gross receipts of corporations. This was not considered a part of the income

[1] For a full statement of the returns, see appendix at the end of this chapter.

tax because in law gross receipts are distinguishable from income. But in reality the tax on dividends and interest was a tax on the income of the security holder, although stopped at the source, while the tax on gross receipts was supposed to hit the ability of the corporation itself. In most of the foreign income taxes at present the tax, as we know, is imposed upon incomes both of individuals and of corporations, even though in some cases an arrangement is made to avoid double taxation by taxing personal incomes from corporate securities only on the surplus over a certain percentage. These taxes on gross receipts amounted to about three and a half millions in 1864, and reached the maximum of over eleven millions in 1866. Even without the gross receipts tax, however, the income tax was a very important part of the whole system of internal revenue. In 1866 when the income tax, as we have seen, yielded about seventy-three millions, the total internal revenue was about three hundred and eleven millions. The income tax thus produced a little less than one-fourth of the entire revenue. While the proportion was not quite so high in the other years, it did not differ very materially. As a fiscal expedient, therefore, the income tax must be declared to have been in its prime a decided success.

The various states, of course, contributed very unequally to this result. New York, for instance, paid about one-third of the entire tax, its percentage ranging in the successive years from about twenty-nine to thirty-nine per cent. Next came Pennsylvania and Massachusetts, which paid respectively from thirteen to fifteen per cent, and from ten to fourteen per cent. Then followed at a respectful distance Ohio, with four to eight per cent; Illinois, three to six per cent; New Jersey, three to five per cent; and California, three to five per cent.[1] In considering these figures it must be remembered that the returns from the southern states were utterly insignificant in the early years because of the war, and in the later years because of the devastations caused by

[1] The exact figures will be found in table III at the end of this chapter.

the war. The same caution applies to the number of persons assessed. The figures in reference to this were not published until 1867, and from this period up to 1870 the number of persons assessed varied from 254,000 to 276,000.[1] After the great increase of exemptions and the increasing leniency of administration in 1870, the numbers fell to 74,000 and 72,000 in 1871 and 1872.

When we come to inquire as to how far the income tax was really successful in reaching the incomes that ought to have been assessed, we enter upon a rather difficult field of inquiry. During the years that the war was in progress it is reasonable to assume that the tax was levied with comparative success. We must not forget the very optimistic statement of Morrill quoted above;[2] and even if allowance be made for so rose-colored a view, the tax cannot be considered a failure. After the war was over, however, the situation changed considerably. Senator Sherman, indeed, tells us that the machinery of the law worked more successfully from year to year.[3] But unfortunately his testimony is contradicted, not only by the diminution of the yield in the face of increasing wealth and population, but also by the common repute in which the tax was held. Frauds and evasions multiplied on every hand until in the closing years the honest taxpayer almost became the laughing-stock of his fellow citizens — a situation quite comparable to that which, as we have seen, is found in Italy to-day. Before, however, proceeding to analyze the reasons for this failure, it must be stated, in common fairness, that the federal income tax, notwithstanding all its imperfections, crudities, and ensuing frauds, was nevertheless more successful than the general property tax in the separate states. Let us test this by taking its fortunes in a typical state, utilizing the returns of the state comptroller and the federal officials.

The special income tax of 1865 was levied at the rate of five per cent on all incomes. Its yield in New York state

[1] For the detailed figures as to these, see table II at the end of this chapter.

[2] *Supra*, p. 449. [3] *Supra*, p. 464.

was $8,765,914, which corresponds to an income of $175,318,280. The state assessment for the general property tax in that year disclosed property to the amount of $1,550,879,685. That is, the self-assessed incomes in New York amounted to over eleven per cent of the property — a preposterously high figure. If we assume that the average rate of profit at that time was seven per cent, the income on New York property should have been $108,561,578. Yet this was not two-thirds of the income actually assessed. The income tax yielded one-third as much again as a corresponding property tax. Of course some allowance should be made for incomes from other sources than property. But the exemption of $600 included almost all the working classes; and the profits from business are practically the income from property invested in the business. So that the only class for which an allowance must be made is that of receivers of professional incomes. The total income of this class is not large enough to make any material difference in the figures given. The success of the income tax as compared with the local property tax was due in part to the fact of the low valuation of real estate. But its main cause was the failure of the state tax to reach personal property. In other words, the federal income tax was able to reach many of those who contrived to escape the personal property tax.

The other years disclose a similar state of affairs. In 1866–1867 the income tax in New York yielded $18,448,664. It was levied at the rate of five per cent and ten per cent. Taking this as approximately equivalent to a uniform tax of seven and one-half per cent, the result would be a real income of $245,982,187. But let us grant, in order to weaken the contention still further, that it was tantamount to a uniform tax of as much as nine per cent on all incomes. That would mean an income of only 205 millions. The property assessed in New York by the state officials is returned at $1,531,229,636. Even assuming that the rate of income on capital was as high as seven per cent, we would have an income of $107,186,074. Yet the income actually returned exceeded this by nearly 100 millions. Even under the least favorable showing incomes appeared as more than thirteen per cent of property — a figure manifestly extravagant. The income tax, therefore, produced almost twice as much as the general property tax. And even if we make the same allowance as before for incomes derived from other sources than property, the disproportion would still be very considerable. Even in 1870, when the limit of exemption had been increased so much as materially to reduce the returns, New York paid $10,420,035 as a five per cent income tax. This corresponds to a taxable income of $208,400,700. The assessment of property for the state tax was $1,967,001,185. This would mean that incomes were eleven per cent of property, which for that period is palpably far too high.

In short, the history of the income tax clearly shows that it was more lucrative than a corresponding property tax, and that it succeeded in many cases where the personal property tax failed. The federal income tax was indeed productive of great frauds, but the state property tax created far more. It was precisely because the income tax reached so many of the mercantile and capitalistic classes who have both previously and since escaped taxation, that it became unpopular and was abolished.

In other parts of the country, indeed, the results may not have been quite so favorable, because of the more primitive economic conditions. Where the value of tangible realty exceeded that of personalty, as in some of the more purely agricultural states, the weakness of the general property tax was less noticeable. And it is possible that in such cases the federal income tax yielded less than a property tax. But wherever the economic conditions approached those of New York, it is probable that the results worked out above would find their counterpart there.

Even, however, if the federal income tax worked better than the state general property tax, it must be confessed that it did not work well. Let us in conclusion discuss the reasons for this comparative failure.

§ 7. *Conclusion*

The shortcomings of the system may be summed up under four heads: mistakes of theory, defective provisions, exaggerated exemptions and administrative methods.

In the first place, the theory of the tax itself was partly a mistaken one. The two chief forms of income tax, as we know, are the lump-sum tax and the stoppage-at-source tax. The Civil War legislation adopted the stoppage-at-source scheme only to a slight extent, applying it only in the case of federal salaries and of the securities of a few specified classes of corporations. The conditions of American life at the time would, perhaps, have rendered impossible any thoroughgoing application of the English scheme. But there is no reason why, in the first place, the stoppage-at-source idea should not have applied to all corporations instead of to only a few classes; and second, why it should not have been applied to the salaries of corporate employes as well as to the income from corporate securities. Had the system of stoppage at source been extended even in these two directions, the history of the tax would have been a very different one.

In the second place, the law itself was very confused in parts and contained mistakes of principle. Such, for instance, were the provisions with reference to the rent and rental value of the homesteads, which led both to large fraud and to considerable diminution of revenue. In the same category of errors must be put the provisions with reference to the sales of real estate, and the details as to farm products which rendered the administration of the law needlessly complicated and exceedingly difficult. As to profits from sales of real estate, the limitation to purchases within one year (or, later, two years), was, to say the least, arbitrary; while all the embarrassments connected with the assessment of farmers' profits might have been avoided by the adoption of the English system of basing the assessment on rental value, — a plan which had been recommended, as we know, by the commissioner of internal revenue.

In the third place, the exemptions were too high. Even if we concede that owing to the different scale of life in the United States, the exemptions ought to have been higher than those existing in England, there was no need of putting the exemption at so large a figure. The European method of abatement or of progressive diminution in the amount of exemption is far preferable to the method followed in the United States. The high exemptions, especially after the amendment of 1870, not only curtailed the revenue, but opened the door wide for evasion and fraud.

Finally, in the fourth place, the administrative methods were inadequate. It would indeed be too much to expect under the existing conditions of American public life that an exception should disclose itself in the income tax. But if good administration is necessary anywhere, it is doubly necessary in so delicate a matter as the assessment of incomes. Every one was, indeed, required to hand in a return of his income, but it was felt on all sides that administrative supervision was necessary. This administrative supervision, however, was not skilfully devised. The chief defect consisted in the great power given to the assistant assessors. These might ask any questions they chose, and might compel the production of books. It is indeed true that the taxpayers were not obliged to answer the questions, but as the commissioner of internal revenue stated, a refusal to do so might lead the assessor to doubt the correctness of the return. "Experience has shown that questions are a great convenience in refreshing the memory of a large class of honest taxpayers who are not accustomed to keep accounts, and who, in many instances, cannot recollect all the sources of their income unless they are thus reminded."[1] But the questions that were put were not always of this character. Moreover, we are told that "the destruction or disappearance of books of account of the persons whose returns are unsatisfactory, is an event which is always a subject of just suspicion. It is hardly possible to give a credible explanation of it; but in most instances

[1] *1 I. R. R.*, p. 145.

assessors will be justified in assuming that it is *prima facie* evidence of fraud, and treating the returns accordingly."[1]

These regulations would, in themselves, perhaps, be unexceptionable, if any reliance could be put upon the assistant assessors. Unfortunately, however, these were merely underlings, at a salary of a few dollars a day, and subject to all the vicissitudes of politics in their appointment and promotion. During a part of the time, at least, the service was in very bad shape. The commissioner of internal revenue tells us, in his report for 1867, that "the number of changes which have occurred during the last fiscal year in the personnel of the service, exceeds that of any year preceding, there being on the average more than three changes even of assessors and collectors in each office, during the year."[2] In the following year the commissioner again referred "to the antagonism between the legislative and executive departments which has so sadly damaged the service of the past two years."[3] Under such circumstances, of course, good administration was out of the question.

As a matter of fact, the American system was inferior to the English in three notable respects. First, there were no representatives of the taxpayers, as in the case of the English Land Tax Commissioners. Secondly, there were no expert and high-class men to do the work of assessment, as in the case of the English Additional Commissioners. Third, in the absence of civil service reform there was no permanent tenure of office, as in England. It is not to be wondered at, therefore, that the administration was so poor. The assessors were indeed given great powers, and in some cases they abused these powers unmercifully, while in others they succumbed to the danger of bargains or compromises with the taxpayers. The situation was rendered still worse by the pub-

[1] *1 I. R. R.*, p. 145.

[2] In two cases there were four and five changes in each office respectively. In 114 districts 369 separate individuals served as collectors, and in 116 districts 370 persons served as assessors. — *Report of the Commissioner of Internal Revenue for the year 1867*, p. xiv.

[3] *Report of the Commissioner of Internal Revenue for the Year 1868*, p. xviii.

licity of the returns. At first, indeed, as we know, the commissioner ruled that the returns should be secret, but in default of any legislation to that effect, the pressure for publicity became so great that before long the commissioner instructed his subordinates to publish the lists "in order that the amplest opportunities may be given for the detection of any fraudulent returns that may have been made."[1] It was not until 1870, it will be remembered, that partial secrecy was provided by the law.

Our conclusion as to the Civil War income tax, therefore, is that it was partly a success and partly a failure. From the fiscal point of view, it achieved notable results. A tax which yielded about one-quarter of the entire internal revenue of the country, at a time when every additional dollar was of the utmost importance, must be declared to have contributed not a little to the successful termination of the struggle, and to the adjustment of the fiscal difficulties thereafter. This consideration is the best answer to those who claim that a federal income tax is not needed even in time of war. During the Civil War every resource of the government was strained to the utmost, and without the very considerable assistance afforded by the income tax the situation would have been far different. As a fiscal engine, the income tax must be pronounced a comparative success.

On the other hand, as we have pointed out, the tax was defective not alone in theory, but also in administration. It started out, just as did the income taxes in England and Germany, with inadequate administrative machinery, and it did not last long enough for the progressive improvement of administrative methods to disclose itself. What was the work of many decades in other countries could not reasonably be expected to be accomplished in a few years in the United States. Moreover, the difficulties of administration were enhanced not only by the proverbial weakness of American administrative methods in general, but also, and especially

[1] Boutwell, *op. cit.*, p. 259.

after the termination of the war, by the hostile public sentiment. This hostility, as we have learned, is always to be observed at the outset of any system of income tax. In England and Prussia it was many decades before the opposition diminished, while in the United States the tax was abolished before there was any real abatement in the feeling of repugnance to the tax. In the face of a hostile public sentiment, even the best administrative methods are powerless; and when we have, as in the United States during the period of the Civil War, a combination of poor administration and of popular prejudice, the result, so far as concerns the fundamental requisite of equality of taxation, was bound to be a comparative failure.

TABLE I

Proceeds of the Civil War Income Tax*

	1863	1864	1865	1866	1867	1868	1869	1870	1871	1872	1873	1874	1875	1876	1877	Total
Income from $600 to $10,000	$ 172,770.35	$ 7,944,153.51	$ 9,697,246.96	—	—	—	—	—	—	—	—	—	—	—	—	$ 17,814,170.82
Income over $10,000	277,461.65	6,855,160.37	9,362,339.46	—	—	—	—	—	—	—	—	—	—	—	—	16,494,961.48
Income from property of citizens residing abroad	1,872.11	58,674.51	169,924.17	—	—	—	—	—	—	—	—	—	—	—	—	230,470.79
Income from interest on U.S. securities	3,637.15	75,373.93	133,402.76	—	—	—	—	—	—	—	—	—	—	—	—	212,413.84
Income from $600 to $5000	—	—	539,143.28	$26,046,759.76	$31,492,694.16	—	—	—	—	—	—	—	—	—	—	58,078,597.20
Income over $5000	—	—	801,941.99	34,501,122.67	25,547,946.51	—	—	—	—	—	—	—	—	—	—	60,851,011.17
Income over $1000	—	—	—	—	—	$32,027,610.78	$25,025,068.86	$27,115,046.11	$10,680,966.69	—	—	—	—	—	—	94,848,692.44
Income over $2000	—	—	—	—	—	—	—	—	3,753,982.70	$ 8,416,685.87	$3,927,252.76	—	—	—	—	16,097,921.33
Income from bank dividends	766,605.85	1,577,010.73	3,991,211.49	4,193,070.61	3,278,322.56	2,914,841.41	3,769,185.69	3,573,272.45	1,542,667.75	2,162,564.31	85,271.76	—	—	—	—	27,854,024.01
Income from bank profits	—	—	25,511.49	47,592.59	496,652.76	709,933.58	—	—	—	—	—	—	—	—	—	1,279,690.42
Income from canal companies' dividends	4,210.40	92,120.69	386,223.13	203,233.77	195,382.19	215,279.96	230,602.81	251,048.75	47,042.89	136,052.35	24,615.17	—	—	—	—	1,785,812.11
Income from insurance companies' dividends	225,485.44	445,366.17	768,770.93	783,882.05	563,473.93	605,489.78	847,668.33	926,519.00	243,205.21	270,531.14	8,678.17	—	—	—	—	5,689,070.15
Income from railroad companies' dividends	338,533.49	927,393.38	2,471,914.39	2,205,852.45	3,379,262.19	2,630,174.08	2,831,140.03	2,898,802.31	1,121,439.59	1,851,296.30	760,930.35	—	—	—	—	21,416,738.53
Income from railroad companies' interest on bonds	253,998.72	596,859.09	847,683.61	1,255,916.98	—	1,259,155.80	1,503,846.51	1,869,369.34	974,345.35	1,291,026.68	135,642.55	—	—	—	—	9,987,844.63
Income from turnpike companies' dividends	1,101.38	17,494.73	28,212.03	27,333.46	30,703.06	49,551.57	22,381.09	32,289.24	11,738.02	14,140.48	2,379.67	—	—	—	—	237,324.76
Income from salaries of U.S. officers and employees	696,181.71	1,705,124.63	2,826,491.82	3,717,394.69	1,029,991.98	1,043,561.40	561,962.52	1,109,526.42	787,262.55	294,564.65	117,541.72	$139,472.09	$232.64	$588.27	$97.79	14,029,994.88
Total	$2,741,858.25	$20,294,731.74	$32,050,017.44	$72,982,159.03	$66,014,429.34	$41,455,598.36	$34,791,855.84	$37,775,873.62	$19,162,650.75	$14,436,861.78	$5,062,311.62	$139,472.09	$232.64	$588.27	$97.79	$346,908,738.56
Special income tax			28,929,312.00	452,550.00												29,381,862 00
Grand Total	$2,741,858.25	$20,294,731.74	$60,979,329.44	$73,434,709.03	$66,014,429.34	$41,455,598.36	$34,791,855.84	$37,775,873.62	$19,162,650.75	$14,436,861.78	$5,062,311.62	$139,472.09	$232.64	$588.27	$97.79	$376,290,600.56

* Compiled from tables in the *Annual Report of the Commissioner of Internal Revenue for the year 1872*, and *ibid*, 1877.

TABLE II

NUMBER OF PERSONS ASSESSED TO THE CIVIL WAR INCOME TAX BY CLASSES[1]

AMOUNT OF TAX	CORRESPONDING TO INCOME OF	1867	1868	1869	1870	1871	1872
$ 20 or less	$ 1,000–1,400	101,219	100,558	107,997	112,874		
20 or less	2,000–2,800					25,479	22,619
20–50	1,400–2,000	68,680	55,949	69,184	68,900		
20–50	2,800–4,000					19,795	18,887
50–100	2,000–3,000	40,899	38,957	41,196	40,839		
50–100	4,000–6,000					12,917	13,335
100–500	3,000–11,000	46,055	51,188	45,002	44,732		
100–250	6,000–12,000					10,742	11,355
250–500	12,000–22,000					3,707	4,264
Over 500	Over 11,000	9,282	7,965	9,464	9,316	2,135	2,489
Over 500	Over 22,000						
	Total	266,135	254,617	272,843	276,661	74,775	72,949

[1] From the *Annual Report of the Commissioner of Internal Revenue for the year 1872*, p. vi.

APPENDIX

THE INCOME TAX IN THE CONFEDERACY

THE history of the Civil War period would not be complete without calling attention to the fiscal experiments made by the Confederate government. The Confederacy was fortunate in having at the head of its finances in C. G. Memminger a secretary of the treasury whose fitness for the position was far greater than that of the statesman who filled a similar position in the North. In fact, had the fortunes of the war been determined by the comparative ability of the statesmen and the generals rather than by sheer economic superiority, there is not much doubt but that the South would have been the victor. Notwithstanding the great ability of Memminger's reports, however,[1] the peculiar situation of the South made a resort to taxation exceedingly difficult, and the fortunes of the war soon undermined the economic basis of the fiscal policy.

The Confederacy, like the Union, started out with a direct tax. On July 24, 1861, Secretary Memminger sent a communication to the provisional Congress, urging that twenty-five millions be raised by taxing real estate, slaves, and all personal property. Congress followed his recommendation, and by the act of August 19, 1861, imposed the so-called war tax of one-half of one per cent on all property. The Confederate constitution contained a provision as to direct taxes analogous to that found in the constitution of the United States; but as the war precluded the taking of any census, the president ruled that the provision as to apportionment of the tax might be dispensed with. The collection of the tax was therefore left to the individual states, with a consequence that only an insignificant amount was collected, and

[1] All of the financial reports of Memminger are printed in the appendix to Henry D. Caper, *The Life and Times of C. G. Memminger*. Richmond, 1893. This volume will hereafter be referred to as *Memminger*.

TABLE III

Percentage of Civil War Income Tax collected in Each State[1]

States and Territories	1864	1865	1866	1867	1868	1869	1870	1871	1872
Alabama	—	—	.0139	.6217	.4449	.2369	.5053	.4258	.2531
Arizona	—	—	—	—	.0164	.0142	.0170	.0323	.0132
Arkansas	—	—	.0121	.0526	.0937	.0973	.2082	.0985	.0568
California	3.2157	2.5909	1.9929	2.7288	5.0155	3.7953	3.2214	3.2746	2.5828
Colorado	.0950	.1312	.1198	.1183	.1033	.0696	.0716	.1098	.2083
Connecticut	2.9736	2.5758	2.9469	3.4447	2.3631	2.7992	2.8656	1.6137	2.5559
Dakota	—	—	—	.0008	.0043	.0024	.0024	.0004	.0006
Delaware	.4621	.4414	.3679	.3087	.3222	.4915	.2388	.3015	.2811
District of Columbia	.8334	.3318	.5415	.6592	.5815	.5939	.6517	.4048	.4374
Florida	—	—	—	.0218	.0656	.0781	.0433	.1138	.0381
Georgia	—	—	.1108	.4933	.8779	.8490	.9868	.9809	.9462
Idaho	—	—	.0378	.0438	.0997	.0813	.0545	.0768	.0234
Illinois	3.6612	3.9164	5.6011	4.6441	5.0642	6.8407	5.3612	2.2334	3.6010
Indiana	1.7830	2.0601	2.4251	1.5803	1.2048	1.4848	1.2870	.8453	1.1523
Iowa	.3706	.5549	.7551	.6537	.6803	.8818	.7485	.1729	.8436
Kansas	.1208	.1855	.2124	.2128	.1525	.1744	.1842	.1251	.1166
Kentucky	2.1702	2.6845	2.3351	1.9699	1.7828	1.6910	1.9865	1.4012	1.7088
Louisiana	.2510	.4609	.3904	.9022	1.2618	.8131	1.5739	1.2863	.7255
Maine	.8036	.6787	.5961	.6026	.6124	.6370	.7648	.4980	.6769
Maryland	3.4019	2.8731	2.9599	2.6092	3.0274	2.6885	3.2738	2.7650	3.4833
Massachusetts	13.1620	12.2529	11.5826	13.6183	12.6423	11.1829	12.2890	10.4042	14.7991
Michigan	.9326	.8161	1.2004	1.0252	1.7863	1.7775	1.5299	2.0486	1.6179
Minnesota	.0845	.1151	.1335	.1631	.2481	.2579	.2969	.1514	.4384

Mississippi	—	—	.0001	.0935	.2687	.0871	.0489	.3925	.1245
Missouri	2.1972	3.4070	2.1379	1.9014	1.7119	2.0896	2.2249	2.1776	1.3223
Montana	—	.0357	.0653	.0318	.0710	.0572	.1117	.0647	.0448
Nebraska	.0393	.0371	.0632	.0621	.0725	.1036	.1734	.0264	.0401
Nevada	.2095	.1987	.1282	.1532	.3015	.3734	.2343	.1994	.1529
New Hampshire . .	.4178	.4371	.4035	.4619	.5783	.5444	.4624	.3780	.3216
New Jersey	2.9580	2.9451	3.6035	3.8659	5.1026	4.8199	4.0536	2.2475	4 2078
New Mexico . . .	.0058	.0645	.0379	.0335	.0498	.0305	.0351	.0443	.0352
New York	34.3457	31.1608	30.5975	30.9421	29.4513	31.3374	28.4185	39.0899	30.5023
North Carolina . .	—	—	.0014	.0961	.1358	.1789	.2186	.2471	.2967
Ohio	7.4278	7.3215	8.2381	7.5124	5.3275	5.9584	6.1 21	4.5223	5.9357
Oregon	.1969	.0815	.1395	.2156	.3900	.1137	.4752	.3069	.2556
Pennsylvania . . .	13.7799	17.6782	15.9335	12.7769	13.1403	11.7174	13.6721	15.5481	14.0158
Rhode Island . . .	2.3984	1.8883	1.9853	2.3633	1.2450	1.7875	1.4630	1.1661	1.6540
South Carolina . .	—	—	.0004	.0957	.5115	.2757	.3907	.4230	.3438
Tennessee	.1473	.4892	.4659	.6099	.6346	.6286	.7770	.5555	.6656
Texas	—	—	.0220	.2390	.4828	.3117	.3015	.3994	.5311
Utah	.0217	.0259	.0378	.0313	.0388	.0670	.0266	.0650	.1633
Vermont	.2989	.3532	.3773	.4164	.3660	.3503	.4214	.4881	.5888
Virginia	.2196	.0717	.2109	.3149	.4406	.5171	.7163	.5312	.8454
Washington . . .	.0398	.0537	.0318	.0445	.0503	.0332	.0876	.0240	.0373
West Virginia . . .	.2296	.3274	.3799	.3201	.2633	.2707	.2684	.1716	.2399
Wisconsin	.7456	.7541	.8035	.9434	.9149	.7998	.8673	1.1590	1.1092
Wyoming	100.0000	—	—	—	—	.0086	.0171	.0082	.0063
Total	100.0000	100.0000	100.0000	100.0000	100.0000	100 0000	100.0000	100.0000	100.0000

[1] From the *Annual Report of the Commissioner of Internal Revenue for the year 1872*, p. 115. The figures are exclusive of the salary tax.

even then most of the sums paid over by the states were raised by loans.[1]

When the Confederate Congress assembled for its regular session in February, 1862, it was seen that the aversion of the people to direct taxation was so great as to have rendered the war tax practically nugatory. Secretary Memminger called the attention of Congress to the matter, and urged the necessity of enforcing the collection of the taxes. "The war tax," he tells us, "has already put in motion all the machinery requisite for levying a tax. It has selected those articles which can best bear the burden, and it levies on their value the very moderate rate of one-half of one per cent. The simplest of all plans, therefore, would be an increase of this tax."[2] The secretary was forced, however, to rely principally upon the sale of bonds, and was met by the difficulty that there was no available floating capital for investment. It was for this reason that he suggested that payment for the bonds might be made in kind. "The inquiry naturally arises where are these lenders to be found? Our people have property in abundance but they have no surplus capital in money. Our plans must be modified to meet this difficulty. We must accept products in exchange for the bonds wherever they can be made available for the wants of the government. The farmer has supplies for the army; the manufacturer has clothing or other commodities; the railroad company has transportation; the miner has coal and iron; all of which the government needs. If these supplies can be obtained in exchange for Confederate bonds, a loan in kind is effected on credit, to the satisfaction of both parties." Thus was inaugurated the so-called produce loan, which paved the way for the later income tax in kind.

The experience of the Confederacy with loans was not more successful than that with the direct tax, and accord-

[1] *Cf.* J. C. Schwab, *The Confederate States of America, 1861–1865, a Financial and Industrial History of the South during the Civil War.* New York, 1901, p. 285.

[2] *Memminger, op. cit.*, p. 436.

ingly, on January 10, 1863, Memminger determined to make an effort to induce Congress to take up the matter of taxation more energetically. In his report of that date he discussed the choice to be made between various kinds of taxes, and declared his preference for taxes on property and income. "It seems to me that a tax upon property and income is so much to be preferred to stamp duties, excises, licenses and other like taxes, which call for a machinery vexatious in its character and expensive in its operation, that there will be little hesitation on the part of Congress in its acceptance. The direct tax heretofore levied has set in operation all the machinery necessary to levy another; and an income tax could be collected by the same means. It seems to me that both these forms of tax should be adopted. To lay a sufficient tax upon property alone would require too large an increase in the rate. Such an increase would operate with peculiar hardship upon property producing no income. On the other hand, a tax upon income is so easily evaded, that of itself it would furnish an insecure resource. It is proper, however, that income should be taxed; otherwise the whole profits of speculation and trade, together with those resulting from skill and labor, would escape contribution. I propose, therefore, that a tax be imposed upon property, and upon the gross amount of incomes of every kind, excepting those below some minimum to be adjusted by Congress."[1]

The secretary estimated the yield of a tax of one per cent on property at about thirty-six millions, and he thereupon proceeded to discuss the probable returns of an income tax. "It may be assumed that the net income of property is measured by the average rate of legal interest of the money which represents its value. If the tax were laid upon net income, and that income were faithfully returned, it could in this way be estimated with some degree of accuracy. But the devices are so many by which a return of net income can be evaded, as to make such returns unreliable. A resort to gross income is, therefore, more expedient. The difference between the

[1] *Memminger, op. cit.*, p. 448.

two must be at least 25 per cent; but, under existing circumstances, and for the purpose of an estimate, it would be prudent to disregard the difference and assume that the returns of gross income will be about equal to the average rate of legal interest. It is believed that even the proceeds of skill, speculation and labor which may be returned where no capital is involved, will not materially vary the result." Calculating the total income at about 280 millions, he figured that a ten per cent income tax would yield 28 millions.[1] Reverting, however, to the idea which underlay the produce loan, he now recommended that the income tax should be payable not only in money, but also in kind.

Congress adopted these suggestions with some modifications, and a few months later enacted a comprehensive tax measure.[2]

The law of 1863 imposed a direct tax of eight per cent on naval stores and agricultural products, as well as a tax of one per cent on securities and capital invested in a business which was not taxed. In the second place the law provided for a series of license taxes on trade, business, and occupation, some of them specific taxes, some calculated according to gross receipts. Then came a series of provisions affecting incomes. A separate section imposed a tax upon "the salaries of all salaried persons serving in any capacity whatever, except upon the salaries of all persons in the military or naval service." The tax was to be at the rate of one per cent on salaries not exceeding $1500 and two per cent above that amount; but recipients of salaries of less than $1000 were exempt.[3] The salaries tax was followed by the so-called income tax proper. It was imposed on "income and profits derived by each person, joint-stock company and corporation, from every occupation, employment or business, and from every investment or labor,

[1] *Memminger, op. cit.*, pp. 449, 450.

[2] Act of April 24, 1863, c. xxxviii, *Public Laws of the Confederate States of America, passed at the Third Session of the First Congress, 1863*. Edited by James M. Matthews. Richmond, 1863, pp. 115 *et seq.*

[3] Sec. 7.

skill, property or money, and the income and profits derived from any source whatever except salaries." The allowable deductions for expenses, repairs, etc., were carefully elaborated in a series of six provisions. In incomes from real estate, other than houses, a deduction not exceeding ten per cent of the gross rent was permitted for necessary annual repairs; in the case of houses the deduction was limited to five per cent. In incomes from manufacturing and mining business, a deduction from "the gross value of the products of the year" was permitted for rent as well as for cost of labor and of raw materials. In incomes from navigating enterprises, deductions from "gross earnings, including the value of freights on goods shipped by the person running the vessel," were allowed to the extent of "the hire of the boat, if not owned by the person running the same, or if owned by him, a reasonable allowance for the wear and tear of same, not exceeding ten per cent per annum, and also the cost of running the boat or vessel." If the income were derived from boat- or ship-building, deductions might be made "from the gross receipts of the occupation, including the value of the ship when finished," to the extent of the cost of labor and "the prime cost of materials." If the income were derived from the sale of property, there might be deducted from the gross sales "the prime cost of the property sold, including the cost of transportation," as well as the salaries of clerks and the rent of buildings. Deductions similar to the last were allowed for other incomes and in the case of mutual insurance companies a further deduction was permitted for the amount of losses paid during the year.

The rate of the tax was progressive, the scale being considerably higher than in the Union. Incomes below $500 were exempt; from $500 to $1500 the rate was 5%; on incomes between $1500 and $3000 5% was levied on the first $1500, and 10% on the remainder; incomes between $3000 and $5000 paid 10%; incomes between $5000 and $10,000 paid 12½%; and incomes of $10,000 and over paid 15%.

In addition to the personal income tax, all joint stock companies and corporations were required to "reserve one-tenth of the annual earnings, set apart for dividends and reserve fund." Where this, however, amounted to more than 10% and less than 20% upon the capital stock paid in, the rate of tax was 12½%; and where the profits were more than 20% the rate was 16⅔%. It was provided, however, that the dividends so paid to the stockholder should not be considered a part of his income.

Every person was required to make a return of his income, and if the assessor was dissatisfied, he was to select "one disinterested citizen in the vicinage as a referee," the taxpayer to select another, and these two to call in a third. The findings of a majority of these referees were to be conclusive.

In addition to the income tax proper, which was payable in cash, the law provided for a tax in kind. This was a tax of ten per cent on all profits made by the purchaser within the Confederate states, or by sale of any flour, corn, bacon, pork, oats, hay, rice, salt, iron, or the manufacture of iron, sugar, molasses (molasses of cane), leather, woollen cloths, shoes, boots, blankets, and cotton cloths. The tax, however, was not to apply to the purchases and sales "made in the due course of the regular retail business." Furthermore, the profits reached by the tax in kind were not to be included in the income subject to the regular income tax. A series of interesting administrative provisions was added. Every farmer and planter, after reserving for his own use fifty bushels of potatoes, one hundred bushels of corn, fifty bushels of wheat, and twenty bushels of peas or beans, was required to deliver to the government for its use one-tenth of all his crops, as soon as the crops were ready for market. In case of disagreement between the taxpayer and the assessor, three referees were to be selected, as in the case of the cash income tax, and these were to estimate "the quantity, the quality, and the value of the produce." The planter was required to deliver the articles so estimated within two months from the time of estimate, at a depot not more than eight miles from the place of production, in default of which he was to suffer a penalty of fifty per cent. The government was to furnish sacks and to allow the cost of barrels.[1] Every farmer, planter, and grazier, moreover, was required to exhibit to the assessor an account of all the hogs he might have slaughtered, and to "deliver an equivalent of one-half of the same in cured bacon, at the rate of sixty pounds of bacon to a hundred weight of pork." In the case of cattle, horses, and mules not used in cultivation, the tax was one per cent upon the value; but if any beeves had been sold, the gross proceeds of such sales "shall be estimated and taxed as income, after deducting therefrom the money actually paid for the purchase of such beeves, if they have been actually purchased, and the value of the corn consumed by them."[2]

In May, 1863, Secretary Memminger issued detailed instructions for the collection of the tax. He called particular attention to the fact that if any person should refuse or neglect to give lists or make returns, the assessor might "enter upon his premises and upon view, or from state tax lists, or any other record or documents, or by any other lawful ways or means, shall make a list" himself, after adding twenty-five per cent.[3] He also directed that if any commission merchant held in store on account of any one else any agricultural products, the former was to pay the tax. The taxes in kind, moreover, were all to be transferred to the duly authorized post quartermaster; that is, they should be subject to the military department. But whenever articles collected by the post quartermaster consisted of cotton, wool, or tobacco, they should be subject to the order of the district collector; that is, to the treasury department.[4]

Such were the provisions of the income tax law passed by the Confederacy. It soon gave rise to much discontent for the reason that the income tax proper was payable in Confed-

[1] Sec. 11. [2] Sec. 12.

[3] *Instructions for Collectors of Taxes. Treasury Department. Confederate States of America.* Richmond, May 15, 1863, p. 7.

[4] *Op. cit.*, p. 14.

erate money, which had now begun seriously to depreciate, while the farmers, subject to the tax in kind, could not avail themselves of this advantage. Numerous meetings of protest accordingly were held in various places, especially in North Carolina. Some of the resolutions passed at these meetings were as follows:[1] "The act of Congress, in secret session, without consulting with their constituents at home, taking from the hard laborers of the Confederacy one-tenth of the people's living, instead of taking back their own currency in tax, is unjust and tyrannical, and we solemnly protest against that act." At another meeting it was resolved "that we pledge ourselves to each other to resist, to the bitter end, any such monarchical tax, — any such contempt to our state — to pay such a tax to a Virginia tithing man." In another place the tax was criticised as "unjust, tyrannical, and oppressive, and a relic of barbarism which alone is practised in the worst despotisms." Most of the resolutions contained a statement that "we are in favor of a just and equitable system of taxation, so that all classes may bear their burdens equally; we are, therefore, opposed to the tithing system . . . discriminating against and taxing the labor and industry of the agricultural classes."

It was largely owing to this discontent, as well as to the need of increased revenues, that the commissioner of taxes, in his report of November, 1863, suggested a decided increase in the income tax. "If necessary a tax of twenty-five per cent should be laid on incomes over $5000, and fifty per cent on all over $10,000, and fifty per cent on the profits of all joint stock companies and corporations, over and above a dividend of twenty-five per cent paid to their stockholders. This may be considered exorbitant, and capitalists may think it oppressive, but it is neither. Every man should be satisfied with a support for himself and family, and all he makes above that should be divided with his country. No man should desire to amass a fortune, or to increase his fortune, if he already has one, from the hard necessities of a bleeding

[1] These quotations will be found in Schwab, *op. cit.*, pp. 295–296.

country. While three-fourths, perhaps, of the men of the Confederacy have dedicated their lives or fortunes, and in many instances, both, to their country's cause, the remaining fraction have no moral right to amass fortunes at their expense."[1] Secretary Memminger, in his report, called attention to the report of the commissioner and adverted to the necessity of more revenue.[2] He pointed out that the direct tax of 1861 had been collected in only three states, but that the new tax of 1863 "is now being rapidly collected. From present appearances the commissioner estimates its probable collections at $100,000,000 in money, and he reports that it is paid with general cheerfulness and alacrity."[3] The Secretary stated, however, that the novelty of many of the provisions of the law had given rise to serious questions.

The protests against the income tax in kind continued, and Congress now endeavored to meet some of the objections by slight modifications. Thus on December 28, 1863, it was provided that the tax on sweet potatoes might be commuted by payment in money, and on January 30, 1864, a similar provision was adopted in the case of tobacco. With these and other slight modifications, however, the tax was continued by the general tax law of February 17, 1864,[4] although an effort was made to meet the wishes of the secretary of the treasury and of the commissioner of taxes by levying new taxes on property and by making a decided increase in the income tax proper. This tax was now increased by ten per cent, raising the maximum rate to twenty-five per cent, and a similarly augmented rate was applied to the profits of all joint stock companies, whether incorporated or not, exceeding twenty-five per cent.

[1] *Report of the Commissioner of Taxes accompanying the Report of the Secretary of the Treasury.* Richmond, 1863, p. 2. *Cf.* Kennan, *Income Taxation.* Milwaukee, 1910, p. 271.

[2] *Memminger, op. cit.*, p. 466.

[3] *Op. cit.*, p. 473.

[4] An act to levy additional Taxes for the Common Defence and Support of the Government. Chap. lxiv. In *Public Laws of the Confederate States of America passed at the Fourth Session of the First Congress, 1863–1864.* Edited by James M. Matthews. Richmond, 1864, p. 209.

This was the last of the income tax acts of the Confederacy. In his report of May 2, 1864, Secretary Memminger discussed the situation. He pointed out that about the only revenue that the government could expect during the coming year was from the tax in kind. "The planting interest, whenever it is beyond the reach of the enemy, is prosperous and can contribute to the public wants as largely as any other." But he stated that under the administration of the tax "the prosperous are favored with a discount, while the unfortunate whose farms have been desolated, are required to pay upon the value of their capital, without any relief from crops."[1] The secretary also called attention to the discrimination arising from the fact that whereas the tax in kind assessed on farmers was deducted from the five per cent tax on capital, the same treatment was not accorded to the owners of non-agricultural property. He asked, therefore, for a reconsideration of this part of the tax act.[2] In another respect, also, as he pointed out, a discrimination was observable, but in the reverse sense. Non-agricultural property was assessed at its value in depreciated currency, while agricultural property was assessed at the values existing at the outbreak of the war, before depreciation had set in. "This inequality creates discontent in the public mind and cannot be maintained as just and equal. In all public, as well as private transactions, it is dangerous to depart from the great principles of justice, with a view to effect present expediency. Doubtless it was supposed that legislation of this kind would reach the speculator and extortioner. But it will be found that most of these classes have escaped the tax by taking refuge in agricultural investments; while thousands of widows and orphans and loyal citizens, who have invested their all in stocks and securities, are deprived of their means of support."[3] Finally, the secretary called attention to the workings of the property and income tax, including the tax in kind, and stated that over eighty-two millions had been received from the internal taxes. He declared, however, that

[1] *Memminger, op. cit.*, p. 484. [2] *Ibid.*, p. 485. [3] *Ibid.*, p. 487.

"the difficulties which are encountered in the collection can only be estimated by any one who will inspect the mass of papers which are required for each return, and the inquiries necessary to be made of each individual taxpayer. The results of the tax will probably confirm the recommendation already made of a resort to a more simple system of taxation. The frauds and evasions, which cannot be discovered under the present system, are a perpetual drain upon the tax, which is necessarily increased by the number of officers who must be employed in its collection. And after all is done by the government which is possible, the result is that the most cunning in devices will escape, whilst only the honest and conscientious pay the full and just demands of the law."[1]

The recommendations of Secretary Memminger, however, could not be put into force. The Confederacy was hastening to its close, and amid the universal confusion incident to the breaking up of the body politic, but little attention could be paid to revenue questions. The experiment of the Confederacy with the income tax thus forms an unfinished chapter in fiscal history. In many respects the provisions were unique, and in some points the laws were more carefully elaborated than the similar legislation of the North. But what might have happened with the Confederate income tax under more favorable auspices is a useless speculation.

[1] *Memminger, op. cit.*, p. 487.

CHAPTER IV

The Income Tax of 1894

§ 1. *The Origin of the Tax*

For almost two decades after the abandonment of the income tax the subject disappeared from the public mind.[1] The demand for a progressive income tax was indeed found in the planks of the Socialist party and of the farmers' groups which afterwards consolidated into the Populist party. But in the country at large these demands were not noticed. The prosperity of the eighties brought to the front the problems of surplus financiering, and the country as a whole approved of the protectionist policy of the dominant party, a corollary of which was the periodical cutting down of the internal revenue taxes. There was therefore no need of any additional federal revenue.

During the beginning of the nineties, however, the situation changed. The great decline in prices which had set in

[1] The greater part of this chapter was published in the *Political Science Quarterly*, vol. ix (1894), pp. 610 *et seq.*, and in a slightly different form in the *British Economic Journal*, vol. iv (1894), pp. 637 *et seq.* For other contemporary articles, see C. F. Dunbar, "The New Income Tax," *Quarterly Journal of Economics*, vol. ix (1895), pp. 26 *et seq.*; A. C. Miller, "National Finances and the Income Tax," *Journal of Political Economy*, vol. iii (1895), pp. 255 *et seq.*; F. C. Howe, "Federal Revenues and the Income Tax," *Annals of the American Academy*, vol. iv (1894), pp. 557 *et seq.* The discussions in Congress are treated by G. Tunnell, "Legislative History of the Second Income Tax Law," *Journal of Political Economy*, vol. iii (1895), pp. 311 *et seq.* For articles that were published before the enactment of the law, see the argument in opposition by D. A. Wells, "The Income Tax: Is it desirable?" in the *Forum*, vol. 17 (1894), pp. 1 *et seq.*; and the argument in favor by U. S. Hall, "The Income Tax: Reasons in its Favor," *ibid.*, pp. 14 *et seq.* For articles that appeared after the passage of the law, but before the decision of the court, see D. A. Wells, "Is the Existing Income Tax Unconstitutional?" in the *Forum*, vol. 17 (1895), pp. 537 *et seq.*; and an article by the present writer, "Is the Income Tax Constitutional and Just?" *ibid.*, vol. 18 (1895), pp. 48 *et seq.*

toward the close of the preceding decade was becoming more and more marked, and the prosperity of the western wheat-grower and of the southern cotton-planter was succeeded by a period of hard times. The immense growth of large fortunes in the industrial and financial centres, and the appearance of the new combinations of capital known as trusts, served to set in still greater relief the difficulties of the agricultural classes. This seeming conflict of interest was responsible for several great political movements, each of which reflected itself in legislation. In the first place, the growing suspicion of the aggregations of capital engendered a movement which resulted not only in the prohibition of railway pooling in the interstate commerce law of 1887, but more especially in the Sherman anti-trust act of 1890. In the second place, the fact that the farmers ascribed the falling prices of agricultural products to the appreciation of gold led to the free-silver movement which came within an ace of entirely controlling the government's policy. In the third place, the bad times among the farmers produced a gradual change in their attitude to the tariff. The protectionists of the East originally found their allies among the farmers of the West, not only because the favors of protection were accorded also to the growers of wool, but chiefly because of the home-market argument, according to which the growth of industrial centres as fostered by protection would afford an increasing demand, and therefore a higher price, for the productions of the soil. The home-market argument, however, slowly lost its force as the foreign demand augmented and as the country entered upon the period of immense exports of agricultural products. This sapping of the farmer's interest in protection was now very materially increased, during the many weary years of hard times, by the reflection that but for the tariff he could secure his clothing and his agricultural implements more cheaply, and that it was the protected manufacturers in the East who were lending their support to the "gold-bugs" of Wall Street whose nefarious machinations, in his opinion, were responsible for the falling prices of agricultural products.

Not only were the farmers beginning to become disloyal to the policy of protection, but they were, partly for the same reasons, growing more favorable to the idea of an income tax. This tendency was accentuated by the changes that were taking place in state and local taxation. As a result of a familiar process, the general property tax throughout the country was fast breaking down. It was becoming, in most places, almost exclusively a real property tax, except in the rural districts where the tangible, visible personalty was to be found. The rich urban investor in securities, the wealthy business men, and the well-to-do professional classes were escaping taxation almost entirely. The weight of state and local taxation was falling more and more on the small farmer, who, under existing conditions of international competition, was unable to shift his burdens to the community. The farmers, and more especially the farmers of the West and South, who constituted the great bulk of the middle classes, as well as the preponderant factor in the voting population, were becoming restless. In the face of a system of state and local taxation which rested with crushing force upon them, and of a system of national taxation which no longer seemed to afford them any protection but which, on the contrary, appeared to benefit the classes responsible, in their estimation, for the fall in prices, it was no wonder that the complaints of the agricultural class should become loud and deep. For some years a progressive income tax was one of the chief planks in the platform, not only of the Populists and of the Anti-monopolists, but of the farmers' conventions throughout the length and breadth of the land.

It was this feeling as to the essential inequality and injustice of the tariff, as well as the movement toward free silver, which resulted in the Democratic victory of 1892. The advent of President Cleveland to power was, therefore, understood to mean a modification of the tariff, and the urgency of fiscal reform was emphasized by the fact that the country was facing a series of deficits. Accordingly, when the President submitted his message to Congress in December, 1893, we find the first suggestion of an income tax, not, indeed, in the shape of a tax on incomes in general, but in the form of a tax on incomes from corporations. The President said: "I am satisfied that the revised tariff duties provided for in the proposed legislation, added to existing internal revenue taxation, will, in the near future, though perhaps not immediately, produce sufficient revenue to meet the indebtedness of the government. The Committee, after full consideration, and to provide against the temporary deficiency which may exist before the business of the country adjusts itself to the new tariff schedules, have wisely embraced in their plans a few additional internal revenue taxes, including a small tax upon incomes derived from certain corporate investments. These new assessments are not only absolutely just and easily borne, but they have the further merit of being such as can be remitted without unfavorable business depression whenever the necessity of their imposition no longer exists."

It is uncertain to which committee the President here referred. Senator Hill stated subsequently that at the date of the measure "neither the full committee of Ways and Means nor the Democratic members thereof, had agreed upon any income tax or other internal taxation,"[1] and he characterized the statement of the President as "both inaccurate and premature." The ways and means subcommittee on internal revenue had, however, been considering an income tax, and had heard various witnesses on the subject, among them, in October, Mr. Shearman, who had suggested a tax on incomes from land and certain corporations.[2] In Secretary Carlisle's report reference is also made to the possibility of an income tax, but limited to incomes from corporations.[3] On Decem-

[1] *Congressional Record containing the Proceedings and Debates of the 53d Congress, 3d Session.* Washington, 1894, vol. 26, p. 3558.

[2] This testimony was published as *A Just and Practicable Income Tax.* By Hon. Thomas G. Shearman, before the Ways and Means Subcommittee on Internal Revenue. Washington, 1893, 21 pp.

[3] *Report of the Secretary of the Treasury for 1893.* Washington, 1893, p. lxxxiii. In November, Secretary Carlisle had received from Smith, the assistant register of the treasury, a document containing his *History of the Income Tax.*

ber 19, in fact, the committee of ways and means submitted a tariff bill which contained no reference to an income tax, and on January 8 the debate on the tariff began. The house adopted a resolution that on January 15 the bill should be read and be open to amendment, and that on January 29 the bill, with all amendments recommended or pending in the committee of the whole, should be reported to the house, and that two hours' debate only be allowed, "whereupon the vote shall be taken."[1]

Although the record shows that three separate income tax bills were introduced, one by Bretz on December 19, to levy an income tax in order to pay pensions, one by Davis on December 20, and one by Johnson, of Ohio, on January 3, designed to impose a tax on the income from invested capital,[2] the chairman reported to the committee of the whole on January 22 that no income tax amendment to the tariff bill had been received by him.[3] On January 29, however, the day fixed for the vote, Mr. McMillin of Tennessee, chairman of the subcommittee, submitted an income-tax amendment to the Wilson Bill, providing for a two per cent tax on all incomes over four thousand dollars, to be payable by individuals and corporations alike.[4]

In his speech explaining the amendment,[5] McMillin presented virtually all the arguments in favor of the tax. He started out by calling attention to the abundant crops and, referring to the aftermath of the crisis of 1893, asked: "Why is it that in the midst of plenty we are starving?" The answer he gave was, the misdeeds of the Republican party and especially their tariff policy. He summed up his indictment against the tariff by stating that "want, not wealth, pays the tax," and that the time had come to "put more tax upon what men have, less on what they need." Referring to the recent growth of revenue and expenditures, he went on to

[1] *Congressional Record*, *op. cit.*, p. 572.

[2] House bills nos. 4861, 4898, and 4955.

[3] *Op. cit.*, p. 1193.

[4] The amendment will be found in *op. cit.*, pp. 1494 *et seq.*

[5] The speech will be found in *op. cit.*, vol. 26, *appendix*, pp. 411 *et seq.*

say: "I ask of any reasonable person whether it is unjust to expect that a small per cent of this enormous revenue shall be placed upon the accumulated wealth of the country instead of placing all upon the consumption of the people. . . . The people of the United States do not ask that all of the revenue shall be placed on accumulated wealth. They do not demand that even one fourth of it shall be placed there. But they do insist that it is not unreasonable or unjust to require that a very small proportion of it shall be. . . . We do not come here in any spirit of antagonism to wealth. . . . It is not a proposition to put an undue embargo upon wealth, but it is to make the wealth that is accumulated in this country pay some share of the expenses of Government. . . . My friends, are we going to put all of this burden on the things men eat and wear and leave out those vast accumulations of wealth? . . . And yet, when it is proposed to shift this burden from those who can not bear it to those who can; to divide it between consumption and wealth; to shift it from the laborer who has nothing but his power to toil and sweat, to the man who has a fortune made or inherited, we hear a hue and cry raised. . . . I would be most reluctant to use the power of government to tax wealth unjustly. But I am also unwilling to let wealth escape all governmental taxation.[1]"

Referring to the "colossal fortunes amassed as were never concentrated at any other age or in any other country of the world," and calling attention to the fact that "in a single lifetime fortunes are gathered together here by protection, and the tribute that it levies on the many for the enrichment of the few," he asked: "Are we to be told, with all this staring us in the face, with all the blessings that have been showered on those who have been able to thus accumulate what would have made Crœsus envy us, that it is a sacred thing that we shall not invade, and that these fortunes shall go untouched for governmental purposes, forever and aye? I do not believe it."

This was the fundamental reason for the tax. And the

[1] *Congressional Record, op. cit.*, p. 415.

result, in his opinion, would be "to diminish the antipathies that now exist between the classes. . . . When each citizen sees that every other citizen is paying to perpetuate the blessings of freedom in proportion to the wealth he possesses, there will be no heed given to iconoclastic complaint, which finds expression in violence, and threatens the very foundations upon which our whole institutions rest."

The minor reason that McMillin gave was what he called the flexibility of the tax, or what is more commonly termed the elasticity of the revenue system. Pointing out that this was the great result achieved by the English tax, he stated that in the United States we must look forward to steady expenditures and fluctuating revenues. "Make the tariff what it should be, and regulate revenues by changing internal revenue taxes. This tax can be raised and lowered without affecting business. Tariff rates can not be." McMillin thereupon proceeded to take up some of the objections to the tax. With reference to the charge of inquisition, he stated that the income tax was not more inquisitorial than certain parts of the tariff, and surely not more so than the entire system by which the state, country, and municipal revenues were collected. "The American people will not accept this as a special reason why we should for a long period put all the federal taxes upon consumption and none upon accumulations." Finally, in answer to the argument that the income tax is a tax upon thrift, he pointed out that, on the contrary, "Every citizen is placed on an equality by this proposition. This law says: 'As you have been prospered, so pay. As you have received the blessings of the government, contribute to its support. As you have been enabled to accumulate this wealth by the blessings of free institutions, contribute something to perpetuate them.' How can that be called a penalty on thrift?"

§ 2. *The Discussion in Congress*

The introduction of the amendment led, as was natural, to a fierce discussion. The opponents of the tax presented vigorous arguments, many of which were well put by Bourke Cockran of New York. Ray quoted with some effect from the Democratic criticism of the tax during the Civil War: "It is not a proposition to tax property, accumulations of wealth, but mind and energy. It is a measure that will encourage shiftlessness and idleness." Ray thought that the weakness of the income tax was sufficiently exposed by characterizing it as "a twin sister of free trade."[1] Walker, of Massachusetts, complained that "the income tax takes from the wealth of the thrifty and enterprising, and gives to the shiftless and the sluggard."[2] Several speakers, like English and Dunn, took refuge in Senator Thurman's objection to the Civil War income tax,[3] that it would ultimately be shifted to the poor, and that they, therefore, would bear the burden. Somewhat inconsistently, however, Dunn contended that "the mad policy of the Democrats would create such a financial revolution in this country as would shake the government to its very foundations."[4] English, in addition, prophesied that "before three years have passed, if this measure shall have become law, you will repeal it amid the jeers and execrations of the people."[5]

Perhaps the strongest language that was used in opposition may be found in the speech of Adams, of Pennsylvania. "An income tax! A tax so odious that no administration ever dared to impose it except in time of war; and you will find that the people will not tolerate it in time of peace. It is unutterably distasteful both in its moral and material aspects. It does not belong to a free country. It is class legislation. Do you wish to put a tax upon thrift and impose a penalty upon success? Do you desire to offer a reward to dishonesty and to encourage perjury? The imposition of the tax will corrupt the people. It will bring in its train the spy

[1] *Congressional Record, op. cit.*, p. 1600.

[2] *Op. cit.*, 1650. Walker's speech was separately published under the title, *The Income Tax.* Remarks of Hon. J. H. Walker. Washington, 1894.

[3] *Cf. supra*, p. 461.

[4] *Op. cit., appendix*, p. 208.

[5] *Op. cit., appendix*, p. 188.

and the informer. It will necessitate a swarm of officials with inquisitorial powers. It is a direct step toward centralization, of which our Democratic friends profess such horror. It is expensive in its collection and cannot be fairly gathered; and finally, it is contrary to the traditions and principles of republican government. Mr. Chairman, pass this bill, and the Democratic party signs its death warrant."[1]

All this opposition, however, was hopeless. Wilson, the author of the tariff bill, and who originally suggested a corporation tax as preferable to an income tax,[2] stated his views as follows: "I did not concur in the policy of attaching an income-tax bill to the tariff bill. I have had some doubt as to the expediency of a personal income tax at the present time, but when the Committee decided otherwise, I threw in my fortunes earnestly and loyally with them because I had never been hostile to the idea of an income tax." He denied that the bill involved either class or sectional legislation. "Why, sir, when for a generation New England has been sending out from her colleges men imbued with the doctrine that an income tax is a wise and equal system of taxation, when through the text books of her great economists, her Sumner, and Walker and Perry, she has taught that doctrine in the colleges of the South and West, she cannot justly complain that her own teachings are used as a sectional weapon against her. But," he added, "I am in close touch with the men of New York,—I am in close touch with the men of the West,—I am bone of the bone of the men of the South. And I can affirm that in all my conferences with them I have heard no man suggest as the motive for this scheme of taxation that he supported it in any sectional spirit, or with any feeling of resentment or hostility to any part of the country."[3]

The other speakers added but little to the points that had been made by McMillin. Hall, of Missouri, however, who,

[1] *Op. cit., appendix*, p. 207.

[2] *Cf.* his article, "An Income Tax on Corporations," in the *North American Review*, vol. 158 (January, 1894), pp. 1 *et seq.*

[3] *Congressional Record, op. cit., appendix*, p. 204.

like many others, made much of the "flexibility" argument advanced by McMillin, emphasized the popular sentiment in its favor. "What the opponents of an income tax have most to dread is the education of the people. If we had been able to put an income tax plank in the Chicago platform, and had had the time to educate the people on this question, there is no question that we would have carried this country, and carried it like a cyclone."[1] The Populists, through Pence and Kem, attempted to introduce a graduated scheme. Kem desired the exemption to be considerably reduced, and the tax to be graduated so that instead of raising the thirty millions estimated by the commissioner of Internal Revenue, it would raise at least one hundred millions.[2]

But the time for discussion was limited. After a short debate in committee of the whole, the bill was reported to the house on January 30, and only three hours' debate was permitted. The general temper of the house is well illustrated by the grandiloquent peroration of De Armond, of Missouri. "The passage of the bill will mark the dawn of a brighter day, with more of sunshine, more of the songs of birds, more of that sweetest music, the laughter of children well fed, well clothed, well housed. Can we doubt that in the brighter, happier days to come, good, even-handed, wholesome Democracy shall be triumphant. God hasten the era of equality in taxation and in opportunity. And God prosper the Wilson bill, the first leaf in the glorious book of reform in taxation, the promise of a brightening future for those whose genius and labor create the wealth of the land, and whose courage and patriotism are the only sure bulwark in the defense of the Republic."[3] The bill passed by a majority of 204 against 140.

On February 2 the bill was sent to the Senate and referred to the committee on finance. On March 20 the chairman, Senator Voorhees, reported it to the Senate with amendments, and shortly thereafter the consideration of its provisions was

[1] *Congressional Record, op. cit.*, p. 1611.

[2] *Op. cit., appendix*, pp. 293 *et seq.*

[3] *Op. cit., appendix*, p. 406.

begun in the committee of the whole. Before the bill was read, Senator Hill attacked the income tax provisions, in a long speech on April 9, in which he marshalled all possible arguments against it. One of these deserves to be quoted: "European professors announce to American professors, who publish and believe it, the birth of a brand new political economy for universal application. From the midst of their armed camps between the Danube and the Rhine, the professors with their books, the Socialists with their schemes, the anarchists with their bombs, are all instructing the people of the United States in the organization of society, the doctrines of democracy, and the principles of taxation. No wonder if their preaching can find ears in the White House."[1] After this outburst of Senator Hill, it was not until June 21 that the income tax provisions were taken up, although on the preceding day Senator Peffer, of Kansas, speaking for the Populists, offered an amendment providing for a graduated tax, and Senator Hoar introduced an amendment exempting the salaries of federal judges.[2]

The debate was opened by Senator Hill, who from now on became the leading opponent of the income tax, and who disclosed his disagreement with his Democratic colleagues. He submitted a petition signed by a number of prominent Democratic business men of New York, against the income tax, which "represents the abandonment of the traditional democratic policy in favor of a socialistic policy, which has failed to receive popular approval."[3] Hill denied that the English income tax was a precedent. "It was instituted as a war tax, and defended as a war tax; it is obnoxious to the English people, and no English statesman of any repute has ever defended it, except as a tax to be levied only in time of war, or to meet subsequent deficiencies traceable to the enormous expenditures of war." Income taxes "seem to be the necessary accompaniment of monarchical governments, but they are justly regarded as odious and unnecessary in free republics. . . . France has no income tax because she has

[1] *Op. cit.*, p. 3564. [2] *Op. cit.*, pp. 6577–6578. [3] *Op. cit.*, p. 6612.

learned to love liberty, to hate inquisitions, to detest class legislation, and to respect the rights of property." In the main, however, the arguments of Senator Hill, Senator Hoar, and the other important opponents of the tax, did scarcely more than elaborate the points that had been made by Adams in the House.

Senator Sherman's attitude, however, is interesting because of his opposition to the abolition of the income tax two decades before. Sherman stated: "I feel precisely as I expressed myself twenty years ago, that it was a tax no man should complain of. If the circumstances and exigencies demanded it, or the interests of our people, the need of revenue or the public credit, or any public interest demanded it, I would vote for it without hesitation. I do not by any means regard the income tax as the worst feature of this bill, and I should have no objection to it, as I say, if there were any real demand for it. But there is not."[1] What he objected to, however, was the high exemption. "In a republic like ours, where all men are equal, this attempt to array the rich against the poor or the poor against the rich is socialism, communism, devilism." He thereupon proceeded to advance the idea that while the income tax is in essence a just tax, it ought to be levied by the states and not by the federal government. "I do not say that an income tax is not a proper and desirable tax to be levied, but only that it is not a proper and desirable tax to be levied now by the United States. It should be left to the states as a source of revenue, to be used by them whenever they choose to do so."

The debate in the Senate continued for six days,[2] and various amendments were proposed. The first, suggested by the committee, was an important one, limiting the operation of the tax to January 1, 1900.[3] This was carried. Senator

[1] *Congressional Record*, *op. cit.*, p. 6695.

[2] For the debate on the successive days, see the *Congressional Record* as follows: June 21, pp. 6610 *et seq.*; June 22, pp. 6684 *et seq.*; June 23, pp. 6764 *et seq.*; June 26, pp. 6804 *et seq.*; June 27, pp. 6865 *et seq.*; June 28, pp. 6920 *et seq.*

[3] *Op. cit.*, p. 6631.

Peffer, who claimed the income tax as a Populist measure, moved, but unsuccessfully, to have it begin with an exemption of one thousand dollars and to have the rate rise progressively from one to five per cent. On the other hand, the Senate adopted a large number of amendments providing for exemptions of various kinds, and also somewhat modifying the administrative provisions. One of the most important amendments was that which deducted from the taxable income of corporations the amounts payable for interest on bonds.

The opponents of the bill knew that their opposition was futile. In vain did Senators Hill and Hoar attempt to raise the bogie of interference with state rights. Said Hill, "No such federal aggrandizement was ever projected," and he referred to this "insidious and deadly assault upon state rights, state powers, and state independence."[1] Hoar declared the "income-tax scheme the most conspicuous, far-going, drastic, sweeping assertion of national power against the state power, state interest, and state functions which can be found in our legislative history."[2] But this attempt to recall the Democratic party to its old constitutional position was unavailing. The bill passed the Senate on July 3 by a vote of 39 to 34. After an unsuccessful endeavor to secure agreement in conference, the House finally receded from its opposition, and on August 13 accepted all the Senate amendments. On August 28 the tariff bill became a law, without having received the approval of the President.

From this consideration of the fortunes of the income tax bill in Congress it is clear what were the real reasons underlying its adoption. The self-imposed mission of the Democratic party was to reduce and equalize taxation. Although the Democrats at first proposed simply to lower the tariff to a revenue basis, it was soon recognized that the reductions would be more radical. Looked at merely from the standpoint of convenience and ease of collection, the simple method of making good a deficit in the tariff revenue would have been to modify the system of internal revenue. This plan,

[1] *Op. cit.*, p. 4351.

[2] *Op. cit.*, p. 6631.

indeed, was advanced by David A. Wells, and at one time it seemed to enjoy a reasonable prospect of meeting with legislative approval. Mr. Wells showed that by leaving the whiskey tax at the original figure, and by slightly raising the tobacco tax and modifying the beer tax, a very considerable increase of revenue might be secured. But the project soon raised a storm of opposition. On the one hand were the immense brewery interests, which objected strenuously to the imposition of any additional burdens on them. On the other hand were the whiskey interests, which desired a nominal increase of the whiskey tax, in order to realize temporary profits, and perhaps also to take advantage of the rate in other ways. And finally, there was the temperance party, which demanded so high a tax on whiskey that in all probability it would have reduced the revenue. As a matter of fact, the new law increased the whiskey tax, raising it from ninety cents to $1.10 a gallon, and furthermore imposed a duty of two cents a pack on playing cards. But neither of these changes materially affected the revenue.

Since, therefore, the proposed tariff schedules would have meant a considerable deficit, and since no relief was to be expected from the internal revenue system, the proposition to make good the difference by introducing the income tax received a hearty welcome.[1] But while the anticipated deficit gave the Western and Southern representatives their opportunity, it was not so much the idea of increasing the revenue as that of correcting inequalities in the tax system that was really in their mind. The truth of this assertion is evident when we reflect on the fortunes of the Wilson bill in the Senate. The Gorman bill put sugar back on the dutiable list, and made many other changes which so weakened the

[1] In April, 1894, Mr. Worthington C. Ford, chief of the Bureau of Statistics in the Treasury Department, submitted an estimate of the probable yield of the tax. He thought that "the revenue from private incomes will be small and will hardly cover the cost of collection; but that the revenue from corporations would range between twelve millions as a minimum and thirty-nine millions as a maximum." —*53d Cong., 2d Sess., Mis. Doc.*, no. 232, p. 9.

radical nature of the House bill that all danger of a deficit seemed to be at an end. The income tax was no longer a fiscal necessity. Yet all attempts to expunge it from the bill were utterly unavailing. The farmers' influence was too strong.

Opposition to the tax came, as was natural, from the great cities of the East. The commercial and financial centres professed to fear that their prosperity might be jeopardized. The large dailies were filled with indignant protests, and the chambers of commerce in New York and other cities voiced their anger in long and vehement resolutions. Even the leading Democratic journals in the North and East did everything in their power to have the income tax sections struck out of the tariff bill.

The contest was analogous to that over the income tax in England. For in England also the opposition was from the very beginning sectional rather than political. In reading the protests of the American chambers of commerce we seem to be reading the manifestoes issued in the first years of the nineteenth century by the corporation of the City of London, and the resolutions adopted by the anti-income tax leagues many decades later in London, Manchester, and Birmingham. For there also the line was drawn not by party affiliation, but by class interests which had not yet found expression in party dogmas.

So it was that here, while the Republican journals in the East opposed the tax, the opposition was due not to the fact that they were Republican, but to the fact that they represented the great industrial centres. In the West there was by no means the same opposition even among Republicans. The sentiment in favor of some form of income taxation was so overwhelming among the mass of the voters that the Republican leaders preferred to preserve silence and not run the risk of opposing a popular measure.[1] Thus the vehement Eastern opposition, instituted by the Republicans and more

[1] Even in the East the Republican platforms of 1894 treated the tax very tenderly, and said nothing about its speedy abolition.

or less openly sympathized with by the Democrats, was wholly ineffectual. No feature of the tariff bill was ever in smaller danger of being successfully opposed than were the income tax sections; for revenue considerations were the pretext for their introduction, not the cause.

§ 3. *An Analysis of the Law*

The new law [1] was copied, with a few important exceptions, almost word for word from the old legislation of the Civil War period. We shall therefore only summarize its chief provisions.

The tax was to begin on January 1, 1895, and to continue for five years. The rate was two per cent on the excess over $4000. It was levied upon all "gains, profits and incomes derived from any kind of property, rents, interest, dividends, or salaries, or from any profession, trade, employment or vocation." The period on which the tax was computed was the preceding calendar year. The tax applied to the entire income of all citizens of the United States, whether resident or non-resident, and to all persons residing within the United States; and it also applied to so much of the income of persons residing abroad as was derived from property or business within the United States.[2]

A long section was devoted to explaining what was to be considered income. The only points that need mention here are the following: Income was deemed to include interest on all securities except such federal bonds as were expressly exempted from taxation by the law of their issue. Profits realized from the sale of real estate were defined to be income only when the real estate had been purchased within two years previous. The amount of sales of all vegetable and animal produce grown or produced by the taxpayer himself was considered income, but the expenses of production were deducted, and the amount consumed directly by the family was not included. All personal property acquired by gift

[1] Act of August 28, 1894, secs. 27–37.

[2] Sec. 27.

or inheritance was declared to be income. In computing income, the necessary expenses actually incurred in carrying on the occupation were deducted. A similar deduction was made for interest on indebtedness, for losses actually sustained, and for worthless debts. But no deduction was permitted for permanent improvements or betterments to real estate. Although taxes might be deducted, the term was held not to include the amount paid for special assessments. In cases where the tax had already been paid by other parties, the individual was not compelled to include that income in his return. This would apply to the salaries of all officials of the United States government, where the government itself was directed to withhold the tax; to the income received in the shape of dividends on corporate stock, where the stock company or association was required to pay the tax in the first instance; and to "any salary upon which the employer is required by law to withhold or pay the tax."[1] It was also provided that salaries due to state, county, or municipal officers should be exempt.[2]

In addition to this tax on individuals the law included a tax on corporations, companies, or associations doing business for profit in the United States, but not including partnerships. This tax was assessed at the same rate, but without any abatements. It was levied on the net profits or income above operating and business expenses, which latter were so defined as to comprise not only ordinary expenses and losses but also interest on bonded or other indebtedness. The income was deemed to include all amounts carried to the account of any fund, or used for construction, enlargement of plant, or any other expenditure or investment paid from the net annual profits.[3] The corporate income tax did not apply to states, counties, or municipalities; nor to charitable, religious, or educational associations; nor to fraternal beneficiary orders; nor to building or loan associations; nor to mutual insurance companies; nor to savings-banks or societies under certain conditions.

[1] Sec. 28. But see *infra*, p. 527. [2] Sec. 33. [3] Sec. 32.

We come now to the administrative features. All persons of lawful age with an income over $3500 were required to make to the collector or deputy collector a return in such form and manner as might be directed by the commissioner of internal revenue, with the approval of the secretary of the treasury. The collector or deputy collector was to require the return to be verified by oath or affirmation. If he had reason to believe that the return had been understated, he might increase the amount. In case no return or a wilfully fraudulent return was made, he was to make the list to the best of his information, adding fifty per cent in the one case and one hundred per cent in the other.[1] Appeal might be taken from the deputy collector to the collector of the district. If still dissatisfied, a taxpayer might, after due notice, submit the case, with all the papers, to the commissioner of internal revenue, whose decision was final. No penalty was to be inflicted upon any one for making a false return or refusing to make a return, except after reasonable notice of the time and place where the charge might be heard. A further section provided that in case a person refused to return his list or made a fraudulent return, the collector might inspect his books and compel the individual, or any one else in charge of the books, to give testimony or answer interrogatories.[2]

Every corporation or business association was required to make a full return of its gross profits, expenses, net profits, amounts paid for interest, annuities and dividends, amounts paid in salaries of less than $4000, and amounts, with name and address of each official, paid in salaries of more than $4000.[3] Whenever the collector or deputy collector thought that a correct return had not been made, he might file an affidavit of such belief with the commissioner of internal revenue, who might then, after notice and hearing, issue a request to have the books inspected. If the corporation refused such request, the collector was to make his own esti-

[1] Sec. 29. [2] Sec. 34, amending sec. 3173 of the Revised Statutes.
[3] Sec. 35.

mate of income, and add fifty per cent thereto.[1] The government was required to withhold the tax from the amount of all salaries over $4000.[2]

The tax was due on July 1 of each year, and was levied on the income for the year that ended on the preceding December 31. The penalty for delay in payment was five per cent on the amount unpaid, together with interest at the rate of twelve per cent. This did not apply to the estates of deceased, deranged, or insolvent persons.

In order to insure the greatest possible secrecy, it was provided that no official of the government was to divulge any fact contained in the income return or to allow any detail to be seen or examined by any person not authorized by law. It was further declared to be unlawful for any one to print or publish in any manner not provided by law any income return or part thereof. The penalty was a fine not exceeding $1000, or imprisonment not exceeding one year. But in case the publication was due to any public official, the offence entailed dismissal from office, with the incapacity thereafter to occupy any position under the government.[3]

Let us now proceed to analyze the provisions which have been recounted in all their baldness.

The first point that arrests our attention is the definition of income. The law differed from those of the Civil War period in that it did not expressly exclude from income the rental value of the residence occupied by the owner. The legislator of the Civil War period, it will be remembered, assumed that income would comprise the rental value of the homestead occupied. A special provision was therefore inserted in the law, excluding this in terms. This was done for the reason that, since a deduction was permitted from income for the amount of rent paid for a dwelling by a tenant, there would otherwise be a gross injustice.[4] But, as was pointed out

[1] Sec. 36. [2] Sec. 33. [3] Sec. 34.

[4] The deduction for amount of rent paid, it will be remembered, was not found in the law of 1862, but in the amendment of 1863. The exclusion of rental value from income was first found in the law of 1864.

repeatedly at the time, the deduction of rent paid was unnecessary. The same equality might have been preserved by including in income the rental value of the property occupied by the owner, and in other cases allowing no deduction for rent paid. In the new law no one was permitted to deduct from income the amount of rent actually paid — which in itself was correct enough. But as nothing was said about including in income the rental value of the dwelling occupied, it is very doubtful whether it would have been included. This was manifestly an injustice.

On other points the explanation of what is to be considered income was copied from the earlier laws. Some of the provisions were quite arbitrary. Such was the requirement that the profits from the sale of real estate should be considered income only when the real estate has been purchased within two years before. Under the law of 1862, which contained no reference to this point, it will be remembered, it was held that profits from the sale of real estate were to be considered income, irrespective of the time when the property had been purchased. The law of 1864 specifically provided that they were to be considered income only if the property had been bought in the same year. Later on, in 1867, the limit was fixed at two years. It is this clause which was followed in the law of 1894. Why the precise period of two years should have been chosen is not clear.

A similar criticism may be urged against the provision that income was to include the sale of all vegetable and animal products, excluding any part consumed by the family. It was frequently pointed out during the earlier period that this deduction was illogical, since an artisan who had to spend his money for provisions was allowed no deduction. If the farmer sold all his produce, and then bought food, he could deduct nothing; but if he reserved from his sales an equivalent amount of food, the deduction was permitted. However, since very few farmers would have been taxed by the law at all, this provision made little difference.

A more important point is the definition of corporate income. From the economic point of view there is a distinction between individual income and corporate income. In the case of individuals, true taxable property consists in the surplus above indebtedness. Net income can therefore be arrived at only by deducting interest on debts. But in the case of corporations the matter is somewhat different. Capital stock represents in many cases only a portion of the property, the remainder being represented by the bonded indebtedness. It is the stock and bonds together that represent the property and the earning capacity of the corporations; and for this reason the most advanced tax laws in America, as well as in Europe, permit an individual to deduct his indebtedness or the interest on his debts, while the corporation is assessed on both bonds and stock, or on both interest and dividends. The bill as it came from the House contained a similar provision; but in the Senate the section was so amended as to permit corporations to include interest on debt among their expenses. It is evident, then, that the income tax on corporations was really not a corporate income tax, but only a tax on corporate profits over and above fixed charges. Thus at one stroke the proceeds from this source were cut down almost one-half.

It may indeed be alleged in extenuation that the corporations, especially the railways, were already taxed so heavily in some states, and that their financial position was in the main so precarious, that the imposition of a tax on both stocks and bonds would have involved many companies in ruin. It may be said further that the provision was not so serious as it seemed, because the individual recipients of the income from corporate bonds were supposed to include those sums in their own returns. On the other hand, it must be conceded that the definition of "income" was certainly an uneconomic one; and that whatever arguments apply to the advisability of making corporations responsible for the tax on dividends apply with equal force to the interest on indebtedness.

The third point of importance is that the law provided, not only for an income tax, but for something over and above an income tax, namely, a tax on successions. As we have learned above,[1] income has come in practice to denote a regular and periodic return. It is for this reason that many income tax laws estimate income at an average of a certain number of years, as the last three or five or seven years. In that way the fat years are balanced by the lean and a greater degree of justice is attained. Although this scheme was not adopted, the new law, nevertheless, was in the main based on the idea of annual recurring profits. It is surprising, then, to find a provision which imposes a tax upon the value of all "personal property acquired by gift or inheritance" during the year. If anything is irregular and unperiodic, it is an inheritance. The income from the inheritance is indeed regular; but the law taxed not only the income from the inheritance, but the inheritance itself. From the standpoint of an income tax, this was not only illogical, but constituted double taxation. In all the other income taxes of the world inheritances are either expressly or impliedly excluded. It may, indeed, have been desirable to impose an inheritance tax in addition to the income tax. But in that case it should have been discussed on its own merits and not smuggled into an odd corner of the bill.

It may be noticed in passing that "inheritance," strictly construed, applies only to real estate passing by descent. The term "inheritance tax" is popularly applied in America to a tax on the devolution of realty, whether by will or by intestacy, and is sometimes applied also to a tax on the devolution of personalty. But the new law used the term in a restricted sense. The provision did not apply to real estate at all, and speaks of "personal property acquired by inheritance." This is very confusing. Passing over this misnomer, however, the exemption of real estate was due to the feeling, alluded to above, on the part of the mass of the small real-estate owners that they were already bearing more than their share of taxation. Whether or not the passage of this succession tax law was wise, we shall consider later. The point which we desire to

[1] Page 20.

emphasize here is that the law of 1894 provided not only for an income tax, but also for a succession tax, and that the inclusion of "gifts and inheritances" in income is unscientific.

The fourth consideration which arrests our attention is that, from the American point of view, the law provided for a corporation tax as well as an income tax. We say from the American point of view, because we are accustomed to make a distinction between a corporation tax and other taxes. Strictly speaking, the antithesis is not between a corporation tax and an income tax or a property tax, but between a tax on corporations and a tax on individuals or, as it is sometimes called, a personal income tax.[1] In England it would make no difference whether the tax were assessed to the individual security-holder or to the corporation. But in the United States the new law combined what during the early years of the Civil War period was embraced in two separate measures. There existed at that time, it will be remembered, not only a tax on corporate dividends and interest, but also a tax on certain corporate gross receipts, in addition to the tax on individual incomes. The corporations were permitted to add the gross receipts tax to the charges made, so that the tax was virtually shifted to the public. In the case of the corporate income tax, however, the corporations were not compelled to deduct the tax from the dividends or interest of each security-holder, and as a matter of fact they generally assumed the tax themselves without withholding it from the bondholder. It became to that extent a tax on the corporation, not on the bondholder. Under the new law the tax was also assessed directly on the corporation. But, as we have seen above, it was not assessed on corporate bonds. So that the question of withholding the tax from the interest due would not arise. Yet so far as it went, it was a corporation tax in addition to the individual income tax.

The fifth point of importance is the $4000 exemption. The merit or demerit of this provision will be discussed below.

[1] The latter term does not represent the distinction with perfect accuracy, because under the American law corporations are also considered persons.

There are, however, several considerations to which attention must be called here. In one sense the system was more logical than the English system. In England, it will be remembered, a certain small amount is absolutely exempted, while incomes up to a higher amount are permitted certain abatements; and it is only on incomes above the latter figure that the full amount is assessed. In the American income tax there was only a single exemption, but the abatement applied to all incomes of whatever amount. The tax was levied only on the excess of incomes over $4000. This is a provision the principle of which was already found in the income tax acts of the Civil War, and which has recently been adopted in some of the Australasian income taxes, where a deduction of a fixed amount is permitted for all incomes. But while it is entirely logical, it is manifestly unjust to permit the man with $4000 income to go entirely free and to impose on his neighbor who has perhaps $4010 income a tax of over $80. The jump is too sudden. It will be perceived, however, that the American system virtually provided for a slightly graduated tax running up from zero to almost two per cent on the entire income. For a proportional tax on the excess over a certain sum necessarily means a graduated tax on the entire amount.

Again, while the exemption was nominally accorded to all incomes, the introduction of the corporate income tax practically nullified the provision in one respect. Since corporations were to pay upon their entire net profits as defined by the law, it is manifest that persons who invested their whole property in corporate stock from which they received less than $4000 income, would nevertheless have the tax withheld from their dividends by the corporation. To the class of small investors the exemption accorded by the law was, therefore, of no use; for no machinery was provided for granting rebates to such taxpayers, as is the case in some other countries. The same inconsistency, as we know, occurred in the acts during the Civil War and was noted at various times. But it was deemed impracticable to remedy the injustice. In the case of official salaries, however, where the tax was advanced by the government, provision was made for the exemption. The government was to withhold the tax only in case the salary exceeded $4000.

It must be noticed also that only one deduction of $4000 was permitted from the aggregate income of all members of any family. This might in some cases render the exemption nugatory. Under the recent development of American law the property interests of a married woman are often entirely independent of those of the husband. Where her income was less than $4000, she would nevertheless still be taxable if her husband's income exceeded that figure. The force of the objection is somewhat weakened, first by the fact that, after all, it is the family income as a whole which serves as the best test of ability to pay, and secondly by the fact that it is very unlikely that married women would have been assessed at all, even though the letter of the law called for the taxation of "all persons of lawful age."

The sixth and final point to which it is well to call attention is what is commonly called double taxation. The law, it will be remembered, applied not only to all citizens resident, but to the entire income, no matter where received, of citizens residing abroad and of aliens residing in the United States; and it also applied to so much of the income of non-resident aliens as was derived from property or business within the United States. Here some interesting questions arise. Even assuming that the first and fourth classes would be reached, it is difficult to believe that the second and third classes could be touched. It might, indeed, be possible to assess the income of a non-resident in so far as it was derived from tangible property situate in this country. But in most cases it would be virtually impossible to reach the non-resident. Still more difficult would have been the task of hitting the entire income of foreigners resident in this country in so far as their income was derived from foreign sources; for the usual means of control would naturally be lacking.

Even assuming, however, that the practical difficulties were not insuperable, there would be grave objections in principle.

If a resident foreigner is taxed on his entire income here, and is again taxed on his income at home, we have manifestly double taxation. Or if a non-resident citizen is taxed by us on his entire income, and is then again taxed abroad in the country in which he happens to reside, we have a not less glaring case of double taxation. Some states, like Prussia, tax foreigners only after they have lived more than a year in the country, except when their income is derived from Prussian property or business. The law of 1894 contained no such provision. Again, while England does in part assess resident aliens, it does not attempt to reach the entire income of non-resident citizens. The Civil War taxes did not at first even tax the income of aliens; but later they did try to reach the entire income of non-resident citizens. The new tax followed the mistaken policy of the later laws. But the practical effect of the provision would have been slight. For this part of the law, it may be conjectured, would almost inevitably have remained a dead letter.

§ 4. *The Alleged Shortcomings of the Law*

What, then, are we to think of this measure? Was it a wise innovation, or was it essentially vicious in principle and destined to be ineffective in practice? We can, perhaps, best approach the problem by discussing some of the objections that were raised against the law.

One of the arguments most commonly advanced by the opponents of the measure was the alleged socialistic character of the tax. To assess people upon their income was said to savor of socialism. The more violent enemies of the measure went so far as to maintain that the state has no right to confiscate any part whatever of a man's earnings. This objection, indeed, scarcely deserves a refutation. It entirely misconceives the relation of the individual to the state. The cry of "socialism" has always been the last refuge of those who wish to clog the wheel of social progress or to prevent the abolition of long-continued abuses. The factory laws were in their time dubbed socialistic. Compulsory education and the post-office system were called socialistic. And there is scarcely a single tax which has ever been introduced which has not somewhere or other met with the same objection. Only a short time ago the new inheritance taxes were vehemently opposed in some of the American commonwealths, as was the new estate duty in England, on the ground of socialism. The same fate befell the property tax before its recent introduction in Holland and Germany. As a matter of fact, if there is any socialism at all to be discovered in these measures, it would be far more obvious in the property tax, which entirely exempts all earnings of the lower classes in so far as they are again expended, than in the income tax, which reaches earnings from other sources than mere property. The property tax hits only the property owner; the income tax, as such, hits the income receiver, whether the income be derived from property or not. Yet we have become so accustomed to the property tax that the idea of its being socialistic seems ridiculous. Nor are we speaking here of the exemption feature of the income tax law, which will be discussed below. The cry of socialism was raised against the income tax *per se*, while the high exemption only served as an additional count against it.

Had the principle of progressive taxation been introduced, some color might have been lent to the charge of socialism. The Populists, it will be remembered, introduced several amendments looking toward graduation, but they were all defeated. As a matter of fact, however, recent investigations have shown that progressive taxation, which to some seems the very quintessence of socialism, and which has undoubtedly often been urged for socialistic reasons, is perfectly defensible in theory on purely economic and fiscal grounds [1] although, for other reasons, its application to the income tax is practically inexpedient.[2] It must be remembered, moreover, that the income taxes of the Civil War period were levied on the progressive principle, and were defended on purely economic

[1] *Cf. supra*, pp. 31–34. [2] *Cf. infra*, *Conclusion*, § 3.

grounds both by the administration and by the legislators. England has not hesitated to introduce, within the last few years, a progressive income tax, and the great extension recently given to the progressive principle in countries like Holland, Switzerland, Germany, and Australia, shows that the legislators are not blinded by mere words. As it was, Congress did not attempt any graduation of the income tax, except in so far as the $4000 exemption provided for a sort of restricted progression. The cry of socialism had no effect.

A still weaker objection was the alleged un-American and undemocratic nature of the tax. The tax was represented as peculiar to monarchic governments and the effete civilization of the old world. Senator Hill roundly asserted that the income tax was unknown in democratic communities.[1] But even if it be conceded that England is the home of hide-bound mediævalism, it is hard to include the cantons of Switzerland or the colonies of Australasia in any such category. No one acquainted with the facts need be told that the income tax has been most fully developed precisely in the most democratic communities, and that the whole tendency toward democracy, even in non-republican states, has gone hand in hand with the extension of direct taxation, and more especially of the income tax. Had this absurd objection not been so widely quoted and copied, it would not deserve mention here.

While the above objections to the income tax law are not of a very serious character, there was perhaps a deeper foundation for the charge that the measure was an expression of sectional animosity. The exemption of $4000 incomes practically meant that the Western and Southern states would gain at the expense of the industrial centres in the East and North. In many of those states individual incomes above the exemption point were comparatively few. And it is undoubtedly a fact that the enthusiasm for the tax came chiefly from those who were thus assured freedom from its burdens. But it must not be forgotten that there was much provocation. The Southern states had for years been compelled to bear the bur-

[1] *Cf.* also his denunciation of the "foreign professors," *supra*, p. 503.

dens of the tariff, the proceeds of which went in great part to the pensioners of the North. It is but natural that when an opportunity came, the tables should be turned. Again, as we have already seen, the Western states felt that they were being unjustly treated by a national revenue system, of which they felt the incubus, but the advantages of which were not so plain. To them also the income tax seemed a piece of retributive justice. So that the sectional animus, which was no doubt present to some degree, despite Wilson's statement to the contrary,[1] may be explained and even partly excused. The sectional feeling itself, however, was considerably exaggerated. For the chief explanation of the income tax is not so much geographical as economic in character. It was not so much a movement of the South and West against the North and East, as of the agricultural class against the industrial and moneyed class. It is simply an accident that the East is the home of the moneyed interest, while the West and South are the home of the landed interest. If any class antagonisms are discernible, they were primarily economic and only incidentally sectional.

The fourth and final objection that was preferred was the old but ever new contention that the income tax, however wise in theory, works badly in practice. That there is considerable truth in this is not to be denied. But it is usually forgotten that in dealing with problems of this character the real inquiry is not what is absolutely good, but what is relatively best. So far as the objection is true, it will be found to be due in great part to certain provisions of the law which, as we shall see, might have been avoided. But of the objection itself too much has been made.

We have seen above[2] that the Civil War income tax, at first, at least, worked more satisfactorily than the contemporaneous local property taxes. And our study of the situation in England and Germany has proved that an income tax does not necessarily work badly in practice. It depends entirely upon the manner in which the tax is administered.

[1] *Supra*, p. 501. [2] *Supra*, pp. 473–5.

It appears from the above review that most of the objections urged against the income tax either entirely lacked foundation or were the results of considerable exaggeration. To those acquainted with the history of the English income tax, the objections will seem quite familiar. Similar points were made year after year, and often in almost the same language; but the tax, nevertheless, commended itself to the people as a whole, and it has persisted and developed. So also it is possible that the new tax, especially in the great industrial centres, would have succeeded better than the present tax on intangible personalty. Imperfect as it undoubtedly was, the income tax might have proved to be a relative good, and to have constituted a considerable improvement over the existing system.

§ 5. *The Real Defects of the Law*

After all has been said, however, it remains true that too much could not be hoped from the practical working of the income tax. A system which rests on a method of self-assessment manifestly opens wide the door to fraud and evasion. The provisions for supplementary revision of the returns in certain cases by official assessments were far from adequate. The methods of checking the returns by utilizing the probate courts and the inventories of property after death, which are customary in Germany and even in democratic Switzerland, would not be possible as yet in America. And although much of the inquisitorial character of the former income tax had been removed by the stringent provisions in the new law calculated to insure secrecy, there can be very little doubt that the effort to secure correct returns of individual incomes would have been far from successful. Above all, there were certain grave defects in the new law, which, in contrast to the more or less imaginary or highly exaggerated objections adverted to above, are deserving of serious consideration.

In the first place, all incomes were treated alike. There was, technically speaking, no differentiation. The tendency of modern income taxation, as we know, is to charge precarious or earned incomes at a lower rate than permanent or unearned incomes. The new national tax made no such distinction. It may be said in reply that the distinction, although not in express terms, was nevertheless virtually provided for. For the very existence of the property tax in the United States implies the non-taxation of labor. If all men are taxed alike on their income, and if an additional tax is imposed on property, the income from property is naturally taxed more severely than income from labor. This was in fact one of the arguments for the introduction of the supplementary property tax in Prussia and Holland. But the force of the argument is weakened in America by the fact that under existing conditions the greater the property, or at all events the personal property, the less does it pay. It might furthermore be contended that the $4000 exemption freed labor incomes from taxation. This argument is good as far as it goes. But under modern conditions there are many labor incomes which exceed that figure, such as the incomes of the professional classes and of officials of large corporations. The injustice of assessing them at the same rate as the recipients of permanent incomes is not removed by making the $4000 exemption applicable to both. The modern theory as well as the modern practice is to pay attention not only to the income itself, but to the source from which the income is derived. The failure of the new law to observe this distinction constituted an undeniable defect.

The second objection is one to which attention has already been called in another connection, viz. the $4000 exemption. It is perfectly true that what is known as the exemption of the minimum of subsistence has become a cardinal demand in the theory of taxation. It is one thing, however, to recognize the justice of the principle in the abstract, and quite another thing to defend the particular shape given to it by the new law. He would be bold indeed who would say that a $4000 income constitutes a minimum of subsistence. When capitalized at the current rate of interest, it is equivalent to property of from $80,000 to over $100,000. This is not a minimum, but a very comfortable subsistence. Under our former income-tax laws, when the exemption was $600, the total number of taxpayers in 1866 was 460,170. With an exemption raised to $1000, the number was reduced in 1867 to 240,134. When the exemption was finally reduced to $2000, the total number of taxpayers in 1872 was only 72,949. Even making allowance for the increase of wealth and population during the last quarter of a century, it is manifest that the number of individual taxpayers under the new law would have been exceedingly small. Regarded from the standpoint of revenue, Congress therefore voluntarily abandoned a rich source.

It must indeed not be forgotten that we should look at the income tax as a branch of the whole revenue system. Much may accordingly be said in mitigation of this seeming injustice. As we pointed out above, the burden of taxation — that is, of the tariff and the local property tax — is borne primarily by the lower middle class, more especially by the farmers. Even though $4000 be not a minimum of subsistence, it nevertheless represents in large part the income of a class which is on the whole unfairly treated at present. Moreover, in England the limit of abatement has recently been raised to £700, which, in view of the different purchasing power of money, is really higher than the proposed American limit. Nevertheless, it is probably true that the limit was fixed too high; for even under the property tax people who earn and spend their own incomes are entirely exempt. In addition, a definite amount of property over and above the annual earnings is also exempt, so that the law of 1894 granted still another exemption. While, therefore, something may be said in explanation, and even in palliation, of the provision, we are forced to the conclusion that the $4000 exemption was too high. Had the law been enforced, it would in all probability have seriously interfered not only with the fiscal success of the measure, but also with the popularity of the tax among those who would surely have thought that they were being unduly burdened in order to free an entire class that was well able to contribute something.

The third objection is one to which we have already alluded, — the incorporation of an inheritance tax into the income tax law. It was discussed above rather from the point of view of the theory of income. To say, however, that the inclusion of inheritances is unscientific does not settle the question whether it was correct to tax inheritances as such. It is, after all, immaterial whether the law provides for a separate inheritance tax or whether it is made a part of a nominal income tax. The real question is: Was it wise to impose an inheritance tax at all?

To answer this query, it is necessary to consider the relations between federal and state taxes. From the very origin of our government it has been the practice to make a difference between the two and to apportion to each government certain sources of revenue upon which the other should not encroach.[1] This principle has been violated only in some periods of extraordinary emergency, or at other times in some minor legislation, as, for instance, in the case of the whiskey taxes in Delaware and Kentucky which conflict with the national internal revenue system. But the introduction of the inheritance tax, even in the modified form of a tax on successions to personal property only, is a serious break with this principle of differentiation or segregation of source. One of the chief steps in the reform of American finance has been the growth of the inheritance tax as a commonwealth tax and its development, together with the corporation tax, as a main, or in some cases almost an exclusive, source of commonwealth revenue, thus permitting the other sources of revenue to be relegated to the local divisions. The imposition of a federal inheritance tax, while perfectly justifiable in itself, would tend to check this salutary development. It

[1] We are only just waking up to the fact that the same salutary principle can and ought to be applied to the state and local governments. The whole tendency of recent tax reform in the United States, as abroad, is to observe the distinction between the sources of state and local revenue.

would supply the commonwealths with a reason for not adopting the inheritance tax as a source of state revenue, and it would render far more difficult a rounding out and logical arrangement of the entire tax system. It may be said that just as an income tax is far better as a national than as a state tax, because so many complicated questions of domicile and double taxation are avoided, so in the same way, and largely for the same reasons, a federal inheritance tax is preferable to a state inheritance tax. But even if this be true, the advantage is dearly purchased at the cost of an entire reversal in the march of progress towards a consistent and logical revenue system for the entire country. It may be possible to find some method of filling the gap created in the commonwealth tax system. But it seems a pity, to say the least, to check a promising movement when the difficulty of making any changes at all are so great as in the local tax systems of the United States at present.[1]

But all these objections to the income tax sink into insignificance when compared with the fourth defect. This is the failure to introduce the principle of stoppage at source.

In the new law we find only two attempts to apply the principle. Corporations were to deduct the tax from dividends, and the government was to deduct the tax from the salaries of public officials. Apart from this, however, the new tax substantially followed the lump-sum idea. Yet it would have been comparatively simple to divide the tax into schedules with the stoppage-at-source principle. For instance, the tax on income from real estate might have been assessed primarily on the occupant, and deducted from the rental paid to the owner. The tax on the income from mortgages might have been levied by treating the income of the mortgagee as a part of real estate, and assessing it primarily on the mortgagor, with provisions for withholding the interest by the mortgagor, and prohibiting contracts to the contrary by the mortgagee, as is the practice in some of the states to-day. The tax on salaries might have been

[1] For a further treatment of this question, *cf. infra*, *Conclusion*, § 2.

reported and withheld by the employer. The interest on corporate bonds might have been withheld by the corporation. And in many other ways the principle of stoppage at source might have been introduced.

Instead of this, the American legislators chose to follow the more primitive and discredited methods. The result would inevitably have been an immense amount of evasion and undervaluation. With no machinery for checking the returns, and with no reliable estimates for gauging the value of the self-assessments, it is unfortunately only too probable that many of the doleful predictions made by the opponents of the measure would have been verified. It may not indeed have been true of the new tax on individual incomes, as it has been said of the state tax on personal property, that it is looked on even by honorable citizens very much in the light of a Sunday-school donation; but it can safely be asserted that the tax on individual incomes would have yielded exceedingly little as compared with those two features of the law in which the stoppage-at-source idea was introduced, namely, the tax on public salaries and that on corporate dividends. It is very much to be regretted that Congress should have deliberately refrained from adopting those measures which alone would have made the tax both lucrative and comparatively efficient. The difficulties were needlessly multiplied; the lessons of experience went unheeded; and the income tax itself would have been held responsible for what is really not the use but the abuse of the principle.

A fifth and final defect in the income tax law was the carelessness with which it was drawn, and the lack of coördination between its various parts. For instance, section 28 deducts from taxable income "that portion of any salary upon which the *employer* is required by law to withhold, and does withhold the tax, and pays the same." Yet section 33 states that "every corporation which pays to an employe a salary or compensation exceeding $4,000 per annum, shall report the same to the collector or deputy collector of his district, and said *employe* [not employer] shall pay thereon," etc. Of course the explanation is that in the original draft the word "employe" read "employer"; but when the law was enacted, the amendment applied only to one of the two clauses, the other being allowed to stand, with the absurd result as stated.

Other incongruities were pointed out several months after the enactment of the law in a speech by Senator Hill on January 11, 1895, in which he objected to the regulations that had in the meantime been issued by the commissioner of internal revenue.[1] He maintained that section 27 was so unclear as to be unworkable. He pointed out further that under section 28 the taxpayers' return of income must be made before March 1, and yet that under section 32 the tax on the profits of corporations was not payable until July 1. "How then can it be possible for an individual to swear in the preceding March that the corporation has paid the income tax in the following July? The law requires of the citizens an impossibility."[2] He also called attention to the words "premiums on bonds, notes and coupons." What that meant no one knows. As Senator Hill stated, "The draftsman has imparted into these days of parity of all our dollars, the lingo of the days of imparity." Finally, he commented on several other glaring inconsistencies like that between sections 32 and 36.

While the law was still being discussed, Senator Platt, of Connecticut, said: "I have been given several severe headaches in trying to read the provisions which relate to the income tax and understand them with the amendments that have been passed."[3] The situation, however, was well summed up by Senator Hill: "I think I understand how it has come to pass that the sections of this income tax law are so conflicting and unworkable. When the measure was framed in the other House it was filled with passionate

[1] This speech was reprinted in *The Income Tax Law and Treasury Regulations relative to its Collection, together with the Speech delivered in Elucidation of the Same.* By Senator David B. Hill, New York, n. d. [1895].

[2] *Op. cit.*, p. 57.

[3] *Congressional Record*, 1894, vol. 26, p. 6577.

resentment against Eastern capital. It was so unreasonable that many of its worst features were expunged by the Senate, but when one section after another had been modified those in the Senate standing sponsors for the measure had not the time or opportunity or disposition to take up the bill as it was finally amended, and put order as well as coherence therein. When it went back to the House, emotion was concentrated on the tariff portion. Had its friends in the House examined the income-tax abortion they would probably have put harmony into its warring sections; but before that had been done the whole bill was swallowed in a lump."[1]

That there is much truth in this statement is undeniable. It is a sad reflection that a measure which, as we know, took in France more than two years to discuss in the chamber of deputies alone, should have been debated in the United States for three hours in the House, and for parts of five days in the Senate. Had the result been anything else but what Senator Hill termed an "abortion" of an income tax, it would have been surprising.

§ 6. *Conclusion*

From the above review it is evident that the act of 1894 fell considerably short of being a perfect measure. The enthusiastic hopes of its admirers were bound to fail of realization. When the time came for the enforcement of the law, comprehensive preparations were made by the commissioner of internal revenue, and offices for the collection of the tax were opened in the principal cities. But scarcely had the declarations of income begun to be made when the tax was attacked as unconstitutional, and within a short time it was declared invalid by the Supreme Court. The grounds upon which this decision rested will be examined in the following chapter. But it may be stated here that whatever be our opinions as to the correctness of the decision, it must be declared, on the whole, not entirely unfortunate that the law

[1] Hill, *op. cit.*, pp. 59–60.

was overturned. So glaring were its shortcomings of principle, and so defective were some of its administrative provisions, that it is safe to say it would have been to a very large extent unworkable, and would in all probability have produced more lawsuits than revenue. Many who believed at the time in the principle of an income tax were keenly disappointed that the experiment was now to be made with so imperfect and partial an application of the principle. Even from their point of view, therefore, the decision of the Supreme Court was not entirely to be deprecated.

Whether the decision, however, was correct in itself is a different matter. It is to this question that we shall now address ourselves.

CHAPTER V

The Constitutionality of the Income Tax

§ 1. *General Considerations*

The constitutionality of the income tax depends upon the interpretation given to certain clauses in the federal constitution. The constitutional provisions in respect to federal taxation are four in number: —

(1) "Representatives and direct taxes shall be apportioned among the several States which may be included within this Union, according to their respective numbers, which shall be determined by adding to the whole number of free persons, including those bound to service for a term of years, and excluding Indians not taxed, three-fifths of all other persons."[1]

(2) "Congress shall have power to lay and collect taxes, duties, imposts and excises, to pay the debts and provide for the common defense and general welfare of the United States; but all duties, imposts and excises shall be uniform throughout the United States."[2]

(3) "No capitation, or other direct, tax shall be laid, unless in proportion to the census or enumeration hereinbefore directed to be taken."[3]

(4) "No tax or duty shall be laid on articles exported from any state."[4]

The two questions that arise are these: First, is the income tax a direct tax within the meaning of the constitution? If so, it must be apportioned in the manner prescribed, and that method of apportionment would, as we shall see later, result

[1] Article 1, sec. 2, clause 3. This clause of the constitution had been modified by the fourteenth amendment, so that the whole number of persons in each state, excluding Indians not taxed, is to be counted.

[2] Article 1, sec. 8, clause 1.

[3] Article 1, sec. 9, clause 4.

[4] Article 1, sec. 9, clause 5.

in such crass inequality as between individuals in different parts of the country enjoying the same amount of income, as virtually to make the tax impossible. If the tax is a direct tax within the meaning of the constitution, it is safe to say that practically it cannot be levied.

Secondly, if the tax is not a direct tax, but a duty, impost, or excise, it must, according to the constitution, be uniform. Does the uniformity prescribed by the constitution preclude either a progressive or a differential rate, or an exemption of the minimum of subsistence? If so, an income tax of a modern kind would again be impossible.

Let us take up first the question of uniformity, as one that has now been definitely settled. In the income tax cases of 1895 the distinguished counsel for the taxpayers, Messrs. Choate, Seward and Guthrie, advanced a vigorous argument that even if the income tax was not a direct tax under the terms of the constitution, it was void as being wanting in uniformity, because of the $4000 exemption, and because of the discriminating treatment of corporations as compared with individuals. In fact, it may be stated that in mere bulk of argument more attention was paid by the counsel to the question of the uniformity than of the directness of the tax. The government claimed, on the contrary, that by uniformity in the constitution is meant only geographical uniformity, and presented a great array of arguments and documents to substantiate its position. As it happened, the court in its decision did not touch upon this point, save to intimate that it was equally divided, and found a discussion of the other point quite sufficient for its purposes. In a later case, however, where a similar question came up, as applied to the inheritance tax, and where one of the same counsel, Mr. Guthrie, repeated virtually the identical argument that had been made in the income-tax case, the court upheld in its entirety the contention of the government that the uniformity predicated in the constitution denotes only geographical uniformity.[1] If, therefore, the income tax is constitu-

[1] Knowlton *vs.* Moore, 178 U.S., 45.

tional in other respects, it is not rendered unconstitutional by the mere fact that it exempts a certain minimum of subsistence, or that it applies the principle either of differentiation or of progression.[1]

The question of constitutionality thus narrows itself down to the problem as to whether the income tax is a direct tax.[2] The question, moreover, is not an economic but a legal one; or rather, it is a question not as to what economists understand by the words "direct tax," but what the words mean as used in the constitution. That there may be a discrepancy between these conceptions is clearly shown by the decisions of the Supreme Court. Thus, at various times, taxes which are everywhere conceded by economic writers to be comprised within the category of direct taxes have been held not to be direct taxes in the purview of the constitution. As early as the end of the eighteenth century a federal tax on carriages was held not to be a direct tax,[3] although to-day, in local and state taxation, a tax on carriages is deemed to be quite as much a direct tax as a tax on any other form of personal property. Again, and more recently, a federal tax on the earnings of corporations was decided not to be a direct tax, although it would everywhere be conceded by economists that such a corporation tax is direct in the ordinary sense of the term. Furthermore, an inheritance tax, which economists would ordinarily class as a direct tax, has been held by the Supreme Court not to fall within that category. We must hence, at the outset, be careful to distinguish between the economic and the constitutional or administrative nomenclature. This is true not alone of the United States, but of other countries; and in addition, what is legally called a

[1] The court indeed leaves it as an open question whether there might not be such an extreme graduation of the tax as to render it repugnant to certain other general clauses of the constitution. *Cf. infra*, chap. vi, § 5.

[2] It is important to make this point clear because in the discussion of the American income tax in the French chamber in 1907–1909, several speakers claimed that the Supreme Court had declared the income tax unconstitutional on the ground that it sinned against the rules of equality and uniformity.

[3] Hylton *vs.* United States, 3 Dallas, 171.

direct tax in one country is frequently excluded from that category in another country.

The question of the constitutionality of the income tax has had an interesting history. When the tax was first suggested in 1815, it was supposed, as we have seen,[1] that it did not fall within the interpretation of the term "direct taxes," as indicated by the Supreme Court in the carriage case in 1796. When the income tax bill was discussed during the Civil War, it was proposed, as we have learned, precisely for the reason that it was not a direct tax, and that it would therefore save the country from the difficulties connected with what was called direct taxation.[2] In a series of subsequent decisions the Supreme Court announced its agreement with this view. In the case of Pacific Insurance Company *vs.* Soule,[3] it was decided that the income tax, as applied to the income of insurance companies, was not a direct tax; in the case of Veazie Bank *vs.* Fenno[4] it was held that a tax on state bank-notes was not a direct tax; in the case of Scholey *vs.* Rew[5] it was decided that a tax on successions was not a direct tax; and in the case of Springer *vs.* United States[6] it was held that the Civil War tax on income from property and professional earnings was not a direct tax. It was accepted as a part of American constitutional law, and was taught without exception by all writers on the subject, that the words "direct taxes," as used in the constitution, signified only land and poll taxes.

In 1895, however, the effort was made to have the Supreme Court put a definitive interpretation upon these words, and in two successive decisions the court now held that the income tax was a direct tax.[7] These cases were differentiated from the earlier ones by the statement that it had never definitely been decided that the income from real estate was not to be included in the phrase "direct tax." As a matter of fact, it happened that the property from which the tax-

[1] See *supra*, p. 430. [2] See *supra*, p. 435. [3] 7 Wallace, 433.
[4] 8 Wallace, 533. [5] 23 Wallace, 331. [6] 102 U.S., 586.
[7] Pollock *vs.* Farmers Loan and Trust Co., 157 U.S., 429; 158 U.S., 601.

payer's income in the Springer case was derived consisted of personalty. The court accordingly now held in the first of the Pollock cases that since a tax on land is a direct tax, a tax on the income from land must also be direct; and in the second case they held that a tax on income not only from real estate, but also from personal property, was a direct tax, and since it is impracticable to differentiate income from property from other incomes, the whole income tax, constituting an entire scheme of taxation, is invalid.

Both of these decisions were made by a divided court, the final judgment being rendered by a bare majority of five to four. This was in marked distinction to the earlier cases, in all of which the judges had been unanimous. It is but natural, therefore, that so close a decision should arouse widespread comment and much criticism. We shall hence, perhaps, be pardoned if we undertake to examine the whole question afresh from the historical and economic points of view; for the legal problem resolves itself into the question of what was actually meant by the term "direct taxes"; and that is at once an historical and an economic question.

In order to answer this question, we must consider several points. First, what is the economic meaning of the words "direct tax," and what light does the answer throw upon the constitutional interpretation? Secondly, what was the origin of the direct-tax clause, and why was it adopted? Thirdly, what did the framers of the constitution mean by the term "direct tax"? And fourthly, what has the Supreme Court really held as to the meaning of the term, and to what extent are its decisions justifiable?

§ 2. *The Economic Meaning of "Direct Tax."*

The words "direct" and "indirect" taxes are of comparatively recent origin.[1] Passing over a few stray and inconclu-

[1] A good summary is found in Professor C. J. Bullock's article, "Direct and Indirect Taxes in Economic Literature," *Political Science Quarterly*, vol. xiii (1898), pp. 442–486.

sive references in the earlier European literature, it may be said that the first scientific distinction is due to the Physiocrats. The Physiocrats, as is well known, taught that land is the only productive factor, and that therefore all taxes must ultimately be paid out of the revenue of land. Consequently, they held, a land tax is the only direct tax, and all other taxes which of necessity fall upon the land indirectly are indirect taxes. Sometimes they also conceded that a poll tax might be put in the category of direct taxes.

The first time that the phrase was used in this sense was in 1757, when the Marquis of Mirabeau wrote a book on the subject.[1] This nomenclature was quickly adopted by Quesnay and his followers, until the distinction soon became a familiar one in France. It spread to other countries, including England, where a translation of Mirabeau soon appeared. Turgot, like the other Physiocrats, declared that the only direct tax is a tax on the landowner; that all indirect taxes may be reduced to three classes: the tax on the cultivator of the soil, the tax on incomes from money or business, and the tax on commodities.[2] In another place, however, Turgot also classed a poll tax as a direct tax, thus taking issue with some of the other leaders of the Physiocratic school. But he held that any kind of a personal tax was an indirect tax.[3] "However," added Turgot, "if the capitation be so graded as to reach the faculties, industry, profits or wages,"—in other words, as we would say, if the poll tax were to develop into an income tax on the income of anything but land,—"then it must be called an indirect tax."[4] The Physiocratic distinction, it may therefore be repeated, was that the only direct tax is a tax on land, or on the revenue from land, and that even a poll tax, or a general income tax, derived in large part from other sources than land, is an indirect tax.

[1] *Cf.* Seligman, *The Shifting and Incidence of Taxation*, 3d ed., 1910, p. 132.

[2] *Op. cit.*, p. 138.

[3] See the quotations from Mercier de la Rivière and Du Pont in Seligman, *op. cit.*, pp. 133, 135.

[4] *Op. cit.*, p. 139.

With the breakdown of the Physiocratic theory of distribution, this interpretation of the phrase "direct tax" gradually disappeared. The distinction itself had, however, become acclimatized, and as the original distinction rested at bottom on the question of ultimate incidence of the tax, it was only natural that a new version of the distinction should arise, based upon a more modern theory of incidence. This was the theory that direct taxes are those where the taxpayer is the tax-bearer, — that is, where the tax is not shifted, — and that indirect taxes are those where the taxpayer is not the tax-bearer, — that is, where the tax is shifted from the one who pays it in the first instance.

In English literature we find the first inkling of this idea in Locke, who speaks of "laying a tax directly where it will at last settle."[1] But neither Locke nor Davenant, who also uses the phrase,[2] makes the distinction so clear as to approve itself to common usage. In 1771 Postlethwayt indeed speaks of people paying taxes directly or indirectly,[3] but makes no further use of the distinction. Adam Smith adopted the term from the Physiocrats, but employed it in a peculiar way. He divided taxes not into direct and indirect taxes, but into taxes on rent, on profits, and on wages. Nor does his use of the term "direct taxes" refer to the question of incidence; for he characterizes as direct, taxes upon profits and upon wages, both of which, according to him, were shifted. By indirect taxes Smith really meant taxes on expenditure, as appears from the following passage: "The state, not knowing how to tax directly and proportionably the revenue of its subjects, endeavors to tax it indirectly by taxing their expense." This was the idea that was gradually, but very slowly, followed in England until, by the beginning of the nineteenth century, indirect taxes came to mean primarily customs and excise duties. Even Ricardo, writing in 1817, did not make the classification into direct and indirect taxes. The later usage

[1] Seligman, *op. cit.*, p. 103.

[2] See the quotation in Seligman, *op. cit.*, p. 104, note 2; see also the anonymous pamphlet of 1730 in *op. cit.*, p. 105, note 3.

[3] Seligman, *op. cit.*, p. 116.

can really be traced to James Mill, who considered direct taxes to comprise those on rents, profits, and wages, and indirect taxes to be those on commodities. Since taxes on commodities are usually shifted, the distinction between direct and indirect taxes came to rest upon a consideration of their shiftability.

It was not long, however, before the weakness of this distinction became apparent, for it was recognized that many so-called direct taxes were just as susceptible of being shifted as the so-called indirect taxes; and, on the other hand, that where the commodity was consumed or utilized by the person who paid the tax in the first instance, a tax on commodities would then also become a direct tax.[1] John Stuart Mill recognized the force of this objection, and attempted to make a new distinction between direct and indirect taxes by relegating the criterion to the mind of the legislator. A direct tax, said he in substance, is a tax which the legislator intends shall be borne by the taxpayer, and an indirect tax is a tax which the legislator intends shall be borne by some one else than the taxpayer. This new distinction for a time satisfied a few writers; but here, again, further reflection showed the inadequacy of the test. For, in the first place, it may be queried whether the legislators have in many cases any intention at all except that of raising a revenue; and secondly, even if they have any idea in regard to the ultimate incidence of the tax, how are we to know what their intention was? Who, for instance, can say what was the intention of the legislators in levying a tax on railway passenger tickets? Did they intend that the tax should be borne by the railway or by the passenger? Of course an answer is impossible.

The relegation of the distinction between direct and indi-

[1] In arguing the income tax cases in 1895 Senator Edmunds gave a definition of direct taxes, based largely on this criterion, in eleven lines, which he thought would be "generally found to be universally true." Cf. 157 U.S., p. 491. It is very fortunate that legal reputation is so entirely divorced from economic knowledge; for, with all respect to Senator Edmunds, it must be said that the merest tyro in present-day economic science could easily puncture almost every successive clause in his definition.

rect taxes to the mind of the legislator, therefore, does not solve the difficulty. Accordingly, some writers reverted to the distinction drawn by the French government at an early period, when they adopted the phrase from the Physiocrats. In an ordinance issued by the Constituent Assembly in 1790, a direct tax was defined as "any tax which is levied by means of a valuation or by an assessment roll."[1] Indirect taxes, therefore, would be those that are levied not at stated periods, but under special circumstances; and not by lists, but by schedules or tariffs of charges. This distinction, however, while undoubtedly valuable for administrative purposes, is not based upon any recognized economic difference; and it fails, moreover, to draw a sharp line. For it not infrequently happens that certain taxes which would everywhere be recognized as indirect, are paid, as in France, through a kind of composition, and would thus fall within the category of direct taxes. The French distinction, accordingly, which at one time influenced quite a number of continental authors, never approved itself to English-speaking authorities.

Since all these criteria of classification are unsatisfactory, others have been advanced by various authors. Thus some writers say that direct taxes fall on possession, and indirect on consumption. Others maintain that direct taxes fall on income, and indirect on expenditure. Others again contend that direct taxes are compulsory, and indirect taxes are voluntary. In English-speaking countries we find two additional distinctions. Thus, in the United States, where the commonwealth revenue was until recently derived almost exclusively from the general property tax, recent reforms have resulted in the utilization of other taxes, like inheritance taxes, taxes on corporations, excise taxes, and the like. All these taxes indiscriminately are now occasionally called "indirect taxes," as over against the only direct tax, which would be the general property tax. But this distinction, as we readily see, is just as illegitimate as the old Physiocratic distinction. Again,

[1] "Toute imposition qui ce lève par les voies de cadastre ou des rôles de cotisation."

the income tax, as we have learned in previous chapters, may be levied either as a lump-sum tax, or as a stoppage-at-source tax. In the case of a lump-sum tax it has occasionally been said to be directly levied on the taxpayer, while in the case of the stoppage-at-source tax it is sometimes said to be levied indirectly. According to this distinction, a direct income tax would be the German type, and an indirect income tax would be the English type. An income tax would, therefore, be either direct or indirect, according to the methods of assessment; and books have been written with the title "Direct and Indirect Income Taxes." [1]

It will readily be seen, therefore, that there are almost as many classifications of direct and indirect taxes as there are authors. It is for this reason that many economists have counselled the complete abandonment of the distinction. Whatever may be the advantages of its retention for popular consumption, it is beyond all doubt that the distinction is not a scientific one. Relying on this fact, almost every country has elaborated an administrative classification of its own, so that what is called a direct tax in one state is not necessarily so called in another. The scientific, or rather, the unscientific, distinctions between direct and indirect taxes are, therefore, not available for the purpose of affording a criterion which has any claim to precision. A definition of a constitutional clause, however, which has no claim to precision is worse than useless. Any appeal to the usage, or lack of usage, among economists is consequently of no value in solving the question as to what is meant by the term in the constitution.

§ 3. *The Historical Antecedents of the Direct Tax Clause*

In order to understand the origin of the direct tax clause in the constitution,[2] it will be necessary to revert to the pe-

[1] *Cf.*, *e.g.*, the excellent work of Ingenbleek, mentioned *supra*, p. 321.

[2] All the important facts upon which this and the following section are based may be found in the *Journals of the Continental Congress*. Washington, 1904 (hereafter referred to as *Journals*); and in the five volumes of Elliot's *Debates*. The first four volumes, of which the second edition, with additions, was published

riod of the confederation. The Continental Congress had no sooner assembled, on Sept. 5, 1774, than it was confronted by the question of voting. John Adams, in his diary, called attention to the importance of this fact in a passage which contains all the rival theories that were to play such a great rôle in the future: "If we vote by Colonies, this method will be liable to great inequalities and injustice; for five small Colonies with one hundred thousand people in each, may outvote four large ones, each of which has five hundred thousand inhabitants. If we vote by the poll, some Colonies have more than their proportion of members, and others have less. If we vote by interests, it will be attended with insuperable difficulties to ascertain the true importance of each Colony. Is the weight of a Colony to be ascertained by the number of inhabitants merely, or by the amount of their trade, the quantity of their exports and imports, or by any compound ratio of both? This will lead us to such a field of controversy as will greatly perplex us."[1] It was moved that

in 1836, are entitled *The Debates in the Several State Conventions on the Adoption of the Federal Constitution, as recommended by the General Convention at Philadelphia, in 1787. Together with the Journal of the Federal Convention, Luther Martin's Letter, Yates' Minutes, Congressional Opinions, Virginia and Kentucky Resolutions of '98–'99, and other Illustrations of the Constitution. Collected and revised from Contemporary Publications.* By Jonathan Elliot. Published under the Sanction of Congress. Second edition, with considerable additions. Washington, 1836. The fifth volume is a supplementary one, containing Madison's *Notes* under the title of *Debates on the Adoption of the Federal Constitution in the Convention held at Philadelphia, in 1787; with a Diary of the Debates of the Congress of the Confederation; as reported by James Madison, a Member and Deputy from Virginia.* Revised and newly arranged by Jonathan Elliot. Washington, 1845. These will hereafter be referred to as *Elliot.* A careful study of this material has been made by Professor C. J. Bullock, in two articles entitled "The Origin, Purpose, and Effect of the Direct Tax Clause of the Federal Constitution," in the *Political Science Quarterly*, vol. xv. (1900), pp. 216, 452. A summary of the discussion will be found in Dwight W. Morrow, "The Income Tax Amendment," *Columbia Law Review*, vol. x (1910), pp. 379–415. A more scientific summary will be found in Foster and Abbott, *A Treatise on the Federal Income Tax under the Act of 1894.* Boston, 1895, pp. 14–30.

[1] *The Works of John Adams, Second President of the United States: with a Life of the Author, Notes, and Illustrations*, vol. ii, p. 366. By his grandson, Charles Francis Adams. Boston, 1850.

each colony should be allowed representation according to its respective importance. This, however, seemed impracticable, and after considerable discussion the motion was carried to give each colony one vote.[1]

The next point was the raising of the necessary supplies. Congress, as is well known, depended at first upon the issue of paper money, and the arrangement was made that a certain proportion of those bills of credit should be allotted to each colony, and redeemed by it. On July 29, 1775, it was resolved "that the proportion or quota of each colony be determined according to the number of inhabitants of all ages, including negroes and mulattoes in each colony." As there was no means of ascertaining the amount of the population, it was determined to make specific requisitions on each colony, which were to be revised later, after the numbers had been ascertained. Each colony was permitted to raise its requisitions in any way that seemed best.[2]

In 1776 a committee was appointed to prepare articles of confederation between the colonies. In the first draft of Article 11, submitted by the committee on July 12, 1776, it was provided that the expenses "shall be defrayed out of a common treasury, which shall be supplied by the several colonies in proportion to the number of inhabitants of every age, sex and quality, excepting Indians not paying taxes"; and article 17 provided that each colony should have one vote.[3] This suggestion led to a warm discussion. The southern colonies objected to having the slaves counted equally with the whites. Chase, of Maryland, moved that the blacks be not counted, on the principle that "negroes should not be considered as members of the state, more than cattle, and that they have no more interest in it." John Adams argued that since numbers were taken as an index of wealth, the slaves should be included; for "the condition of the laboring poor in most countries — that of the fishermen, particularly, of the

[1] *Journals*, vol. i, p. 25. The discussion will be found in Adams, *op cit.*, vol. ii, pp. 366–368.

[2] *Journals*, vol. ii, p. 221.

[3] *Journals*, vol. v, pp. 548, 550.

Northern States — is as abject as that of slaves." Harrison, of Virginia, suggested that two slaves be counted as one freeman, because they did not do any more work. Wilson agreed with Adams on the ground that otherwise "the southern colonies would have all the benefits of slaves, while the northern ones would bear the burden." Witherspoon, of New Jersey, desired to avoid the difficulty by suggesting the basing of the requisitions upon the value of lands and houses instead of on population, for those, he said, were the "true barometer of wealth." The same controversy occurred on the question as to the method of voting. Franklin thought that "if we vote equally we ought to pay equally." Wilson maintained that "taxation should be in proportion to wealth, and that representation should accord with the number of freemen." [1]

It was not until 1777 that the matter was settled. On October 7 the small states won their contention, and it was decided that each state should have one vote.[2] On October 14, after the rejection of a plan for basing requisitions upon the value of all property, Witherspoon's original suggestion was adopted, and it was resolved that the quota of each state should be "ascertained by the value of all land with the buildings and improvements thereon." [3] The committee report was adopted as a part of the articles of confederation, and attempts that were made during 1778, especially by Massachusetts and Connecticut, to change the basis, were unsuccessful.[4] Several years later, one of the southern members, Clark, in referring to this controversy, stated that the southern states would have agreed to numbers in preference to the value of land, if one-half of their slaves only would have been included; but he added that the eastern states would not agree to this.[5]

The articles of confederation were not signed until 1781. Both before and after that date, however, it was recognized

[1] Jefferson's *Notes of Debate on Confederation* in *Elliot*, vol. i, pp. 70–78.

[2] *Journals*, vol. ix, p. 782.

[3] *Journals*, vol. ix, p. 801; and *Elliot*, vol. i, p. 81.

[4] *Elliot*, vol. i, pp. 86–88.

[5] *Elliot*, vol. v, p. 79.

that the scheme was unworkable. Congress was not in a position to make a valuation of the real estate, and the separate commonwealths were extremely remiss in sending in their quotas. Repeated efforts were made to give Congress an independent power of raising money. Proposals were introduced in turn for a general impost on trade, for a poll tax, for a land tax, and for a house and window tax.[1] But all of these proved unsuccessful. Finally, on June 31, 1783, the subcommittee of the grand committee declared that it was expedient to appoint one commissioner for each state, who should make the valuations. But much opposition was manifested, and one member, Mr. Dyer, facetiously proposed to add the words, "and that each of the states should cheat equally."[2] Considerable discussion ensued as to whether the states should be called upon to make a return of anything else except the mere value of the lands, and it was finally resolved in grand committee, in February, 1783, that Congress should request the states to make the necessary valuation. Nothing, however, was done, and on March 7, 1783, the committee on revenue recommended an amendment providing that requisitions should be based upon population and not upon valuation of land. This led to a repetition of the old discussion. Some suggested that one-half of the slaves should be counted; others one-fourth, and still others three-fourths. Madison finally moved that five slaves should be considered as equal to three freemen, and thus the famous three-fifths provision was introduced.[3] On April 18, the report, as amended, re-

[1] *Elliot*, vol. v, pp. 34-38. For the opposition of the South to the land tax, see *ibid.*, p. 67.

[2] *Elliot*, vol. v, p. 44.

[3] Madison sums up the discussion as follows: "The arguments used by those who were for rating slaves high were that the expense of feeding and clothing them was as far below that incident to freemen as their industry and ingenuity were below those of freemen; and that the warm climate within which the states having slaves lay, compared with the rigorous climate and inferior fertility of the others, ought to have great weight in the case; and that the exports of the former states were greater than of the latter. On the other side, it was said that slaves were not put to labor as young as the children of laboring families; that, having no interest in their labor, they did as little as possible, and omitted every exertion

ceived the favorable votes of the representatives of ten states.

According to the constitution, however, it was necessary to submit the amendment to each of the separate states, and it proved to be impossible to secure universal consent. In 1786 the effort was again made to obtain the acceptance of the amendment,[1] but without success. Real estate thus remained the basis of the requisitions until the end of the confederation.[2]

The federal convention began on May 25, 1787. The Randolph, or Virginia, resolutions were introduced on May 29. The second resolution provided that "the rights of suffrage in the national legislature ought to be proportioned to the quotas of contribution, or to the number of free inhabitants, as the one or the other rule may seem best in different cases." As this would have precluded the imposition of any import or excise duties by the general government, King and Madison objected to the words "quotas of contribution," and succeeded in having them expunged.[3] The resolutions were then referred to a committee of the whole, and were reported back to the convention on June 13, in the form that the rights of suffrage in both houses of the legislature "ought not to be according to the rules established in the Articles of Confederation, but according to some equitable ratio of representation namely, in proportion to the whole number of white and other free citizens, and inhabitants of every age, sex, condition, including those bound to servitude for a term of years,

of thought requisite to facilitate and expedite it; that if the exports of the states having slaves exceeded those of the others, their imports were in proportion, slaves being employed wholly in agriculture, not in manufactures; and that, in fact, the balance of trade formerly was very much more against the Southern States than the others." —*Elliot*, vol. v, pp. 79, 80.

[1] *Elliot*, vol. v, pp. 79, 81.

[2] In the income tax case of 1895 the court fell into error in stating that the change had actually been made. Edmund Randolph tells us that only twelve of the thirteen states assented. — *Elliot*, vol. i, p. 484. King states that only eleven had agreed. — *Elliot*, vol. v, p. 290. Wilson made the same statement as late as December 3, 1787. — *Elliot*, vol. ii, p. 452.

[3] *Elliot*, vol. v, p. 134.

and three-fifths of all other persons not comprehended in the foregoing description except Indians not being taxed in each state."

In the meantime Paterson had submitted, on June 15, resolutions granting to the new federal government power to raise revenues from duties on imports, stamp duties and postal charges, in addition to requisitions upon the several states, according to population and in accordance with the three-fifths rule. This plan would give the general government far less powers than that contemplated in the sixth of Randolph's resolutions, which conferred upon the new Congress power to legislate "in all cases in which the separate states are incompetent," and which gave to the federal government the right to "call forth the force of the Union against any member of the Union, failing to fulfil its duty to the articles thereof."[1] Paterson's proposal to restrict the powers of the federal government were voted down by the convention. So vivid were the recollections of the sad experience of the confederation that the convention was not in a mood to impose any important limitations upon the power of the federal government to collect a revenue of its own.

In only three points — apart from the question of direct taxes, which, as we shall see, must be interpreted in a very different way — was there any discussion as to the propriety of restricting the fullest powers of taxation on the part of the national government. The one was the prohibition of levying a tax on exports. This prohibition was inserted at the request of Pinckney, on the ground that the tax would hit especially the tobacco, rice, and indigo produced by the southern states. After a long discussion, in which the South made it clear that a tax on exports was virtually a blow at slavery, the prohibi-

[1] This sixth resolution was reported by the committee in the following form: "That the national legislature ought to possess the legislative rights vested in Congress by the Confederation ; and moreover, to legislate, in all cases, for the general interests of the Union, and also in those in which the states are separately incompetent, or in which the harmony of the United States may be interrupted by the exercise of individual legislation." — *Elliot*, vol. i, p. 221, and vol. v, p. 375.

tion was enacted by a vote of seven against four, Massachusetts and Connecticut voting with the five southern states.[1]

The second prohibition dealt with the import duty on slaves. The original clause reported by the committee, on August 6, prohibited the imposition of an import duty on slaves, and was opposed to the right of Congress to interfere with the slave-trade. In this respect the southern states finally made a compromise, and accepted the arrangement whereby the right of the federal government to impose an import duty on slaves was granted, although limited to ten dollars a head, and whereby a prohibition of the slave-trade was permitted after the year 1808. In the third place, the principle of uniformity of taxes was adopted. This was due to a consideration of the powers of Congress over commerce. On August 24 the committee appointed to consider the slave-trade and the regulation of commerce had reported that Congress ought to be given the right to pass navigation acts by a simple majority vote. This led to a discussion in which some apprehension was expressed lest Congress might favor some ports over others. As a result of a resolution introduced to meet this difficulty, the grand committee, on August 28, reported a clause as follows: "Nor shall any regulation of commerce or revenue give preference to the ports of one state over those of another, or oblige vessels bound to or from any state to enter or pay duties in another, and all tonnage, duties, imposts and excises laid by the legislature shall be uniform throughout the United States." This was adopted on August 31 by the convention, after striking out the word "tonnage." Subsequently, when the final draft of the constitution was considered, the resolutions were divided, and the latter clause was now added to the section of the constitution which gives Congress general power to levy taxes. Accordingly, the general power of taxation conferred upon Congress is followed by the restrictive words, "But all duties, imposts and excises shall be uniform throughout the United States."[2]

[1] The discussion will be found in *Elliot*, vol. v, pp. 432–434 and 454–456.

[2] This simple statement of facts is sufficient to prove the correctness of the decision of the Supreme Court in Knowlton *vs.* Moore, and the fallacy of the con-

These three restrictions on the taxing power of Congress are, as we see, all of an entirely subordinate nature, and do not in any important way limit its revenue rights. Of an entirely different character, however, is the direct tax clause, which, as we shall learn, had its origin not in the question of the general tax powers of government, but in the dispute over the problem of representation.

§ 4. *The Introduction of the Direct Tax Clause*

The critical question in the convention was that of the basis of representation. The larger states naturally demanded a representation which should be proportioned either to wealth or to population, or to some similar criterion; the smaller states, on the other hand, held out strongly in favor of equal representation. The first contest took place over the representation in the upper House. On June 11, 1787, by a vote of six to five, the committee of the whole recommended that the representation in the upper House should be the same as in the lower. On June 29 the convention voted that the right of suffrage in the lower House ought not to be according to the rule established in the articles of confederation, but according to some equitable ratio of representation. The smaller states thereupon made a vigorous fight for equal representation in the upper House, but this was defeated by a tie vote, the delegates of Georgia being divided. The matter was then referred to a grand committee, which on July 5 reported Franklin's scheme for equal representation in the upper House, and proportionate representation in the lower House. This was called the Great Compromise. On July 6 the question of representation in the lower House was, on motion of Gouverneur Morris, referred back to a special committee of five, while the contention of the smaller states for equal representation in the upper House was accepted on July 7 as a necessary concession.

tention of Messrs. Choate and Guthrie in the income tax cases that the uniformity required by the constitution means anything else than territorial uniformity.— See *infra*, chap. v, § 9.

Then began the battle on the question of representation in the lower House. Here the centre of the controversy shifted from that between the large and the small states to that between the northern and the southern states. As Madison stated a few days later: "It seemed now to be pretty well understood, that the real difference of interest lay, not between the large and small, but between the northern and southern, states. The institution of slavery and its consequences formed the line of discrimination."[1] On July 9 the special committee of five referred to above made its report, which assigned a number of representatives in the first Congress to each state, and then provided that in future the legislature should "regulate the number of representatives upon the principles of wealth and numbers."

This led to a heated discussion as to whether the future representation should be based upon property or upon numbers, and if upon numbers, how slaves should be counted. It was soon recognized that the principle of numbers alone would not suffice, and it was here that some jealousy of the western states was manifested. Gorham, of the committee of five, claimed that a representation based upon both wealth and numbers was necessary, as otherwise the East would ultimately be outvoted by the West. Although Gouverneur Morris, as well as King and Gerry, took the same position, the majority of the members did not share these fears. On July 14 Gerry moved that the number of representatives should be so regulated that states subsequently admitted could never outvote the original members of the Union. But this was voted down by a large majority, and we hear very little more about the jealousy of the western states.

The real fight came not over West and East, but over North and South. The committee of five recommended the apportionment in the first legislature of twenty-six members to the South and thirty members to the North. This recommendation was referred back to another committee composed of one representative from each state, and the report of this

[1] *Elliot*, vol. v, p. 315.

committee on July 10 changed the numbers to thirty-five to the North as against thirty to the South. After vain efforts on the part of the southern states to increase their numbers, the recommendation was adopted. Then arose the question of future representation. According to the report of the committee of five, the matter was to be left in the hands of the legislature. But as a majority of the legislature had now been decided to consist of northern members, the North would have the whip-hand. Randolph accordingly proposed an amendment whereby the legislature should "cause a proper census and estimate to be taken once in every term of —— years." This, however, failed of adoption. On July 11 Williamson, of North Carolina, introduced a substitute motion providing that a periodical census should be taken of the free inhabitants of each state, "and three-fifths of the inhabitants of other description," and that representation should be apportioned accordingly. The three-fifths clause was thus again brought to the attention of the convention, and was attacked by the radicals, both northern and southern. For the extreme southerners now wanted to have all the slaves counted equally with the whites, and the extreme northerners were equally insistent upon having none of the slaves counted. Through a combination of these radicals, both North and South, Williamson's resolution was voted down, and the convention seemed to have arrived at a dead-lock.

It was at this juncture that, on the morning of July 12, when the whole fate of the convention appeared to hang upon the decision as to the representation of slaves, Gouverneur Morris introduced his famous motion to add to the clause empowering the legislature to vary the representation according to the principles of wealth and numbers of inhabitants, a proviso "that taxation shall be in proportion to representation." This was an entirely new suggestion, although the proposition in its reverse form — that representation should be proportioned to taxation — had occasionally been advanced, both in the Continental Congress and in the convention.[1]

[1] See the quotations in Bullock, *op. cit.*, p. 233, note 3.

The aim of Morris was to overcome the objections of the extremists on both sides. He hoped that the southerners might be induced to accept the three-fifths proposition, rather than to insist upon full representation, because it would then proportionately diminish their quota of contribution; and that, on the other hand, it would appeal to the extremists of the North, on the ground that if the three-fifths clause passed, the South would have to pay something, at all events, for their slaves. As Madison puts it: "The object was to lessen the eagerness on one side for, and the opposition on the other side to, the share of representation claimed by the Southern states on account of the negroes."[1] Morris himself, who was a strong nationalist, and not disposed to restrict the powers of the new government in any way, stated subsequently that he had "only meant the clause as a bridge to assist us over a certain gulf."[2]

It was, however, at once pointed out by Mason, who admitted the justice of the principle, that the clause was badly worded, in that it might drive Congress to resort to the discredited plan of requisitions. Morris, who thereupon conceded that his motion was open to these objections, "supposed they would be removed by restraining the rule to direct taxation,"[3] and added: "With regard to indirect taxes on exports and imports, and on consumption, the rule would be inapplicable." Wilson as well as Pinckney approved of the suggestion, and Morris, having varied his motion by inserting the word "direct," the convention unanimously accepted it so that it read "provided always that direct taxation ought to be proportioned to representation."[4]

[1] *Elliot*, vol. v, p. 363.
[2] *Ibid.*

[3] Later on, Morris was by no means sure that the objections would be so removed. On May 8, 1789, after the adoption of the constitution, he stated: "There is a further inconvenience, which arises from the necessity of apportioning direct taxes in a manner fixed by the Constitution. This, which seems to force Congress into requisitions, leads thereby to perpetuate that ineffective system." — Sparks, *Life of Gouverneur Morris*, vol. iii, p. 471. *Cf.* Morrow, *op. cit.*, p. 393.

[4] *Elliot*, vol. v, p. 304.

From this recital of the facts two points are clear. First, the introduction of the words "direct taxes" had no reference to any dispute over tax matters, but was designed solely to solve the difficulty connected with representation; and secondly, direct taxation, according to Morris' motion, was to be proportioned, not to population alone, but to wealth as well as population.

After the adoption of the amendment, the southerners desired to have the matter more precisely determined. Pinckney stated that he wanted the rule of wealth to be ascertained, and not left to the pleasure of the legislature. Randolph lamented that such a species of property as slaves existed; but inasmuch as it did exist, the holders of it would require this security. He thereupon made a motion which, after a slight amendment by Wilson, was adopted by the convention. This made Morris' clause read as follows: "Provided always that the representation ought to be proportioned according to direct taxation; and in order to ascertain the alterations in the direct taxation which may be required from time to time by the changes in the relative circumstances of the states, *Resolved* that a census be taken within two years from the first meeting of the legislature of the United States, and once within the term of every —— years afterwards, of all the inhabitants of the United States, in the manner and according to the ratio recommended by Congress in their resolution of the 18th of April, 1783, and that the legislature of the United States shall apportion the direct taxation accordingly."[1] The ratio referred to, it will be remembered, was that of counting a negro as three-fifths of a freeman.

On the next day final action was taken. The original proposition, it must not be forgotten, had been to regulate representation according to wealth and numbers. In the meantime that convention had just adopted Randolph's resolution that representation should be proportioned to direct taxation, and that direct taxation should be proportioned to

[1] *Elliot*, vol. v, p. 304.

population. Randolph therefore now moved that the original motion be amended by striking out the word "wealth." Gouverneur Morris objected strongly to the amendment, but it was adopted by an almost unanimous vote. Thus the matter was settled that representation should be proportioned to direct taxation, and that direct taxation should be proportioned to population, counting a negro as three-fifths of a freeman.[1] On July 16 the report of the grand committee, which contained this amendment, was adopted by a bare majority, and thus the great compromise was effected. But Gouverneur Morris was now not satisfied with his own proposition. On July 17 he moved to reconsider the whole compromise resolution, and on July 24 he expressed the hope that at least the committee "would strike out the whole of the clause apportioning direct taxation to representation. He had only meant it as a bridge to assist us over a certain gulf; having passed the gulf, the bridge may be removed. He thought the principle laid down with so much strictness liable to strong objections."[2] But the convention having once settled this most delicate matter, refused to take it up again.

The principle having been settled, the matter was referred to the committee of appeal which, on August 6, reported back its first draft of a constitution. This draft gave Congress power "to lay and collect taxes, duties, imposts and excises." The committee reported in favor of separating the resolutions relating to representation and direct taxes. On August 8, when the question of the census came before the convention, Morris made a final effort against the clause for which he himself had been responsible. He delivered a savage attack upon slavery, and concluded that "he would sooner submit himself to a tax for paying for all the negroes in the United States than saddle posterity with such a Constitution."[3] But Sherman contended that the compromise, as adopted, was unexceptionable, for "it was the farmers of the southern states who were, in fact, to be represented, according to the tax paid by them, and the negroes are only included in the

[1] *Elliot*, vol. v, p. 309. [2] *Ibid.*, p. 363. [3] *Ibid.*, pp. 392–393.

estimate of the taxes." The arrangement was changed by the committee on style, which reported on September 12. The committee again brought together the two clauses as to representation and taxation, and used the words "direct taxes" instead of "direct taxation." Article I, section 2, was make to read that "representatives and direct taxes shall be apportioned among the several states which may be included within this Union according to their respective numbers, which shall be determined by adding to the whole number of free persons, including those bound to servitude for a term of years, and excluding Indians not taxed, three-fifths of all other persons." When the report came up for discussion on September 13, Dickinson and Wilson moved to strike out the words "direct taxes" as being improperly placed. But after a defence of the point by Gouverneur Morris, the report was adopted by a large majority.

The term "direct tax" is used in one other clause of the constitution, where it is put in connection with the capitation tax. On August 6 the committee on detail reported a resolution that "no capitation tax shall be laid unless in proportion to the census hereinbefore provided to be taken." This originated in the contest over the slave-trade and the possible import duty on slaves. The southerners evidently feared that Congress, with its northern majority, might decide to make an arbitrary computation of population, and thus saddle the south with an undue share of taxation through a tax on slaves. It was in order to prevent this that the capitation clause was introduced. It awakened no objection at all, since it was practically a confirmation of the compromise that had been adopted, and it came before the convention for final vote on September 14. In the meantime various suggestions had been made looking toward the securing from the delinquent states payment of the old requisitions for which they had been liable under the Confederacy. Reade, of Delaware, in order to obviate this, or to use his own words, in order to prevent the attempt "to saddle the states with the readjustment by this rule of past requisitions of Congress," moved that the words "or other direct tax" be inserted after the word "capitation." He maintained "that his amendment, by giving another cast to the meaning, would take away the pretext," and his motion was adopted without any discussion.[1]

§ 5. *The Purpose of the Direct Tax Clause*

From the above review of the origin of the direct-tax clause it is clear that it was due simply and solely to the attempt to solve the difficulty connected with the maintenance of slavery. But for that struggle Gouverneur Morris would never have introduced the term "direct tax," and there would have been no reason to introduce it anywhere else.

It is true that the counsel in the income tax cases of 1895 advanced a different doctrine. Mr. Choate, in his argument, stated that the clause was the result of a compromise designed to protect, on the one hand, the states in general against the federal government, and on the other hand, the richer states against the poorer. He tells us that "there was a surrender by the States to Congress of the exclusive power to levy taxes on imports. . . . Then, too, the States surrendered forever afterwards the right that they had had of taxing and regulating commerce between the States. . . . Then came the grant to Congress of power to lay indirect taxes, as we now call them." All these were an "essential part of the compromise" whereby the power of the federal government to levy taxes was restricted.[2] Moreover, the rule of apportionment results "in a law of protection for the benefit of the holders of such property as was contemplated as the subject of direct taxes. . . . There had occurred an accumulation of wealth *per capita* in certain states to a greater extent than in other states. This disproportion existed then, as it exists now, only different in degree. It was just this disproportion that the provi-

[1] *Elliott*, vol. v, p. 545.

[2] *Closing Argument by Mr. Choate in the Pollock Case*, 1895, p. 34. The argument is summarized in 157 U.S., p. 543.

sion as to apportionment was intended to protect. . . . It was then understood perfectly well to be a rule of inequality, on the strength of which was bought the assent of the States then owning such property." Mr. Choate closed by stating: "The question to-day is whether that bargain shall be repudiated. Your Honors know what the seaboard States gave up for it. . . . Now the question is whether the other States, in whose behalf and for whose benefit that was given up, shall take back the price for which it was given." [1] And to clinch his argument Mr. Choate added that the introduction of the term "direct taxes" in the clause prescribing that no capitation or other direct tax should be levied according to the census was due to the same cause. The framers of the constitution "were fresh from the struggle about representation going hand in hand with taxation, and it was for the protection of this property, this accumulated property in the States, as against the inroad of the vote of mere numbers, that they stipulated and insisted upon the guaranty of apportionment." [2]

This argument approved itself to the court. Chief Justice Fuller, in the opinion, stated: "Thus was accomplished one of the great compromises of the Constitution, resting on the doctrine that the right of representation ought to be conceded to every community on which a tax is to be imposed, but crystallizing it in such form as to allay jealousies in respect to the future balance of power.[3]" In the separate opinion of Justice Field the same view is contained: "The States bordering on the ocean were unwilling to give up their rights to lay duties upon imports, which were their chief source of revenue. The other States, on the other hand, were unwilling to make any agreement for the levying of taxes directly upon real and personal property, the smaller States fearing that they would be overborne by unequal burdens forced upon them by the action of the larger States. . . . But hap-

[1] *Closing Argument by Mr. Choate in the Pollock Case*, 1895, p. 35.
[2] *Ibid.*, p. 36.
[3] Pollock vs. the Farmers Loan & Trust Company, 157 U.S., p. 563.

pily a compromise was effected by an agreement that direct taxes should be laid by Congress by apportioning them. . . . This compromise protected every State from being controlled in its taxation by the superior numbers of one or more other States."[1] In the second Pollock case the court restated its position as follows: "The reasons for the clauses of the Constitution in respect of direct taxation are not far to seek. The States, respectively, possessed plenary powers of taxation. . . . They gave up the great sources of revenue derived from commerce; . . . they retained the power of direct taxation, and to that they look as their chief resource; but even in respect of that they granted the concurrent power. . . . Therefore, they did not grant the power of direct taxation without regard to their own condition and resources as States. . . . If, in the changes of wealth and population in particular States, apportionment produced inequality, it was an inequality stipulated for, just as the equal representation of the States, however small, in the Senate, was stipulated for."[2]

In the light of actual history, as it has been explained above, all these statements must be characterized as essentially erroneous. It is true that when the constitution was submitted to the different states for ratification, some jealousy of the powers granted to Congress was in a few instances manifested. But there was no difficulty in overcoming this objection. In the convention itself, however, which framed the constitution, there was no trace of any such conflict in connection with the taxation clause, just as we have seen that there was no effort and no disposition on the part of the convention to restrict the general tax powers of the government. The states did not even question the advisability of abandoning their rights to impose import duties, and every one agreed that the old system of requisitions must be done away with. There was no jealousy of large states on the part of small states that manifested itself at all in the discussion over the tax provisions; the sporadic allusions to the future development of the western states were found, as we have seen, only

[1] 157 U.S., p. 587. [2] 158 U.S., 620–621.

in the discussion of the original clauses affecting representation, and they played no rôle at all in the tax discussion. The introduction of the words "direct tax" in the phrase "no capitation or other direct tax" had, as we know,[1] nothing whatever to do with the compromise of which Mr. Choate and the court speak. Far from being a question of the small states against the large states, or of the seaboard states against the western states, or of the states in general against the federal government, the compromise was due solely to an effort of the slave states to protect the three-fifths rule.

That the Supreme Court of the United States was misled by the counsel into an historical interpretation which is beyond all doubt erroneous, is deplorable; but that in view of the material that has since come to light, and of the later investigations on the subject that have been made, this interpretation should still be advanced, is still more deplorable. In a memorandum submitted to the legislature of the state of New York, in opposition to the proposed sixteenth constitutional amendment, signed by six eminent lawyers, two of whom argued this very point in the income tax cases, the same statement is repeated as almost a self-evident fact. "As all students know, the provisions of the constitution as to representation and apportionment of taxes were the result of a compromise after a fierce contest. If the smaller states were to be given a representation in the Senate equal to the populous states, it was understood that the smaller states must agree to observe some rule which would protect the other states against the possible abuse of the taxing power. The question now is whether that compromise shall be abandoned and its protection thrown away without any consideration or any check against possible abuse."[2] It is to be hoped

[1] *Supra*, p. 554.

[2] *Memorandum submitted to the Legislature of the State of New York in Opposition to the Proposed Sixteenth Article of Amendment to the Constitution of the United States.* By Joseph H. Choate, William D. Guthrie, Victor Morawetz, Austen G. Fox, John G. Milburn, F. L. Stetson (who concurred only in part). The same statement is repeated in a still more indefensible form in Mr. Guthrie's speech, entitled "No Taxation without Representation," in *The Journal of*

that no serious student of history or economics will ever again be led astray by what is a no doubt unconscious, but none the less lamentable, misapprehension of historical fact. The direct-tax clause was inserted into the constitution simply and solely as a concession to slavery, and with the disappearance of slavery and the adoption of the fourteenth amendment the very reason of its existence passed away.

§ 6. *The Constitutional Meaning of "Direct Tax"*

Now that the origin and the purpose of the term "direct tax" have been elucidated, it remains to ascertain what the founders of the constitution really meant by the term. In what sense did they use the words? Did it have any definite meaning, and if so, what?

It may be pointed out in the first place that the words in the constitution, "taxes, duties, imposts and excises," were used without any precise signification. The nomenclature of taxation — even the legal nomenclature — has changed from century to century and from country to country. As has been pointed out elsewhere, there were no less than seven different stages in the etymological growth of the terms used to designate taxes. Benevolence, aids, subsidies, contributions, duties, imposts, and rates were all at one time or another generic terms for tax.[1] In the England of the eighteenth century, while imposts and excises had come to possess a more restricted meaning, the word "duty" was a generic term applied to every source of revenue except the land tax.

Accountancy, vol. 10 (1910), pp. 13–14. He there says: "The great question was, shall we, the strong states that have borne the brunt of the Revolution, whose treasury has been poured out that the Union might live, shall we place our fortunes and our property at the mercy of perhaps an irresponsible majority. . . . The compromise was . . . that the men who were voting to impose direct taxes should be compelled to impose these taxes proportionately upon their constituents." As a matter of fact, Virginia did not vote with, but against, the other large states like New York, Massachusetts, and Pennsylvania in the contests that preceded the compromise.

[1] Seligman, *Essays in Taxation*. 5th ed., 1905, pp. 6, 7.

Thus we find the "house duty" and the "window duty," as well as the "tea duty" and the "tobacco duty." When the income tax was introduced, it was also officially designated as the "duty on profits," or the "income duty." So when the inheritance tax was introduced, it was called the "succession duty," or the "death duties." This is still the legal usage of England. "Duties" still comprise most of the general taxes, including many an impost that the average American would call a direct tax. According to the present American usage, "duties" are restricted to customs duties; but in the Civil War the income tax was officially called the "income duty," and in the eighteenth century the term had a still wider meaning. It is used in the debates on the constitution to include not alone stamp duties, but also other internal duties or taxes on goods and merchandise which elsewhere would often be called excises.[1] In a Pennsylvania law of 1783 the carriage tax is officially called a "duty,"[2] and in the federal internal revenue system, at the end of the eighteenth century as well as during the War of 1812, many of the internal taxes were called duties. A careful research would no doubt disclose the fact that its wider use in the English sense as equivalent to taxes was by no means uncommon.

The word "impost" was ordinarily used in the sense of "import duties"; but it is frequently employed in the debates in the convention in the sense of taxes on trade;[3] although the still wider use of imposts, as equivalent to taxes in general, seems to have disappeared. Again, while "excise" is used in the eighteenth century in the sense of ordinary taxes on manufactures, there was a great diversity of custom, imposts on particular classes of property being called taxes in some states and excises in others.[4] Finally, in the various

[1] See the passage in *Elliot*, vol. i, p. 368; vol. ii, p. 333.

[2] Pennsylvania, act of July 10, 1783, chap. xii.

[3] *Cf.*, for instance, *Elliot*, vol. v, pp. 38–42 and p. 299. In one place we find even the phrase "taxes on imposts"; *ibid.*, p. 305.

[4] See *infra*, p. 567.

state constitutions that were adopted in the eighteenth century we find a rather indiscriminate collection of terms, such as power to levy "assessments, rates and taxes," "subsidies, charges, taxes, imposts and duties," and "taxes, customs or contributions."[1]

We see, then, that there was no settled usage anywhere on the American continent; that the most generic term, next to tax, was duty; and that there was no clear line of demarcation between a tax and a duty.

With this general uncertainty as to the use of the older terms, it need not surprise us to find that there was no agreement at all as to the use or meaning of the newer term, "direct tax." As a matter of fact, the term was scarcely employed at all before 1787. We have found only one instance of its use in the United States before that date, namely, in a Massachusetts act of 1786. In the preamble of this law, which imposed an excise duty upon carriages,[2] it is stated: "Whereas every well-wisher to the peace and happiness of this commonwealth will most cheerfully acquiesce in all these measures adopted by the government which will tend to establish their public faith and honour; and ease the people as much as possible of direct taxation, and to encourage the agriculture, manufactures and population of the country." But no clew is given as to what is meant by the term "direct taxation," except that it there stands in opposition to an excise upon carriages, — an interesting fact in view of the consideration that at the present time in Massachusetts a tax on carriages is considered a part of the general property tax.

Inasmuch as this is the only example that has been discovered in legislation or literature of the use of the words "direct tax," what shall we say of the repeated contention of the distinguished counsel in the income-tax case that "at the date of the Constitution, the words 'direct taxes' and 'indirect taxes' were household words. They were borrowed

[1] See, *e.g.*, the constitutions of Massachusetts, New Hampshire, and Pennsylvania.

[2] Act of November 15, 1786.

from the literature and practice of Great Britain and the Continent of Europe. They are to be found in the literature of the period. They had been used in Europe as meaning taxes which fell directly upon property and its owner, like a land tax or a tax on incomes. . . . The inquiry now is, whether, when adopted in this country, they carried with them the signification which universally obtained elsewhere."[1] As a matter of fact, it would be difficult for almost any one to pack into such small compass an equal number of misstatements. On the contrary, the distinction had scarcely begun to be made. The only literature on the subject consisted of the writings of Adam Smith and Turgot. Adam Smith, as we remember, had made no clear-cut distinction; all that he intimated was that indirect taxes were taxes on expenditure, and even here, as we know, he was not at all in agreement with the later writers, who distinguish between direct and indirect taxes on expenditure. The other alleged authority is Turgot. Turgot had given the usual Physiocratic explanation in a small memoir that was written in 1764; but it was very unlikely that this was known in the United States, as it had never even been published in France, much less translated in the United States.[2] More-

[1] *Argument of Mr. Seward in the Income Tax Cases.* 1895, pp. 18, 19. This argument is summarized in 157 U.S., 452. See esp. p. 455. The statements are repeated by the other counsel and accepted by the court.

[2] Mr. Seward, in his argument in the Income Tax cases, stated that Turgot published in 1764 a work on taxation, and that in the *American Museum* for January, 1787, "this work is quoted, as showing that it was then in circulation in America."—Seward's *Argument, op. cit.*, p. 17. Almost every statement in this passage is erroneous. In the first place, the production of Turgot in question was not a "work," but a simple memorandum; in the second place, it had never been published in France. In the third place, the reference in the *American Museum* is not to this production of Turgot, nor to any matter connected in the remotest degree with direct or indirect taxation. It is a general quotation referring to his political ideas, in which, indeed, the word "taxes" happens to be mentioned. But that is the nearest approach to Mr. Seward's amazing misstatement. See the *American Museum*, January, 1787, p. 16. As a matter of fact, the only economic writings of Turgot which were published during his lifetime, or for that matter during the eighteenth century, were two articles entitled *Foires et Marchés* and *Fondations*, in the *Encyclopédie* in 1756; the translation of

over, the classification given by Turgot does not at all carry out the contentions of the counsel in the income-tax cases. Turgot, we remember, spoke of a direct tax as being one *sur les fonds.* The counsel in the income-tax case innocently translated this as "a tax on the funds," thus hoping to bolster up their contention that according to Turgot a tax on personal property was also a direct tax. Of course *fonds* or *bien fonds* means lands, not funds, and Turgot's contention was that the only direct tax was a tax on lands — just the opposite of what the counsel thought it meant. If the counsel, however, had gone a little farther and stated the fuller and subsequent classification made by Turgot, they would have found small comfort in their conclusion that Turgot's idea of direct tax included an income tax. The only country in the

Tucker's *Important Questions on Trade* in 1755; and the *Reflections on the Formation of the Distribution of Wealth*, which appeared in the *Éphémérides du Çitoyen* in 1767. In none of these works is there the slightest reference to taxation. All of Turgot's writings on taxation consisted of official memoirs preserved in manuscript in the French archives, until they were published by Du Pont de Nemours in 1809.

This glaring misstatement of Mr. Seward has been widely copied. So Mr. Morrow says: "They [the counsel] went to the extent of showing that a work on taxation written by Turgot, with a certain definition of 'direct taxes' was in America in 1787 and therefore might have been consulted by the framers of the Constitution." — Dwight W. Morrow, "The Income Tax Amendment," in *Columbia Law Review*, vol. x (1910), p. 407.

It was perhaps Mr. Seward who is responsible for the passage in Mr. Guthrie's argument in the income tax cases: "Were the members of the Convention likely to use terms they did not understand: Had they never seen the term 'direct tax' before; and if so, where? In the books that were in every man's hand. Many had studied Turgot in the original or in translations of particular passages and they knew his clear definition of 'les impôts directs.'" — *Opening Argument by W. D. Guthrie, on behalf of Appellants in the Income Tax Cases.* 1895, p. 7. Equally unfounded is Mr. Guthrie's statement that "Turgot to-day is still the great work put in the hands of French students of the Science of Finance and Government." We should be glad to learn to which "work of Turgot" Mr. Guthrie refers.

All this would not have been so deplorable had it not been blindly accepted by the court. Chief Justice Fuller calls special attention to the fact that "Turgot had published in 1764 his work on taxation, and in 1766 his essay on 'The Formation and Distribution of Wealth.'" Unfortunately, the first statement is incorrect; and the second utterly devoid of the significance attached to it.

world which at that time possessed a general income tax was France, and it so happened that the income tax was known under the name of "capitation."[1] In this other and fuller passage, written several years later, Turgot distinctly states that if the capitation comprises what are called all forms of faculty, industry, commerce, wages or profits, the tax is an indirect tax.[2] According to Turgot, an income tax is an indirect tax.

So far, therefore, as any of the framers of the constitution may have been acquainted with the views of Turgot and accepted them, their understanding of a direct tax must have been entirely different from that of Adam Smith. We are forced to confess that for the counsel to jumble together such conflicting views and for the court to follow them, does not reflect the greatest credit on their economic acumen, their historical learning or their knowledge of finance.

If, then, we proceed to discuss the sense in which the framers of the constitution use the term, we must abstract entirely from Adam Smith and Turgot, with their completely contradictory opinions, and seek to ascertain what the members themselves thought.

§ 7. *The Use of the Term in the Constitutional Convention*

The words "direct taxes" and "indirect taxes" were used only a very few times in the convention. In some cases there is no doubt that the phrase refers to the mode of assessment. The old plan of supporting the general government was by a system of requisitions on the states. The new method was to be that of direct action of the federal government upon the individual. Direct taxes would therefore simply mean taxes imposed not by the states, but by the federal government

[1] See *supra*, p. 50.

[2] See the passage quoted above, p. 536. It may be added that these passages from Turgot were supplied by the present writer to the opposing counsel in the income tax cases, but the second passage was handed in by the government counsel too late to produce any effect in the course of the argument.

upon the individual. Thus, for instance, on July 13, 1787, Gerry moved that "all moneys to be raised for supplying the public treasury by direct taxation shall be assessed on the inhabitants of the several states according to the number of their representatives." When this motion was lost, Gerry stated that he had ascertained that the failure "had proceeded from an objection, with some, to the proposed assessment of direct taxes on the inhabitants of the states." He thereupon varied his motion, so "as to authorize the assessment on the states, which leaves the mode to the legislature"; and he accordingly put his motion in the form that "all moneys for supplying the public treasury by direct taxation shall be raised from the several states, according to the number of their representatives." The motion, so amended, was accepted.[1] Again, on August 21, when the matter was taken up by Martin, he stated that "direct taxation should not be used but in cases of absolute necessity; and then the states will be the best judges of the mode."[2] In the debates in the separate states also we find this use of the term, as, for instance, by Dana in Massachusetts, and by Randolph in Virginia.[3] It is, however, a well established fact that in some of the states, like New York, where state taxes were apportioned to the counties instead of being levied upon the individuals as such, this method was termed "indirect taxation," and the words "direct taxes" were limited to taxes directly levied upon the individual. So that the term denoted in some states just the opposite of what it denoted in others.

In a number of other cases, however, the term "direct taxes" was used in the convention, irrespective of the question whether the tax was to be levied on the state or other political body, or on the individual. Thus the term "direct tax" was employed in some cases as opposed to "taxes in trade,"[4] and in other cases as opposed to "exports, imports and excises";[5] and both there, as well as in the case

[1] *Elliot*, vol. v, pp. 306–307.

[2] *Ibid.*, p. 453.

[3] *Ibid.*, vol. ii, p. 43; vol. iii, p. 122.

[4] *Ibid.*, vol. v, p. 320.

[5] *Ibid.*, p. 393.

of the phrase "no capitation or direct tax," the term evidently refers to a particular category of taxes.

When we consider the use of the term "direct tax" in the different legislatures that ratified the constitution, we find no less than five different uses of the term. In the first place, as just explained, it is sometimes used to signify a tax on the states. Secondly, it is employed to mean only a land tax.[1] Thirdly, it is used to signify a land and a poll tax.[2] Fourthly, it is employed to mean a poll tax, together with a general assessment on property.[3] In the fifth place, it is used in the sense of a tax on land, together with the specific articles of personal property. Thus Livingston, in New York, said, "They must have recourse to direct taxes, that is, taxes on land and specific duties";[4] and Jay, of New York, stated that "It ought to be considered that direct taxes are of two kinds — general and specific" — and he instanced, as an example of the latter, a tax on coaches.[5] So also Marshall, in Virginia, said: "The objects of direct taxes are well understood; they are but few; what are they? Lands, slaves, stock of all kinds, and a few other articles of domestic property."[6]

The only conclusion from the above survey is that almost every speaker used the term "direct taxes" in a different way. It is particularly to be noticed that the very tax which was afterwards to form the subject of the first decision of the

[1] *Cf.* the speech of Dana in the Massachusetts convention, *Elliot*, vol. ii, p. 42.

[2] *Cf.* the speech of Mason in the Virginia convention, *Elliot*, vol. iii, p. 264.

[3] *Cf.* the speech of Williams in the Massachusetts convention, *Elliot*, vol. iii, p. 330. "Under this clause may be imposed a poll tax, a tax on houses, and buildings, on windows and fireplaces, on cattle, and on all kinds of personal property." See also the speech of Spencer, in the North Carolina convention. — *Elliot*, vol. iv, p. 76: "How are direct taxes to be laid? By a poll tax, assessment on land or other property?" See also Monroe in Virginia, who says: "What are the objects of direct taxation? Will the taxes be laid on land? . . . Will the taxes be laid on polls only? . . . How then will it be laid? On all property?" — *Elliot*, vol. iii, pp. 215–216.

[4] *Elliot*, vol. ii, p. 341.

[5] *Ibid.*, p. 381. *Cf.* the statement of Smith, *ibid.*, p. 393.

[6] *Ibid.*, vol. iii, p. 229.

Supreme Court, namely, the carriage tax, which existed both in Virginia and in Massachusetts, was in 1787 called a direct tax in Virginia, where it was comprised among the other articles of property mentioned by Marshall, and yet was at the same time, in Massachusetts, as we have seen above, officially called an excise, and especially distinguished from the direct taxes.

Nor is any further light thrown upon the subject by the use of the term "indirect taxes." In the debates in the convention we find in one place the term "indirect taxes" used by King simply in opposition to the old land tax of the confederation.[1] In another place Gouveneur Morris opposes direct taxation to indirect taxes on exports and imports, and on consumption.[2] This was, however, not an exclusive definition, because it allows no room for such taxes as stamp duties, which are certainly not taxes on exports or imports or on consumption, and which at the same time presumably would not have been called direct taxes by Morris. Finally, in the Connecticut convention, Elsworth used "indirect taxation" in the sense of taxes on consumption, but he did not indicate what constituted direct taxation.[3]

[1] *Elliot*, vol. v, p. 312.

[2] *Ibid.*, p. 302.

[3] "Direct taxation can go but little way towards raising a revenue. To raise money in this way, people must be provident; they must constantly be laying up money to answer the demands of the collector. But you cannot make people thus provident. If you would do anything to the purpose, you must come in when they are spending, and take a part with them. This does not take away the tools of a man's business, or the necessary utensils of his family; it only comes in when he is taking his pleasure, and feels generous. . . . I will instance two facts which show how easily and insensibly a revenue is raised by indirect taxation. . . . In England and Holland prodigious taxes . . . are levied chiefly upon articles of consumption." — *Elliot*, vol. ii, pp. 191–192.

In a brief submitted in the income tax cases of 1895 this quotation from Elsworth is followed by the interpolation of counsel, "This was the income tax pure and simple, and brought within the phrase 'direct taxation.'" — *Extracts from the Evidence proving the Historic Facts . . . bearing upon the question whether the words 'Direct Tax' . . . embrace a Tax upon Incomes, etc.*, p. 42. As the income tax was not in existence at this time in Connecticut or anywhere else, the pertinency of the interpolation is not obvious. But perhaps it served its purpose in impressing the court.

The above are the only references in the debates to the terms "direct taxes" or "indirect taxes." It is clear that, far from having any settled meaning, the terms were employed by each speaker in a different sense. It must therefore not surprise us to learn that when the clause in question came before the convention for final action, on August 20, and when Mr. King asked, "what was the precise meaning of *direct* taxation," we are told, in the significant words of Madison, that "no one answered."[1] No one answered, because no one could answer. Yet the phrase was allowed to remain because it had served the invaluable purpose of effecting the great compromise.

The same uncertainty continued for another decade. A few years later the Hylton case arose and was argued by Hamilton and decided by judges, all of whom had taken a distinguished part in the deliberations of either the constitutional or state ratifying conventions. Hamilton tells us, in his brief: "What is the distinction between direct and indirect taxes? It is a matter of regret that terms so uncertain and vague in so important a point are to be found in the Constitution. We shall seek in vain any antecedent, settled legal meaning to the respective terms — there is none." Of the judges who decided the case, only one was positive, another simply "thought," while a third was doubtful as to the general meaning of the term. Justice Chase said, "I am inclined to think, but of this I do not give a judicial opinion, that the direct taxes contemplated by the Constitution are only two, to wit: a capitation or poll tax, simply, without regard to property, profession or any other circumstance, and a tax on land." Justice Iredell said, "Perhaps a direct tax in the sense of the Constitution can mean nothing but a tax on something inseparably annexed to the soil." While Justice Paterson said, "I never entertained a doubt that the principal, I will not say the only, objects that the framers of the Constitution contemplated as falling within the rule of apportionment were a capitation tax and a tax on land." Yet at the same time

[1] *Elliott*, vol. v, p. 451.

Albert Gallatin, who confessed that the words had no "general acceptation or technical meaning," and who thought it very important that a fixed interpretation be given to the terms "for the sake of preventing future controversies, which may be not more fatal to the revenue than to the tranquillity of the union," suggested that Adam Smith's distinction be observed, and that accordingly "the most generally received opinion is that by direct taxes in the Constitution, those are meant which are raised on the capital or revenue of the people; by indirect such as are raised on their expense."[1] Parenthetically remarked, it may be stated that Gallatin, like Morris quoted above, would have found great difficulty in deciding whether, under this definition, stamp duties were direct or indirect.

Amid this diversity of opinion only one thing is sure, namely, that no one knew exactly what was meant by a direct tax, because no two people agreed. What, then, shall we say of the statement of the counsel which was accepted and repeated by the court in the first Pollock decision that "the distinction between direct and indirect taxation was well understood by the framers of the Constitution, and those who adopted it." This is just the reverse of the truth. The exact distinction between direct and indirect taxation, such as is necessary for purposes of precise classification, was beyond peradventure of doubt *not* understood by the framers of the Constitution and those who adopted it.[2] All that can be said is

[1] *A Sketch of the Finances of the United States*, by Albert Gallatin, New York, 1796, p. 11.

[2] Mr. Samuel B. Clarke thinks that he has discovered the precise meaning of the term. According to him, the constitutional test is this: "operation of the tax statute through the medium of the wills of the persons upon whom the liability to be deprived of property or property resources is imposed, in the matter of the total amount of the liability. . . . If you find that whatever you do or refrain from doing, you are affected with the same unvarying amount of liability, the tax is direct; but if you find that the amount varies as your conduct varies, it is indirect." — Samuel B. Clarke, *Memorandum on the Taxes described as "Direct" in the Constitution of the United States.* New York, 1910, pp. 14–16. *Cf.* also *Letters debating a Memorandum on the Taxes described as 'Direct' in the Constitution of the United States.* New York, 1910, 36 pp. It may be asked, however, how Mr.

that, in a general way, import and export duties were considered indirect taxes, and that land and poll taxes were considered direct taxes; but farther than that it is impossible to go. Even certain taxes on specific articles of property which would to-day generally be considered direct taxes, were, as we have seen, variously called in the different states direct taxes, or duties, or excises, the two latter terms being employed in contradistinction to direct taxes.

The question, therefore, as to whether the term 'direct taxes,' as used in the constitution, included in the minds of the framers an income tax, is impossible of solution, first and foremost because of the fact that income taxes did not at that time exist, either in England or in the United States. Of two very significant facts, however, we may be certain. The first is that the only tax at all akin to the income tax existed in a few of the northern colonies, under the name of the "faculty tax." As to these taxes, however, we have the distinct statement of Secretary Wolcott, which has been quoted above in another connection,[1] that they were not meant to be included under the term "direct taxes." Secondly, the income tax as such existed at the time in only one country of the world, namely, France. But according to the classification of taxes made by Turgot, which the counsel and the court believe to have been as familiar as household words to the American people, the income tax is specifically declared to be an indirect tax. If, therefore, any inference at all were to be drawn from these facts, it would be that the framers of the constitution specifically desired to exclude income or faculty taxes from the category of direct taxation. But such an inference would really be unwarranted, first, because in all probability no one thought of the "faculty tax"; and secondly, because without much doubt almost no one knew anything about Turgot or the French capitation.

The only safe conclusion from this whole discussion is

Clarke would, according to his definition, justify the decision of the Supreme Court that an inheritance tax is indirect.

[1] *Supra*, p. 386.

that it is utterly useless to speculate what the founders of the constitution would have thought of the income tax. They dealt only with the taxes with which they were familiar, and they could not possibly have attempted to put into the category of direct taxes imposts which did not yet within their knowledge exist. Neither a tax on corporations, nor a tax on successions, nor a tax on inheritances, nor a tax on incomes, was in existence. With none of these were the framers of the constitution familiar. It is therefore idle, from a scientific point of view, to speculate into which category they might have put these taxes if they had existed. When these taxes did actually develop, however, it became necessary for the Supreme Court to take some position on the question, and in the decision of each question the court, as may easily be shown, was swayed at bottom by considerations of political exigency and opportunism. To these decisions we must now turn our attention.

§ 8. *The Earlier Decisions of the Supreme Court*

In 1794 the United States government levied a tax on carriages "for the convenience of persons which shall be kept by or for any person for his or her own use, or to be let out for hire, or for the conveying of passengers." The constitutionality of this tax was attacked by the political opponents of Hamilton, during the discussion of the bill, and when the case finally came before the Supreme Court, Hamilton was no longer Secretary of the Treasury to argue in its favor. This tax happened to be one which, as we have seen, not only existed, but was treated differently in several states. It so happened that the chief opponents of Hamilton at the time came from the South, where the carriage tax was considered a tax on specific property, whereas in some of the northern states, as we have seen, it was called a duty or an excise tax, in contradistinction to a direct tax. The tax, moreover, illustrates the difficulty of any precise classification because, from the very terms of the law, as recited above, it might be considered a tax on consumption (when the carriage was used by the owner) or, on the other hand, a tax on earnings or on property used for productive purposes, as in the case of carriages let out for hire. The case came up in 1796, and was argued before a court, every member of which had taken a prominent part in the constitutional convention or in the state ratifying conventions, and who therefore might be presumed to have understood what the convention really intended to enact. All that is left of the argument, however, is a fragment of Hamilton's brief.

Hamilton showed that there was no well-settled legal meaning attached to the term, and also called attention to the unsatisfactory economic usage based on the criterion of shiftability. He adverted to the Physiocratic distinction, but contended that obviously the term "direct taxes" meant more than merely the Physiocratic land tax, because the constitution specifically speaks of a capitation tax as a direct tax. Hamilton then went on to say: "But how is the meaning of the Constitution to be determined? It has been affirmed, and so it will be found, that there is no general principle which can indicate the boundary between the two. The boundary, then, must be fixed by a species of arbitration, and ought to be such as will involve neither absurdity nor inconvenience." Hamilton therefore continued: "The following are presumed to be the only direct taxes: capitation or poll taxes; taxes on lands and buildings; general assessments, whether on the whole property of individuals, or on their whole real or personal estate. All else must of necessity be considered as indirect taxes." Yet as Hamilton himself had previously stated in referring to the absence of any settled meaning of the respective terms, "We shall be as much at a loss to find any disposition of either which can satisfactorily determine the point." He concluded that, on the basis of his suggestion, a carriage tax must be declared to be indirect.

The judges unanimously agreed with him. Justice Chase put his decision on the following ground: "The Constitution evidently contemplated no taxes as direct taxes, but only such as Congress could lay in proportion to the census. The rule of apportionment is only to be adopted in such cases where it can reasonably apply, and the subject taxed must ever determine the application of the rule. If it is proposed to tax any specific article by the rule of apportionment, and it would evidently create great inequality and injustice, it is unreasonable to say that the Constitution intended such tax should be laid by that rule."[1] Justice Paterson based his decision upon somewhat similar grounds. "The Constitution," he stated, "has been considered as an accommodating system; it was the effect of mutual sacrifices and concessions; it was the work of compromise. The rule of apportionment is of this nature; it is radically wrong; it cannot be supported by any solid reasoning. Why should slaves, who are a species of property, be represented more than other property? The rule, therefore, ought not to be extended by construction." So again Justice Iredell said: "As all direct taxes must be apportioned, it is evident that the Constitution contemplated none as direct, but such as could be apportioned. If this cannot be apportioned, it is, therefore, not a direct tax in the sense of the Constitution. That this tax cannot be apportioned is evident. Such an arbitrary method of taxing different States differently . . . would lead if practiced, to such dangerous consequences, that it will require very powerful arguments to show that that method of taxing would be in any manner compatible with the Constitution."

It is evident from these quotations that the judges desired to uphold the internal revenue system of Hamilton, and that they called the carriage tax indirect because this afforded the only possible method of permitting its continuance.

The next case did not arise until many years later. From now on the question was not as to the constitutionality of taxes which had been known at the time of the framing of the constitution, but of taxes which did not exist at all at that period.

In 1868 the question arose as to the constitutionality of the Civil War income tax, or more specifically, as to the legality of

[1] Hylton *vs.* United States, 3 Dallas, 171.

the act of 1866 imposing taxes on the incomes of insurance companies. This was the case of Pacific Insurance Company *vs.* Soule.[1] The court, however, held that the tax was an indirect tax and therefore constitutional, basing their conclusion on the following grounds: "The consequences which would follow the apportionment of the tax in question among the States and Territories of the Union, in the manner prescribed by the Constitution, must not be overlooked. They are very obvious. Where such corporations are numerous and rich, it might be light; where none exist, it could not be collected; where they are few and poor, it would fall upon them with such weight as to involve annihilation. It cannot be supposed that the framers of the Constitution intended that any tax should be apportioned, the collection of which on that principle would be attended with such results. The consequences are fatal to the proposition. To the question under consideration it must be answered that the tax to which it relates is not a direct tax, but a duty or excise." Here, again, it will be seen that the income tax was declared to be an indirect tax because to declare it anything else would either render the tax impossible, or involve annihilation to individual interests.

The next case was that of Veazie Bank *vs.* Fenno, where the question arose as to the constitutionality of the federal tax on state bank-notes. Chief Justice Chase stated the opinion of the court as follows: "Much diversity of opinion has always prevailed upon the question what are direct taxes? Attempts to answer it by reference to the definitions of political economists have been frequently made, but without satisfactory results." He maintained that "it may be rightly affirmed that in the peculiar construction of the Constitution by Congress direct taxes have been limited to taxes on land and appurtenances, and taxes on polls, or capitation taxes." After quoting the insurance company case he concluded that "the tax under consideration is a tax on bank circulation, and may very well be classed under the head of duties. Certainly it is not, in the sense of the Con-

[1] 7 Wallace, 433.

stitution, a direct tax. It may be said to come within the same category of taxation as the tax on incomes of insurance companies."[1]

Here, again, it is obvious that it was the desire of the court to maintain the existence of a tax that had been considered necessary by the Secretary of the Treasury, who had now become the chief justice of the supreme court.

A few years later the question of the constitutionality of the inheritance tax arose in the case of Scholey *vs.* Rew.[2] The particular question involved was the validity of the tax imposed by the United States on the right to take real estate by inheritance. The counsel argued that if ever there were a direct tax on land, this was a tax. Yet the court unanimously decided that the inheritance tax was an indirect tax. "Whether direct taxes, in the sense of the Constitution, comprehend any other tax than a capitation tax and a tax on land, is a question not absolutely decided; nor is it necessary to determine it in the present case, as it is expressly decided that the term does not include the tax on income, which cannot be distinguished in principle from a succession tax, such as the one involved in the present controversy." Thus here, again, the court set its foot against the attempt to restrict by inference the tax powers of the United States, and upheld the inheritance tax on the ground that it could not be distinguished in principle from an income tax, which had been declared constitutional.

Finally, in the case of Springer *vs.* the United States, decided in 1880,[3] the question of the validity of an income tax imposed on an individual came up for discussion, and the court, by a unanimous vote, upheld the tax. After going over the history of the convention the court stated: "It does not appear that any tax like the one here in question was ever regarded or treated by Congress as a direct tax. This uniform practical construction of the Constitution touching so important a point . . . is a consideration of great weight." Referring to the Hylton case, it went on to say:

[1] 8 Wallace, 533. [2] 23 Wallace, 331. [3] 102 U.S., 586.

"It was well held that where such evils would attend the apportionment of a tax, the Constitution could not have intended that an apportionment should be made. This view applies with even greater force to the tax in question in this case. Where the population is large and the incomes are few and small, it would be intolerably oppressive." After quoting the other cases mentioned above, the decision concludes: "All these cases are undistinguishable in principle from the case now before us, and they are decisive against the plaintiff in error. The question, what is a direct tax, is one exclusively in American jurisprudence. The text-writers of the country are in entire accord upon the subject. Our conclusions are, that direct taxes, within the meaning of the Constitution, are only capitation taxes as expressed in that instrument, and taxes on real estate, and that the tax of which the plaintiff in error complains is within the category of an excise or duty."

§ 9. *The Income Tax Cases of 1895*

It would seem impossible to go farther than this. Yet notwithstanding the unanimous decisions of the supreme court on the question, the attempt was again made to attack its constitutionality when the income tax law of 1894 was enacted. What had been borne with more or less equanimity in time of war was regarded with apprehension and determined opposition in time of peace; and some of the important financial interests now engaged a notable array of eminent counsel to essay the arduous task of persuading the supreme court that it might declare the income tax a direct tax without reversing its previous decisions. The effort was made with the most astonishing degree of ability and ingenuity, and the briefs and arguments of the opposing counsel fill several large volumes.[1]

[1] The chief documents in the case are as follows: —

(1) *Brief on behalf of Appellants in support of Contention that the Provisions as to the Income Tax embodied in the Tariff Act of August 28, 1894, are Unconstitutional.* By Joseph H. Choate, Clarence A. Seward, Benjamin

A large part of the argument was taken up with a discussion of the question of uniformity, the counsel contending that the word "uniformity" in the federal constitution had the

H. Bristow, William D. Guthrie, David Willcox, and Charles Steele. 113 pp.

(2) *Additional Brief and Argument for Appellants on Question of Direct Tax.* By Seward, Guthrie, Morawetz, and Steele, Solicitors, and Joseph H. Choate and Charles F. Southmayd of Counsel. 42 pp.

(3) *The Teachings of Political Economists defining Direct and Indirect Taxes.* By Max West, Ph.D. Submitted by Seward, Guthrie, Morawetz, and Steele. 38 pp.

(4) *Extracts from the Evidence proving the Historic Facts from the general Literature, and from the Authorities, bearing upon the Question whether the Words "Direct Tax" and "Direct Taxes," as used in the Federal Constitution, embrace a Tax on Incomes, or are limited to a Tax on Land only.* Submitted by Seward, Guthrie, Morawetz, and Steele. 71 pp.

(5) *Brief for the Continental Trust Company of the City of New York, Appellee.* By James C. Carter and William C. Gulliver. 48 pp.

(6) *Brief for Appellant John G. Moore.* By Samuel Shellabarger and Jeremiah W. Wilson, Attorneys, and George F. Edmunds of Counsel. 38 pp.

(7) *Brief on Behalf of the United States.* By Richard Olney, Attorney-General, and Edward B. Whitney, Asst. Attorney-General. 99 pp.

(8) *Opening Argument by W. D. Guthrie on Behalf of Complainants, in support of the Contention that the Income Tax Law of 1894 is Unconstitutional.* 49 pp.

(9) *Mr. Seward's Argument upon the Question whether the Words "Direct Tax" and "Direct Taxes," as used in the Federal Constitution, embrace a Tax on Income, or are limited to a Tax on Land only.* 89 pp.

(10) *Oral Argument of Hon. Richard Olney,* Attorney-General. 21 pp.

(11) *Argument of Mr. James C. Carter, for the Appellees.* 61 pp.

(12) *Closing Argument by Mr. Choate on Behalf of Complainants, in support of the Contention that the Income Tax Law of 1894 is Unconstitutional.* 82 pp.

(13) *Opinion of the Court and Opinions of Justices Field, White, and Harlan.* 151 pp.

In the rehearing, additional documents were filed. These are as follows:—

(14) *Petition for Rehearing by Appellants.* 7 pp.

(15) *On Petition for Rehearing by the Attorney-General.* 3 pp.

(16) *Brief for Appellants in support of Contention that the Provisions as to Income Tax embodied in the Tariff Act of August 28, 1894, are Unconstitutional.* [By same Counsel.] 117 pp.

(17) *Brief for the United States on Petition for Rehearing.* 73 pp.

(18) *Appendix to Brief on Behalf of the United States.* 18 pp.

(19) *Extracts from Turgot submitted by the United States.* 5 pp.

(20) *Brief for Appellant John G. Moore in no. 915, filed by leave of the Court in*

same meaning as in the state constitutions, and that the income tax was therefore unconstitutional because lacking in uniformity. Mr. Whitney, the assistant attorney-general, devoted the greater portion of one of his arguments to the attempt to prove that, on the contrary, uniformity meant only geographical uniformity. In its decision the court, however, entirely ignored this question on the ground of an even division of opinion, only eight judges having sat; but Justice Field, in a supplementary opinion, adopted the view of the counsel. As has been stated above, the contention of the government as to the meaning of uniformity was completely approved in the inheritance tax case decided a few years later.

The other argument, however, was the one which the counsel pressed home with remarkable ingenuity and with telling force. It was to the effect that the supreme court had never specifically held a tax upon the income from land to be an indirect tax. For in the insurance company case the point of the ownership of real estate by the company was not expressly made. While in the Springer case it so happened, unfortunately for the government, that the income of Springer was derived partly from professional earnings and partly from United States bonds. The counsel now argued that income

numbers 893 and 894. By Samuel Shellebarger and Jeremiah M. Wilson, attorneys; George F. Edmunds, Counsel. 25 pp.

(21) *Reply to Brief filed on Behalf of John G. Moore.* Submitted by the United States Government. 3 pp.

(22) *Historical Argument upon Meaning of Words "Direct Tax" and "Duty" in Constitution.* Submitted by the United States. 91 pp.

(23) *Opening Argument by Mr. W. D. Guthrie, on Behalf of Appellants.* 70 pp.

(24) *Oral Argument of Hon. Richard Olney, Attorney-General.* 19 pp.

(25) *Argument of Edward B. Whitney, Assistant Attorney-General on Behalf of the United States, upon the Uniformity Question.* 11 pp.

(26) *Closing Arguments by Mr. Choate.* 84 pp.

(27) *Decision of the Court on the Rehearing.* 114 pp.

A large part of the material contained in no. 4 and no. 22 was based, to a great extent, upon a manuscript study which had been made by the present writer, and which was put at the disposal of both sides. No. 19 was also submitted by him. The author of no. 3 was a student of the writer, and the greater part of that document was based upon statements contained in his lectures.

from land cannot be distinguished from land itself, and that if, as every one concedes, a land tax be a direct tax, a tax on the income from land must also be direct, irrespective of the question whether the tax be levied specifically on the income from land, or as a part of a general income tax. This argument, admirably elaborated, convinced the court, and by a close vote it decided in the first Pollock case that the income tax was to that extent a direct tax. Even from this, however, several judges dissented, while as to the question whether the rest of the income tax would fall with the decision as to the real estate part of it, the court was evenly divided. The court also held — and here there was no difference of opinion — that so much of the tax as fell on the income from state bonds was unconstitutional, not because it was a direct tax, but because the federal government had no power to tax the agencies of said government.[1]

This decision emasculated the income tax, leaving it in a most unsatisfactory condition. A rehearing was therefore applied for, and granted by the court; and the counsel, on the allegation of new material that had been discovered, made a fresh argument. Starting from the point that a tax on the income of real estate had now been adjudged to be a direct tax, the counsel contended that a tax on personal property, or on the income of personal property, is also a direct tax. Here, again, they were able to carry with them a bare majority of the court. Although the ninth judge, Justice Jackson, who had arisen from what soon turned out to be his death-bed in order to hear the argument, voted in favor of the constitutionality of the law, another judge in the meantime changed his mind. Thus by a vote of five to four was the income tax declared unconstitutional because it was not apportioned according to the rule of direct taxation.

The second decision rested largely upon the interpretation of the historical facts. A careful and unbiased study of the documentary evidence shows, however, that both the government and the opposing counsel made extreme claims, which

[1] As to this particular argument, see *infra*, chap. vi, § 4.

cannot be substantiated. The argument of the government, for instance, that the meaning of the terms "duty" and "direct taxation" was perfectly clear at the time of the constitutional convention, and that the word "duty" was intended to cover such a tax as the income tax, goes farther than the actual facts warrant. That is, however, almost the only exaggeration in the government's contention. On the other hand, the counsel's arguments abound in historical errors and economic inaccuracies. To expect that great lawyers should also be great economists is perhaps unreasonable; but it is not unreasonable to protest against such a statement as this: "A tax on personal estate held for the purpose of income is directly imposed upon the owner, and ultimately borne by him without possibility of shifting it upon any one else. The owner's subjection to it is absolute and imperative, with no choice on his part or possibility of escape from it, short of abandoning his property."[1] This completely indefensible statement in the brief was repeated in substantially the same words in Mr. Choate's closing argument and hammered in upon the court.[2] Mr. Seward's misstatement about the references to Turgot in the *American Museum* and Mr. Guthrie's mistaken allegation as to Turgot have been mentioned above.[3] Senator Edmunds emphasized the old economic fallacy that taxes upon consumable goods differ from direct taxes in that they are voluntarily paid.[4] Finally, well-nigh all the counsel harped upon the point that it was entirely feasible to have a fairly equal income tax, even if it were apportioned according to the constitutional mandate!

But if the counsel may perhaps be excused for not being sound economists, we cannot make the same allowance for their errors of historical fact. Among these misstatements

[1] *Additional Brief and Argument for Appellants on Question of Direct Tax.* p. 17.

[2] *Closing Argument by Mr. Choate*, etc. [in first case], p. 30. Also in 157 U.S., p. 541.

[3] *Supra*, pp. 562-563.

[4] That some lawyers can also be good economists is apparent from the effective answer to this in the *Argument of Mr. James C. Carter for the Appellees*, p. 5.

are the following: First, we are told that "there has been an income tax in England since 1435," and "the income tax, therefore, was in force in Great Britain at the time that Mr. Madison spoke."[1] Secondly, it is alleged that in 1783 the eighth article of confederation was changed so as to alter the basis of direct taxation from land to population.[2] Thirdly, it is stated that incomes were taxed in the New Netherlands.[3] Fourthly, Mr. Seward contended that at the date of the constitution the terms "direct taxes" and "indirect taxes" were household words.[4]

But such errors and misstatements, which might be multiplied, pale into insignificance compared with the glaring misinterpretation put upon the origin and the purpose of the direct-tax clause — a misinterpretation which, like most of the preceding mistakes, was adopted bodily by the majority of the court, who evidently had found no time for an independent investigation of the subject. So important, indeed, did this point seem, that the reporter of the second Pollock case, Mr. J. C. Bancroft Davis, naturally made it in his syllabus the very centre of the decision, in the following words: "In distributing the power of taxation, the Constitution retained to the States the absolute power of direct taxation, but granted to the Federal government the power of the same taxation upon condition that, in its exercise, such taxes should be apportioned among the several States according to numbers; and this was done, in order to protect to the States, who were surrendering to the Federal government so many sources of income, the power of direct taxation, which was their principal remaining source." The entire falsity of this statement, which was the very basis of the decision, has been so fully explained above[5] that we may here pass it by, with the mere reflection that even supreme court justices are human, and that there is nothing sacrosanct about any one's

[1] *Extracts from the Evidence proving the Historic Facts*, etc., pp. 16, 49.

[2] *Ibid.*, p. 19. As to this error, see *supra*, p. 545.

[3] *Ibid.*, p. 20. As to this error, see *supra*, p. 372.

[4] *Mr. Seward's Argument*, p. 18.

[5] *Supra*, p. 558.

opinions when they are founded not on the bed-rock of fact, but on the shifting sands of historical error.

The opinion of the court, hence, in both the first and the second cases, calls for no special mention, as it practically accepted the views of the counsel in all respects except on the question of uniformity, on which point the only statement made was that the court was evenly divided. Justice Field, however, in the first case delivered the remarkable supplementary opinion which has aptly been called "his tirade against the income tax,"[1] devoted almost entirely to the effort to prove that the tax was so grossly lacking in uniformity as to make it, in his opinion, unconstitutional. He spoke of the act as constituting a usurpation. "The present assault upon capital is but the beginning. It will be but the stepping-stone to others larger and more sweeping till our political conditions will become a war of the poor against the rich; a war constantly growing in intensity and bitterness." And he quoted the statement of an anonymous authority, who is well known to have been the late David A. Wells, that "if the court sanctions the power of discriminating taxation, and nullifies the uniformity mandate of the Constitution, it will mark the hour when the sure decadence of our present government will commence." If Mr. Wells and Justice Field are correct, the decadence of our government is in full progress, for "discriminating taxation" is now the law of the land, as it is the custom everywhere else in the civilized world.

In the second case, pronounced dissent was manifested by four of the judges, not only to the general view of the majority, but also to the extremely conservative opinion of Justice Field. Because of the commanding reputation of the judges and the weight of their arguments, the dissenting opinions merit careful attention.[2]

[1] Bullock, in *Political Science Quarterly*, vol. xv (1900), p. 453.

[2] In the first case, the opinion of the court occupied sixty pages, the opinions of the dissenting judges sixty-one pages. In the second case, the figures are twenty pages for the decision and seventy-seven pages for the dissenting opinions.

§ 10. *The Dissenting Opinions*

In the first income tax case Justice White, speaking for himself and Justice Harlan, posited the following dilemma: "If the framers understood the meaning of the word 'direct' in the Constitution, the practical effect which they gave to it should remain undisturbed; if they were in doubt as to the meaning, the interpretation long since authoritatively affixed to it should be upheld." He pointed out that the opinion of the court "virtually annuls its previous decisions in regard to the powers of Congress on the subject of taxation, and is therefore fraught with danger, to the Court, to each and every citizen and to the republic." And he concluded that "if the permanency of its conclusions is to depend upon the personal opinions of those who, from time to time, may make up its membership, it will inevitably become a theatre of political strife."

In the second case, where four dissenting opinions were filed, Justice Harlan stated: "In my judgment—to say nothing of the disregard of the former adjudications of this court, and of the settled practice of the government—this decision may well excite the gravest apprehensions. It strikes at the very foundations of national authority, in that it denies to the general government a power which is, or may become, vital to the very existence and preservation of the Union in a national emergency. . . . It tends to re-establish that condition of helplessness in which Congress found itself during the period of the Articles of Confederation."[1] He thereupon referred to the practical impossibility of levying an income tax by way of apportionment: "No such apportionment can possibly be made without doing gross injustice to the many for the benefit of the favored few in particular States. Any attempt upon the part of Congress to apportion among the States, upon the basis simply of their population, taxation of personal property or of incomes, would tend to arouse such indignation among the freemen of America that it would never be repeated." He concluded, "I cannot assent to an interpretation of the

[1] 158 U.S., p. 671

Constitution that impairs and cripples the just powers of the National Government in the essential matter of taxation, and at the same time discriminates against the greater part of the people of our country. . . . The practical effect of the decision to-day is to give to certain kinds of property a position of favoritism and advantage inconsistent with the fundamental principles of our social organization, and to invest them with power and influence that may be perilous to that portion of the American people upon whom rests the larger part of the burdens of the government, and who ought not to be subjected to the dominion of aggregated wealth any more than the property of the country should be at the mercy of the lawless."[1]

Justice Brown, in referring to the opinion of the counsel and the court that an apportioned income tax was perfectly feasible, said: "If the States should adopt a similar system of taxation and allot the amount to be raised among the different cities and towns, or among the different wards of the same State, in proportion to their population, the result would be so monstrous that the entire public would cry out against it. Indeed, reduced to its last analysis, it imposes the same tax upon the laborer that it does upon the millionaire."[2] And after going fully into the legal as well as the economic aspects of the case, he contended that a tax on rents is an indirect tax on lands.[3] Calling attention to the fact that "even the spectre of socialism is conjured up to frighten Congress from laying taxes upon the people in proportion to their ability to pay them," he concluded: "It is certainly a strange commentary upon the Constitution of the United States and upon a democratic government that Congress has no power to lay a tax which is one of the main sources of revenue of nearly every civilized State. It is a confession of feebleness in which I find myself wholly unable to join. While I have no doubt that Congress will find some means of surmounting the present crisis, my fear is that in some moment of national peril this decision will rise

[1] 158 U.S., p. 685. [2] *Ibid.*, p. 689. [3] *Ibid.*, p. 693.

up to frustrate its will and paralyze its arm. I hope it may not prove the first step toward the submergence of the liberties of the people in a sordid despotism of wealth. As I cannot escape the conviction that the decision of the court in this great case is fraught with immeasurable danger to the future of the country, and that it approaches the proportions of a national calamity, I feel it a duty to enter my protest against it."[1]

Justice Jackson pointed out that "we cannot attribute to the framers of the Constitution an intention to make any tax a direct tax which it was impossible to apportion. If it cannot be apportioned without gross injustice, we may feel assured that it is a tax never contemplated by the Constitution as a direct tax. . . . The fact that a tax cannot be so apportioned without producing gross injustice and inequality among those required to pay it should settle the question that it was not a direct tax within the true sense and meaning of those words as they are used in the Constitution."[2] And he concluded: "This decision, in effect, relieves the citizens having the greater ability, while the burdens of taxation are made to fall most heavily and oppressively upon those having the least ability. It lightens the burden upon the large number, in some States subject to the tax, and places it most unequally and disproportionately on the smaller number in other States. Considered in all its bearings, this decision is, in my judgment, the most disastrous blow ever struck at the constitutional power of Congress."[3]

Finally, Justice White stated that "the injustice of the conclusion points to the error of adopting it. It takes invested wealth and reads it into the Constitution as a favored and protected class of property, which cannot be taxed without apportionment, whilst it leaves the occupation of the minister, the doctor, the professor, the lawyer, the inventor, the author, the merchant, the mechanic and all other forms of industry, upon which the prosperity of a people must depend, subject to taxation without that condition. And where

[1] 158 U.S., p. 695. [2] *Ibid.*, p. 703. [3] *Ibid.*, pp. 705–706.

it works out this result, which, it seems to me, stultifies the Constitution, by making it an instrument of the most grievous wrong, it should not be adopted, especially when, in order to do so, the decisions of this court, the opinions of the law writers and publicists, tradition, practice and the settled policy of the government must be overthrown." [1] He closed by the statement: "It is, I submit, greatly to be deplored that, after more than one hundred years of our national existence, after the government has withstood the strain of foreign wars and the dread ordeal of civil strife, and its people have become united and powerful, this court should consider itself compelled to go back to a long repudiated and rejected theory of the Constitution, by which the government is deprived of an inherent attribute of its being, a necessary power of taxation." [2]

§ 11. *The Effect of the Decision*

When it is considered that all the preceding decisions of the court on the question of direct taxation were unanimous, and that this decision was rendered by the barest of majorities; when it is remembered that the decision is based upon glaring historical errors and undoubted misinterpretations of what actually took place a century and a quarter ago; and finally, when we recollect that all of the dissenting opinions, while taking up different phases of the legal argument, agree in considering the decision of the court to be fraught with the utmost danger to the perpetuation of the republic, it is not to be wondered at that the country did not acquiesce in the decision. There soon appeared a flood of articles and pamphlets, a few of which upheld the court, but the great majority of which sharply criticised the findings, although mainly on general grounds.[3] The echo of these criticisms reached Con-

[1] 158 U.S., p. 712.

[2] *Ibid.*, p. 715.

[3] Among the most important of these articles were the following: George F. Edmunds, "The Salutary Results of the Income Tax Decision," *The Forum*, vol. xix (1905), pp. 513 *et seq.*; Edward B. Whitney, "The Political Dangers of the Income Tax Decision," *ibid.*, pp. 521 *et seq.*; Sylvester Pennoyer, "The Income Tax Decision and the Power of the Supreme Court to nullify Acts of Con-

gress, and every few years the question came up again. As a type of the current criticisms we select the speech of Fleming, of Georgia, in the House of Representatives, on April 28, 1898.[1]

Fleming called attention to the practical consequences of the decision. He pointed out that, tested by the income tax figures of 1866, as compared with the existing situation, if the taxes were levied according to what had now been declared to be the sole constitutional method, a citizen in Massachusetts would pay 2.8 per cent on his income and a citizen of Minnesota 32.9 per cent. "Any man with the smallest capacity for practical affairs can see at a glance," he said, "that it is utterly impracticable for Congress to raise money by a direct tax on land or personalty or on incomes in the manner required by the decision of the court. Congress has been stripped of effectual power to place a tax on wealth, and it is limited in raising revenue to putting taxes on consumption." . . . "The nation has grown in all other attributes of sovereignty, but has lost its once-admitted power of taxation."[2] Fleming pointed out that the situation in 1894 differed materially from 1866. "In the meantime wealth, especially corporate wealth, had waned in patriotism and waxed in power. It was no longer willing to bear its just share of governmental expenses, and with great ability, marvelous ingenuity and supreme audacity, it undertook to convince the highest court of the nation that it ought to reverse

gress," *American Law Review*, vol. xxix (1895), pp. 550 *et seq.;* L. Allen, The Income Tax Decision; an Answer to Governor Pennoyer," *North American Review*, vol. clx (1895), pp. 84 *et seq.;* G. S. Boutwell, "The Income Tax; the Decision of the Supreme Court, *ibid.*, pp. 589 *et seq.;* J. K. Beach, "The Income Tax Decision," *The Yale Review*, vol. v (1896), p. 58; E. L. Godkin, "The Income Tax Decision," the *Journal of Political Economy*, vol. iii (1895), pp. 509 *et seq.;* C. G. Tiedemen, "The Income Tax Decisions as an Object Lesson in Constitutional Construction," *Annals of the American Academy of Political and Social Science*, vol. vi (1895), pp. 268 *et seq.*

[1] *Congressional Record*, vol. 31, *appendix*, pp. 381 *et seq.* This speech was reprinted, with the title, *The Income Tax—its Relation to Political Economy, to the Constitution, and to the Supreme Court Decision.* By William H. Fleming Washington, 1898.

[2] *Op. cit.*, p. 11.

a decision it had upheld for a century. The battle raged anew with hair-splitting distinctions around that little word 'direct,' although its legal meaning had been definitely fixed and accepted for a century." [1]

Referring to the decisions of the supreme court, Fleming went on to say: "No member of this high tribunal who has a proper appreciation of the relations he sustains to the people, will claim that the court or its decisions are above respectful criticism." He quoted with telling effect the statement of one of the supreme court justices himself: "It is a mistake to suppose that the Supreme Court is either honored or helped by being spoken of as above criticism. On the contrary, the life and character of its justices should be the objects of constant watchfulness by all, and its judgments subject to the freest criticism." [2] Fleming continued: "It is not too much to say that in both decisions of the income tax cases under the act of 1894 those printed opinions which uphold the constitutionality of the law are considered by the profession at large as stronger expositions of the true principles involved than the printed opinions in favor of the contrary doctrine. Besides, broad-minded men cannot but think that in passing upon such an issue the justices should not have relied so much on verbal niceties and technical legalisms, but should have followed the example of their illustrious predecessors, when facing similar issues, by basing their decisions more firmly on long established precedents, and on broad principles of constitutional construction, keeping also in mind the tremendous political and economic results." He concluded: "Let us hope for relief through the court, seeing as we do, that the decision was a judicial anomaly, a political anachronism and an economic blunder."

From year to year the feeling grew that something must be done to extricate the nation from an awkward, if not a perilous, situation.[3] The income tax was commonly referred to as

[1] *Op. cit.*, p. 13.

[2] *Op. cit.*, p. 12.

[3] Cf. the excellent article by Max West, "The Income Tax and the National Revenues," *Journal of Political Economy*, vol. viii (1900), pp. 433 *et seq.* For

"the Dred Scott decision of government revenue." Gradually, however, the conviction was strengthened that it was in vain to hope for a change in the supreme court which would convert the minority into a majority, and which would reverse the decision; for it was felt that such a proceeding would undoubtedly impair its prestige. The only alternative, however, was an amendment of the constitution, which would permit what the court had stated is now prohibited. The alternative was the plan finally determined upon, although it took almost fifteen years of agitation and of development of public sentiment before Congress was able to submit such an amendment. With this amendment we shall now have to deal.

later articles, see Wayne MacVeagh, "Graduated Taxation of Incomes and Inheritance," *North American Review*, vol. 182, pp. 823 *et seq.;* and the discussion on the subject of the income tax at the Sixth Annual Meeting of the National Civic Federation, by Andrew Carnegie and others in the *National Civic Federation Review*, vol. ii (1907), pp. 14 *et seq.*

CHAPTER VI

The Proposed Sixteenth Amendment to the Constitution

§ 1. *The Origin of the Amendment*[1]

We have stated the reasons why, if an income tax was to be made possible, an amendment of the constitution was imperative. For a time, indeed, it seemed as if the supreme court might recede from its position, especially when it held that the inheritance tax imposed during the Spanish War was not a direct tax, and that the earlier case of Scholey *vs.* Rew[2] had not been overruled by the Pollock case. In reality, however, the court did not attempt to alter the decision in the Pollock case, which it restated as being to the effect that "a tax which was in itself direct, because imposed upon prop-

[1] This chapter, excepting sections one and five, originally appeared in the *Political Science Quarterly* for June, 1910. The advance copies, however, were published and circulated early in March. In April appeared the *Memorandum submitted to the Legislature of the State of New York in Opposition to the Amendment*, by six of the leading lawyers of New York. The full title of this will be found *supra*, p. 558. Two weeks later appeared a defence of the amendment by another distinguished lawyer, J. Hampden Dougherty, *The Proposed Sixteenth Article of Amendment to the Constitution of the United States. Memorandum containing a Criticism of Objections to the Amendment, and some Reasons for its Adoption.* At the end of March the New York Economic Club held a meeting at which four addresses on the subject were delivered, all of which were printed in the *Journal of Accountancy* in May, vol. x (1910), pp. 18–42. The addresses opposed to the amendment were: William D. Guthrie, "No Taxation without Representation"; and Austen G. Fox, "Insert no Ambiguity into the Constitution." The addresses in favor of the amendment were: Lawson Purdy, "The Income Tax Amendment should be Ratified"; and Senator William E. Borah, "The Income Tax Sound in Law and Economics." For other articles on the subject, see Dwight W. Morrow, "The Income Amendment," *Columbia Law Review*, vol. x (1910), pp. 379 *et seq.*; and W. E. Borah, "The Income Tax Amendment," *North American Review*, vol. 191 (1910), pp. 755 *et seq.*

[2] 23 Wallace, 331.

erty solely by reason of its ownership, could not be changed by affixing to it the qualification of excise or duty." And in another passage the court gave still more precision to the existing rule by stating: "First, that no sound distinction existed between a tax levied on a person solely because of his general ownership of real property, and the same tax imposed solely because of his general ownership of personal property. Secondly, that the tax on the income derived from such property, real or personal, was the legal equivalent of a direct tax on the property from which said income was derived, and hence must be apportioned."[1]

Very shortly after this the court again had occasion to take up the question of direct taxation. When the internal revenue was increased in 1898, during the Spanish War, it was proposed to tax corporations on their gross earnings. When the bill emerged from committee, however, it became "a special excise tax on the gross receipts of companies refining petroleum or refining sugar," and as such became law. This act was attacked as obnoxious to the income-tax decision, but was upheld by the court.[2] Although the decision was again in harmony with the Pollock case, hopes were nevertheless aroused in the minds of some that the court would see its way clear to make further distinctions. The opportunity for this, however, did not arise. As late as 1906, indeed, President Roosevelt in his annual message stated that, a "graduated income tax of the proper type would be a desirable feature of federal taxation, and it is to be hoped that one may be devised which the supreme court will declare constitutional."

By 1908, however, this had become so doubtful that the Democratic platform included a resolution that "we favor an income tax as part of our revenue system, and we urge the submission of a constitutional amendment specifically authorizing congress to levy and collect a tax upon individual and corporate incomes, to the end that wealth may bear its

[1] *Op. cit.*, p. 82.

[2] Spreckels Sugar Refining Company *vs.* McClain, 192 U.S., 397.

proportionate share of the burdens of the federal government." The candidate of the Republican party, Mr. Taft, did not, however, agree with this. In his speech of acceptance on July 28, 1908, he said: "In my judgment an amendment to the constitution for an income tax is not necessary. I believe that an income tax, when the protective system of customs shall not furnish income enough for individual needs, can and should be devised which, under the decisions of the supreme court will conform to the constitution." After the victory of the Republicans at the polls, Mr. Taft's views seemed to have changed, for in his inaugural address, while not opposing an income tax, he said nothing about it, but suggested, obviously in its stead, an inheritance tax. "Should it be impossible to do so [secure sufficient revenue] from import duties, new kinds of taxation must be adopted, and, among these I recommend a graduated inheritance tax as correct in principle and as certain and easy of collection."

In conformity with this recommendation, an inheritance tax provision was introduced into the new tariff bill that was discussed in the spring of 1909. It soon became apparent, however, that the movement in the West in favor of some kind of income taxation had become exceedingly strong. So loud was the opposition of the insurgents to the proposed Payne-Aldrich tariff that the leaders of the Republican party recognized the impossibility of securing enough votes to carry the tariff unless some concessions were made on the question of the income tax. As early as April 15, Senator Bailey, of Texas, had moved an amendment for a general income tax,[1] at the rate of three per cent of incomes over $5000, and six days later, Senator Cummins, of Iowa, proposed a graduated income tax[2] on all incomes over $5000, the rates ranging from two up to six per cent on all incomes over $100,000. These two amendments were later on consolidated, and became known as the Bailey-Cummins amendment. A general discussion now ensued, in which many of

[1] *Congressional Record*, vol. 44 (1909), p. 1351.

[2] *Op. cit.*, p. 1468.

the progressives of both parties spoke in favor of an income tax.[1]

The strength which the income-tax proposition developed alarmed the Republican leaders considerably. When, therefore, the inheritance-tax provision was dropped, very largely because of the opposition of the various states, an attempt was made to placate the insurgents by agreeing to enact at once a tax on corporate incomes, and to couple with this the submission of an income-tax amendment to the states. President Taft, who was in part responsible for this, stated in a special message of June 16, 1909: "Although I have not considered a constitutional amendment as necessary to the exercise of certain phases of this power [to tax incomes], a mature consideration has satisfied me that an amendment is the only proper course for its establishment to its full extent. I therefore recommend that both Houses . . . shall propose an amendment to the constitution, conferring the power to levy an income tax upon the national government without an apportionment among the states. . . . I have become convinced that a great majority of the people of this country are in favor of vesting this national government with power to levy an income tax."

The programme was accordingly carried out. The corporation tax was adopted, but in the form of a tax only on corporate dividends at the rate of one per cent. Senator Aldrich stated, on June 29, "I shall vote for the corporation tax as a means to defeat the income tax,"[2] and Senator Root said: "Gentlemen may assume I am for the corporation tax to beat the income tax. I care not. I am for the corporation

[1] Among these speeches are especially to be noted those of Hitchcock on February 20, *op. cit.*, vol. 43, p. 2842; of Hull on March 31, *op. cit.*, vol. 44, p. 502; of Bailey on May 3 and 4, *op. cit.*, pp. 1692 and 1749; of Borah on May 5, *op. cit.*, p. 1363; of Sutherland on May 19, *op. cit.*, p. 2243; of Newlands on May 27, *op. cit.*, p. 2518; and of Cummins on July 7, *op. cit.*, p. 4285. In the House of Representatives also a number of speeches were delivered in favor of the income tax, especially by Dixon, Hobson, Dies, Sharp, Hamlin, Cline, and Hinshaw. *Op. cit.*, pp. 4524–4685.

[2] *Congressional Record*, vol. 44, pt. iii, p. 3929.

tax because I think it is better policy, better patriotism, and higher wisdom than the general income tax, at this time, and under these circumstances." The other part of the agreement, however, was the submission of the constitutional amendment.

It would naturally occur to an unbiased observer that the simplest way out of the difficulty would be entirely to eliminate from the constitution the clause or clauses referring to direct taxes. We have learned that the only reason of its original insertion was to effect a compromise on the slavery question. Now that slavery had long been abolished, there was no further reason for retaining the clause in the constitution. We have learned what difficulty was caused by a proper interpretation of the direct clause, not only as affecting the income tax, but as affecting many other measures enacted by Congress. We must not forget that as long as the words "direct taxation" are retained in the constitution, similar difficulties will arise in the future, even if the income tax matter is disposed of. Hamilton's prophecy that we shall be at a loss to find any disposition of the matter which can satisfactorily determine the point has not only come true but will remain true in the future. As it has been well said by Judge Whitney: "Apportioned taxes have turned out a failure. They are difficult enough to assess within the limits of a state and under control of a state board of equalization. They have been tried by the nation, and each trial was a failure. The last direct tax levied was paid back again. There will probably never be another. Whatever taxes are levied in the future will be levied under the rule of uniformity. If we are to amend the constitution, a matter now so often discussed, we should not try to tinker it by introducing a specific exception to a broken down general rule." [1]

Congress, however, was unfortunately not much interested in the larger question. What gave it immediate concern

[1] Edward B. Whitney, "The Income Tax and the Constitution." *Harvard Law Review*, vol. xx (1907), p. 296.

was the disposition of the pending imbroglio. It was therefore decided to arrange the matter by an amendment to the constitution which would affect only the income tax. A proposition by Senator McLaurin, on July 5, to strike out the words "direct taxes" in the respective clauses of the constitution was not even debated.[1]

On April 28 Senator Brown, of Nebraska, had proposed an amendment in the following words: "Congress shall have power to lay and collect taxes on incomes and inheritances, from whatever sources derived, without apportionment among the states, without reference to any census or enumeration." This was, however, withdrawn, and it was not until June 17 that a new amendment was introduced in accordance with the understanding with the leaders of the House. This new amendment read as follows: " Congress shall have power to lay and collect direct taxes on incomes without apportionment among the several states, according to population." It was referred to the committee on finance, and reported back on June 28. In the meantime a change had been made, striking out the word "direct" and inserting the words "from whatever source derived," so that the amendment now read: "Congress shall have power to lay and collect taxes on income from whatever source derived, without apportionment among the several states, and without regard to any census or enumeration." No explanation was made of the change, and when Senator Aldrich reported the amendment, he asked to have it disposed of without debate. It was indeed debated, but the discussion was exceedingly slight. In the House the discussion was a little longer, but still occupied only four hours, and one of the members protested in the following words: "I imagine that nothing which I may be able to say will defeat the prearranged programme, and prevent the passage of the joint resolution; but for the House to perform its part in such a solemn transaction as amending the Constitution of the United States without having the form of the amendment seriously considered by one of its committees, strikes

[1] *Congressional Record*, vol. 44, pp 4109, 4120.

me as a proceeding of extraordinary levity."[1] Nothwithstanding this protest, however, the joint resolution (no. 40) was passed by the Senate on July 5, by unanimous vote,[2] and in the House a week later by the overwhelming vote of 318 to 14.[3]

Thus the amendment started on its way. In the following winter, as the legislatures of several of the states convened, the path seemed to be clear to an acceptance of the amendment, when the country was startled by a message of the reform governor, Hughes, to the legislature of New York, objecting to its passage.

In the judgment of Governor, now Justice, Hughes, the power to levy an income tax ought assuredly to be given to the national government, but the amendment proposed by Congress labored under the fatal defect that it would empower the federal legislature, by taxing state and municipal bonds, to strike at the very vitals of state credit and state independence.[4]

Justice Hughes is so excellent a lawyer and so great a statesman that his opinion is not lightly to be controverted. But in our judgment it is erroneous in three respects: —

(1) His interpretation of the legal force of the amendment is incorrect.

(2) Even were his legal interpretation correct, he fails to take account of economic facts which would prevent the consequences which he fears.

(3) Even were his view correct, that the constitutional amendment would operate to change the law in the direction indicated, there are valid reasons why the law should be so changed and the amendment prevail.

Let us take up each of these points in order.

[1] Mr. McCall, of Massachusetts, in *Congressional Record*, vol. 44, part iv, p. 4391.

[2] *Op. cit.*, p. 4121.

[3] *Op. cit.*, p. 4440.

[4] *Special Message from the Governor submitting to the Legislature a Certified Copy of a Resolution of Congress entitled, "Joint Resolution proposing an Amendment to the Constitution of the United States."* Albany, 1910.

§ 2. *The Meaning of the Amendment*

A long series of decisions has established the doctrine that there are limitations implied as well as expressed upon the power of taxation, both of the federal and of the state governments. In the case of McCulloch *vs.* Maryland,[1] decided in 1819, it was held that a state tax on the Bank of the United States was unconstitutional. Chief Justice Marshall, in this case, stated: "That the power to tax involves the power to destroy; that the power to destroy may defeat and render useless the power to create; that there is a plain repugnance in conferring on one government a power to control the constitutional measures of another, which other, with respect to those very measures, is declared to be supreme over that which exerts the control, are propositions not to be denied. . . . The states have no power, by taxation or otherwise, to retard, impede, burthen, or in any manner control, the operations of the constitutional laws enacted by Congress to carry into execution the powers vested in the general government."

A few years later, in 1824, the same proposition was advanced in the case of Osborn *vs.* United States Bank.[2] The next step was taken in 1829, when, in the case of Weston *vs.* Charleston,[3] a local tax on federal bonds was declared unconstitutional. The court said: "The tax on government stock is a tax on the contract, a tax on the power to borrow money, on the credit of the United States, and consequently repugnant to the Constitution. . . . The right to tax the contract to any extent, when made, must operate upon the power to borrow before it is exercised and have a sensible influence on the contract. The extent of this influence depends upon the will of a distinct government. To any extent, however inconsiderable, it is a burthen on the operations of government." Again, in 1842, in the case of Dobbins *vs.* Commissioners of Erie County,[4] it was held that a local tax

[1] 4 Wheaton, 316.
[2] 9 Wheaton, 738.
[3] 2 Peters, 449.
[4] 16 Peters, 435.

was invalid so far as the salaries of federal officers were concerned. And finally, in 1862, in the case of Bank of Commerce *vs.* City of New York,[1] it was decided that a state tax on the capital stock of a bank, when such capital stock consisted, in whole or in part, of United States bonds, was unconstitutional.

Beginning at a later period, another series of decisions declared that the federal government was likewise restrained from taxing state operations and agencies. In the case of Collector *vs.* Day,[2] decided in 1870, the federal Civil War income tax was held to be unconstitutional so far as it applied to the salaries of state judicial officers. The court said: "It is admitted that there is no express provision in the Constitution that prohibits the general government from taxing the means and instrumentalities of the states, nor is there any prohibiting the states from taxing the means and instrumentalities of that government. In both cases the exemption rests upon necessary implication, and is upheld by the great law of self-preservation; as any government, whose means employed in conducting its operations, if subject to the control of another and distinct government, can only exist at the mercy of that government. Of what avail are these means if another power may tax them at discretion?"

In United States *vs.* Baltimore and Ohio Railroad Company,[3] decided in 1872, it was held that the United States government cannot tax "the agencies and instruments" of the states. In Mercantile Bank *vs.* New York,[4] decided in 1886, which held that a state tax on the shareholders of national banks was valid for special reasons, not necessary here to discuss, it was stated, although indeed *obiter*, that bonds issued by a state, "or under its authority by its public municipal bodies, are means for carrying on the work of government, and are not taxable even by the United States." And finally, in Pollock *vs.* Farmers' Loan and Trust Company,[5] decided in 1895, the foregoing dictum was cited with

[1] 2 Black, 620.
[2] 11 Wallace, 113.
[3] 17 Wallace, 322.
[4] 121 U.S., 138.
[5] 157 U.S., 429.

approval, and it was distinctly held that a tax upon incomes from municipal bonds was unconstitutional. The court said: "It was long ago determined that the property and revenues of municipal corporations are not subjects of federal taxation. The same want of power to tax the property or revenue of the states or their instrumentalities exists in relation to a tax on the income from their securities.[1]" It is accordingly an established rule of constitutional interpretation that state and municipal bonds are not subject to federal taxation.

The question which now confronts us is: Will the adoption of the proposed amendment change this situation? The amendment states that Congress "shall have power to lay and collect taxes on income, from whatever source derived, without apportionment among the several states, and without regard to any census or enumeration." What does this mean? It is obvious that the government now has power to levy an income tax; but in attempting to levy such a tax it is met by those provisions of the constitution which declare, first, that "no capitation or other direct tax shall be laid unless in proportion to the census or enumeration hereinbefore directed to be taken"; and secondly, that "representatives and direct taxes shall be apportioned among the several states according to their respective numbers." If these provisions apply to the taxation of income, they mean that if state A, with the same population as state B, has five times the wealth, the income tax payable by a citizen of state B will be five times as large as that payable by an equally wealthy citizen of State A. So monstrous an inequality would, of course, prevent Congress from imposing an income tax as a direct tax. To make a federal income tax practicable, it is necessary either to declare it to be an indirect tax, — the sole restriction as to which is that it shall be uniform, — or expressly to permit the levying of an income tax without apportionment.

For many years the income tax was supposed to be an in-

[1] 157 U.S., pp. 584, 585.

direct tax in the sense in which the term is used in the constitution. Toward the close of the War of 1812, the secretary of the treasury, as we know, brought in a scheme for an income tax and, had peace not been suddenly declared, the scheme would have been adopted. Many signers of the constitution were still living, and no one raised the objection that the income tax was direct in the constitutional sense. During the Civil War the income tax was levied, as we remember, precisely for the reason that it was not a direct tax, and in order to obviate the necessity of a direct tax, levied by apportionment. This Civil War tax moreover was upheld in the first cases adjudicated. Taking each of these cases as decisive only of the precise question before the court, it was settled in Pacific Insurance Company *vs.* Soule[1] that a tax on the premiums received by an insurance company is not a direct tax, and in Springer *vs.* United States[2] that a tax on the income which an individual derives in part from professional earnings and in part from the interest on bonds is not a direct tax. In the Pollock case,[3] on the other hand, it was decided that a tax on the income from real estate is a direct tax, valid only when apportioned, while a tax on municipal bonds was declared to be, like a tax on the salaries of state officers, entirely invalid for lack of power to impose it.

The supreme court of the United States has thus held that certain kinds of income taxes are indirect, that certain other kinds of income taxes are direct, and that still other kinds of income taxes are invalid, irrespective of whether they are direct or indirect. So far as the first two classes are concerned, therefore, the court has stated the law to be that a tax on incomes from certain sources, being direct, can be levied only through apportionment, and that a tax on incomes from other sources, being indirect, can be levied without apportionment. The object of the pending constitutional amendment is simply to remove this discrimination and to make it possible to tax incomes without apportionment,

[1] 7 Wallace, 433 (1868).
[2] 102 U.S., 586 (1880).
[3] 157 U.S., 429 (1894).

whether the sources of the incomes are regarded as falling within the one category or the other. That is, the amendment declares that an income tax can henceforth be levied without apportionment, no matter what the source may be, *i.e.*, no matter whether the source is one that at present necessitates apportionment or one that at present does not necessitate apportionment. When the amendment states that the government shall have power to levy a tax "on incomes, from whatever source derived, without apportionment," chief emphasis is to be put upon the words "without apportionment." The words "from whatever source derived" are indeed no mere surplusage.[1] On the contrary, their real import is to remove the existing discrimination between the various sources of income, so far as apportionment is concerned, and to put those sources which, under the existing interpretation, can be taxed only through apportionment in the same category as those sources which can now be taxed without apportionment. To say "from whatever source derived" is simply another way of saying "irrespective of the source," or a shorter way of saying "from all sources alike, whether the source be one that previously made apportionment necessary or not." So that the amendment is equivalent to the statement that "Congress shall have power to lay and collect a tax on incomes, whether previously laid by apportionment or not, without apportionment." It is accordingly a mistake to assume that the words "from whatever source derived" give the government the power to tax the income from state or municipal bonds, for such a tax falls within the third category of income taxes mentioned above as being entirely beyond the taxing power of the federal government.

[1] It is here that I venture to differ from the position taken by Senator Root in his letter to Senator Davenport of New York on the income tax. *Cf. The Letter of United States Senator Root on the Income Tax Amendment written to Senator Davenport. Presented by Senator Davenport to the Senate and read also in the Assembly.* 1910, 13 pp. Senator Root contends that the phrase "from whatever source derived" is innocuous, because mere surplusage. The present chapter it may be well to state, was written before the appearance of Senator Root's letter.

This has been clearly recognized by the supreme court. In the Pollock case[1] it was expressly held that the objection to the taxation of municipal bonds was lack of power on the part of the general government to interfere with the operations of state government.[2] When the Pollock case was reheard,[3] the court said, in reference to the grounds of the decision in the original hearing: "As to the income from municipal bonds, that could not be taxed because of want of power to tax the source, and no reference was made to the nature of the tax as being direct or indirect."[4] Both on the original hearing and on the rehearing, dissenting opinions were read, but on the point which we are now considering there was no dissent. Justice White said: "The decisions of this court, holding that the federal government is without power to tax the agencies of the state government, embrace such bonds [*i.e.*, those of municipal corporations]. . . . Where there is no power to tax for any purpose whatever no direct or indirect tax can be imposed. . . . The levy whether direct or indirect, is beyond the taxing power."[5]

Justice Harlan, who concurred with the views expressed by Justice White, added: "It is immaterial to inquire whether the tax [on the income of municipal bonds] is, in its nature or by its operation, a direct or an indirect tax; for the instrumentalities of the states . . . are not subjects of national taxation in any form or for any purpose."[6] And Justice Brown stated that a tax upon the income of municipal bonds was, in his opinion, a "tax upon something which Congress has no right to tax at all, and hence is invalid. Here is a question, not of the method of taxation, but of the power to subject the property to taxation in any form."[7]

It is clear, therefore, that a change in the method of assessing an income tax, from that of apportionment to that of direct levy cannot make any difference as to the power of the government to tax the income of state or municipal bonds.

[1] 157 U.S., 429.
[2] *Ibid.*, pp. 584, 585.
[3] 158 U.S., 601.
[4] *Ibid.*, p. 618.
[5] 157 U.S., 652.
[6] *Ibid.*, p. 654.
[7] 158 U.S., 693.

If the federal government is precluded by the very nature of the constitutional pact, as we are told in Collector *vs.* Day,[1] from imposing any tax on state agencies, power to do this will not be conferred upon it by an amendment which simply changes the method of levying a particular kind of tax. What is now non-taxable will remain non-taxable. A change in the method of taxation does not constitute a change in the subject of taxation.

Any other interpretation of the amendment, moreover, would result, in the event of its adoption, in a situation which may well be characterized as absurd. The existing inability of the federal government to tax the property of a state or the instrumentalities of its government will of course continue, for the amendment clearly does not empower Congress to tax property as such. If it were to be held that the amendment gave the federal government power to tax the income of state bonds, we should then have the awkward result that the federal government could not tax the bonds themselves but could tax the income from the bonds. Or, to take a still more absurd case, if a state or municipality possessed some revenue-yielding property, like a piece of real estate, it would be competent for the federal government to tax that real estate if it assessed the tax *eo nomine* on the income, while it would be incompetent for the federal government to tax the real estate if the tax were levied on the property as such. In view of the fact that the market value of any piece of property is due only to its present and prospective income, it will readily be perceived in what a maze of contradictions we should be involved by the acceptance of so strained an interpretation of the amendment. When two interpretations of a clause are possible, of which the one is not only, as the supreme court has asserted, in direct opposition to the spirit of the constitution, but is also calculated to bring about the most awkward practical situation, while the other is in complete harmony with the trend of judicial decisions and at the same time is likely to obviate all fear of fiscal

[1] 11 Wallace, 113.

contradictions or complications, is it not reasonable to assume that the court will prefer the second and more natural interpretation? Such an interpretation is the one which puts the emphasis on the words "without apportionment," and regards the amendment as legalizing a change simply in the method of levying the tax — a change from apportionment to direct assessment.

We are therefore justified in concluding that the essential character of the implied restrictions in the constitution will not be altered one whit by the amendment. State and municipal bonds will henceforth, as before, be exempt from federal taxation, whether the tax be imposed on the property, or whether it be imposed on the income from the property.

§ 3. *The Effect on the Borrowing Power of the States*

If now, for the sake of argument, it be assumed that the contrary view is legally correct, and that the effect of the proposed constitutional amendment would be to legalize the taxation of state and municipal bonds, it may still be shown that the consequences mentioned in the message of Governor Hughes would not follow. We are told that the amendment might "place the borrowing capacity of the state and of its governmental agencies at the mercy of the federal taxing power," and that it might "place such limitations upon the borrowing power of the state as to make the performance of the functions of local government a matter of federal grace."

This opinion, as I hope to show, is erroneous, and the error is traceable to the lack of an adequate economic analysis on the part of the governor — an analysis, indeed, which is equally absent from the legal decisions which have misled him. In other words, even if the governer's law be sound, his economic reasoning is unsound, and his final position is still untenable. Let us leave for a time the whole domain of legal contention and discuss the question of the economic effect of the amendment.

The objection to a tax on governmental securities rests on

the presumption that their market value will be affected by the tax. As the supreme court said in 1829, in Weston *vs.* Charleston:[1] "The tax on government stock is a tax on the contract, a tax on the power to borrow money, on the credit of the government. . . . The right to tax the contract to any extent, when made, must operate upon the power to borrow before it is exercised, and have a sensible influence on the contract." Of course this sensible influence on the contract can register itself only in the lower market price of the securities. This is the result of the familiar economic principle known as the capitalization or amortization of taxation.

The theory of the capitalization of taxation is, in effect, that when a recurring tax of virtually the same amount is imposed upon the capital or selling value of some durable or permanent property, the selling value of that property will be reduced by a sum equal to the capitalization of the tax.[2] If, for instance, the normal rate of interest on securities is five per cent, and a five per cent bond has been selling at par, and if a new tax of one per cent per annum be imposed upon that particular class of securities, the price of the bond will fall from 100 to about 80.[3] The new purchaser of the bond will

[1] 2 Peters, 449.

[2] The whole subject of the capitalization of taxation is fully treated in Seligman, *The Shifting and Incidence of Taxation*, 3d. ed., 1910.

[3] As a matter of fact, whether the price of the security upon which the new tax is imposed will fall exactly to 80 depends very largely upon the amount of these securities, compared with the total amount of capital in the country. If the amount of these newly taxable securities is comparatively large, the price will not fall quite to 80, but perhaps only to 81; for the imposition of a tax on so large a part of the outstanding capital of the country will probably have an influence, even though slight, on the general rate of interest, and may reduce that general rate from five per cent to perhaps four and seven-eighths or four and fifteen-sixteenths. If a large amount of capital is transferred from these newly taxed bonds to other securities, the increasing demand for these other securities, previously selling at par, will enhance their price to a little above par. As, however, the net return on these other securities remains at five dollars, this is equivalent to saying that the rate of interest on the investment will now be a little below five per cent. If the general rate of interest falls to a little below five per cent, the market value of the taxed securities will now be a little over 80. If, as is usually

net only four dollars on the hundred, since he has to pay one dollar in taxes. If, however, he can look forward to a net return of only four dollars, and if the general rate of interest still remains at five per cent, he will naturally pay only eighty dollars for that bond. There is no reason why he should pay more, since he can continue to invest his money in enterprises which are not taxed and which will still net him five per cent. In other words, the annually recurring tax of one per cent will be capitalized into a sum which is automatically deducted from the market value of the securities, thus bringing about an amortization of these securities. At any given time the discrepancy between the taxed and the untaxed securities will be precisely such as to make the net income from each equal the normal rate of interest, and the difference in the market value of the two classes of securities will always be exactly equal to the capitalization of the tax.

The influence of tax exemption is the very reverse of that exercised by taxation. If all securities have hitherto been subject to taxation, and if one particular class of securities be suddenly exempted, the value of these tax-exempt securities will rise by an amount equivalent to the capitalization of tax. If five per cent bonds, like all other forms of capital that are subject to a tax of one per cent, should sell at par, it means that the normal rate of interest is four per cent, since investors net four dollars on every hundred dollars. If this particular class of bonds be now exempted from taxation, the price of the bonds will appreciate to 125, since five dollars bear the same relation to $125 as four dollars do to $100. Thus, whatever way we look at it, taxation will diminish the market value of bonds just as exemption will increase their market value.

Where an annual tax is actually enforced, and where other conditions remain the same, the difference between taxable and non-taxable securities is indeed precisely in accord with

the case, the taxed security forms only an insignificant part of the whole amount of capital, the influence on the general rate of interest will be inappreciable, and the price of the security will fall to 80.

the capitalization theory.[1] In the United States, however, the influence of taxation is sensibly modified by prevailing conditions, and the discrepancy between taxable and non-taxable bonds is far less than might be expected. The rate of the local property tax varies in the United States from one and one-half per cent to over two per cent. Let us take two per cent as the normal figure. Let us also assume that the current rate of interest is four per cent, so that four per cent bonds will sell at about par. If there were no property tax, and if these bonds were now subjected to the two per cent tax, they would manifestly fall to 50, since one-half of their yield would be eaten up by the tax. If, on the other hand, we take the actual law under which all property is taxable at the rate of two per cent, then if the four per cent bonds were exempted from taxation their price on the market ought to rise from par to 200; for instead of the holder netting two dollars on each one hundred dollars (four dollars interest minus two dollars tax), he would now net four dollars, or double the amount. A doubling of the income, however, would involve a doubling of the market value.

As a matter of fact, the disparity between taxable and tax-exempt securities in our American states falls far short of reaching this point. This is true not only of exemption from a special tax, but and in still larger measure, of exemption from a general tax. A good example of the influence of a special exemption is afforded by the New York State canal bonds.[2] When these bonds were authorized, to provide for

[1] An excellent illustration is found in the mortgage bonds of the Northern Railway in France, part of which are issued on its French line and part on the Belgian stretch, although the security is the same in both. In the case of the bonds on the French stretch, however, a special tax is imposed and levied up to the hilt by the French government. In the case of the securities of the Belgian stretch there is no such tax. The difference in the market price of the bonds, on the Paris stock exchange, is exactly equivalent to a capitalization of the French tax. *Cf.* Edgar Milhaud, *L'Imposition de la Rente*. Paris, 1908, pp. 29, 30.

[2] For many of the facts in this section I am indebted to the courtesy of Mr. McKee, of Messrs. N. W. Harris and Company, of New York City, one of the largest American houses dealing in state municipal securities.

the enlargement of the Erie Canal, the constitutional amendment limited the rate of interest to three per cent. By the time that it had become necessary to issue the bonds, the market had fallen to such a point that they were not salable, and in order to change the rate another constitutional amendment became necessary. To arrange for the state finances in the interval, a law was passed granting to the three per cent bonds a special exemption of one per cent, to be applied against the franchise tax of similar amount, payable by savings-banks, trust companies and insurance companies. The three per cents, as a result, sold around a 2.90 per cent basis, and the four per cents around a 3.45 per cent basis. Even here, therefore, the difference in the price of the bonds was only about one-half of the capitalization of the tax.

The case of general exemption is illustrated in Massachusetts. In that state all municipal bonds issued after May 1, 1908, are exempt from taxation. The old taxable three and one-half per cent Boston bonds sold in 1910 in Massachusetts on about a 3.80 per cent basis, the new tax-exempt bonds sold on about a 3.40 per cent basis, *i.e.*, at 101.83 as compared with 94.76. The tax rate was about 1.65, almost one-half of the income of the bonds. In other words, a tax exemption of almost fifty per cent of income made a difference of only seven per cent in selling value. Even this difference, moreover, is largely due to the fact that the chief purchasers of Boston bonds are the Massachusetts savings-banks, which are subject to a fixed tax of one-half of one per cent — a tax that is collected with comparative efficiency.

Where the bonds command a wider market, the influence of tax exemption is naturally far less marked, because the exemption applies only within the state. In Pennsylvania, for instance, bonds are subject to a tax of four mills on the dollar, and some corporations and municipalities pay the tax without deducting it from the interest. In the case of the smaller municipalities, whose bonds are sold only locally or within the state, this tax produces a difference in price between taxable and tax-exempt bonds, but a difference that is far less than a capitalization of the tax. In the larger cities, however, like Philadelphia, Pittsburg and Scranton, where the bonds are a local investment for New York savings-banks, and thus reach a wider market, the difference in value is exceedingly slight. A bond which sells on a 3.90 per cent basis, tax exempt, would in such cases, if taxable, sell only on about a four per cent basis. In the case of general corporate securities which have a still wider market, the difference due to tax exemption is almost inappreciable. A tax security selling at 100 will frequently compare with a tax-exempt security at 102 or 103 — a difference which, when spread over the years prior to the maturity of the bond, represents only the merest fraction of the four mills tax.

In most of the states, however, the tax rate is not four mills, as in Pennsylvania, but, as stated above, from one and one-half to two per cent. Even where a serious attempt is made to enforce the personal property tax, as was formerly the case in Ohio with its tax inquisitor law, the only result is that tax-exempt bonds — Cincinnati bonds, for instance — sell on a 3.80 per cent basis in the local market, while in the general outside market they sell at a lower price — namely on a 3.90 or 3.95 per cent basis. The actual tax, or the risk of taxation of two per cent, hence means a difference of only a few points in the value of the securities.

Even within the area of tax exemption, the larger the amount of the tax-exempt securities, the smaller will be the difference in value between them and the taxable securities. In New York, for instance, so long as tax-exempt bonds were rare, they commanded somewhat of a premium: the New York City two and one-half per cent bonds at one time sold above par, because they were much sought after by savings-banks, trust companies and insurance companies, in order to escape the franchise tax. Since 1908, however, all municipal bonds are exempt from general taxation throughout the state; and the result has been a progressive disappearance of the difference in price between taxable and tax-exempt bonds. Of course two other factors have been coöperating:

the one, that the market in New York City bonds now transcends the capacity of New York City investors; the other, that the assessment of taxable securities in the hands of individuals, under the local general property tax, is becoming even more infrequent than it was formerly. Undoubtedly, however, the chief factor in the progressive elimination of the premium on tax-exempt bonds is the increase in their quantity. It is instructive to note, how, through the inevitable operation of economic law, the very multiplication of tax-exempt state and municipal bonds is gradually defeating the object of the exemption. The greater the area of tax exemption, the less does its influence become.

It appears, accordingly, that, under present American conditions, exemption from a tax which in some cases amounts, nominally, to twenty-five or even fifty per cent of the income of the bonds actually makes no. difference in their market value, or a difference so slight as to be negligible. This at least is the result of the exemption of state and municipal bonds from the general property tax, as levied in the American states. Let us now consider the bearing of this fact upon the results to be anticipated from the imposition of a federal income tax.

The income tax contemplated by the constitutional amendment is very different from the general property tax. A general property tax of two per cent is, we have seen, equivalent to a fifty per cent income tax, if the prevailing rate of interest is four per cent. The federal income tax of 1894 provided for a tax, not of fifty per cent, but of two per cent. If a tax of fifty per cent makes, as we have seen, virtually no difference, what significance can we ascribe to a tax of two per cent? Even if we assume that a federal income tax will be more effectively enforced than a state general property tax, the margin is still so enormous as to rob the income tax of much of its supposed danger. The practical effect of subjecting the income of state or municipal bonds to federal taxation would be so slight as to render the tax virtually innocuous.

We come now, however, to the central point of the argument. In the entire preceding discussion we have assumed the existence of an exclusive tax or of a special exemption. The theory of capitalization or amortization applies only in such cases. If a special tax is permanently imposed on a class of property, it can be capitalized because of the existence of a taxless field to which the taxpayer can repair and in which he can invest his money. If a special class of property is exempt from taxation, the influence will be felt only because the exemption applies to it alone, and not to other classes of property. But if the tax applies to all classes of property alike, there can be no amortization; and if the exemption applies to all classes alike, there can be no capitalization. The very basis of the theory is the exclusiveness or uniqueness of the proceeding. When a tax is a general tax and not an exclusive tax, the theory ceases to apply.

Now the income tax contemplated by the amendment is not a special tax but a general tax. By the very terms of the amendment it applies to all kinds of income, from whatever source derived. This is the true purpose of the measure. It is conceded that if a special tax were imposed *eo nomine* on state and municipal bonds, it would, theoretically at least, have some influence on their market value, although, as we have seen, the practical effect of such a tax would be less than might be expected. But if incomes derived from state bonds are taxed at the same rate as incomes from other bonds, how can the tax have any influence on their value? There is no taxless field to which the bondholder can repair if he seeks to make a different investment. In whatever kind of property he puts his capital, his income will be equally diminished by the tax. But if all incomes are equally diminished, there can be no change brought about in the relative superiority or inferiority of the different sources of income. If five per cent government bonds are selling at par, and if a general income tax of one per cent is imposed on all incomes, the price of government bonds as compared with other securities in general will not be affected one iota. We may go farther, and say that there will be no change at all in the actual values of any securities, unless the tax is so high as to cause a perceptible exodus of capital to foreign countries, with a resulting slight change in the domestic rate of interest, which change in the rate of interest would, of course, reflect itself in the market values of the securities.

The ordinary view is to be traced to the adoption by the supreme court of what it mistakenly conceived to be the opinion of Chief Justice Marshall. In explaining the decision of the court in Weston *vs.* Charleston, Chief Justice Marshall said: "The right to tax the contract to any extent, when made, must operate upon the power to borrow before it is exercised and have a sensible influence on the contract." And again: "To any extent, however inconsiderable, it is a burthen on the operations of government." This reasoning, in these very terms, was applied in the Pollock case to the federal income tax. It is evident, however, that this application is erroneous; for if the tax is a part of a general income tax, there can be no capitalization and no change in the value of the bonds; and hence it cannot "operate on the power to borrow" and cannot be a "burthen on the operations of government." Marshall's statement was justified, in the case which he had before him, for two reasons: first, because the tax in question was, in part at least, *eo nomine* on government bonds; and secondly, because it was a state tax on federal securities. In the Pollock case, however, not only was the court discussing a federal tax on state bonds, but the tax in question was a general tax. Passing over, for the moment, the distinction between a state tax on federal securities and a federal tax on state securities, which will be treated below, the difference between a special tax and a general tax is in itself sufficient to show that Marshall's reasoning does not apply to the Pollock case. In this later case, the failure of the court to estimate the inexorable operation of economic law led it astray; and implicit reliance on the economic views of our later jurists has misled so eminent a statesman as Governor Hughes.

We may accord the fullest authority to the legal reasoning of the supreme court; but when a legal conclusion is based on an economic argument which is plainly fallacious, it is time to call a halt. In this instance the economic reasoning of the supreme court is so obviously defective that it invalidates the entire conclusion. A specific and exclusive tax on state bonds would indeed have the consequences ascribed to it by the court; a general tax could not possibly have those consequences. A tax on the income of state or municipal bonds as a part of a general income tax would leave everything as it was before the tax. If the operations of state governments were previously not burthened, they would not be burthened by such a tax. If the power of the state to contract was not affected before the imposition of the tax, it would not be affected by the imposition of the tax. The economic situation would be unchanged.

It may be claimed, however, that, even if the preceding argument is valid, and even though state and municipal bonds will not suffer in price by being subjected to a general income tax, a special exemption of state and municipal bonds from taxation will enhance their price. Therefore a failure to exempt them might be regarded as virtually tantamount to an attack on the state's credit. This claim is specious, but it is not valid.

In the first place, the actual enhancement of prices due to special exemption will be far less than is usually imagined; for not only will an income tax or an exemption from such a tax have, as pointed out above, no significant influence on the capital value of the security, but the mere fact of the general exemption of all state and municipal bonds would, in itself, tend to mimimize even this slight influence. The exemption of the bonds of a particular municipality might well be expected to exert an influence on their price. But in proportion as other municipal bonds in the state, and state and local securities in other states, come to enjoy the same privilege, the advantage would tend to be neutralized. If the exemption were to apply to all state and local bonds, amounting to many hundreds, or perhaps in the near future even thousands, of millions of dollars, we should see the same development which, as explained above, has actually worn away the original advantage attaching to the tax-exempt bonds of New York City. The broader the exemption area, the less the value of the exemption.

The argument that tax exemption is especially needed in times of crisis is thus robbed of most of its force; for if tax exemption has little value under normal conditions, it can have no great value in times of crisis. At such times, indeed, it will have no value; for in crises bonds are almost completely unsalable. The drop in their price is so great that the question of their taxation or exemption becomes immaterial.

It may be urged, further, that even if the exemption of state securities from a federal income tax were of real advantage to the states, there seems to be no reason why the federal government should confer upon them this advantage. The constitutional inhibition, if it means anything, means only that the national government shall not discriminate against the states by injuring their power to borrow. It does not mean that the national government should discriminate in favor of the states by enhancing their power to borrow. A special exemption of state bonds from a general income tax would, if it increased the market price of these securities, be tantamount to a gift from the national government to the state government. Such a relation, however, is not contemplated by the constitution. It is not the function or the province of the national government to confer gifts or favors upon the state governments. The states can look after themselves, and all that they have a right to ask from the national government is that there shall be no unconstitutional interference with their powers. Equality under the constitution they have a right to claim; special favors they have no right to demand.

Moreover, such an exemption of state and municipal bonds would be inconvenient to the national government and unjust to the individual citizen. Federal securities have at times been taxed by the federal government. It may again become desirable that they shall be so taxed; all the important

European countries now find it, on the whole, advisable to tax their own securities. If the bonds of the United States were taxed under a general income-tax law, and if at the same time state and municipal bonds were exempt, it will be readily seen that this would in effect be subordinating the credit of the United States to that of the local divisions. Such a contingency can be contemplated only with apprehension. Of still greater importance is the consideration that, if state and local bonds were especially exempt as over against the whole mass of private and corporate securities, the individual citizen would have a just cause for complaint. Not only would it mean an escape from taxation for all those who chose to invest in state or local bonds; but, if the advantage were at all appreciable, the increasing demand for these state and local bonds would mean such a transfer of investments as to cause a sensible depreciation in the market value of other securities, and the unfortunate possessors of those other securities would have to suffer a loss, the corresponding gain accruing to the happy possessors of the tax-exempt state and local bonds.

Thus, from every point of view, the special exemption of state bonds from a general income tax is indefensible. It would in all likelihood not accomplish the object which it is designed to attain; but in so far as it did accomplish this object, it would create a glaring inequality, inimical alike to the maintenance of the national credit and to the interests of the mass of the individual taxpayers.

§ 4. *The Immunity of State and Municipal Bonds from Taxation.*

We come now to the final consideration. Even if it were true, as it is not, that the proposed constitutional amendment empowers the national government to tax the income of state bonds, there are valid reasons to justify such a change in the law. Even if the amendment may be so interpreted as to give the federal government this new power, it ought still to prevail.

On what ground, however, it may be asked, can we defend the immunity of national bonds from state taxation, and at the same time uphold the possible legitimacy of the federal taxation of state bonds? Does not the same principle, the independence of each government within its own sphere, apply in both cases? Let us look into this question.

If we examine the successive legal decisions on the subject, we shall find that there have been three stages in the development of the doctrine that the states may not tax the agencies of federal government. In the case of McCulloch *vs.* Maryland, in 1819, the objection was to a special and exclusive state tax on an agency of the federal government; for the tax in question was levied on "all banks, or branches thereof, in the state of Maryland, not chartered by the legislature," and the only bank at that time fitting the description was the Bank of the United States. In the case of Weston *vs.* Charleston, in 1829, the second step was taken by declaring unconstitutional a state or local tax which was indeed not exclusively levied on the instrumentalities of the national government, but which specifically and by name included federal bonds in a list of taxable securities. The third and final stage was reached in the case of Dobbins *vs.* Commissioners of Erie County, decided in 1842, in which it was held that a local tax, entirely general in character and making no special mention of government salaries, was nevertheless invalid so far as it affected the salaries of federal officers. And in the same way, a few decades later, in 1862, it was decided in Bank of Commerce *vs.* New York City that a state tax on federal bonds was unconstitutional even if the tax were entirely general in character and did not mention federal bonds at all. Thus we have a gradual evolution of the doctrine, from the initial stage of exclusive taxation through that of specific mention to the final stage of general taxation.

On the other hand, in the reverse case of the attempt of the federal government to tax state agencies, there was no such gradual evolution of the doctrine. The theory which had reached its complete formulation in 1842 and in 1862, with reference to state taxation of federal agencies, was now, in 1870, taken over bodily to apply to the federal taxation of state agencies. In the case of Collector *vs.* Day it was decided that a general federal income tax was unconstitutional so far as the salaries of state judicial officers were concerned, even though they were not at all specifically mentioned in the law. And in the Pollock case this reasoning was applied to a general federal income tax so far as it reached the income of municipal bonds.

On what grounds, now, can we justify the rule of non-interference with agencies of government in the first set of cases and withhold our approval from its application to the second set of cases? It may at once be conceded that a tax on the agencies of state government which really impairs the operations of state government would be just as obnoxious to the constitution as a similar state tax on federal agencies. It may further be conceded that a special federal tax on state bonds or on the income of state bonds would be just as indefensible as a similar state tax on federal bonds. The question at issue, however, is a different one — it is whether the taxation of federal bonds under a general state tax law is to be put in the same category as the taxation of state bonds under a general federal tax law. In our opinion the two cases are not on a par, and for the two following reasons, the one political, the other economic.

The political ground on which a distinction may be drawn between the two cases is this: a state legislature may frequently find it in the interest of the state to follow a policy which is different from that of other states, and which may even be distinctly opposed to that followed in federal legislation. The states, acting through their legislatures, may regard only their peculiar narrow interests, and may consider them superior to those of the country as a whole. On the other hand, Congress is composed of representatives from all the states, and in the Senate, in particular, equal voice is given to the wishes of each state. There is hence no likelihood of a federal tax law interfering with the states, except where it is the well-considered opinion of a majority of all the states that the interests of any particular state ought to be subordinated to the welfare of the whole. In other words, while the federal government would, without the restrictions which the supreme court has read into the constitution, have no protection against hostile action on the part of state legislatures, the state governments have, from the very nature of the case, a far greater measure of protection against the acts of Congress.

It must, moreover, not be overlooked that all sound constitutional interpretation should keep pace with the changing needs of political and social life. The conditions which existed when the constitution was framed are no longer existent. At that time the political and economic interests of the separate states were so distinct and the sense of state sovereignty was so strong that it was only with extreme difficulty that a federal government was established at all. During the last century, however, the development of the underlying economic and social forces has created a nation, and this development calls for uniform national regulation of many matters which were not dreamed of by the founders. In all the federal states which have been created during the nineteenth century, under the influence of these newer economic forces, in Canada, in Germany, in Australia and in South Africa, we find no such problems as those which vex us, because of the greater authority initially granted to the central government. In Canada, for instance, we find just the reverse of our system. With us all powers not expressly conferred upon the federal government are reserved to the states or to the people; in Canada the powers not expressly conferred on the states or provinces are reserved to the federal government. It is idle to say that this centralization of powers, where centralization is needed, is injurious either to democracy or to self-government. There is at least as much true democracy and as much real self-government in Canada and in Australia as there is in the United

States. Let us not make a fetich of "self-government," and let us not oppose central authority in those cases where self-government means retrogression rather than progress.

The supreme court of the United States has already been influenced by these considerations. In the case of Veazie Bank *vs.* Fenno[1] it was held that a federal tax on state bank-notes was valid, because of the necessity of upholding a national system of currency. In the recent and very important case of South Carolina *vs.* United States[2] it was held that a federal tax on a state dispensary was constitutional. On the other hand, it is certain that the supreme court would never uphold the validity, without the express consent of Congress, either of a state tax on national bank-notes or of a state tax on a federal business or a federal monopoly. In other words, we are gradually working out, in detail, the distinction that Marshall formulated many years ago in McCulloch *vs.* Maryland: "The difference is that which always exists and always must exist between the action of the whole on a part and the action of a part on the whole." Sooner or later it will be realized that this distinction applies also as between a state tax on federal bonds and a federal tax on state bonds. Sooner or later we shall outgrow many of the notions of extreme individualism and of exaggerated state rights which dominated the country at the time of the formation of the constitution. They are bound to disappear in the United States as they have disappeared in every other great federal republic.

If this political argument does not appeal to those who are still enmeshed in the web of extreme individualism and exaggerated state rights, there remains another argument of an economic character which is of decisive importance. Even though we assume that from the political point of view no distinction ought to be made in the matter of taxation between the state and the national government, it is susceptible of proof that valid economic reasons will justify the distinction between a general state tax on federal bonds and a general

[1] 8 Wallace, 533 (1870). [2] 199 U.S., 437 (1905).

federal tax on state bonds. The general state tax to which allusion is made is the general property tax. The general federal tax to which allusion is made is the general income tax. Now a state tax on government bonds, as part of a general property tax, not only is unconstitutional but ought always to remain unconstitutional. State A, which imposes the tax in question, would, of course, from the very nature of the case, tax all other moneyed capital as well as the capital invested in federal bonds. But its neighbor, state B, might see fit not to impose a general property tax. There are several states in the Union which to-day do not impose a general property tax. Or, even if state B imposed a general property tax, its methods of assessment might be so lax that it would not reach all other moneyed capital. Consequently, if state A included government bonds in its taxable general property and actually assessed the bonds, the bonds would undoubtedly be affected in value through the lack of uniformity in the various states. The power of the general government to borrow money might thus be seriously impaired, and this risk would, beyond cavil, constitute a sufficient reason for withholding the power from the states. On the other hand, if the federal government were to impose a general income tax which, under the very terms of the constitution must, as we shall see, necessarily be uniform throughout the country, the income from state bonds would be reached in precisely the same way as the income from all other moneyed capital; and, as we have abundantly shown above, there would be no alteration in the value of the bonds, and therefore no influence exerted on the power of the states to borrow.

The supreme court of the United States went off on a wrong tack, not in the case of Dobbins *vs.* Commissioners in 1842, but in the case of Collector *vs.* Day in 1870. The cases, from the economic point of view, were not on a parity. Had Collector *vs.* Day presented a situation like that in McCulloch *vs.* Maryland, *i.e.*, had it been a question of an exclusive federal tax comparable to the exclusive state tax, the economic basis of the argument would have been the same. But when

Collector *vs.* Day attempted to apply by inversion Dobbins *vs.* Commissioners, — when, in other words, a general federal tax was declared equivalent to a general state tax, — the judges were misled by a superficial analogy which had no basis in economic fact. In the same way the supreme court erred when, in deciding the first Pollock case, it thought that it was applying the principle involved in Weston *vs.* Charleston. Weston *vs.* Charleston dealt with a state tax on federal securities; the Pollock case involved the question of a federal tax on state securities. As we have seen, the economic conclusions which apply in the one case do not apply in the other.

In the long run, however, the economic interests of a community must prevail; for law is nothing but the crystallization of economic and social imperatives. Sooner or later, therefore, the underlying fallacy in the more recent decisions of the supreme court will be recognized by the court itself, or the mistake will be corrected by constitutional amendment. The law cannot permanently lag behind the economic truth.

Entirely apart, therefore, from any legal or political considerations that might be invoked, an economic analysis shows clearly that the inclusion of state bonds under a general federal tax is a very different thing from the inclusion of federal bonds under a general state tax. Since the economic results are or may be so entirely different, the legitimacy of the action of the respective governments is entirely different. From the economic point of view the states ought not to have the right to tax the bonds of the federal government at all; but the federal government might well be justified in including state bonds in a general income tax. Hence, even if the constitutional amendment were to have the legal consequences which are predicated of it, it ought still to prevail, in order to subserve the best economic interests of the whole country.

§ 5. *The Question of Uniformity*

There remains one other point which deserves a word of comment. This refers to the question of uniformity. It might be claimed, and in fact it has been claimed, that under the proposed amendment there will be no assurance of uniformity, for the constitutional provision as to uniformity specifically applies only to "all duties, imposts and excises." Since the amendment, while changing the method of levying the income tax, in so far as it has been held to be a direct tax, leaves unaltered its nature or appellation as a direct tax, it might be contended that the income tax as a direct tax is not necessarily subject to the constitutional inhibition as to uniformity.

This contention, however, is clearly erroneous. The constitution gives a double classification of taxes — one according to their nature, the other according to the mode of levy. According to their nature, taxes are divided into the four classes of direct taxes, duties, imposts and excises. According to the mode of levy, however, taxes are divided into two classes only — those subject to the rule of apportionment and those subject to the rule of uniformity. If, now, the income tax is by constitutional amendment taken out of the first category, it necessarily falls into the second. There is no third category into which it could fall. To assume that an income tax could be levied without uniformity would be to make of the tax neither fish nor flesh — to keep it, as it were, suspended in mid-air between the two solid posts of apportionment and uniformity. These are the only methods contemplated by the constitution. Every tax, no matter what its application, must be levied in one of these two ways. If the one way is barred by the constitutional amendment, it must necessarily be levied in the other way. To assume that under the amendment we could have anything but a uniform income tax would be to do violence to every rule of constitutional construction.

Chief Justice Fuller, in the first Pollock case, makes this clear. He says: "Although there have been from time to time intimations that there might be some tax which was not a direct tax nor included under the words 'duties, impositions and excises,' such a tax for more than a hundred years of national existence has as yet remained undiscovered, notwithstanding the stress of particular circumstances has invited thorough investigation into sources of revenue."[1] Is it reasonable to suppose that the court would fly in the face of the experience of a century in order to create such an abortion? Moreover, any such interpretation of the amendment would lead to a manifest absurdity. For under the existing decisions an income tax levied on business or on professional incomes is still to be classed as an excise or duty, and therefore subject to the uniformity clause. How, then, could we have a general income tax a part of which should be uniform and a part of which should not be uniform? Such a tax would indeed be theoretically possible, but is it conceivable that any legislature composed of sane human beings would attempt to enact such a measure? Moreover, apart from any such considerations, it is scarcely open to doubt that the other clauses, such as the fifth amendment, as well as the implied restrictions of the constitution, would avail to prevent any serious derogation from the principles of equality in taxation.[2]

The six New York lawyers, in their *Memorandum*, seem to doubt this. "It should be realized," say they, "that under the proposed Sixteenth Amendment congress, in exercising the power to lay and collect income taxes, would not be restrained by any constitutional rule; that is to say, that no rule of apportionment nor any other rule of restriction is made applicable and that it could act oppressively."[3] The chief example of such possible oppression is, in their opinion, the danger of graduated taxation.[4]

As to this danger, however, three considerations must be borne in mind. In the first place, all the imaginary perils referred to are already incurred by the United States, for in

[1] 157 U.S., p. 557.

[2] This whole subject is well treated by James M. Gray, *Limitations of the Taxing Power, including Limitations upon Public Indebtedness. A Treatise upon the Constitutional Law governing Taxation, etc.* San Francisco, 1906. See esp. chap. 1, and chap. 8, p. 357.

[3] *Op. cit.* (*supra*, p. 558), p. 14.

[4] *Op. cit.*, pp. 18–21.

the inheritance tax cases[1] the supreme court disagreed with these identical arguments presented by some of the very same counsel, and upheld the principle of progressive taxation. If the country is in danger from that principle, the danger will not be enhanced by the authorization of an income tax; for if there were really any desire on the part of the Congress to confiscate property, it could be far more readily done by a system of graduated inheritance taxes than by a system of graduated income taxes.

In the second place, the counsel make an unfortunate invasion into the field of economics, and present what they consider an irresistible array of opinion opposed to the principles of progressive taxation. This same array of authorities was presented unavailingly to the supreme court both in the income-tax case and in the inheritance tax cases. Had the counsel been as eminent in economic lore as in legal learning, they would have realized that the overwhelming opinion of modern economists is in favor of the very principle which they deprecate,[2] however much all may be agreed as to the undesirability of any extreme application of the principle. To deprecate the abuse, however, is not to oppose the use of a principle.[3] The chief reliance of the six lawyers, moreover, is upon Mr. Lecky, who, as is well stated by the opposing counsel in the first inheritance tax case, "is known as a historian and not as an economist, and who wrote the work cited very much in the character of a partisan apologist for reactionary Toryism in Great Britain."[4]

In the third place, it must not be forgotten that in the very

[1] Magoun *vs.* Illinois Trust and Savings Bank, 170 U.S., 283; and Knowlton *vs.* Moore, 178 U.S., 41.

[2] In the book by the present writer on *Progressive Taxation in Theory and Practice*, 2d ed., New York, 1908, the distinguished counsel could have found a hundred authorities in favor of progressive taxation for every one that they quote in opposition.

[3] *Cf. supra*, p. 34.

[4] *In re* Drake *vs.* Kochersberger, *Brief and Argument for Defendant in Error and Appellee.* By T. A. Moran, Robert S. Iles, Edward C. Akin and Frank L. Shepard. Chicago, n. d. [1898], p. 60.

cases in which the legitimacy of the general principle of graduation is upheld, the supreme court of the United States pointed out the existence of implied restrictions on the power of government to introduce any glaring inequality in taxation. In the first inheritance tax case, where the constitutionality of a graduated inheritance tax imposed by a state was upheld, the court declared the principle of graduation not to be repugnant to the fourteenth amendment, which requires the states to observe due process of law and to follow the principle of equality. But the court was careful to point out that the rule, even with this interpretation, "is not without limitations under the equality clause of the fourteenth amendment,"[1] and proceeded to quote from another recent tax case that "clear and hostile discriminations against particular persons and classes, especially such as are of unusual character, unknown to the practice of government, might be obnoxious to the constitutional prohibition."[2]

The same principle which was stated to be operative on the state governments was declared, in the second inheritance tax case, to be applicable as restrictive of the power of the federal government. The court decided that the meaning of the federal law of 1898 was that the progressive rate applied only to the separate shares, and not to the entire legacy, *i.e.*, that two recipients of a legacy of $20,000, for instance, should be taxed at the same rate, irrespective of whether the legacy was in the one case a part of a hundred thousand dollar estate, or in the other, a part of a million dollar estate. The court intimated that if the contrary interpretation, which it discarded, should be given to the act, it would be unconstitutional as "bringing about a profound inequality which would transcend the limitations arising from those fundamental conceptions of free government, which underlie all constitutional systems."[3] This was certainly a sufficiently conservative doctrine, although Justice Harlan was alone in upholding the other inter-

[1] Magoun *vs.* Illinois Trust and Savings Bank, 170 U.S., p. 294.

[2] Bell's Gap Railroad *vs.* Pennsylvania, 134 U.S, p. 237.

[3] Knowlton *vs.* Moore, 178 U.S., p. 77.

pretation and contending that it did not involve any constitutional inequality.[1]

Finally, in a later passage, the court squarely faced the question of graduated taxation in itself. "Some authoritative thinkers and a number of economic writers contend that a progressive tax is more just and equal than a proportional tax. . . . The grave consequences which it is asserted must arise in the future, if the right to levy a progressive tax be recognized, involves in its ultimate aspect the mere assertion that free and responsible government is a failure, and that the grossest abuses of power are foreshadowed unless the courts usurp a purely legislative function. If a case should ever arise where an arbitrary and confiscating exaction is imposed, bearing the guise of a progressive or any other form of tax, it will be time enough to consider whether the judicial power can afford a remedy by applying inherent and fundamental principles for the protection of the individual, even though there be no express authority in the constitution to do so."[2] The court held, however, that the graduation imposed by the law of 1898 was so reasonable as not to expose the act to any such charge of arbitrariness or confiscation. There was only one dissentient from this opinion, and he put himself on record as entirely opposed to the whole principle of progression.

In view of all these considerations, is it not clear that the uniformity objection is a mere bugaboo?

§ 6. *Conclusion*

In order thoroughly to discuss all the problems raised by the constitutional amendment it would be necessary to go at some length into two further problems: first, to what extent is the taxation of government securities advisable, even by the power that issues them? and secondly, how far is the general scheme of an income tax in itself to be welcomed? These matters, however, would lead us too far astray here,

[1] 178 U.S., p. 111.

[2] *Op. cit.*, p. 109.

and they have, strictly speaking, only an indirect connection with the specific questions that are raised by the amendment. It may be stated, however, that in so far as the question of the taxation of government bonds is concerned, there are good arguments on both sides, and that this question finally resolves itself into a choice between upholding the credit of the government and maintaining exact impartiality as between individual taxpayers. Most of the European countries, after a long period of wavering, have now come to the conclusion that the exemption of government securities from the income tax is on the whole inadvisable, and they are willing to subordinate the slight advantages which would accrue to the borrowing power of the government to what they conceive to be the far greater benefits of complete uniformity and equality as among the various classes of taxpayers. The tendency throughout the civilized world is away from, and not in the direction of, the exemption of government securities.

So far as the problem of a general income tax is concerned, there is perhaps less room for discussion. Many thoughtful citizens, indeed, still have their doubts as to the practicability of an income tax and as to the possibility of the United States government creating a really successful income-tax measure. These points will be taken up in the next chapter. But all these doubts must fade away when the question is presented in all its baldness: "Shall the government of the United States be precluded from even making the attempt to levy an income tax?" To deny to a great empire like the United States the possibility of utilizing so powerful a fiscal engine in times of national stress would be almost equivalent to advocating national suicide. At all events, it amounts to a deliberate decision to put the national government at an enormous disadvantage at the very time when no possible advantage can safely be neglected. To withhold from the government of the United States a power which is possessed by the smallest of its competitors would be a monstrous folly.

Whether an income tax is a desirable supplement to the ordinary tax system of the United States in times of peace is a far-reaching question which will be discussed later. But surely no patriot can afford to object to conferring upon the United States a power which until recently it was always supposed to possess, and without which its prosperity — nay, even its very existence — might possibly be menaced. The pending constitutional amendment seeks to secure this result, and its adoption ought not to be impeded by arguments that place upon it an erroneous interpretation and conjure up dangers which a more careful economic analysis shows to be wholly non-existent. The pending constitutional amendment, even though it does not go so far as some might think wise, is not only legally defensible and politically innocuous, but it is, above all, economically sound. It is therefore from every point of view eminently desirable.

CONCLUSION

A PRACTICABLE PROGRAMME

CONCLUSION

A Practicable Programme

Now that we have studied the historical development of the income tax at home and abroad and have called attention to some of the general considerations which apply to the topic, it remains to draw the conclusion as to the actual problem confronting the American people. This problem is really three-fold. In the first place, we must decide whether, in the light of existing conditions, an income tax is in itself desirable as an adjunct to our tax system. In the second place, assuming that the answer is affirmative, the next query is whether the income tax should be a state or a federal tax, or, perchance, a combination of the two; and in the third place, the final and most important question is what kind of an income tax should we have and how should the administrative features be elaborated in order to insure success.

§ 1. *Is an Income Tax Desirable?*

In approaching the question as to the desirability of an income tax under actual conditions, we must carefully consider the American fiscal system as a whole. Partly as a result of constitutional restrictions, but chiefly as a consequence of a natural evolution, there has been in the main a separation between the sources of state and of national revenue. The commonwealths started out with a general property tax, or a land tax which soon developed into a general property tax. The national government began with a system of import duties, which were exclusively reserved to it. For a long time these two sources of revenue sufficed and developed independently of each other. During almost a decade, at the close of the eighteenth century, the tariff was supplemented by an internal revenue system ; but this was abolished in 1802, and was revived for only a few years during the period of the war of 1812. With the advent of the Civil War, however, the internal revenue became, and has since remained, an integral part of the national fiscal system. For the most part the internal revenue has been derived from indirect taxes or excises. The experiment with the so-called direct tax levied on real estate, which worked fairly well in 1798, was less successful in 1813, and aroused such complaints during the Civil War that the tax was subsequently repaid. A century ago, amid primitive conditions, real estate values and population were fairly proportional to each other; in modern times, under the influence of industrial changes, this proportion has been so greatly altered that the constitutional method of apportioning a direct tax would involve an enormously greater burden upon the landowner of an agricultural state like Mississippi than upon the owner of a precisely similar amount of land in an industrial state like Massachusetts. The direct real estate tax has thus lost its original equality, and is as a consequence not likely to be repeated. The only other case where the federal government entered upon what has come to be considered the reserved fiscal domain of the states, was that of the inheritance tax, levied during the Civil War and again during the Spanish war. In the main, then, it may be said that the national government has chosen sources of revenue which are not employed by the state governments.

On the other hand, the states have almost uniformly refrained from trenching on the field of excises or internal revenue occupied by the federal government. In the case of excises there are exceedingly few instances of commonwealth activity, as, for instance, in Delaware and Kentucky. So far as license taxes are concerned, we find a somewhat more widespread activity on the part of the commonwealths, especially in the southern states. Such licenses, however, have been gradually abandoned by the federal government, and have come to be reserved only for special exigencies. The same observation may be made with reference to the only other point of conflict, namely, the stock-exchange tax in New York, which is analogous to the similar taxes imposed by the federal government during the Civil War and the Spanish war.

Taking it all in all, therefore, the fiscal practice of the United States has been to distinguish, for normal purposes at least, rather sharply between federal and state sources of income, the federal revenue tending more and more to limit itself to that derived from customs duties and excises on commodities, while the state revenue has been, to an overwhelming extent, secured from direct taxes on property, both individual and corporate.

In considering, therefore, whether an income tax is a desirable adjunct to the American tax system, we must approach it from both the fiscal and the social point of view; or, to be more precise, since the fundamental object of every tax is really fiscal, we must study not only its direct results as a producer of revenue but also its incidental consequences on social and economic progress. And this study must furthermore be prosecuted from the point of view successively of federal and of state revenue, without, however, attempting in this stage of our inquiry to decide as to whether it ought to be a state or a federal tax. We are, therefore, really confronted by four distinct questions: Is the tax needed for revenue? Is it needed for elasticity? Is it needed for purposes of compensation? Is it needed for purposes of local tax reform?

In the first place, then, what are the revenue considerations attaching to the income tax? So far as national taxation is concerned, it will scarcely be doubted that the income tax is not needed — at all events not for purposes of normal revenue. For over half a century before the Civil War, all the necessities of the federal government were met by the tariff; and since then the internal revenue, which was imposed to defray the war expenses, and retained to pay the interest and principal of the debt, has been continually reduced in the rate of tax and restricted in the choice of commodities subject to tax. For several decades before the Civil War the tariff was primarily a tariff for revenue; since then it has become a tariff for protection, with incidental revenue. This is not the place to consider the merits of protection versus so-called free trade; but it is reasonably certain that in the form either of a protective or of a revenue tariff, the customs duties, in addition to a moderate and restricted application of internal revenue taxes, will continue to suffice for ordinary purposes. If in future it should become desirable somewhat to diminish the revenue from the tariff, it would be a simple matter to make good the deficiency by a slight increase in the rates of the existing excises, or by a small addition to the articles subject to excise. We do not often stop to think what an immense potential resource is afforded by the excise system. In a country of the prodigious wealth of the United States it is no exaggeration to say that the entire expenses of the national government could be easily met by a system of internal excises which would even then be moderate in both rate and extent. Instead of reckoning our internal revenue by the few hundreds of millions, we could; without great difficulty, reckon it almost by the thousands of millions.

Even when the need for extraordinary revenue arose, it might in large measure be supplied by further extending the excises, and supplementing them by stamp and transportation taxes. It is only in the rare exigency, when the resources of government are strained to the utmost in a foreign war, necessitating a resort to every conceivable sort of revenue, that a good argument might be framed for a national income tax simply as a revenue-producer. Such an exigency, however, arose during the Civil War, and might easily recur. It is this argument which, as we have seen,[1] is the convincing one as to the desirability of the passage of the sixteenth amendment; for when worst comes to worst, no government ought to be without the power of tapping every imaginable resource. The question, however, that we are here considering is not whether the government should possess the constitutional

[1] *Supra*, p. 627.

power to impose an income tax, but whether a national income tax is really needed for ordinary revenue purposes. Put in this way, the question must clearly be answered in the negative. As a part of the regular tax system of the national government, the income tax is assuredly not needed for revenue purposes.

If, however, it is not needed for national purposes, is it needed for state purposes? It cannot be too often emphasized that what we are discussing here is not whether the income tax is a better or fairer tax than any other, but whether the existing tax system works so unsatisfactorily from the point of view of revenue that the income tax is needed as a supplement. It is obvious that if we frame the question in this way the answer again is not doubtful. Whatever may be the objections to the general property tax, it cannot be claimed that it has failed to secure revenue. The questions of a possible inadequacy of state revenue have arisen not so much in those states which still levy the general property tax as in those which, like New York, have virtually abandoned the property tax for state purposes and are securing the necessary revenues in other ways. Even in such states, however, an ample fund may be found in the corporation, the inheritance, the mortgage, the liquor-license, and the stock-exchange taxes. Whatever force, accordingly, there may be in the demand for an income tax on the part of either the state or the nation, it is not to be found in the purely revenue argument.

The second possible argument is that the income tax, although not needed for revenue, is still desirable for purposes of flexibility or elasticity of income. This function of the income tax, as we know, has until recently been the chief characteristic of the British income tax. The strength of this position in general is undoubted. It is clear, however, that the argument is of slight consequence so far as state income taxes are concerned, especially where, as in the great mass of cases, the general property tax still exists. For if there is any one good point about the system of the general property tax for state purposes, it is precisely its inherent elasticity. In our various states the process of raising a revenue is simple. The amount of revenue needed is known as soon as the appropriation bills have been passed. All that is necessary is to divide the amount of revenue required by the valuation of property in the state, or in the respective subdivisions, and the result is the tax rate. Nothing could be simpler. Even in those few states where the general property tax has been abandoned as a source of state revenue, the missing elasticity could be reintroduced through one of the other taxes. The income tax is therefore not needed for purposes of elasticity in the states.

In the federal government the argument, although of somewhat more weight, is really not strong, since we have virtually no budget at all. Under existing methods no attempt is made to calculate closely and to bring about a balance between expenditure and revenue such as exists in other civilized countries. Under our form of government, with the strict separation of powers and the dominance of committee management in Congress, we have become accustomed to a series of surpluses followed by a series of deficits, and we pursue the wasteful practice of making good the deficits out of the accumulated surplus. Until an entirely different and more modern method of budgetary practice is introduced into the national government, the need of some elastic tax to secure an equilibrium between income and outgo is not evident. Even when that time comes, however, it does not follow that the end can be achieved only by the income tax. In France and Germany close budgetary calculations are made, and in neither country is there any national income tax.

We may therefore conclude that while the elasticity argument for the income tax is a fairly good one, it is applicable only to a national income tax, and even there only in part.

We come in the third place to a more important problem. If the income tax is not needed for purely revenue purposes, and if it is not greatly needed for the purpose of elasticity, is it needed for purposes of justice?

Here again we must distinguish between state and national finance. Let us take up first the national situation.

It has become customary in modern times to frame a general indictment against the entire scheme of customs duties and internal revenue as unjust because it constitutes a system of taxes on expenditure. It is this feeling which led Lassalle, a half century ago, in his famous work entitled *Indirect Taxes and the Workingman*, to oppose such imposts; and it is somewhat the same idea which induced Shearman a generation later to speak of *Crooked Taxation*, by which he meant indirect taxation.[1] To this general indictment exception may, however, be taken, for two reasons. In the first place, the scheme of taxation must be considered as a whole. When the burden finally rests upon the individual, it makes very little difference to him who receives the proceeds. Whether he pays the amount to one official or several is immaterial to him as long as the amount does not vary. In estimating the expediency of federal taxes on expenditure we must therefore consider the state and local taxes, which are primarily levied not on expenditure, but on property. If we assume—and for the purposes of this argument it may be assumed—that these taxes really effect their purpose, a strong defence may be made for federal customs and internal revenue. For all publicists and statesmen agree that exclusive reliance on either direct or indirect taxes is impossible. To secure the entire revenue for all the various kinds of government—local, county, state, and national—from direct taxes alone would under present conditions require such an augmentation of the rate as to exaggerate the difficulties, to foster evasion, and to engender inevitable dissatisfaction. Indirect taxes therefore may be upheld on the simple ground that without their aid the burden of direct taxes would become a crushing one. It is not so much the crookedness as the burdensomeness of a tax which is really important.

But indirect taxes may be defended for a second reason. The contention that, because direct taxes alone respond to the principle of faculty or ability to pay, they must be exclusively utilized for fiscal purposes, involves a misconception. The

[1] *Natural Taxation.* By Thomas G. Shearman. New York, 1895, chap. ii.

principle of faculty has indeed, as we have seen all through this volume, a very decided strength of its own. But, as we have pointed out elsewhere,[1] it is not adequate to explain the entire problem of public revenue. The principle of faculty or ability is primarily an individual principle. It attempts to interpret the fiscal relations of the government to the individual. Side by side with the individual principle, however, there has come into the foreground in modern times the social principle, — the principle, namely, that the government, in laying any particular tax, should be guided by the social consequences, — that is, by the results upon groups or classes rather than upon individuals; or, to express it in another way, that attention should be paid not simply to the immediate results upon the individual, but also to the wider consequences that ensue from the fact of his being a part of society.

From this point of view much may be said in favor of a system of customs duties and internal taxes, provided they are taxes of the right kind. A correctly devised tariff, for instance, could, without difficulty, be so adjusted that the burden would fall with comparative equality upon the community as a whole. Even a protective tariff could conceivably be so framed that there would be no undue or special favors to enterprises that did not deserve them, so that whatever of truth there is in the diversified-industry argument could be realized, thereby spreading the benefits of an intelligent protection over the community as a whole, and fostering the prosperity of all classes rather than increasing the profits of a few favored individuals. Again, if the tariff were one for revenue only, the duties could be so devised as not to press with undue severity upon the consumption of the poorer classes, but might be levied primarily upon articles of luxury and of middle-class consumption.

Much the same may be said of a system of internal revenue taxes. There is, indeed, no doubt that in the Middle Ages,

[1] "Pending Problems in Public Finance," in *Proceedings of the Congress of Arts and Sciences, Universal Exposition, St. Louis, 1904*, vol. vii, pp. 191 *et seq.* Boston, 1906.

under aristocratic influences, some of the most hideous fiscal enormities were found in this category, even though it may be doubted whether the abuses of the indirect taxes on consumption in France or Italy were really much worse than the abuses of the direct taxes on the poor. In the face, however, of general excises or of the multiplicity of taxes on commodities the weight of which rested primarily on the poor, it was but natural that the reaction should take the form of an attempt to develop direct taxes. But the modern democratic movement in all civilized countries has succeeded in framing a system of internal revenue taxes which preserves most of the good points and eliminates most of the bad points of the older system. Everywhere the tendency is to concentrate the excises upon a very few articles which, like tobacco and spirituous liquors, combine in a marked degree the seemingly opposite qualities of luxury and of mass consumption. Such taxes, as in the United States to-day, are not only susceptible of affording an immense revenue, but accomplish this result in a way which does not contravene any principle of justice. In so far as the tax tends to restrict consumption, the argument in favor of these taxes is specially strong, since here if anywhere the restrictive effect of taxation is to be welcomed; while the prodigious revenue derived from such sources renders to that extent unnecessary the resort to the higher rates or the more burdensome kinds of direct taxes.

The general argument, then, that an income tax is needed for federal purposes in order to countervail the weight of the customs duties and the internal revenue taxes, is doubly weak. For in the first place, if these national taxes require a compensation, the compensation already exists, or can easily be made to exist, in the state and local property taxes; and in the second place, entirely apart from this, a system of customs duties and internal revenue taxes may be so arranged as to require little, if any, compensation at all to the direct taxes. Our internal revenue taxes are already for the most part on the proper basis, and it is not entirely hopeless to expect that the tariff duties may gradually be so changed as to retain the good, and to eliminate the evil, features.

In the preceding argument there is, however, one important gap. We have proceeded on the assumption that even if the tariff be so changed as to remove some of its objectionable features, a makeweight to the indirect taxes on expenditure exists, or can be made to exist, in the state and local system of property taxes. Here, however, is the difficulty. In theory the system of state and local taxation is calculated to reach the respective abilities of the property-owners; but in practice, as has repeatedly been pointed out, the general property tax has broken down completely; and, especially so far as personal property is concerned, the wealthier classes stand from under. Everywhere we meet the growing complaint that great wealth does not bear its share of the public burden. If, then, the tariff, as it actually exists, imposes too large a share of the burden on the expenditure of the poorer classes, and if the state and local revenue systems do not succeed in reaching the abilities of the more well-to-do classes, the argument becomes exceedingly strong in favor of some form of tax which will redress the inequality.

It is this argument which, as we have seen, was really at the bottom of the movement for the income tax of 1894, and which explains the great development of income taxes abroad. Although we may well concede that the principle of faculty is not the only one to be borne in mind by the fiscal administrator, it is none the less undeniable that a general movement which runs counter to the principle of faculty is doomed to failure. Under existing conditions in the United States the burdens of taxation, taking them all in all, are becoming more unequally distributed, and the wealthier classes are bearing a gradually smaller share of the public burden. Something is needed to restore the equilibrium; and this something can scarcely take any form but that of an income tax. Without prejudicing the question whether it should be a state or a federal tax, it is difficult to escape the conclusion that some form of income taxation is needed to redress existing inequalities.

We come finally to the fourth possible argument in favor of an income tax. We have called attention to the breakdown of the general property tax in state and local taxation. In almost all our states there is such a diversity between the legal system and the practical situation that the attempt to assess personal property gives rise to the most striking abuses and the most shocking injustice. The efforts on the part of tax-reformers to bring about a change in the law have heretofore failed, very largely because of the perfectly explicable feeling on the part of the great mass of the voters that the wealthier classes, with their great ownership of personal property, should in some way be made to bear their share of the burden. Unfortunately the attempt to accomplish this laudable result by a strict enforcement of the local property tax has turned out to be a dire failure. If now the average citizen could see that the wealthier classes were actually subject to some form of income taxation, even if they paid this tax to the state or to the federal government, rather than to the local government, the opposition to a reform of local taxation on sound lines would very largely disappear, and it would doubtless be far easier to effect a readjustment of the entire fiscal system without the present complications of a general property tax. It is significant that this is precisely what happened in England. There the local taxes were for a long time assessed on personalty as well as realty, and the attempt to confine the local rate to real estate met with somewhat the same difficulty that is encountered at present in the United States. It was not until shortly before the middle of the nineteenth century that the local taxes, or rates, as they are called, were limited to real estate; and it was only a few years thereafter that the national income tax was imposed. To ascribe to these events the character of cause and effect would doubtless be extravagant; but it is scarcely open to doubt that the opposition to the change in the system of local taxation would have been far more pronounced had there not been in prospect some method of reaching the income from personal property. Is it too much to hope that a similar result will ensue in the United States?

To sum up: We have seen first that the income tax is not needed for purposes of revenue in either the state or the nation; and in the second place, that the elasticity argument does not hold good at all in the state, and is of very slight weight in the nation. We have seen, in the third place, that the compensatory or makeweight argument has been considerably exaggerated, and that if the tariff were altered on correct lines, and if the system of state and local taxation could be changed, as might well be the case, the income tax would then not be needed for either state or local purposes.

But on the other hand, it is obvious that there is no immediate likelihood of a revolutionary change in the tariff, and we have learned that the system of state and local taxation is becoming in some respects progressively worse rather than better. In the face of this situation the argument for some kind of an income tax becomes very strong. When we join to this argument the further consideration that the adoption of an income tax would not only tend to redress existing inequalities, but would also in all probability make a reform of our entire system of state and local taxation more easy of accomplishment, the arguments in favor of the adoption of an income tax acquire additional weight. When, finally, we add to these considerations the reflection that the income tax is in harmony with a pronounced tendency throughout the civilized world, and that wherever we find the spread of democracy, we find the growth of income taxation, the argument for the adoption of some form of income tax becomes well-nigh irresistible.

§ 2. *Shall the Income Tax be a State or a Federal Tax?*

If, then, an income tax is a desirable adjunct to the American fiscal system, the next problem is, shall it be a federal or a state tax? This question is now becoming an acute one because of the emergence of the demand for a state income tax in one or two of our western commonwealths. In a previous chapter,[1] we have already touched upon this question to a certain extent; but it seems wise to consider the problem here from a somewhat broader point of view.

In order to help us to form a conclusion, four sets of considerations must be borne in mind. First, what is the basis of the tax? Second, what are the chances of administrative success? Third, how far is the problem complicated by considerations of double taxation? And fourth, are there any dangers involved to the fiscal autonomy of the states? Let us take up these points in order.

In the first place, the problem of the basis of taxation involves the question as to whether a given source of revenue is naturally more suitable for utilization by one tax jurisdiction rather than by another. It is obvious that in proportion as the basis of a tax is more widely extended, the argument in favor of its utilization by the broader tax jurisdiction becomes correspondingly stronger.[2] One of the chief reasons, for instance, why a tax on real estate is not employed by the central government is because the basis is so narrow. And it is largely because the tax on real estate is unsuitable even for state revenue that it is in many places gradually being relegated to the local jurisdictions. In the United States, at all events, there is no doubt that a tax on real estate is obviously unfitted for the federal government. We have had but three instances of such a federal tax, and the last experiment was so unsuccessful that its repetition is exceedingly doubtful.

While real estate, with its narrow basis, stands at one extreme of the scale, we find at the other extreme, with a very

[1] *Supra*, p. 426 *et seq.*

[2] For an elaboration of this point see the article by the present writer, "The Relations of State and Federal Finance," in *State and Local Taxation. Third International Conference. International Tax Association*, Columbus, 1910, pp. 212 *et seq.*

wide basis, articles of general consumption. The widest possible basis is afforded by commodities of so-called mass consumption, like tobacco and spirituous beverages; and we accordingly find that in the United States, as everywhere else, taxes on these commodities are reserved for the use of the broadest tax jurisdiction. Almost without exception the American states have voluntarily refrained from utilizing this source of revenue because of the obvious unsuitableness for state purposes of taxes on consumption. The same is true to a still greater extent of customs duties, which are almost everywhere kept for national or federal use. So strongly were these conditions of suitability present in the minds of our forefathers that the constitution not only expressly reserved the employment of import duties to the federal government, but provided that the indirect taxes should be uniform throughout the country. It is clear that this desirable uniformity would be completely lost if the separate states were to arrogate to themselves this important source of revenue.

In between the land tax on the one hand and the indirect taxes on consumption on the other, lie the general property and income taxes. So far as the general property taxes are concerned, these everywhere started out, as we know, as local taxes, and for a long time remained suitable for such purposes. For not only did the general property tax comprise land, which is an especially good source of local revenue, but the remaining constituent elements of property consisted very largely of articles of personalty which were visible and tangible, and thus had a local situs. We have learned, however, how, with the development of commerce and industry and with the splitting up of personalty into property no longer found in the immediate neighborhood of the owner, and especially with the appearance of intangible personalty on a considerable scale, the local property tax became less and less successful, until it everywhere broke down. In the United States today we are in this unsuccessful stage of the general property tax very largely because of the fact that we employ the old local administrative methods, which have become entirely unsuitable to modern conditions.

The same may be said of the income tax. If there is anything that may be considered a well-settled induction from experience, it is that an income tax is less successful as the basis of the tax becomes narrower. In former times a local income tax was fairly workable, because incomes were chiefly local in character. In modern times, however, the income of the taxpayer, and especially the income of the large taxpayer, has very little to do with the locality in which he happens to live. If local property taxes have broken down in America largely because of the narrowness of the basis, local income taxes would be still more likely to be unsuccessful.

But, it may be asked, conceding that the locality is too narrow a basis for the income tax, would not a state income tax be perfectly feasible? It may indeed be granted that a state income tax — that is, a tax levied and assessed either by a state board or by local officials, adequately controlled by state authorities — would constitute a considerable improvement. It may be observed, however, that state centralization of assessment in the case of the income tax would have to be something far different from the present state boards of equalization employed in connection with the general property tax. It would be necessary for the state authorities not simply to equalize local assessments, but to exercise from the very outset a very effective control over the original local assessment.

The difficulty with the whole theory, however, is this: If a state income tax is preferable to a local income tax because of the more extended basis of the tax, cannot the argument be carried a step further, so as to result in the conclusion that a federal income tax would be still better than a state income tax, because of the still greater widening of the basis? In fact, if we once depart from the principle of the local basis for the income tax, there is really no good halting-place until we reach the national basis. Incomes nowadays, through the working out of economic forces over which we have no control, have become national, and even international, in character, or, at all events, have far transcended state lines. A man may live in one state, and may secure his income partly from real estate holdings situated in another state, and partly from investments in securities of corporations whose earnings are derived in many other states. How would it be possible for any state administration successfully to ascertain, or adequately to control, such income of its resident citizens? There is, indeed, a distinction to be observed between the newer or more agricultural and slightly developed states, as compared with the great commonwealths which contain the busy marts of industry and commerce, and the homes of capitalists deriving their incomes from all over the country. It is not impossible that in some states of the former category a state income tax, so far as this particular argument of basis is concerned, might work fairly well; just as there are communities to-day where the local property tax works fairly well. But it is exceedingly probable that in the more developed centers a state income tax would be relatively unsuccessful, because of the disparity between the base of the tax and the control of assessment.

Moreover, with the passing of every successive year, as the conditions in the more primitive and undeveloped communities began to approximate those in the older and more industrial states, the difficulties would soon appear. Instead of becoming from year to year a better tax, according to the principle that old taxes are good taxes, it would, on the contrary, tend to become continually worse. The broader the basis, the broader should be the control of assessment; the more individuals living within a state who have economic relations outside of the state, the more unsuitable does an income tax become for state purposes. In the United States economic life is fast becoming almost everywhere a national economic life, and as a consequence incomes are coming more and more to be national in character. An attempt to control national incomes by state methods does not promise much success. If a state income tax is better than a local income tax, a federal tax is better than a state income tax.

In the second place, let us consider the problems connected with double taxation. One of the chief embarrassments that are found in every federal government, and which are themselves another result of the disparity of base mentioned above, are those arising out of conflicts of tax jurisdiction. It is well known, for instance, that the practical injustice connected with the American general property tax is largely due to this fact. Owing to the existence of the legal fiction *mobilia sequuntur personam*, a man's personal property is supposed to be taxed in the place of his domicile. This rule, however, has suffered amendment in two important particulars. If the personalty in question is capable of a situs, it is sometimes taxed where it is situated. In such a case it would be taxed twice — once by the state which follows the first rule, and again by the state which adopts the second rule. Or, as is sometimes the case, the property would not be taxed at all, because of the reverse rules adopted by each state in the frequently erroneous belief that the opposite rule was adopted by its neighbor. Secondly, when we come to the question of intangible personalty, and more especially corporate securities, the difficulties multiply. One state may tax a corporation where it is legally domiciled, that is, where its principal place of business is to be found; another state may tax the same corporation where its property happens to be; and a third state may tax the stockholder where he chances to reside. The same property may, therefore, be taxed three times over, and there may be all manner of variations of this principle. In the case of the inheritance tax, as it has developed of recent years, the opportunities of complication are still more numerous: a man may die in one state, his legal residence may be in a second, and his property may be located in another state. In the case of a state income tax the embarrassments would be greater, rather than less. A man might reside in one state, his legal domicile might be in a second state, his income might be derived from railroad securities which may be in a safe deposit vault in a third state; the railway itself may have its chief office in a fourth state, and its track may traverse several other states. Where and how should this income be taxed? There are all possibilities of inequality, ranging from the complete escape from taxation, which may arise on the erroneous belief by one state that the income would be assessed in some other state, down to the simultaneous taxation of the identical income by half a dozen different states. The possible combinations are almost terrifying in their complexity; and with more adequate administrative methods on the part of the separate states, the possibility might become a reality.

It may be contended, indeed, that these dangers of duplicate taxation may be averted. In some countries like Germany the conflicts of state jurisdiction have been minimized, as we know,[1] by the enactment of a national law which imposes upon the separate states a certain degree of uniformity of action. It is clear, however, that the American commonwealths would not brook such national interference, even if it were constitutional; and it is scarcely open to doubt that the accomplishment of the desired end would require a constitutional amendment which it would be well-nigh impossible to secure. The other method of avoiding the embarrassment would be by interstate agreements, based on considerations of interstate comity, whereby each state would bind itself to refrain from levying more than its equitable and proper share of the tax. While this consummation would be exceedingly desirable, it may well be doubted whether it is at all feasible. For in the first place, it would be necessary to elaborate some general system of equitable apportionment which would have to approve itself to all the states concerned; and secondly, even if such a principle were accepted in theory, it would be virtually impossible to secure its accomplishment in practice. American experience in many other domains of an economic character has unfortunately driven home the lesson that the separate commonwealths cannot be

[1] *Supra*, p. 270.

depended upon voluntarily to relinquish any weapons which may constitutionally be employed in the struggle of local and sectional interests for economic advantage. Even if the majority of the states could be induced to enter into such a compact, the defection or refusal of a few would be sufficient to defeat the whole scheme. And even if all these difficulties were eliminated, the attempt to levy a state income tax, so far as corporations are concerned, would still encounter the constitutional obstacles connected with interstate commerce.

In view of all these considerations, is it not hopeless to expect that any state income tax could solve the difficulties of interstate double taxation? And is it not a reasonable conclusion that the income tax ought to be a national tax, if for no other reason than that all these difficulties would at once vanish into thin air?

The third consideration that confronts us is that of administrative efficiency. Irrespective of the difficulties adverted to above, would the administration of a state income tax be as successful as that of a federal income tax?

Administration is one of the sore points of American public life. It is a trite saying that we have solved many of our constitutional problems, but have scarcely begun to attack the administrative problems. Administration in a democracy is proverbially difficult. In a community where every one considers himself as good as his neighbor, respect for expert knowledge is not likely to be so great as in an aristocracy or autocracy. The university professor, for instance, occupies a far higher position, socially and financially, in Russia than he does in the United States. Not only is democracy less favorable to the dominance of the expert, but it is also less favorable to administrative efficiency in other respects. Permanence of tenure, with all the knowledge that results therefrom, is difficult to secure. "To the victors belong the spoils" is a principle which it is not easy entirely to eradicate. And finally, the general attitude of the average citizen to the government official is more likely to be that of superior to inferior, rather than the reverse. Where the official knows that he is dependent for his continuance in office upon the good will of the individuals with whom he comes into immediate contact, he is apt in any doubtful case to decide the question in favor of the citizen, rather than of the government. Democratic administration, in short, is apt to be lax and inefficient administration.

This is, of course, not necessarily or permanently true. It represents rather the dangers inherent in democracy — dangers over against which are to be set the inestimable advantages of a democratic form of government. But even these dangers can be met and resolutely overcome. A more enlightened and intelligent democracy will learn to value expert knowledge, and, through various devices, to minimize the perils. The last quarter of a century has seen in many domains a very marked improvement in American administrative methods, and what has been so auspiciously begun will, without doubt, be carried forward in the future.

The progress that has been made, however, has thus far been most noticeable in national administration, somewhat less so in state administration, and not yet so pronounced in local administration. So far as the relations of local and central government are concerned, there are in the civilized world to-day three main types, the characteristics of which have recently been admirably portrayed by Sidney Webb.[1] "On the European continent we find the local administration entrusted in the main to salaried officials of special training and high professional qualifications, whose work is closely supervised by, and completely subordinate to, the various departments of the executive government. . . . The functions and powers of the local councils are narrowly limited; and their actual interferences with the day by day administration are, in almost all cases, subject to the control and

[1] In his preface to J. Watson Grice, *National and Local Finance. A Review of the Relations between the Central and Local Authorities in England, France, Belgium, and Prussia during the Nineteenth Century.* London, 1910, pp. vii *et seq.*

approval of the central executive departments." This Mr. Webb calls the Bureaucratic System.

At the other extreme stands the organization of local government in the United States. Here "there is nothing in the nature of an administrative hierarchy, and nothing in the nature of a national system, whether in education, sanitation, or means of communication. This, which has its merits as well as its characteristic drawbacks, may be termed the Anarchy of Local Autonomy. It has given the United States the worst local government of any State claiming to be civilized." Finally, in England, they "have, by characteristic good luck, stumbled on a third arrangement," which lies midway between the other two.[1]

So far as financial administration is concerned, there is no doubt that the United States is suffering from this "anarchy of local autonomy." The attempts to secure a somewhat

[1] Between 1590 and 1640 an organized national system was in process of development in England, but "when this (with much else) got knocked on the head in 1642, there remained only an Anarchy of Local Autonomy, lasting from 1660 to 1835, which was strictly comparable with much in the United States to-day." Then England set to work "to find some way of securing national inspection and audit, and the amount of national supervision and control that was required in the interest of the community as a whole, without offending the susceptibilities of local autonomy, and without losing the very real advantages of local initiative and local freedom to experiment. Without theory, almost without the notice of political students, a solution has been found in the device of the Grant in Aid. The National Government, in the course of the past three-quarters of a century, has successively 'bought' the rights of inspection, audit, supervision, initiative, criticism, and control in respect of one local service after another, and of one kind of local governing body after another."

Mr. Webb goes on to point out that "in reality the Grant in Aid is the necessary hinge in the flap. The elected local council, administering its own business in its own way, is far too valuable an element in British freedom to be superseded. On the other hand, the poorer localities need aid to prevent the cost of government falling upon them as a crushing burden; the smaller authorities require the counsel and information of wider experience; the negligent or apathetic authorities have to be incited to bring their administration up to the national minimum that is called for by the interests of the community as a whole, and all local authorities are the better for an entirely independent audit of their accounts. How to get these advantages is still an insoluble problem in the United States." — *Op. cit.*, p. x.

greater centralization of administration have been only partially successful. In the few cases, however, where the experiment has been tried, it has been successful. The transfer of the liquor licenses, for instance, from local to state administration in New York proved to be an undoubted success from every point of view.

But while the state administration is, in certain respects, undeniably superior to the local administration, it is only relatively good; and the same reasons which make local administration inferior to state administration render state administration in some respects inferior to federal administration. The corruption and inefficiency in our American municipalities have become a byword, but while striking improvements have recently been effected, the situation is not very much better in the state than in the city. The frauds connected with the building of the state capitols in Harrisburg and Albany and the notorious influence of the state machine on administrative methods in almost all our commonwealths are cases in point. The federal administration, on the other hand, although by no means beyond criticism, is greatly superior to state administration. Compare, for instance, the administrative methods of the enlargement of the Erie Canal under state auspices with the construction of the Panama Canal under federal auspices. From the very nature of the case, in fact, federal administration is apt to be more successful than state administration. Not only is it easier to secure expert assistance for the larger problems involved in national expenditure, but the contact between official and citizen is not so likely to have that intimate relationship which would exist in the smaller administrative sphere. Above all, the influence of the party boss and of machine methods is obviously less pronounced in proportion as the sway of governmental operations becomes broader. The income tax needs for its successful operation a far greater degree of administrative efficiency than any other source of revenue, and it may be added, than almost any other branch of government activity. Where the relations with the individual are so delicate and where the opportunities for connivance and fraud are so immense, the steadiness and reliability of the administrative machinery become of especial importance.

Bearing these considerations in mind, it is clear, therefore, that a local income tax, considered purely from the point of view of administrative efficiency, would be the least successful of all; that a state income tax, while indubitably superior to the local income tax, would still be relatively unsatisfactory; and that to secure the best results it would be necessary either to have a very strong national control over the state administration — a control which is, in all probability, impossible under our constitution — or, as an alternative, a direct federal administration of the tax. Entirely apart, therefore, from any other reason, the purely administrative argument seems to point clearly to a national, rather than to a state, income tax.

We come, fourthly, to the last consideration, namely, the dangers that might accrue to the fiscal situation of the states themselves by the adoption of a state income tax.

It has been repeatedly pointed out that owing partly to the growth of modern expenditure, and partly to the gradual breakdown of the general property tax, the American states are relying, to a continually increasing extent, upon the revenues derived from the corporation and the inheritance taxes. In some states, as in New York, where the general property tax is no longer utilized for state purposes, the corporation and the inheritance taxes have become entirely indispensable. In other states, where less and less reliance is being put upon the state general property tax, any diminution in the yield of the inheritance tax, and more especially of the corporation tax, would involve serious difficulties. It may be laid down as a general proposition that under the present development of American finance, both the corporation tax and the inheritance tax are needed as sources of state revenue.

If, now, the income tax were to be levied by the states, rather than by the federal government, it is scarcely open to doubt that the federal government would resort, as an alternative, to either the corporation tax or the inheritance tax, or both. It was only with great difficulty that the danger of a federal inheritance tax was averted in 1909 by the vigorous objection on the part of the various states. But the other side of the prediction has already come true. We now have a national corporation tax, and we know that this was imposed in 1909 simply because of the political difficulties connected with the enactment of a national income tax.[1] To any one, however, who realizes the difficulties and complexities of our state finance, the permanent retention by the national government of a corporation tax in its present shape, levied without regard to analogous state taxes, would seem in the highest degree undesirable. Sooner or later the entering wedge would be pushed farther in, until the corporations would ultimately be almost entirely removed, for revenue purposes, from the activity of the states.

A state income tax, if enacted, would take the place of the general property tax or of a part of it, so that aside from the greater administrative difficulties connected with an income tax as compared with a property tax, no serious increase of revenue could be expected from it; and in those states where the property tax has been relegated to the local divisions, it is unlikely that the localities would permit the state to retain much, if any, of an income tax that might be levied by it. There would, therefore, in all probability, be the same need of a state revenue from these other sources, like corporations and inheritance. If, however, as would almost inevitably be the case, the national government should take over one or both of these taxes, the finances of the states would be thrown into the utmost confusion. Thus, from the point of view of the state fiscal conditions themselves, it seems highly desirable that there should be a national income tax.

To recapitulate: The four reasons why the income tax should be federal rather than state in character are, first, the basis of the tax; second, the avoidance of double taxation;

[1] *Supra*, p. 593.

third, the administrative difficulties; and fourth, the probable ensuing embarrassments to the state finances. Any one of these arguments would in itself be sufficient; taken together their cumulative force must be pronounced overwhelming. If there is to be an income tax in the United States, the chances of success are incomparably greater as a federal than as a state tax.

The above exposition, however, overlooks one important point, — namely, the question of fiscal necessity. The income tax, as we have seen, is really not needed by the federal government, and although it is in itself not needed by the state governments, it would be needed to the extent that it might lead to the abolition of the general property tax, or at least of the tax on personal property. Moreover, in so far as the proceeds of the income tax might be utilized to satisfy, in part, at all events, the almost insatiable demands of our localities, and especially of our cities, its fiscal significance would be far from negligible.

How, then, are we to escape from these two horns of the dilemma? According to the arguments advanced above, the income tax should be a federal tax. According to the considerations just mentioned, the income tax is needed as a source of state or local revenue. What is the way out of the difficulty?

The solution is really not complicated. Why is it not possible to secure all the ends of general suitability by having the tax administered by the national government under direct national supervision, and to secure all the ends of adequacy and fiscal necessity by having the proceeds apportioned, to a large extent at least, to the various states, perhaps to be further apportioned by the states in part or whole to the localities? This seems to be the real solution: Let the national government assess the tax, and let the state and local governments share in the proceeds of the tax.

The same argument applies to the corporation tax and to the inheritance tax, for in all three taxes the difficulties of conflicting tax jurisdictions are becoming, as we have seen, daily more pronounced. Let the federal government collect the income tax, the corporation tax, and the inheritance tax; and thus, at one blow, eliminate all the difficulties connected with the escape of the taxpayer from the tax jurisdiction. If the federal government then needs, for any special exigency, a part of one or more of these taxes, let it keep that part, and let it distribute the remainder among the various states, according to rules and criteria that can without difficulty be elaborated. Even if the national government were to keep a part of the proceeds for normal purposes, the states would not suffer; for the far greater administrative success of federal assessment would lead to such an enhanced yield, that the revenue accruing to the separate states from a portion of the tax, under the new system, would surely be larger than the proceeds of the whole of the tax under the old system. From the fiscal point of view, as well as from every other, the states have really nothing to lose.[1]

This is by no means so new or revolutionary a suggestion as it may appear. It is found, in some form or other, in many countries, and in not a few of the American commonwealths. In England, for instance, the inheritance tax is assessed by the central government, and a part of the proceeds of what is known as the estate duty is allotted to the local government. Before this plan was adopted in 1888, Mr. Goschen had originally contemplated the scheme of allotting to the localities additions to the national income tax. The principle of apportionment is continued by the act of 1907. In France the revenue from all of the four leading direct taxes is apportioned between state and localities by the device of the *centimes additionnels;* and the same principle is applied in part in Italy. In Germany the proceeds

[1] This suggestion as to a division of the proceeds between federal and state governments was first made by the present writer some ten or fifteen years ago, in testifying before a government commission on the corporation tax. The principle there declared applicable to the corporation tax was subsequently extended by him in various essays to the inheritance tax and the income tax. See especially "The Relations of State and Federal Finance," mentioned *supra*, p. 643, from which a part of the following paragraph is taken.

of certain indirect taxes are divided between the federal and the state governments, and one of the important features in the recent budgetary scheme of the late Chancellor von Bülow was to have a federally administered inheritance tax, a part of the revenue to go to the state. The project now pending for a national unearned-increment tax contemplates a division between the nation, the state, and the locality. In Canada it is well known that a large part of the provincial revenues is derived from the proceeds of taxes that are levied by the federal government. Other instances might readily be mentioned, as in the recent fiscal arrangements of the Australian commonwealth. In the United States, also, many of our separate commonwealths raise revenues which are apportioned to the local administrations. Even the federal government, in the one familiar instance of the distribution of the surplus, apportioned to the various states the proceeds of federally assessed taxes. The principle of apportionment of revenues between central and local authorities is hence one that is entirely familiar to students of finance. It may be objected, indeed, that the constitutionality of the scheme is doubtful. Our opinion, expressed with all due diffidence, is that a constitutional method can be devised of accomplishing this result, especially if the federal government retain a portion of the revenue. But our additional opinion, expressed without any diffidence, is that if constitutional methods cannot be devised, the sooner a constitutional amendment is procured the better it will be. There is really no other avenue of escape from the difficulties that are looming up on all sides.

This method of federal administration and state and local apportionment will accomplish everything that is needed. It will conform to the principle of efficiency and of suitability, because the income tax, like the inheritance tax or the corporation tax, can best be administered by the federal government, and because in that way alone the gross inequalities of state assessment can be overcome. While, on the other hand, these important incidental gains will be achieved:

the separate states will secure the revenue which they need; the localities will no longer be open to the charge that personalty escapes assessment; and there will be a lessening of the resistance to the application of so-called unearned-increment taxes to the real estate of our cities. Thus from a threefold point of view our states and localities will be enabled to continue in the path of tax reform upon which they have recently and so auspiciously entered. The important point is that some adjustment be reached whereby the legitimate demands of equality and uniformity may be satisfied without sacrificing the ends of efficiency and adequacy. The interests of the states must, at all costs, be safeguarded; but the difficulties inherent in a state administration of what has become national in character must be avoided. The plan outlined above will accomplish this end. In this way and in this way alone can we do justice to the underlying principles of fiscal and social reform. In this way and in this way alone can the relations of local, state, and federal finance be put on an enduring and a completely satisfactory basis. Let the income tax be a national tax; let the proceeds go, in part or in whole, to the separate commonwealths, to be utilized as the necessities or convenience of each state may prescribe.

§ 3. *How Shall the Income Tax be Administered?*

We come, then, to the final inquiry, namely, what kind of an income tax shall we have, and what are the administrative provisions most likely to make it a success?

In the introduction to this investigation we called attention to the three chief types of income tax: the presumptive, the lump-sum, and the stoppage-at-source tax. The rich experience of the various countries that we have passed in review enables us without difficulty to draw a conclusion as to the type best suited to American conditions.

The presumptive income tax — that is, the tax founded on presumptions or external indicia of income — manifestly possesses certain advantages. It requires but slight troublesome investigation; it exposes the taxpayer to little inquisitorial procedure; and it is comparatively easy to collect. It is well suited to a community where the administration is proverbially weak, where the differences of wealth are not too great, and where public sentiment is unfavorable to a rigid application of personal taxation. But, as we have learned, especially from a study of the French conditions, it has serious shortcomings. Unless the presumptions are exceedingly simple, the discretion afforded to the officials is liable to abuse. In addition, the more complicated the society becomes, the more deceptive are the criteria of income, until in the highest grades of income they are almost entirely bereft of significance. Thus, while the presumptive income tax is, at best, only a very rough and ready method of apportioning burdens according to ability to pay, it becomes more and more inadequate, until it finally reaches the point of creating practical injustice as between individuals and classes. While, therefore, presumptions or external criteria may be utilized to a certain extent in order to check the returns and to help us over some of the difficulties of the exact ascertainment of individual income, the time has gone by when a system of income taxation can be erected on this basis alone.

The lump-sum income tax avoids the theoretical weakness of the presumptive income tax, and in several countries has formed its logical successor. But the administrative difficulties connected with the ascertainment of the entire income of the individual in a lump-sum are exceedingly great, and the system as a consequence requires for its successful operation not only a high degree of administrative efficiency, but wide and inquisitorial powers conferred upon the officials. In only one country of the world can the lump-sum income tax be said to be successful, namely, in Germany; and we have studied the peculiar conditions which explain its success there — conditions which reflect both favorably and unfavorably upon the social and political life, and which it would be difficult to reproduce, for good or for evil, in other countries. In the two other states of importance where the lump-sum income tax has been tried, namely, Austria and Switzerland, it has proved to be a failure; and it is Austria and Switzerland, rather than Germany, whose conditions are analogous to those of the United States. For in Austria, as in the United States, public sentiment is not so much inclined to personal taxes as in Germany; and in Switzerland, like the United States, the prevalence of democracy has engendered an attitude of the ordinary citizen to the government very different from that which obtains in Prussia.

Two other significant facts must not be lost from sight. The English tax was originally levied according to the lump-sum idea, until the introduction of the stoppage-at-source method doubled the revenue. The universal testimony of all British administrators, as we know, is to the effect that their system is incomparably superior to the German, which they had tried and discarded; and that it would be a deplorable mistake to revert to the lump-sum method. Furthermore, it will be recollected that the French Chamber, after an exhaustive discussion of the lump-sum idea, decided that it was unworkable in a democracy and especially inapplicable to French conditions. Finally, the experience of the United States during the Civil War, with what was in essence a lump-sum income tax, only serves to emphasize the lesson. A lump-sum income tax would strain American administrative methods to the breaking point; it would probably be ineffective as a producer of revenue; and it would surely be impotent to secure the relative justice which is the primary desideratum of an income tax. The lump-sum idea might indeed be utilized in a subordinate way, as is the case both in the English super-tax and in the French complementary tax; but, as the chief element of the system in an American income tax, it would be to the highest degree undesirable.

There remains, then, only the stoppage-at-source or schedule income tax. The advantages of this method have been fully stated in our account of the English conditions. It also affords the reason why the Italian income tax is more successful than the Austrian or the Swiss. Even in Italy, it will be remembered, only about four-tenths of the revenue is derived through the stoppage-at-source method; but since, in these schedules, almost the entire amount of taxable income is collected, while in the other schedules the tax is very much of a farce, it is no exaggeration to say that in all probability not more than a quarter of the real income of the country is secured by the stoppage-at-source method. Even this small percentage, however, serves to make the Italian tax more successful than the Swiss or Austrian tax. On the other hand, according to the careful calculations that have been made by the French government, the accuracy of which in this respect has not been seriously disputed, at least three-fourths of the large revenues that are to be expected from the French income tax would be raised according to the stoppage-at-source idea.

In the United States the arguments in favor of the stoppage-at-source income tax are far stronger than in Europe, because of the peculiar conditions of American life. In the first place, nowhere is corporate activity so developed, and in no country of the world does the ordinary business of the community assume to so overwhelming an extent the corporate form. Not only is a large part of the intangible wealth of individuals composed of corporate securities, but a very appreciable part of business profits consists of corporate profits. In the second place, in no other important country are investments to so great an extent domestic in character. The one great difficulty in England, as we have learned, is that connected with foreign securities. And in France, where the same difficulty exists, we have learned that the projected control of these foreign investments through the French bankers and agents forms the one difficult and complicated point in the scheme. In the United States, on the other hand, the situation is the reverse. Instead of our capitalists seeking investments abroad, it is the foreign capitalist who purchases American securities. We are, therefore, fortunately exempt from the chief embarrassment which confronts Europe; and there is every likelihood that this situation will not be changed for some time to come. The arguments that speak in favor of a stoppage-at-source income tax abroad hence apply with redoubled force here. The stoppage-at-source scheme lessens, to an enormous extent, the strain on the administration; it works, so far as it is applicable, almost automatically; and, where enforced, it secures to the last penny the income that is rightfully due. Can there really be any doubt as to the preference to be given to the stoppage-at-source income tax over either the lump-sum or the presumptive income tax under American conditions?

If, then, the income tax must take the form of the stoppage-at-source tax, the question arises, how can such a tax be worked out in detail, so as to conform to American conditions?

The first element in the scheme would be the taxation of incomes through corporations. Corporations could be utilized for this purpose in a threefold way: In the first place, the tax could be imposed on corporate incomes as such. The machinery for such a tax is already in operation in the federal corporation tax. One necessary and fundamental change, however, would be the abolition of the privilege of deducting interest on bonded indebtedness. The tax on corporate income should, of course, be one on the real profits or gains of the corporation, and the tax on such profits would, if assessed at the same rate, yield just about double what is now secured from the federal corporation tax.

In addition to the tax on corporate incomes, there should be a tax on the individual incomes secured from corporations. The simplest method of accomplishing this result would obviously be to have the tax charged to, and paid by, the corporation, to be thereupon deducted from the sums due the security-holder. The objection will, of course, at once be made that this is double taxation; that it is not legitimate to tax the corporation and again to tax the holder of the security. This objection, however, is valid only in part. It is not valid at all, so far as the holders of corporate bonds are concerned. A tax on the corporation as such may indeed diminish the profits of the owner, — that is, may reduce the rate of dividends on the stock. But since the interest on bonds is a fixed and not a contingent remainder, a tax on corporate profits would have no effect on it, except, indeed, in the very unlikely event that the rate of taxation should be so confiscatory as to leave nothing available for fixed charges, or so high as seriously to impair the underlying security of the bondholders. As such contingencies are, however, not to be expected, it may be laid down as a general proposition that a tax on the corporation is not a tax on the bondholder. If, therefore, we desire to reach the income of the bondholders, an additional tax must be assessed on the corporation, with the obligation to subtract it from the interest. The privilege granted to railroad corporations during the Civil War to assume this tax themselves ought not to be allowed, for the result of such action would be to make the tax on the bondholder really payable by the stockholder.[1]

What, however, shall we say as to the tax on the stockholder? If a tax on the corporate income is a tax on the stockholder, then this additional tax would indeed be double taxation. Even here, however, the situation is not quite so simple. It is by no means a fact that the entire income of a corporation, after paying fixed charges consisting of interest on bonds, is distributed in dividends. Some of the profits may be put into a surplus account; another part may be devoted to investments in other corporations; and so on. Ultimately, of course, the earnings will reach the stockholder, but in any given year this may be far from being the case. To say, therefore, that because a corporation advances the income tax for its stockholders, it should be exempt from a tax on corporate income, would be inadmissible. At best, the corporation should be allowed to deduct from its tax only so much

[1] Many bonds now issued by corporations contain a stipulation that the interest shall be payable without deduction for any taxes which the corporation may be required to retain or deduct. This difficulty can, however, be met in all probability by appropriate legislation.

as had actually been advanced in payment of the tax on stockholders. In some of the European countries, as we know, this result is reached by a rough approximation, the corporations being taxed only on the surplus over a sum arbitrarily fixed at three and a half or four per cent of the income, which is supposed to represent the income of the shareholder. But if the shareholder's tax is advanced by the corporation, there is no reason why we should not prefer exact to arbitrary figures. The net result of the situation, therefore, would be that the corporation should advance the income tax on all interest and dividends, and that it should, in addition, be held to pay a tax on its corporate income, not deducting interest on debt, but being allowed a deduction for the actual amount of tax advanced for its stockholders. This method, moreover, should be applied to all corporations, with a few exceptions of an educational, scientific, and philanthropic character; and even here the exceptions should not attach to such security-holders as seek to secure a profit therefrom.

The third method of utilizing corporations would be to reach the officials and employees. We have found that in various countries corporations are required to send in the names and salaries of all employees; but in only one or two cases has the further step been taken of requiring the corporations to advance the tax and to deduct it from the salaries. There is, however, no reason why this should not be done; and in the United States, where business salaries are to so large an extent corporate in character, the advantage would be especially great. Every argument that applies to the retention by the government of the tax on official salaries would apply with redoubled force to corporate salaries.

This threefold utilization of corporations through the corporation tax proper, the tax on corporate securities, and the tax on corporate officials would greatly simplify the administration, and would result in yielding a very substantial portion of the entire income tax — a portion which in the United States would be far greater than anywhere else.

In another schedule might be put the tax on government salaries, the government being required to withhold the tax from the salaries, and to pay it over to the proper fiscal authorities. This plan was actually in operation during the Civil War. The only complication here would arise from the salaries of state and local officials. Under our constitution we have seen that it is doubtful whether the federal government has the right to impose such a tax, and the doubt will not be entirely dispelled by the adoption of the sixteenth amendment. If, however, it turned out to be impracticable to levy such a tax, the deficiency in the revenue would, after all, not be very great. On the other hand, if such a tax were ultimately declared constitutional, which, as we have seen, ought to be the case, the machinery could without great difficulty be devised for enlisting the coöperation of the state and municipal governments in collecting the tax.

Another schedule would embrace the income derived from government securities. If it were decided to levy such a tax, it could be easily and automatically collected, so far as federal securities are concerned. The question as to the desirability of taxing government bonds played quite a rôle, as we remember, in the early period of the English income tax; and it received a full discussion during the deliberations on the French income tax. Although much may be said on either side, the weightier arguments which need not be here repeated are, on the whole, in favor of the inclusion of income from government bonds within the purview of the tax. In so far, however, as state and municipal bonds are concerned, the same question would arise as in the case of state and municipal salaries. The decision either way would not make any very material difference in the revenue.

After these schedules had been disposed of, there would remain four other chief classes of income: income from real estate; income from securities other than corporate securities; income from business; and income from professions. How should these be treated?

So far as concerns real estate, the conditions of American

life would not make it necessary to distinguish, as does the French scheme, between property in land and property in houses. Nor would it seem advisable to rely entirely on the English or the French model in assessing "statutory," or constructive, rather than real income. At the same time, the difficulties involved in ascertaining the exact income, especially in the case of agricultural property, would be almost insurmountable, as was shown by the experience of the Civil War. Our farmers do not keep books of account, and any attempt to introduce this method would probably fail. Accordingly, the best plan would seem to be to utilize a combination of constructive and actual income; that is, to calculate the income roughly as a certain percentage of the rental value (or of the selling value), but to permit proof that the actual income differs from the constructive income. Where it is customary to rent property, as is frequently true in our cities, and in not a few sections of the country, a certain proportion of the rental value would afford a reasonably good criterion of income; where it is not customary to rent property, the assessed valuation of the premises for the local tax, after making correction for the local standards of assessment, would form a fairly satisfactory indication. In some American cities, for instance, real estate experts now calculate very closely the proportion of net to gross rent.

The tax, moreover, ought always to be collected from the occupier, who, if he was not the owner, should be authorized to deduct the tax from the rent paid. If, on the other hand, the occupier was the owner, and if there was a mortgage outstanding on the property, the owner should not be allowed any abatement of tax because of interest, but should be authorized and expected to deduct the proportionate amount of tax from the interest due to the mortgagee. Finally, if in any one year the actual income was less than the constructive income, as ascertained on the basis of rental or selling value, the owner should be permitted to prove this fact, and thus secure a reduction of the tax. In this way not only would the administration of the schedule be much simplified, but there would be a practical assurance that the government would secure the entire amount of income derived from the ownership of real estate.

Whether it would be desirable to have a separate schedule, as in England and France, for agricultural profits as divorced from the ownership of the property, is somewhat doubtful. The custom of renting agricultural property is far less common in this country than abroad, and even where it exists it is probable that the exemption which would no doubt be permitted in any income tax law would cover the great mass of agricultural profits derived from rented property. If, however, this should not be the case, it would be a simple matter to construct an additional schedule, basing the tax on the constructive income of the tenant farmer according to a certain lower percentage of the gross rent paid by him, but with a similar privilege to substitute the actual income. Taking it all in all, the income tax on land can be administratively so arranged as to be operated with almost the same ease and simplicity that would be the case in the preceding schedules.

The method that has been suggested for assessing land would, at the same time, solve the problem connected with the taxation of the income from securities other than corporate securities. In the United States, about the only class of securities of any importance, in addition to corporate securities, are mortgages on real estate. The tax on the mortgage might be paid, as in England, through the real estate schedule; that is, if the real estate tax were paid by the owner, he would advance the tax on the mortgage and deduct it from the interest. If the tax were paid by the occupier, he would deduct it from the rent due to the owner, who would thereupon deduct it from the interest payable to the mortgageor. As the income tax would be a general tax, applicable to all forms of investment, there would be no shifting of the tax to the borrower in the shape of an increased rate of interest, as now happens in the United States where the tax on mortgages is, in practical operation, a partial or excessive tax.[1] In this way one of the great difficulties connected with the ascertainment of intangible personalty would be avoided and the tax on securities would be stopped at the source, with slight chance of any defection of revenue.

We come now to the important category of business incomes. Here it is clear that the principle of stoppage at source cannot be applied. This schedule is accordingly apt to be the weak point in any income tax. It must be remembered, however, that this schedule, while doubtless important, would play a less significant rôle in the United States than elsewhere. For a great part of business incomes would already have been automatically secured through the corporation tax. In fact, it is safe to say that the schedules that we have hitherto been considering would yield at least three-fourths of the entire revenue to be expected from an income tax. So far, however, as relates to the assessment of business incomes derived from individual enterprises, certain devices could be employed to render the tax less unsuccessful than would otherwise be the case. The rate in this schedule might for instance be made lower than in the case of the property incomes; and with a tax rate which would in itself be moderate, the further concession afforded to business men would doubtless be productive of good results. In the second place, we might take another leaf out of the book of the English practice. In England, it will be remembered, much use is made, especially in the larger towns, of the Additional Commissioners, selected from the prominent business men, willing to serve without pay. During the period of the Civil War much dissatisfaction, as is known, resulted from the employment of assistant assessors and special agents who were for the most part ordinary, inexpert, and untrustworthy underlings, employed at a few dollars a day. To put the business interests of a great nation at the mercy of such men would be the height of folly. On the other hand, it is not at all chimerical to suppose that, especially in our larger towns,

[1] Cf. Seligman, *The Shifting and Incidence of Taxation*, 3d edition, 1910, pp. 333–337.

business enterprises might be arranged in broad classes, and that one or two prominent representatives of each class, presumably acquainted with the conditions of their trade, might be prevailed upon to accept honorary positions as advisers to the chief assessor in each locality. We are now able to secure our best citizens without compensation for our school boards. Why should we not be able to obtain men of similar standing for our assessment boards? Is it hopeless to expect that what has been so successfully accomplished in other domains of administration in this country, and in this particular field in England, cannot also be accomplished here? But whether this device or some other be employed, every care must be taken, at the outset at least, to combine prudence with firmness, and to avoid arbitrary and inquisitorial treatment of the taxpayer, without an undue sacrifice of the revenue. If we are to have an income tax at all in the United States, we must be prepared to devote much thought and attention to the administrative details of this schedule. But even at the worst, this schedule would form, under American conditions, so small a part of the whole, that even a comparative lack of success here would not imperil the entire tax.

There remains, finally, the subject of professional incomes. Here again it must be remembered that a large part of such incomes in the United States is derived through the medium of corporations, institutions, and government service, and would therefore be reached in full through stoppage at source. So far as other professional incomes are concerned, the same devices might be employed as in the case of business incomes, namely, low rates, and the utilization of honorary assessors from the various professions. Here again, moreover, the aggregate of such independent professional incomes would be comparatively unimportant.

If, then, the stoppage-at-source principle were applied, and if improved administrative methods were employed in the schedules to which stoppage at source is not applicable, the yield of a federal income tax would, in our opinion, compare not unfavorably with that secured in England. But any attempt to introduce into the United States the methods employed in Prussia, for instance, would most assuredly lead to dismal failure. The American legislator has far more to learn from a careful study of the details of the British law and of the French bill than from any other measure, American or European.

Three questions still remain for solution — that of exemption, of differentiation, and of progression.

That an exemption of moderate amount is demanded by modern conditions will be disputed by no one; and we have learned how the tendency in all countries has been gradually to raise the limit. With the standard of life as it exists in the United States, the exemption ought to be higher than that found elsewhere. But to make it as high as was contemplated in the law of 1894 would, in our opinion, be a grievous error. For if the income tax is to be utilized for revenue purposes, such an extravagant exemption would seriously impair the fiscal possibilities. It is like cutting off a large slice from the base of a pyramid and leaving only the half which tapers to a point. Furthermore, so great an exemption would expose the tax to the charge of sectional prejudice, for there would then be large portions of the country which would virtually pay no tax at all. An exemption of one or two thousand dollars ought to be adequate. If that, however, prove unsatisfactory, we might at least introduce the English principle of abatement in order to permit a gradually diminishing reduction of tax between the limit of absolute exemption and the point of normal charge. If a thousand dollars, for instance, were completely exempt from taxation, progressively diminishing abatements might be made for each successive five hundred or one thousand dollars, until the normal rate might begin with four or five thousand dollars. The exact figures indeed are arbitrary, but the principle is clear. Let there be a comparatively low limit of complete exemption, supplemented by a system of abatements reaching to a comparatively high maximum.

The next point is that of differentiation. A differential

rate of income tax is advisable for two reasons. In the first place, as we have seen, a lower rate on business and professional incomes would be of great administrative help. In the second place, differentiation is demanded by considerations of justice. It might even be queried as to whether, in the United States, we are not ready for a further application of the differential principle than that recently adopted in England. The distinction between earned and unearned incomes is assuredly a good one, so far as it goes. But we have become accustomed in the United States, in economic analysis at least, and to a certain extent in public recognition, to make further distinctions with reference to the social justification of various classes of income. Thus, for instance, the incomes of public-service corporations are gradually being put on a somewhat different footing from others; and the same consideration would apply to cases where individual and corporate incomes depend, to a large extent, upon other forms of privilege. It will manifestly be a considerable time before such distinctions in the nature of income are worked out with sufficient precision to warrant their incorporation into law. But we are perhaps even now ready for a distinction between public-service and other corporations. Even though it would probably be advisable to make only slight distinctions of rate in the income tax at the beginning, the wedge might gradually be pushed further in.

Finally, so far as progression is concerned, it is clear that the adoption of the stoppage-at-source scheme is incompatible with the general plan of a graduated income tax. If we divide the tax into schedules, there is no way of ascertaining the entire income of the individual, and there would therefore be no justification in imposing a graduated tax upon the higher incomes. We could well afford to be content with a successful income tax, even if it be a proportional tax. After the tax had been in operation for some time, it might indeed be possible cautiously to introduce the principle of graduation, through a device similar to the English super-tax or the French complementary tax. For when the administrative provisions of the stoppage-at-source income tax were once in full operation, so that the government might be assured of its desired revenue, there would perhaps be no insuperable objection to requiring a compulsory declaration of entire income from all individuals whose income exceeded, let us say, ten or twenty thousand dollars, and assessing a somewhat higher rate of tax upon them. Under existing American conditions, however, not much could be hoped from such a device. At best, if it were utilized only as a supplementary measure, it would not do much harm and might result in some additional revenue; at worst, it would in practice be a tax only upon the conscientious and patriotic millionaires, to their manifest disadvantage as compared with those of an opposite type. But unless graduation be utilized only as a supplementary principle, it would, under actual conditions, in all probability play havoc with the entire scheme of the income tax from the point of view both of revenue and of justice.

We have come to the end of a long and laborious study; and it is perhaps worth while, in conclusion, to emphasize the three chief lessons that we have learned. In the first place, the income tax is coming. Sooner or later the constitutional or political difficulties will be surmounted, and the United States will fall in line with every other important country of the world. Economic conditions have everywhere engendered a shifting of the basis of taxable faculty, and democracy has declared that the best criterion, on the whole, is to be found in income. Whether we like it or not, the development is irresistible, and the income tax will come to stay until some new criterion of ability approves itself to the democracy of the future.

In the second place, wherever an income tax has been introduced under conditions that were obviously not fatal to success, the tax has worked better from year to year or from decade to decade. This is due partly to the fact that business conditions are apt to adjust themselves to long-continued laws, partly to the fact that in progressive communities a gradual improvement in administrative methods may be expected, and partly to the fact that public sentiment slowly accommodates itself to a *fait accompli*. For the present generation in England or Germany to read of the imprecations heaped upon the income tax by an earlier generation is almost to read an unfamiliar language, so completely has both the governmental and the individual attitude changed. Is it unreasonable to expect that the similarly extreme opposition which is still manifested by certain individuals or classes in France and in the United States will be regarded with the same feelings of wonder by a future generation?

Finally, the success of an income tax depends, perhaps more than almost any other modern institution, upon administrative machinery. Simply to adopt the principle of an income tax and to enact a law providing for its imposition is by no means adequate. If we select the correct machinery and elaborate a scheme which is in harmony with administrative possibilities and public sentiment in any particular country, the tax will work. If we choose the opposite course, and attempt too much, the result is bound to be disastrous. Certain methods, which promise well from the point of view of the symmetry of the tax, work badly amid a democratic environment. We must decide between ideal perfection of theory which cannot be made to work in actual life, and a less ambitious, but more realizable, programme of practical efficiency. The United States has had a sad trial with the first alternative; shall we not profit now by the lessons of experience and choose the second?

APPENDIX

The Income Tax of 1913

The enactment of the income tax law of October 3, 1913 marks a new stage in the history of American finance. As in the case of England with its first income tax of 1798, our Civil War income tax was avowedly a temporary measure; and just as the English income tax was reintroduced in 1842 in order to make good the loss in revenue occasioned by the repeal of the Corn Laws, so the American law was enacted to compensate for the loss of revenue due to the new tariff. The English tax, indeed, was not intended to be a permanent part of the revenue system, but the force of circumstances soon gave it that position. The American tax, on the other hand, was designed from the very outset as an integral and permanent part of the fiscal arrangements.

The chief argument which was responsible for the passage of the Sixteenth Amendment and for the enactment of the law was, as we have elsewhere pointed out,[1] that wealth is escaping its due share of taxation. Again and again in the course of the discussion attention was called to the fact that our federal system of taxes on expenditure puts an undue burden on the small man; and when the objection was made that the principle of ability to pay is recognized in state and local taxation, the ready answer was found that in actual practice our state and local revenue systems fail almost completely to reach those taxpayers who can best afford to contribute to the public burdens. It is true that some of the more extreme supporters of the income tax based their advocacy on the ground of opposition to the tariff alone; but

[1] *Supra*, p. 640.

the more influential legislators did not tire of stating that, far from purposing to make an attack on wealth as such, their aim was solely to redress the inequality of taxation which was a predominant feature of the American fiscal system as a whole.[1]

In our consideration of the measure, it will be convenient first to consider what the law actually provides and then to call attention to its shortcomings. Under the first head the chief points are: who is taxed; what is taxed; how much is taxed; and how is the tax imposed? In other words, the main problems are: on whom is the tax levied; what is meant by income; what are the rates and exemptions; and what are the administrative methods pursued? Let us consider these in turn.

I. *Who is Liable to the Income Tax?*

Under the provisions of the statute the tax is imposed upon the entire income of every American citizen, whether residing at home or abroad, as well as upon that of every person residing in the United States although not a citizen thereof. In the case of non-citizens of the United States residing abroad, the tax is assessed upon the income from all property owned, and from every business, trade, or profession carried on, in the United States. It will be noticed from these provisions that no attempt is made to avoid double taxation. Under the law, an American citizen living abroad and subject to an income tax there, or a resident alien who has already paid the income tax in his own country, is again subject to the tax here. It is to be noted, however, that the rigor of these provisions is somewhat abated by the clause, to be considered later, which virtually exempts the foreign holder of the bonds of American corporations. It is still to be regretted that the United States failed to lead in the movement

[1] See especially the speech of Senator Borah, who ascribes to the present writer the unmerited honor of responsibility for the impetus given to the income tax. *Cf. Congressional Record*, 63d Congress, 1st sess., pp. 4260–4261, Aug. 28, 1913.

to do away with this undoubted infraction of international justice.

In the second place, the law applies not only to individuals but to corporations. The income tax is payable by every corporation, joint stock company, or association, and every insurance company organized in the United States, with a few exceptions.[1] This part of the law contains provisions similar to those of the corporation or excise tax law of 1909. The chief differences between the two, apart from the matters which will be considered later under other heads, are that the former specific deduction of $5000 is no longer permitted and that corporations are now allowed to make a return for their fiscal year when this does not coincide with the calendar year. The objection that the taxation of both individual and corporation on the same income involves double taxation is sought to be met by the provision which permits individuals to deduct from their taxable income the amount of corporate dividends or other income on which the tax has been paid by the corporation. The American law, therefore, seeks to avoid double taxation by the same jurisdiction, while making no effort to prevent double taxation by competing jurisdictions.

II. *What is Taxable Income?*

As we have observed elsewhere[2] it is easy to say that income should be taxed, but it is not so easy to define what is meant by income. The law of 1913 states that net income "shall include gains, profits, and incomes derived from salaries, wages, or compensation for personal services of whatever kind, and in whatever form paid; or from professions, voca-

[1] The exceptions are: labor, agricultural or horticultural associations; mutual savings banks not having capital stock; fraternal beneficiary societies, orders or associations, operating under the lodge system; domestic building and loan associations; cemetery companies operated exclusively for the mutual benefit of members; associations operated exclusively for religious, charitable, scientific or educational purposes; business leagues, chambers of commerce, boards of trade, and civic leagues and organizations not organized or operated for profit.

[2] *Supra*, p. 19 *et seq.*

tions, businesses, trade, commerce, or sales or dealings in property, whether real or personal, growing out of the ownership or use of or interest in real or personal property; also from interest, rents, dividends, securities, or the transaction of any lawful business carried on for gain or profit, or gains or profits and income derived from any source whatever, including the income from, but not the value of, property acquired by gift, bequest, device, or descent." In this comprehensive definition several points are to be noticed: first, that no endeavor is made to introduce a new conception of income; second, that the idea of income as a regular and periodic return is accepted; third, that a slight attempt is made to distinguish between capital and income; and fourth, that a somewhat more careful attempt is made to distinguish between gross and net income. Let us take up each of these points.

We have said that no endeavor is made to introduce a new conception of income. This new conception of income, to which the new law pays no homage, may be regarded from a double aspect: that of psychic or benefit income and that of disposable income. The problem of psychic income involves the question as to whether the conception of income is to be limited to that received in the form of money or whether it should be extended to include the satisfactions for which money stands. Since it is manifestly impossible to gauge in terms of money the varying degree of general satisfaction that individuals receive, the only practical question is as to whether that particular satisfaction which comes from living in one's own house, and which can be fairly well measured in terms of rent, ought to be included in income. Suppose that A lives in his own house, worth $50,000, and pays perhaps $1000 in taxes and $1000 in repairs. B, who has had a precisely similar house, sells it for $50,000 but continues to live in it, at a rental of $5000. His position is virtually the same as that of A, because he gets $3000 as six per cent return on his $50,000 and saves the $2000 on taxes and repairs. Yet B now has to pay a tax on his $3000 additional income. It might be urged that in order to attain exact equality the net rental value of the residence ought to be included in A's income. It will be remembered that this rental value was so treated in the Civil War income tax. The framers of the present law, however, thought it wise to follow the almost universal European example and to confine the term "income" to the ordinary conception of actual money income.

The other aspect of this new conception of income relates to the question of savings. Many years ago John Stuart Mill thought that he had discovered a flaw in the theory of the income tax. He pointed out that unless savings were exempted we should be imposing double taxation; that is, the tax would be imposed, first, on the amount of income actually saved and secondly, upon the future income from that amount considered as capital. Although the fallacy of this contention was subsequently pointed out, it has remained for a recent Italian writer to take up the subject anew and to maintain that the only way of avoiding gross inequality in taxation of income is to exempt savings. It is remarkable, however, that at the same time that this theory was rehabilitated, a German author should have devised a precisely contradictory theory, namely, that all that should be included in the conception of income is the balance of receipts over expenditures, and that the term expenditures should comprise not only those incurred in securing the income but personal expenditures as well. Equal taxation hence involves not simply equality of income received but equality of surplus available. The new Italian theory would result in taxing nothing but expenditure; the new German theory would result in taxing nothing but savings.[1]

[1] The Italian work is *Intorno al concetto di reddito imponibile e di un sistema d' imposte sul reddito consumato*, published as a memoir of the Turin Academy of Sciences in 1912 by Professor Luigi Einaudi. The German work is *Die Besteuerung nach dem Ueberfluss (nach der Ersparnissmöglichkeit)*. Von Bürgermeister H. Weissenborn in Halberstadt, 1911. The Italian book has given rise to a discussion carried on in a series of articles in the *Giornale degli Economisti* for 1912 and 1913. The argument rests on the distinction between "earned" and "realized" income propounded by Professor Irving Fisher in 1906 in *The*

It is evident not only that these two theories are mutually contradictory, but that the wisdom of attempting to carry out either of them would be highly questionable. To levy a tax solely on expenditure, even if the expenditure were limited to so-called luxuries, would ultimately bring us back to the evils of the mediæval system from which modern progress has extricated us. On the other hand, to lay a burden only on savings or the possibility of savings would controvert some of the most firmly established principles of economic progress. It must be said, therefore, that the framers of the new law were well advised in refusing to be led astray by either of these recent vagaries.

The second point to be noted with reference to the theory of income implied in the new federal law is its attitude toward irregular receipts. It will be remembered that in the law of 1894, in contradistinction to the well-nigh universal practice abroad, inheritances were taxed as income.[1] The general view, as explained elsewhere,[2] is that income consists only of regular and periodic returns, irregular returns in the shape of inheritances being reached by the inheritance tax. In the new law this conception is adopted, although no additional tax on inheritances is imposed by the federal government. As inheritances are usually reached by the separate states, however, and as it is not improbable that the federal income

Nature of Capital and Income. This distinction has, however, found little acceptance among American economists, and its validity has been vigorously denied, especially from the standpoint of its applicability to taxation. See the review of Professor Fisher's book by Professor H. R. Seager in the *Annals of the American Academy of Political and Social Science*, vol. xxx, p. 175 (1907); and the discussion on the subject "Are Savings Income," by Professors Fetter, Daniels, and Robinson in *Papers and Discussions of the Twentieth Annual Meeting of the American Economic Association at Madison, Wis.*, Third Series, vol. ix, no. 1 (1908), pp. 48–58.

[1] Senator Cummins must have overlooked this when he stated: "I do not think that there is any man in America who would contend that . . . a devise or bequest of property . . . is income. I never heard of it being so construed, and it is not possible that it could be so construed." *Congressional Record*, p. 4264, Aug. 28, 1913.

[2] *Supra*, p. 20.

tax may before long be supplemented by a federal inheritance tax, there is much to be said for this provision of the act. The law of 1913, moreover, is still further and favorably distinguished from that of 1894 by excluding from the conception of income, property acquired by gift *inter vivos*.

The third element to be considered in the conception of income is the distinction to be drawn between capital and income. The two chief problems under this head are the treatment of profits from sales of property, and the disposition made of certain receipts of life insurance companies.

In respect to the former, the law states that taxable net income comprises "gain, profits and income derived from . . . dealings in property whether real or personal. . . ." It is obvious that in the case of persons engaged in the real estate or bond business, profits from the sales of real estate or of securities are included in taxable income. The question arises, however, whether the purchaser of a piece of property who after the expiration of several years sells it at an enhanced price ought to regard the difference as a part of his income in that year. If the letter of the law be followed, this is the obvious result. The injustice, however, of such a procedure is apparent from the fact that there is no provision made for deducting losses arising from a similar transaction. Of course a real-estate dealer in figuring up his income for the year can set off losses on some transactions against profits on others. But an ordinary individual who sells at a loss a piece of real estate that he has held for a number of years has no way of setting off that loss against profits from other sources. It is simply a diminution of his capital. Why, then, should any possible profit derived from a similar transaction be considered as income rather than accretion to capital?

It will be remembered that in the original income tax such profits were counted as income. This, however, created such dissatisfaction that the law of 1867 limited such profits to those from sales on real estate purchased within two years.[1] In the

[1] *Supra*, p. 512.

discussion of the present bill Mr. Cordell Hull, its framer, stated: "In construing all these laws . . . unless the unearned increment is expressly made income, it is not considered income in any sense of the word, but simply increase of value or capital."[1]

When pressed still further, he added: "My judgment would be that as to the occasional purchase of real estate not by a dealer or one making the buying and selling a business, this bill would only apply to profits on sales where the land was purchased and sold during the same year."[2]

As this section was adopted in the light of Mr. Hull's explanation, it is not unlikely that it will be so interpreted as to carry out the evident intention of its framers. If so, the same rule will apply also to profits from the sales of securities or other personal property. This would seem to be a fairly satisfactory solution of an undoubted difficulty.

The other aspect of this problem is connected with insurance and especially mutual life insurance companies. The payments from life insurance companies to the policy holders include, as is well known, death claims, annuities, endowments, surrender values, and so-called dividends. Since, however, a part of these payments is made from premiums received it is clear that this involves merely a return of capital. In the heated discussion that took place on this topic it was pointed out that a large part, at all events, of the dividends ought really not to be included in income. An amendment to the bill was finally adopted, whereby it was provided that life insurance companies should not include as income "such portions of any actual premium received from any individual policy holder as shall have been paid back or credited to such individual policy holder or treated as an abatement of premium of such individual policy holder within such year." And in the same way mutual fire and marine insurance companies are not compelled to include refunds of premium deposits to policy holders in their taxable income, a provision

[1] *Congressional Record*, April 26, 1913.

[2] Such a provision, it will be remembered, was contained in the law of 1864.

of great importance in the case of so-called "factory mutuals" which pay to their policy holders "dividends" amounting in some cases to ninety or ninety-five per cent of the premium received. It is fortunate that this amendment prevailed, as in a recent decision of the Supreme Court it has been held that the inclusion of such "dividends" in the income of corporations under the corporation tax law of 1909 was invalid. The elimination of "dividends," however, does not dispose of all the difficulty, as there still remain some so-called earnings of insurance companies which are really nothing but a return of capital to the policy holders.[1] Mr. Hull was quite emphatic in his statement that there was no intention of taxing capital rather than income, but he was not thoroughly clear in his own mind as to the exact distinction to be made, and he maintained that the accounts of the insurance companies were not so kept as to permit the legislature to distinguish between the two conceptions.

The fourth difficulty connected with the concept of income is presented in determining the deductions to be made from gross income in order to arrive at net income. With respect to certain of these items, there is no controversy. Such are the provisions of the law for deducting necessary business expenses, interest on personal indebtedness, losses actually sustained during the year, including worthless debts charged off, and a reasonable allowance for exhaustion, wear and tear of the property arising out of its use in the business (not ex-

[1] The objections of the insurance companies are presented in a series of memoranda printed in *Tariff Schedules. Briefs and Statements filed with the Committee on Finance, United States Senate.—Income Tax and Customs Administration.* Washington, 1913. See esp. pp. 1947–1986, 2119–2126. This whole subject is well treated by K. K. Kennan in a monograph entitled *The Federal Income Tax in its Relation to Life Insurance Companies*, Milwaukee, 1913.

The accountant's point of view is summed up in W. A. Staub, *Income Tax Guide*, 1913, p. 50, as follows: "Only the income derived from the investment of premiums between the time they are received from the policy holders and the time they are returned to them or their beneficiaries in the form of death claims, annuities, endowments, surrender values, 'dividends,' less the expense of conducting the business, represents real income derived from the amounts placed in a company's hands by the policy holders for insurance purposes."

ceeding in the case of mines five per cent of the gross value of the year's output at the mine). Nor is there room for dispute as to the propriety of the permission to deduct from gross income of individuals, not only dividends from corporations which have paid a tax on their net income but also any income on which, as will be explained later, the tax has been withheld at the source. The real difficulty in the matter, apart from the question of actual fact as to the difference between repairs and permanent improvements, relates to the question of taxes and of interest on corporate debts.

As to the former, the law permits deduction for all taxes, not including, however, in the case of individuals, assessments for local benefits. Why this deduction should be allowed is not clear. It might indeed be claimed that so far as taxes on business are concerned, this ought to be put on a par with other outlays incurred in order to secure a net profit. But where the income is derived from other sources than purely business transactions, the legitimacy of the deduction seems questionable. It is to be conceded, however, that herein lies a real difficulty in the theory of income.

In considering the deduction of interest on corporate debt, it should be remembered that the theory of corporate indebtedness differs, as we have elsewhere pointed out,[1] in some important respects from that of individual indebtedness. In the case of the individual, taxable property consists in the surplus above indebtedness, and the taxable income consists in the corresponding surplus of receipts. Capital stock of a corporation, however, usually represents only a portion of the property, while the remainder is represented by the bonded indebtedness. Strictly speaking, indeed, the proper distinction is not between corporate and individual credit, but between production and consumption credit. In the case of corporations, however, while debts are sometimes contracted to meet pressing exigencies and may thus in a way be considered a kind of consumption credit, mortgage bonds, at least, are al-

[1] Seligman, *Essays in Taxation*, 8th edition, 1912, pp. 106–107; and *supra*, p. 513.

most exclusively issued in order to provide capital. Economically speaking, the corporate capital consists of the bonds and the stock. Theoretically, therefore, the income from interest on corporate bonds ought not to be deducted. As a matter of fact, it is not so deducted in European income-tax laws. In the corporation tax law of 1909, however, interest on indebtedness was deducted, but only on an amount of debt not exceeding the capital stock. In the present law we find a compromise. Interest paid is allowed as a deduction from income on an amount of indebtedness not exceeding one-half the sum of the corporation's interest-bearing debt and its paid-up capital stock. Thus it will be seen that the new tax is more favorable to the corporations than was the excise tax. The compromise, however, is entirely arbitrary. Either there should have been no deduction at all, or the deduction should have been permitted on all the indebtedness which might be regarded as a result of purely consumption credit.

Another point, and one in which the corporations appear to have a just cause for complaint, is the disappearance of that provision of the law of 1909 which permitted corporations to deduct from gross income the dividends received from the stock of other corporations held by them. The result of the disappearance of this provision will be a great burden on the so-called holding companies, as the same income will be taxed once to the subsidiary companies and again to the parent company. The reason for this change was obviously to interpose obstacles to the formation or to the continuance of holding companies. While this is not the place to express any opinion as to desirability or the economic legitimacy of holding companies in general, it is quite clear that, in the case of railroads at least, some form of holding company of non-competitive lines may be entirely compatible with the best public interests; and in any event the attempt to combine fiscal and prohibitive ends in the same measure is of doubtful wisdom.

III. *The Tax Rates*

In discussing the question of tax rates the two chief problems are those of exemption and of graduation.

The most important point to be noted under the head of exemption is the fact that the tax applies to individual incomes only when they exceed $3000. In the law of 1894, it will be remembered, the exemption was placed at $4000, and in this bill, as originally drafted, the exemption was also kept at the higher figure. In the course of the discussion, however, and partly as a concession to the feeling that the limit was excessive, it was reduced to $3000, with additional exemptions of $500 or $1000 for children. In the final draft, while the figure of $3000 was retained, the exemption for children was eliminated and was replaced by an additional exemption of $1000 for a married couple. A total exemption, however, of $4000 only is permitted in the case of the aggregate income of husband and wife when living together. It is to be noted, moreover, that the exemption applies to the first three or four thousand dollars respectively of any amount of income; that is to say, three or four thousand dollars respectively are always to be deducted from the net income, in order to reach the taxable income.

In the discussion of the law, several attempts were made to reduce the exemption to a lower limit. It was repeatedly pointed out, however, that this exemption did not mean so much the minimum of subsistence, as a minimum of comfortable existence according to the desirable American standard of life. An American family of from three to five children living in decent comfort, and desirous of giving the children a college education would, it was maintained, need all of $4000, or in the case of a widow, certainly all of $3000, for meeting the necessary family expenses. It was further urged that the recipients of smaller incomes are already bearing more than their share of the burden, through the federal indirect taxes, and that this comparatively high exemption would only redress the inequality. Finally it was argued that the administrative advantages of the high exemption in averting needless expense and endless complications, such as are found in the English system, would far outweigh any objections to the higher exemption. While, however, these considerations were prominent in the minds of the framers of the measure, there is little doubt that the controlling reasons for so high an exemption were primarily political. One of the congressmen ingenuously asked, in reply to a proposition to reduce the exemption: "Does the gentleman not think it would defeat every member who would vote for this amendment if the fact were known at home?"[1] And another member said: "I venture the assertion that if Congress at the first opportunity which it has had of levying a direct tax upon the people without apportionment, should levy a tax which would fall upon every citizen of the land, that tax would not stay upon the statute books longer than the first election which followed the first call of the tax collector."[2] In justice, however, to the majority, we must quote the statement made by Mr. Murray, of Oklahoma: "There are those who would say that we should begin at $1000, in lieu of $4000. They forget the principle upon which this tax is founded, and that is that every man who is making no more than a living should not be taxed upon living earnings, but should be taxed upon the surplus that he makes over and above that amount necessary for good living. We also recognize the assumption that $4000 will reach the highest grade of good living. . . . The purpose of this tax is nothing more than to levy a tribute upon that surplus wealth which requires extra expense, and in doing so, it is nothing more than meting out even-handed justice."[3]

The other exemptions may be passed over rapidly. The salaries of the present President of the United States and of the federal judges now in office are exempt out of regard for the constitutional provision prohibiting any diminution of their compensation while in office. This, however, does not

[1] *Congressional Record*, p. 1215, May 6, 1913. [2] *Ibid.*, p. 1218.
[3] *Ibid.*, p. 1219.

apply to future presidents or federal judges. The salaries of all officers and employees of a state or a political subdivision thereof, and the interest on bonds or other obligations of a state or any political subdivision thereof, are also exempted. It was indeed claimed that according to the contention of former Governor Hughes, the Sixteenth Amendment empowered the federal government to levy such taxes. The framers of the bill, however, while specifically disclaiming any opinion on this point, maintained that, as long as there was any doubt, no opportunity should be given to contest the constitutionality of the law for this reason. The provision therefore prevailed, although it was emphatically asserted that from the standpoint of equality of taxation such an exemption was illegitimate. It is, in our opinion, not at all unlikely that at some future time this exemption will be removed by special amendment to the statute, the constitutionality of which can then be tested.

The exemption of interest on bonds or other obligations of the United States or its possessions did not arouse any comment. This was partly due to the fact that the federal debt is so small and is so largely held by national banks. If the time should come when the national debt, in the hands of individuals, should again assume large dimensions, it is not unlikely that we shall have a controversy here comparable to the one that has been responsible for the recent fall of the French ministry. The issue will then be the equality of taxation versus the maintenance of the national credit.

Finally, it is to be noted that the exemption of $5000 accorded to corporations in the law of 1909 is eliminated in the present law.

The consideration of tax rates involves not only the question of exemption, but that of graduation. It is significant that the principle of progressive taxation evoked almost no discussion. The legitimacy of the theory was taken for granted, and in the few cases where it was mentioned, it was assumed to be a corollary of the theory of ability to pay. This shows the development which has taken place since the discussion of the law of 1894. In considering the question of graduation, only two difficulties confronted the framers of the bill. The one was how to make a workable system of progressive taxation harmonize with the administrative methods employed; the other, how to oppose with success the demands of the radicals.

The former difficulty is connected with the principle of stoppage at source, to be discussed below. It is clear that if a tax is paid at the source by the income payer, rather than by the income recipient, it is not easy to introduce a graduated scale. The bonds of a corporation, the tax on the income of which is withheld by the corporation, may be owned by a person of very small or of very large total income.

This problem had, however, recently been solved in England, and a similar solution was adopted in the bill which passed the Chamber of Deputies in France a few years ago, and is now pending in the Senate.[1] In England a uniform rate is imposed upon all tax-payers, and is assessed on the principle of stoppage at source. This remains the backbone of the tax. Then on all individual incomes above a certain figure, a so-called super-tax is levied upon the income as a whole. So in the French bill, the uniform tax levied according to the stoppage-at-source principle is supplemented by a "complementary" tax levied upon the entire income. The same plan has been adopted in the new American law. The uniform tax levied upon all incomes, primarily by the method of stoppage at source, is called the normal tax, and is assessed at the rate of one per cent. The extra tax is called the additional tax or the surtax and is assessed on the entire income of individuals, according to a graduated scale. The advantage of this ingenious scheme is that the constituent parts of the income of any individual will be reached in large measure by the normal tax, and in such a way that the government will be able to ascertain the facts. The returns made by individuals for the additional tax can, to a considerable degree, thus be checked up, and the fiscal interests of the government be

[1] *Supra*, p. 324.

protected. This protection is, however, not complete; for, as we shall see, the principle of stoppage at source does not apply to all incomes within the United States, and applies only in an imperfect way to incomes received abroad. To a very large extent, however, the protection is undoubted. Thus it may be said that the old problem of the incompatibility of graduated taxation with stoppage at source has been attacked with a fair prospect of success.

The other difficulty with which the framers of the bill had to cope was the danger of an exaggerated application of the progressive scale. In the original bill, the clause relating to the "additional" tax was so framed as to impose one per cent on incomes from $20,000 to $50,000, two per cent on incomes from $50,000 to $100,000, and three per cent on incomes above $100,000. In the course of the discussion, however, many amendments were introduced calling for much higher scales. It will suffice to mention the plan of Mr. Copley, who suggested a scale rising to no less than sixty-eight per cent on incomes over $1,000,000, a proposition so manifestly extravagant that it was voted down by a large majority. Another rather extreme proposition was subsequently advanced in the Senate. Senator Williams disposed of it with the statement that "the object of taxation is not to leave men with equal incomes after you have taxed them."[1] The general feeling was, however, that the graduated scale contained in the bill was not high enough. Senator LaFollette proposed a scale which ran up to ten per cent. Senator Bristow suggested a somewhat more moderate scale and scouted the idea of possible future complications:

"I am not worrying about where we are going to stop. I believe the American people are capable of self-government. I believe their purpose is to do what is right to every citizen. The American people, as a whole, would not do an injustice to a rich man any quicker than they would to a poor man. . . .

[1] *Congressional Record*, p. 4225, August 27, 1913. As to the leave-them-as-you-find-them theory of taxation, see Seligman, *Progressive Taxation*, 2d ed., 1908, p. 231.

I would rather trust the honesty of the American people as a whole in dealing with a rich man, than to trust a good many rich men in their dealings with the American people. If there is any prejudice in this country against the rich, it is because the rich have not been just in their dealings with the public. There is no fundamental prejudice in the Anglo-Saxon race against property or the rights of property. It is the very basis upon which every Saxon nation has been builded in the history of our civilization. Yet here in this, the most enlightened nation of all in my opinion, we are afraid to enter upon a system of taxation which England has been following for years, because, forsooth, the American people may confiscate the property of their well-to-do citizens. Such a suggestion is abhorrent to me. . . . In endeavoring to work out this amendment, I have tried to be conservative and just, so that no man could say it was a radical measure, and no man has declared here that it was an unjust measure. The only objection to it has been from those who were afraid that in the future somebody else might do an injustice."[1]

And Senator Williams, who was in charge of the measure in the House, stated in a similar strain, after speaking of the dangers of large fortunes: —

"I realize another thing: No honest man can make war upon great fortunes, *per se*. The Democratic party never has done it, and when the Democratic party begins to do it, it will cease to be the Democratic party and become the Socialistic party of the United States; or better expressed, the Communistic party, or Quasi-Communistic party of the United States. . . . The war that an honest man makes upon accumulated wealth must be a war upon the manner in which the wealth was accumulated. . . . I am not going to attempt to make this bill a great panacea for all the inequalities of fortune existing in this country; nor would it do any good if we did, because we would be doctoring the symptoms, and not the cause of the disease."[2]

[1] *Congressional Record*, p. 4236.

[2] *Ibid.*, p. 4239.

As a result of the discussion the Finance Committee of the Senate saw that some concession was inevitable. Under the law as it was finally enacted, the rates of the "additional" tax are as follows: —

Per Cent	On Amount Exceeding	And Not Over
1	$20,000	$50,000
2	50,000	75,000
3	75,000	100,000
4	100,000	250,000
5	250,000	500,000
6	500,000	

The maximum rate of the income tax as a whole, therefore, under the new law, is somewhat under seven per cent. This is somewhat lower than either the English maximum (1*s*. 8*d*. on the £), or that of the recent German *Wehrsteuer* (eight per cent on incomes over half a million marks).[1]

IV. *Stoppage at Source*

The provisions in the new law which deal with the methods of assessment and collection involve a fundamental departure from the theory of all preceding income taxes in the United States. As has been frequently pointed out, the two chief types of income tax are the personal or lump-sum tax, where every one is compelled to make a return of his entire income from whatever source derived, and the stoppage-at-source tax, the theory of which is that it should be collected from the person or agency paying the income, rather than from the individual who receives it. The argument in favor of payment at source is the double one of protecting the honest taxpayer, and of safeguarding the interests of the treasury. Whatever may be true of a country like Germany where the administrative and political conditions are unique, there is little doubt

[1] As to the German tax, see F. Stier-Somlo, *Wehrbeitrag und Besitzsteuer. Die Reichssteuergesetze vom 3 Juli, 1913*.

that a purely personal lump-sum income tax, resting primarily on the declaration of the individual, would be as much of a failure in the United States as was the original income tax in England or the American income tax in the years subsequent to the Civil War, and as are those parts of the income tax in Austria, Italy, and Switzerland, which rest upon the same principle. It was to avoid these evils, that England adopted the principle of stoppage at source, to a certain extent at least, and that some other countries have in a minor degree followed this example. It was reserved, however, for the United States to apply the principle in a more thoroughgoing fashion than is the case anywhere else.

The law provides that "all. persons or firms, co-partnerships, companies, corporations, joint-stock companies or associations, in whatever capacity having control, receipt, disposal, or payment of fixed or determinable annual or periodical gains, profits, and income of another person, subject to tax" are required to deduct and withhold the annual tax of one per cent from all "interest, rent, salaries, wages, premiums, annuities, compensation, remuneration, emoluments or other fixed or determinable annual gains, profits and income of another person exceeding $3000 for any taxable year." In the case of payment of interest on bonds and mortgages or of trusts or other similar obligations of corporations, as well as in the case of collections of interest and dividends on foreign bonds and stocks not payable in the United States, the tax is to be deducted on all sums irrespective of whether or not the payments amount to $3000. The obligation to withhold the tax is not applicable to three cases. First it does not apply to the dividends on the stock of corporations (except foreign corporations not doing business in the United States) for the reason that all such corporations are subject to the tax on their net income, irrespective of whether they pay out this income as dividends or allow it to accumulate as surplus and undivided profits. Secondly, the obligation to withhold the tax does not apply to the interest on bonds, mortgages, equipment-trust, receiver's certificates or similar obligations of which the bona fide owners are citizens of foreign countries and residing abroad. Thirdly, it does not apply to the payments to a corporation, the reason for this obviously being that all corporations are required to file a complete return of all of their income, and that the books of the corporation are open to inspection by the revenue authorities.

It will be observed that the provision for payment at source is exceedingly broad. With the exceptions mentioned, it applies virtually to every one through whose hands there may go money or money's worth belonging to any one else, provided that the payments are "fixed or determinable." If the income is not fixed or certain or payable at stated periods, or if it is indefinite or irregular either in the amount or the time at which the income is paid, the provision does not apply. A failure to deduct the tax makes the individual or corporation personally liable. Moreover, any one who collects foreign payments of interest or dividends by means of coupons, checks or bills of exchange must procure a license from the Commissioner of Internal Revenue, and give bonds. All licensees must keep records open to inspection by the government officials, and must file monthly with the district collector of internal revenue a list of the names and addresses of persons from whom any items have been received, the amounts of tax deducted, and the sources thereof. Failure to conform to these regulations involves a fine not exceeding $5000, or imprisonment not exceeding one year.

In connection with this general problem of stoppage at source, two points deserve consideration: first, is the principle itself sound; and second, what administrative regulations have been issued to facilitate the execution of the law?

Among the criticisms directed against the principle of stoppage at the source, the first to be noted is the contention that there is no warrant for imposing upon the so-called "withholding agents" the expense connected with the withholding of the tax and the rendering of the accounts to the government. In this contention there seems to be some merit. It must be remembered, however, that in so far as the withholding agents are corporations, they all enjoy a privilege which is not granted to corporations in Europe, namely, that of deducting interest on debt from their gross income. Apart from this consideration, however, it would seem proper for the government to allow some compensation to withholding agents for the expense involved. This might be done by amending the law, or perhaps by a mere administrative provision. In any event, the matter does not seem sufficiently important seriously to compromise the principle of the law.

The next criticism is more weighty. It is well known that as a result of a decision of the Supreme Court in the eighties, almost all of the American railroads, and many of the larger industrial corporations, have issued their bonds with the so-called "tax-free" clause; that is, the corporations have obligated themselves to pay any taxes that might be imposed upon the bonds or coupons. The consequence is that as the present law compels these corporations to withhold the income tax on the coupons, the corporations under the tax-free clause have no option but to pay the tax themselves. As a result, the government is hitting the wrong man. It seeks to impose the tax upon the bondholder; in effect, it mulcts the corporation. Under the present situation, the tax due by such corporate bondholders is paid by the stockholders.

The framers of the bill were well aware of this complication. They accordingly introduced a section rendering void any tax-free provision in corporate bonds to be issued in the future. They did not, however, deal with existing bonds, as they feared thereby to expose the law to a charge of unconstitutionality. It may be stated, indeed, that so far as bonds to be issued in the future are concerned, it makes little difference, from the economic and fiscal points of view, whether the tax-free provision is contained therein or not. The only result of the tax-free provision in future bonds will be that the bonds will sell at a higher price than would otherwise be the case, the tax being capitalized into a difference in the market price. So far as the corporation is concerned, it makes no essential difference because the corporation will sell its tax-free bonds at a price sufficiently high to compensate it for the payment of the annual tax; and so far as inequality of taxation among individuals is concerned, it also makes no difference, because the purchasers of tax-free bonds, instead of paying the income tax on the coupons, will capitalize this annual tax into the additional price they pay for the bonds. This consideration, however, does not affect the thousands of millions of existing corporate bonds where the result of the present system is to impose an additional burden on the corporation and to exempt the security holders.

It was a consideration of this nature which led the representatives of the withholding corporations to suggest during the pendency of the discussion an alternative scheme.[1] They conceded that the chief object to be attained by the payment-at-source method ought to be kept in view, namely, the prevention of tax evasion. They contended, however, that the needs of government in this respect would be met by the receipt of information as to details of payment, ownership, addresses, etc.; and they declared themselves quite ready to present such reports. This suggestion was not entirely novel. Such reports form a part of a system originally introduced by Italy when it imposed upon the corporations the duty of supplying the government with certain facts. For this scheme the present writer suggested the name of "information at source," a name that was at once adopted as a convenient appellation. The framers of the bill acknowledged its legitimacy and were willing to substitute, in part at least, information at source for payment at source. The doubts of the majority of the Conference Committee, however, as to the efficacy of the proposed substitute in completely accomplishing the desired results were not entirely dispelled, and the principle of stoppage at source was therefore retained.

[1] See the memoranda of the Guaranty and other Trust Companies, and of Professor Bullock in *Briefs and Statements* (quoted above, p. 683), pp. 2004–2013 and 2071–2075. The former memorandum was also separately published under the title *Income Tax Bill. Memorandum on behalf of certain Trust Companies.*

The validity of these doubts must indeed be acknowledged, in part at least. To the extent that they are justifiable, it must be conceded that the Conference Committee was correct in refusing to permit any general acceptance of the information-at-source principle. Yet in so far as tax-free bonds are concerned, there is little doubt that the information-at-source method would have been an acceptable compromise between the impracticable lump-sum personal tax and the stoppage-at-source scheme, which virtually results, for the present at least, in some inequality. It must be remembered, however, that with the passage of every year and the gradual disappearance of tax-free bonds, the objections will diminish. Our conclusion must therefore be that, with this one exception, the stoppage-at-source principle is defensible, but that the information-at-source method deserves serious consideration as a possibility of the future. At all events, the elimination of the old lump-sum personal income tax constitutes an undeniable advance.

The other phase of the stoppage-at-source question is that of the administrative regulations issued to enforce the law. The Treasury Department, which was given great latitude in the matter, has struggled with the difficult task of interpreting some obscure passages in the law and making them workable. In the first place, the Bureau of Internal Revenue has provided for the attachment of certificates by all withholding agents. In case of bonds and similar obligations, it has been settled that if the debtor corporation or its fiscal agent does not deduct the tax, the first bank, trust company, banking firm, individual or collecting agency receiving the coupons for collection or otherwise shall withhold the tax and attach a certificate stating for whom the tax is deducted, the person from whom the coupons were received, the bonds from which the coupons were cut, and the amount of interest. All such certificates, which may be signed by a bank or other responsible collecting agency, as well as those prepared by persons licensed to collect foreign incomes, must be filed with the district collector by the 20th of the following month. The authorities are now engaged in an attempt greatly to reduce the number of forms and certificates. So far as income from sources other than corporate interest is concerned, the situation has been rendered much simpler by a regulation that the tax shall not be withheld until the aggregate of the payments during the year amounts to more than $3000. The tax is then to be paid upon this aggregate unless the person to whom the income is payable files with the withholding agent a claim for the three or four thousand dollar exemption, respectively, in which case the tax is to be withheld only on the excess above the exemption claimed. The tax payer may present his claim for exemption to the revenue officers, rather than to the withholding agent. In a great majority of the cases, of course, this will be done, because in order to take advantage of the deductions, the tax payer must file a statement of his annual income from all other sources. After the tax has once been withheld, any one may subsequently pass on the money involved without incurring any liability for further withholding or payment. It must also be remembered that the obligation on the part of the withholding agent to deduct the tax does not apply where the payment is made to corporations. Owing to this provision, as well as to the regulation governing the $3000 exemption, most of the complications which had been anticipated, so far as concerned rentals of real estate or the interest on real estate mortgages, will be effectively removed. There are still left, however, not a few minor administrative difficulties to be overcome.

Finally, it is to be stated that the law took effect, so far as the date of taxable income is concerned, as of March 1, 1913. Manifestly, however, the provision requiring payment at the source could not be made retroactive, and was enforced only from November 1st. Were it not for the fact that the treasury regulations provided that during November and December, 1913, the tax was to be withheld only on payments aggregating $3000 during these two months, the confusion which occurred when the law went into effect would have been far greater than it actually was.

V. *Other Administrative Features*

There remain for consideration some of the miscellaneous administrative provisions of the law.

Of these, perhaps the most interesting is that which provides for secrecy. The law states that it shall be unlawful for any officer or employee of the United States to divulge any detail set forth in any income return, nor shall he permit any details to be seen or examined by any person except in the manner to be mentioned; nor shall any person print or publish in any way any detail connected with the income returns. The returns of corporations, however, constitute public records, open to inspection upon the order of the president, under rules and regulations to be prescribed. It is further provided (and this is due to Senator LaFollette) that the proper officers of any state imposing a general income tax may, upon the request of the governor thereof, have access to such corporate returns. The secrecy imposed in the case of individuals is in bold contrast to the publicity of returns under the earlier Civil War income-tax acts.

Every individual with an income exceeding $3000 during the preceding calendar year must file a return on or before March 1st under oath or affirmation, with the collector of the internal revenue for the district in which he resides or has his principal place of business. The only exception is in the case of individuals whose income does not exceed $20,000 all of which has been derived from corporate dividends, or from sources where the tax has already been withheld.[1] Neglect or refusal to make the returns involves a penalty of from $20 to $1000, and an increase of fifty per cent in the tax. A false or fraudulent return made with intent to evade the tax is punishable with a fine not exceeding $2000, or imprisonment not exceeding one year, or both, together with the costs of prosecution. The commissioner of internal revenue is empowered

[1] For the year 1913 the returns are only to include the income that has accrued between March 1st and December 31st, after deducting five-sixths of the statutory exemptions and deductions.

to amend the return upon the discovery of fraud at any time within three years after it is due. It is to be observed that although the return is called for from the individual, the assessment itself is to be made by the commissioner of internal revenue or his assistants. It is only when no return has been rendered, or when a return is rendered which in the opinion of the collector is false or fraudulent or contains any undervaluation or understatement, that the collector is permitted to proceed further. He may then summon the individual or any other person having possession of the books, or any person that he deems proper, to appear before him, to produce the books, and to give testimony, or to answer interrogatories under oath "respecting any possible liability to tax or the returns thereof." The tax is payable on or before June 30th of every year.

Corporations are permitted to make a choice between two methods. They may file a return for the calendar year, in which case they are notified of the tax assessed against them by June 1st, and are then liable to pay the tax before June 30th. If, however, they prefer to file a return for a fiscal year which does not coincide with the calendar year, they are compelled to pay the tax within one hundred and twenty days after the date upon which they are required to file a return. Taxes remaining unpaid after the due date together with ten days' additional notice from the collector, are increased by five per cent of the amount of the tax together with interest added also. Corporations neglecting or refusing to make returns at the stated time, or making a false return, are liable to a penalty not exceeding ten thousand dollars. Moreover, in the case of refusal or neglect, the return is increased fifty per cent, and in case of fraud, one hundred per cent. Any officer of a corporation who makes a false or fraudulent return is subject to a fine of two thousand dollars or to imprisonment for one year or to both. It will be seen, therefore, from the above regulations that the provisions for the collection of the tax are not only ample but rigid.

VI. *Conclusion*

The income tax law of 1913 is not perfect. It is not in all respects well drawn, and there are not a few obscure points which will require interpretation by the administrative authorities or the courts. Moreover, it contains defects of omission as well as of commission.

Many of the criticisms urged both before and after the passage of the law are indeed not valid. Thus it was maintained that if an income tax should be imposed, there would surely be discrimination against New York and the other wealthier states. As a matter of fact, there is no discrimination in the present law except that which arises from the fact that New York is wealthier than other states, and therefore ought to pay a larger sum. No one would think of protesting against the justice of customs duties because as a matter of fact so large a proportion is collected from the port of New York. It is interesting to notice that in the year 1871, the year before the abolition of the Civil War income tax, when residents of New York state paid slightly over thirty-nine per cent of the entire tax, they paid actually more than that percentage of other federal taxes — for instance, forty-one per cent of the tax on gas, and forty-two per cent of the taxes in Schedule A. In 1867, indeed, New York paid no less than fifty-six per cent of the tax on sales. If New York pays more than thirty-nine per cent of the present income tax, it will simply mean that there has been in the intervening years a greater concentration of wealth in that state.

In the same way the charge that the tax is socialistic can be brushed aside. It is true that we now have a graduated scale of taxation, but the extremes of graduation are lower than in other countries. It is also true that the exemption is placed at a figure which may seem excessive. It must be remembered, however, in addition to the three reasons mentioned above,[1] that this is, on the whole, in accord with the conception of taxation that has long obtained in America.

[1] *Supra*, pp. 686–687.

For many decades the great mass of state and local revenues has rested on the basis of the general property tax, the accepted principle of which is to exempt all those who have not accumulated property. Now if it is true, as is claimed, that the recipients of an income of $3000 ordinarily spend the greater part of their income and lay by little or nothing, the exemption of $3000 from an income tax would amount to the usual exemption involved in the imposition of a general property tax. For if a man saves nothing from a $3000 income, he will not be subject to a property tax. Whether or not it is accurate that the recipients of $3000 income ordinarily spend all of it, it is probable that with the rising standard of life in this country, much, if any, saving is unlikely; and to the extent that this is true, the argument for a comparatively high exemption seems to be defensible. Those who urge that there should be no exemption at all or a very slight one, forget that they are running counter to the whole theory of the general property tax which has hitherto been at the basis of American fiscal policy. The $3000 exemption, then, does not involve any serious departure from accepted principles of fiscal justice.

The real defects of the income-tax law are entirely different. In the first place, no attempt has been made to introduce a differentiation of taxation; that is, to distinguish between the rate on earned and unearned incomes. This scheme was indeed suggested during the discussion, in the shape of a formal amendment.[1] But its full import seems to have been misunderstood, and in the haste of the elaboration of the bill, the matter was allowed to drop. It must be remembered, indeed, that the question of differentiation of taxation was agitated in England for half a century; but it is also true that differentiation was finally accepted before graduation — the one in 1907, the other in 1910. In our present law, on the other hand, the principle of graduation has been accepted, but it still remains to introduce that of

[1] By Senator Crawford, approved by Senator Cummins. *Congressional Record*, pp. 4233, 4280, Aug. 27, 29, 1913.

differentiation. It is to be hoped that this will not long be delayed.[1]

The second defect in the law is the failure to introduce proper administrative methods, so far as ordinary business incomes are concerned. The principle of stoppage at source is not applicable to most of these. It is well known how England has had to struggle with Schedule D. Instead, however, of utilizing the lessons which can be drawn from the English experience, the framers of our law have preferred to leave the matter alone on the ground that too much must not be attempted at once. It remains to be seen whether a simple declaration by the tax payer, even as amended by the government officials, will suffice to prevent a repetition of the enormous frauds and evasions which were common to our income-tax laws of the Civil War period. It is indeed true that the far greater part of the tax is to be collected according to the principle of stoppage at source; but there seems to be no good reason why such an enormous loophole should have been left open in the case of ordinary business returns.

These, however, are the only important criticisms to be urged against the law. So far as the stoppage-at-source principle is concerned, we have seen that in the main it is not only defensible, but constitutes a distinct advance, even though it might have been desirable to substitute, in part at least, the information-at-source principle.

Taking it all in all, the law must be pronounced an intelligent and well-considered effort. It will need amendment in detail to make it completely equitable in principle, and fairly smooth in operation. But when we compare it with our preceding ventures in this field, we may be proud of what has been accomplished. Indeed, the law may be declared to be in many respects superior to any other existing income-tax law. With the passage of time, and with the settlement by economic science of some of the moot points in the theory of

[1] Senator Williams mentioned this as well as other possible improvements in a speech beginning: "What we are doing with this income tax is a totally different thing from what we hope to do some day." *Congressional Record*, p. 4189.

income, it may be expected that the law will gradually win its way to public recognition.

Of the wider question involved as to the probable future of the federal income tax and its position in the whole field of public revenue, this is no place to speak. The gradual development of income taxes in some of our states and the feeling that a large revenue from personal property or its income is needed by our states and municipalities rather than by our federal government, are weighty considerations that must not be overlooked. It is interesting to observe that even during the discussion of the present law the proposal was made that a part of the proceeds, at least, be returned to the states. Had not this suggestion emanated from a source that was undisguisedly hostile to the very idea of a federal income tax, it is not impossible that it would have received fuller recognition.[1] Whatever the future may have in store as to the interrelations of federal and state revenue, it is probable that the income tax has come to stay. Let us be thankful that it has come in such a shape, and let us look forward with hopeful anticipation to a future in which the income tax, improved and amended, will play its important part in bringing about greater justice in American taxation.

[1] According to the proposition of Senator Dillingham, who presented a joint resolution introduced into the Vermont legislature, the entire proceeds were to go to the states. *Congressional Record*, Sept. 8, p. 4881. In Mr. Copley's scheme for a highly graduated tax, the surplus only was to go to the states. *Ibid.*, p. 1214.

BIBLIOGRAPHY

BIBLIOGRAPHY[1]

ENGLAND

A. Signed Works.

Allen, J. E. "A Graduated Income Tax." *The Economic Review*, vol. xv (1905).

Atwood, M. *Speech on the Income Tax, in the House of Commons, on Wednesday, March 23rd, 1842.* London, 1842.

Aucland, Lord. *The Substance of a Speech in the House of Peers, on Tuesday, the 8th Day of January, 1799, on the Third Reading of the Bill for Granting Certain Duties upon Income.* London, 1799.

B., R. S. *Two Letters to a Member of Parliament; containing Suggestions for a Property Tax upon an Improved Basis; with Remarks upon the Principal Speeches in Defense of the Present Income Tax, during the late Debates.* London, 1848.

Babbage, Charles. *Thoughts on the Principles of Taxation, with Reference to a Property Tax, and its Exceptions.* London, 1848.

Beal, James. *Direct Taxation. London Financial Reform Association. Observations addressed to the Members of the Westminster Reform Union.* London, 1862.

Beeke, Rev. H. *Observations on the Produce of the Income Tax, and on its Proportion to the Whole Income of Great Britain: including Important Facts respecting the Extent, Wealth and Population of this Kingdom. Part the First.* London, 1799.

Blunden, G. H. "The Position and Function of the Income Tax in the British Fiscal System." *The Economic Journal*, vol. ii (1892).

Blunden, G. H. "A Progressive Income Tax." *The Economic Journal*, vol. v (1895).

Blunden, G. H. "A New Property Tax." *The Economic Journal*, vol. vii (1897).

Blunden, G. H. "The Future of the Income Tax." *The Economic Journal*, vol. xi (1901).

Booth, Dr. "On the Principles of an Income Tax." *Journal of the Statistical Society*, vol. xxiii (1860).

Boult, Francis. *Taxation: Direct or Indirect. An Essay intended to be read to the Economic Section of the British Association.* Liverpool, 1861.

Browning, Reuben. *The Finances of Great Britain considered. Comprising an Examination of the Property and Income Tax, and Succession Duty Act of 1853. Part I.* London, 1859.

Buchanan, David. *Inquiry into the Taxation and Commercial Policy of Great Britain; with Observations on the Principles of Currency and of Exchangeable Value.* Edinburgh, 1844.

[1] This bibliography does not include the general works on taxation and finance, many of which are quoted in the body of this book.

Buckingham, J. S. *Outlines of a New Budget, for raising Eighty Millions, by Means of a justly Graduated Property Tax; with Suggestions on the Representative System, the National Debt, etc. Prepared for the Consideration of the Reformed Parliament of England.* London, 1831.

Buckingham, J. S. "The Superiority of an Income and Property Tax to every other Source of Revenue." *The Parliamentary Review*, vol. v (1834).

Buckingham, J. S. *Plan of an Improved Income Tax and Real Free Trade. With an Equitable Mode of Redeeming the National Debt.* London, 1845.

Buckingham, J. S. See *Debate in the House of Commons.* London, 1853.

Burns, James. "A Graduated Income Tax." *Westminster Review*, vol. cxlvi (1896).

Burt, J. Gurney. *The Incidence of Taxation and Debt on Industry.* London, n. d. (1871).

Clarke, Thomas. *Essay on Taxation, Direct and Indirect, with Suggestions for its Revision.* Liverpool, 1851.

Coad, Joseph. *A New Plan of Taxation. This Plan will render the Custom and Excise Duties useless, abolish the Income Tax, take off all the Assessed Taxes, and reduce Provisions more than Seventy Per Cent, etc.* London, 1807.

Cobbett, William. *A Letter to the Chancellor of the Exchequer on the Relative Political Merits of Beer, Wine, and Tea; shewing the Effects of Taxes on those Articles, and Substitutes for Those Taxes and also for the Income Tax.* London, 1863.

Cooke, N. *The Just Proportion which Each Class of the People, from the Peasant to the Peer, have in the Support and Prosperity of the State. Or Test of Taxation; and a Schedule for Assessment on Income, resulting from a Mathematical Investigation of the Value of Property acquired, and that Fluctuating in Trade. Addressed to every Individual of the British Empire.* London, 1798.

Court, Major M. H. *A Review of the Income Tax in its Relations to the National Debt; with Suggestions for Removal of its Present Inequalities, by a more Uniform Mode of Assessment.* London, 1853.

Courtenay, Thomas Peregrine. *Observations upon the Present State of the Finances of Great Britain; suggested by Mr. Morgan's Supplement to his "Comparative View," and by Mr. Addington's Financial Measures.* London, 1803.

Easton, Josiah. *A Plan for Commuting and Abolishing Taxes on the Necessaries of Life, and All the Assessed Taxes, to the Amount of £25,000,000 per Annum, etc.* Taunton, 1833.

Farr, William. "The Income and Property Tax." *Journal of the Statistical Society*, vol. xvi (1853).

Fox, Charles J. *The Speech (at length) on the Third Reading of the Bill for Increasing the Assessed Taxes.* London, n. d. (1798).

Frend, William. *Principles of Taxation.* London, 1799.

Frend, William. *The Principles of Taxation: or Contribution according to Means; in which it is shewn that if Every Man pays in Proportion to the Stake he has in the Country, the present Ruinous and Oppressive System of Taxation, the Custom House, and the Excise Office may be abolished, and the National Debt gradually and easily paid off.* London, 1804.

Fry, T. Hallet. *Income Tax Anomalies.* London, 1903.

Fry, T Hallet. *The Income Tax Burden.* London, 1904.

Fry, T. Hallett. *The Recovery and Adjustment of the Income Tax; What to do and how to do it.* London, 1905.

Fry, T. Hallett. "Income Tax Adjustment." *The Magazine of Commerce,* vol. ix (1906).

Fry, T. Hallet. *Income Tax. Its Return, Assessment and Recovery.* London, 1909.

Fry, T. Hallet. "The Income Tax Problem." *The Magazine of Commerce,* vol. x (1907).

Furnivall, Thomas. *Taxation Revised and National Progress.* London, 1847.

Gibbon, Alexander. *Taxation: its Nature and Properties, with Remarks on the Incidence and the Expediency of the Repeal of the Income Tax.* London, 1851.

Gibbon, Alexander. See *A Familiar Treatise on Taxation, Free Trade, etc.* London, 1846.

Gibbon, Alexander. *The Income Tax; in Causes and Incidence: showing by Analysis that it is a Land Tax, a House Tax, a Tax upon Commodities and a Repudiation of Public Debt.* London, 1860.

Gisborne, Thomas. *Thoughts on an Income Tax and on a Property Tax; principally founded on the Evidence taken by the House of Commons Committee in the Session 1851.* London, 1852.

Gladstone, Right Hon. W. E. *The Financial Statements of 1853, 1860–1863.* London, 1863.

Glover, Rev. George. *Thoughts on the Character and Tendency of the Property Tax, as adapted to a Permanent System of Taxation.* London, 1816.

Goddard, J. G. "Graduated Taxation." *Economic Review,* vol. v (1895).

Gray, John. *The Income Tax scrutinized, and Some Amendments proposed to render it more Agreeable to the British Constitution.* London, 1802.

Grey, John. *A Letter Addressed to a Member of the House of Commons on the Subject of the Liability of the Pay of the Officers of the Navy and Army to the Tax upon Property.* London, 1810.

Haywood, G. R. *Direct Taxation and how it may be applied.* Liverpool, 1883.

Heathfield, Richard. *Means of Extensive Relief from the Pressure of Taxation, on the Basis of a Charge of Five Per Cent on all Property in the United Kingdom, Real and Personal.* London, 1849.

Hemming, G. W. *A Just Income Tax, how Possible. Being a Review of the Evidence reported by the Income Tax Committee, and an Inquiry into the True Principle of Taxation.* London, 1852.

Heron, Denis Caulfield. *Three Lectures on the Principles of Taxation, delivered at Queen's College, Galway, in Hilary Term, 1850.* Dublin, 1850.

Heyworth, Lawrence. *Direct and Indirect Taxation contrasted; or, the immeasurably Preferable Policy of an Income Tax to Customs and Excise Duties, elucidated.* London, n. d. (1861).

Hilditch, Richard. See *Aristocratic Taxation.* London, 1842.

Hilditch, Richard. *Aristocratic Taxation, its Present State, Origin and Progress, with Proposals for Reform; comprising Proofs of the Justice and Expediency of a Land Tax for Redemption of National Debt; Strictures on the Income Tax and the Idea of a System of Taxation not only without Burthen, but absolutely in itself Beneficial.* London, 1842.

Hilditch, Richard. *The Income Tax criticised and epitomized, containing some*

Plain Statements on the Income and Property Tax, showing that it falls most heavily on the Industrious Classes; with Full Instructions for Filling up the Tax Papers. London, 1843.

Hill, Joseph A. "The English Income Tax with Special Reference to Administration and Method of Assessment." *Economic Studies, American Economic Association.* New York, 1889.

Hourglass, Humphrey. *The Mouse-Trap Maker and the Income Tax; A Tale supposed, by Anticipation, to be written in the Year 2000; with an Introductory Allegory addressed to a Man in Office.* London, n. d. (1799).

Hook, A. "Earned and Unearned Incomes and the Income Tax." *Westminster Review,* vol. 165 (1906).

Hubbard, John Gellibrand. *How should an Income Tax be levied? Considered in a Letter to the Right Honourable Benjamin Disraeli, Chancellor of the Exchequer.* London, 1852.

Hubbard, John Gellibrand. *Reform or Reject the Income Tax. Objections to a Reform of the Income Tax considered, in Two Letters, to the Editor of the Times, with Additional Notes.* London, 1853.

Hubbard, John Gellibrand. *A Lecture on Currency, Taxation and Finance, delivered at the Town Hall, Buckingham, on the 21st of April.* N. p., n. d. (1859).

Hubbard, John Gellibrand. *Local and Imperial Taxation. A Speech, the Delivery of which on Tuesday the 20th of July, was precluded by the Counting out of the House at 9 P.M.* London, 1875.

Hubbard, J. G. "Forty Years of Income Tax." *National Review,* February, 1884.

Hubbard, J. G. *Gladstone on the Income Tax. Discussion of the Income Tax in the House of Commons on 25th April, 1884. With Preface and Historical Sketch, including a Proposed Bill.* London, 1885.

Hume, Joseph. *The Draft Report proposed by the Chairman of the Select Committee on the Income and Property Tax.* Liverpool (1852).

Huneke, Ernst. *Die Entwicklung von Einkommensteuer und Einkommen in England in den letzten zwanzig Jahren.* Breslau, 1904.

Lauderdale, Earl of. *A Letter on the Present Measures of Finance; in which the Bill now depending in Parliament is particularly considered.* London, 1798.

Leake, P. D. *Income Tax on Capital. A Plea for Reform in the Official Method of Computing Taxable Profits.* London, 1909.

Lecky, W. E. H. "Mr. Gladstone and the Income Tax." *Nineteenth Century,* vol. xxii (1887).

Levi, Leone. "On the Reconstruction of the Income and Property Tax." *Journal of the Statistical Society,* vol. xxxvii (1874).

Lubbock, Sir John. "The Income Tax in England." *North American Review,* vol. 158 (1894).

MacGregor, John. *Financial Reform: a Letter to the Citizens of Glasgow, with an Introduction and Supplementary Notes.* London, 1849.

MacLeod, John MacPherson. *Remarks on Some Popular Objections to the Present Income Tax.* London, 1849.

M'Laren, Duncan. *Indirect Taxation: Its Wasteful and Burdensome Nature, as compared with Direct Taxation, in necessarily causing the Public to pay much more than the Amount imposed by Parliament; and the most Equitable Mode of imposing Direct Taxes on Property.* Edinburgh, 1860.

M'Laren, Duncan. *Report to the Edinburgh Chamber of Commerce, proposing a Just and Simple Mode of Laying on the Income and Property Tax.* Edinburgh, 1862.

Maitland, J. G. See *Property and Income Tax, Schedule A and B.* London, 1852.

Maitland, J. G. *Property and Income Tax. The Present State of the Question.* London, 1853.

Makepeace, William. *Taxation, in its Operation, by Means of the Income and Assessed Taxes, considered. Together with Suggestions for its Alteration and Amendment.* London, n. d. (1840).

Matson, John. *Repeal of all Taxes with Security to the Fund Holder, in a Letter, shewing also the Great Advantages to the Land-Owner and all Other Classes of his Majesty's Subjects. Addressed to the Duke of Wellington.* London, n. d. (1829).

Miller, Samuel. *Suggestions for a General Equalization of the Land Tax and the Abolition of the Income and Real Property Taxes, and the Malt Duty.* London, 1848.

Morgan, William. *A Comparative View of the Public Finances, from the Beginning to the Close of the Late Administration.* London, 1801.

Morgan, William. *A Supplement to a Comparative View of the Public Finances, containing an Account of the Management of the Finances to the Present Time.* London, 1803.

Newbatt, Benjamin. "The Income Tax." *Journal of the Institute of Actuaries,* vol. 28 (1890).

Newbery, Francis. *Observations on the Income Act; particularly as it relates to the Occupiers of Land: with Some Proposals of Amendment. To which is added a Short Scheme for Meliorating the Condition of the Labouring Man.* London, 1801.

Peel, Robert. *The Income Tax. Speech in the House of Commons, on Friday Evening, March 18, 1842.* London, 1842.

Pellett, Stephen. *Constitutional Aids. Progress of Taxation, with New Plan of Finance.* London, 1817.

Phipps, Edmund. *A Few Words on the Three Amateur Budgets of Cobden, MacGregor and Watson.* London, 1849.

Pitt, William. *Speeches in the House of Commons.* 2d ed. London, 1808.

Price, W. H., "The British Income Tax in recent years." *Quarterly Journal of Economics,* vol. xx (1906).

R. *Redemption of the National Debt by Composition of Income Tax.* London, 1891.

Ranby, John. *An Examination of Mr. Wakefield's Reply to the Bishop of Landaff's Address.* London, 1798.

Richardson, James. *Unequal Taxation, the Chief Cause of the Misery now suffered by the Industrious and Middle Classes of Society; and its Remedy, a Graduated Tax upon Property.* London, 1833.

Rickman, Thos. Clio. *Mr. Pitt's Democracy manifested; in a Letter to him, containing Praises of, and Strictures on, the Income Tax.* London, 1800.

Roberts, C. A. "Sketch of the History of the English Income Tax." *Bankers Magazine.* New York (1866).

Rogers, J. E. Thorold. "On the Statistical and Fiscal Definitions of the Word Income." *Journal of the Statistical Society,* vol. xxviii (1865).

Rose, George. *A Brief Examination into the Increase of the Revenue, Commerce and Manufactures, of Great Britain, from 1792 to 1799.* 4th ed. London, 1799.

Rose, George. *Speech in the House of Commons on the 20th of February, 1815, on the Subject of the Property Tax.* London, 1815.

Russell, R. W. *Financial Reform. A Digest of the Reasons for and against a Tax upon Permanent Property, in Lieu of Some of the Present Taxes, especially those on Commodities.* London, 1842.

Sargant, William Lucas. "An Undiscriminating Income Tax reconsidered." *Journal of the Statistical Society*, vol. xxv (1862).

Sargant, William Lucas. "Some Observations on the Fallacy of the Warburton Argument in favor of an Indiscriminating Income Tax." *Journal of the Statistical Society*, vol. xxiv (1861).

Sayer, Benjamin. See *An Attempt to shew the Justice, etc.* London, 1833.

Scott, E. Erskine. *The Property and Income Tax the best Tax for the Community.* London, 1852.

Smee, William Ray. *The Income Tax; Its Extension at the Present Rate proposed to all Classes; abolishing the Malt Tax, Window Tax, and other Taxes, with some Observations on the Tea Duties.* London, n. d. (1846).

Smith, George Henry. *The Rights of Rich and Poor: Just Taxation; Abolition of all Duties on the Necessaries of Life, etc.* Liverpool n. d. (1861).

Stamp, J. C. "Economic Aspects of Income Tax Change." *The Economic Review*, vol. xix (1909).

Stansfeld, Hamer. *Outline of a System of Direct Taxation for superseding Customs and Excise Duties, and establishing Perfect Freedom of Trade.* London, n. d. (1859).

Tennant, Chas. *The People's Blue Book: Taxation as it is, and as it ought to be.* London, 1853.

Vaux, Thomas. *Relative Taxation; or Observations on the Impolicy of Taxing Malt, Hops, Beer, Soap, Candles, and Leather; with a View of the Manner in which the Duties imposed upon them affect the Different Kinds of Land, whether in Grass or Tillage, and their Constant Tendency to increase Pauperism; with Reasons for substituting a Tax on Property, etc.* London, 1833.

Vocke, W. *Geschichte der Steuern des Britischen Reichs. Ein Finanzgeschichtlicher Versuch.* Leipzig, 1866.

Wakefield, Gilbert. *A Reply to Some Parts of the Bishop of Landaff's Address to the People of Great Britain.* London, 1798.

Wakefield, Daniel. *An investigation of Mr. Morgan's Comparative View of the Public Finances, from the Beginning to the Close of the late Administration.* London, 1801.

Watson, R., Lord Bishop of Landaff. *An Address to the People of Great Britain.* London, 1798.

Whitock, Richard. *An Inquiry into the Cause of the Present Depression of Trade, and a Remedy proposed, in a Measure calculated at the Same Time to obviate the Necessity of an Income Tax.* Edinburgh, 1842.

Wilkinson, Harrison. *The Principle of an Equitable and Efficient System of Finance: Founded upon Self-evident, Universal and Invariable Principles capable of diminishing Taxes and Poor-Rates; reviving and permanently supporting Agriculture, Trade, Commerce, Wealth and Happiness. Demonstrating that the Existing System of Finance is Capricous, Impolitic and Im-*

provident; Injurious to Liberty, Property and Legislation; Proving the Necessity of Repealing all Existing Taxes both General and Local; and adopting One Simple, Equitable, and Efficient, grounded upon a Scale Just, and Unchangeable. By the Adoption of this Plan the Dread of the Rich would be removed, the Distress of the Poor relieved, and the Confidence of All restored; etc., etc. London, 1820.

Willich, Charles M. *Letters on the Income Tax; Conversion of Consols; Savings Banks and Friendly Societies.* London, 1852.

Wilson, Iames. *The Revenue; or, What should the Chancellor do?* London, 1841.

B. ANONYMOUS WORKS (arranged chronologically).

An Address to the People of Great Britain, extracted from the Bishop of Landaff's Pamphlet. Leeds, 1798.

An Address to the Right Hon. William Pitt, etc., on Some Parts of his Administration; occasioned by his Proposal of the Triple Assessment in the House of Commons in November, 1797. London, n. d. (1798).

An Appeal to the Head and Heart of Every Man and Woman in Great Britain, respecting the Threatened French Invasion and the Importance of immediately coming forward with Voluntary Contributions. London, 1798.

A Plan for Raising the Supplies during the War, humbly submitted to the Two Houses of Parliament, the Landed and Monied Interest, and to all Ranks and Conditions of the People, capable of Contributing to the Expenses of the State. London, 1798.

Consolatory Thoughts on Taxation or Contribution, in Three Letters to a Member of the House of Commons. By the author of *Thoughts on Taxation and a New System of Funding.* London, 1798.

Observations, etc., upon the Act for Taxing Income; in which the Principle and Provisions of the Act are fully considered, with a View to facilitate the Execution, both with Respect to Persons chargeable, and the Officers chosen to carry it into Effect. With the Act at Large. Together with the Substance of the Clauses of the Assessed Tax Act that have a Reference to this, and a Copious Index, referring both to the Act and Observations. London, 1799.

Observation upon the Amended Act for taxing Income. London, n. d. (1799).

Three Essays on Taxation of Income, with Remarks on the Late Act of Parliament on That Subject. On the National Debt; the Public Funds; on the Probable Consequences of the Law for the Sale of the Land Tax; and on the Present State of Agriculture in Great Britain. With a Scheme for the Improvement of every Branch of it, and Remarks on the Difference between National Produce and Consumption. [By Benjamin Bell.] London, 1799.

Review of the Arguments advanced in the House of Commons in Support of the Bill for Granting an Aid and Contribution for the Prosecution of the War, by imposing Certain Duties upon Income. London, 1799.

Strong Reasons for the Continuance of the Property Tax. To which is added an Estimate of the National Income recently made by Patrick Colquhoun. By a Friend to his Country. London, 1814.

Three most Important Objects Proposed. York, 1815.

Two Letters to the Right Honourable Viscount Castlereagh, on the Present Situation of the Landed Interest, and the Intended Partial Repeal of the Income Tax. London, 1816.

Resist or be Ruined! The Property Tax must be abolished now, or a State Inquisition will be established in England for ever. The immediate Resistance of the Whole Nation shewn to be the only Means of averting an Inquisitorial and Perpetual Income Tax, from which Mr. Vansittart has declared no Class of Society will be exempted. With a full Account of the Proceedings in London. London, 1816.

Thoughts on Taxation. Dedicated with the Most Profound Respect to the Right Honourable the Speaker and Gentlemen of the Commons House of Parliament. London, 1827.

A Letter to the Earl of Wilton on the Commutation of Existing Taxes for a Graduated Property and Income Tax; connecting therewith a Plan of Parliamentary Reform. By an Englishman. 2d ed. London, 1830.

Property (not Income) the only Just Ground of Taxation. N. p., n. d. (1831).

Suggestions for Combining an improved System of Taxation, with a wide Diffusion of the Elective Franchise. London, 1831.

A Practical Plan for the Immediate Annihilation of Taxes, and Equitable Liquidation of the National Debt. By a Capitalist. London, 1832.

A Scheme for a Graduated Property Tax. London, 1832.

The Property Tax the only Effectual Remedy for the Present Embarrassment of the Country. Birmingham, 1832.

An Attempt to shew the Justice and Expediency of substituting an Income or Property Tax for the Present Taxes, or a part of Them; as affording the Most Equitable, the Least Injurious, and (under the Modified Procedure suggested therein) the Least Obnoxious Mode of Taxation; also, the Most Fair, Advantageous, and Effectual Plans of Reducing the National Debt. [By Benjamin Sayer.] London, 1833.

British Taxes Dissected. Being a Plain Letter addressed to the Workingmen of Great Britain and Ireland; explaining how fifty Millions are yearly raised to pay these fifty Millions; how they ought to be raised and who ought to pay them. By one of the Council of the Nat'l Political Union. London, 1833.

Outlines of a Plan for Amending the System of Taxation. Birmingham, 1833.

Tax on Capital and Fixed Duty on Corn. London, 1833.

A Property Tax. The Justice and Utility of a Property Tax, as a means of Restoring the Revenue, Placing it upon a Permanent Basis, and Affording Facilities for the Development of the Commercial and Manufacturing Resources of the Country. By a true Conservative. London, n. d. (1839).

Argument for the General Relief of the Country from Taxation, and eventually from the Corn Laws, by an Assessment on Property. London, 1839.

Aristocratic Taxation; Its Present State, Origin, and Progress, with Proposals for Reform. [By Richard Hilditch.] London, 1842.

Income Tax. A few Words to the Operative and Lower Classes of the People of England, upon Sir R. Peel's Proposed Income Tax. By One of Themselves. London, 1842.

Tory Taxes. London, 1842.

A Familiar Treatise on Taxation, Free Trade, etc. Comprising Facts usually unnoticed or unconsidered in Theories of Those Subjects. With Notes on Subjects arising incidentally. [By Alexander Gibbon.] London, 1846.

Reasons for a Tax on Property, in Substitution for Duties of Excise and Customs. London, 1846.

A Letter to Charles Babbage, Esq., in Reply to "Thoughts on the Principles of

Taxation, with Reference to a Property Tax and its Exceptions." *Liverpool Financial Reform Association.* Liverpool, 1852.

A Few Words on Behalf of the Middle Classes of England, on the Subject of the Income Tax. London, 1852.

Equitable Taxation and Representation on a Fixed, General and clearly Defined Principle. London, 1852.

Property and Income Tax, Schedule A and Schedule D. [By J. G. Maitland.] London, 1852.

Debate in the House of Commons on the Gradual Extinction of the National Debt, and of the True Principles of a Property and Income Tax. Republished for comparison with Gladstone's Proposition. [By J. S. Buckingham.] London, 1853.

Elements of Taxation; to which are added a Summary of the Evidence adduced before the Parliamentary Committee on the Property and Income Tax. And also a complete Analysis of the Finance Accounts of the United Kingdom, for the year 1851. By X + Y, Authors of the Prize Essay on Direct Taxation. London, n. d. (1853).

Address of the Income Tax Reform Association established at Birmingham, May 28, 1855. Birmingham, 1855.

Address on the Present Anti-Income Tax Agitation; showing how and why Direct Taxation is preferable to Customs and Excise Duties. By the Liverpool Financial Reform Association. New Series, no. 19. Liverpool, 1856.

Address of the Birmingham Income Tax Reform Association to the Electors of Great Britain and Ireland, Feb. 1857. Birmingham, n. d. (1857).

The Property and Income Tax Association to the Taxpayers of the United Kingdom. London, n. d. (1857).

The Shade of Cocker and the Chancellor of the Exchequer. A Dialogue on the Income Tax. London, n. d. (1858).

Taxation: Gross Injustice of the present System. Direct Taxation the true Remedy. By a Mill Owner. Edinburgh, 1859.

"The Income Tax and its Rivals." *Quarterly Review*, vol. 109 (1861).

"Income Tax Reform." *Westminster Review*, vol. lxxvii (1862).

Shall the Tax be Permanent? By the author of *Our Deficient Revenue and the Income Tax.* London (1877).

On the Incidence of Taxation, as Affecting Different Classes in the United Kingdom at the Present Time. By Investigator. London, 1883.

"The Tyranny of the Income Tax." *Blackwood's Magazine*, vol. 178 (1905).

"Anomalies of Income Tax Collection." *Chambers's Journal.* 1907.

C. Official Documents and Commentaries.

A Plain, Short, and Easy Description of the Different Clauses of the Income Tax so as to render it Familiar to the Meanest Capacity. London, 1799.

Income. The New Schedule, as corrected and altered by the Amended Act for Taxing Income. Together with an Abstract of the Clauses of the Original Act, that relates to the Mode of estimating Income, and a Brief Notice of the Provisions of the Amended Act; with a Variety of Examples calculated to shew the Mode of Estimating the Different Descriptions of Income, and making the Deductions according to the Cases in the Schedule. London (1799).

Taxes on Income. A Correct Abridgement of the Act imposing a Tax on All Income, containing Those Clauses which principally affect Landlords, Tenants, etc., exhibited in a Clear and Methodical Manner, etc., with a Schedule for Estimating the Income of Persons liable to be Assessed. London (1799).

An Exposition of the Act for a Contribution on Property, Professions, Trades, and Offices; in which the Principles and Provisions of the Act are fully considered with a View to facilitate in Execution both with Respect to Persons Chargeable, as Persons Liable, to the Tax by Way of Deduction, and the Officers chosen to carry it into Effect. London, 1803.

First Report from the Select Committee on the Income and Property Tax; together with the Minutes of Evidence and Index. London, 1852.

Second Report from the Select Committee on the Income and Property Tax; together with the Proceedings of the Committee, Minutes of Evidence, Appendix, and Index. London, 1852.

Report from the Select Committee on Income and Property Tax; together with the Proceedings of the Committee, Minutes of Evidence, and Appendix. London, 1861.

Twenty-eighth Report of the Commissioners of Her Majesty's Inland Revenue on the Duties under their Management for the Year ending 31st March, 1885, with some Retrospective History, and Complete Tables of Accounts of the Duties from 1869–70 to 1884–5 inclusive. London, 1885.

Forty-third Report of the Commissioners of Inland Revenue. London, 1900.

Papers respecting the Local Taxation of Personal Property in Certain Foreign Countries and British Possessions. (Cd. 2098). London, 1904.

Report of the Departmental Committee on Income Tax. London, 1905.

Appendix to the Report of the Departmental Committee on Income Tax with Minutes of Evidence taken before the Committee. London, 1905.

Reports from His Majesty's Representatives Abroad respecting Graduated Income Taxes in Foreign States. Foreign Office, Misc., no. 2. London, 1905.

Graduated Income Tax (Colonies). Return to an Address of the House of Commons, dated August 11, 1904. Colonial Office, 196. London, 1905.

Report from the Select Committee on Income Tax; together with the Proceedings of the Committee, Minutes of Evidence, and an Appendix. London, 1906.

Berry, Jabez. *Index to Income Tax Acts; being a Complete Guide to the Statutes relating to Income Tax, from the Income Tax Act, 1842, to the Finance (1909–10) Act, 1910.* London, 1910.

Dowell, Stephen. *The Acts relating to the Income Tax.* 6th ed., by John Edwin Piper. London, 1908.

Ellis, A. M. *Guide to the Income Tax Acts for the Use of the Income Tax-Payer.* London, 1886.

Nicholson, William. *The Income Tax Act, Epitomized and Simplified.* London, 1842.

Paget, John. *The Income Tax Act, 5 and 6 Victoria, c. 35, with an Explanatory Introduction and Index.* London, 1842.

Peacock, H. St. George and Campbell, R. F. G. *The Income Tax Acts, with Introduction, Notes, and Cross References.* London, 1901.

Pratt, J. T. *Income Tax Law.* 8th ed. by J. H. Redman. London, 1910.

Spicer, E. E. and Pegler, E. C. *Income Tax in Relation to Accounts.* 2d ed. London, 1910.

ADDITIONS TO THE SECOND EDITION

A. Signed Works.

Adams, Francis. *A Plan for raising the Taxes impartially and almost free of Expense in War and in Peace for paying off the National Debt.* London, 1797.

Coleman, S. *Some Observations on Direct Taxation in reference to Commercial Reform.* London, 1853.

Fry, T. Hallet. *The Income Tax Incubus and the Budget.* London, 1909.

Jones, Edward. *Reflections on a Graduated Property and Income Tax to raise the sum of £17,822,000.* London, 1833.

Morris, W. *Three Letters to the Rt. Hon. Sir Robert Peel on the Repeal of the Present System of Revenue and Protection, Imports, Excise, Stamps, and the Adoption of a Great System of Income Taxation.* Exeter, 1843.

Y., J. O. *Proposed Reform in the Income Tax and Extension of the Franchise to the Payers of the Same.* London, 1863.

B. Anonymous Works (arranged chronologically):

Occasional Letters upon Taxation; upon the Means of Raising the Supplies within the Year, to answer the Expences of a Necessary War; and upon such Measures as would probably tend to secure Great Britain and its Natural Dependencies the Blessings of Peace upon a Durable System. By an Independent Man. London, 1780.

Hints towards an improved System of Taxation, extending to all Persons in exact Proportion to their Property and without any kind of Investigation or Disclosure of their Circumstances. London, 1798.

Thoughts on Taxation, in the course of which the Policy of a Tax on Income is impartially investigated. London, 1798.

A Defense of the Landowners and Farmers of Great Britain and an Exposition of the heavy Parliamentary and Parochial Taxation under which they labour. By an Agricultural Gentleman. London, 1814.

A Pat from the Lion's Paw, inflicted in the Name of Common Sense, upon the Railers against the Property Tax. By Leo Britannicus. London, 1815.

Considerations addressed to the People of England on the Expediency of continuing the Property Tax a certain number of years. London, 1815.

The Property Tax considered with reference to its Renewal. London, 1816.

An Equitable Property Tax: a Financial Speculation and a Fair Rate of Wages to the Labouring Poor. By a Loyal Briton. London, 1831.

The Expediency of a Property Tax considered in relation to the Objections of Earl Grey and Lord Brougham. London, 1831.

Thirty Years Observations on the Effects of taxing Provisions instead of Income, with a just Scale to tax Income. By a Farmer. London, 1836.

UNITED STATES

A. Signed Works.

Abbott, Austin. "The Income Tax. How it should be paid by the Honest Citizen." *Banker's Magazine*, vol. 50 (1895).

Allen, L. "The Income Tax Decision; an Answer to Governor Pennoyer." *North American Review*, vol. clx (1895).

Beach, J. K. "The Income Tax Decision." *The Yale Review*, vol. v (1896).

Borah, William E. "The Income Tax Amendment." *North American Review*, vol. 191 (1910).

Borah, William E. "The Income Tax Sound in Law and Economics." *The Journal of Accountancy*, vol. 10 (1910).

Boutwell, G. S. "The Income Tax; the Decision of the Supreme Court." *North American Review*, vol. clx (1895).

Bullock, C. J. "The Origin, Purpose, and Effect of the Direct Tax Clause of the Federal Constitution." *Political Science Quarterly*, vol. xv (1900).

Bullock, C. J. "Direct and Indirect Taxes in Economic Literature." *Political Science Quarterly*, vol. xiii (1898).

Carnegie, Andrew and others. "Discussion on the Subject of the Income Tax at the Sixth Annual Meeting of the National Civic Federation." *National Civic Federation Review*, vol. ii (1907).

Carter, James C. *Argument for the Appellee. Income Tax Case.* Washington, 1895.

Carter, James C. and Gulliver, William C. *Brief for the Continental Trust Company of the City of New York, Appellee. Income Tax Case.* Washington, 1895.

Choate, Joseph H. *Closing Argument on behalf of Complainants, in support of the Contention that the Income Tax Law of 1894 is Unconstitutional.* Washington, 1895.

Choate, Joseph H. and others. *Brief on behalf of Appellants in Support of Contention that the Provisions as to Income Tax embodied in the Tariff Act of August 20, 1894, are Unconstitutional.* Washington, 1895.

Choate, Joseph H.; Guthrie, Wm. H.; Morawetz, Victor; Fox, Austen G.; Milburn, John G.; and Stetson, Frances Lynde. *Memorandum submitted to the Legislature of the State of New York in Opposition to the Proposed Sixteenth Article of Amendment to the Constitution of the United States.* (New York, 1910.)

Clarke, Samuel B. *Memorandum on the Taxes described as "Direct" in the Constitution of the United States.* New York, 1910.

Dougherty, J. Hampton. *The Proposed Sixteenth Article of Amendment to the Constitution of the United States. Memorandum containing a Criticism of Objections to the Amendment, and some Reasons for its Adoption.* (New York, 1910.)

Dunbar, C. F. "The New Income Tax." *Quarterly Journal of Economics*, vol. ix (1895).

Dutton, W. T. "The Income Tax." *The American Journal of Politics.* May, 1894.

Edmunds, George F. "The Salutary Results of the Income Tax Decision." *The Forum*, vol. xix (1905).

Fleming, William H. *The Income Tax — its Relation to Political Economy, to the Constitution, and to the Supreme Court Decision.* Washington, 1898.

Fox, Austen F. "Insert no Ambiguity into the Constitution." *The Journal of Accountancy*, vol. x (1910).

Godkin, E. L. "The Income Tax Decision." *Journal of Political Economy*, vol. iii (1895).

Guthrie, W. D. *Opening Argument on Behalf of Complainants, in Support of the Contention that the Income Tax Law of 1894 is Unconstitutional.* Washington, 1895.

Guthrie, William D. "No Taxation without Representation." *The Journal of Accountancy*, vol. x (1910).

Hall, U. S. "The Income Tax: Reasons in its Favor." *The Forum*, vol. 17 (1894).

Hill, David B. *No Income Tax! Great Speech on the Tariff Bill and Income Tax.* New York, 1894.

Hill, David B. *The Income Tax Law and Treasury Regulations together with the Speech delivered in Elucidation of the Same.* New York, n.d. (1895).

Hill, Joseph A. "The Civil War Income Tax." *Quarterly Journal of Economics*, vol. viii (1894).

Howe, F. C. "Federal Revenues and the Income Tax." *Annals of the American Academy of Political and Social Science*, vol. iv (1894).

Hughes, Charles J. (Governor). *Special Message from the Governor submitting to the Legislature Certified Copy of a Resolution of Congress entitled, Joint Resolution proposing an Amendment to the Constitution of the United States.* Albany, 1910.

Kennan, K. K. *Income Taxation.* Milwaukee, 1910.

Kinsman, Delos O. "The Income Tax in the Commonwealths of the United States." *Publications of the American Economic Association*, 3d series, vol. iv, no. 4. New York, 1903.

Kinsman, Delos O. "The Present Period of Income Tax Activity in the American States." *Quarterly Journal of Economics*, vol. xxiii (1909).

Lewis, William Draper. "The Constitutionality of the Income Tax." *The American Law Register and Review*, vol. ii (1895).

MacVeagh, Wayne. "Graduated Taxation of Income and Inheritance." *North American Review*, vol. 182 (1906).

Miller, A. C. "National Finances and the Income Tax." *Journal of Political Economy*, vol. iii (1895).

Morrow, Dwight W. "The Income Tax Amendment." *Columbia Law Review*, vol. x (1910).

Olney, Richard. *Oral Argument of the Attorney-General. Income Tax Case.* Washington, 1895.

Olney, Richard, Attorney-General, and Whitney, Edward B., Asst. Attorney-General. *Brief on Behalf of the United States. Income Tax Case.* Washington, 1895.

O'Neill, John J. "The Graduated Income Tax." *The American Journal of Politics*, vol. iii, 1893.

Pennoyer, Sylvester. "The Income Tax Decision and the Power of the Supreme Court to nullify Acts of Congress." *American Law Review*, vol. xxix (1895).

Purdy, Lawson. "The Income Tax Amendment should be Ratified." *The Journal of Accountancy*, vol. x (1910).

Root, Elihu. *Letter on the Income Tax Amendment written to Senator Davenport. Presented by Senator Davenport to the Senate and read also in the Assembly.* Albany, 1910.

Seligman, Edwin R. A. "The Income Tax." *Political Science Quarterly*, vol. ix (1894).

Seligman, Edwin R. A. "The American Income Tax." *Economic Journal*, vol. iv (1894).

Seligman, Edwin R. A. "Is the Income Tax Constitutional and Just?" *The Forum*, vol. 18 (1895).

Seligman, Edwin R. A. "The Income Tax in the American Colonies and States." *Political Science Quarterly*, vol. x (1895).

Seligman, Edwin R. A. "The Sixteenth Amendment." *Political Science Quarterly*, vol. xxv (1910).

Sewell, Robert. "The Income Tax: Is it Constitutional?" *The American Law Review*, vol. 28 (1894).

Seward, Mr. *Argument upon the Question whether the Words "Direct Tax" and "Direct Taxes," as used in the Federal Constitution, embrace a Tax on Income, or are limited to a Tax on Land only. Income Tax Case.* Washington, 1895.

Seward, Guthrie, Morawetz and Steele, Solicitors, and Joseph H. Choate and Charles F. Southmayd of Counsel. *Additional Brief and Argument for Appellants on Question of Direct Tax. Income Tax Case.* Washington, 1895.

Shellabarger, Samuel, and Wilson, Jeremiah M., attorneys; Edmunds, George F., counsel. *Brief for Appellant John G. Moore in no. 915, filed by leave of the Court in numbers 893 and 894. Income Tax Case.* Washington, 1895.

Shelton, William A. "The Income Tax in Georgia." *Journal of Political Economy*, vol. xviii (1910).

Sherman, John. *Selected Speeches and Reports on Finance and Taxation from 1859 to 1878.* New York, 1879.

Smith, Henry H. *Income Tax.* Washington, 1893.

Tiedemen, C. G. "The Income Tax Decisions as an Object Lesson in Constitutional Construction." *Annals of the American Academy of Political and Social Science*, vol. vi (1895).

Trickett, N. "The Income Tax: Is it Constitutional? A Rejoinder." *The American Law Review*, vol. 29 (1895).

Tunnell, G. "Legislative History of the Second Income Tax Law." *Journal of Political Economy*, vol. iii (1895).

Wells, David Ames. "An Income Tax: Is it desirable?" *The Forum*, vol. 17 (1894).

Wells, David Ames. "Is the Existing Income Tax Unconstitutional?" *The Forum*, vol. 18 (1895).

West, Max. "The Income Tax and the National Revenues." *Journal of Political Economy*, vol. viii (1900).

West, Max. *The Teachings of Political Economists defining Direct and Indirect Taxes. Income Tax Case.* Washington, 1895.

Whitney, Edward B. *Argument of the Assistant Attorney-General on Behalf of the United States, upon the Uniformity Question. Income Tax Case.* Washington, 1895.

Whitney, Edward B. "The Political Dangers of the Income Tax Decision." *The Forum*, vol. xix (1905).

Whitney, Edward B. "The Income Tax and the Constitution." *Harvard Law Review*, vol. xx (1907).

B. Anonymous Works.

Appendix to Brief on Behalf of the United States. Income Tax Case. Washington, 1895.

Brief for the Appellants in Support of Contention that the Provisions as to Income Tax embodied in the Tariff Act of August 28, 1894, are Unconstitutional. Income Tax Case. Washington, 1895.

Brief for the United States on Petition for Rehearing. Income Tax Case. Washington, 1895.

Extracts from the Evidence proving the Historic Facts from the General Literature, and from the Authorities, bearing upon the Question whether the Words "Direct Tax" and "Indirect Taxes," as used in the Federal Constitution, embrace a Tax on Incomes, or are limited to a Tax on Land only. Income Tax Case. Washington, 1895.

Historical Argument upon Meaning of Words "Direct Tax" and "Duty" in Constitution. Submitted by the United States. Income Tax Case. Washington, 1895.

Reply to Brief filed on Behalf of John G. Moore. Submitted by the United States Government. Income Tax Case. Washington, 1895.

C. Official Documents and Commentaries.

Report of the Commissioner of Taxes accompanying the Report of the Secretary of the Treasury. Richmond, 1863–1865.

Instructions for Collectors of Taxes. Treasury Department. Confederate States of America. Richmond, 1863.

Internal Revenue Record and Customs Journal. Washington, 1865–1873.

Report of the Commissioner of Internal Revenue. Washington, 1864–1872.

Report of the United States Revenue Commission. Washington, 1866.

Report of the Special Commissioner of the Revenue upon the Industry, Trade, Commerce, etc., of the United States, for the Years 1866–1869. Washington, 1866–1869.

Report of the Commissioners appointed to inquire into the Expediency of Revising and Amending the Laws relating to Taxation and Exemption therefrom. Boston, 1875.

Report of the Maryland Tax Commission to the General Assembly. Baltimore, 1888.

Report of Special Committee on Taxation. Boston Executive Business Association. Boston, 1889.

Report of the Special Tax Commission of Maine, 1889. Augusta, 1890.

Message of the Mayor transmitting Report of the Special Commission on Taxation. Boston, 1891.

Hearing before the Joint Special Committee appointed to consolidate, arrange and revise the Statutes of this Commonwealth relating to Taxation. Boston, 1893.

Report of Counsel to revise the Tax Laws of the State of New York, 1893. Albany, 1893.

A Full Report of the Joint Special Committee on Taxation, Recommendations and Codifications relating to the Laws of Taxation. Boston, 1894.

Report of the Commission appointed to inquire into the Expediency of Revising and Amending the Laws of the Commonwealth relating to Taxation. Boston, 1897.

Report of the Commission on Revenue and Taxation of the State of California, 1906. Sacramento, 1906.

Report of the Special Tax Commission of the State of New York. Albany, 1907.

Boutwell, George S. *Manual of Direct and Excise Tax System of the United States.* Boston, 1863.

Estee, Charles F. *The Excise Tax Law, approved July 1, 1862; and all the Amendments, together with the Intructions and Blank Forms, Decisions and Regulations of the Commissioner, with Full Marginal Notes and References.* New York, 1863.

Redfield, A. A. *A Hand-Book of the United States Tax Law, with all the Amendments, Comprising the Decisions of the Commissioner of Internal Revenue together with Copious Notes and Explanation.* New York, 1863.

Bump, Orlando F. *Internal Revenue Statutes now in Force with Notes referring to all Decisions of the Courts and Departmental Rulings, Circulars, and Instructions reported to October 1, 1870.* New York, 1870.

Foster, Roger & Abbot, Everett V. *A Treatise on the Federal Income Tax under the Act of 1894.* Boston, 1895.

GERMANY

A. Signed Works.

Baumstark, E. *Zur Einkommensteuerfrage.* Greifswald, 1850.

Birnbaum, K. *Uber die Anwendbarkeit der Einkommensteuer und Steuerreformen überhaupt.* Leipzig, 1873.

Bomboy, Réné. *L'Impôt sur le Revenu en Prusse.* Paris, 1908.

Bornemann, Dr. *Die Einkommensteuerfrage.* Berlin, 1850.

Borst, A. *Die Grund- und Einkommensteuer des Grossherzogthums Sachsen-Weimar.* Jena, 1879.

Breitenstein, Dr. *Nur eine Steuer und deren Catastrirung, Erhebung und Verrechnung, mit vorausgeschickter praktischer Betrachtung aller bisherigen directen und indirecten Auflagen.* Gotha, 1826.

Dieterici, C. *Zur Geschichte der Steuer-Reform in Preussen von 1810–1820.* Berlin, 1875.

Dinglinger, Friedrich. *Die Staatliche und Kommunale Einkommens-besteuerung der Aktiengesellschaften und Kommanditgesellschaften auf Aktien in Preussen und Baden.* Berlin, 1905.

Emminghaus, K. B. A. *Ueber die Steuerfrage.* Bremen, 1862.

Enneccerus, B. *Vermögensteuer, Fundirte Einkommensteuer oder Erbschaftssteuer.* Marburg, 1893.

Fuisting, B. *Die Einkommens-Besteuerung der Zukunft in Anknüpfung an das Preussische Einkommensteuer-Gesetz.* Berlin, 1903.

Fuisting, B. *Geschichtliche Entwickelung der Preussischen Steuersysteme und Systematische Darstellung der Einkommensteuer.* Berlin, 1894.

Gerstner, S. *Das Bayrische Einkommen- und Kapitalrentensteuergesetz.* Erlangen, 1858.

Glattstern, S. *Die Steuer vom Einkommen. Eine finanzwissenschaftliche Studie.* Leipzig, 1876.

Gneist, Rudolf. *Die Preussische Finanz-Reform durch Regulirung der Gemeindesteuern.* Berlin, 1881.

von Graffenried, Dr. *Uber die Einkommensteuer.* Zürich, 1855.

Gratzer, R. *Zur Geschichte der Preussischen Einkommen- und Klassensteuer, 1812–1851.* Berlin, 1884.

Hagedorn, C. *Die klassificirte Einkommensteuer in Preussen . . . unter Berücksichtigung der neuesten Gesetze.* Düsseldorf, 1885.

Heckel, Max von. *Die Einkommensteuer und die Schuldzinsen; ein Beitrag zur Kritik und Reform der deutschen Einkommensteuern.* Leipzig, 1890.

Held, Adolf. *Die Einkommensteuer. Finanzwissenschaftliche Studien zur Reform der Directen Steuern in Deutschland.* Bonn, 1872.

Henrich, L. "*Ein Lug und Trug-system.*" *Die Reform der Directen Steuern, insbesondere die Einführung der Selbsteinschätzung in Preussen. Ein Mahnwort an die Preussischen Landtagswähler.* Berlin, 1889.

Hill, J. A. "The Prussian Income Tax." *Quarterly Journal of Economics*, vol. vi (1892).

Hoffmann, J. G. *Die Lehre von den Steuern als Anleitung zu gründlichen Urtheilen über das Steuerwesen mit besonderer Beziehung auf den preussischen Staat vorgetragen.* Berlin, 1840.

Howard, Dr. Hermann. *Wie hat sich der Landwirt zur progressiven Einkommensteuer zu verhalten.* Leipzig, 1889.

Jastrow, J. "Die Vermögenssteuer und ihre Einfügung in das Preussische Steuersystem." *Conrad's Jahrbücher*, Dritte Folge, vol. 59 (1892).

Judeich, A. *Die Rentensteuer im Königreiche Sachsen.* Dresden, n.d. (1857).

Kellermann, J. G. *Das Besitzsteuersystem, die künftige, einzige, direkte Steuerquelle aller Rechtsstaaten.* 1889.

Kloos, J. *Die Entwickelung der direkten Steuern in Elsass-Lothringen.* Leipzig, 1908.

Knapp, F. *Ertragssteuer oder Einkommensteuer.* Leipzig, 1872.

Kries, Dr. "Grundzüge und Ergebnisse der Englischen Einkommensteuer." *Zeitschrift für die Gesammte Staatswissenschaft*, vol. x (1854).

Kries, C. J. "Ergebnisse der Preussischen Einkommensteuer." *Zeitschrift für die Gesammte Staatswissenschaft*, vol. xi (1855).

Kries, C. J. "Die Preussische Einkommensteuer und die Mahl- und Schlachtsteuer." *Zeitschrift für die Gesammte Staatswissenschaft*, vol. xii (1856).

Lips, A. *Ueber die allein Wahre und Einzige Steuer, die Einkommentaxe und ihre Ausführbarkeit.* Erlangen, 1812.

Lucius, Dr. *Plan zur Einführung einer Steuer im Königreiche Sachsen.* Leipzig, 1833.

Maatz, Dr. "Die Novelle zum preussischen Einkommensteuer- und Ergänzungs-steuergesetz." *Finanz Archiv*, vol. xxiii (1906).

Müller, Otto. Die Einkommenbesteuerung in den verschiedenen Ländern. Halle a. S., 1902.

Neumann, Fr. J. *Ertragsteuern oder Persönliche Steuern vom Einkommen und Vermögen. Ein Wort zur Steuerreform.* Freiburg i/B, 1876.

Neumann, Fr. J. *Die Progressive Einkommensteuer im Staats-und-Gemeinde-Haushalt.* Leipzig, 1874.

Neumann, Fr. J. *Die persönlichen Steuern vom Einkommen, etc.* Tübingen, 1896.

Quarizius, Dr. *Die Einkommensteuer.* Weimar, 1853.

von Raumer, Friedrich. *Das Britische Besteuerungs-System, insbesondere die Einkommensteuer, dargestellt mit Hinsicht auf die in der Preussischen Monarchie zu treffenden Einrichtungen.* Berlin, 1810.

Rouffie, Marcel and Momméja, Fernand. *L'Impôt sur le Revenu en Alsace-Lorraine. Histoire d'une Réforme des Contributions Directes.* Paris, 1910.

Schanz, G. "Die direkten Steuern Hessens und deren neueste Reform." *Finanz Archiv*, vol. ii (1885).

Schanz, G. "Der Einkommensbegriff und die Einkommensteuergesetze." *Finanz Archiv*, vol. xiii (1896).

Schmidt, H. *Die Steuerfreiheit des Existenziminimums. Ein Beitrag zur Theorie der Einkommensteuern.* Leipzig, 1877.

Schuhler, Henri. *L'Impôt sur le Revenu en Prusse.* Paris, 1898.

Seeger, Dr. *Ueber das vorzüglichste Abgabensystem.* Leipzig, 1815.

Sinnhold, Dr. *Die Klassensteuerverfassung des Preussischen Staats.* Liegnitz, 1831.

v. Sparre, Karl. *Die allgemeine Einkommensteuer als einzige gerechte directe Abgabe, aus Theorie und Erfahrung nachgewiesen.* Giessen, 1848.

Steinitzer, E. *Die Entwickelung zur Einkommensteuer in Bayern.* Munich, 1909.

Strutz, G. *Die Direketen und Indirekten Steuern.* Berlin, 1902.

Vocke, W. "Beiträge zur Geschichte der Einkommensteuer in Baiern," *Tübinge. Zeitschrift*, vols. 20 and 21 (1864–1865).

W. R. *Die Einkommenssteuer als Einzige Abgabe, aus staatsrechtlichem, national-ökonomischem und finanziellem Gesichtspuncte und mit besonderer Beziehung auf den vom Gerichts-Director Lucius herausgegebenen Planentwurf beleuchtet.* Leipzig, 1833.

Weygold, Dr. *Zur Steuerreformfrage in P eussen mit besonderer Rücksicht auf die Ausführbarkeit einer allgemeinen Einkommensteuer.* Leipzig, 1872.

Wilke, R. *Vorschlag zu einem Einkommensteuergesetz und zur Ausdehnung des Erbschaftsteuergesetzes.* Berlin, 1891.

B. Anonymous Works.

Die allgemeine und die partielle Einkommensteuer, verglichen mit der bisherigen Steuertheorie und Praxis. Zweite Auflage, Frankfurt a/M, 1854.

Ueber verhältnissmässige Besteuerung oder wie jeder Staatsangehörige nach der Grösse seiner finanziellen Kraft zu den Allgemeinlasten beitragen würde. Leipzig, 1834.

C. Official Documents and Commentaries.

Denkschriftenband zur Begründung des Entwurfs eines Gesetzes betreffend Aenderungen im Finanzwesen. Herausgegeben vom Reichsschatzamt. Berlin, 1908.

Kolisch. *Das Einkommensteuergesetz vom 24. Juni 1891 für die preussische Monarchie.* Glogau, 1891.

Fuisting, Bernhard. *Kommentar zum Einkommensteuergesetz.* Fünfte Auflage. Berlin, 1910.

FRANCE

A. Signed Works.

Aimond, M. *La Réforme Fiscale et le Projet Caillaux.* Paris, 1908.

Arnaud, L. "L'Impôt sur le Revenu appliqué à Verviers." *Revue Politique et Parlêmentaire* (1896).

Aubry. *L'Impôt sur le Revenu sans Déclaration ni Inquisition, basé sur le Rapport de la Valeur Locative du Foyer Domestique de chaque Contribuable avec l'Ensemble de son Revenu.* Paris, 1873.

Baudrillart, H. "L'Impôt sur le Capital et l'Impôt sur le Revenu." *Journal des Économistes* (1858).

Beauregard, Paul. *L'Impôt sur le Revenu et l'Income Tax.* Paris, 1904.

Besson, M. *L'Impôt sur le Revenu.* Paris, 1884.

Braniçki, Xavier de. *L'Impôt sur le Capital Libérateur de la Contribution de Guerre. Moyens pratiques de l'appliquer.* Paris, 1871.

Brouillard, R. *Des Impositions Extraordinaires sur le Revenu pendant la Révolution.* Bordeaux, 1910.

Caillaux, J. *L'Impôt sur le Revenu.* Paris, 1910.

Canon, M. *L'Impôt sur le Revenu, son Tasse, ses Modes d'Application, ses Effets sur la Rente et les Valeurs Étrangères.* Paris, 1906.

Catalan, A. de. *De la Transformation de l'Impôt. L'Unitaxe. Impôt sur l'Avoir de Chacun et sur les Éléments Constitutifs des Bénéfices et du Revenu.* Paris, 1890.

Catalan, Etienne. *L'Impôt et la Famille. Projet de Réforme de l'Impôt Mobilier.* Argenteuil, 1892.

Catalan, Etienne. *L'Impôt Direct.* Argenteuil, 1894.

Chailley, Joseph. *L'Impôt sur le Revenu. Législation Comparée et Économie Politique.* Paris, 1884.

Chardon, M. *Projet d'un Impôt Unique établi en raison du Capital.* Paris 1875.

Charton, A. Pierre. *La Réforme fiscale en France et à l'Étranger. Historique. Théôrie, Assiette et Incidence de l'Impôt.* Paris, 1901.

Chatelain, Emile. "Une nouvelle Formule d'Impôt sur le Revenu. L'Impôt, par Classes Conjugées." *Revue Politique et Parlêmentaire*, vol. 49 (1906).

Couron, M. *L'Impôt sur le Revenu.* Paris, 1899.

Crotard, M. *L'Impôt sur le Revenu, son Objet et sa Législation dans les Pays qui l'ont adopté.* Paris, 1871.

Davidson, D. "L'Impôt sur le Revenu." *Revue d'Économie Politique* (1891).

Doumer, P. *L'Impôt sur le Revenu.* Paris, 1896.

Duclos, M. *L'Impôt sur le Revenu.* Paris, 1904.

Duguies, Henry. *Le Projet d'Impô sur le Revenu.* Paris, 1888.

Dupont, M. *Le Projet d'Impôt sur le Revenu.* Paris, 1896.

Eybert, M. *L'Impôt sur les Revenus Commerciaux et Industriels.* Paris, 1907.

Faucher, Léon. *De l'Impôt sur le Revenu.* Paris, 1849.

Faure, M. *Le nouveau Projet d'Impôt sur le Revenu.* Paris, 1907.

Ferret, Abbé. "L'Impôt sur le Revenu." *L'Association Catholique* (1895).

Fouquet, M. *L'Impôt sur le Revenu Global ou la Taille Ressuscitée.* Paris, 1897.

Frédéricksen, N. "Les Principes et la Pratique de l'Impôt sur le Revenu et la Propriété." *Le Monde Économique* (1896).

Garnier, Joseph. "Du Rapport sur les Propositions de M. Sainte-Beuve relatives à l'Impôt sur le Revenu, etc." *Journal des Économistes*, vol. 26 (1851).

Gaston-Gros, M. *L'Impôt sur le Revenu, Essai d'Économie Financière.* Paris, 1907.

Gauthier, A. E. *La Réforme Fiscale par l'Impôt sur le Revenu.* Paris, 1908.

Geraud-Bastet, M. *Une Transformation Sociale. M. Caillaux et l'Impôt sur le Revenu expliqués.* Paris, n.d. (1910).

Gide, C. "La Psychologie et l'Impôt sur le Revenu." *Revue d'Économie Politique* (1889).

Girardin, Émile de. *Le Socialisme et l'Impôt.* Paris, 1849.

Gourgas, M. de. "De l'Impôt sur le Revenu." *Journal des Économistes* (1858).

Guigard, J. A. *De l'Impôt sur le Revenu, le Capital, la Propriété, l'Industrie, le Commerce.* Paris, 1850.

Guyot, Yves. *L'Impôt sur le Revenu.* Paris, 1887.

Haristoy, Just. *L'Impôt sur le Revenu.* Paris, 1910.

Hébert, J. B. *De l'Impôt sur les Créances Hypothécaires de l'Income Tax ou Impôt Progressif admis en Principe par le Citoyen Garnier Pagès, Ministre des Finances, etc.* Paris, 1848.

Henricet, J. "L'Impôt sur le Revenu et la Justice Gratuite." *Journal des Économistes*, Sér. 6, vol. 20 (1908).

Henricet, J. "Les inutiles Complications de l'Impôt sur le Revenu." *Journal des Économistes*, Sér. 6, vol. 22 (1909).

Heuschling, M. *L'Impôt sur le Revenu.* Brussels, 1873.

Houques-Fourcade, M. *Les Impôts sur le Revenu en France au XVIII Siècle. Histoire de la Dixième et de la Cinquantième. Leur Application dans la Généralite de Guyenne.* Paris, 1889.

Ingenbleek, M. *Impôts Directs et Indirects sur le Revenu.* Bruxelles, 1908.

Jenot, M. *De l'Impôt sur le Revenu.* Paris, 1885.

Kergall, M. *L'Impôt Démocratique sur le Revenu.* Paris, 1896.

Koenig, G. *Un Nouvel Impôt sur le Revenu. Memoire qui a inspiré le Projet du Gouvernement relatif à la Réforme de la Contribution Personnelle-Mobilière déposé sur le Bureau de la Chambre, par M. Dauphin, Ministre des Finances, le 26 Février, 1887.* Paris, 1887.

Laroche-Joubert, M. *L'Impôt sur le Capital.* Paris, 1874.

Laroche-Joubert. *La Réforme Fiscale.* Paris, 1873.

Laroche-Joubert, M. *Du Relatif et de l'Absolu en matière de l'Impôt ou Étude Comparative du Principe des Impôts Directs et des Impôts Indirects, 1872; Réponse aux Objections faites contre l'Impôt sur le Capital à la Séance de la Société d'Économie Politique.* Paris, 1872.

Lasseau, Amadée. *Sur diverses Questions relatives à l'Impôt.* Paris, 1876.

Lasteyrie, Charles de. "L'Impôt sur le Revenu sous l'Ancien Régime." *Revue des Deux Mondes* (1910).

Lechopie, Alfred. *L'Impôt Unique et Indirect sur le Revenu par la Taxe Proportionnelle sur les Quittances.* Paris, 1886.

Lefèbvre, Thibault. *De l'Impôt sur le Revenu Mobilier.* Paris, 1849.

Liesse, A. "L'Impôt sur le Revenu et les Socialistes." *Le Monde Économique* (1896).

Leroy-Beaulieu, P. "La Mystification du Projet d'Impôt Général sur le Revenu." *L'Économiste Français* (1896).

Luçay, M. *L'Impôt Général sur le Revenu, dans le Passé et le Présent.* Paris, 1896.

Malarce, Augustin de. "L'Impôt sur le Revenu d'après l'Expérience." *Journal des Économistes*, Sér. 5, vol. 56 (1903).

Manchez, M. *L'Impôt Général sur le Revenu.* Paris, 1899.

Marion, Marcel. *L'Impôt sur le Revenu au dix-huitième Siècle principalement en Guyenne.* Toulouse, 1901.

Martinet, M. *Les Différentes Formes de l'Impôt sur le Revenu.* Paris, 1888.

Maujan, M. *La Réforme Générale de l'Impôt.* Paris, 1891.

Menier, M. *Théorie et Application de l'Impôt sur le Capital.* Paris, 1874.

Meyer, Hermann. *Die Einkommensteuerprojecte in Frankreich bis 1887.* Berlin, 1905.

Meyer, Hermann. "Ein Ueberblick über die französischen Einkommensteuer-projecte in Frankreich bis 1887, nach Annahme der Resolution vom 10 Febr. 1887." *Finanz Archiv*, vol. 32 (1906).

Michel, M. *Impôts sur les Revenus.* Paris, 1907.

Montégut, R. de B. *Un Mécanisme de Transformation Sociale. L'Impôt Progressif sur le Revenu.* Paris, 1910.

Moreau, R. *L'Impôt Global et Progressif sur le Revenu.* Poitiers, 1910.

Nabos, Henri. *Impôt Unique et Proportionnel sur le Revenu. À Messieurs les Membres de l'Assemblée Nationale.* Auch, 1851.

Parieu, Esquirou de. "Examen des Avantages et des Inconvénients des Impôts Généraux sur la Propriété ou le Revenu." *Journal des Économistes* (1857).

Pelletan, M. *L'Impôt sur le Revenu.* Paris, 1907.

Pelletan, M. *L'Impôt sur le Revenu: où en sommes-nous?* Paris, 1908.

Philippe, C. *L'Impôt sur le Revenu.* Paris, 1894.

Philippe, Charles. *Le Probleme Fiscal — de l'Impôt sur le Revenu.* 6th ed., Paris, 1898.

Proudhon, Pierre Joseph. *Proposition relative à l'Impôt sur le Revenu présentée le 11 Juillet, 1848.* Paris, 1848.

Raynaud, M. *Les Réformes Fiscales. Révolution Pacifique par l'Impôt sur les Revenus. Système de M. Jacques Lorrain premier Lauréat.* Paris, 1888.

Révillon, Albert. "L'Impôt sur le Revenu et la Liberté Individuelle." *Journal des Économistes*, Sér. 6, vol. 13 (1907).

Rochard, M. *Réforme Radical de l'Impôt par l'Adoption de l'Impôt sur le Revenu.* Paris, 1894.

Rochard, M. *De l'Impôt Direct sur le Revenu.* Paris, n.d. (1877).

Roche, Jules. *Contre l'Impôt sur le Revenu.* Paris, 1896.

Roche, Jules. "L'Impôt sur le Revenu à l'Étranger." *Revue des Deux Mondes*, 5 Sér., vol. 25 (1905).

Sarrault, M. *L'Impôt Progressif sur le Revenu.* Paris, 1898.

Say, Leon. "Les Réformes Projetés dans le Système d'Impôts en France. La Proposition de M. Gambetta. L'Impôt sur le Revenu." *Journal des Économistes* (1877).

Siegfried, Jules. *L'Impôt sur le Revenu et les Droits de Douane.* Havre, 1871.

Staehling, Charles. *L'Impôt sur les Revenus.* Paris, 1876.

Staehling, Charles. *De l'Impôt sur le Revenu.* Paris, 1877.

Swarte, V. de. *L'Impôt sur le Revenu: Historique et Législation Comparée.* Nancy, 1893.

Tellier, M. *L'Impôt Unique et l'Invasion de 1870; La Libération par l'Impôt Proportionnel sur les Factures. Avec Projet de Loi et Commentaires à l'Appui.* Paris, 1872.

Thiers, M. *Rapport, precédé de la Proposition du Citoyen Proudhon relative à l'Impôt sur le Revenu et suivi de son Discours prononcé à l'Assemblée Nationale le 31 Juillet, 1848.* Paris, 1848.

Thiers, M. *Discours contre l'Établissement d'un Impôt sur le Revenu. Prononcé le 26 Décembre, 1871, à l'Assemblée Nationale.* Paris, 1896.

Vidal, Emmanuel. "L'Impôt sur le Revenu." *Revue Internationale du Commerce*, vol. vi (1904).

Vigne, M. *L'Impôt Général sur le Revenu. Rapport présenté au Conseil Communal de Gand.* Gand, 1903.

Willis, H. Parker. "Income Taxation in France." *Journal of Political Economy*, vol. iv (1896).

Wolowski, M. *L'Impôt sur le Revenu. Discours (Séances des 22 et 27 Décembre, 1871) avec des Observations et des Annexes sur l'Impôt du Revenu aux États-Unis et en Angleterre.*

Worms, E. de. "De l'Impôt sur le Revenu." *Revue Politique et Parlémentaire* (1895).

B. Anonymous Works. (arranged chronologically).

L'Impôt Unique représentatif et possessif, appliqué et contrôlé par le Suffrage Universel. [Par M. Adelante.] Havre, 1870.

L'Impôt sur le Revenu. Delivérance du Territoire. [Par M. Adelante.] 1871.

De l'Impôt et de la Production. Lettre à Messieurs les Députés à l'Assemblée Nationale. Par un Industriel. Paris, 1871.

Un Système Pratique d'Impôt sur le Revenu. Paris, 1872.

De la Transformation de l'Impôt. L'Unitaxe. Impôt sur le Capital et sur les Éléments Constitutifs des Bénéfices et du Revenu. Saint Quentin, 1877.

Étude sur l'Organisation d'un Impôt Unique et de Répartition. [Par E. Chaix.] Marseilles, 1890.

Le Projet d'Impôt sur le Revenu devant la Presse Économique et Financière. Paris, 1903.

"Quelques Conséquences de l'Impôt sur le Revenu." *Journal des Économistes*, Sér. 6, vol. 14 (1907).

Protestations de 1500 Syndicats contre le Projet Caillaux. Paris, 1908.

C. Official Documents (arranged chronologically).

Périer, Casimir. *Rapport fait au nom de la Commission sur le Budget rectifié de l'Exercice 1871.* Paris, 1871.

Leydet, M. *Proposition de Loi ayant pour Objet d'établir un Impôt sur le Revenu, proportionnel et progressif.* Paris, 1883.

Ballue, M. *Rapport fait au nom de la Commission chargée d'examiner . . . la Réforme de l'Assiette de l'Impôt.* Paris, 1886.

Guyot, Yves. *L'Impôt sur le Revenu. Rapport fait au nom de la Commission du Budget sur les Questions soulevées par diverses Propositions relatives à l'Impôt sur le Revenu.* Paris, 1886.

Laur, Francis. *Rapport Sommaire fait au nom de la Première Commission d'Initiative Parlémentaire chargée d'examiner la Proposition de Loi de M.*

Ballou et plusieurs de ses Collègues, ayant pour Objet la Réforme de l'Assiette de l'Impôt. Paris, 1886.

Chevalier, Charles. *Rapport Sommaire fait au nom de la 21° Commission d'Initiative Parlêmentaire chargée d'examiner la Proposition de Loi de M. Planteau.* Paris, 1888.

Dupuy-Dutemps, M. *Rapport fait au nom de la Commission chargée d'examiner la Proposition de Loi de M. Maujan et un grand nombre de ses Collègues ayant pour Objet la Réf rme Générale de l'Impôt.* Paris, 1892.

L'Impôt sur le Revenu et l'Impôt sur les Revenus dans les Pays Étrangers. Notes réunies par la Direction Générale des Contributions Directes. Paris, 1894.

Coste, Adolphe. *Rapport Général présente au nom de la Commission Extraparlêmentaire de l'Impôt sur les Revenus.* Paris, 1895.

Commission Extraparlêmentaire de l'Impôt sur les Revenus instituée au Ministère des Finances. Procés-Verbaux. Paris, 1895.

Delombre, Paul. *Rapport au nom de la Commission du Budget chargée d'examiner le Projet de Loi portant Fixation du Budget Général des Dépenses et des Recettes de l'Exercice, 1897. (L'Impôt sur le Revenu.)* Paris, 1896.

Krantz, Camille. *Rapport fait au nom de la Commission du Budget chargée d'examiner le Projet de Loi relatif aux Impôts Directs sur les Revenus et aux Taxes y assimilées de l'Exercice 1897.* Paris, 1897.

Merlou, Pierre. *Rapport fait au nom de la Commission de l'Impôt sur le Revenu chargée d'examiner les Projets et Propositions de Loi portant Établissement d'un Impôt général sur le Revenu.* Paris, 1901.

Renoult, Réné. *Rapport fait au nom de la Commission Fiscale chargée d'examiner le Projet et les Propositions de Loi tendant à l'Établissement d'un Impôt sur le Revenu.* Paris, 1907.

Caillaux, J. *Exposé des Motifs. Projet de Loi adopté par le Chambre des Députés, portant Suppression des Contributions Directes et Établissement d'un Impôt Général sur les Revenus et d'un Impôt Complêmentaire sur l'Ensemble du Revenu, Présenté au nom de M. Armand Fallières, Président de la République Française.* Paris, 1909.

Impôt sur le Revenu et Impôt Complêmentaire sur l'Ensemble du Revenu. Texte complet du Projet de Loi voté par la Chambre des Députés le 9 Mars, 1909. Notice Historique du Projet de Loi et Table par Article des Débats de la Chambre. Paris, 1910.

L'Impôt sur le Revenu. Le projet Caillaux devant la Chambre. Textes, Discussions, Commentaires. Paris, 1910.

AUSTRIA

Berg, Leopold. *Die Oesterreichischen Steuerträger.* Vienna, 1898.

Fürth, E. von. *Die Einkommensteuer in Oesterreich und Ihre Reform.* Vienna, 1892.

Lesigang, M. "Die besherigen Versuche zur Reform der Direkten Steuern in Oesterreich." *Finanz Archiv*, vol. vi (1889).

Mann, O., and Jedlicka, H. *Das Oesterreichische Personal-Steuergesetz nach dem derzeitigen Stande der Praxis.* Vienna, 1904.

Marcé, V. *L'Impôt sur le Revenu en Autriche.* Paris, 1907.

Meyer, R.; Pensch, R.; Mann, O.; Vlasák, B.; and Drachovsky, J. *Die direkten Personalsteuern.* Vienna, 1907.

Myrbach, Franz, Freiherr von. "Die Reform der direkten Steuern in Oesterreich. Die Personaleinkommensteuer." *Jahrbuch für Gesetzgebung*, vol. 22 (1898).

Nitschke, Kurt. "Die neuen Einkommensteuern in Preussen und Oesterreich, nach Veranlagung, Statistik und Ergebnissen." *Zeitschrift für Socialwissenschaft*, vol. v (1902).

Pensch, Rudolph. *Wie das Personaleinkommensteuer-Bekenntniss verfast werden soll.* Vienna, 1908.

Rauchberg, H. *Steuererklärung und Steuerauflage auf dem Gebiete der direkten Personalsteuern in Oesterreich.* Vienna, 1907.

Sieghart, Dr. "Die Steuerreform in Oesterreich." *Finanz Archiv*, vol. xiv (1897).

Steinitzer, E. " Gegenwart und Zukunft der Direkten Steuern in Oesterreich." *Conrad's Jahrbücher*, Dritte Folge, vol. 35 (1908).

Von Wieser, F. *Die Ergebnisse und Aussichten der Personal-Einkommensteuer in Oesterreich.* Leipzig, 1901.

Zebo, K. " Zur Reform der Personaleinkommensteuer." *Zentralblatt für die juristische Praxis*, vol. 27 (1909).

ITALY

Beaufond, A. Papin Labazordière Ruillier. *L'Impôt sur les Revenus de la Richesse Mobilière en Italie.* Paris, 1906.

Broglio, Emilio. *Dell' Imposta sulla Rendita. Lettera al Conte Camillo di Cavour.* Turin, 1856–57.

Bruni, Enrico. *L'Imposta sui Reditti di Richezza Mobile.* Milano, 1894.

Canestrini. *La Scienza e l' Arte di Stato, desunta dagli Atti officiali della Repubblica Fiorentina e dei Medici. Ordinamenti Economici. — Della Finanza. Parte I, L'Imposta sulla Richezza Mobile e Immobile.* Florence, 1862.

Flora, F. *L'Imposta sui Reditti di Richezza Mobile.* Milan, 1898.

Garelli, A. *Le Imposte nello Stato Moderno.* Milan, 1903.

Lia, A. *L'Imposta Mobiliare e la Riforma dei Tributi Diretti in Italia. Ordinamento, Funzione, Proposte.* Turin, 1906.

Magrini, M. *L' Imposta di Richezza Mobile nei Rapporti con le Società Commerciali obbligate alla Presentazione dei Bilanci.* Milan, 1903.

Perdrieux, Pierre. *Les Fraudes dans l'Impôt Italien sur les Revenus de la Richesse Mobilière, avec une Lettre-Préface de M. Luigi Luzzatti.* Paris, 1910.

Quarta, O. *Commento alla Legge sull' Imposta di Richezza Mobile.* 3 vols. Milan, 1902.

de Spoelberch, Le Vicomte Olivier. *L'Impôt sur le Revenu en Italie.* Brussels, 1908.

Tivaroni, J. *Le Imposte Dirette sulla Richezza Mobiliare e sul Reddito.* Rome, 1904.

Vessélowsky, M. *L'Impôt sur le Revenu Mobilier en Italie.* St. Petersburg, 1879.

Vinci, Giuseppe. *L'Imposta di Richezza Mobile in Italia nel suo Funzionamento.* Palermo, 1893.

SWITZERLAND

Bücher, Karl. *Basel's Staatseinnahmen und Steuervertheilung*. Basel, 1888.

Bullock, C. J. "The General Property Tax in Switzerland." *State and Local Taxation, Fourth International Conference under the Auspices of the International Tax Conference*. Columbus, 1911.

Cérenville, Max de. *Les Impôts en Suisse*. Lausanne, 1898.

Cohn, Gustav. "Income and Property Taxes in Switzerland." *Political Science Quarterly*, vol. iv (1889).

Cohn, Gustav. "Die Einkommensteuer im Kanton Zürich." *Jahrbücher für Nationalökonomie und Statistik*. Neue Folge, vol. i (1881).

Ernst, H. *Die Direkten Staatssteuern des Kantons Zürich im neunzehnten Jahrhundert*. Winterthur, 1903.

Esslen, Dr. *Die direkten Steuern im Kanton Zurich*. Zurich, 1910.

Gerloff, W. *Die Kantonale Besteuerung der Aktiengesellschaften in der Schweiz*. Bern, 1906.

Schanz, G. *Die Steuern der Schweiz in ihrer Entwickelung seit Beginn das 18 Jahrhunderts*. Stuttgart, 1890.

Von Scheel. *Ueber einige Fragen betreffend die Reform des Steuerwesens im Kanton Bern*. Bern, 1876.

Steiger, J. *Grundzüge des Finanzhaltes der Kantone und Gemeinden*. 2 vols. Berlin, 1903.

Weiler, Peter Hans. *Direkte Staats- und Gemeindesteuern in der Schweiz. Die heutige Belastung physischer Personen durch direkte Staats- und Gemeindesteuern in der Schweiz, mit besonderer Berücksichtigung der Progression*. Zurich, 1910.

Wolf, Julius. *Steuerreform im Kanton Zürich*. Zurich, 1897.

INDEX

T

www.ingramcontent.com/pod-product-compliance
Lightning Source LLC
Chambersburg PA
CBHW020641110726
47901CB00001B/3

* 9 7 8 1 6 1 6 1 9 1 6 4 1 *